Mitterrand, the End of the Cold War and German Unification

BERGHAHN MONOGRAPHS IN FRENCH STUDIES

Volume 1
The Populist Challenge: Political Protest and Ethno-nationalist Mobilization in France
Jens Rydgren

Volume 2
French Intellectuals against the Left: The Antitotalitarian Moment of the 1970s
Michael Scott Christofferson

Volume 3
Sartre against Stalinism
Ian H. Birchall

Volume 4
Sartre, Self-Formation and Masculinities
Jean-Pierre Boulé

Volume 5
The Bourgeois Revolution in France 1789–1815
Henry Heller

Volume 6
God's Eugenicist: Alexis Carrel and the Sociobiology of Decline
Andrés Horacio Reggiani

Volume 7
France and the Construction of Europe 1944–2006: The Geopolitical Imperative
Michael Sutton

Volume 8
Shades of Indignation: Political Scandals in France, Past and Present
Paul Jankowski

Volume 9
Mitterrand, the End of the Cold War and German Unification
Frédéric Bozo

Mitterrand, the End of the Cold War and German Unification

Frédéric Bozo

Translated from the French by Susan Emanuel

Berghahn Books
New York • Oxford

Published by
Berghahn Books
www.berghahnbooks.com

French edition
© 2005 Editions Odile Jacob
Mitterrand, la fin de la guerre froide et l'unification allemande.
De Yalta à Maastricht
by Frédéric Bozo

English-language edition
© 2009 Berghahn Books

All rights reserved.
Except for the quotation of short passages
for the purposes of criticism and review, no part of this book
may be reproduced in any form or by any means, electronic or
mechanical, including photocopying, recording, or any information
storage and retrieval system now known or to be invented,
without written permission of the publisher.

Library of congress cataloging-in-publication data

Bozo, Frédéric.
 [Mitterrand, la fin de la Guerre froide et l'unification allemande. English]
 Mitterrand, the end of the Cold War, and German unification / Frédéric Bozo ; translated from the French by Susan Emanuel. — Eng. language ed.
   p. cm. — (Berghahn monographs in French studies ; 9)
 Includes bibliographical references and index.
 ISBN 978-1-84545-427-2 (hardback : alk. paper)
 1. Mitterrand, François, 1916–1996—Influence. 2. France—Foreign relations—1981–. 3. France—Foreign relations—Europe. 4. Europe—Foreign relations—France. 5. Cold War—Diplomatic history. I. Title.
 DC423.B69 2009
 327.44009'048—dc22   2009025221

British Library cataloguing in publication data

A catalogue record for this book is available from
the British Library.

Printed in the United States on acid-free paper

ISBN 978-1-84545-427-2

Contents

Acknowledgements	vii
Abbreviations	ix
Prologue: France and the End of the Cold War: A Reappraisal	xi
Introduction: France in East-West Relations, 1981–1988	1
Chapter 1 The End of 'Yalta' (Spring 1988 to Summer 1989)	29
Chapter 2 Return of the German Question (August to Early November 1989)	83
Chapter 3 The Fall of the Wall (9–10 November – 31 December 1989)	111
Chapter 4 The Breakthrough toward German Unity (January–February 1990)	165
Chapter 5 The Great Bargaining (March–June 1990)	208
Chapter 6 From London to Paris (Summer and Autumn 1990)	278
Chapter 7 French Diplomacy and the New European Architecture (1990–1991)	310
Conclusion: Mitterrand and the End of the USSR	377

Epilogue: Twenty Years After	388
Chronology	393
Bibliography	401
Index	409

Acknowledgments

My thanks first go to the institutions with whose support I carried out my research. In granting me a sabbatical year in 2001–2002, the University of Nantes, my former university, enabled me to make progress in the very absorbing archival work. During this same period, my colleagues in the History Department showed themselves to be understanding with regard to a project that inevitably distracted me from more collective tasks. By inviting me for a research stay in the spring of 2002, the Nobel Institute in Oslo provided me with exceptional work conditions and gave me the opportunity to present preliminary findings in a stimulating atmosphere, for which I thank its personnel and especially its director, Geir Lundestad, and its director of research, Olav Njølstad.

This work would not have been completed successfully without the very large access it received to French archival collections. I am grateful to the successive directors of the Archives de France, Philippe Bélaval and Martine de Boisdeffre, and to Dominique Bertinotti, who allowed me to consult the collection of the Mitterrand presidency. I thank the heads of the twentieth century section, Paule René-Bazin and Isabelle Neuschwander, as well as the archivists in charge of the collection, Agnès Bos and Damien Vaisse, for their help. As for the archives of the Quai d'Orsay, I am grateful to then Minister of Foreign Affairs Hubert Védrine for authorizing the consultation. I thank Hervé Dejean de La Bâtie, Frédéric Baleine du Laurens and Pierre-Jean Vandoorne for their support in that regard. I am also grateful to the directors of the Archives diplomatiques, Louis Amigues and Yvon Roé d'Albert, to the deputy director, Monique Constant, and to the archivists in charge of the relevant series, particularly Véronique Godefroy and Olivia Perez, for their cooperation. Finally, I am indebted to former advisers to François Mitterrand for allowing me to unofficially consult the documents that they personally kept from their time at the Elysée. I also thank Françoise Carle for having allowed me to benefit from her intimate knowledge of the Mitterrand archives.

Even if I cannot list here all of those who took part, I would like to emphasize that the numerous exchanges I had with colleagues or friends as I carried out my research and pursued the writing of this book significantly contributed to my work. I thank Jean Klein, who never limited his time in allowing me to enjoy his extraordinary erudition on the German question and who agreed to read, with his customary care, a first draft of my manuscript. I am also indebted to Jean-Yves Haine, Marie-Pierre Rey and Hans Stark for having allowed me the benefit of their knowledge on a variety of issues, including, respectively, American foreign policy, Soviet foreign policy and European construction. My thanks also go to Hans-Hermann Hertle and Helga Haftendorn for having conveyed useful information to me. Finally, I am grateful to the forty-odd French and foreign individuals whose names are listed as sources at the end of the book, for having taken the time to respond to my questions as witnesses or former actors, thus making available to me the resources of oral history.

This book was first published in French in 2005 by Editions Odile Jacob. Its translation and publication in English in 2009 are the result of the efforts and tenacity of several individuals. First of all, I thank my publisher, Marion Berghahn, for having agreed to publish a demanding book on a difficult subject. The always friendly confidence that she placed in me was a decisive factor in the culmination of this work. I am also indebted to Irwin Wall, general editor of the monographs in French studies at Berghahn Books, who did not spare his support or encouragement. Finally, I thank Ann Przyzycki and Melissa Spinelli for having followed the production of the work.

This is the translation of my 2005 book. I have not made any major addition or correction. However, when useful, I have acknowledged new evidence and/or recent scholarly work by referring to it in endnotes or in the bibliography. The translation was in large part carried out with financial support granted by the Institut François Mitterrand. I thank the Institute's president, Hubert Védrine, its general secretary, Gilles Ménage, and its scientific director, Georges Saunier, for their help and support.

Susan Emmanuel had, yet again, the courage to transpose into English an often difficult text. Irwin Wall was kind and patient enough to reread the whole manuscript with a view to perfect legibility. Tracy Adam and Cemohn Sevier tackled the chore of translating the sometimes dry material in the endnotes. I am also indebted to Christophe Carle for his valuable recommendations. May they all be thanked.

Finally, this book would not exist without the encouragement or patience of all those who were subjected to it indirectly. May Jane, Pauline, André and Clémence forgive me for the excessive number of evenings or weekends devoted, in spite of myself, to this work.

Abbreviations

ABC	Atomic, Biological, and Chemical (weapons)
AD	Archives diplomatiques (Archives of the French foreign ministry)
AN	Archives nationales (French national archives)
CAP	Centre d'analyse et de prévision (French foreign ministry policy planning staff)
CDE	Conference on Disarmament in Europe
CDU	Christian Democratic Union
CEEC	Central and Eastern European Countries
CFE	Conventional Forces in Europe
CFSP	Common Foreign and Security Policy
CIS	Community of Independent States
CPSU	Communist Party of the Soviet Union
CSCE	Conference on Security and Cooperation in Europe
CSU	Christian Social Union
EBRD	European Bank for Reconstruction and Development
EEC	European Economic Community
EFTA	European Free Trade Area
EMU	Economic and Monetary Union
ESDP	European Security and Defence Policy
EU	European Union
FDP	Free Democratic Party
FFA	Forces françaises en Allemagne (French Forces in Germany)
FOTL	Follow-on to *Lance*
FRG	Federal Republic of Germany
GATT	General Agreement on Tariffs and Trade
GDR	German Democratic Republic

HSWP	Hungarian Socialist Workers' Party
IFRI	Institut français des relations internationales (French institute of international relations)
IGC	Intergovernmental Conference
IMEMO	Institute of World Economy and International Relations (Moscow)
IMF	International Monetary Fund
INF	Intermediate-Range Nuclear Forces
LRINF	Longer-Range Intermediate Nuclear Forces
MAE	Ministère des Affaires étrangères (French foreign ministry)
MBFR	Mutual and Balanced Forces Reductions
MID	Ministerstvo Innostrannikh Del (Soviet foreign ministry)
MRE	Ministère des relations extérieures (French ministry of external relations)
NAC	North Atlantic Council (NATO's supreme body)
NACC	North Atlantic Cooperation Council
NATO	North Atlantic Treaty Organization
NPT	[Nuclear] Non-Proliferation Treaty
NSC	National Security Council
OSCE	Organization for Security and Cooperation in Europe
PDS	Partei des Demokratischen Sozialismus (ex-SED)
PUWP	Polish United Workers' Party
RRF	Rapid Reaction Force
SACEUR	Supreme Allied Commander Europe
SDI	Strategic Defense Initiative
SED	Sozialistische Einheitspartei Deutschlands (Communist Party, GDR)
SGCI	Secrétariat général du comité interministériel (Coordinating Committee on European Affairs)
SHAPE	Supreme Headquarters Allied Powers Europe
SNF	Short Range Nuclear Forces
SPD	Sozialdemokratische Partei Deutschlands (Social Democratic Party, FRG)
SRINF	Shorter-Range Intermediate Nuclear Forces
UN	United Nations
USSR	Union of Soviet Socialist Republics
WEU	Western European Union

Prologue

FRANCE AND THE END OF THE COLD WAR
A Reappraisal

Almost twenty years ago, in the night of 9–10 November 1989, the Berlin Wall came down, at least metaphorically. This scene, displayed via television all over the world, instantly became the most powerful symbol of the end of the 'Yalta' system, summing up the chain of events that in a mere few months would put an end to more than forty years of Cold War and the East-West division. In short order there took place no less than the peaceful liberation of Eastern Europe from Communism and its emancipation from the Soviet bloc, the return of Germany to unity and full sovereignty following a process both democratic and peaceful, and the redefinition of the European system and its institutional 'architecture' with, in the background, the decomposition and then splintering of the USSR. Several characteristics rank this period among the most extraordinary and fascinating of recent history: the intrinsic importance of events that liquidated a situation dating back more than four decades, if only by definitively settling the 'German question'; the unexpected nature of the end of the East-West conflict, predicted by hardly anyone a few years or even months before; and finally, the sheer speed of these events and their effective shaping by international diplomacy and by the major powers, starting with the Federal Republic of Germany, the United States, and the Soviet Union, but not forgetting France and Great Britain.

Notes for this section begin on page xxvii.

A History Yet to be Written

From the start this period aroused fascination, first among the general public, as witnessed by the many journalistic accounts, television series and productions of all kinds devoted to it, a phenomenon fed by a mixture of the play of memory and captivation by the often spectacular character of these events; then among scholars animated by a desire to understand these events, whence emerged the impressive mass of publications devoted since then to the Cold War in general and to its end in particular.[1] Drawing on readily available sources and first-hand testimony, a first wave of scholarship quickly addressed the events of 1989–1991, resulting in a series of books that remain points of reference.[2] Witnesses and actors themselves soon began to publish their memoirs, documents, or diaries, thus making first-hand sources accessible.[3] Next, an important development influenced scholarship: the possibility – exceptional so short a time after events – offered to some writers to gain access to archives, resulting in the publication of works using original documents very soon after the facts. In the forefront of these is the 1995 book by Philip Zelikow and Condoleezza Rice, considered to this day to be an unrivaled work of reference.[4]

Of course, this early literature on German unification and the end of the Cold War, like all historical writings, is marked by the conditions under which it was produced. To this day, access to archives has remained selective, thus introducing a bias, and even in some cases (when authors are themselves former protagonists) producing a confusion of genres. By the same token, most of that first wave of literature makes for a particular reading of the end of Yalta, a reading that is essentially American-Soviet centered – corrected solely by the necessary accounting of the German factor – and underpinned (at least implicitly) by the idea of a Western (if not American) victory in the Cold War, an interpretation obviously nurtured by the political context of the 1990s and the U.S.'s assertion of itself as the sole superpower.[5] On the whole, less than twenty years after the facts – an amazingly short period – we possess an already considerable body of documentation and written history. Still, one cannot consider the history of the end of the Cold War as definitively written.

It is with this situation in mind that one has to tackle the role of France in these events, the subject of this book. French diplomacy has not occupied a major role in the books so far devoted to this period, and such treatment as it has received is scarcely favorable. In the best of cases, France's role in the end of the Cold War is considered marginal, like that of Great Britain, with which it is generally associated: 'London and Paris reacted and followed; they did not lead', aver Zelikow and Rice.[6] Often, authors' attitudes are critical if not outright negative with regard to France's record in these events. For a majority of writers, French or foreign, there is no doubt that France was caught short by the events of 1989–1991. Worse yet, it is commonly alleged that Paris tried to slow down if not altogether block certain ineluctable evolutions: German unification, against which Mitterrand purportedly attempted to make an alliance with Mikhail Gorbachev's USSR and Margaret Thatcher's Great Britain; the disintegration of the Soviet Union, which French diplomacy allegedly sought to avert up until the end; and finally the integration of the former people's democracies into the European Community, which Paris reputedly tried to postpone indefinitely by means of a European confederation proposed by Mitterrand.[7] An apt illustration of these criticisms is a book published in 1998 after a colloquium organized by the French political scientist Samy Cohen, which concluded with the verdict that Mitterrand's 'lack of foresight' had led to a 'succession of errors', supposedly attributable to a faltering decision-making process under an 'omniscient presidency'.[8]

Such remains the dominant opinion today, whether among academics, in the media, or in informed circles, not least in France. The idea that French diplomacy, after having profited from a long period of comfort thanks to the Cold War, in essence 'regretted' the end of this situation and even tried to oppose this historic evolution is indeed hardly questioned in France or elsewhere.[9] With hindsight, this unflattering reputation may be explained. As we shall see, the negative image of France's role at the end of the Cold War and vis-à-vis German unification began to emerge at the time of the events as a result of the misperceptions brought about by French policy, in particular in the domestic and international press, not least the German press. It has also been fueled by the revelations and polemics that accompanied the end of Mitterrand's presidency (whether on financial scandals or his role during the Vichy years), which had the effect of tarnishing his presidential record, including in foreign policy. But more importantly, it was nourished by the highly controversial publication of the last volume of his former special advisor Jacques Attali's diary for the years 1988 to 1991, in which many comments and documents – although of dubious authenticity – contribute to dramatizing Mitterrand's alleged hesitations, if not his anxiety, when faced with German unification and the end of the Cold War.[10] To the extent that a number of later works rely largely on Attali's toxic *Verbatim*, it is no exaggeration to state that the negative image of French policy in this period arises to no small extent from an 'Attali problem'.[11]

Of course, Mitterrand and his advisors quickly tried to alter the poor reputation that followed their policy. From the fall of the Berlin Wall onwards, the Elysée was preoccupied with its treatment in the French and foreign press; Mitterrand, during his meetings with Helmut Kohl in the fall and winter of 1989–1990, regularly complained about the German press in particular. Scarcely had German unification occurred, when Mitterrand's entourage tried to dissipate the impression of a French diplomacy that had supposedly spoiled its exit from 'Yalta'. Hubert Védrine, the Elysée spokesman and Mitterrand's strategic advisor, responded personally to Zbigniew Brzezinski, the former national security advisor to Jimmy Carter, who had called France, along with the USSR, nothing less than one of the 'two defeated [powers] of the Cold War'. France, replied Védrine, recalling French doctrine regarding East-West relations from de Gaulle to Mitterrand, 'never behaved like a country that tried to take advantage of the Cold War and to perpetuate it'.[12] Soon after the events, President Mitterrand, conscious of this problem, tried manifestly to put forth his own version of the truth, as documented by notes that his collaborators wrote to him in 1991 about his controversial trips of December 1989 to Kiev and the GDR as well as on the '2 + 4' process regarding the external aspects of German unity in the spring and summer of 1990.[13] By 1991–1992, as he began to entertain the thought of writing his memoirs, Mitterrand was particularly concerned with the issue of German unification, asking Védrine to gather the necessary documentation.[14] Prevented by the exigencies of his office and then by illness from producing his complete memoirs, Mitterrand's last efforts before his death in January 1996, in fact, were devoted to a manuscript exclusively concerned with his attitude in the face of events in 1989–1990. A few months later a posthumous book did appear that bore his name and his style but suffered from incompleteness and all too often read like a plea *pro domo* to convince critics.[15] Thereafter, those closest to the deceased president inherited the task of defending the Mitterrandian brief, principally Védrine, whose 1996 memoir on Mitterrand's foreign policy from 1981 to 1995 includes a valuable insider's account of French policy faced with the events of German unification and the end of the Cold War. Yet whatever his credibility, Vedrine's testimony is that of an actor (although surely an important one) and not the work of a scholar.[16] The same remark holds true for a four-volume account of the Mitterrand presidency by two AFP reporters, Pierre Favier and Michel Martin-Roland, which despite its narrative and documentary qualities is mainly a journalistic probe (the last two volumes, covering the period from 1988 onwards, appeared in 1996 and 1999).[17] Finally, one must mention the 2002 book by the German political scientist Tilo Schabert: focused exclusively on Mitterrand and German unification, it is informed by the consultation of numerous documents that Mitterrand himself authorized Schabert to see in the Elysée during his term in office. This book is thus the first truly documented one on the subject, and it denounces the 'legend' that Mitterrand's France tried to 'stall' if not 'block' German unification. Schabert seeks to radically correct the negative image of French policy that prevailed until then, and he goes so far as to defend the thesis of Mitterrandian prescience about German unity going as far back as 1981.[18] His thesis, however, has raised a number of questions among German and French historians who have been both critical of the author's modes of access to archives and skeptical about some of his analyses and conclusions.[19]

The present book, then, has a dual point of departure: the still highly controversial nature of the subject, and the absence until now of a work able to convince all parties. Hence the need for a historical investigation that can overcome the sterile division between a literature that is systematically hostile, due either to methodological bias or ulterior motives, and works that on the contrary are committed to defending and illustrating Mitterrand's policy but do not pass the test of scholarship. Such a work must have a threefold aim: first and above all, to reconstruct as precisely and objectively as possible the course of French policy in this particularly dense period – an indispensable effort, given the absence to this day of such an uncontested account. Then, on the basis of this factual narrative, we must try to explain French actors' choices when faced with the events under consideration or at least to try to reconstitute their own logic, and not, as is too often done, to infer alleged motives from a narrative that is itself questionable. Finally, we will assess the balance sheet of French policy from the perspective of its own objectives, as well as against the more general background of this period.

What really *was* Mitterrand's policy with regard to the emancipation of Eastern Europe, German unification, the disintegration of the USSR, and the redefinition of the European order after the Cold War? Was French diplomacy guided by the ambition, constantly proclaimed from de Gaulle to Mitterrand, to move beyond 'Yalta'? Or on the contrary, once this perspective carried the day, was France conservative and wary of leaving the 'Cold War niche' it had comfortably occupied since the 1960s by denouncing the East-West status quo while at the same time benefiting from security against the USSR and from primacy over a divided Germany?[20] To what extent did France attain its objectives at Cold War's end, whether in the resolution of the German question, in its relations with Eastern Europe and with the USSR, in the relaunching of European construction, in the redefinition of transatlantic relations or in the establishment of a new pan-European architecture? Finally, and as a corollary, did France contribute in a significant way to events of this period, or did it play only a marginal role in the transformations that marked the end of the Cold War? These are among the questions that this book proposes to answer.

Time for Reconsidering

The moment has come to try to reconsider the French role for two reasons. The first is that, twenty years after the facts, these events and their principal protagonists have truly entered into history. This was not the case in the 1990s, for in many respects, the first decade after the Cold War had the effect of prolonging it. Many European and international issues, such as the affirmation of the European Union, the enlargement of Western institutions, the stability of the Old Continent, and even the respective roles of the U.S. and Russia, were then still being essentially articulated around questions opened by the upheavals of 1989–1990. This page has now been turned. The 'post–Cold War' has now been replaced by the 'war against terror' as the organizing principle of the international system. The 11/9 1989 fall of the Berlin Wall has been largely superseded by the 9/11 2001 attacks on New York and Washington. As a result, the events of the years 1989–1991 may now be analysed from a more distanced perspective: while it is not yet a 'closed' history, it is incontestably approaching that status. Moreover, many of the principal actors have quit the scene: after Thatcher in 1990, Gorbachev in 1991, George H. W. Bush in 1992, and Mitterrand in 1995, the last to do so was Helmut Kohl in 1998, and the political implications of the writing of history are now therefore significantly blunted. As for Mitterrand, more than ten years after his death, the controversy if not polemic that long surrounded the man and his politics – well beyond the events that interest us here – have partially ebbed, allowing a calmer assessment that is all the less hazardous for the historian.

And here lies the second reason for this work: extensive access to French archives, public and private, has enabled careful study of the contents of hundreds of cartons. These archival documents are gathered in three main depositories. First and foremost, there are the archives of the Presidency of the Republic, deposited at the French National Archives, whose use was authorized for the period 1988–1991.[21] This is quite evidently a major source for this history: no archive collection so accurately reflects the politics of Mitterrand's diplomacy, since it is composed of the working dossiers of the principal collaborators of the former president. Thus it allows the historian to reconstitute as nearly as possible the process of decision-making at the Elysée, and, more generally, in Paris. Consultation of this archive was essential, in particular in the effort to reconstruct Mitterrand's policies in the face of the double problematic of German unification and the relaunch of European construction between 1989 and 1991, which is at the heart of this book and for which the author was able to gain access to the most important files.[22] To be sure, this archive is not without its shortcomings. While it is the best source for reconstructing the decision-making process in the Elysée, it is also a reflection of how the Mitterrand presidency functioned, as has been well described by former staff. It was an often informal process, characterized both by a certain compartmentalization and competition among the president's advisers, sometimes leading to incoherence if not lacunae in the archives. In addition, one should emphasize that these same archives very much reflect the chronic lack of personnel from which the Élysée suffers – or at least suffered in that period – and in certain cases, a lack of rigour in the collection, despite the efforts of the archivists.[23]

The situation is different with the second collection of documents consulted, i.e. the diplomatic archives kept by the Quai d'Orsay (the French Ministry of Foreign Affairs), to which access was also obtained.[24] This, too, is an essential source: complementary to the presidential archives, the archives of the Quai d'Orsay are in effect indispensable to reconstructing the role of French diplomacy properly speaking, since they hold the working dossiers of senior civil servants of the Ministry of Foreign Affairs. This allows us to discern the daily workings within the foreign policy apparatus while evaluating the state of mind, the quality of the information, and the reactions of the French diplomats involved, whether they be ambassadors in Bonn, Moscow, Washington or London, or those responsible in the offices of the Quai d'Orsay. Consulting these cartons proved particularly useful from the standpoint of bilateral relations, in particular between France and the Soviet Union and between France and Germany, but also regarding the dossier of German unification and its diplomatic aspects, as well as the major multilateral dossiers like NATO or the CSCE and, of course, the European Community and the future European Union.[25]

The third archive consulted is different from the preceding ones, even if the content is quite often similar: it gathers documents conserved personally by former officials at the Élysée, to which the author had access informally thanks to permission from the people concerned. Admittedly, these archives – which may be termed private, and which shadow the public archives, particularly the presidential ones – must be handled with precaution for at least two reasons: for one thing, they contain photocopies rather than originals; for another, the documents have been selected and classified according to criteria that are scarcely scientific, since they were gathered during the Mitterrand presidency more for the purpose of writing memoirs than for facilitating the future work of historians.[26] These two difficulties have been attenuated, however, by recourse to this source only as a complement to the two preceding ones – with which it largely intersects – familiarity with the 'official' sources permitting judgment as to the reliability and quality of the 'private' sources. The utility of the latter is thus and especially to fill possible lacunae in the former, which obviously constitute the documentary bedrock of the research.[27] Overall, even if one cannot claim exhaustiveness in the matter, the author believes that the cumulative consultation of these archives constitutes a solid base for undertaking a study with proper historical methods.

Nonetheless, its must be borne in mind that the archives are subject to a phenomenon more and more notable as one approaches the current period: a growing amount of data is missing due to the evolution of the means of communication or simply due to working methods, a phenomenon from which the Mitterrand presidency was not immune.[28] The inquiry into archives must therefore be complemented by other sources, starting with oral history, which is made possible by the still recent nature of the events under consideration, as well as the now routine aspect of this practice for historians and for the persons concerned: hence the forty-odd interviews conducted for the preparation of this book, which allowed the author to question witnesses and actors in this history, sometimes on several occasions. These include former French officials of course, but also Germans, Americans and ex-Soviets who lent themselves to this exercise, bringing information or perspectives that – as with any source – should be examined and sifted by taking account of possible biases (whether arising from lapses in memory or ex post facto reconstruction of events). Finally, research was completed thanks to published sources (in the German case, the important volume gathering together Chancellery documents for the year 1989–1990) and the innumerable memoirs, diaries and testimony of all kinds written by the protagonists of this history (German, American, British, French, ex-Soviet).[29]

Having access to primary sources and in particular to archives is a necessary but not sufficient condition: one still needs to use them appropriately. Here the author must be more precise about the approach taken to writing this history on the basis of the massive documentation used. Three imperatives were observed. First, all efforts were made to reconstruct the thread of French policy by establishing as precisely as possible the statements, positions and decisions of various actors: the enduring controversy over certain facts or events (e.g. the meeting in Kiev and the visit to the GDR in December 1989) indeed calls for particularly methodical work in that regard. Then, care has been taken to insert these elements into an exact chronology, knowing that the extreme density of the period and the precipitousness of events necessitates more than ever respecting their sequence and being attentive to the risk of retrospective history-writing: thus, as we shall see, Mitterrand's trip to the GDR changes its meaning according to whether it is assessed, as it should be, in light of its context at the time, or ex post facto, in view of the subsequent acceleration of events (only in January 1990 did it become clear – including to the West Germans themselves – that the GDR was doomed in the very short term). Finally, every attempt has been made to reconstruct the perceptions of different actors, both at different moments and as a function of the multiplicity of vantage points: the degree of information, schemes of analysis, and political preoccupations brought to bear were evidently not the same for Kohl or Hans-Dietrich Genscher, Mitterrand or Bush, and thus there intruded inevitable distortions in their respective perceptions, as the historian needs to remain constantly aware.

These imperatives of method have, in turn, involved choices in the making of this book: first, a resolutely narrative, event-based writing – an indispensable decision given the complexity of the material and the controversial nature of the subject; then, a rigorously chronological frame and a linear progression of chapters; finally, the insertion of the thread of French policies within the larger frame of international diplomacy, whence derives the often polyphonic character of the narrative. These choices reflect the ambition of this book: indeed, this is above all a study of French diplomacy, which implies first and foremost analysing the discourse and practice of Mitterrand's foreign policy and restoring both to the more general framework of international politics.

At the same time, the author must be precise about what this book is *not*. First, it is not the umpteenth book on Mitterrand. Certainly the former president is the main protagonist of French policies faced with these historic events, and these events could not be written about without integrating this factor into the equation, nor, more generally, the personal or cultural data that influenced French decision makers and leadership circles as a whole. That these facts mattered in Mitterrand's choices is evident: born in 1916 – the year of Verdun – Mitterrand reached manhood against the background of the ascent of the Hitler menace, before being caught up – from Vichy to the Resistance – in the whirlwind of World War II, then becoming one of the most prominent politicians of the Fourth and then Fifth Republics, and once president, working for Franco-German reconciliation and for the construction of Europe. Could such a Frenchman escape his own personal history when faced with an event as significant as the unification of Germany?[30] Evidently not! But how much has one said after positing this fact? For if these personal data explain the hesitations and at times the anguish – although undoubtedly exaggerated in most of the literature – on the part of French leaders who were suddenly faced with the so-called return of history, they also testify, perhaps more importantly, to these leaders' remarkable ability to transcend them. This is the dialectic that in the final analysis was at the heart of Franco-German relations during the greater part of the second half of the twentieth century, up to and including the events of 1989–1990. Besides, can one really fathom hearts and minds and reconstruct the deep thinking of individuals? This is why this book chose not to dwell extensively on the 'psychology' of French leaders. As Védrine justly states, 'the deep thinking of a statesman are his acts'[31] – and these are indeed what most interest us in this book.

Nor is this a book about France and the French people confronting the end of the Cold War and German unification. These are certainly important aspects of this history: public opinion reactions in the larger sense or informed opinion in a narrower sense, the attitude of the media and the positions adopted in the political class did influence official policy. However, these questions are not treated as such in this book as they would have necessitated extensive research plunging into a vast corpus of sources (the press, opinion polls, etc.) that would have added to the already considerable mass of archival materials consulted. Such a study has been largely done by other authors and it would have been useless to repeat this effort, all the more so because most works devoted to these aspects essentially confirm two elements that were already apparent at the time of events, in particular concerning German unification. One was the very wide support of French opinion for it, which obviously reflects the positive effects of reconciliation between France and Germany and of European construction (this marks a clear difference from the British case – where public opinion was far less supportive – and makes the French case quite similar to the American in terms of popular feelings toward German unity), and the other was a somewhat more ambivalent attitude among some sectors of the political class, the media, and pundits, which proved less supportive than the French people as a whole.[32] So while refraining from duplicating previous works, the author has nevertheless constantly tried to integrate their findings, if only because these aspects directly influenced French policy: it will be seen that the Élysée during this period was particularly attentive to the opinion polls as well as to the declarations and attitudes of the political class, and this factor played an indisputable – and, in the end, a positive – role in the formulation of Mitterrand's policy at key moments.[33] To be sure, history is never written in advance and one must beware of any kind of determinism. Yet it is not forbidden to the historian to reason in terms of historical development: how can one not see that the Franco-German reconciliation and European construction – a double reality solidly anchored in France and the French at the end of the 1980s – played a decisive and positive role in this history?

From Facts to an Assessment

We now come to the main results of this study, starting with the plain facts. Three major questions have remained so far at the heart of the controversy. Was Mitterrand's diplomacy, first, caught short by the end of the Cold War and especially by German unification? No doubt it was, as were other diplomacies, including that of the U.S. – later reconstructions notwithstanding. Of course, French diplomacy since de Gaulle had postulated the inevitable break-up, in time, of the bloc system, and Mitterrand had essentially adopted this approach after his 1981 election. In fact, from the new Cold War under Ronald Reagan to the new détente under Gorbachev, Mitterrand's diplomacy during his first seven-year term was able to find a dynamic equilibrium between recognition of East-West realities and the desire to overcome them. Reelected in the spring of 1988, the president was determined to give French diplomacy a major role in the international transformation induced by the acceleration of changes in Eastern Europe, which by then had become clearly perceptible. So on the eve of the 'revolutions' of the autumn of 1989, there did exist a Mitterrandian conception – at least in the long term – of overcoming 'Yalta' and the division of Germany, a vision largely inherited from de Gaulle, but also, as we shall see, much influenced by Willy Brandt.

Yet by the same token, the upheavals of the end of 1989 would inevitably challenge French expectations that had been all the more reassuring because they had belonged to a certain pattern – that of a gradual convergence between the two parts of Europe – and because they were measured in years and not in months. As elsewhere, no doubt – including Bonn – the fall of the Berlin Wall was a complete surprise in Paris; but the event and its aftermath, by challenging these same expectations, perhaps preoccupied French leaders slightly more than it did those in some other capitals – e.g. Washington. Faced with successive accelerations in the unification process – from Kohl's ten-point plan at the end of November to the announcement of the monetary union between the FRG and GDR in February, via the collapse of the GDR and the 'green light' from Gorbachev in January – the French, briefly, found themselves outstripped by events.

Hence a second key, indeed central, question: did French diplomacy then try to slow if not halt these same events, as has often been said and written? By no means. Of course Mitterrand and those close to him, starting in the last weeks of 1989, would have preferred that events – and in particular the march toward German unity – take a more moderate turn and a slower rhythm, in particular after the acceleration provoked by the ten-point plan. Mitterrand did not try to hide (including from the Germans themselves, with whom he remained quite frank throughout the process) his preference for a process of unification that would be controlled and stretched over time. The trips to Kiev and especially to the GDR in December 1989 obviously belonged to this line of thought (it must be remembered that they occurred when the fate of East Germany did not yet appear to be sealed once and for all). Meanwhile, the absence, in the last months of 1989 and the early months of 1990, of a resounding or solemn public statement from the French president in favor of German unity – earning him reproach from his critics and regrets from his supporters – cannot be reduced to a sheer error of communication. It was indeed because he did not wish to sanction and still less to encourage what he perceived as Kohl's precipitation and forced march toward German unity during these months that Mitterrand refrained from such a statement and avoided such strong symbolic gestures as participation in the opening ceremony of the Brandenburg Gate at the end of December 1989.[34] However, *at no moment did French diplomacy seek to slow down, let alone impede, German unification.* This is the key finding that emerges from plumbing hundreds and hundreds of archival documents, not one of which can be seriously interpreted as evidence of such an attempt – an attempt whose futility, and even danger, was perfectly realized by Mitterrand. The idea of an *'alliance de revers'* between France and the USSR against Germany had long ago lost any pertinence, and the hypothesis of a Franco-British entente to prevent the unity of Germany scarcely existed, except in the dreams of Thatcher. After all, can one imagine that the French president would have taken the risk of irreparable damage to forty years of relations between France and Germany and European construction in the illusory hope of preventing German unity – which, it should never be forgotten, was, for France as for its Western allies, a goal proclaimed since the 1950s? Had not de Gaulle solemnly reaffirmed this as early as 25 March 1959 by describing 'the reunification of the two fractions' of Germany as 'the normal destiny of the German people'?[35]

So – and this is the third question – what *was* the key objective of Mitterrand's diplomacy in that period? The answer is quite straightforward: it was about setting the process of German unification, and more generally the exit from the Cold War, within a strong European and international framework. In declaring as early as the end of July 1989 that German unity was 'legitimate' but that 'it could only be realized peacefully and democratically',[36] Mitterrand – who was, it should be noted, among the first to take a forthcoming position on unification – indeed formulated two preconditions that were indispensable from that perspective. With the principle of democratic elections in the GDR rapidly won – they took place on 18 March 1990 – the second precondition was met in effect; so it was on the first that French diplomacy was to concentrate. Hence the French insistence on the necessary international supervision of the German unification process in the name of respect for European stability and equilibrium, in particular through the '2 + 4' talks that took place in the spring and summer of 1990. Mitterrand's view of the international preconditions for German unification, in fact, was strikingly in line with the doctrine set by de Gaulle in his famous press conference of 4 February 1965, twenty years to the day after the Yalta Conference: the definitive confirmation of the German-Polish border and renunciation by Germany of ABC weapons, the emergence of a pan-European security framework and the pursuing and deepening of European construction.[37] The flip side of the coin was that this strong French desire to channel the process – badly received by the Germans, who were then mostly eager to maximize their national margin of maneuver in the pursuit of unification – would inevitably feed the misrepresentation according to which French diplomacy was seeking to effectively hinder it, whether by setting the precondition of strengthening the European Community or by requesting Germany's definitive recognition of the Oder-Neisse line beforehand.

How, then, can one explain the French and Mitterrandian choices when faced with the end of the Cold War and German unification? How in particular can one account for this desire to impose a strong international and European framework on the revolutionary events of 1989–1990 – sometimes with the effect of distorting perceptions of French policies on the part of Germans and others? By three factors, essentially. The first arises from the weight of history, omnipresent in the attitude of a Mitterrand who was prone, according to Védrine, to 'thinking of the future in the light of the past'.[38] For the president and French leaders in general, the exit from the Cold War and the end of the Communist block were undeniably, from the start, portentous opportunities. Yet they were also full of risks linked to the resurgence of the tragic history of the first half of the twentieth century. Hence, starting in 1989, constant references were made to such risks in his speeches, as typically when he evoked a 'return to 1913', which for him expressed the danger of fragmentation and of nationalism; hence also he was convinced that German unification should not be performed 'with forceps', and that the emancipation of Eastern Europe had to be channeled, and that a chaotic explosion of the USSR had to be avoided. This weight of the past in apprehending 'post-Yalta' has sometimes been judged 'excessive', contributing to the reputation of an excessively prudent diplomacy, overly attached to the status quo, if not conservative.[39] Whether justified or not, this occasionally obsessive preoccupation with the return of history – which, it should be underlined, was far from absent among the other actors, starting with Bush and Kohl – largely explains the major French options in the face of the upheavals of the end of the Cold War, whether they be the concern to monitor the process of German unification internationally, the project for a European Confederation to anchor the countries of the East, or the attitude to the disintegration of the USSR and – starting in the summer of 1991 – of Yugoslavia.

The second factor, deriving from the necessity to take into account the pressing realities of the moment, was the French diplomats' concern to best manage events so as to avoid a dangerous backlash, especially with regard to the situation in the USSR. To not destabilize Gorbachev nor take the risk of jeopardizing *perestroika* by imposing too many concessions (or even unacceptable losses) on the USSR was indeed a major preoccupation behind Mitterrand's policy until the final collapse of Soviet power in 1991. This logic of preserving Gorbachev's experiment played a preponderant role in the German affair, promoting a certain wait-and-see attitude on the part of the French until Gorbachev gave the 'green light' to the East German leader Hans Modrow at the end of January 1990. This then augmented the importance attached to the 2 + 4 process, which was seen in Paris as instrumental in order to assuage the Soviet worries about German unification (French diplomacy, as we shall see, was to play a constructive role in this process). It led, finally, to the French attitude in the debate over European 'architecture' in the post–Cold War era, marked by its concern not to clash head-on with Soviet interests (this was a clear worry when it came to a unified Germany's belonging to the Atlantic Alliance – which Mitterrand supported, provided Soviet concerns were taken into account – but also with respect to the European Confederation, one aim of which was to anchor the USSR in Europe).

But this too had a flip side: the preoccupation with Gorbachev that so influenced Mitterrand's policies contributed to the distorted image of a France having trouble accepting the end of the Yalta order, to the point of perhaps regretting the disappearance of the USSR – even though the worry about jeopardizing the Gorbachev experiment was in fact fully shared by Bush and Kohl. To be sure, the attempted putsch of August 1991 and its fallout would eventually confirm how right Mitterrand was to be worried, but the Americans and Germans had meanwhile proved to have a better appreciation of the Western powers' capacity to obtain decisive Soviet concessions in exchange for compensations, both strategic (over NATO) and economic (through credit loans), which they were respectively prepared to grant Moscow. These different evaluations underline the relatively limited role that France was to have in the 'great bargaining' with the USSR over the strategic and financial aspects of German unification, at least in comparison with the FRG and the U.S. Still, France's role was far from nonexistent, as is illustrated, for example, by Mitterrand's impact on Gorbachev's thinking with regard to a unified Germany's membership in NATO during his Moscow visit on 25 May 1990.

Whatever the weight of the past and present, however, the central explanatory factor hinges more on what the future held in store. As for all major players, it was in the name of a certain vision of the post–Cold War era and of the role and interests of France within it – a vision, again, largely inherited from de Gaulle – that Mitterrand's diplomacy advanced a strong desire to manage and channel these same events. First and foremost in that vision was Mitterrand's grand European design – in other words, his ambition with regard to European construction, which was the alpha and omega of French policy during the upheavals of 1989–1991. His brief worry over Kohl's attitude in that regard explains his determination at the end of 1989 to obtain from the chancellor a confirmation of his definitive agreement the following year to launch an economic and monetary union (EMU), which since 1988 had become the priority of his European policy – a confirmation, it should be remembered, that the chancellor had very much seemed to shy away from in the preceding months. This determination was proclaimed at the risk of appearing to favor European unification over German unification, or even appearing to make one conditional on the other, to the point that a 'deal' was suspected (incorrectly as will be seen) at the European summit in Strasbourg in December 1989: acceptance of German unification by France and the Twelve in exchange for Germany's agreement to the pursuit of European construction.

But it was also and especially this same grand European design that, ultimately joined with Kohl's, put an end to the transitory misunderstandings between Paris and Bonn by laying the bases for the relaunch of Europe that would result, at the Maastricht summit, in creating the European Union. It would require, noted Joachim Bitterlich, Kohl's European affairs advisor, 'three or at most four months' for the Franco-German tandem to adapt to the new situation and again 'find itself with a common responsibility for European unification'.[40] Maastricht, in this sense, represents the destination point of French policy in the period 1989–1991: a policy almost entirely oriented toward the imperative of European integration, an imperative that the end of the Cold War and German unification could only make even more categorical. This is attested by the central place of European construction in Mitterrand's conception of the institutional architecture of the post–Cold War era, whether in the pan-European dimension (hence the Confederation project) or in the transatlantic dimension (France's European ambitions would factor strongly into its positioning in the great debate over the future of the Atlantic Alliance). This conception, as we shall see, was rapidly to come into conflict with that of the Americans. This, in turn, no doubt contributed to further distortion of the image of Mitterrand's diplomacy – to the extent that, until now, the dominant reading of German unification and the end of the Cold War privileged the American vision to the detriment of the French.[41]

In putting back-to-back the dominant narrative of the 'missed exit' from Yalta and the somewhat hagiographic reading of Mitterrand's prescience, the present book thus seeks to offer a balanced reading of French policy faced with the upheavals of 1989–1991. Admittedly, Mitterrand's diplomacy envisaged another scenario for exiting from the Cold War and for German unification – which accounts for why it was to some extent caught off guard at first by the course of events – but it certainly did not try to slow down, let alone hinder, these evolutions. After a brief period of fluctuation, French leaders were able to pull their acts together and to contribute constructively to the international settlement, and indeed to the definitive solution of the German question, while defending a certain vision of the post-Yalta European order organized around European construction. And this vision succeeded to some extent. Granted, the Europe that emerged from the debris of the blocs did not fully correspond to Mitterrand's designs, as shown in 1991 by the failure of his idea of a Confederation as well as by the renewal of American leadership within the Atlantic Alliance. However, the success of Maastricht incontestably marked the achievement of the main French objective at the end of the Cold War, to wit, strengthening European construction, which the French have historically seen as the principal anchor of a post-Yalta Europe.

By the same token, France's role in this history appears far less secondary than has been generally recognized until now. The dominant interpretations to date cast the United States, Germany and, to a lesser extent, the USSR, in the leading roles. But would the end of the Cold War have constituted such a success for international diplomacy without the European factor to which France, in concert with the Federal Republic, contributed more than any other? Would the democratic and economic transition of Eastern Europe, the return of Germany to unity and full sovereignty, the disintegration of the USSR and the recomposition of the European order all have happened in an orderly and stable manner without the major contribution of European construction and the Franco-German relationship? Almost twenty years after the fact, has not the enlarged European Union effectively become the main structuring element of the Old Continent?

Beyond the French case, we hope this book will contribute also to illuminating the wider historical debate over the end of Yalta by leading to a reconsideration of the one-sided interpretations that have prevailed until now. Has not the moment come to get past the somewhat caricatural reading of an American or Western 'victory' in the Cold War that still dominates the literature on the subject? Should we not dig deeper than the essentially bipolar schemes by whose standard the events have most often been interpreted? Should we not integrate into the analysis the plurality of actors and the diversity of factors, which came together at first to unleash the upheavals, then internationally to channel the process of exiting from the Cold War, and finally, to refashion Europe after Yalta? Is it not suitable to give a place not only to the Atlantic Alliance, but also to European construction, as well as to the pan-European process and what has been called the 'Helsinki Effect'?[42] Is it not indispensable to reintroduce into this picture not only the role of the great powers but also that of individuals, societies and, last but not least, ideas? The history of the end of the Cold War is still being written and will progress only if there is an increase in the number of points of view from which it is apprehended. I hope that this work will contribute to that effort.

Notes

1. On the impact of the end of the Cold War on the writing of Cold War history, see John L. Gaddis, *We Now Know: Rethinking Cold War History* (Oxford: Clarendon Press, 1997), and *The Cold War: A New History* (New York: Penguin Books, 2005).
2. See in particular, on German unification: Karl Kaiser, *Deutschlands Vereinigung. Die internationalen Aspekte* (Bergisch Gladbach: Gustav Lübbe, 1991); and Stephen F. Szabo, *The Diplomacy of German Unification* (New York: St. Martin's Press, 1992); on Soviet-American relations and the end of the Cold War: Michael R. Beschloss and Strobe Talbott, *At the Highest Levels: The Inside Story of the End of the Cold War* (Boston: Little & Brown, 1993); and on Eastern Europe: Jacques Lévesque, *1989, la fin d'un empire. L'URSS et la libération de l'Europe de l'Est* (Paris: Presses de la FNSP, 1995).
3. See typically the book (in diary form) by Helmut Kohl's main international adviser, Horst Teltschik, *329 Tage. Innenansichten der Einigung* (Berlin: Siedler, 1991).
4. These two former senior aides in the George H. W. Bush White House were able to base their research on government archives: see Philip Zelikow and Condoleezza Rice, *Germany Unified and Europe Transformed: A Study in Statecraft* (Cambridge, MA: Harvard University Press, 1995). In the FRG, the same kind of access to government documents was given to Werner Weidenfeld, *Außenpolitik für die deutsche Einheit. Die Entscheidungsjahre 1989/90* (Stuttgart: DVA, 1998); in addition, a selection of key documents from the Chancellery was published by Hanns Jürgen Küsters and Daniel Hofmann, eds., *Deutsche Einheit. Sonderedition aus den Akten des Bundeskanzleramtes 1989/90* (Munich: R. Oldenburg, 1998).
5. For all their scholarship, Zelikow and Rice can hardly claim complete objectivity. Although they had both returned to academia when they wrote their 1995 book, they never lost touch with politics (as their subsequent careers made clear), and yet they were allowed exclusive access to the files of their own former administration, arguably a unique case of confusion between scholarship and politics that raises methodological, if not ethical questions: to what extent can such writing of contemporary history be distinguished from official history? The same question applies to Weidenfeld's 1998 book and the volume of documents edited that same year by Küsters and Hofmann, which after all were made possible thanks to access granted to archives by Kohl himself at a time when he was clearly tempted to use his image as the 'Chancellor of Unity' for political purposes: see e.g. 'Helmut im Glück', *Der Spiegel* 24 (1998). On all this, see Kristina Spohr, 'German Unification: Between Official History, Academic Scholarship, and Political Memoirs', *The Historical Journal* 43(3) (2000): 869–888.

6. Zelikow and Rice, *Germany Unified*, p. 367 (although they clearly minimize France's role, the authors, it must be recognized, offer a relatively balanced and objective presentation of French policy).
7. This unfavorable reading of French diplomacy – often poorly supported by the evidence and prompted by clichés or the search for ulterior motives – emerges early on in the literature, whether journalistic or scholarly; see in particular Elizabeth Pond, *Beyond the Wall: Germany's Road to Unification* (Washington, D.C.: Brookings Institution Press, 1993); and Robert L. Hutchings, *American Diplomacy and the End of the Cold War: An Insider's Account of U.S. Policy in Europe, 1989–1992* (Washington, D.C.: Woodrow Wilson Center Press, 1998). For a critical analysis of this literature, see Frédéric Bozo, 'Mitterrand's France, the End of the Cold War, and German Unification: A Reappraisal', *Cold War History* 7(4) (November 2007): 455–478.
8. Samy Cohen, ed., *Mitterrand et la sortie de la guerre froide* (Paris: Presses universitaires de France, 1998), p. 372. This first truly academic conference on the subject had the merit of bringing together scholars and actors and to prompt a useful debate; yet the contributions essentially relied on secondary sources, and the analysis was conducted with a bias, the stated objective of the book being to explain the reasons for what was a priori considered to have been a failed diplomacy.
9. The perception of France's reluctance to accept German unification is particularly widespread in Germany; see e.g. 'Einheit? Jein, Danke,' *Die Zeit*, November 4, 2004.
10. Jacques Attali, *Verbatim*, Vol. 3 (Paris: Fayard, 1995). The book is ostensibly a diary in which the author gathered his own recollections and impressions as well as his personal notes and documents, yet many of his assertions or quotations are unverifiable and sometimes doubtful, and whoever has had access to original archival documents may see that Attali falsely attributes to himself documents that he had not written and that he often transcribes them with approximations, omissions and at times even additions. See the comments by Françoise Carle, *Les Archives du Président* (Paris: Editions du Rocher, 1998), pp. 111 and 308. Attali's book has been described as a pure and simple 'imposture' by two journalists: see Pierre Favier and Michel Martin-Roland, *La Décennie Mitterrand*, vol. 3, 'Les Défis' (Paris: Seuil, 1996), p. 38. Pierre Joxe, a former defense minister and Mitterrand associate, is even blunter: 'Whoever uses Attali's books as a scientific source runs the risk of making the gravest errors. These books are full of mistakes in some instances and of lies in other instances ... Anyone may lie, but anyone may say that liars lie'; see his statement in Cohen, *Mitterrand*, p. 426.
11. The quote is from Pierre Hassner, who rightly asks 'how it is that so unprofessional an author has had such an eminent position as Mitterrand's close associate': see Cohen, *Mitterrand*, p. 455. According to some, Attali projected on Mitterrand his own anxieties or doubts with regard to German unification, at times making unauthorized statements on his behalf and thereby blurring perceptions of French policy at key junctures, in particular at the time of the Mitterrand-Gorbachev meeting in Kiev in December 1989: see below, chapter 3, note 131. Attali contaminated not only most of the subsequent literature, but also, in some instances, memoirs of actors: see the recollection of Helmut Kohl himself, whose surprisingly negative evocation of his 'friend' Mitterrand in his recent memoirs (in which he frequently alludes to information on Mitterrand's attitude obtained after the facts and quotes 'diaries' of 'close advisors' of the president) has clearly been influenced by the reading of Attali's controversial book. See Helmut Kohl, *Erinnerungen 1982–1990* (Munich: Droemer Verlag, 2005), e.g. pp. 954–955, where a whole paragraph of an alleged Mitterrand declaration in the Council of Ministers, to be found on p. 322 of Attali's *Verbatim*, is reproduced uncritically; other implicit quotations of *Verbatim* and of Attali appear e.g. on pp. 984 and 1042.

12. Letter from Védrine to Brzezinski, 31 July 1990, Archives nationales (AN), 5AG4/7010. Brzezinski had given an interview along these lines in *Le Figaro* a few days earlier.
13. See e.g. Caroline de Margerie, note pour le président de la République, 23 January 1992, Votre déplacement à Kiev le 6 décembre 1989, AN, 5AG4/CDM 33; and Ministère des affaires étrangères, le directeur de cabinet du ministre d'Etat, note pour Hubert Védrine, 23 November 1991, AN, 5AG4/CDM 36.
14. See Carle, *Les Archives*, p. 240.
15. François Mitterrand, *De l'Allemagne, de la France* (Paris: Odile Jacob, 1996); although the book is unquestionably by Mitterrand, a note from the publisher suggests that the historian Dominique Bertinotti (who had served on the Elysée staff at the end of Mitterrand's second mandate) had contributed to the book and that Mitterrand's interpreter Brigitte Sauzay-Stoffaës had also helped.
16. Védrine, *Les Mondes*. Other memoirs by former Mitterrand associates include those of his foreign affairs minister, but this book is of lesser importance: see Roland Dumas, *Le Fil et la pelote. Mémoires* (Paris: Plon, 1996).
17. Favier and Martin-Roland, *La Décennie*, vol. 3 and vol. 4, 'Les déchirements' (Paris: Seuil, 1996 and 1999): these books are based on documentation that the authors had access to during Mitterrand's term in office and on many interviews, and they offer a generally credible and balanced narrative of Mitterrandian diplomacy.
18. Tilo Schabert, *Wie Weltgeschichte gemacht Wird. Frankreich und die deutsche Einheit* (Stuttgart: Klett-Cotta, 2002), p. 11. Schabert's book deals only partly with the events covered by the present book, for its focus is on German unity, leaving aside other aspects such as the debates over European architecture in 1990–1991, which are covered in the last chapter of the present volume.
19. See e.g. Martin Mantzke, 'Plaudereien an französichen Kaminen,' *Internationale Politik* 4 (2003): 56–58; and the review by Jacques Bariéty, *Politique étrangère* 2(2004): 441–445.
20. The notion of a 'Cold War niche' was suggested by Hubert Védrine, 'France: le piano et le tabouret,'*Le Débat* 95 (May–August 1997): 165–170.
21. The 1979 French law on archives establishes a general thirty-year accessibility rule for government documents (which is brought up to sixty years for documents relating to national security), but it also allows for derogations to this rule on an individual basis. Although the legislation has given rise to debates and controversies in the past few years – in particular with regard to the alleged lack of transparency in the granting of derogations – it has allowed many historians to work in satisfactory conditions before the elapse of the thirty-year period. On the general situation of the French archival system, see Guy Braibant, *Les Archives en France* (Paris: La documentation française, 1996); and Sophie Coeuré and Vincent Duclert, *Les Archives* (Paris: La Découverte, 2001). The archives of the Mitterrand presidency, as far as they are concerned, are accessible to historians by derogation under the 1979 law, but the authorization process involves, as for all presidencies since de Gaulle, the agreement of the former president or his representative (Bertinotti in the case of Mitterrand) in addition to that of the Archives nationales. This 'dual key' arrangement – from which the author has benefited like other historians – has given rise to a controversy on the conditions under which access has been granted, but the archivists in charge of the collections have argued persuasively that the system has been made more transparent and effective in the past few years, thus allowing access to an increasing number of historians (386 files were consulted in 2002 and 2003, and 70 percent of the requests have received a positive response): see Agnès Bos and Damien Vaisse, 'Les archives présidentielles François Mitterrand,' *Vingtième siècle* 86 (February 2005): 71–79.
22. These include the working files of two of Mitterrand's closest associates: Elisabeth

Guigou, whose influence in European affairs at the Elysée was decisive in the 1988–1990 period (until she was appointed minister for European affairs in October 1990); and Caroline de Margerie, who followed in particular the negotiations on the international aspects of German unification in the spring and summer 1990 before taking over the European and Franco-German dossiers from Guigou in the autumn (de Margerie thus followed the negotiations leading up to the conclusion of the Maastricht treaty in December 1991). Although some of the requests to consult the files of the Elysée's 'cellule diplomatique' were turned down by the Archives nationales on grounds of national security, many documents emanating from the Elysée diplomats may be found in the files to which the author was granted access, including minutes of Mitterrand's conversations with his foreign counterparts and memos from his diplomatic advisers Védrine, Loïc Hennekinne and Pierre Morel, as well as those of Guigou and de Margerie. In addition, documents gathered in these files are frequently annotated by Elysée Secretary General Jean-Louis Bianco, who was quite influential in these issues, and sometimes by the president himself. Finally, these files typically include many documents from the main concerned ministries, especially the Quai d'Orsay (e.g. diplomatic telegrams or dispatches, or memos by high officials in the ministry).
23. On the functioning of the Mitterrand presidency, see Védrine, *Les Mondes*, p. 30ff., and Carle, *Les Archives*, in particular p. 101ff. A reflection of the fact that the Elysée was undermanned is the sizeable number of conversation transcripts that have remained in manuscript form as a result of lack of time (see e.g. the transcript of the conversation during the key visit by Polish leaders to the Elysée on 9 March 1990, below, chapter 5, footnote 2). In some cases, though, the lacunae may reflect inappropriate behaviour: hence Carle suspects that Attali kept for himself the original transcript of the Kiev meeting, which cannot be found in the archives but appeared in his book.
24. Access to this collection is normally given by the ministry's director of diplomatic archives. In this instance, however, the request – because of the exceptionally recent character of the documents – had been submitted directly to the minister (now Védrine) in 2000, who had personally agreed to it.
25. The most important files consulted in the diplomatic archive are those of the political directorate, of the European directorate and of the strategic directorate (remarkably, no request was turned down on the grounds of national security, even for sensitive issues like NATO). Here also, this archive reflects the institution that has produced it: on the one hand, the files are abundant and well kept, reflecting the excellent organization of the ministry; on the other hand, one detects a certain effacement of the political leadership, a reflection of Dumas' style and his penchant for informal dealings between the minister, his entourage and the Quai d'Orsay bureaucrats; see e.g. the testimony by the political director from 1988 to 1991, Bertrand Dufourcq, '2+4 ou la négociation atypique', *Politique étrangère* 2 (2000): 467–484.
26. Françoise Carle thus summarizes the directive she was given to that effect by Mitterrand in 1991: 'to gather appropriate documents with a view to narrate the key events' of the presidency; see Carle, *Les Archives*, p. 140. Of course, the existence of this 'parallel' archival collection has been strongly disapproved of by those in charge of the official collections: see Bos and Vaisse, 'Les archives.'
27. The works that have been published so far on the subject – including the book by Schabert – have exclusively relied on this 'parallel' archival collection, hence the heavy criticism from historians: see e.g. the review of Schabert's book by Bariéty, quoted above.
28. Carle mentions an 'awesome quantity of unwritten material', referring in particular to the president's telephone conversations or personal meetings (but this also applies, of course, to ministers and aides): *Les Archives*, p. 134.

29. For memoirs or testimonies in Russian, the author has relied on English or German translations.
30. On these biographical elements, see Pierre Péan, *Une Jeunesse française. François Mitterrand, 1934-1947* (Paris: Fayard, 1998); and Jean Lacouture, *Mitterrand. Une histoire de Français*, 2 vols. (Paris: Seuil, 1998). As for Dumas, the son of a member of the French Resistance who had been shot by the Gestapo, he would later write that '[his] personal history was no inducement to indulge in any kind of passion for the European community or in an intense rapprochement with Germany'. Dumas, *Le Fil*, p. 327.
31. Védrine, *Les Mondes*, p. 445.
32. See Marie-Noëlle Brand Crémieux, *Les Français face à la réunification allemande, automne 1989–automne 1990* (Paris: L'Harmattan, 2004). See also the earlier work by Ingo Kolboom, *Vom geteilten Deutschland zum vereinten Deutschland. Deutschland-Bilder in Frankreich* (Bonn: DGAP, 1991).
33. Thus, against the backdrop of an acceleration in the German unification process at the beginning of February 1990, the Elysée staff – Guigou first and foremost – emphasized the strong support that prevailed within French public opinion for German unity and for continuing European construction and underlined the risk that French policy might be perceived as 'ambivalent' as a result of the reluctance of some politicians vis-à-vis German unification. The aim was to convince Mitterrand to give a positive answer to Kohl's offer of a fresh Franco-German initiative with regard to the European community; see chapter 4 of this volume, pp. 183–184.
34. Védrine acknowledges that Mitterrand failed to explain his policies to the French people and thus 'to manage the *symbolic* dimension of German reunification'; see Védrine, *Les Mondes*, pp. 455–456.
35. Press conference, 25 March 1959, in Charles de Gaulle, *Discours et messages*, 5. vols. (Paris: Plon, 1970), vol. 3, pp. 84–85.
36. Interview with five European newspapers, 27 July 1989, in *Politique étrangère de la France* (July–August 1989): 78–82.
37. Press conference, 4 February 1965, in de Gaulle, *Discours et messages*, vol. 4, pp. 341–342.
38. See Védrine, *Les Mondes*, p. 464 (Védrine's remark applies to Mitterrand's handling of German unification and of the Yugoslav disintegration).
39. See typically Cohen, *Mitterrand*, p. 374.
40. Joachim Bitterlich, 'Frankreichs (und Europas) Weg nach Maastricht im Jahr der deutschen Einheit,' in Werner Rouget, *Schwierige Nachbarschaft am Rhein: Frankreich-Deutschland* (Bonn: Bouvier, 1998).
41. This is most clear in Zelikow and Rice, *Germany Unified:* the authors almost exclusively emphasize the Atlantic dimension and ignore the European one, asserting that the relaunch of European construction was 'the product of French dismay and frustration' with regard to German unification, leading to 'hasty' decisions as a result of Bonn's desire to give 'credentials as good Europeans' (p. 365).
42. Daniel C. Thomas, *The Helsinki Effect: International Norms, Human Rights, and the Demise of Communism* (Princeton, NJ: Princeton University Press, 2001).

Introduction

FRANCE IN EAST-WEST RELATIONS
1981–1988

One cannot tackle French policy with regard to the events of 1988–1991 without going back to François Mitterrand's first seven-year presidential term (1981–1988), which evolved against the backdrop of a profound transformation of East-West relations. Of course, nobody then could have anticipated these dramatic events. If there was a shift over barely a few years from the 'new Cold War' to a 'new détente', the fundamentals of the East-West conflict did not seem to be in question in that period, at least for the foreseeable future. Yet although the end of 'Yalta' was at best a very distant prospect, those years were marked by events and tendencies that would give rise to more spectacular developments later on, thereby contributing to the end of the Cold War. Thus, in the first half of the 1980s, the Euro-missile crisis, which marked the high point of the 'new Cold War', in effect highlighted the impasse in the arms race and gave new salience to the German question; meanwhile, turmoil in Poland fostered East-West tensions even as it revealed the fragility of Soviet domination of Eastern Europe. The second half of the 1980s, especially the three-year period following the rise to power of Mikhail Gorbachev in March of 1985, was characterized by the impact of *perestroika* in the USSR and its growing effects on East-West relations. Of course, Gorbachevian policy in this early period mostly expressed a desire for domestic modernization and for a fresh dynamic in Soviet diplomacy along rather traditional lines. But

---

Notes for this section begin on page 22.

a rupture with the Soviet system was already in the making underneath, thus creating a challenge to the international status quo whose effects would appear more fully later.

Mitterrand's diplomacy in this period was in line with this particular context: French foreign policy from 1981 to 1988 very much reflected, and was overwhelmingly influenced by, the reality of the East-West division. And yet it was by no means merely a status quo policy: heir to a Gaullist vision that was fundamentally about challenging 'Yalta', Mitterrand's diplomacy, which also resulted from the president's own intuitions and assumptions, proclaimed from the outset a prudent desire to move beyond the established order. This quickly led it to search for an exit from the new Cold War, to gamble on the Gorbachev factor and to make France the strong advocate of a new détente.

France in the New Cold War

Mitterrand's France had initially given the impression of a sort of conversion to the new Cold War. This impression was fed to a large extent by a strong contrast with the policy of his predecessor Valéry Giscard d'Estaing (1974–1981), who had been concerned to limit the damage caused by the deterioration of East-West relations at the end of the 1970s. While sharing the preoccupation expressed by West German Chancellor Helmut Schmidt in the autumn of 1977 regarding the deployment of SS20 missiles by the Soviets, and while contributing to the elaboration of the Western response, Giscard had in effect abstained from formally associating France with the 'dual track decision' taken by NATO in December 1979.[1] Similarly, while condemning the Soviet invasion of Afghanistan at the end of December 1979, French diplomacy had refused to see it as a death sentence for détente in Europe – hence Giscard's controversial meeting with Leonid Brezhnev in Warsaw in May 1980, where the French president had tried, in vain, to persuade the Soviet premier to begin a withdrawal of the Soviet army.[2] In addition, Giscard had shown great restraint with respect to the protests in Poland after the strikes of the summer of 1980: one had 'to take into account the geographical and strategic realities,' he declared in the first weeks of 1981.[3] There was, of course, a logic in all this: foremost in Giscard's policy was preserving the accomplishments of a détente that had become, for France as for its partners (particularly the FRG), a structural component of security. One also had to equilibrate an American policy that, starting in 1978–1979, was now considered too confrontational with respect to the USSR after having been too lax earlier, hence the re-launching of Franco-German cooperation and, beyond that, of the European strategic project as a way to balance the U.S. Finally there was, of course, a domestic motivation: by maintaining privileged relations with the USSR, which since de Gaulle had become a central component in France's politics of 'rank', Giscard – the first non-Gaullist president of the Fifth Republic – manifestly sought to acquire Gaullist credentials in foreign policy matters.[4]

After the presidential election of May 1981, French diplomacy broke with this logic: the former center-right president's restraint in East-West relations was for a while replaced – somewhat paradoxically – by the very 'new Cold War' accents of his Socialist successor.[5] The support that Mitterrand proclaimed from the start for NATO's dual track decision was 'the founding act'[6] of this new course, which was to find its strongest expression in his famous speech in the German Bundestag sixteen months later. The hardening of France's East-West stance was also clear with respect to the situation in Afghanistan, which was seen as incompatible with the maintenance of 'normal' relations between Paris and Moscow, but also with respect to Poland, where the crisis resulted in the proclamation of a 'state of war' in December 1981. Hence the so-called 'detoxification cure' that Mitterrand's diplomacy imposed upon itself in the further conduct of Franco-Soviet relations. While there was no complete interruption in contact, which continued at ministerial level and below, the intention was to put an end to the 'ritual', developed under Georges Pompidou (1969–1974) and especially under Giscard, of regular summits punctuated by joint statements.[7] Finally, as a corollary of this hardening toward the East, the new President wanted to reaffirm Western solidarity: hence his dramatic rapprochement with the Atlantic Alliance, underpinned by an ambitious defense policy which gave priority to the modernization of nuclear deterrence and to the restoration of strong conventional forces – to the point that the French now firmly believed that, 'the United States aside', they were the only ones in the alliance to be 'serious'.[8]

Several factors explain this shift of French policy in 1981. Aggravation of the East-West conflict, most importantly, disqualified any complacent attitude in Mitterrand's eyes: faced with the rupture in equilibrium implied by the deployment of SS20s by the Soviets, détente at all costs was simply no longer possible. Then there was the Western situation. While the renewal of East-West tension was a challenge that was simultaneously military (responding to the SS20s), strategic (maintaining the Euro-American 'coupling') and especially political (winning over the public opinion), contributing to maintaining Atlantic cohesion was something for which the French felt that their position of independence within the alliance – which sheltered the country from the pacifist wave–was a prime asset. Finally, domestic factors played an equally strong role. Fueled by the return of repression in the USSR and Eastern Europe in the aftermath of the Helsinki conference, 'the Solzhenitsyn effect' throughout the 1970s had caused many French intellectuals to convert to 'anti-totalitarianism', thereby fostering a sort of anti-Soviet consensus in the intelligentsia and general public. Hence Mitterrand's virulent critique of Giscard's 'complacency', which probably contributed to his winning the presidential election. Domestic politics, in this sense, amplified the perception of a major turn in French diplomacy in 1981, if not that of France's alignment with Ronald Reagan's America.[9]

New Cold War and Old Dilemmas

This impression was misleading, though: beyond the change in tone, it was in fact continuity that prevailed underneath. The East-West context, which steadily deteriorated after Mitterrand's election, continued to weigh on French policy, thus hampering its margin of maneuver and aggravating its dilemmas.[10] First there were the Atlantic dilemmas. Spared by the pacifist wave, France did appear more staunchly pro-Western than its neighbors, but this stance, by the same token, exposed it to an overbearing American leadership. Thus on the Euro-missile issue, support from Paris threatened to lead to an alignment with Washington. While Mitterrand held to a balanced interpretation of the dual track decision, the Reagan interpretation indeed privileged the 'modernization' component of the decision – i.e. the deployment of new U.S. missiles in Western Europe–to the detriment of the 'negotiation' component – i.e. arms control talks with the Soviets – thus leading the French president quickly to make his position clear. 'Everyone thinks that I am for the Pershings', he told Schmidt, 'but it is more complicated'.[11] Despite the opening of Soviet-American negotiations on Intermediate-Range Nuclear Forces (INF) in Geneva in November 1981, the difficulty persisted. Mitterrand indeed believed that the 'zero option' put forth by the U.S. administration was really a cover for refusing serious negotiations, which pushed him to distance himself from Washington while becoming increasingly frustrated at the difficulty of making a nuanced voice heard.[12] The same schema pertained to the 'sanctions' that Washington was trying to impose on the USSR and that French leaders, like their European partners, objected to. With the Euro-Siberian gas pipeline affair looming in the background in 1982–1983, this subject provoked a lively French and Euro-American tension. In short, the French experienced the perverse effects of a proclaimed solidarity with the U.S. that made all the more difficult any expression of a French 'difference': Reagan's anti-Soviet crusade, the Élysée lamented, reinforced the hand of the Americans in the Western bloc and comforted them in a 'conception of leadership' that contradicted the very 'notion of alliance'.[13]

For the French and their Western partners alike, the new Cold War, by placing Germany at the heart of the East-West confrontation, by the same token put the German problem at the top of the international agenda.[14] One must of course avoid any anachronism: German unification could not appear then as a serious hypothesis, at least in the foreseeable future; the very intensity of the East-West confrontation, added to three decades of partition, simply precluded it. Mitterrand nevertheless appeared more prompt than some Germans themselves to evoke the question of German unity: in October 1981, as Schmidt shared his skepticism on the subject, the French president replied that it was 'inscribed in History' and that he saw it as an affair 'lasting a generation'.[15] Three years later, it was again Mitterrand who would broach the subject with Schmidt's successor, Helmut Kohl (who, it must be underlined, proved more determined than his predecessor to assert that the German question remained 'open'): 'You cannot decree reunification', Mitterrand told Kohl, 'but you have to start from the principle that all that is not impossible is possible'.[16] It is therefore undeniable – as he would later stress to his detractors – that Mitterrand did envisage openly, from the start of the decade, a hypothesis that he judged inevitable in the long term. And yet it is also clear that the question of Germany's unity was scarcely salient in the context of that time. Without being dodged, it was tackled only very occasionally – and in private– as a distant prospect. It did not, therefore, represent a real stake in French-German relations at that time, nor until 1989.[17]

The East-West crisis nevertheless did lead, as the French ambassador in Bonn realized, to the 're-emergence of the German question' in German consciousness.[18] This phenomenon was evidently perceived in France, where speculation about the famous *Angst* abounded, speculation nourished by the German leaders themselves: 'All Europeans feel comfortable in their nation-states except for the Germans', confided Schmidt in October 1981, adding that 'this anxiety among my people makes me nervous'.[19] In short, West Germany was then traversing an identity crisis that worried the French, who rediscovered the famous 'German uncertainties'. The dominant feeling, including at the Élysée, was of a 'major and multiform trial' of a nation whose 'psyche' was 'effectively ill'.[20] But beyond this existential crisis, what French leaders – like their Western partners – feared much more concretely was the vulnerability of the Federal Republic over the Euro-missile issue, which could challenge its Western orientation. Seen from Paris and other Western capitals, the German question, in other words, was and would remain throughout the 1980s more a matter of the FRG's European and Atlantic anchoring than a matter of unification. In fact, throughout the year 1982 the growing pacifist wave in the FRG was taken very seriously in Paris, where it was thought possible that the proponents of a 'neutralist' line might carry the day in Bonn.²¹ Schmidt, in particular, appeared less and less capable of containing the 'drift' in public opinion and especially in the SPD, thus endangering the implementation of the NATO dual track decision and hampering the possibility of deploying American missiles.

Of course, Kohl's arrival in power in October 1982 was reassuring: the new chancellor proved more vigilant in relations with the East and more determined to defend Western positions.²² Mitterrand nevertheless seized the occasion of his speech to the Bundestag on 20 January 1983 to put up a show of support for the Bonn government. The perceived risk of 'the FRG's slide' thus led to a position statement that the Élysée judged 'the most important in foreign policy since the start of the president's term'.²³ The reasoning behind the speech was quite clear: in order to reinforce the Western anchoring of Germany, France should in effect solemnly reaffirm political and strategic solidarity between the two countries and accomplish a quantum leap in that realm, which the speech was to signal. The significance of the event was therefore considerable: pronounced on the occasion of the twentieth anniversary of the Élysée Treaty, which de Gaulle had signed with Konrad Adenauer, the Bundestag speech marked the veritable launch of the deeper bilateral cooperation Schmidt and Giscard had begun to sketch a few months earlier. Along with the revival of European construction, this endeavor would from then on become the centerpiece of Mitterrand's foreign policy: 'anchoring the FRG to the West through Franco-German friendship' and 'strengthening the assertion of Europe in security matters' were indeed two faces of the same coin, a reality that would weigh more than any other at the end of the decade.²⁴ In the meantime, the electoral victory of the CDU-FDP coalition in March 1983 came as a relief in Paris: the FRG thus remained firmly tied to the West, as was confirmed by the Bundestag vote in favor of deployment of U.S. missiles under the dual-track decision the following November. Even if the French remained attentive to the FRG's vulnerability to the East in the following years, what remained of the 'German uncertainties' was henceforth compensated for by the solidity of the Western and European character of the FRG, of which Mitterrand remained personally convinced. This fact – inseparable from the strong personal relation that developed between the president and the chancellor from the start of 1983–would also constitute a determining factor in what followed.

In the meantime, the new Cold War placed France before its most constant dilemma: what was the right balance between independence and solidarity? On the one hand, for Paris not to take sides in the INF matter would have encouraged a 'neutralo-pacifist' drift of the FRG that could have been fatal for the West and hence for France, which could not alone resist Soviet pressure in Europe. Such was the realization that inspired the Bundestag speech.[25] On the other hand, to adopt a line of systematic solidarity with the alliance in the matter also appeared perilous, given the risk of the French posture being assimilated to that of NATO and hence resulting in a de facto French 'reintegration'. What would then remain of the justification for a security policy founded on the need for an autonomous strategy? And how could one then avoid the danger of French nuclear arms being included in negotiations between the Soviets and the Americans? This last point would remain prime in French calculations as long as there remained anxiety that France's partners – the U.S. to begin with – would give way to the Soviet demand to 'take into account' its nuclear force in arms control negotiations.

In sum, the new Cold War placed French policy on a tightrope: it had to preserve the effectiveness of nuclear deterrence in Europe without exposing French nuclear weapons to arms control negotiations, to support the deployment of American missiles without returning to the NATO fold, and to back up the FRG's Western orientation without renouncing an autonomous French posture. If Mitterrand managed to transform it into a major initiative whose importance for the future was incontestable, the Bundestag speech was thus above all a reflection of the narrow constraints in which the East-West crisis enclosed French policy.

Continuity Underneath Change

Far from 'converting' to the U.S.-led new Cold War, Mitterrand's France soon proved keen to keep its distance from Reagan's America. While the French president shared the goal of reestablishing a strategic balance with the USSR, France and the United States diverged profoundly on other aspects of East-West relations. There were disagreements, first of all, in evaluating the strengths and weaknesses of the USSR and of the Soviet bloc. French analyses appeared much more pragmatic than American ones on this score. To be sure, there is no evidence that Mitterrand anticipated the implosion of the USSR itself, which would effectively occur ten years later. Yet, the Soviet empire in Eastern Europe was evidently not seen as eternal in Paris. As early as October 1981, Mitterrand confided to Schmidt his certainty that the weakening of the Soviet bloc – which he saw as a precondition for German unification–'would occur within fifteen years'.[26] Of course, Mitterrand's policy – as French restraint vis-à-vis the situation in Poland illustrated – remained prudent with regard to Eastern Europe. Paris was indeed keen to avoid any provocation while wagering on endogenous evolution in 'the other' Europe: a 'national-liberal current' was developing in the people's democracies, Mitterrand told Reagan in March 1984.[27] Consequently there were also divergences in how to react: the French in particular rejected the American tendency to extend the Cold War from the strategic to other aspects of East-West relations, notably the economic ones. Like their European partners, they feared the consequences of an interruption of East-West exchanges not only for obvious reasons of interest, but because such a policy might result in strengthened Soviet domination of Eastern Europe. French diplomacy was keen to preserve the benefits of more than a decade of intensifying East-West relations so as to 'keep open the paths of communication with the countries of Eastern Europe'.[28]

Under these conditions, one understands why the French discourse – beyond a very circumstantial pro-Western and anti-Soviet inflection – quickly resumed its traditional tone: 'Everything that will allow an exit from Yalta will be good', declared Mitterrand on 31 December 1981, appropriating the Gaullist mantra and thus asserting the fundamental continuity of French policy in East-West relations.[29] Of course, this 'exit from Yalta' advocated by Mitterrand appeared then to be a distant objective, for the logic of confrontation was reaching its high point. Without questioning *hic et nunc* a bipolar system that the new Cold War seemed to perpetuate, it was mostly a matter of preserving the political, economic and human gains – the three Helsinki 'baskets' – of East-West cooperation achieved by détente since the 1970s. A French priority from the start, the Conference on Security and Cooperation in Europe (CSCE) remained a major orientation in Mitterrand's diplomacy.[30] Even if the French always proved watchful lest the CSCE drift toward a logic of collective security that would challenge the Atlantic Alliance or prevent the emergence of a European defense, the pursuit of a pan-European process still remained a priority.

However, it was first and foremost from within the Western ensemble that France, under Mitterrand and his predecessors alike, tried to contest the bloc system. To be sure, this attitude arose to a significant extent from France's desire to defend its national independence: 'France's sovereignty cannot be compromised', warned Mitterrand against the backdrop of his quarrel with the U.S. over the gas pipeline affair.[31] But for Mitterrand's diplomacy (as formerly for de Gaulle's), resisting what was perceived as an inherent tendency of American policy to impose a logic of blocs was also and especially conceived as a contribution to moving beyond the Cold War. Hence the constant French opposition to Washington's desire to increase NATO's role beyond its strictly defensive function and to extend its geographical scope to make it a 'global' alliance. But it was above all the Western European project that was now at the core of the French ambition to challenge the status quo. For Mitterrand as for de Gaulle, a Western Europe constituted as a political and strategic actor (which had been the objective of the Fouchet Plan in the early 1960s) would not only strengthen France's international status and challenge American 'hegemony' in the alliance, but also contribute to getting past 'Yalta'. A Europe emancipated from the United States – hence less disturbing for Moscow – might even bring the USSR in time to abandon the logic of confrontation, and perhaps release its hold over Eastern Europe. At least, this was Mitterrand's schema for getting out of the East-West impasse over the following years.

Searching for an Opening to the East

Far from accommodating itself to the new Cold War, Mitterrand's diplomacy was thus impatiently waiting for the conflict to end. As early as the spring of 1983, some already believed in Paris that Moscow's aggressive policies were being defeated by Western steadfastness.[32] By the fall, Mitterrand was beginning to anticipate the end of the East-West standoff: 'If we hold good on the missiles, we will be in a position to lend a hand to the Soviets', he confided to British Prime Minister Margaret Thatcher.[33] Because it made possible a return to 'equilibrium', the beginning of deployment of U.S. Pershing II missiles in the FRG at the end of 1983 was a decisive moment, from the French standpoint. The year 1984, it was hoped, would offer the prospect of an increased margin of maneuver for French diplomacy in East-West relations. First, vis-à-vis the United States: after the turbulence of 1982–1983, Franco-American relations indeed returned to 'serenity', as illustrated in March by the trip to the United States of a Mitterrand still enjoying the afterglow of his Bundestag speech.[34] Second, within Europe: with the French presidency of the EC during the first half of 1984 and the success of the Fontainebleau summit in June, the European project was becoming a central objective of French diplomacy, while in parallel, political and strategic cooperation between France and Germany was taking on a European dimension with the relaunch of the Western European Union (WEU) in the fall. Third, and even more importantly, toward the East: since the Soviets would, sooner or later, try to break the deadlock in which they found themselves, French diplomacy indeed hoped to take a new initiative in the course of 1984. The capital accumulated since 1981 due to French firmness vis-à-vis Moscow would, it was believed in Paris, allow France to resume its place in East-West relations. In March, Mitterrand informed Reagan that he would soon go to Moscow, and he tried to convince the American president to be ready to resume dialogue with the Soviets 'on the inevitable day when the Soviet Premier wants to discuss things'.[35]

In the spring of 1984, Mitterrand no doubt congratulated himself on being able to return to a longtime facet of French diplomacy. For him as for his predecessors, the Franco-Soviet relationship was an instrument for affirming France's 'rank' and, at the same time, a significant component of the European equilibrium. And yet, for him there was no question of returning to the 'old' pattern of relations between Paris and Moscow, in which French diplomats discerned a motivation that they believed was now outmoded: previously, they noted, the search for a 'tacit entente with Moscow' had been carried out against 'the resurgence of a certain Germany', but this motivation now ran counter to the 'major axes' of Mitterrand's foreign policy goals, to wit, European construction and Franco-German cooperation.[36] This point became central later on: if the Franco-Soviet relation was indeed for Mitterrand, as Védrine wrote, a 'complementary assurance', the idea of an *'alliance de revers'* with Moscow clearly belonged to the past.[37] For the rest, the French were careful not to give the impression of an abrupt turnaround, or give credit to the idea of a French 'gift' to the Soviet regime – hence, until the last moment, the lingering uncertainty over Mitterrand's visit to Moscow, scheduled for the end of June 1984.[38] And once in Moscow, the French president avoided the trap of appearing too conciliatory: in evoking the fate of the dissident Andrei Sakharov during a toast made at the Kremlin during the official banquet, he conveyed a strong message, i.e. that firmness of conviction was not incompatible with dialogue. Of course, Mitterrand's visit did not in itself bring anything new: the conversations in Moscow proved most conventional.[39] But for French diplomacy it was a matter of staking out a position in the expectation of a new détente once the page of the Cold War was turned as anticipated. Mitterrand, in fact, came back from Moscow convinced of the Soviet leaders' desire to reestablish strategic dialogue with the West – provided Washington proved its moderation and renounced pushing its advantage further, once 'equilibrium' was reestablished after the Pershing deployment.[40]

The Gorbachev Factor

Mikhail Gorbachev's rise to power in March 1985 was not really a surprise: Constantine Chernenko was known to be ill and Gorbachev figured as the probable successor.[41] Nevertheless, the event represented a major new parameter for Mitterrand's diplomacy. Having met Gorbachev in Moscow in June 1984, the French president had been struck by the frankness of his analysis of the difficulties of the Soviet system, an impression subsequently confirmed by Thatcher, who had received him in December 1984. Having decided to seize the occasion of Chernenko's funeral, on the evening of 13 March 1985 Mitterrand became the first Western leader to converse with the new general secretary.[42] Mitterrand, no doubt, immediately developed an interest in, if not an attraction to, such an interlocutor: Gorbachev's 'very lively personality', he stressed the next day, represented a break with his predecessors. From the start, Mitterrand appeared to believe that Gorbachev incarnated a transformation of the nature of Soviet power – but would this mean a 'renunciation' of the foreign policy that Andrei Gromyko (who would be replaced as head of MID in July 1985 by Eduard Shevardnadze) continued to direct? The French president remained circumspect on this point.[43] These first impressions were confirmed in the following months. Mitterrand did not depart from his initial judgment of Gorbachev: 'He is a direct man, in touch with the major problems, attentive and capable of prompt responses', he wrote to Reagan.[44] But the French president remained prudent about the political consequences of Gorbachev's arrival. At least in the initial phase of *perestroika*, he thought the new Soviet leader for the most part simply embodied 'an intelligent way' of 'perpetuating' the Soviet system.[45]

Gorbachev's arrival in the spring of 1985 nevertheless represented a chance that Mitterrand was all the more eager to seize because the context – which had changed since his Moscow visit the preceding year – pushed in that direction. As he had anticipated, in the previous several months the Soviet leaders had expressed interest in resuming strategic talks, and Reagan wanted his second term to be remembered for an easing of tensions. Thus U.S.-Soviet negotiations, suspended since the Pershing deployment, were restarted in March 1985, and France could not turn a blind eye to the resumption of an arms control process that it had called for but that might affect its interests – hence the importance of a continued independent French dialogue with Moscow, more interesting now that Gorbachev was in power. This meanwhile coincided with new Franco-American friction: starting in the first months of 1985, Washington set out to rally the Europeans to the Strategic Defense Initiative (SDI) launched by Reagan in 1983, popularly known as 'star wars'. Not only did the French regard the program as a challenge to the logic of nuclear deterrence, but it threatened to destabilize the strategic balance and foster a renewal of the arms race. Above all, it might strengthen the United States' technological hold over, as well as dominance of, the Western alliance while increasing the risk of Euro-American strategic 'decoupling'.[46] In short, at a time when other controversies with Washington were resurfacing (monetary problems, GATT), which culminated in the summit of the G-7 in Bonn in May 1985, Paris – classically – hoped to balance American hegemonic temptations with better relations with Moscow: the new dynamic of Soviet policy, thought the Élysée, 'might have the advantage of bringing the United States to a less imperial attitude'.[47]

A final factor was Franco-German relations and European construction. Two years after the Bundestag speech, strategic rapprochement between Paris and Bonn seemed stalled. The disparity of status between a nuclear

France, autonomous within the Atlantic Alliance, and an FRG that was non-nuclear and integrated into NATO limited the possibilities for cooperation between the two countries, and the pressure exerted by the United States regarding the SDI aggravated these difficulties. The spring of 1985 saw no progress on the issue of bilateral cooperation.[48] In parallel, European divisions and transatlantic misunderstandings compromised the relaunch of the political Europe that Mitterrand and Kohl now wanted to promote more actively. To be sure, the summit of the Ten in Milan in June led some months later to the signing of the Single European Act, which produced modest progress, but it also marked the limits of Franco-German voluntarism in this area.[49] In order to advance further, Paris thought, the European project needed a calmer transatlantic climate and consequently a less strained East-West environment: only a return to détente would permit the relaxation of the American hold over Europe as well as the USSR's acceptance of a Western European political and strategic project that it had opposed up to now. To keep an eye on the resumption of the Soviet-American dialogue, to balance Reaganite 'hegemonism', to develop Franco-German cooperation, and to foster affirmation of Western Europe became motivations for Mitterrand to engage further with Gorbachev.

USSR-France: 'Great Possibilities'

As it happened, the Soviet Number One was available. Having mentioned, on that 13 March evening, some 'great possibilities' for Franco-Soviet relations, he accepted Mitterrand's invitation to come to France in October 1985. Gorbachev's motivations did not escape the French president: the Soviet leader 'dreamed of taking some trips' abroad, and France, due to its particular position within the alliance and its disagreements with the United States, was a 'convenient' destination. But French diplomacy remained cautious, not playing Moscow's game at a juncture when the Soviets were trying to regain international credit by advocating a pure and simple return to a détente of which both countries had been the 'pioneers' in the 1960s.[50] This prudence was explained by political considerations: as illustrated in December 1985 by the backlash around the Paris visit of the Polish leader General Wojtech Jaruzelski, French public opinion remained marked by the anti-Soviet attitudes of the 'new Cold War', so one had to avoid giving the impression of an abandonment of Mitterrand's earlier tough policy. But this vigilance also reflected a basic analysis: despite the change in style, in Paris Moscow's policies were still believed to be unchanged in their inspiration – hence the concern to not endorse Soviet aims as long as the Soviets had not given commitments to really change their line, whether over human rights, Afghanistan, or security issues.[51]

Still, the conversations in Paris (2 to 4 October 1985) gave rise to exchanges of real intensity.[52] Gorbachev ably tried to play on convergences between France and the USSR; he tried to proclaim a joint desire to 're-establish détente' between France and the USSR, wanted to associate Mitterrand with a denunciation of SDI, and hoped to entrain the French onto the ground of direct negotiations over nuclear weapons. Mitterrand, for his part, wanted to announce the renewal of Franco-Soviet dialogue, but without endorsing the USSR's objectives: he was willing for the word 'détente' to be pronounced by both during the press conference and for each to say why they were opposed to SDI, but he declined any common declaration and watched over traditional French interests like a hawk, reserving a polite silence about the proposal for Franco-Soviet nuclear negotiations. For the rest, the French president was intent upon passing a certain number of messages to Moscow, the most significant of which concerned his European and Franco-German projects. Knowing the Soviet reservations about them, he tried to convince his interlocutor that they could be acceptable to the USSR. Thus, while clearly stating his determination for closer military cooperation between France and Germany, Mitterrand categorically excluded any 'sharing' in the nuclear domain, which, he emphasized, 'would imperil the whole European equilibrium'. This declaration was well received by Gorbachev, who judged this point to be 'as important as the inviolability of borders' (we shall see how much the nuclear and the border issues were to count in the German question in 1989).[53]

Finally, the French president sketched for the Soviet chief a long-term vision of East-West relations: 'There is a situation in Europe inherited from the war' that one might 'correct' by 'expanding' relations between Eastern Europe and Western Europe, he concluded, encouraging Gorbachev to 'take the hand' of the European Community. To persuade the USSR of the legitimacy of European construction, and, when the time came, make the EC the lever of a whole-scale recomposition of the Old Continent in the framework of the Helsinki Process: in the autumn of 1985, these constituted the elements of the scheme that the Frenchman delivered to the Russian in order to provide a means of exit from 'Yalta'.

France, Spearhead of Détente

With his visit to France – which was his first trip abroad as Soviet leader – Gorbachev made a successful entrance onto the international scene, using to good effect a resolutely 'modern' appearance and communications skills, which three years later were to arouse a veritable 'Gorby-mania' in Western Europe.[54] Aware of the motivations of a Soviet diplomacy still reliant on traditional schemas and heavily in need of improving its image, Mitterrand was nevertheless able to use this occasion to place France at the forefront of East-West relations while also knitting a personal relationship that would henceforth be meaningful. In the first months of 1986, France thus reclaimed its role as privileged interlocutor of the USSR in Western Europe and placed itself in a position to lead the new détente that was appearing on the horizon. At the same time, the French president, in a preface to a published collection of his main foreign policy speeches, delivered a statement on East-West relations that made his policy clear, and in which we find echoes of his recent conversations with Gorbachev.

Mitterrand started with a realistic assessment of the current situation. 'We are living in the era of Yalta', he argued, and 'this reality' dictated the major objectives of French policy: securing a balance of power between East and West, being a member in a 'defensive' Atlantic Alliance, and maintaining an autonomous deterrent. But he added that this situation was not satisfactory: 'Militarily dependent, politically disunited, economically anachronistic', Western Europe was proving 'each day more vulnerable to the enticements that sway it: submission to the American *imperium* or abandonment to neutrality'. Hence his prescription: 'The gradual affirmation of Western Europe's autonomous personality, the promotion of its complementarities with Eastern Europe, the obligation of the USSR to re-establish a more trusting climate with Community countries in order to stimulate its exchanges and to foster its development, and the assurance that it should obtain from these countries in return that the independence of Europe will not become a war machine against the USSR' – all this, he claimed, 'could slowly displace the immobile horizons of the last forty years' and give rise to 'awareness after a half century of ignorance of [our] belonging to the same continent, expressing the same civilization', thus hastening 'the hour of the true Europe, that of history and of geography'.[55] There was no doubt that the French president had a design – largely inherited from de Gaulle – to get past the Cold War, and that he was already wagering on the new Soviet leader to start to realize it.

However, Mitterrand's visit to Moscow from 7 to 10 July 1986 was more disappointing. Clearly more sceptical than the Élysée about the reality of changes in Soviet policy, the Quai d'Orsay – just after the installation of a conservative government of 'cohabitation', as we shall see – proved anxious to closely monitor the presidential trip. For French diplomacy, in fact, Moscow's intentions appeared not to have changed: Soviet diplomacy was still eager to promote the idea that détente was back for good, although the reasons that had led to its interruption – namely, Soviet aggressive behavior – had not disappeared. Moscow, the Quai thought, was, as usual, trying to weaken Western cohesion and vigilance, as illustrated by Gorbachev's offensive on disarmament that was launched on 15 January 1986, when the Soviet leader announced a plan for the elimination of nuclear weapons within fifteen years.[56] As a result, the exchanges during Mitterrand's visit were without surprise. The Soviets wanted to speak about SDI and disarmament, continued to insist on taking French nuclear weapons 'into account' in Soviet-American negotiations, and tried to convince the French to 'act together' to return East-West relations to détente. But Mitterrand stuck to French positions, particularly on the 'non-inclusion' of national forces: 'There are difficulties, divergences, and that is normal and healthy', he concluded: 'let's take realities as they are and squarely tackle them.'[57]

Yet the visit was not without consequence, coming as it did at an important juncture in East-West relations. The day after Gorbachev's speech on 15 January, Mitterrand had encouraged the American president to make a 'serious' response; then, meeting Reagan in New York a few days before leaving for Moscow in July, he had exhorted him to choose disarmament rather than the arms race, which he believed was indispensable if the Soviet leader's reform program were to be successful. Convincing the Western powers to support Gorbachev rather than to profit from Soviet difficulties was thus becoming a priority Mitterrand would never relinquish.[58] In Moscow, inversely, he tried to persuade Gorbachev to speak with Reagan: the latter, he emphasized, was not the plaything of the military industrial complex, not an 'automaton' but a 'human being' – statements that appear to have effectively contributed to erasing 'Soviet stereotypes' about the American president.[59]

In short, in the summer of 1986 Mitterrand tried to contribute to the renewal of dialogue between Soviets and Americans by playing the honest courtier: 'I say the same thing in Moscow as in New York,' he emphasized to the Soviets.[60] And not without success: the day after his meeting with Mitterrand, Gorbachev proposed meeting Reagan, which would result in the Reykjavik summit in October.[61] Thus the French president's early intuitions proved correct, and he was therefore starting to see in Gorbachevian policy something other than a mere altered façade. Even if Moscow's diplomacy continued to be marked by traditional goals, he confided to Hans-Dietrich Genscher upon his return from Moscow, the Soviet leader embodied a lasting generational change and was 'capable of unleashing an *aggiornamento*'.[62]

New Détente and its Dilemmas

Yet even while this evolution was taking place, the dynamics of French policy were paradoxically turning the other way: the search for an opening to the East desired by Mitterrand since 1984 was succeeded between

1986 and 1988 by two years of reticence over East-West relations. Domestic policy played a significant role. Deprived of his exclusive influence on foreign policy in the aftermath of the March 1986 elections as a result of cohabitation with a conservative government, Mitterrand now had to deal with a prime minister, Jacques Chirac, who chose a less forthcoming position in relations with the East and demonstrated mistrust of Gorbachev's policy.[63] At the same time, the diplomatic establishment continued to be reserved, thinking it necessary to 'soberly' judge Soviet evolution, since 'a country like the USSR cannot change from one day to the next' – a sceptical viewpoint that very much reflected the state of mind of leadership circles as well as public opinion in France in 1986 and 1987.[64] In other words, the 'Solzhenitsyn effect' in France still prevailed over the 'Gorbachev effect'. Added to this was the international context: because the two superpowers were talking again – the Reykjavik summit of 11–12 October 1986 would mark a turning point – France's intermediary role was bound to diminish.[65] In addition, while also resuming dialogue with the United States, Gorbachevian diplomacy, starting in 1987, tried ostensibly to diversify its European contacts in the direction of Italy, Great Britain, and lastly and especially, the FRG, with which relations were gradually resuming. While the 'new détente' was becoming a reality, France was now thus to a large extent marginalized in East-West relations.

The difficult trip that Chirac made to Moscow (14–16 May 1987) and his conversations with the Soviets illustrate this. Predictably, Gorbachev regretted that relations with the French 'were no longer what they had been in the time of General de Gaulle' and deplored the fact that the French were trying to 'throw spokes in his wheels' by taking hostile positions, notably over disarmament; to which Chirac replied by raising the situation in Afghanistan and Poland and by rejecting any inclusion of French nuclear forces in the arms control process.[66] To be sure, relations did not further deteriorate after the trip: the French prime minister came back from Moscow convinced of Gorbachev's sincerity and of his 'determination to reform his country', while Moscow, for its part, was now anxious to improve relations with France.[67] As for Mitterrand, he tried to maintain direct contact with the Kremlin. Informed of Soviet complaints with regard to Chirac's policy (Moscow, of course, did not hesitate to play on differences between the Elysée and Matignon), he discreetly passed messages in which he both asserted his presidential prerogatives in foreign policy and demarcated himself from the government over major East-West issues, notably disarmament.[68] Cohabitation, moreover, rapidly approached its end as a result of forthcoming presidential elections in which Mitterrand clearly intended to stand for a new term of office. The French president thus appeared increasingly determined to take the upper hand in East-

West relations and assert himself as an unreserved partisan of the 'new détente'.

Dilemmas of Disarmament

French-Soviet relations would nevertheless remain tepid until Mitterrand's actual reelection in May 1988. Disarmament problems, now at the forefront of East-West relations, largely contributed to this situation. Though the Mitterrand policy had until then maintained a line favorable to arms control, Reykjavik and cohabitation changed that. At Reykjavik, Reagan, in rallying to the Soviet objective of denuclearization and then rejecting an accord that Gorbachev made conditional on the U.S. abandonment of SDI, had committed a double fault in European eyes: the American president had indeed shown himself ready to trade off the nuclear deterrence to which the Europeans were wholeheartedly attached, and then stopped short of doing so as a result of his own attachment to 'Star Wars', a project to which the Europeans strongly objected.[69] After Reykjavik, European disquiet was confirmed: quickly, the Soviets and Americans agreed to concentrate their efforts on INF, a move that led the Russians (who then gave up linking this issue to SDI and strategic weapons) to put forth a series of disarmament proposals that were all the more difficult for the U.S. to reject because they had been formerly defended by the West: hence, having proposed in February 1987 a first zero option on LRINF (above 1,000 km in range), Gorbachev added a second one in April on SRINF (500 to 1,000 km), thereby arousing hesitation and division within the alliance. Finally achieved in the summer, Western acceptance opened the way to the Washington Treaty of December 1987, thus consecrating the 'double zero' option and therefore the complete elimination of INF – and posing the question of the remaining SNF (less than 500 km range) and therefore of a possible 'triple zero' option, which would be the big topic in 1988–1989, once again dividing the allies.

From the start, the Chirac government was reticent toward Soviet proposals, sharing if not amplifying its Western partners' objections. In their view, the series of zero options appeared merely to serve Moscow's old objective, the denuclearization of Europe; moreover, American extended deterrence would be seriously threatened by the withdrawal of the Pershings, which would involve the risk of 'decoupling' the U.S. and Europe. Finally, pressure on the French and British forces to be included in negotiations would increase despite Soviet renunciation of the prior condition of taking 'third' forces into account. These arguments were shared by experts and the French media, who rivalled each other in scepticism about Soviet proposals, considering them as traps for the West. As for public opinion in France, although increasingly sensitive to the theme of disarmament, it remained clearly more reluctant to accept the new détente than were other European countries, at least until 1987.[70] In short, government policy reflected, here again, the ambient consensus, still marked by the new Cold War of the early 1980s. True, Chirac's foreign affairs minister, Jean-Bernard Raimond, was rather moderate – in contrast to his own staff, who were vocally denouncing Moscow's intentions – but the defense minister, André Giraud, stated his serious reservations about the Soviet proposals in no uncertain terms, even labelling the acceptance by the West of the zero option as a new 'Munich'.[71]

Mitterrand's line was different. Since Reykjavik, the French president (who had welcomed Gorbachev's initiative of 15 January 1986, as we have seen), adopted a calm attitude toward the Soviet proposals.[72] He approved successively of the first and then second zero options; he then fully supported the signing of the Washington Treaty in December 1987 and played a significant role in finding a compromise between the Western countries over the SNF question during the NATO summit of 2–3 March 1988.[73] Mitterrand responded to the prevailing distrust regarding Gorbachev's designs with cold calculation: 'If Gorbachev makes such an effort', he confided to Genscher in October 1987 with reference to the forthcoming INF agreement, 'it is because he needs it'.[74] Without denying the permanence of traditional Soviet objectives, Mitterrand judged the risk of a denuclearized Europe to be negligible (even a triple zero option on SNF, he argued, would leave Europe with American nuclear bombs but also French and British weapons). He also rejected the argument that NATO strategy would be doomed by the INF agreement and its consequences. (At any rate, he proclaimed his scepticism about flexible response, of which he thought the French, who fundamentally objected to it, should certainly not become the advocates). Moreover, he thought the preoccupation with the risk of French or British weapons being taken into account in Soviet-American negotiations was excessive: 'We only have to say no', he hammered.[75] Finally and especially, he thought it unrealistic to reject an agreement that the West had originally wanted very much and thereby oppose European opinion – starting with German opinion – which only wanted a successful outcome to negotiations; and he thought it illusory to knock heads with the United States, which had manifestly now decided to conclude things with the Soviets.[76]

Thus disarmament became during 1987 a major issue in rivalry between the Élysée and Matignon, leading at the beginning of 1988 to a confrontation in the corridors of the cohabitation.[77] At this stage, the debate went beyond disarmament to bear on French security policy in general and on nuclear strategy in particular. Against the background of the presidential campaign, a Socialist president who presented himself as the trustee of the Gaullist heritage paradoxically faced a neo-Gaullist conservative prime minister whose positions were in the Atlanticist camp. Of course, the dilemmas of disarmament were not exclusively French. Whether in the United States (where the INF treaty was attacked by conservative Republicans), in the FRG (where the ruling coalition was divided) or even in Great Britain (where Thatcher was torn between her reservations and her wish to preserve the 'special relationship' with Washington), the debate on the response to give to the Gorbachev initiative set the partisans of seizing the occasion against the proponents of vigilance. Yet the French case was distinguished by a visible contradiction between the official ambition to 'get past' Yalta and reservations about arms control. At a time when disarmament had become the decisive stake in East-West relations, France, in 1988, despite Mitterrand's personal positions, paradoxically presented the image of a country hesitant to challenge the established order.

France and Germany in the New Détente

The French attitude toward the German issue in this period contributed to this perception. As seen above, the new Cold War had replaced the German question at the heart of East-West relations, and this was amply confirmed by the return of détente. Of course Gorbachev's coming to power in 1985 did not immediately change the situation. At a nadir since the Pershing deployment late in 1983, German-Soviet relations remained cool for more than a year after his nomination. Things at long last began to change in 1986, but the process was interrupted by an interview with Kohl in *Newsweek* in October, in which he awkwardly compared Gorbachev to Josef Goebbels for his art of propaganda; only when President Richard von Weizsäcker visited Moscow in July 1987 did things begin to warm up.[78] Genscher's role was preponderant in this evolution, and it was clearly accentuated as a result of his personal rivalry with Kohl – a fact that resurfaced in 1989. The German foreign minister was indeed becoming the principal advocate of détente and disarmament as well as the privileged interlocutor of the Soviets: 'You have to take Gorbachev "at his word",' he famously declared at Davos in February 1987, an expression that would stir Western chancelleries, where 'Genscherism' was perceived with increasing suspicion as the manifestation of an overly complacent policy toward Moscow.[79] As a result, with Franco-Soviet relations deteriorating, the respective situations of the FRG and France in East-West relations were reversed in comparison to earlier years, thus involving a return to the usual French questions. True, France's public opinion was hardly critical of Bonn's activism in the East, but 'in political and intellectual circles', the Quai d'Orsay noted, 'unacknowledged fears' about 'a German drift toward neutrality, if not to the East', remained vivid.[80] Position-takings to that effect proliferated throughout 1987, whence a clear contrast (an important fact later on) emerged between the serenity of the French people as a whole toward German evolutions and the often excessive disquiet among some politicians and the media about the new profile of the Federal Republic in East-West relations.[81] French diplomacy, too, harked back to 'German uncertainties'. True, the Quai d'Orsay did not want to believe in a German 'drift', but it did not hide its reservations about a policy judged increasingly inclined to concessions toward the USSR, in particular over disarmament.[82] These reservations were shared at the governmental level: while Giraud denounced Genscher's 'very dangerous Ostpolitik', Raimond emphasized the necessity of taking Gorbachev at his word *and* deed.[83] But Mitterrand, here again, played a different tune: he had nothing critical to say about the phrase used in Davos by Genscher, who was 'one of the Germans most favorable to the European Community and to France,' he objected to Giraud.[84] In fact, the president clearly showed understanding for Bonn's policy toward the East: 'The French must understand that Germany, placed between the Soviet world and France, on the border of Western Europe, is naturally led to look to the East.'[85] Still, Mitterrand was an exception here again, and his comprehension of Bonn's Eastern policy did not compensate for the reservations in governmental circles: France, seen from across the Rhine, had become in the spring of 1988 'a brake on Ostpolitik'.[86]

Does fear of a challenge to the German status quo explain French hesitation in those years, as has been sometimes suggested? One has to avoid any anachronism: if Bonn in this period was attached to defending the idea that an evolution in Soviet policy might attenuate the rigorous division of Europe, and hence of Germany, and that the German question was consequently 'not closed', the French – just like their Western partners – scarcely saw in this more than the statement of an abstract principle.[87] Aware that the USSR had entered into a phase of seducing the FRG (witness in 1987 the return of a classic theme of Soviet diplomacy, accepting the unification of Germany in exchange for its neutrality, which was the subject of rumors fed by Moscow), they also, here again rightly, judged that the Kremlin was in reality very far from envisaging a challenge to the German status quo, at least in the foreseeable future.[88] In this context, a renewal of the debate in Germany over the 'national question' scarcely brought about Franco-German difficulties. French diplomacy held to the classic line in this matter: it was 'clear that there will not be a normal situation in Europe as long as Germany is not reunified', declared the French director of political affairs to his West German homologue the day after the historic visit of Erich Honecker to the FRG at the end of 1987 (a visit long postponed due to the Soviet veto), adding that 'progress of the inter-

German dialogue diminished tension in Europe' and made it possible 'to overcome the effects of separation'.[89] The same note was being sounded at the highest level: as we have seen, Mitterrand and Kohl had discussed the problem of unification several times since 1982, and the return of the German question in West German internal debates was leading them to do so anew. Mitterrand, summarized Védrine, understood that unification 'was at the center of Bonn leaders' thinking', and he 'was going along with this slow movement' – although without imagining that 'he would actually see its result'.[90] Yet things did not go much beyond this rather passive understanding. One finds in this period scarcely any expression of *active* French support for the long-term objective of German unification.[91] Mitterrand's statements on the German question were limited to cautious responses to German journalists: 'I think that the Germans must possess the right to settle their own destiny, though I remain mindful that the conditions of pacific development of this process must be respected', he declared on the eve of his state visit to the FRG in October 1987.[92] The division of Germany 'is a separation of circumstance', he said a few months later, adding: 'I wish that one day the Europe of Yalta can be left behind, but as the process must be both peaceful and democratic, this will require time, patience, and tenacity.'[93] Gradually taking shape was the discourse that he would offer during the 1989 events by emphasizing both the principles of self-determination and the need to maintain European stability.

For the French as for their Western partners, the German question, at the end of the 1980s, thus remained that of the FRG's anchoring to the West, not that of unification. As a result – as had been the case during the Euro-missile confrontation – there was a renewed thrust of cooperation between the two countries, which the French, against the backdrop of the changing East-West environment and of the FRG's increasing international assertiveness, saw as *the* response to this challenge. Cohabitation in France in fact functioned to the advantage of Franco-German rapprochement, whose importance, with the INF issue in the background, was a subject of consensus among the French political elite. Hence there was substantial progress after 1987 in the political and strategic cooperation between Paris and Bonn, which would lead to the key creation of a Franco-German council on defense and security on the occasion of the twenty-fifth anniversary of the Élysée Treaty in January 1988.[94] At the same time, Paris and Bonn were aware of the risks of being split over how to react to Gorbachev and tried to bring their viewpoints closer together. In the spring of 1987, the Chancellery proposed a 'common diplomatic action' to the Élysée that would take the form of a meeting of Kohl and Mitterrand with Gorbachev, and in the autumn the Auswärtiges Amt suggested to the Quai d'Orsay the undertaking of a joint review of policy toward the USSR. In fact, the protocol adopted on the occasion of the twenty-fifth anniversary of the Élysée Treaty included increased cooperation on Eastern policy, and in the following months a working group of the two foreign affairs ministries was effectively set up on this topic.[95] Finally and above all, there was a common desire to intensify European construction. The European Community, at the end of the first Mitterrand presidency, had clearly become the French solution to the German 'problem': 'There is only European construction', said Mitterrand in February 1987. '[I]f not, Germany will play between East and West.'[96] Of course, at the time of Mitterrand's reelection in May 1988, Franco-German harmony could not be definitively taken for granted. With the acceleration of East-West changes, as we shall see, the succeeding months would demonstrate the limits of cooperation and collaboration with respect to Eastern policy, as well as the difficulties of the European project. Still, the relationship between France and Germany now represented the major axis of French foreign policy against the backdrop of a Cold War that was winding down, and European construction had become the central element of Mitterrand's vision of getting beyond Yalta. This would be amply confirmed by the events of 1988–1989.

Notes

1. NATO's dual track decision included (a) the proposal to negotiate with the USSR on intermediary nuclear forces and (b) the deployment of U.S. Pershing II and Cruise missiles in Europe in case the negotiations failed. It resulted from a compromise between the German preference to negotiate and the American one to deploy. The French president had contributed to this compromise at the Guadeloupe summit (United States, France, Great Britain, FRG) held on his initiative in January 1979: see Valéry Giscard d'Estaing, *Le Pouvoir et la vie*, vol. 2, 'L'affrontement' (Paris: Compagnie 12, 1991), p. 263ff.
2. The idea of a meeting with Brezhnev seems to have come from Giscard's assumption that the Soviet leaders might soon look for an 'exit door' in Afghanistan. True, in Warsaw Giscard did not indulge in appeasement diplomacy with Brezhnev; but a few weeks later during a G-7 summit in Venice he would make the imprudent announcement of a future partial withdrawal of the Soviet Army, which then allowed Mitterrand to famously portray Giscard as Brezhnev's 'little telegraphist'. See Henri Froment-Meurice, *Vu du Quai. Mémoires 1945–1983* (Paris: Fayard, 1998), p. 560ff. (The author was then France's Ambassador in Moscow).
3. Press conference held on 27 January 1981, quoted by Froment-Meurice, *Vu du Quai*, p. 580.
4. See Froment-Meurice, *Vu du Quai*, p. 559.
5. On all of this, see Pierre Grosser, 'Serrer le jeu sans le fermer. L'Elysée et les relations franco-soviétiques, 1981–1984', in Serge Berstein, Pierre Milza, and Jean-Louis Bianco eds., *François Mitterrand. Les Années du changement, 1981–1984* (Paris: Perrin, 2001).

6. In the words of Hubert Védrine, *Les Mondes de François Mitterrand. À l'Élysée 1981–1995* (Paris: Fayard, 1996), p. 93.
7. An exposition of this new line may be found in MRE, sous-direction d'Europe orientale, note a.s. Les relations franco-soviétiques en 1981, 1 December 1981, Archives nationales (AN), 5AG4/11385.
8. Note de Jean-Marie Mérillon, sommet de Bonn, 1 June 1982, AN, 5AG4/2627; about all this, see Frédéric Bozo, 'La France, fille aînée de l'Alliance? La politique atlantique de François Mitterrand 1981–1984', in Berstein et al., *François Mitterrand*.
9. Védrine, *Les Mondes*, p. 102ff. Was Mitterrand, thanks to the hardening in regards to the USSR, seeking to clear his name from the designation of communist ministers in June 1981? This factor likely played but a limited role, even if the president did try to reassure American representatives about this: see Pierre Favier and Michel Martin-Roland, *La Décennie Mitterrand*, vol. 1, 'Les Ruptures' (1981–1984) (Paris: Seuil, 1990), p. 241.
10. It was the 'method' of Giscard's policy, not its orientation, that Mitterrand denounced; see Védrine, *Les Mondes*, p. 110. Indeed, whether concerning the dual track decision (which Giscard, as seen above, had contributed to formulating) or Afghanistan (on which the former president had taken a tough stand in Warsaw), there was no real break with respect to the principles of France's position.
11. Meeting between Mitterrand and Schmidt, Latché, 7 October 1981, private papers.
12. Mitterrand's reservations with respect to the 'zero option' were not a matter of principle (as early as 1979 he had supported the formula 'neither Pershing nor SS20', and he would support it again in 1987) but of circumstance: within the context of 1981–1983, he thought it unacceptable for the Soviets since it would lead them to dismantle their SS20s whereas the Americans would not have to concede a withdrawal because the Pershing and Cruise missiles had not yet been deployed (in his January 1983 Bundestag speech, he supported the deployment of U.S. missiles, but he also made clear that 'the level of [this] deployment' should depend on the result of the Geneva negotiation).
13. Védrine, note a.s. Relations Franco- et euro-américaines, 28 July 1982, AN, 5AG4/11437.
14. On all this, Froment-Meurice, *Vu du Quai*, p. 603ff. (The author was then the ambassador in Bonn).
15. Meeting between Mitterrand and Schmidt, Latché, 7 October 1981.
16. Meeting between Mitterrand and Kohl, Bad-Kreuznach, 30 October 1984, private papers. (The Chancellor agreed, adding that unification would become a 'relative problem' thanks to Franco-German cooperation.)
17. I disagree on this point with Tilo Schabert's analysis: see Tilo Schabert, *Wie Weltgeschichte gemacht wird. Frankreich und die deutsche Einheit* (Stuttgart: Klett-Cotta, 2002), p. 125. If at that time the question of German unity had been on the agenda for Mitterrand, as Schabert affirms, it would have given rise to more frequent and substantial exchanges between French and Germans as well as to public declarations, which was not the case. (Some, like Froment-Meurice, deplored it, judging that French leaders did not understand, in this critical period, the importance that a solemn expression of French support for the goal of German unity would have for Germany and Franco-German relations. The Bundestag speech, in which he had suggested such a stand without being heard in the Elysée, constituted in his eyes a missed opportunity that, according to him, would weigh negatively in 1989: cf. Froment-Meurice, *Vu du Quai*, pp. 660–662).
18. Froment-Meurice, *Vu du Quai*, p. 659.
19. Meeting between Mitterrand and Schmidt, Latché, 7 October 1981.
20. Pierre Morel, note pour Jean-Louis Bianco, Discours au Bundestag: Nécessité et modalités d'une grande initiative, 17 January 1983, AN, 5AG4/6523.

21. See Hélène Miard-Delacroix, 'Les relations franco-allemandes', in Berstein et al., *François Mitterrand*, p. 304.
22. See MRE, Sous-direction d'Europe orientale, note, a.s. Les relations inter-allemandes, 6 October 1982; note a.s. Est-Ouest, 13 October 1982; and Sous-direction des affaires stratégiques et des pactes, note a.s. Sommet franco-allemand. Questions stratégiques, 8 octobre 1982, AN, 5AG4/2627.
23. Morel, note, Discours au Bundestag, 17 January 1983. Transcript of the speech in *Politique étrangère de la France* (PEF), January–February 1983, pp. 41–47.
24. Védrine, note pour le président de la République, Perspectives des relations Est-Ouest en 1984, après le début du déploiement. Rôle de la France, 1 December 1983, AN, 5AG4/4066.
25. Morel, note, Discours au Bundestag, 17 January 1983.
26. Meeting between Mitterrand and Schmidt, Latché, 7 October 1981. (The Elysée did not exclude a "Finlandisation" of the people's democracies that would take the form of desovietized regimes but without ending the geopolitical control of the USSR: see handwritten note from Jean-Michel Gaillard for Hubert Védrine, AN, 5AG4/11385; on all this, see Grosser, 'Serrer le jeu'.)
27. Meetings between Mitterrand and Reagan, the White House, 22–23 March 1984, I. Thursday 22 March Meeting, private papers.
28. TD Diplomatie 11089, DSL, 17 March 1982, AN, 5AG4/2317.
29. Mitterrand's New Year Address, 31 December 1981, *PEF*, November-December 1981, p. 85.
30. MRE, note de la direction d'Europe, La CSCE et la réunion de Madrid, 29 September 1982, AN, 5AG4/2627.
31. *Le Monde*, 26 November1982; see also letter from Mitterrand to Reagan, 20 November 1982, AN, 5AG4/11437.
32. MRE, note du directeur des affaires politiques, Relations Est-Ouest, 26 May 1983, AN, 5AG4/4329.
33. Meeting between Mitterrand and Thatcher, London, 20 October 1983, private papers.
34. Jean-Louis Gergorin and Bernard Dorin, note, Relations franco-américaines: éléments pour l'étape de Washington du voyage présidentiel (no date, March 1984), AN, 5AG4/11441; see also Védrine, *Les Mondes*, p. 251ff.
35. Meetings between Mitterrand and Reagan, the White House, Washington, 22 and 23 March, 22 March meeting, private papers.
36. MAE, Centre d'analyse et de prévision, Note a.s. Caractères du dialogue franco-soviétique au sommet (1966–1980), 16 mai 1984, secret, MAE, archives diplomatiques (AD), Europe, URSS 1981–1985, box 5694.
37. Mitterrand, he writes, certainly did not reject the century-old tradition of the Franco-Russian entente, but this factor, though it remained 'latent', was for him neither a 'priority' nor 'essential' any longer: Védrine, *Les Mondes*, pp. 373–374.
38. On the June 1984 visit to the USSR, see Grosser, 'Serrer le jeu'.
39. See transcripts of the conversations in TD Moscow 1555, 1562–1563 and 1569, DSL, 21, 22 and 23 June 1984, meeting between Mitterrand and Constantine Chernenko, Moscow, 21 June 1984; and French Embassy in Moscow, meeting between Mitterrand and Andrei Gromyko on 22 June 1984, 23 June 1984, secret, private papers.
40. Meeting between Mitterrand and Henry Kissinger, 28 June 1984, private papers.
41. Védrine, note pour le président de la République, 27 February 1985, private papers; see also Jean-Bernard Raimond, *Le Quai d'Orsay à l'épreuve de la cohabitation* (Paris: Flammarion, 1989), p. 26ff. (Raimond was then the ambassador to Moscow.)

42. One detects a real impatience with the approaching contact, which Mitterrand's aides predicted would be 'all the more interesting because the USSR is going to come out with [Gorbachev] of the immobilization that was theirs for five or six years'; see Védrine, note pour le président de la République, a.s. Obsèques de M. Tchernenko, 11 and 12 March 1985, private papers; and Védrine, *Les Mondes*, p. 369ff. (During his meeting with Mitterrand, Gorbachev spoke without a prepared text, and with skill, authority, and a sense of repartee; see TD Moscow 761 and 762, 14 March 1985, private papers; cf. also Raimond, *Le Quai d'Orsay*, p. 30.)
43. Conseil des ministres, 14 March 1985, private papers.
44. Letter from Mitterrand to Reagan, 12 October 1985, private papers
45. Interview to *Globe*, March 1986, quoted in Védrine, *Les Mondes*, p. 380.
46. On all this, cf. Favier and Martin-Roland, *La Décennie*, vol. 2, "Les Épreuves", 1984-1988, Paris, Seuil, 1991, p. 234ff; Védrine, *Les Mondes*, p. 352ff.
47. Védrine, note a.s Funérailles de M. Tchernenko, 12 March 1985.
48. On these aspects, see Urs Leimbacher, *Die unverzichtbare Allianz. Deutsch-französische sicherheitspolitische Zusammenarbeit 1982–1989* (Baden-Baden: Nomos, 1992), and Georges-Henri Soutou, *L'alliance incertaine. Les rapports politico-stratégiques franco-allemands, 1954–1996* (Paris: Fayard, 1996).
49. On this, see Favier and Martin-Roland, *La Décennie*, vol. 2, pp. 200–218.
50. TD Moscow 761 and 762, 14 March 1985; Conseil des ministres, 14 March 1985; and letter from Gorbachev to Mitterrand, 30 April 1985, private papers.
51. MRE, Le directeur des affaires politiques, Pierre Morel, note pour M. Védrine, 4 October 1985, private papers.
52. Meeting between Mitterrand and Gorbachev, Paris, 2 October 1985; Meeting between Mitterrand and Gorbachev, 3 October 1985; Meeting between Mitterrand and Gorbachev, Friday 4 October 1985, private papers.
53. Concerning the 'German problem', Mitterrand declared himself 'divided': 'On one hand, I don't desire anything else than to get along fraternally with the Germans', but 'on the other hand, I cannot desire the reconstitution of a dominant pole in the center of Europe', he conceded, meanwhile highlighting that France and Russia had been 'almost continuously allies and friends' and that 'history and geography dictate constants to us'. If one detects here echoes of the old theme of the *'alliance de revers'*, this was but a residual factor in Mitterrand's policy toward the USSR – as a matter of fact, until the summer of 1989 the German question would remain almost absent from the Franco-Soviet dialogue. In the context of the fall of 1985, one can rather interpret these words as expressing some kind of reassurance for Gorbachev, whose worries about the intensification of Franco-German strategic cooperation Mitterrand was trying to ease. It is in any case not justified to affirm that Mitterrand then 'hinted that he was for maintaining the division of Germany'; see Soutou, *L'Alliance*, p. 385.
54. On Gorbachev's diplomacy and Western Europe, see Marie-Pierre Rey, 'Europe Is Our Common Home: A Study of Gorbachev's Diplomatic Concept', *Cold War History* 4(2) (January 2004): 33–65.
55. François Mitterrand, *Réflexions sur la politique étrangère de la France* (Paris: Fayard, 1986).
56. MAE, dossier de synthèse, visite du président de la République en URSS, (no date, June 1986), AD, Europe, URSS 1986–1990, box 6677. It was necessary, the Quai thought, to be all the more wary because the presidential visit coincided with the twentieth anniversary of de Gaulle's, which Moscow would seek no doubt to use: MAE, sous-direction d'Europe orientale, note pour le ministre, 20ème anniversaire de la visite en URSS du

général de Gaulle (20 juin–1er juillet 1966), 20 May 1986, AD, Europe, URSS 1986–1990, box 6670.
57. Meeting between Mitterrand and Gorbachev, 9 July 1986, AD, Europe, URSS 1986–1990, carton 6684.
58. Letter from Mitterrand to Reagan, 28 February 1986, private papers. In New York, Mitterrand asked Reagan: 'Should we ... help [Gorbachev] make economic reforms a success by making military concessions [to him]? Or, on the contrary, should we allow him to become further embroiled by forcing him to reduce civilian spending?' – an allusion to the notion that U.S. leaders might want to use SDI to lead Gorbachev into an arms race that would end up bringing the USSR to its knees; see the transcript of the meeting in Védrine, *Les Mondes*, p. 381.
59. Mitterrand's visit was looked on as a 'major event' in Moscow: cf. Anatoly S. Chernyaev, *My Six Years with Gorbachev* (University Park: Pennsylvania University Press, 2000), pp. 75–76.
60. Meeting between Mitterrand and Gromyko, 8 July 1986, AD, Europe, URSS 1986–1990, box 6676.
61. Back from Moscow, Mitterrand had written to Reagan to convince him of the dispositions of the Soviets: 'For economic, personal, and political reasons', he emphasized, Gorbachev 'is truly interested in coming to an agreement with you': letter from 31 July 1986, private papers.
62. Meeting between Mitterrand and Genscher, 18 July 1986, private papers.
63. On the impact of *cohabitation* in foreign policy, see Frédéric Bozo, *La Politique étrangère de la France depuis 1945* (Paris: La Découverte, 1997), pp. 90–93.
64. MAE, note du chef adjoint du CAP, a.s. Quel langage tenir à Moscou ? Éléments de réflexion, 22 April 1987, AD, Europe, URSS 1986–1990, box 6678.
65. It is effectively after Reykjavik that a 'downturn' occurred in Franco-Soviet relations: cf. Mikhaïl Gorbatchev, *Mémoires* (Monaco: Éditions du Rocher, 1997), p. 542.
66. See TD Moscow 1830–1832, DSL, secret, 19 May 1987, AD, Europe, URSS 1986–1990, box 6678. Gorbachev keeps the memory of 'a frank explanation with Chirac': *Mémoires*, p. 543.
67. Letters from Chirac to Reagan and Thatcher, 26 May 1987, private papers; MAE, note de la sous-direction d'Europe orientale, a.s Entretiens avec M. Ligatchev, 25 November 1987; and note à l'intention du Premier ministre, a.s Compte-rendu de la visite Ligatchev (no date, early December 1987), AD, Europe, URSS 1986–1990, box 6684.
68. Meeting between Mitterrand and Soviet Ambassador Riabov, 19 December 1986; and meeting between Mitterrand and Yuli Vorontsov, 7 March 1987, private papers.
69. The Quai d'Orsay considered the Reykjavik 'slip up' to be 'very preoccupying': see MAE, Service des affaires stratégiques et du désarmement, note a.s. Reykjavik: premières leçons politiques, 16 October 1986, AD, Directeur politique (DP), box 263.
70. MAE, CAP, note, a.s. L'opinion française, l'URSS et l'option zéro, 9 July 1987, AD, Europe, URSS 1986–1990, box 6670.
71. Conseil des ministres, 4 March 1987, private papers. The same André Giraud stated several weeks later that the double zero option 'would be the final stage of Finlandisation': Conseil des ministres, 28 April 1987, private papers. (In the Quai d'Orsay, the influence of Deputy Director for Political Affairs Benoît d'Aboville was then considerable in the disarmament issue. D'Aboville counselled 'vigilance' facing proposals from Moscow: see for example MAE, le directeur adjoint des affaires politiques, note pour le ministre, a.s. L'après Reykjavik et la sécurité de l'Europe, 26 October 1986, AD, DP, box 263.)
72. See handwritten note from Mitterrand for Védrine, 15 October 1986; and handwritten note from Mitterrand on a note from Védrine, 27 April 1987, private papers.

73. While Thatcher, supported by Chirac, hoped for a firm decision to modernize short-range missiles to mark a stop to the zero options, Mitterrand supported Kohl, who considered such a decision premature and wanted to leave the possibility open to negotiation on SNF. Compromise was reached at the summit around the notion, defended by the French, that SNF modernization (as well as a future negotiation) should depend on the effective progress of conventional disarmament: see Védrine, note pour le président de la République, a.s. conclusions du sommet de l'OTAN des 2 et 3 mars derniers, 15 April 1988, private papers; or MAE, sous-direction des affaires stratégiques et des Pactes, Fiche, La RFA et la question des SNF, 24 juin 1988, AD, Affaires stratégiques et désarmement (ASD), 1985–1990, box 14.
74. Meeting between Mitterrand and Genscher, 20 October 1987, private papers.
75. Meeting between Mitterrand and Thatcher, Bénouville (Calvados), Monday 23 March 1987, private papers.
76. Conseil des ministres, 4 March 1987; note de Hubert Védrine pour le président de la République, a.s. Remarques sur les négociations americano-soviétiques, 9 April 1987, private papers.
77. The two men had a heated exchange after a Mitterrand statement contesting the urgency of SNF modernization, a position disapproved of by Chirac: see letter from Chirac to Mitterrand, 29 February 1988, and letter from Mitterrand to Chirac, 29 February 1988, private papers.
78. MAE, sous-direction d'Europe orientale, Les relations germano-soviétiques après la visite du président von Weizsäcker à Moscou, 21 July 1987, AD, Europe, RFA 1986–1990, box 6770.
79. The word 'Genscherism' was coined by the journalist John Vinocur; see Christian Hacke, *Die Außenpolitik der Bundesrepublik Deutschland. Weltmacht wider Willen?* (Berlin: Ullstein Buchverlag, 1997), p. 312ff. and p. 352.
80. MAE, sous-direction d'Europe orientale, note pour le Ministre, Situation des relations franco-allemandes, 26 March 1986, AD, Europe, RFA 1986–1990, box 6776.
81. See Jean Hohwart, *Nécessités franco-allemandes et défense en Europe* (Paris: FEDN, 1988); see also Ingo Kolboom, *Vom geteilten Deutschland zum Vereinten Deutschland. Deutschland-Bilder in Frankreich* (Bonn: DGAP, Arbeitspapiere zur internationalen Politik, n° 61, April 1991), and 'L'histoire et l'avenir des politiques respectives à l'égard des pays de l'Est', in André Brigot et al., eds., *Défense, désarmement et politiques à l'Est. Perspectives franco-allemandes* (Paris: FEDN, 1988).
82. MAE, notes de la sous-direction d'Europe orientale, L'Union soviétique, la RFA et la relation franco-allemande, 17 February 1987; Développements des relations de l'URSS et de la RFA, 26 March 1987; L'état des relations germano-soviétiques après la visite du président von Weizsäcker à Moscou, 21 July 1987; and L'attitude de l'URSS à l'égard de la RFA, 8 October 1987, AD, Europe, RFA, 1986–1990, box 6770.
83. Conseil des ministres, 16 February 1987, private papers; see Jean-Bernard Raimond, 'Le fait et le mot', *Politique internationale* (spring 1987): 21–39.
84. Meeting between Mitterrand and Genscher, 6 February 1987, private papers; Conseil des ministres, 16 February 1987.
85. Interview granted to *Die Welt*, 18 January 1988, *PEF*, January–February 1988, p. 32; see also Meeting between Mitterand and Kohl, Chambord, 28 March 1987; Conseil des ministres, 22 April 1987; and Meeting between Mitterrand and Genscher, 20 October 1987, private papers.
86. Kolboom, 'L'histoire et l'avenir', 129.
87. Von Weizsäcker having emphasized in Moscow in July 1987 that the long-term goal of the FRG was still unification, the French observed that Gorbachev had stuck to the

official line in response: the German question, Gorbachev said, had been settled by history. True, the Soviet Number One had admitted that what would happen in the next hundred years could not be predicted, and this remark was interpreted by the Germans as the sign of a new opening, but the French were sceptical: see TD Bonn 1417, 15 July 1987, Europe, RFA 1986–1990, box 6770. Soviet leadership was then, in effect, very far from envisioning German unity: see on this Hannes Adomeit, *Imperial Overstretch: Germany in Soviet Policy from Stalin to Gorbachev* (Baden-Baden: Nomos, 1998), p. 215ff.

88. MAE, note de la sous-direction d'Europe orientale, L'attitude de l'URSS à l'égard de la RFA, 7 October 1987. Mitterrand highlighted as early as the month of May that such a proposal – unity versus neutrality – could be expected, because 'it would be surprising that the Soviet Union didn't play with this determining element of German policy': Conseil des ministres, 13 May 1987, private papers.
89. MAE, Direction d'Europe, compte rendu de la réunion des directeurs français et allemands à Bonn le 1er octobre, 5 October 1987, AD, Europe, RFA 1986–1990, box 6795.
90. Védrine, *Les Mondes*, p. 406.
91. Just as in 1983 (see above, note 17) though in a different context, the year 1987 could have provided opportunities for such a position to be taken, starting with Mitterrand's state visit in the FRG in October. The visit, it was suggested by the Quai d'Orsay, 'could be an opportunity to recall the importance that we give to the necessity to overcome the division of Europe and notably Germany', but this idea was barely taken up at the Elysée, where the priorities, as far as Franco-German relations were concerned, dealt far more with defense and Europe, which in effect would be the major themes of the president's speeches during his visit: see MAE, note de la sous-direction d'Europe orientale, L'attitude de l'URSS à l'égard de la RFA, 8 October 1987; and Jean-Louis Bianco, note pour M. le Président, a.s. Votre visite d'État en République fédérale d'Allemagne, 7 September 1987, private papers.
92. Interview granted to the German TV channel ZDF, 16 October 1987, private papers.
93. Interview granted to the German newspaper *Die Welt*, PEF, January–February 1988, p. 32.
94. In September 1987, the decision to create a Franco-German brigade was announced on the occasion of the Franco-German large-scale military maneuver 'Moineau hardi/ Kecker Spatz'. On all this, see Leimbacher, *Die unverzichtbare Allianz*, p. 136ff.; Schabert, *Wie Weltgeschichte gemacht wird*, p. 224ff.; and Soutou, *L'Alliance incertaine*, p. 391ff.
95. J. Attali, note pour le président, déjeuner avec M.Telschik (*sic*) à Bonn le 7 avril, 8 April 1987, private papers; TD DFRA New York 1431, 21 September 1987; MAE, Sous-direction d'Europe orientale, note a.s. Entretien du Ministre avec M. Genscher (22 janvier). Politique à l'Est et coopération franco-allemande, 20 January 1988; and Note a.s. La RFA, la France et la politique à l'Est, 18 mai 1988, AD, Europe, RFA 1986–1990, box 6782.
96. Conseil des ministres, 11 February 1987, private papers.

Chapter 1

THE END OF 'YALTA'
(Spring 1988 to Summer 1989)

Even if contemporaries were not aware of it, the year 1988–1989 was the last chapter in the Cold War and the prelude to the events of autumn 1989. The evolution of Soviet policy was of course the decisive factor: while the dominant interpretation until then was that Gorbachev's policies were continuous with Moscow's traditional objectives, it was no longer possible after the spring or summer of 1988 to ignore the breadth of the change. By then, the 'new thinking' had resulted in a thorough ideological revision that translated into a profound transformation of Soviet foreign policy. While previously the reality of the 'new détente' was a topic of speculation, this term was outmoded by the end of 1988. The new tone of Soviet diplomacy, the new direction in Moscow's disarmament policy and, more spectacularly, the evolution of the situation in Eastern Europe would all lead in the following months to a questioning of the division of Europe inherited from the Cold War. While nobody could foresee the breadth or rapidity of the upheavals of the autumn, the end of the bipolar confrontation had become a certainty by the spring of 1989.

How did French diplomacy react to these events? Reelected in May 1988 after two years of 'cohabitation' with a prime minister of the opposition party, François Mitterrand began his second mandate with major advantages in the realm of foreign policy. Over the years, he had asserted himself as the guardian of the Gaullist heritage and – more than in 1981 –

Notes for this section begin on page 69.

he now incarnated a national consensus on France's role in the world. He was again in control of all the instruments of diplomacy, and he could take advantage of his expertise and the international status recognized by his peers. Mitterrand's priority was to close the two-year parenthesis during which France had held back from any initiatives in East-West relations. While French diplomacy during cohabitation had shown reservations about the new course of Soviet policy to the point of appearing as a guardian of the status quo, he was now determined to reassume a leading role. Hence, from the autumn of 1988 to the spring of 1989, there occurred a relaunch of Franco-Soviet relations and especially of French policy toward the East that included a presidential tour of Eastern European capitals. At the same time, new French positions on disarmament, formerly marked by serious reservations, now helped redynamize East-West negotiations, playing a significant role in the turn taken in the spring of 1989 by the Bush administration, which was initially wary of Gorbachev. In parallel, French diplomacy was keen to hasten Franco-German rapprochement and West European integration, the major business of which was becoming the project for an economic and monetary union (EMU). Against the backdrop of a crumbling bloc system, the acceleration of European construction appeared increasingly to be the French route to moving beyond the established order. Overall, a year after Mitterrand's reelection, French diplomacy seemed to have renewed its ambition to exit 'Yalta'; in any case, it was in this state of mind that French leaders would tackle the decisive events of the second half of 1989.

Paris-Moscow: A New Departure?

Aware of the considerable changes that had occurred in Moscow over the past two years, the reelected president aimed to catch up and make the Paris-Moscow axis a priority of French diplomacy again. While the impulse came from the Élysée, it was up to the Quai d'Orsay – where Roland Dumas returned in the spring of 1988 – to put it into operation. The tone at the Quai clearly changed after the presidential election: 'At the moment when the USSR is opening up more,' French diplomats thought they should drop their 'wait-and-see' policy and 'develop our relations with the USSR so as not to let ourselves be marginalized'.[1] As an ambitious program to reactivate French diplomacy to the East was being elaborated, the reestablishment of a 'substantial and diversified Franco-Soviet dialogue' seemed a precondition.[2] Past reservations were no longer in order: the perceived risk was no longer being entrained by Moscow into a return to the 'specific and privileged relations' of the détente period, but rather that bilateral relations might become 'banal'. In short, even if the Quai d'Orsay could still not be suspected of 'Gorby-mania', the bottom line was that the moment had come to 'vigorously' relaunch relations with Moscow.[3]

The Soviets were also asking for a strengthening of ties. Some weeks after the election, Shevardnadze divulged to Dumas that Moscow very much wanted France to be involved 'fully' in the East-West dialogue, in which Paris was seen as the partner of choice.[4] They did not hide their principal goal: at a time when the USSR was becoming aware of the importance of European integration, they wanted to establish a dialogue with Western Europe through France as the designated privileged interlocutor, a message that even became 'particularly insistent' at the end of the summer of 1988.[5] The two ministers met in New York at the end of September, but the coming of Shevardnadze to Paris at the start of October clearly marked an important stage, and so there was intense preparation on the French side.[6] As the first official visit of a Soviet foreign affairs minister since 1980, this confirmed in French eyes 'the Soviet interest in a rapid and strong relaunch of our relations' as well as the 'priority that the USSR presently intends to give to Europe'.[7] Welcomed at the Élysée, the Soviet minister insisted on the need for a 'more active dialogue' after two years of immobility. Mitterrand agreed to go to the USSR the following month to attend the Franco-Soviet space launch at Baikonur, and he invited Gorbachev to return to France in 1989. At the Quai d'Orsay the talk was of a 'new departure' in Franco-Soviet relations.[8]

The relaunch of Franco-Soviet relations took place against the background of rapid transformations in the USSR. The summer and fall of 1988 were indeed a decisive stage in *perestroika*. The 19th CPSU Conference at the end of June led to the consolidation of the party leadership as well as a series of major political decisions, including a reduction of the tutelage of the party over the state, the establishment of parliamentary institutions, and the principle of multiple candidacies. At the end of September, Gorbachev imposed the retirement of conservatives (like Gromyko) and the promotion of reformers (in the forefront, Alexander Yakovlev, now in effect number two of the CPSU), thereby considerably increasing his power in the party apparatus. This internal evolution henceforward resulted in considerable changes in the USSR's international policy. In the autumn of 1988, French diplomacy noted that the USSR had renounced a 'messianic' foreign policy founded on class struggle transposed to international relations, in favor of a conception aimed at 'realizing interests common to all humanity'.[9] Gorbachev's speech to the UN on 7 December – in which, as we shall see, he announced important decisions about disarmament – confirmed this change. The Quai d'Orsay considered the Soviet Number One to have understood the need to redefine the international role of his country 'by moving away from its revolutionary inspiration'.[10] Yet the evolution of Soviet policy after mid 1988 was not merely theoretical. On points formerly posing obstacles to resuming dialogue, the change throughout the year was becoming increasingly perceptible. The withdrawal of forces from Afghanistan, begun in the spring (it would end in February 1989), was a major factor: because it had been a precondition for a return to normal East-West relations, Paris could now improve relations with the Soviet Union without having to contradict itself.[11] And because human rights had been another French requirement (Mitterrand, we recall, had brought up the Sakharov case at the Kremlin in June 1984), the relative improvement in the situation in the USSR also permitted a resumption of dialogue with more equanimity.[12] These changes in Soviet attitudes, in turn, contributed to further changes in Mitterrand's estimation of the situation. The French president had confided to Reagan as recently as June 1988 that the Soviet leader, while having 'made the choice for peace', remained the 'product of a system'.[13] But after the autumn, he went much farther: he now thought it was possible 'for the system to soften and (why not?) to democratize itself'.[14]

November 1988: Mitterrand in Moscow

Still, Mitterrand's evaluation of the change in the USSR remained markedly ahead of the dominant viewpoint in France. French public opinion's reservations were not entirely dissipated, in particular over the human rights issue, and so the decision was taken to organize a meeting with representatives of the 'new dissidence' during Mitterrand's visit to Moscow.[15] There also remained a gap between the Élysée and the Quai d'Orsay: whereas Dumas was in unison with Mitterrand, members of his staff were still far from having overcome their reservations. In October 1988, the director of political affairs, Bertrand Dufourcq, thought that 'one must be careful that public opinion in our countries not be dazzled by the Gorbachev mirage'.[16] The same tone transpired in the analyses of the French Embassy in Moscow. Of course Gorbachev had undertaken a vast transformation of the USSR, but the results remained 'largely reversible', and while his foreign policy was able to replace intimidation with seduction, the 'traditional designs of Soviet diplomacy' were still 'valid' (although in a revised form): decoupling Europe from the U.S., denuclearization, opposition to a political Europe, a quest for a system of pan-European security dominated by Moscow, etc.[17] In short, the theory and means might have changed, but the old objectives and policies remained – this , at least, was still the Quai d'Orsay's interpretation at the end of 1988 (an interpretation that, as a matter of fact, was rather close to that of other Western diplomacies, with the growing exception of West Germany).

In this context, French diplomats struggled to give substance to a new meeting between Mitterrand and Gorbachev, which mainly appeared as the occasion to formally consecrate the bilateral initiative.[18] The Moscow meetings on 25 and 26 November, which were rather brief, confirmed this. They marked a renewal of ties after two and a half years: the two heads of state congratulated each other on the quality of their exchanges and agreed on the principle of regular annual summit meetings and biannual foreign ministers' meetings.[19] However, the visit was not the success the French had hoped for. The conversations showed the limits of the Franco-Soviet rapprochement. On disarmament, Mitterrand called Gorbachev's goal of a denuclearized world 'romantic', reiterated the traditional French position, and emphasized the priority of conventional arms reduction only. On the European 'common home' (a goal that he said he shared) he refused to 'hide the difficulties'. Finally, on human rights, he made the conference that Moscow wanted to host on this subject in the CSCE framework contingent on improvement on that score within the USSR.[20] And so it was difficult to hide a certain disappointment, especially in comparison to Kohl's visit a few weeks earlier, which was perceived in Paris as a 'turning point' in German-Soviet relations.[21] The disappointment was discernible between the lines in the press statement distributed by the Élysée a few days after the visit. No, it was argued, Paris was not lagging behind the United States or the FRG in relations with the USSR, for France represented an 'imperative' partner for the USSR; she was simply not easily manipulated by Moscow, for 'both public opinion and the French government were resisting with a certain scepticism the discourse on denuclearization' and they 'were not subject to the "Gorby-mania" observed in Germany'.[22] Clearly, despite Mitterrand's goodwill, relations between Paris and Moscow at the end of 1988 remained marked by the perceptions of the preceding period.[23]

July 1989: Gorbachev in Paris

When the Soviet leader arrived in France seven months later, the context had totally changed. The events of that spring, the acceleration of the democratic transition in Eastern Europe and a new Western initiative on disarmament, to which we shall return, left no doubt about Moscow's acceptance of an overhaul of the 'system' and the capacity of the West to respond to the Gorbachev 'challenge'. True, attitudes were not homogeneous in all capitals. Succeeding Reagan, whose second term had ended in the euphoria of détente, George H. W. Bush wanted to mark a 'pause' in relations with the USSR when he arrived in the White House in January and called for a thorough review of U.S. policy, which concluded that prudence was in order. Even if, as will be seen, it took a more positive attitude toward disarmament in the spring of 1989, the new American administration remained reserved about Gorbachev. By contrast, the FRG was now leading the rapprochement with Moscow, as shown by the Soviet leader's visit to Bonn in mid June 1989.

As France prepared in turn to welcome Gorbachev at the start of July 1989, French diplomacy occupied a position midway between American reserve and German enthusiasm. Against the background of substantial transformation in East-West relations, Paris wanted a balanced but dynamic approach to relations with the USSR. Gorbachev's visit to France (4 to 6 July) came at a key moment: former Western distrust toward the USSR was being replaced by Western disquiet. Worries were now concentrated on the issue of Gorbachev's chances of success. This gave rise to contrasting analyses: some pointed to Gorbachev's personal strength, while others pointed to the fragility of the domestic situation (the problem of nationalities, the gap between political reform and economic stagnation and the rise in internal opposition groups).[24] This dual perception would later play a role in French policy, which was given both to overestimating the solidity of the Soviet leader's position and to worrying about 'destabilizing' him. For the time being, Mitterrand proved increasingly insistent on the need for Western support for *perestroika*. As a matter of fact, Gorbachev's growing difficulties in the summer of 1989 complicated preparations for his visit. According to the French ambassador to Moscow, Jean-Marie Mérillon, domestic preoccupations were at their height in the Kremlin, where 'it was felt at that moment that the fate of the USSR was being played out' – hence an atmosphere of 'political psychodrama' that almost led, he believed, to the cancellation of the visit, which was eventually maintained out of consideration for Mitterrand and so as not to expose these difficulties.[25]

Despite these chaotic preparations, the visit took place with good auspices. France had just taken over the half-year presidency of the European Community, and the bicentenary of the French Revolution and the Summit of the Seven at the Arche of La Défense were to take place a few days later, so this 'spectacular revitalization of Franco-Soviet relations' in a promising East-West context helped make Paris the planet's center of attention.[26] Yet French diplomats seemed unclear about the real significance of Gorbachev's coming visit, for it was, as the European director at the Quai d'Orsay, Jacques Blot, pointed out, neither a 'première' as in 1985, nor a 'unique event' like Gorbachev's recent trip to Bonn, and no 'major outcome' depended on it. Of course Paris, holding the presidency of the European Community, could show Soviet diplomacy the determining importance of the Europe of the Twelve, but did this not mean recognizing that (unlike the FRG) France had little weight in East-West relations except via Europe? France might also point to its vision of a 'reconciled Europe' and offer the Soviets strengthened cooperation between the two countries in working toward this, but was the French vision of a grand Europe ordered around the Community compatible with Gorbachev's vision of the 'common home'? These questions were not explicitly formulated, but they were present in filigree in an analysis that revealed a questioning of the relative weight of France compared to the Federal Republic at a time when the latter was occupying an increasingly central position in East-West relations. Thus France was tempted to emphasize its 'global' role, in contrast with that of the FRG; Gorbachev's visit, it was argued, 'should furnish the occasion to recall that France and the Soviet Union were two powers with world interests'. How better to distinguish oneself from a Germany that remained a leading power at the European level?[27]

The event unfolded according to the 'script'. Seen from the Quai, the balance sheet was positive: the visit marked a Franco-Soviet revival and 'laid the foundation for renewed and ambitious cooperation'.[28] True, it was acknowledged, comparison with Gorbachev's visit to the FRG might appear disadvantageous, but this was not in fact the case, for the German visit had 'drawn a line under the postwar period', whereas the Soviet leader's visit to France consecrated the 'renewal' of relations between two world powers. Indeed, it was emphasized, *Pravda* had called the result exceptional and recalled 'the particular role played by our country in relations between East and West' since General de Gaulle.[29] This positive official assessment was not purely pro forma: the East-West context of the summer of 1989, the festive atmosphere of the French bicentennial, and finally the 'exceptionally frank and profound tone' of the conversations all contributed to place the visit, according to Gorbachev, 'among the most important'.[30]

Mitterrand's diplomacy could feel itself at the heart of East-West relations once again. As with Reagan formerly, the French president was indeed playing the role of 'honest courtier' between the Soviet leader and the new American president, whose distrust of the Soviet leaders disturbed Gorbachev. Mitterrand reassured the Russian: beyond the statements required by domestic politics, Bush (whom he had met at his home in Kennebunkport in May) was intent on not resuming the Cold War, and he strongly encouraged Gorbachev to meet with him. Some days later, Mitterrand would defend Gorbachev to Bush, arguing that the Russian was overwhelmed by his domestic difficulties and in need of help, and advising Bush to see him as soon as possible. These good offices may well have led to the statement, made shortly afterward by the American president, that he would soon meet his Soviet counterpart (the summit would take place in December in Malta).[31] In any case, Mitterrand henceforth made himself the defender of a policy of active support for the Soviet leader: the summit was an occasion for him to plead in favor of Gorbachev's request for 'full participation' by the USSR in the global economy and for Western aid to help him achieve it.[32] Mitterrand's conviction that everything should be done to sustain Gorbachev and the USSR's reforms, and his feeling that he had his own role as advocate of this case among the Western powers, would be a decisive factor in his later attitude. Even if some were already wondering whether unconditional support for *perestroika* might not artificially prolong what they considered a doomed regime, the Élysée noted a consensus on this issue in France.[33] One year after the decision to reinvigorate relations with Moscow, these relations reassumed their traditional importance in the French policy of searching for an exit from 'Yalta'. This would constitute an important development during the events of the following months.

France and Eastern Europe: A Grand Ambition?

The start of the new presidential term coincided with the beginning of profound changes in Eastern Europe. Until 1988, *perestroika* and the new thinking had produced scarcely any effects; Gorbachev's arrival even coincided at first with a desire to strengthen the unity of the Socialist camp.[34] Between 1986 and 1988, it was clear that Moscow's goal remained the 'cohesion' of the bloc, although the Soviet resumption of control with 'flexibility and efficiency', French diplomats noted, also facilitated the propagation of Gorbachevian ideas in Eastern Europe.[35] Still, by mid 1988 the Quai d'Orsay had come to recognize that 'the other Europe', as shown by events in Poland and especially in Hungary, was traversing a 'relatively favorable phase' marked by the affirmation of 'national specificities' – in other words, that the situation in Eastern Europe was 'no longer frozen'.[36] From the start Mitterrand measured both the possibilities and potential dangers of this situation: the probable challenge to 'Soviet hegemony' was 'a great risk', but it was 'nevertheless the logic of history', he confided to Italian Prime Minister Ciriaco De Mita in June 1988, adding that the Europeans should 'behave so that the situation evolves slowly, without creating difficulties for the USSR'. This pinpointed a dilemma that would remain at the heart of Mitterrand's approach to change in the East: 'One may wish for the dissolution of the empire – surely, it cannot last', he commented a few weeks later during a meeting of the Defence Council, 'but one may also fear the consequences of this dissolution'.[37]

Still, these transformations could not be met with indifference by French diplomacy, for the relaxation of Soviet control over Eastern Europe had been its proclaimed goal since de Gaulle. Mitterrand, as discussed earlier, had long intuited Eastern Europe's probable evolution toward more autonomy. Then, anticipating the changes subsequent to Gorbachev's rise to power, he had been early to envisage a reactivation of French policy in the East – hence, risking public and political disapproval, his controversial meeting in December 1985 with General Vojtech Jaruzelski, whom he saw first and foremost as a Polish patriot.[38] Yet, as he later recognized, the time was then 'not yet ripe' for such dramatic initiatives.[39] In the two or three years that followed, French diplomacy therefore stuck to a mostly incantatory desire for 'an active policy toward the countries of Eastern Europe' founded on France's 'historic relations' with them, while at the same time recognizing the worrying 'erosion' of its own influence there (notably cultural and linguistic) in comparison with Germany.[40] By the spring of 1988, the realization was painful: while France should more than ever encourage the Eastern countries 'to exist for themselves' and thus contribute to 'overcoming the division of Europe', the Quai d'Orsay remarked that it had 'become commonplace to say that France has no policy toward the East', for 'the means put at the service of our discourse appear utterly insufficient and sometimes ill-suited.'[41] In these circumstances, evidence of the existing changes under way in Eastern Europe was obviously well received in Paris in mid 1988: 'Changes in the East offer possibilities for increased action in all domains', noted the Quai d'Orsay, 'and we should seize them'.[42]

The idea of reactivating French policy in Eastern Europe had been ripening before the presidential election. Dumas had been convinced of its necessity since 1986–1987, especially as a result of conversations with Genscher: West Germany's engagement in the East would go on increasing, he reckoned, and France should not be left out. Mitterrand was also thinking along these lines in the first months of 1988. Judging that Gorbachev had renounced the use of force to maintain Soviet domination, he was impatient to observe for himself the changes he had forecast some years before.[43] Soon after his reelection, the project took shape. From the start, possible Franco-German cooperation was discussed. In May 1988, Elisabeth Guigou envisaged joint visits by Mitterrand and Kohl to Eastern Europe, preceded by a trip by Dumas.[44] Rather quickly, though, priority was given to a national, French-only approach. By July, Védrine had sketched out the specifics of the approach, the objective being for France to 'be more present in the East' during Mitterrand's second term, and although this might call for coordination with Bonn, he argued that it presupposed above all the prior reconstitution 'of our own game' in Eastern Europe through a program of systematic activity over two or three years.[45]

At the Quai d'Orsay the urgency of such a reactivation of French presence in the East was also very clear: France had lost its status as principal political partner of the Eastern countries and had sunk from fourth to seventh place in commercial dealings; meanwhile, its cultural influence was stagnating in comparison with German – or even American or Italian – dynamism. In short, it was now a matter of defending France's 'rank as a European and a world power', which would require actions with 'political and media impact,' 'condensed in time' and exposing 'our conception of the European future'.[46] By mid 1988, the stakes of a grand initiative appeared very clear: to recapture terrain lost to the German rival-and-partner, to profit from the favorable context in the East, to encourage change, and to illustrate the prospects for Europe and for East-West relations.

A New Season in the East

By the start of the summer, a program was elaborated. The principal goal was to renew political dialogue with a schedule of high-level visits and sharpened efforts at French cultural and economic presence in the East.[47] In mid September, Dumas went to Prague as head of a large delegation to mark the desire 'for a new impetus'.[48] Then from 17 to 19 November, Mitterrand received Hungarian Prime Minister Karoly Grosz in Paris. Grosz had succeeded Kadar as head of the HSWP in May and appeared to be 'the most Gorbachevian of the East European leaders'.[49] The discussion was very open: Mitterrand responded to his guest's desire for dialogue with the West by bringing up 'the end of Yalta', meaning 'a return to full decision-making by the countries of Europe'.[50] A few days before Mitterrand's departure for Moscow, this was an opportunity for him to announce his intention to visit all the Eastern countries, recalling that he was 'one of those who thought that one of the great affairs of the end of this century and the beginning of the next was the rapprochement of the separated Europes'.[51] 'Early signs of a new season are surging up everywhere', he added: 'I dream of a Europe reconciled and independent. I dream of this and work for it.'[52] It was indeed in the Gaullist spirit of overcoming blocs that Mitterrand promoted his new policy in the East in the fall of 1988.

Of course there were difficulties. The internal situation of the countries concerned was still far from satisfactory. While Mitterrand said he had decided to visit 'each country of Eastern Europe, or almost all' in the coming months, he had to recognize that the 'Polish problem, the Czech hardening, the Romanian follies, the Bulgarian followership – all these complicate things', not to mention East Germany.[53] In addition, Moscow's policy remained restrictive: despite the hopes of a softening of Soviet control, noted the embassy, 'we must realize that the *aggiornamento* is relative'. In short, the Quai d'Orsay thought 'it is still too early to say whether the doctrine of limited sovereignty [i.e. the Brezhnev doctrine] has been abandoned or still exists'.[54] Finally, there remained the problem, already mentioned with regard to Franco-Soviet relations, of a public opinion still marked, especially among intellectuals, by the events of the last two decades in Eastern Europe, and scarcely prepared to accept the return to close relations with regimes that continued to be condemned for their human rights violations. In this respect the choice of Mitterrand's first destination – Czechoslovakia, whose regime was particularly resistant to *perestroika*, followed by Bulgaria in January – posed a problem of which the Élysée was aware. For this reason a schedule that 'represents the maximum compatible with the [Czech] regime's capacity for tolerance' was designed. This included a breakfast meeting at the French embassy in Prague with the most visible dissidents, including Vaclav Havel – 'an absolute first-ever at this level', according to the presidential entourage.[55]

Mitterrand's visit to Czechoslovakia on 8–9 December 1988 was thus a sort of test, all the more so because Havel (in an article published shortly beforehand in *Le Monde*) evoked the risk of seeing the regime's 'legitimacy' thereby endorsed.[56] Yet Mitterrand found the right tone in Prague. He did not hesitate to tackle the human rights issue with Gustav Husak and his successor Milos Jakes, declaring that 'it is not the change taking place that today threatens Europe' but rather 'perpetuation of the status quo'.[57] Meeting with dissidents at the embassy, where Havel painted a somber picture of the situation, he recognized the dilemma raised by the resumption of contact with current regimes. Yet Mitterrand's message got through: for Jiri Hajek, 'the French initiative fosters Czech evolution toward democracy', while Jiri Dienstbier declared that Mitterrand was the first to push 'a concept of a united Europe as opposed to a Europe divided by the Cold War'.[58] In sum, Mitterrand acquitted himself rather well in a difficult exercise; as in Moscow back in June 1984, he succeeded in reconciling the defense of principles and the recognition of realities, putting forth a message that was well received in the press. Of course, noted Védrine after the Prague visit, a new issue now arose: did France have the means to back up its new ambition, in either human or financial terms? It was urgent, he told the president, to do what was necessary 'to make this essential axis of foreign policy concrete in your second term.'[59] Still, at the end of 1988, French diplomacy appeared once more on the move: 'You are ahead of your time', declared Lech Walesa, received in Paris by Mitterrand upon his return from Prague, while Bronislaw Geremek thanked him for having announced the end of Yalta, and expressed satisfaction that 'this was France's message'.[60]

A New Springtime of Peoples?

The evolution of the Eastern bloc accelerated sharply during the first half of 1989. Gorbachev's reaffirmation of 'freedom of choice', combined with the unilateral withdrawal of Soviet forces announced at the UN on 7 December, was interpreted as signaling a possible disengagement by the USSR. At the start of the year, French diplomacy cautiously predicted that 1989 would extend the evolution begun in 1988.[61] Events quickly confirmed this. In Warsaw, round table negotiations between the government and Solidarnosc that had been planned since the summer of 1988 finally commenced on 6 February; they would lead in April to a historic agreement, and in June to the first free election of the postwar era in Poland. In Budapest, the central committee of the HSWP, meeting in extraordinary session on 10 and 11 February, adopted the principle of multiple political parties; a few days later, the major outline of a constitution that did not mention the Communist Party's leading role was proclaimed. Four years after the arrival of Gorbachev, Eastern Europe thus passed from the status quo to a 'certain fluidity' – a situation that, seen from the Quai d'Orsay at the start of 1989, presented risks of 'speeding' but that essentially validated French policy toward the East.[62] This was all the more so because the new U.S. administration still appeared to hesitate over its Eastern Europe policy; the French noted that democratization in the East had scarcely any place in Washington's thinking.[63] Henry Kissinger's idea of an American commitment to respect Soviet influence in Eastern Europe in exchange for a Soviet commitment not to intervene there (an idea that the Bush team appeared to adopt for a while) seemed 'strange' to the Élysée, for 'it misrecognize[d] the revolutionary character of the Eastern situation' and showed that the new U.S. administration lacked 'audacity and a positive vision'.[64] Seen from Paris, all this confirmed the unfortunate tendency of the Americans and Soviets to co-manage European affairs, even at a time when the Community was acting as a 'magnet' vis-à-vis Eastern Europe and when the Twelve appeared best able to reestablish links with the other Europe.[65] In this context, French leaders naturally thought their own approach was validated by events: with the first round of elections having been held on 4 June, Mitterrand's visit to Poland (14–16 June 1989) was presented as aiming to bring France's 'full and complete cooperation' to the democratic process.[66] Mitterrand's diplomacy indeed regarded the Polish situation as an exemplar of a balanced and gradual transition that was taking geopolitical realities into account: as he confided to Jaruzelski, the French president thought he had been justified in his intuition dating back to 1985 that Polish policy from then on would be about 'taking facts into account while wanting to modify them'.[67]

By mid 1989 the Élysée felt that the French 'revival' of relations with the East was justified by the changes that had taken place there.[68] Nevertheless, questions remained that would assume increasing significance in the coming months. Had the French presence and influence – economic, commercial, cultural – in the 'other' Europe really progressed? Only slightly: apart from the limited effect of the presidential visits, France had not really caught up, especially with the FRG, and this relative failure would weigh on its ambitions later. In sum, the renewed French presence in the East in 1988–1989 had been more political than anything else.[69] For the rest, Paris was now wagering on the European Community's increased engagement in Central and Eastern Europe; hence its satisfaction over Washington's acceptance at the Arche summit of the European Commission's role in coordinating Western aid to Hungary and Poland. But while this preference for a strong Community role corresponded to the ambition to see the Twelve become a major actor in East-West rapprochement, did it not also reflect awareness of a limited French (as opposed to European) margin of maneuver? More importantly, the increasing pace of change in the East (which preoccupied Mitterrand from the start) was threatening to pose problems. A fresh and strong acceleration was perceptible at the start of the summer of 1989. In Poland, Solidarnosc's triumph in the second round of elections on 18 June rendered the continuation of Communist power uncertain. In Hungary, the round table began its work at the end of June and rapidly agreed that the anticipated elections in 1990 would be completely free. In this context, Gorbachev decided upon a formal renunciation of the Brezhnev doctrine: 'Any interference of any kind in the internal affairs to limit the sovereignty of states is inadmissible', he declared in a speech to the Council of Europe on 6 July.[70] The U.S. administration, abandoning its initial wait-and-see attitude, now proclaimed a policy of active engagement in favor of democracy in Eastern Europe, which was becoming the litmus test of the end of the Cold War, as confirmed by Bush's trip to Poland and Hungary (9–12 July).[71]

But this new acceleration, however welcomed, confirmed the existence of the dilemma enunciated by Mitterrand the previous year: how far could one encourage change without risking a backlash? French diplomats were rather skeptical about what the USSR was ready to tolerate in its sphere of influence. Gorbachev was disposed to 'dynamization' but not 'de-satellization', it was thought in Paris before his visit (which would confirm in French eyes that while Moscow recognized 'a certain freedom of choice', there was no question for him of accepting the 'elimination' of the Communist system in the East).[72] In short, Mitterrand's diplomacy privileged prudence: 'The Western powers should not over-react', Védrine said, for 'this would be the best way to push things into tragedy and provoke the counter-reaction or a sharp brake in the USSR or in Eastern Europe which would halt the current evolution for several years'. He summarized the approach he judged 'the most favorable to the interests of the people of Eastern Europe' thus: 'Gradual tightening of all kinds of links with the

Europe of the Twelve, whose rhythm of construction should by no means slow down; refusal of all provocation to the Soviet system.'[73] On the eve of the decisive events of the second half of 1989, this approach – which postulated an ordered and gradual transition in the East – was the one that French policy was betting on.

Détente versus Alliance

In 1988–1989, disarmament was more than ever at the center of East-West concerns. With the conclusion of the INF agreement in 1987, the issue of SNF came to the forefront, making the Western strategic dilemmas even more acute. The NATO Brussels summit in March 1988 had led to a compromise (strongly favored by Mitterrand's diplomats) consisting of postponing the question of modernizing short-range NATO missiles (as well as any talks about them with the USSR) until after the results of the negotiations on conventional forces, thus putting the SNF question 'on the backburner'.[74] But the problem remained of how to reduce this remaining category of weapons – which were all the more dangerous as their range was limited – without risking a denuclearization of the Western 'posture'. In the summer of 1988, the controversy continued between the Americans and British, both of whom emphasized the need for maintaining the credibility of deterrence, and the Germans, who refused to be 'singled out' as the only NATO country keeping tactical nuclear missiles. As a result the FRG was proving increasingly receptive to Soviet arms control proposals.[75] By the autumn the positions were fixed: while Genscher, reflecting the changing opinion of German politicians, was now personally favorable to a third zero option previously excluded by Bonn, the Americans and British were opposed to any negotiation and were determined to obtain a formal decision to modernize the Lance missiles as early as 1989.[76] The Mitterrand diplomacy in this affair demonstrated comprehension of the German viewpoint. Still, the president's entourage was uneasy: 'To do nothing is to unilaterally disarm NATO', warned Védrine.[77] During the meetings in Moscow at the end of November, the president remained cautious: recalling France's position (it could not 'disarm unilaterally until the arsenals [of all countries concerned] really became comparable'), he emphasized to Gorbachev the necessity of maintaining tactical nuclear weapons 'at the technical level', a way of alluding to modernization without saying the word.[78] But it was especially at the Quai d'Orsay that people were concerned: irrespective of the issue of modernization, they dreaded negotiations that would almost certainly lead to a third zero option, which Gorbachev was certain to propose; this would open the way to the denuclearization of Europe, undermine the strategy of flexible response and, worst of all, risk 'singling out' French short-range weapons (i.e. the Pluton and the future Hadès, whose range placed them among the SNFs), thus jeopardizing their maintenance. For all these reasons, the Quai warned, French interests were 'not served' by such negotiations.[79]

The French attitude to conventional disarmament, now in the foreground, was less guarded. The coming negotiations over conventional forces in Europe (CFE) – whose mandate had been discussed in Vienna since 1987 – were indeed in line with the priorities traditionally proclaimed by Paris in the realm of disarmament.[80] They also corresponded to a certain political vision put forth by French diplomacy. At a time when changes in Eastern Europe were accelerating, France indeed saw in future conventional negotiations 'from the Atlantic to the Urals' the means of constraining the USSR to give up its political and military hold over the popular democracies by reducing the number of Soviet forces stationed within their borders.[81] Moreover, such negotiations would permit the defusing of the SNF problem, since a rebalancing of classical forces would make the fate of tactical nuclear arms (which were justified mostly by Soviet conventional superiority) less determining. For these reasons, throughout 1988 Mitterrand hammered that nuclear disarmament must not take priority over classical disarmament, on which he called for an immediate new initiative.[82] French diplomats, however, remained more circumspect over this issue, as compared with the Élysée. In fact, in its obsession with preventing the inclusion of nuclear weapons in the CFE negotiations and avoiding these negotiations being conducted 'bloc-to-bloc' (the French wanted these negotiations to be linked instead to the CSCE) the Quai d'Orsay risked lending credence to the idea of a fundamental French unwillingness to negotiate altogether.[83] This guarded attitude, in fact, was comparable to the policies of the other Western powers (again, with the exception of the FRG), and it reflected the persistence of a certain distrust of Soviet motives. Gorbachev's speech before the United Nations on 7 December 1988, however, marked a major turning point. By announcing a unilateral reduction of 500,000 men in their armed forces (including 50,000 in Eastern Europe), the Soviets demonstrated the seriousness of their intentions. French diplomacy recognized this, describing Gorbachev's proposals as 'encouraging new directions'.[84] With the pending opening of CFE and the SNF issue threatening to unleash a crisis within the Atlantic Alliance, the intensification of the Soviet offensive on the terrain of disarmament represented a serious challenge for the West.

The West on the Defensive

As a direct consequence of the above, the year 1989 began in a climate of nascent crisis within NATO. As U.S. Secretary of State James Baker noted, confirmation of détente and the disarmament dynamic made it difficult to maintain Western cohesion over defense priorities.[85] In the face of Gorbachev's disarmament offensive, opinion polls showed that NATO appeared increasingly anachronistic – to the Bush administration's consternation.[86] In Atlantic Alliance circles, people were wondering how the institution could come to be seen as a motor for transforming East-West relations instead of a prop for the established order. How, in particular, could the legitimacy of nuclear deterrence be preserved, and how could public opinion be convinced, notably in Germany, of the necessity of maintaining it?[87] To these questions new queries were added about the revival of European construction: could one maintain the status quo in transatlantic relations while Western Europe was unifying and might one day take charge of its own defense? Inversely, was it possible to preserve the Atlantic Alliance if the Twelve really became an economic and political bloc?[88] As NATO celebrated its fortieth anniversary in April 1989, the debate over how the end of the Cold War would impact it was thus already underway. Proponents of keeping a strong NATO despite the changes in the East advanced their arguments against those who thought it should be radically reformed or abolished. Secretary-General Manfred Woerner responded that the alliance remained irreplaceable as 'the magnetic pole of stability' in international affairs; only NATO, he argued, could allow 'pacific change in the East' and the establishment of a 'just and durable order of security' that would overcome 'artificial divisions, notably that of Germany'.[89] Thus in broad outline, the plan to renovate NATO that would be adopted by the allies in 1990–1991 against the background of German unification and the end of the Cold War was already in place by the spring of 1989.

Still, the future of the alliance appeared mostly dependent on the outcome of the SNF 'test'. In the first months of 1989, the SNF affair indeed threatened to lead to a veritable transatlantic clash. The U.S. hardening on East-West relations, perceptible since the Bush administration took control, was felt foremost over disarmament. The new president feared that 'Gorbachev might incite us to disarm without the USSR radically changing' its own military posture. Bush advisers considered the issue of short-range nuclear weapons 'the decisive question of the coming two years', and they wanted to be as firm on this issue with the allies – starting with the Germans – as with the Soviets.[90] Washington (and more so London, where Margaret Thatcher demonstrated total intransigence) thus underlined the need to modernize NATO's tactical nuclear weapons and insisted that SNF negotiations were not opportune.[91] Meanwhile German positions were changing on both these issues, but in exactly the opposite direction from the one the Americans and British wished for. In Bonn in February 1989, Baker was told that the question of Lance modernization could wait, and that talks with the Soviets should start quickly on SNF. Kohl's declaration to the Bundestag on 27 April provoked special consternation in the alliance: not only did Bonn effectively demand a 'quick' opening of negotiations and call for postponing modernization until 1992, but under pressure from Genscher, the FRG no longer excluded the possibility of a third zero option, a position clearly unacceptable to the Americans, who were prone to equate it with a *fait accompli* on the part of their German allies.[92] Even if the chancellor tried to calm things the next day, Washington held that Kohl, in order to avoid a crisis inside his coalition, had risked provoking a 'major crisis' within the alliance.[93] The Quai d'Orsay thought the same, worried to see the Federal Republic question 'fundamental principles' of security and thus give a 'blank check' to the Soviets.[94] And although the Élysée was unsurprisingly much more sympathetic to Bonn's position and advised against any 'dramatic reaction' (e.g. evoking a risk of denuclearization or of a 'German drift'), Mitterrand's advisors were concerned that the affair might eventually 'lead to a profound deterioration in relations between the United States, Great Britain, and the FRG'.[95]

As the NATO summit planned for the end of May 1989 approached, the French therefore dreaded a 'blocked situation'.[96] This was even less desirable, inasmuch as France was in an uncomfortable position: to support the German demand for negotiations would provoke a grave crisis with the United States, while to oppose such negotiations on principle would lead to just as serious a crisis with the FRG. The SNF issue only accentuated France's own dilemmas. The French wanted nothing done that might compromise pursuing disarmament and confirming détente, but they also wanted to assure the efficacy of defence and the credibility of deterrence. And although France did not share the doctrine of flexible response, NATO did not possess a replacement strategy for it, and so Paris had no interest in its obsolescence; hence in French eyes, there remained a need to maintain a minimum of American nuclear weapons in Europe.[97] Finally, while France was not directly implicated in a debate that essentially concerned the NATO 'integrated' allies, it could not remain indifferent to an issue that involved its own security, if only due to the issue of the French Hadès missiles. So the question arose: 'Should we stay outside the debates or contribute more actively to thinking about the future of the Alliance?'[98] Such considerations pushed Paris to seek ways of helping to defuse the crisis: 'Without wanting to pose as mediators', said the Quai d'Orsay, 'we want to try to contribute to the appearance of a compromise based on convergences among the partners'.[99]

The Alliance Resumes Control

The spring 1989 summit thus appeared crucial for the Atlantic Alliance and East-West relations alike. As was often the case, this event itself served as a catalyst: as the summit approached, the Bush administration measured the breadth of the difficulties it would be confronting and tried ways of reassuming the initiative. While the 'strategic review'undertaken since January resulted in March in conservative recommendations, the White House realized that the 'status quo plus' proposed by the bureaucracy with regard to East-West and disarmament issues was simply not tenable. With CFE talks having effectively started in March and the SNF question becoming central, Bush – increasingly criticized in public opinion for his passivity – became impatient at seeing Gorbachev keep the initiative while the West remained on the defensive. Meanwhile, Washington was becoming aware of the possible impact upon German-American relations and the need to keep the entente with Bonn as a priority. Hence the decisive choice was made to support Kohl actively in order to avoid the risk of a victory by the SPD with its anti-nuclear positions during the 1990 elections, a choice that involved being understanding about the chancellor's concessions to Genscher. Now these two preoccupations converged: in seizing the momentum from Gorbachev over disarmament, the Bush administration hoped to take the upper hand in the alliance and to reassert American leadership based on a dynamic approach to East-West relations. Meanwhile, a daring initiative on CFE would diminish pressure over the SNF issue and consequently contribute to resolving the differences between Germans, British and Americans. Three months after its inauguration, the Bush administration was thus leaning toward major shifts with respect to both East-West and West-West relations.[100]

Washington was thereby converging with Paris's preoccupations. Seeking the terms for a balanced compromise before the alliance summit, Mitterrand's diplomats judged it desirable to 'push disarmament forward without contributing to the crisis' in NATO or 'granting to the Soviets the enormous advantage of NATO denuclearization' in ground-based weapons. As during the preceding summit, the Élysée wished to 'relativize' the quarrel over SNF by postponing both modernization and negotiation until 1992, which meant giving priority to conventional disarmament and recognizing that Soviet proposals, although still distant from Western ones, were to be taken seriously.[101] The German factor was the determining one, in French reasoning: when Thatcher wrote to Mitterrand to beg him to use his influence 'with Helmut' and bring him to reason in the SNF affair, the Élysée thought that the British prime minister was 'tackling the problem very maladroitly'; it would be better 'not to confront German expectations head on' but rather to bring Bonn 'to take again a priority interest in conventional disarmament as opposed to nuclear disarmament'.[102] With this scheme in mind, Mitterrand met Bush at Kennebunkport on 20–21 May. Since June 1981, when the latter had visited the Élysée (Mitterrand had reassured the then vice president about the presence of Communist ministers in the newly appointed French government), their relationship had remained trusting. At Kennebunkport, the American president proved very attentive to Mitterrand's statements, questioning him at length about the major topics of the day. Mitterrand said he was disturbed by the turn taken by the Lance issue and Thatcher's counterproductive fierceness over it: even though it appeared much less important in the light of the East-West changes now underway, the affair, he dreaded, might compromise the alliance summit. He thus recommended to Bush that the latter support Kohl, who represented the best West German partner possible. Even if he was obliged to make apparent concessions for domestic reasons, Kohl, Mitterrand assured Bush, was personally hostile to a third zero option. Mitterrand, therefore, petitioned Bush for substantial progress in negotiations over conventional forces so as to be able to postpone the SNF question.[103]

The Americans judged the Maine meeting as 'extraordinarily useful', a confirmation of the good relations between the two presidents that would play a significant role in the months and years to come. Even if Mitterrand only echoed Bush's personal thinking, it is manifest that his plea contributed to shifting the American position at a time when it was still fluid and when the Pentagon was still resisting a major disarmament initiative.[104] In the following days the White House finally imposed its views, and on the eve of the NATO summit it unveiled its major outlines: moving far beyond its previous hesitation, the Bush administration made daring proposals (posing incidentally some new problems for the French and British) that aimed at concluding negotiations over conventional forces in six to twelve months.[105] As a result, the NATO summit in Brussels, which had risked producing a split, achieved a spectacular success on 30 and 31 May: the allies welcomed the American initiative on CFE and the Germans accepted that SNF negotiations (which would exclude a third zero option) be postponed until the conclusion of an agreement on conventional forces. Mitterrand was the first to express his satisfaction during the summit and to 'congratulate' Bush on a balanced initiative that 'also marks a victory over the conservatism of the bureaucracies' and thus permitted 'avoiding a crisis damaging to the Alliance'; he praised the 'imagination and audacity' of the American proposal.[106] The day after the summit, the Quai d'Orsay noted that 'the compromise was effected at a balance point very close to the French position' and (forgetting its own former reservations) expressed satisfaction over a proposal 'that meets the priority that we give to [the CFE talks] and our concern to appear as imaginative and ambitious'.[107] The press mentioned the conciliatory role played by Mitterrand in Brussels, even if this role remained discreet due to the particular status of France within NATO.¹⁰⁸ And George Bush addressed his thanks to Mitterrand on 2 June for his contribution to the 'very great success' of the summit.¹⁰⁹

The Brussels summit did mark an important stage. It was the first real foreign policy success of an American administration until then paralyzed by an extreme prudence verging on immobility. Bush was able to reassert American leadership at a decisive moment for East-West relations and for relations among the Western nations. As a result, the crisis feared within NATO was avoided; better still, the alliance now presented itself no longer as a brake but as a motor of détente and disarmament. Moreover, relations between the U.S. and Germany, troubled for long months by the SNF affair, were strengthened and consolidated. On 31 May in a major speech given at Mainz, Bush proposed to the Germans becoming 'partners in leadership', a proposition that illustrated the rediscovery of the German priority in American policy (which would not fail to annoy London, where it was feared that this would challenge the Anglo-American 'special relationship'), and he presented the emergence of a 'Europe whole and free' as the 'new mission' of the Atlantic Alliance. Whether or not these events constituted a veritable American strategy to end the Cold War (as was later claimed), Washington's reaffirmation of its Atlantic leadership, the consolidation of the partnership with Bonn, and the adoption of an audacious policy in the realm of disarmament did constitute landmarks whose importance would more fully appear in the following months.

Meanwhile, the immediate effect on East-West relations was tangible as well: between Gorbachev's visit to Bonn in June and the meetings in Paris in July, the climate was euphoric. French diplomacy noted that the Soviets recognized the importance of these developments: after the NATO summit, Shevardnadze stressed to Dumas 'the positive elements in the Bush proposal', which opened the way to rapid negotiations over conventional forces in Europe.¹¹⁰ Even if the consequences of four decades of military confrontation could not be offset from one day to the next, the Vienna talks were now at the heart of the disarmament process and of the sea change in East-West relations. By the same token, the Brussels summit and its aftermath were a source of satisfaction for Mitterrand's diplomacy.¹¹¹ The Élysée saw in the relaunch of conventional disarmament and the postponement of the SNF question a confirmation of French priorities (and a respite for Hadès), and it wanted to share the diplomatic success attained by the Bush administration. After all, Mitterrand too had imposed on French diplomats and the military a more dynamic approach to disarmament, marking a change from the three years during which France had appeared reluctant. This had contributed to a synthesis between British foot-dragging and German haste and, by encouraging the American initiative, made compromise possible within the alliance. The French policy of independence in the alliance also appeared validated by this whole episode: in a context of détente and disarmament, the SNF affair as seen from Paris indeed proved the political and strategic erosion of NATO's doctrine of flexible response, by the same token validating French-style 'minimal' deterrence and the Gaullist strategic 'model' that Mitterrand had made his own. It was in this state of mind that the French president would tackle the strategic upheavals of the autumn.[112]

The Difficult Franco-German Dialectic

The reelection of François Mitterrand allowed the pursuit of the rapprochement between France and Germany begun in 1983. On the threshold of a new seven-year presidential term, relations between the Élysée and the Chancellery had indeed become increasingly close, if not 'organic'.[113] However, in the period from the summer of 1988 to the summer of 1989, difficulties did appear: whether over East-West relations, strategic cooperation, or even European construction, the Franco-German couple – in the context of a growing assertion of German power – encountered friction that presaged in some respects the misunderstandings of the autumn.

The clearest failure was of the common Ostpolitik proposed by Bonn in 1987. Despite initial analyses that were rather remote from each other, the working group set up at the beginning of the year had by the summer of 1988 achieved a common document, but things had scarcely gone beyond that, despite the German wish to follow up on the exercise.[114] It was at this juncture that the reactivation of French policy toward Eastern Europe took place. The Élysée had first thought that it could combine the *'relance'* of its Eastern policy with the stepping up of Franco-German cooperation, but the former quickly trumped the latter in priority, which the French did not try to hide from the Germans. While Kohl's advisor Horst Teltschik at the end of September 1988 regretted that the chancellor's suggestion of a joint Ostpolitik had not received 'many echoes', his Élysée counterpart, Jacques Attali, was quite frank: the French were 'certainly in favor of close cooperation with the FRG', but 'our German friends [should] know that in the immediate future we [will] try to make our own major effort to catch up'.[115] The French had the feeling that the Germans, under the cover of the joint Ostpolitik, were trying to press their own ambitions, especially economic, in Central and Eastern Europe without a real spirit of sharing.[116] They fully realized that France could hardly compete there with an increasingly assertive Germany. It was difficult in these conditions to envisage a veritable joint approach going beyond minimal coordination. True, when in the autumn Kohl and then Mitterrand were expected to visit Moscow a few weeks apart, the French were favorable to such coordination in order to avoid giving the impression of a 'beauty contest', and they agreed with the Germans during the 52nd Franco-German summit at the start of November on the need to emphasize the parallelism of their respective steps toward the USSR.[117] Mitterrand's visit to Moscow at the end of November in fact illustrated the overall good climate between the two capitals with respect to policy on Eastern Europe: French moves, it was thought in Bonn, could have only positive effects for the Federal Republic and confirm the utility of both countries having a joint Ostpolitik.[118] Yet they were far from this goal: if the French and Germans managed at the cost of minimal cooperation to avoid giving the impression of a race toward Moscow, it was in fact a case more of parallel than of common policies.[119]

The first months of 1989 would confirm this perception, as witnessed at the end of January by a meeting among senior officials of the Quai d'Orsay and of the Auswärtiges Amt. The German representatives emphasized their desire to exploit in common the improvement in the East-West climate and the fact that the Paris-Bonn relation was the 'backbone' of German policy toward the East, but the secretary-general of the Quai d'Orsay, François Scheer, poured cold water on the idea: 'Those less familiar with German policy', he responded, might 'wonder about the firmness of Germany's engagement in Europe and the Franco-German relationship due to the importance attached by the FRG to its relations with the East'. France, he added, was 'determined to conduct a policy of openness to the East' and attached 'value to doing so in cooperation with the Federal Republic', but not to the detriment of her priority of constructing Western Europe.[120] It would be difficult to state more clearly the persistent misgivings of French diplomats about Bonn's Ostpolitik and their doubts about the possibility of a joint approach that took account of French concerns. Hence the process of cooperation launched a year previously made no headway. After the joint study on changes in the USSR, Bonn had hoped that the work of the Franco-German group would lead to 'positions and even initiatives in common' and to 'implementation of convergent policies' – but there was no follow-up to this wish.[121] In a March speech in Bonn, Teltschik regretted that cooperation was running out of steam and that France had 'never responded to German offers of an Ostpolitik conducted in common'.[122] In the spring of 1989, with strategic cooperation stalled and European issues leading to difficulties in the bilateral relationship, the failure of coordination with respect to Eastern policy did not help.[123] Of course, the fault was shared: if the French feared an unequal partnership and wanted first to reconstitute their own influence in Central and Eastern Europe, the Germans unsurprisingly wanted to legitimize their Eastern policy and were not disposed (given their advantage) to parity sharing. Be that as it may, in the light of the misunderstandings that later appeared between Paris and Bonn, the Germans would retrospectively regret that the French had not managed to seize the occasion to deepen Franco-German cooperation in the face of changes in the East.[124] Here again, the events of 1988–1989 can be read as a prelude to those of the autumn of 1989.

The Bomb...

The limits of Paris-Bonn cooperation also appeared in the strategic dimension.[125] Six years after the revival of the Franco-German strategic cooperation desired by Mitterrand and Schmidt and then Kohl, the French congratulated themselves on many achievements. From the Bundestag speech in January 1983 to the creation of a common council on defense and security, ratified during the twenty-fifth anniversary of the Élysée Treaty in January 1988, the tally was 'considerable'. Still, in the summer of 1988, questions remained: if the Euromissile crisis had pushed the two countries closer earlier in the decade, this cooperation had 'more difficulty progressing in an undeniably more relaxed East-West climate'. In addition, the Quai d'Orsay thought the orientation the FRG was trying to give this cooperation called for 'particular vigilance and prior reflection on goals and modes'.[126] Despite a common desire to progress, the East-West context and the differences between Paris and Bonn made strategic rapprochement difficult.

These problems resulted, as always, from the persistent difference between the two countries in relation to NATO and nuclear weapons. At the end of the 1980s, Franco-German strategic cooperation indeed still ran up against the disparity between a FRG integrated into NATO and a France that held itself outside the alliance's military apparatus, a principle on which, as we know, Mitterrand demonstrated a quite Gaullist intransigence. '[I will accept] nothing that could insert us further into NATO', he proclaimed, objecting regularly to any proposition that might bring France closer to the integrated organization.[127] Hence, in the short term, difficulties stemmed from the definition of how to employ the mixed Franco-German brigade created in the autumn of 1987; hence also, in the long term, disagreements remained on the ultimate goal of bilateral cooperation, conceived by the French as contributing to the construction of a truly European defence and by the Germans as allowing a reduction of the gap between France and the integrated organization of NATO.[128] But it was especially the two countries' different statuses with regard to atomic weapons that limited the possibilities of strategic cooperation, something that the context of the end of the 1980s, with its focus on nuclear disarmament, could only exacerbate.

The insistent question of consultation in case of recourse to nuclear weapons remained central: while Bonn had for years wished to be involved in a possible French decision to use nuclear weapons on FRG territory, Paris wanted a strictly minimal engagement in this domain for the sake of strategic autonomy.[129] Despite his wish to pacify German fears (hence his declaration in the fall of 1987 that the 'ultimate warning' would not necessarily be delivered in the FRG), this principle was nonnegotiable for Mitterrand. In addition, the French president held that French nuclear weapons could not be substituted for NATO deterrence in order to guarantee the security of the FRG and a fortiori of Western Europe.[130] Finally, even if the French president could understand the German position on disarmament, in the spring of 1989 the SNF question (and as a corollary, the issue of the French Hadès missile, which was increasingly contested by the Germans) crystallized the contradictions between a Germany obsessed by its nonnuclear status and increasingly reticent about the nuclear weapons of others, and a France attached to its status as an atomic power and opposed to denuclearization. In short, the disagreement between the two countries – whether over arms control or strategy – presented an obstacle to pursuing their rapprochement and risked becoming instead a bone of contention. In diagnosing Germany's 'small latent jealousy' about French nuclear weapons (but was not France itrself 'jealous' over its own atomic power?), Mitterrand put his finger on one of the principal unspoken aspects of the Franco-German relationship that still persisted on the eve of the upheavals of the autumn of 1989.[131]

Of course, Franco-German cooperation aimed to overcome these contradictions. Yet the year 1988–1989 was marked by no major initiative, with the two partners mostly focusing on the implementation of the decisions of January 1988, in particular the establishment of the defence and security council, whose aim was precisely to allow the two countries to adopt common positions. But the difficulties were manifest: while the Germans tried to push their strategic conceptions (in particular in the realm of nuclear consultation), the French wanted inversely to restrict the scope and powers of the council.[132] By the spring of 1989, the Elysée noted that persistent divergences over disarmament were giving rise to 'real malaise' and casting a cloud over 'the reality of Franco-German cooperation'. In that context, the first meeting of the council on 24 April 1989, in Paris, presided over by Kohl and Mitterrand, exposed the limitations of the new body.[133] Without excessive enthusiasm, the French president described it as an 'important novelty' that ought to demonstrate its relevance in its effective work; as for the chancellor, he remained silent about the debates going on in Bonn about SNF, and – although questioned on this subject by Mitterrand – he refrained from making the French aware of the new governmental position that he would announce three days later in the Bundestag.[134] Paris, like Washington, was thus confronted with a *fait accompli* in the declaration of 27 April calling for a quick opening of SNF negotiations, which shortly afterward occasioned a frank talk between Dumas and Genscher.[135] True, the affair left almost no trace, and the SNF question, as seen above, was satisfactorily resolved at the NATO summit a few weeks later. It was nevertheless revealing, in the spring of 1989, of the limits of Franco-German strategic coordination and of continuing divergences between the two countries.

... and the Deutschemark

The same was true of European integration, which was now the French president's principal ambition. His reelection was of course a favorable factor, for the Kohl-Mitterrand tandem had been for several years identified with the two countries' will to push the European project. By the beginning of Mitterrand's second term, French diplomacy more than ever advanced the necessity of responding to East-West changes by accelerating European construction: as Dumas explained to a Genscher confidant, Otto Lambsdorff, in the summer of 1988, 'the more the dialogue with the Eastern countries intensifies, the more the European community must be solid'.[136] By then, the French increasingly identified progress in the European project with the economic and monetary union (EMU) idea, which was now in the foreground. Advanced by Genscher in February 1988, the creation of a European currency soon became the beacon project of the Twelve. At the European summit in Hanover at the end of June, Commission President Jacques Delors was entrusted with the preparation of a report on EMU. Mitterrand realized what this step represented for the FRG, since it implied the eventual abandonment of the deutschemark, symbol of its power but also in certain respects its national identity. 'The deutschemark is like its nuclear weapon', he noted after Hanover, stressing the idea of an equilibrium between an economically powerful Germany and an atomically powerful France.[137] To rally Kohl, whom he knew to be hesitant for domestic reasons – the right wing of the CDU-CSU was very hostile to the project – Mitterrand was therefore ready to accept, despite his own convictions, that the future European central bank (ECB) might be modeled on the Bundesbank and hence function independently of governments. These were the terms of the bargain sketched in the autumn of 1988 for what became the principal European project.[138]

In the first months of 1989, however, the French began to worry about the firmness of Bonn's European commitments. The theme was not new: Paris had for some time been concerned about the FRG's 'disaffection' with the European Community.[139] But the French worries were now expressed more openly against the background of a growing and premonitory debate in Germany about compatibility between European integration and German unification.[140] Receiving Lambsdorff, National Assembly President Laurent Fabius stated that 'today the questions France asks about the evolution in Germany have changed: they relate to Germany's intentions with regard to European integration' at a moment when there are 'signs of a turn in [German] public opinion about Europe'.[141] The remark was telling: more than the desire for a German unification that remained hypothetical, it was the FRG's possible disinterest in, or even hesitation over, European construction that disturbed French leaders and nourished alarmist commentaries among opinion makers (who, as always, were clearly more suspicious than decision makers) for whom the 'German drift' was reflected in this hesitation.[142] The events of the autumn of 1989 would later crystallize this Franco-German misunderstanding, but it was already quite perceptible in the spring with regard to the EMU, which was then becoming for Paris the touchstone of progress on European construction.[143] Against the backdrop of the latent crisis about SNF, Bonn, in a series of national decisions with important consequences for Europe (in particular regarding interest rates and taxes on savings), effectively multiplied negative signals, revealing both the realities of German economic power and the chancellor's hesitations about EMU in a difficult domestic context. In the wake of the governmental declaration of 27 April, the effects of the two issues (nuclear disarmament and monetary union) were combined. Paris was concerned: 'Despite his personal engagement in favor of Europe', noted Guigou, Kohl for the first time was constrained 'to take a set of decisions that will make a joint Franco-German position very difficult and perhaps impossible' on both security and community matters.[144]

As the Summit of the Twelve in Madrid (26–27 June) approached, along with the start of the French presidency of the European Community (1 July), relations between France and Germany were somewhat strained, already heralding the difficulties at the end of the year. Yet for the time being a full-blown crisis was avoided, with Kohl eventually committing himself to the EMU objective and reaffirming his European engagement. Even if he did not wish for a decision to convene an intergovernmental conference (IGC) on EMU to be made at the coming Madrid summit, Guigou, by mid May, thought that he might accept such a decision being made during the summit at the end of the year under the French presidency.[145] True, the Bonn government remained split between the proclaimed hostility to EMU of Finance Minister Theo Waigel and the advocacy of Genscher, but the excellent relationship between Dumas and Genscher counted for a great deal: in the run-up to Madrid, the two ministers agreed that the Delors Report, which had been submitted in April, should be adopted as 'a working basis' by the Twelve and that its three stages should be considered a 'single process' leading, by means of a new treaty prepared by an IGC, to a full-blown economic and monetary union, which should become 'the prime objective of the Community'.[146] Kohl accepted this scheme, thereby rallying to the objective of a European currency – even if, unlike Genscher, he did not want to see an intergovernmental conference effectively start in 1990, the year of elections in the FRG (this factor would continue to weigh for the rest of 1989) and refused therefore to set a deadline for the completion of preparatory work.[147]

As for Mitterrand, who wanted Madrid to go as far as possible by fixing 1 January 1990 as the start of the first phase of the Delors Plan (after which the IGC might begin) he accepted a few months' postponement. Thus a compromise – although an ambiguous one, as we shall see – was reached in Madrid: the start of the first phase was fixed as of 1 July 1990, after which an IGC could begin upon completion of the preparatory phase. Kohl was satisfied: he could hope the debates on the EMU would not interfere with his electoral campaign. Meanwhile Mitterrand, although he had not obtained the setting of a firm date for launching the IGC, was intent on using the French EC presidency to secure a decision to convene it as soon as possible after 1 July 1990.[148] Still, although the 'tandem' had functioned once again, it was manifest that the pursuit of the process would not be easy: both the 'bomb' (which symbolized the disparity between a France jealous of its sovereignty and a Federal Republic less and less inclined to accept its political inferiority) and the 'deutschemark' (which reflected the growing gap between the two countries' economies) appeared now as possible brakes to Franco-German cooperation.

Return of the Greater Germany?

While the Federal Republic asserted itself more and more in the Western alliance and within the European Community, it had now also become a dominant actor in the East-West game in Europe. Kohl's visit to the USSR from 24 to 27 October 1988 was an important stage: the result of the rapprochement begun two years before, it reflected Moscow's wish to turn the page on confrontation and Bonn's determination to assert itself as the principal partner for Gorbachevian diplomacy in the West. But it marked, above all, the start of a close and trusting relation between Gorbachev and Kohl that would be decisive later.[149] The importance of the event did not escape the Quai d'Orsay. From the economic standpoint, the agreements signed in Moscow confirmed the place of the FRG as the USSR's prime partner; from a political standpoint, the visit marked a long deferred 'normalization' in the bilateral relationship between the USSR and West Germany and opened the way to a real 'reconciliation' between them.[150] But it was Gorbachev's visit to the FRG from 12 to 15 June 1989 that appeared to be a historic event: taking place in an ambience of 'Gorby-mania', its impact would loom in the retrospective light of German unification barely a year later. As we will see, French diplomacy remained circumspect about the real consequences of the event for the German question, but its significance was understood in France, both for Gorbachev, who enjoyed a large public opinion success, and for Kohl, whose country was thus granted a central role in East-West relations, as illustrated by the joint declaration in which Bonn and Moscow promised to seek means to overcome the division of Europe.[151] This declaration, commented the French ambassador in Bonn, Serge Boidevaix, amounted 'almost to a sort of charter of principles for East-West relations', to which other European states were invited to subscribe. Only days after Bush's own visit and his offer of a 'partnership in leadership', the French had thus to recognize that Gorbachev's visit consecrated the pivotal role of the FRG between the two great powers.[152]

Did the irresistible rise of the Federal Republic of Germany's power in East-West relations trouble the French? The answer must be nuanced. Of course, German activism in the East, combined with an open wish for national assertion, fed the usual disquiet in the media and among many commentators.[153] The Quai d'Orsay, as seen above, had not abandoned all of its reservations, either. True, differences with Bonn were less tense than in 1986 or 1987, and despite the failure of a joint Ostpolitik or even a coordinated approach, the two capitals were now more in phase with each other. Still, the French diplomatic apparatus retained certain concerns that were perceptible in the spring of 1989: hence the joint German-Soviet declaration was closely examined and the French noted without pleasure that Gorbachev's 'European home' and the *'Friedensordnung'* dear to the Auswärtiges Amt were contained there side by side.[154] But they had to adjust to the situation, so French diplomacy stuck to simple ideas: the FRG's policy did not challenge the anchoring of Bonn in the West, and overall the best response would be for France to be just as active as the FRG in its own relations with the East.[155] This was indeed Mitterrand's line: 'There is nothing threatening in relations between Germany and the USSR', he replied to those who were worried about Kohl's visit to Moscow, and this rapprochement 'should stimulate us'.[156] A little later, on the occasion of Willy Brandt's birthday, he stressed that the FRG's Ostpolitik had never cast doubt in his eyes on the engagement of the Federal Republic in the West.[157] While he noted in the spring of 1989 that 'the difficulty arises when it is a matter of integrating Germany's preoccupations into relations among Western states', he thought that the best response to this challenge was a French policy to the East 'that allows us to place the Franco-German couple on a new footing'.[158] For Mitterrand, in short, the Eastern ambitions of the Federal Republic could be accommodated if its European and Western ties were assured, and as long as French diplomacy proved capable of a healthy emulation.

Still, the spectacular amelioration of German-Soviet relations in 1988–1989 could but feed the speculation about the German question that had resurfaced since 1987. For Bonn, reestablishment of dialogue with Moscow could by no means take place at the cost of renouncing the proclaimed objective of unity: quite to the contrary, improvement in relations with the USSR as well as with the GDR went hand in hand with reassertion of the official discourse on unification.[159] The Germans, and Kohl first and foremost, were therefore more attached than ever to stressing their national objectives before their Soviet interlocutors. Kohl (like President von Weizsäcker before him) had done so with Gorbachev on the occasion of a Kremlin toast during his autumn 1988 visit to Moscow.[160] Yet the main occasion for recalling the ever-open character of the German question was Gorbachev's visit to West Germany in June 1989. His arrival was preceded by new rumors of a Soviet initiative on the German question, which (despite Bonn authorities' denials) evidently contributed to making the issue topical again.[161] In this context West German diplomacy was prone to emphasize its success as represented by the joint German-Soviet declaration, notably the mention of the right to self-determination, in which Bonn was willing to see the 'premise of a recognition' by Moscow of the right of the German people as a whole to choose its destiny.[162] In his public statements during the visit, Kohl did not fail to recall the goal of 'unity and liberty' and described the division of the country as an 'open wound'.[163] Later, of course, he famously made his conversation with Gorbachev by the Rhine the point of departure for the process that would lead to unity in a few months.[164]

The German Question: French Scepticism

The French were skeptical, however, about this presentation of things. As seen from Paris and other Western capitals, the rapprochement between Germany and the USSR, spectacular as it was, did not fundamentally modify the terms of the German situation. In the summer of 1988, when Bonn had announced Kohl's forthcoming visit to Moscow, wagering on an evolution in the Soviet position on the German question, the Quai thought that Gorbachev was in fact maintaining 'the most rigid orthodoxy about the irreversible character of the division of Germany'.[165] Kohl's trip to the USSR in the fall confirmed this diagnosis: after the Soviet leader's response to Kohl's toast, 'it ought now to be clear on the German side', Paris thought, 'that the USSR rejects any idea of revising the German territorial situation as fixed in the aftermath of the Second World War'.[166] As for Mitterrand, he then declared himself convinced that nothing would make 'Moscow evolve on the problem of the reunification of Germany' since it would represent a 'real threat' to the USSR.[167] His opinion remained unchanged in the spring of 1989, as he confided to Bush at Kennebunkport: 'Never will the USSR accept [unification] as long as it is strong ... [T]he Soviet Empire will be dislocated, but Germany will remain [its] major problem', he asserted.[168] So the French were scarcely convinced of the importance of the progress about which the Germans boasted after Gorbachev's visit. From Bonn, Serge Boidevaix noted that recognition of the right to self-determination in the joint declaration was accompanied by the assertion of other principles that significantly reduced its scope, such as respect for 'international law' and 'the integrity and security of each state' as well as its right to choose freely its political and social system – a clear reference to the existence of the GDR.[169] From Moscow, Jean-Marie Mérillon confirmed that Gorbachev 'has made no particular concession on the German question', although he did recognize the major role of the FRG 'in a Europe which admittedly cannot remain fixed'.[170] In short, as the Quai d'Orsay summarized it, 'one can wonder in light of the euphoric reception' given Gorbachev, whether the Germans 'are not feeding extravagant hopes ... about the prospect of solving the German problem'.[171]

The sentiment that the German question had little chance of being reopened in the foreseeable future was in fact confirmed by the state of mind of the West German leaders, at least as the French perceived it. Paris had reason to believe that behind the conventional speeches, the tendency in the Bonn political establishment at the end of the 1980s was more toward recognizing realities than challenging them. This was not surprising within the SPD, whose representatives now went quite far in their acceptance of the status quo: hence Egon Bahr confided to Dumas shortly before Gorbachev's arrival in Bonn that 'if one wants stability one cannot do otherwise than maintain two German states'.[172] More novel was the fact that many in the CDU were now inclined to accord unification only slight urgency.[173] The French embassy in Bonn noted in the spring of 1989 that, behind the persistent official position on the right to self-determination, 'it was pointed out in private that the CDU also admits that facts must be recognized' and that 'the SPD cannot boast exclusivity in the matter'.[174] The French in fact were not the only ones to hear it said that the German question was not on the agenda: convinced from his arrival in Bonn in the spring of 1989 of the probability of a forthcoming unification (a very rare prescience), the American ambassador Vernon Walters encountered firm scepticism among his German interlocutors.[175] It is true that unspoken views abounded and that at this time the Germans did not reveal all their thinking despite the closeness of relations between Paris and Bonn or Washington and Bonn. Be that as it may, the dominant perception in Paris as elsewhere in mid 1989 was indeed of a durably settled German question, whether due to the (effective) opposition of Moscow or the (presumed) acceptance of the situation by the Germans themselves.

The German question, as a matter of fact, was now practically absent as a stake in relations between France and the Soviet Union. This was the product of a tendency that, as seen above, had been perceptible since the start of the 1980s: by 1989, preserving the German status quo was no longer a motivation for the entente between Paris and Moscow, if it ever had been since de Gaulle. As noted in a Quai d'Orsay memo in the summer of 1988, whereas 'the "German question" had been initially an essential aspect' of the Franco-Soviet dialogue, this aspect 'has gradually diminished' due to both the Franco-German rapprochement and the evolution in Soviet policy toward the FRG.[176] 'Managing the German problem', noted the French director of political affairs (in a remark that would be key later), no longer meant seeking from Moscow an understanding to prevent possible unification, but rather 'tying the Federal Republic of Germany firmly down to the Community'.[177] It was significant that when Gorbachev was expected in France in July 1989 after a visit to the FRG that had been marked by speculations about the German question, it still did not figure among the subjects that the French wanted to discuss as a priority.[178] True – and this point has already been mentioned as proving important later – there remained between the French and Soviets elements of understanding on *specific* aspects of the German problem: in addition to the border issue, Paris and Moscow continued to share the same hostility toward any West German access to nuclear weapons.[179] Mitterrand mentioned to Gorbachev during his visit to Paris that 'concerning the German problem, there is no escape from managing things together', adding: 'It has been solved with violence, and now should be solved in harmony.'[180] But in no way does it appear the two men thought the issue was central, or even salient.

A Resolved Issue?

In this context, the French attitude remained essentially unchanged. On the one hand, Mitterrand maintained the attitude he had held for several years, stressing the 'understandable' nature of the German aspiration to unity; on the other, there was a clear holding back on a subject where prudence remained advisable. Until the summer of 1989, he kept his reserve: if unification was a legitimate goal, it was not conceivable for the time being. When Bush asked him in Kennebunkport if he was favorable to such an eventuality, he replied that he 'was not against it because of the changes in Eastern Europe' and added: 'If the German people want it, it cannot be opposed' – but, as seen above, he said that he was skeptical about this eventuality, given the Soviet position.[181] Bush, in fact, proved equally cautious: while a first version of his speech in Mainz on 31 May clearly mentioned the goal of German unification, his National Security adviser Brent Scowcroft cut the passage in question: the problem had not been discussed beforehand with Bonn and the administration had no precise position on the subject; in these conditions, the White House feared 'needlessly stimulating German nationalism'.[182] In short, if American rhetoric could seem more open on the German question (the Mainz speech would be retrospectively interpreted in this way despite its being at best allusive in that regard), Washington and Paris in the spring of 1989 were not in very different positions. Caution was all the more in order because the question was not considered as open – and because it was felt at the same time that it might well return to the agenda and thus perturb a fragile equilibrium. While some in the spring of 1989 suggested active American support for the objective of unification, Scowcroft imposed a much more reserved line within the NSC, a line shared by the State Department, careful not to make more of it than the Germans themselves.[183] The Germans, too, were inclined to discretion to avoid a backlash: 'Always think but never speak about it', wrote Mitterrand later to describe the German attitude, paraphrasing Léon Gambetta on the Alsace-Lorraine question a century earlier.[184] In fact, in his meetings with Mitterrand a few days after his famous conversation with Gorbachev on the Rhine, Kohl, characteristically, did not breathe a word of this allegedly decisive exchange.[185]

In these circumstances, Mitterrand's declaratory policy remained marked until the start of the summer of 1989 by caution and continuity, and it remained essentially reactive. It was because he was asked about the subject during his joint press conference with Gorbachev on 5 July that he expressed himself publicly on the matter. Mitterrand pointed out the legitimacy of the aspiration of the Germans to unity and the 'determining' character of their choice, but also the need for the process 'to unfold in peace' and not be 'a factor in new tensions': 'I will not adopt a more imprudent attitude than that of the German leaders themselves, who are still very patriotic Germans', he soberly concluded.[186] Nevertheless thinking he should return to the subject, he did so three weeks later on the occasion of an interview that he granted to five European newspapers at the end of July, repeating that the goal was 'legitimate' but that unification could only be realized 'peacefully and democratically' – two adverbs that would henceforth summarize the French attitude to a German question soon to be reopened. And he specified that 'the inalienable right' of people to self-determination 'should not materialize with forceps': neither of the two

Germanys should 'impose its views on the other' and the process should be conducted without increasing 'Europe's internal tensions', he added.[187] With the German question returning to the top of the news in that summer of 1989, Mitterrand's discourse on the subject was thus gradually becoming more proactive: he was in fact the first Western leader to publicly acknowledge the legitimacy and the possibility of German unification, under certain conditions.

Still, for French diplomacy as for its Western partners, the German problem, on the eve of the upheavals of the second half of 1989, was less about a still improbable unification than about a real desire for national assertion: more than unity, it was full sovereignty to which the West Germans seemed to aspire. Even before the autumn's events, signs of a rejection of the supposed inferior status of the FRG were perceptible: hence Germany's wish to weigh more heavily in the West and assert its national interests, its impatience about the presence of foreign troops on its soil and hostility towards the presence of nuclear weapons, which were resented as a symbol of inferiority, and its contestation of everything that might express singularity or special status.[188] As the head of the planning staff of the Quai d'Orsay, Jean-Marie Guéhenno, put it, it was its 'humiliating dependence' that 'exacerbated the nationalism of a country that aspires to normality'. He added: 'Rather than a hypothetical drift to the East', it was a matter of West Germany's 'desire to assert itself'.[189]

Of course, this aspiration could in some respects be seen as contradicted by a certain fragility, for the Bonn government appeared quite weakened by its internal divisions and low support in public opinion. In fact, before the summer of 1989, Kohl's days seemed numbered and his chances of success in the 1990 elections compromised. Yet it was precisely this same political fragility that obliged Kohl to take decisions that his partners judged disconcerting, whether his alignment with Genscher's positions over SNF or his hesitations in European issues under pressure from his right wing. To be sure, the chancellor's diplomatic successes at the end of the spring (the NATO summit, visits by Bush and Gorbachev) allowed him to take back the upper hand; still, French diplomacy remained skeptical about the long-lasting character of this consolidation, for the underlying problems remained.[190] In short, in the spring of 1989, the French felt that the Federal Republic would be a less obliging partner in future and that the bilateral relationship should be adapted as a consequence. This relationship 'might [continue to] play a decisive role' in the future, Guéhenno thought, but on condition that France can offer a long-term perspective that 'would show the German people ... that a strong, sovereign, and responsible Germany had a central place in the French vision of Europe'.[191] As for Mitterrand, he thought philosophically that 'the result of all this is that relations between

France and Germany are not always very easy'.[192] Events of the coming months would amply confirm this.

France and the 'Exit' from the Cold War

Retrospectively, the first half of 1989 was a decisive moment. The European status quo appeared doomed even if nobody could foresee the ways, pace and still less the result of the now probable 'exit' from the Cold War and the return to a Europe 'whole and free'. Still, while everything appeared up for grabs, nothing was yet foreordained: 'Everyone has the feeling', said the political director of the Quai d'Orsay in a note written in February 1989, 'that the organization of Europe as it resulted from the Second World War is about to give way to something new without anyone knowing clearly where we are going'.[193] What, at that juncture, was the vision of a French diplomacy that from de Gaulle to Mitterrand had made the overcoming of 'Yalta' its grand design? How did it conceive of what a post–Cold War Europe might look like in the long run? By what paths and means and in what timescale could it be reached? Such questions need to be addressed at the end of this first chapter: we must situate French diplomacy at the end of a decade marked by a profound transformation in the logic of East-West relations, and also understand with which assumptions, expectations and schemas French diplomacy would approach the events in the last months of 1989 (still unforeseeable in the summer) that would effectively put an end to the Cold War. The answers are not obvious: the diplomatic apparatus, like the political leaders in this period, was more concerned with the daily aspects of international affairs than with long-term thinking. Yet the acceleration of history constrained diplomats and decision makers to project themselves into the future and to imagine the contours of a future Europe. True, one would be hard pressed to find a systematic exposition of the French vision of the post-Yalta scenario, yet the notes and analyses of some and the speeches and conversations of others allow us to form an idea of what that French vision was.

Grand Europe?

Since 1981, the Mitterrandian discourse on the need to 'exit from Yalta' had not varied. But what might have appeared a slogan became a powerful reality starting in 1988 and still more in 1989. The thawing of Eastern Europe indeed meant envisaging a practical way to overcome the division of the Old Continent; this would be the 'grand affair' of the century's end, according to the French president. How did his diplomacy imagine the 'other Europe' beyond the Cold War? First, as a democratized Europe: despite the criticisms that surrounded his visits to Prague, Sofia and Warsaw and French diplomacy's sometimes negligent tradition in this domain, the democratic transition in the East – even if he recognized its necessarily gradual character, as he did with Jaruzelski in June 1989 – was in his eyes the precondition for challenging 'Yalta'; hence he proposed in the spring of 1989 to admit the nascent democracies of Eastern Europe to the Council of Europe.[194] On the other hand, one suspects that Mitterrand would accommodate himself to an Eastern Europe that, while having broken with a Communism of Marxist-Leninist inspiration, would continue to practice some type of Socialist system. The French president in the spring of 1989 was far from envisaging the rapidity with which the Eastern countries would adopt market economies in the following years – this would weigh on the project for a European confederation, as we shall see.[195] In fact, for Mitterrand's diplomacy (heir to the Gaullist vision of a Europe 'from the Atlantic to the Urals'), the real touchstone of change in the East was less a return to the liberal model in Central and Eastern Europe than the reassertion of 'nations' beyond blocs, meaning their return to 'full decision-making', as he had said to the Hungarian leaders in 1988. True, at this stage it was not a matter of questioning alliances, properly speaking, even if one hoped to push them into the background. The Élysée thought it 'useless' to challenge immediately the political and military separation between the two Europes, even if 'the combination of negotiations over conventional disarmament and over new security and confidence-building measures' might contribute to erasing 'the logic of blocs'.[196] More modestly, the goal for French diplomacy was 'to reintroduce real fluidity to the continent, in political relations among States as well as in all kinds of contact among people'.[197]

Socialist but democratic countries, linked to the USSR but once more free in their choices and able to resume their place in the Europe of nations: such was the Mitterrandian vision of the transition in Eastern Europe on the eve of the upheavals of 1989. For him, this transition was the condition for the desired rapprochement between a de-Sovietized Eastern Europe and an increasingly integrated Western Europe, each conserving its socioeconomic and geopolitical identity but sharing the same democratic principles and seeking convergences so as to 'surmount existing borders in practical life, in economic and cultural exchanges, in the circulation of people and ideas'.[198] It was within this pan-European framework that French diplomacy envisaged the evolution of the German problem in the medium to long term: the rapprochement between East and West, the Quai d'Orsay thought, would offer 'certain prospects for rapprochement' between East and West Germany, thereby helping the two countries to 'surmount the division – if not political, at least human – from which the German people suffered'. The evolution of the German problem, then, was conceived by the French not in the mode of state unification (at least not in the foreseeable future) but as a process that would allow the effects of the break to be attenuated. In short (as de Gaulle had once postulated), the German problem and the European problem were inseparable and their solution should progress in tandem; this appraisal (which mostly converged with Brandt's Ostpolitik) would be the key to Mitterrand's later policy.[199] Finally, let us repeat that the gradual character of this evolution was essential: in the analysis of French leaders, starting with Mitterrand himself, this process would take a decade at least. But it was also and especially a matter of prescription: as we saw, the awareness or fear of a risk of instability (return of nationalisms in the East, failure of the Gorbachev experiment) became after 1988 a preponderant factor in Paris, were it was thought that 'we have no interest in forcing the pace'.[200] This concern would obviously weigh in the coming months.

In what 'architectural form' did French diplomacy conceive of this reconciled *grande Europe* that the end of the Cold War allowed people to hope for? First and foremost, of course, it was to exist within the framework of the CSCE, which was seen as the best way of bypassing 'the divisions that separate the European countries' and of building 'real confidence among them'.[201] For Paris, the Helsinki Conference remained the best instrument to allow European states to free themselves from the logic of blocs. Moreover, the CSCE had the advantage of maintaining an interaction favored by the French between the security, economic and human dimensions (the three 'baskets') of East-West relations. In 1989, it was incontestably the first dimension that appeared to them the most promising for change in the East (it was expected that the CFE talks would limit the Soviet capacity for intimidation in Eastern Europe) and in East-West relations (the talks would break the logic of military confrontation by establishing a balance at the lowest level between the two alliances). For these reasons, the French insisted on maintaining the CFE within the CSCE framework and were opposed to any bloc-to-bloc negotiations.[202]

But although French diplomacy privileged the CSCE, its attachment to the Helsinki process, as we will see, was not unlimited. On the one hand, the French wanted to avoid any 'drift' toward a collective security organization that would replace alliances and challenge the transatlantic link and the American guarantee while preventing the emergence of a separate Western European defense. On the other hand, Mitterrand's policy considered the CSCE to be a framework unsuited to the European cooperation that it strongly wished for in concrete domains like energy, technology or culture – for which the Helsinki process was inadequate due to the presence of the United States and Canada.[203] Thus there was an ambivalent

French attitude to Gorbachev's idea of the 'common home', which aroused both distrust over its security implications (the French saw it as a rehash of old Soviet ideas on collective security) and genuine interest in its other dimensions, with Mitterrand trying by all accounts to respond to Gorbachev on that terrain.[204] Védrine warned that 'this sympathetic expression' signified for the Soviets 'a Europe without Americans, without the Atlantic Alliance, without European defense', whereas 'we would rather dream of a Europe of 32 nations (Western Europe without the United States and Canada plus Eastern Europe without the USSR).'[205] Here is already posed the whole problematic of the European confederation, Mitterrand's future response to the common home: cooperative (but not collective) security within the CSCE framework, residual alliances freed from their bloc character, and concrete cooperation organized within what would become known as the Confederation. This was the essence of the French vision of a '*grande Europe*' beyond the Cold War before the upheavals of the autumn of 1989.

The Community Imperative

In this vision, the European Community self-evidently occupied a central place: French diplomacy's 'first objective' was to 'strengthen the cohesion of the Community, the core of any organization of a Europe from the Atlantic to the Urals'.[206] 'The Twelve', noted Védrine in the spring of 1989, 'are the best placed to conceive and put into operation … a regular, constant and smooth reestablishment of links between the two Europes'.[207] French diplomacy thought it was up to the Community to foster the 'gradual rapprochement' between Western Europe and a de-Sovietized Eastern Europe, to serve 'as magnet to the various parcels of a Soviet Empire on its way to being Ottomanized'. To do so, the Community should be surrounded by a 'second circle' composed of countries of the Council of Europe so that cooperation would be jointly organized with the countries of the East (the 'third circle') in domains like culture, the media, social issues or even technology (on the basis of Eureka, a program that exceeded the contours of the Community). This Europe of concentric circles (the Twelve, then the Western countries not belonging to the Community, and finally the Eastern countries) – which was also among Commission President Jacques Delors' ambitions – prefigured the future Mitterrand-style confederation.

Last but not least, of course, the strengthening of the European Community should, in French eyes, contribute to the solution of the German problem. Against the background of rapprochement between the two Germanys and between the two Europes, 'managing the German problem', the French believed, signified 'tying the Federal Republic strongly to the

Community, with Franco-German relations being the privileged means' to that end.[208] Overall, Mitterrand regarded the Community imperative, on the eve of the revolutionary events of the fall, as the condition sine qua non of a stable transition toward post–Cold War Europe. Inversely, the end of 'Yalta' was perceived as the occasion to make the Community the cornerstone of the *grande Europe* beyond blocs: '[P]ursuing the construction of the Europe of Twelve and working to reestablish the unity of our continent are two projects that, far from being opposite, complement and reinforce each other.'[209]

The end of the Cold War, by the same token, was perceived as a challenge for European construction, for while they saw the former as an opportunity, French leaders were also worried about a possible calling into question of the latter. 'The strengthening of the Community's cohesion, the preservation of its potential political and defense dimensions', they believed, were thus 'an absolute priority'.[210] Even before the acceleration of the second half of 1989 the French no doubt feared 'dilution', in a post-Yalta grand Europe, of what the Community had accomplished – this concern would become the focus of Mitterrand's policy in the following months. Hence it was imperative to postpone any new enlargement of the European Community in favor of accomplishing its necessary deepening first. Regarding enlargement, for French diplomacy the very success of the Community in the wake of the European Single Act of 1986 and the approach of the 1992 deadline conferred on it 'a considerable power of attraction', but any new memberships, notably of EFTA states like Austria, would increase the risk of a dilution in both the economic and the political dimension. The French therefore believed that even if the door was not closed forever, one should 'clearly and quickly state that there will be no new members in the ten or twenty years to come' and that it would be best to organize the 'second circle' accordingly and make it a veritable 'buffer zone' around the Twelve. As for deepening, it had to be fostered by a 'dynamization of political cooperation' of the Twelve, leading in due course to 'a political union and in turn, quite naturally, to a defense policy' (this latter goal reinforced the need to avoid in the foreseeable future the accession of neutral countries – like Austria – whose presence in the 'second circle' was judged more useful from the perspective of East-West rapprochement).[211] A European Community that would be durably limited to its current contours and would gradually assert itself as an international power – such was then the French vision that events of the autumn of 1989 would put to the test.

The question of relations with the superpowers also arose. Of course, there was no real symmetry, let alone equivalence, between the USSR and the United States in French perceptions. Still, France's European ambitions represented a challenge to both sides. With regard to the USSR, Paris was aware of the persistence of Soviet reticence about European integration despite Moscow's now manifest interest in the project. The 'common home', as mentioned above, appeared to French diplomats as 'revealing fears aroused in the USSR by the progress of European construction': the fear of breaking with the most economically and technologically dynamic part of Europe, the concern about the attraction exercised by the EEC over the countries of the East, and of course the danger it felt over the emergence of a political and military ensemble built around Franco-German cooperation, a project that continued to arouse distrust in Moscow and ran against its own traditional pan-European designs.[212] Inversely, Mitterrand's vision of post-Yalta Europe postulated (as had de Gaulle's) that a Western Europe more politically united and militarily autonomous would indeed become in time the fundamental element of the European equilibrium. Convincing the USSR of the innocuousness of Franco-German cooperation and of a Western Europe that would be capable of asserting itself politically and militarily thus appeared as one of the major objectives of French diplomacy even before the events of the fall of 1989.[213]

Simultaneously, the French ambition to see such a Western European entity emerge also raised the question of the Atlantic Alliance and the relationship between Europe and the United States. French leaders indeed thought the Western Alliance was bound to change profoundly as a result of conventional disarmament and the lowering of military expenditure as well as the reduction in American troops in Europe and the United States' desire for a better 'burden sharing'.[214] Of course, there was no calling into question an alliance that remained one of the foundations of French security and defense policy. By the end of the 1980s, Mitterrand remained skeptical (perhaps more so than his own diplomats) about the possibility of a truly autonomous European defense that could in the near future be substituted for the American guarantee. Still, the rebalancing of the transatlantic relationship and a certain military self-assertion by Western Europe (the mechanical consequence of an American disengagement judged inevitable now that the Soviet threat was fading) naturally figured among the French expectations for the post–Cold War era. These objectives would play a major role in France's European and Atlantic policy of the following months and years.

France in the New European Order

What role would France have in post-Yalta Europe? On the eve of the autumn events, there was no doubt that those responsible for French diplomacy envisaged it as central, if only because the country kept some of the serious advantages of a great power. As a nuclear state and permanent member of the UN Security Council, France, it was thought, had no reason to fear a recasting of European politics. True, the French were aware that such a recomposition might first and foremost benefit the FRG, now the dominant European power, but they were confident that France's status as a world power would not be called into question. France was one of the four victors of 1945 and therefore co-responsible, along with the United States, Great Britain and the USSR, for the fate of Germany – and nothing allowed people to think that Germany's international status would change in the short term. In a Europe gradually freed of blocs, France, it was believed, might renew its old contacts to the East and resume its traditional positions there while entertaining complex-free relations with a Germany that was increasingly assertive, but whose state unification remained merely a distant hypothesis. Mitterrand's diplomacy, in sum, seemed to have little to fear from post-Yalta, as it was envisaged in the summer of 1989. This was all the more so because its Western European priority (France, it should be recalled, was set to assume the presidency of the Community in the second half of 1989) seemed to guarantee it an influence that would be increased by wielding the lever of the Community: in this new Europe 'that carries as many risks as opportunities', the Quai d'Orsay thought, 'France, which is probably the only one among the Twelve to have a coherent European vision' appeared 'the best placed to take the initiative'.[215] The euphoric atmosphere of July 1989 (from Gorbachev's visit to the Arche Summit to the bicentennial celebrations of the French Revolution) confirmed this: far from being worried, Mitterrand's diplomacy was surfing on the wave of change and proclaiming its confidence in European transformations that it had ceaselessly called for, and in which it had no doubt it would find its interests satisfied.

On the eve of upheavals whose breadth, speed and outcome nobody could foretell, there existed, therefore, a 'French path' to exit from the Cold War. Of course, the expectations, preferences and especially the priorities of Mitterrand's diplomacy for 'post-Yalta' were not identical to those of others. While some privileged the Atlantic dimension (obviously the case with the Americans and the British or even West Germans, at least as incarnated by Kohl), and while others put the accent on the pan-European dimension (as did Gorbachev and Genscher, each in his own way), the French above all advanced the Western European dimension. This, for them, was a priority over the organization of the grand Europe and still more over the maintenance of an Atlantic Alliance that the French saw more as the last recourse of European security than as an instrument of East-West change. We will see how this EC priority contributed, only a few months later, to the impression of a French policy of trying to put the brakes on German unification until after Europe was unified first. We will also see how, beyond German unity, this same Western European project would earn France the stigma of opposing the flow of history because it was attached to a vision of the European Community that was now judged as outmoded by the proponents of building a grand Europe and opposed as harmful by those unconditionally wedded to the larger Atlantic Community. In the summer of 1989, however, Mitterrand's diplomacy could not be reduced to a pure and simple policy of preserving the status quo. It remained to be seen to what extent the acceleration of events in the autumn, and how things turned out in the following months, would actually coincide with the French 'scenario' for exiting from Yalta.

Notes

1. MAE, Direction d'Europe, Sous-direction d'Europe orientale, note a.s. L'URSS fin mai 1988 et les relations franco-soviétiques, 31 May 1988, Archives diplomatiques (AD), Europe, Série URSS 1986–1990, box 6670.
2. MAE, Direction d'Europe, Sous-direction d'Europe orientale, note a.s. Relance de la politique à l'Est : dossier technique, 28 June 1988, AD, Europe, Série Communisme et eurocommunisme 1986–1990, box 6095; see also Note du directeur d'Europe (Jacques Blot) pour le Ministre, a.s. Relance de notre politique à l'Est, 21 July 1988; and Hubert Védrine, note pour le président de la République, a.s. Le développement de nos rapports avec l'Europe de l'Est, 13 July 1988, private papers.
3. MAE, Direction d'Europe, Sous-direction d'Europe orientale, note a.s. Relations franco-soviétiques, 8 September 1988, AD, Europe, URSS 1986–1990, box 6674.
4. The message was passed on by Ambassadeur Riabov: TD Diplomatie 13061, DSL secret, 24 June 1988, AD, série Europe, URSS 1986–1990, box 6673. Riabov was also received by Mitterrand on 7 June: see Hubert Védrine's handwritten notes (n.d.), private papers.
5. MAE, CAP, note, a.s. Entretiens de planification franco-soviétiques (Paris 20–21 septembre 1988), 29 September 1988, AD, Europe, URSS 1986–1990, box 6674. To be sure, statements by members of the Soviet delegation showed that Moscow had not yet overcome its habit of intimidation. Soviet diplomacy, they said, had to 'decide in the coming 12 months' which one of the three great European powers (France, Germany and the United Kingdom) it was in its interest 'to favor', and it was 'a pity' that one 'was in a situation of hesitation', because 'a few years ago, the answer was self evident'. Be that as it may, the French were aware of Moscow's new interest in the European community starting in 1988, which manifested itself, amongst other ways, in the creation of a new institute of Western Europe: see TD Moscou 460, 4 February 1988, AD, Europe, URSS 1986–1990, box 6674. On Gorbachev and his entourage becoming aware of the importance of the dynamics of European integration, see Anatoly S. Chernyaev, *My Six Years with Gorbachev*, University Park, Pennsylvania University Press, 2000, p. 105ff.; Marie-Pierre Rey, 'Europe' is Our Common Home : A Study of Gorbachev's Diplomatic Concept', *Cold War History*, vol. 4, n° 2 (01/2004), pp. 33–65; and Jacques Lévesque, *1989, la fin d'un empire. L'URSS et la libération de l'Europe de l'Est*, Paris, Presses de la FNSP, 1995.

6. TD Ministre 6, DSL secret, 26 September 1988, AD, Europe, USSR 1986–1990, box 6674; see also a thick dossier in preparation of Shevardnadze's visit; and Note de synthèse, a.s. Visite officielle de M. Chevardnadze à Paris, (10–12 octobre 1988), n. d., AD, Europe 1986–1990, box 6684.
7. Jean Musitelli, note pour le président de la République, Votre entretien avec M. Chevardnadze (lundi 10 octobre, 15h), 10 October 1988, private papers.
8. MAE, note a.s. Visite de M. Chevardnadze à Paris, conférence de presse, no date, AD, Europe, URSS 1986–1990, box 6684; Fiche, 'Groupes de travail franco-soviétiques', 18 November 1988, AD, Europe, URSS 1986–1990, box 6680.
9. MAE, CAP, note, a.s. Entretiens de planification franco-soviétiques, 29 September 1988.
10. MAE, Sous-direction d'Europe orientale, note a.s. Discours de M. Gorbatchev devant l'AGNU (7 décembre 1988), AD, Europe, URSS 1986–1990, box 6649. In Moscow, Gorbachev's entourage thought that the speech 'had brought us to a new level in world politics' and that 'now we can't afford concessions to the policies of the past': see Chernyaev, *My Six Years*, p. 148. It was this deep intellectual renewal that led Gorbachev and his entourage to give priority to the Old Continent in their international thinking, a change that resulted in their advancing the concept of a European 'common home', which a few years before was but a slogan of Brezhnev's diplomacy: see above all Rey, 'Europe', and Lévesque, *1989*, pp. 55ff. and 101ff.
11. Le directeur d'Europe, note pour le Ministre, a.s. Relance de notre politique à l'Est, 21 July 1988.
12. Hence French diplomacy showed itself to be less hostile, in the fall of 1988, to the idea of a meeting on the 'human dimension' of the CSCE taking place in Moscow by 1991; see Note du directeur adjoint d'Europe, a.s. Conférence sur la dimension humaine, 24 October 1988, AD, Europe 1986–1990, URSS, box 6650 (Mitterrand, however, remained guarded on this topic when he visited Moscow the following month).
13. Meeting between Mitterrand and Reagan, Toronto, 19 June 1988, handwritten report, private papers.
14. Interview with *Libération*, 23 November 1988, Ministère des affaires étrangères, *Politique étrangère de la France. Textes et documents* (*PEF*), November-December 1988, pp. 50–57.
15. The Élysée noted that acceptance by Paris of the idea of a conference on the 'human dimension' that would take place in Moscow (see above, note 12) was interpreted as complacency by the press: Musitelli, note pour le président de la République, Moscou. Droits de l'Homme, 14 November 1988, private papers.
16. MAE, Direction d'Europe, Fiche a.s. Situations et perspectives en URSS et dans les pays d'Europe de l'Est : conclusions susceptibles d'être tirées de la réunion de nos ambassadeurs à l'Est, 14 October 1988, AD, Europe, Communisme et eurocommunisme 1986–1990, box 6092.
17. TD Moscou 5211–5212 and 5345–5347, 17 and 21 November 1988, AD, Europe, URSS 1986–1990, box 6680.
18. Annoucing the establishment on a permanent basis of the Franco-Soviet working groups created the previous month, as well as the calendar of future meetings, was for the Quai the main goal of the presidential visit: see MAE, Direction d'Europe, Fiche a.s.Visite de M. le président de la République en URSS (25–26 novembre), conception générale: propositions, 8 November 1988, AD, Europe, URSS 1986–1990, box 6680; and fiche a.s. Groupes de travail franco-soviétiques, 18 November 1988.
19. Report in TD Moscou 5619 and 5620, 2 December 1988, AD, Europe 1986–1990, URSS, box 6680; and Meeting between Mitterrand and Gorbachev, Moscow, 25 November 1988, private papers. Védrine 'didn't find the atmosphere between the two men this

time to be very pleasant': see Hubert Védrine, *Les Mondes de François Mitterrand. À l'Élysée 1981–1995,* Paris, Fayard, 1996, pp. 390–391. Back in Paris, he deplored the bad treatment given to the French press by Soviet authorities, which some journalists interpreted as a desire of some of Gorbachev's foes to humiliate France: Védrine, note pour le président de la République, 28 November 1988, private papers.

20. During his meeting with dissidents a day later, he recognized that Gorbachev was still far from giving the same meaning to the words 'rights' and 'liberty', even if dialogue with him on this subject was now possible: see Ambassade de France en URSS, petit déjeuner du président de la République avec des personnalités non officielles, résidence de l'ambassadeur de France, 26 November 1988, AD, Europe, URSS 1986–1990, box 6680.

21. MAE, Direction d'Europe, note a.s. Visite de M. le président de la République en URSS (25–26 novembre), Conception génerale, propositions, 8 novembre 1988.

22. 'Argumentaire' distributed on 2 December 1988, private papers.

23. The French diplomats' reluctance to enter into more intense relations with Moscow was met with impatience at the Élysée. See a memo in which Védrine complained that the majority of French diplomats posted in Moscow were hostile to *perestroïka* and a more active French policy in the East: Védrine, note pour le président de la République, 14 December 1988, private papers.

24. See for example MAE, Service des affaires stratégiques et du désarmement, note a.s. Visite de M. Gorbatchev. Affaires politico-militaires, désarmement, 29 June 1989; and dossier de synthèse, a.s. Visite de M. Gorbachev (4–6 juillet 1989), no date, AD, Europe, URSS 1986–1990, box 6685.

25. TD Moscou 4065, 2 July 1989, DSL, Secret, AD, Europe, URSS 1986–1990, box 6685; and Musitelli, note pour le président de la République, Visite de M. Gorbatchev, 3 July 1989, private papers; see also Musitelli, note pour le président de la République, Visite de M. Gorbatchev, 28 June 1989; and Védrine, note pour le président de la République, Réponses soviétiques à propos du programme du voyage de M. Gorbatchev, 30 June 1989, archives nationales (AN), 5AG4/CDM 48.

26. Dossier de synthèse, a.s. Visite de M. Gorbachev (4–6 juillet 1989), no date.

27. MAE, Direction Europe, le directeur, J. Blot, Note, a.s. Visite de M. Gorbatchev en France, 30 juin 1989, AD, Europe, URSS 1986–1990, box 6685. Cambodia, the Near East, Lebanon and Southern Africa were quoted as examples of a Franco-Soviet dialogue.

28. TD Diplomatie 14103, 7 July 1989, AD, Europe, URSS 1986–1990, box 6685.

29. TD Moscou 4327, 12 July 1989; and MAE, Direction d'Europe, Sous-direction URSS, note a.s. Éléments de comparaison entre les visites de M. Gorbatchev en France et en RFA, 18 July 1989, AD, Europe, URSS 1986–1990, box 6685.

30. Mikhaïl Gorbatchev, *Mémoires,* Éditions du Rocher, 1997, p. 631. Gorbachev declared the day after his visit to Paris that 'We have to devote primary attention to France': quoted in Hannes Adomeit, *Imperial Overstretch: Germany in Soviet Policy from Stalin to Gorbachev,* Baden-Baden, Nomos, 1998, pp. 399–400.

31. Pierre Favier and Michel Martin-Roland, *La Décennie Mitterrand,* vol. 3, 'Les Défis', 1988–1991, pp.172–173; Védrine, *Les Mondes,* pp. 482–483; Gorbatchev, *Mémoires,* p. 634; and George Bush and Brent Scowcroft, *A World Transformed,* New York, Vintage Books, 1999, p. 132.

32. Letter from Gorbachev to Mitterrand, 15 July 1989; letter from Mitterrand to Gorbachev, 26 July 1989, private papers.

33. Védrine, note pour le président de la République, 6 July 1989, private papers.

34. MAE, Sous-direction d'Europe orientale, note a.s. Les pays de l'Est et l'URSS depuis l'avènement de M. Gorbatchev, 23 June 1986, AD, Europe, Communisme et eurocom-

munisme 1986–1990, box 6092. On Soviet policy in Eastern Europe, the work of reference is Lévesque, *1989;* see also Vladislav M. Zubok, 'New Evidence on the Soviet Factor in the Peaceful Revolutions of 1989', and Jacques Lévesque, 'Soviet Approaches to Eastern Europe at the Beginning of 1989', *Cold War International History Project Bulletin* 12/13 (fall/winter 2001): 5–23 and 49–72.

35. MAE, Sous-direction d'Europe orientale, note a.s. Deux années de Gorbatchev: relations avec les alliés d'Europe de l'Est, 13 March 1987; CAP, note a.s. L'Europe de l'Est à l'heure Gorbatchev, 19 October 1987 AD, Europe 1986–1990, Communisme et eurocommunisme, box 6092; and Sous-direction d'Europe orientale, fiche a.s. L'URSS et les pays d'Europe de l'Est, 8 March 1988, AD, Europe 1986–1990, URSS, box 6650.
36. MAE, Sous-direction d'Europe orientale, note a.s. Les évolutions en Europe de l'Est, 3 June 1988; and note a.s. Les évolutions en URSS et en Europe de l'Est, 23 June 1988, AD, Europe 1986–1990, Communisme et eurocommunisme, box 6092. Things started to change deeply in the summer of 1988. The turning point of the 19th CPSU conference was particularly important for Eastern Europe, as it was from then on that Gorbachev established the sociopolitical 'freedom of choice' as a 'universal principle' and a 'key concept' of Soviet policy. Even if it was not a question of abandoning the sphere of influence, it was about making it evolve toward an agreed Soviet preeminence: see Lévesque, *1989*, p. 106.
37. Meeting between Mitterrand and De Mita, 3 June 1988; Conseil de défense, 20 July 1988, private papers.
38. Dumas, *Le Fil*, pp. 365–366.
39. This is what he confided to Lech Walesa and Bronislaw Geremek at the end of 1988: meeting on 10 December 1988, private papers.
40. MRE, note a.s. La France et 'l'autre Europe', 19 March 1986, AD, Europe, Communisme et eurocommunisme 1986–1990, box 6095.
41. MAE, Sous-direction d'Europe orientale, note a.s. Relance de la politique à l'Est, 27 June 1988, AD, Europe 1986–1990, RFA, box 6795.
42. MAE, Sous-direction d'Europe orientale, note a.s. Les évolutions en URSS et en Europe de l'Est, 23 June 1988.
43. Favier and Martin-Roland, *La Décennie*, vol. 3, p. 167; Dumas, *Le Fil*, p. 372; and Jean Lacouture and Patrick Rotman, *Mitterrand. Le Roman du pouvoir*, Paris, Seuil, 2000, p.208.
44. Elisabeth Guigou, note pour le président de la République, Une proposition d'initiative commune avec le chancelier Kohl, 30 May 1988, private papers.
45. Védrine, note pour le président de la République, a.s. Le développement de nos rapports avec l'Europe de l'Est, 13 July 1988, private papers.
46. Note du Directeur d'Europe pour le Ministre, a.s. Relance de notre politique à l'Est, 21 July 1988.
47. Note du Directeur d'Europe pour le Ministre, a.s. Relance de notre politique à l'Est, 21 July 1988; and Sous-direction d'Europe orientale, note a.s. Relance de la politique à l'Est: dossier technique, 28 June 1988; amongst other goals: a plan to invite new elites and visits from personalities, increasing the portion relative to Eastern Europe in the budget of the DGRSCT (the Quai's directorate for cultural exchanges), etc.
48. MAE, Sous-direction d'Europe orientale, note de synthèse, a.s Visite en Tchécoslovaquie du ministre d'État (15–17 September 1988), 12 September 1988, private papers.
49. Musitelli, note pour le président de la République, Vos entretiens avec M. Grosz (jeudi 17 novembre, 12h30), 16 November 1988, private papers.
50. Meeting between Mitterrand and Grosz, 17 November 1988, Musitelli's handwritten notes, private papers.

51. Mitterrand and Grosz's joint press conference, Palais de l'Élysée, 18 November 1988, *PEF*, November–December 1988, pp. 39–41.
52. Interview granted to *Libération*, 23 November 1988.
53. Conseil des ministres, 26 October 1988, private papers. At this stage, a visit to Czechoslovakia and one to Bulgaria were scheduled for December 1988 and January 1989 respectively; a visit to Poland (where dialogue between the government and the opposition was slow to start) was being considered (it would take place in June 1989); moreover, Mitterrand had accepted the idea of a visit to the GDR upon Honecker's invitation (who had come to Paris in January 1988) and to Hungary (returning Grosz's in November) but the dates were not fixed yet (they would take place respectively in December 1989 and in January 1990). Only Romania was excluded from this schedule because of the Ceausescu regime, considered '*infréquentable*'.
54. TD Moscou 5211, 17 November 1988, AD, Europe 1986, URSS 1986–1990, box 6680; MAE, Direction d'Europe, Fiche a.s. Situations et perspectives en URSS et dans les pays d'Europe de l'Est, 14 October 1988.
55. Musitelli, note pour le président de la République, Votre visite à Prague. Droits de l'homme, 5 December 1988, private papers. Paris had to threaten to cancel the visit at the last minute if the meeting wasn't authorized by the authorities: see Musitelli's and Éric Danon's testimonies in Samy Cohen (ed.), *Mitterrand et la sortie de la guerre froide*, Paris, PUF, 1998, pp. 219 and 221. In the same book, Jacques Rupnik harshly criticizes the choice of Prague and Sofia as early destinations, which he saw as a credit given to disreputable regimes, echoing retrospectively the fears then expressed by Václav Havel (see next note). This critique, however, underestimates the importance given by Mitterrand to human rights during these visits. It also overestimates the meaning of these destinations: the possibility of starting the tour with the most 'acceptable' of Eastern Europe's capitals was limited because the Hungarian leader had just gone to Paris, and because a visit to Poland was difficult to envisage as long as the 'round table' betwen government and opposition had not started effectively. (Rupnik was less removed from reality when he mentioned a possible 'improvisation': Mitterrand, evidently, wanted to quickly start his tour of Eastern Europe in the fall of 1988, even if this meant beginning in Prague and Sofia.)
56. Václav Havel, 'La Tchécoslovaquie, le masque et le visage', *Le Monde*, 2 December 1988.
57. Speech at the diner offered by Gustav Husak at Prague Castle, 8 December 1988, *PEF*, November–December 1988, pp. 128–130.
58. Mitterrand's breakfast with Czechoslovak dissidents, French Embassy, Prague, 9 December 1988, private papers.
59. Védrine, note pour le président de la République, 14 December 1988, private papers. Among the questions Védrine raised: were French diplomats stationed in the East well prepared? Was the financial effort adequate? (A budget increase requested by the Quai to ensure the relaunching in the East, notably for the DGRCST, had recently been refused by the ministry of finances.)
60. Meeting on 10 December 1988.
61. MAE, le directeur adjoint d'Europe, note a.s. Visite officielle de M. Qian Qichen, 3 January 1989; sous-direction d'Europe orientale, fiche d'entretien, a.s. Situation et perspectives des relations Est-Ouest, 16 January 1989, AD, Europe, Communisme et eurocommunisme 1986–1990, box 6097.
62. MAE, Sous-direction d'Europe orientale, fiche d'entretien, a.s. Situation et perspectives des relations Est-Ouest, 16 January 1989; and Note a.s. L'URSS et ses alliés est-européens, 8 March 1989, AD, Europe, Communisme et eurocommunisme 1986–1990, box 6092; TD Moscou 1329, 14 March 1989, AD, Europe, URSS 1986–1990, box 6650.

63. MAE, CAP, note de Nicole Gnesotto, a.s. Impressions de Washington, 9 March 1989, AD, Europe, Communisme et eurocommunisme 1986–1990, box 6097.
64. Védrine, note pour le président de la République, 29 March 1989, private papers.
65. Védrine, note pour le président de la République, 6 April 1989, private papers.
66. MAE, Sous-direction URSS, fiche a.s. Relations Est-Ouest : situation et perspectives, 8 June 1989, AD, Europe, Communisme et eurocommunisme 1986–1990, box 6097.
67. Meeting between Mitterrand and Jaruzelski, 14 June 1989, Musitelli's handwritten notes, private papers. The day following the elections in Warsaw, the Quai d'Orsay wanted 'this movement to continue at its own pace and spread to other advanced countries': MAE, note, Les relations entre l'URSS et les pays de l'Est, 20 June 1989, Europe AD, URSS 1986–1990, box 6685.
68. Védrine noted that, despite the initial hesitations and fears expressed by some that this policy might reinforce the existing regimes, 'The idea that France should be more present in all of Eastern Europe now prevailed.' see Védrine, note pour le président de la République, 6 July 1989.
69. Several top actors, at the Élysée as well as the Quai d'Orsay, do not seem to recall that the 'relance à l'Est' was, in this period, a real operational priority, apart from the scheduling of presidential visits: personal meetings; see also the memoir of Védrine, *Les Mondes,* which doesn't make any mention of it.
70. Quoted in Lévesque, *1989,* p. 153.
71. In a speech in Hamtramck, Michigan, on 17 April, Bush declared that the Cold War had started in Eastern Europe and that it would come to an end there. As for his visit to Warsaw at the beginning of July, it seems to have played a significant role in assuring the election of Jaruzelski as president of the republic several days later: see Hutchings, *American Diplomacy,* p. 38ff. and 48ff., and Lévesque, *1989,* pp. 158–159.
72. MAE, Les relations entre l'URSS et les pays d'Europe orientale, 20 June 1989, and TD Diplomatie 14103, 7 July 1989. Characteristically, in Gorbachev's Strasbourg speech the Élysée did not read a clear refutation of the Brezhnev doctrine, but rather an affirmation that 'surmounting the division of Europe does not mean to surmount socialism', a remark interpreted as a response to American activism; see Védrine, note pour le président de la République, a.s. Discours de M. Gorbatchev à Strasbourg, 6 July 1989, private papers. In Washington too, the import of the speech was seen as limited: if the Soviets were favorable to change in theory, they were worried in practice; see Hutchings, *American Diplomacy,* p. 61. Before Gorbachev's departure for Strasbourg at the end of his Paris visit, Mitterrand assured the Soviet premier, who was worried about the new tone of the U.S. Administration regarding Eastern Europe (Washington having called for a withdrawal of Soviet troops from Poland), that he had advised Bush to pursue moderation: see meeting between Mitterrand and Gorbachev, 6 July 1989, private papers.
73. Védrine, note pour le président de la République, 6 July 1989.
74. MAE, Sous-direction des affaires stratégique et des pactes, note a.s. L'affaire SNF; historique, 20 décembre 1988, AD, Affaires stratégiques et désarmement (ASD) 1985–1990, box 15; see above, prologue, note 73.
75. MAE, Sous-direction des affaires stratégique et des pactes, Fiche a.s. La RFA et la question des SNF, 24 June1988, and Fiche a.s. État des travaux concernant un 'concept global de maîtrise des armements et de désarmement', 6 July 1988, AD, ASD 1985–1990, box 15.
76. Védrine, note pour le président de la République, Modernisation des armes à courte portée de l'OTAN, 23 September 1988, private papers.
77. Védrine, note pour le président de la République, 19 November 1988, private papers.
78. TD Moscou 5619–5620, 2 December 1988; meeting between Mitterrand and Gorbachev, Moscow, 25 November 1988.

79. MAE, Direction des affaires stratégiques et des pactes, note, a.s. L'affaire SNF : problématique et enjeux, 21 December 1988, AD, ASD 1985–1990, box 15.
80. France had given special attention to the question of conventional arms negotiations since reactivating its disarmament policy in 1978, a move that contributed to holding, starting in 1984, the Stockholm conference on disarmament in Europe (CDE). After the conclusion of the CDE in 1986, the CSCE, which was gathered in Vienna, discussed the terms of a negotiation on conventional weapons, whose mandate would be finally adopted in January 1989 at the end of the CSCE meeting. (The beginning of negotiations on conventional forces in Europe (CFE) in March 1989 brought about the end of the MBFR negotiations between NATO and the Warsaw pact, which Paris had always rejected, believing that it would in fact perpetuate military blocs). On all this, see Jean Klein, *Sécurité et désarmement en Europe*, Paris, IFRI, coll. 'Travaux et recherches', 1987.
81. The argument was constantly used by French diplomats: see e.g. meetings in Bonn of Benoît d'Aboville, in TD Bonn 734, 14 April 1988, AD, Europe, RFA 1986–1990, box 6782.
82. See e.g. the meeting between Mitterrand and NATO Secretary General Manfred Woerner, 22 July 1988, private papers, and meeting between Mitterrand and Gorbachev, Moscow, 25 November 1988.
83. The French were on the defensive about defining the mandate of the negotiation, notably in contrast to the Germans, who were a lot more relaxed: see MAE, le Directeur des affaires politiques (B. Dufourcq), fiche a.s. Réunion de travail à la Chancellerie. Bonn (23.9.88), 3 October 1988, confidential, AD, DP, box 281; see also Benoît d'Aboville, 'The French Approach to Conventional Arms Control', in Uwe Nerlich and James A. Thomson (eds.), *Conventional Arms Control and the Security of Europe* (Boulder, CO: Westview Press, 1988).
84. See TD Diplomatie 24590, 8 December 1988, AD, Europe, URSS 1986–1990, box 6649.
85. James A. Baker III and Thomas M. DeFrank, *The Politics of Diplomacy: Revolution, War and Peace 1989–1992*, New York, Putnam, 1995 p. 43ff.
86. Michael R. Beschloss and Strobe Talbott, *At the Highest Levels: The Inside Story of the End of the Cold War*, Boston, Little & Brown, 1994, p. 37.
87. MAE, le chef du CAP, Fiche a.s. Conférence d'Ebenhausen sur les 'tâches de l'Alliance', 27 February 1989, AD, ASD 1985–1990, box 130 bis.
88. See TD Washington 778–779, 6 April 1989, AD, ASD 1985–1990, box 130 bis.
89. TD RPAN Bruxelles, 4 April 1989, AD, ASD 1985–1990, box 133.
90. Bush and Scowcroft, *A World Transformed*, p. 14; Beschloss and Talbott, *At the Highest Levels*, p. 36.
91. Bush and Scowcroft, *A World Transformed*, p. 58ff.; Margaret Thatcher, *The Downing Street Years*, New York, Harper Collins, 1993, p. 784; and MAE, Sous-direction des affaires stratégiques et des pactes, note a.s. Affaire SNF; point de la situation, 9 March 1989, private papers.
92. TD Bonn 15 February 1989; MAE, Service des affaires stratégiques et du désarmement, note a.s. Discours du chancelier Kohl au Bundestag (27 avril 1989), 28 April 1989, AD, ASD 1985–1990, box 15; and Fiche a.s. Affaire SNF, 10 mai 1989, AD, ASD 1985–1990, box 13.
93. Bush and Scowcroft, *A World Transformed*, p. 70.
94. MAE, fiche a.s. Sommet de l'Alliance atlantique (consultations franco-britanniques, Chevening, 15–16 mai), 10 May 1989, AD, ASD 1985–1990, box 13.
95. Védrine, note pour le président de la République, 28 April 1989, private papers.
96. MAE, Note du directeur des Affaires politiques, Bertrand Dufourcq, pour le ministre d'État, a.s. SNF : position française, 11 May 1989, AD, DP, box 305.

97. Védrine, note pour le président de la République, 28 April 1989; fiche a.s. Affaire SNF, 10 May 1989; and Védrine, note pour le président de la République, 17 May 1989, private papers.
98. Védrine, note pour le président de la République, 28 April 1989.
99. MAE, Note du directeur des Affaires politiques, Bertrand Dufourcq, pour le ministre d'État, a.s. SNF : position française, 11 May 1989.
100. On all this, see Beschloss and Talbott, *At the Highest Levels*, p. 43ff.; Bush and Scowcroft, *A World Transformed*, p. 57ff.; and Hutchings, *American Diplomacy*, p. 27ff.
101. Védrine, note pour le president de la République, 17 May 1989.
102. Message from Thatcher to Mitterrand, 9 May 1989; Védrine, note pour le président de la République, 16 May 1989, private papers. Thatcher seems to have overestimated Mitterrand's agreement with her own stance on the SNF question: see Thatcher, *Downing Street Years*, p. 788.
103. Meeting between Mitterrand and Bush, Kennebunkport, 21 May 1989, Musitelli's handwritten notes, private papers; American account in Bush and Scowcroft, *A World Transformed*, pp. 74–79; personal interviews.
104. Personal interviews; see also Beschloss and Talbott, *At the Highest Levels*, p. 77.
105. The Bush proposal included limiting American and Soviet troops in Europe to 275,000 men on both sides (which would lead the Soviets to decrease their troops in this region by about half, versus only 10 percent on the American side) and the inclusion of fighter airplanes in the negotiation. This last point, which the Soviets had constantly called for, caused a problem to the French and British because, due to the nuclear capability of certain aircrafts, it contradicted the notion that nuclear weapons were excluded from CFE. It thus gave rise to strong reluctance on the part of French diplomats and military men, on whom the Élysée had to impose its point of view, which was supportive of the American initiative; see Beschloss and Talbott, *At the Highest Levels*, p. 78.
106. See TD RPAN Bruxelles 433–434, 30 May 1989, AD, ASD 1985–1990, box 215, and handwritten notes from Védrine, private papers.
107. MAE, Fiche, a.s. Bilan du sommet Atlantique, 2 June 1989, AD, ASD 1985–1990, box 130 bis.
108. *Le Monde*, 2 June 1989; Védrine, note pour le président de la République, 31 May 1989, private papers.
109. Letter from Bush to Mitterrand, 2 June 1989, private papers.
110. TD Diplomatie 10761, 1 June 1989, AD, Europe, URSS 1986–1990, box 6684.
111. See Conseil des ministres, 31 May 1989, private papers.
112. See Conseil de défense, 2 June 1988; and Védrine, note pour le président de la République, a.s. Avenir des stratégies française et otanienne de dissuasion nucléaire, 7 June 1989, private papers.
113. Védrine, *Les Mondes*, p. 416.
114. MAE, Groupe de travail franco-allemand sur la politique à l'Est, Le changement en URSS trois ans après l'arrivée au pouvoir de Gorbatchev, 15 July 1988; and TD Bonn 2114, 20 October 1988, AD, Europe, RFA 1986–1990, box 6782; MAE, Sous-direction Europe orientale, note, a.s. Réunion du groupe de travail franco-allemand sur la politique à l'Est, le 12 septembre 1988 à Bonn, AD, DP, box 281.
115. MAE, le directeur des Affaires politiques (B. Dufourcq), note a.s. Réunion de travail à la Chancellerie. Bonn (23.9.88), 3 October 1988.
116. Personal interviews; the French had the feeling that the Germans were keeping the promising countries for themselves (Hungary) and leaving them with the least economically interesting ones (Romania).
117. Musitelli, note pour le président de la République, Votre entretien avec M. Chevard-

nadze (lundi 10 octobre, 15h), 10 October 1988, private papers; MAE, le directeur des Affaires politiques (B. Dufourcq), note a.s. Réunion de travail à la Chancellerie. Bonn (23.9.88), 3 October 1988; MAE, Sous-direction d'Europe orientale, note, a.s. Les relations entre l'URSS et la RFA (résumé), 18 October 1988, AD, Europe, RFA 1986–1990, box 6770.
118. TD Bonn 2431, AD, Europe, URSS 1986–1990, box 6680.
119. On all this see Urs Leimbacher, *Die unverzichtbare Allianz. Deutsch-französische sicherheitspolitische Zusammenarbeit 1982–1989*, Baden-Baden, Nomos, 1992, p. 264ff.
120. TD Bonn 144, DSL secret, 19 January 1989, AD, Europe, RFA 1986–1990, box 6782.
121. TD Diplomatie 1956, 30 January 1989, AD, Europe, RFA 1986–1990, box 6772.
122. See Caroline de Margarie, note, Remous en RFA à la suite de l'ouverture des négociations sur le désarmement conventionnel, 31 May 1989, private papers.
123. Guigou, note pour le président de la République, Compte-rendu des discussions avec les collaborateurs du chancelier Kohl sur les questions européennes (mercredi 17 mai, après-midi), 17 May 1989, private papers.
124. Horst Teltschik, 329 *Tage. Innenansichten der Einigung*, Berlin, Siedler, 1991, pp. 31, 106 and 369.
125. This aspect can not be discussed in detail. On this subject, see Leimbacher, *Die unverzichtbare Allianz*, and Tilo Schabert, *Wie Weltgeschichte gemacht wird. Frankreich und die deutsche Einheit*, Stuttgart, Klett-Cotta, 2002, notably pp. 95 *ff.* and 224 *ff.*
126. MAE, Sous-direction des affaires stratégiques et des pactes, note, a.s. Entretien du Premier ministre et du chancelier fédéral. Coopération franco-allemande en matière de défense et de sécurité, 8 July 1988, AD, Europe, RFA 1986–1990, box 6798; and Fiche a.s. Le point sur la coopération bilatérale franco-allemande en matière de défense et de sécurité, 11 July 1988, AD, DP, box 281.
127. Mitterrand's handwritten annotation on a note from Védrine, a.s. Force d'action rapide franco-allemande, 31 March 1987, private papers.
128. MAE, Sous-direction des affaires stratégiques et des pactes, note, a.s. Entretien du Premier ministre et du chancelier fédéral. Coopération franco-allemande en matière de défense et de sécurité, 8 July 1988.
129. The commitment given in this regard by Mitterrand in February 1986 had always been considered too restrictive by the Germans, but the French refused to go further, fearing a German 'droit de regard' on French strategy; this issue continued to weigh on Franco-German cooperation in 1988–1989: see e.g. MAE, fiche pour le directeur politique, a.s. Proposition allemande de consultation sur les questions nucléaires au sein du conseil franco-allemand de défense et de sécurité, no date (late 1988–early 1989), AD, DP, box 281.
130. Mitterrand explained this to Thatcher during the G7 summit in Venice in June 1987, an exchange that he would often mention later on: see Védrine, *Les Mondes*, p 725ff; see also the analysis in Schabert, *Weltgeschichte*, p. 224ff.
131. Conseil des ministres, 26 April 1989 (report from Jean-Louis Bianco), private papers. If Mitterrand appeared, on the whole, understanding in regard to the Germans in this area, others were more critical; hence the Minister of Defense, Jean-Pierre Chèvenement, wrote that 'Germany's desire to not be singularized comes down in fact to banalizing France and suppressing its nuclear specificity': Chèvenement, note à l'attention du président de la République, 29 March 1989, private papers.
132. MAE, Service des affaires stratégiques et des pactes, Fiche a.s. Bilan de la coopération franco-allemande en matière de défense et de sécurité, 22 September 1988, AD, DP, box 281; MAE, le Directeur des affaires politiques (B. Dufourcq), fiche a.s. Réunion de travail à la Chancellerie. Bonn (23.9.88), 3 October 1988.

133. De Margerie, note, Remous en RFA à la suite de l'ouverture des négociations sur le désarmement conventionnel, 31 March 1989.
134. MAE, Direction des Affaires politiques, Première réunion du conseil franco-allemand de défense et de sécurité, 24 April 1989, AD, DP, box 305.
135. MAE, Le ministre d'Etat, note à l'attention de Monsieur le président de la Republique, Visite de M. Genscher, 2 May 1989, AN, 5AG4/CDM 33.
136. MAE, Cabinet du ministre, Compte rendu, Entretien du ministre d'État avec le comte Lambsdorff (22 juin 1988), 24 June 1988, AD, Europe, RFA 1986–1990, box 6782.
137. Conseil des ministres, 17 August 1988, private papers.
138. On all this, Favier and Martin-Roland, *La Décennie*, vol. 3, p. 160ff; see also Pascal Riché and Éric Aeschimann, *La Guerre de sept ans. Histoire secrète du franc fort 1989–1996*, Paris, Calmann-Lévy, 1996; Schabert, *Weltgeschichte*, p. 355ff., and Hans Stark, *Kohl, l'Allemagne et l'Europe. La politique européenne de la République fédérale 1982–1998*, Paris, L'Harmattan, 2004, p. 83ff.
139. See e. g. MAE, CAP, note, 'La RFA et la communauté européenne', 11 May 1987, AD, Europe, RFA 1986–1990, box 6769 (the author of the note remarked: 'It is because the political component [of integration] is missing and particularly because the EEC is today incapable of bringing a solution to the most crucial problem of the FRG, meaning its defense, that the community factor has lost its priority status.')
140. TD Bonn 169–171, 24 January 1989, AD, Europe, RFA 1986–1990, box 6769. The debate gained momentum in the CDU as a result of a draft resolution introduced by deputies from the right wing of the party, aiming to ensure that, in case of unification, the GDR could automatically have access to the EEC. This debate, which caused difficulties for Kohl – if only because it tarnished the reputation of Bonn's European commitment abroad – ended on a compromise formula: the German question could only be resolved in a European context and, on the other hand, the community must clearly show the goal of German unity. Less than a year later, this hypothetical scenario became a reality: see chapter 4 of this volume, pp. 184–185.
141. Assemblée nationale, Présidence, compte rendu de l'entretien avec M. Otto Lambsdorff, 31 January 1989, AD, Europe 1986–1990, RFA, box 6800. A survey done several weeks earlier nuances these fears without dissipating them: if the West Germans in their greater majority considered building Europe as a given, they tended more and more to think that the FRG was already powerful enough to resolve its problems on its own; see Ambassade de France à Bonn, dépêche a.s. Les Allemands et la Communauté européenne, 16 May 1989, AD, RFA, Europe 1986–1990, box 6769.
142. See typically Alain Minc, *La Grande Illusion*, Paris, Grasset, 1988.
143. Guigou, note pour le président de la République, Union économique et monétaire. Vos entretiens avec MM. De Mita, Gonzalez et Kohl, 29 March 1989, private papers.
144. Guigou, note pour le président de la République, Quelques réflexions à la suite du discours du chancelier Kohl devant le Bundestag, 28 April 1989, private papers.
145. Guigou, note pour le président de la République, Compte-rendu des discussions avec les collaborateurs du chancelier Kohl sur les questions européennes (mercredi 17 mai après-midi), 17 May 1989.
146. Projet de conclusions approuvé par R. Dumas et H.-D. Genscher à Paris le 19 juin, Secret, private papers.
147. Guigou, note pour le président de la République, UEM, 24 June 1989, private papers. See also meeting between Kohl and Mitterrand, Paris, 22 June 1989, in *Deutsche Einheit. Sonderedition aus den Akten des Bundeskanzleramtes 1989/90* (Munich: R. Oldenburg, 1998), pp. 307–309.
148. Favier and Martin-Roland, *La Décennie*, vol. 3, pp. 164–166.

149. On the meaning of the event from the Soviets' side, see Chernyaev, *My Six Years*, p. 198ff.
150. MAE, Sous-direction d'Europe orientale, note, a.s. Premier bilan de la visite à Moscou du chancelier Kohl (24–27 octobre 1988), 28 October 1988, AD, Europe, RFA 1986–1990, box 6770.
151. TD Moscou 3657, 16 June 1989, AD, Europe, RFA 1986–1990, box 6771.
152. TD Bonn 1386–1387, DSL Secret, 21 June 1989, and MAE, note, Bilan de la visite de M. Gorbachev en RFA (12–15 June 1989), 27 June 1989, AD, Europe, URSS 1986–1990, box 6685.
153. See Védrine, note pour le président de la République, 3 April 1989, private papers. Védrine reported on a conversation with Jacques Julliard, an influential journalist and intellectual; while disapproving Minc's alarm (here above, note 142), Julliard was worried about an 'increasingly emotional, neutralist, and anti-European' climate in the FRG.
154. TD Bonn 1307, 13 June 1989, AD, Europe, RFA 1986–1990, box 6771.
155. See e.g. MAE, Sous-direction d'Europe orientale, note, a.s. Les relations entre l'URSS et la RFA (résumé), 18 October 1988, AD, Europe 1986–1990, RFA, box 6770.
156. Conseil des ministres, 26 October 1988.
157. Speech given for Willy Brandt's birthday, 20 January 1989, private papers.
158. Conseil des ministres, 3 May 1989, private papers.
159. At the CDU congress in Wiesbaden in June 1988, Kohl, building on Gorbachev's declarations during von Weizsäcker's visit to Moscow the previous year, typically affirmed that the German question remained open for the USSR, too: MAE, Sous-direction d'Europe orientale, note a.s. Relations germano-soviétiques, 20 June 1988, AD, Europe, RFA 1986–1990, box 6770; and TD Bonn 1346 to1350, 30 June 1988, AD, Europe, RFA 1986–1990, box 6772.
160. MAE, Sous-direction d'Europe centrale, note a.s. Visite du chancelier Kohl à Moscou. Question allemande et Berlin, 7 November 1988, AD, Europe, RFA 1986–1990, box 6770; for Soviet testimony see Chernyaev, *My Six Years*, p. 200.
161. TD Bonn 1449, 30 June 1989, AD, Europe, RFA 1986–1990, box 6771.
162. TD Bonn 1273–1275, 9 June 1989; TD Bonn 1307, 13 June 1989, AD, Europe, RFA 1986–1990, box 6771.
163. Bilan de la visite de M. Gorbatchev en RFA (12–15 June 1989), 27 June 1989.
164. Gorbachev, he later reported, didn't contradict him when he compared the unavoidable nature of German unity with the Rhine moving forward toward the sea: Helmut Kohl, Kai Diekmann and Ralf Georg Reuth, *Je voulais l'unité de l'Allemagne*, Paris, De Fallois, 1997, p. 42.
165. MAE, Sous-direction d'Europe orientale, note a.s. Relations germano-soviétiques, 20 June 1988.
166. MAE, Sous-direction d'Europe centrale, note a.s. Perspectives des relations germano-soviétiques au lendemain du voyage à Moscou du chancelier, 7 November 1988, AD, Europe, RFA 1986–1990, box 6770.
167. Conseil des ministres, 26 October 1988.
168. Meeting between Mitterrand and Bush, Kennebunkport, 21 May 1989; and Bush and Scowcroft, *A World Transformed*, p. 78. If Bush didn't take a position on this question in his discussion with Mitterrand, there is no reason to think that the American president and his entourage had at this stage a very different analysis: see Zelikow and Rice, *Germany Unified*, p. 32ff. Passing through Paris at the end of June 1989, Zbigniew Brzezinski didn't say anything different: 'The Soviets will not allow the reunification of Germany for a long time,' he confided; see Chevènement, Compte-rendu, a.s. Entretien avec M. Brzezinski (Mardi 27 juin-15h.), 3 July 1989, private papers.
169. TD Bonn 1307, 13 June 1989.

170. The ambassador asked nonetheless if there was not 'something deeper' in the Bonn declaration and concluded that 'the evolution of the coming months and years will tell': TD Moscou 3657, 16 June 1989. Still, Gorbachev's visit, seen from Moscow, essentially confirmed the German status quo: hence Nicolaï Portugalov, one of the 'Germanists' on the Central Committee, interpreted the Bonn declaration as the recognition by a conservative German government of the validity of the 1970 Moscow Treaty: see TD Moscou 3961, 27 June 1989, AD, Europe, RFA 1986–1990, box 6649.
171. Bilan de la visite de M. Gorbatchev en RFA (12–15 June 1989), 27 June 1989. This analysis is echoed in Adomeit's book: 'The fact that the FRG ... had become the Soviet Union's most important partner in Europe in practice meant that Gorbachev was prepared to cooperate more closely with that country than with any other in Europe, including East Germany. Cooperation with West Germany, however, meant within the framework of two separate German states. It did not mean that he [Gorbachev] accepted Kohl's idea of actively working toward ending the division of Germany:' Adomeit, *Imperial Overstretch*, p. 400.
172. MAE, cabinet du ministre, compte rendu de l'entretien entre le ministre et M. Egon Bahr (mercredi 7 juin de 8h à 10h), 9 June 1989, AD, Europe, RFA 1986–1990, box 6782. By 1989, Bahr, the architect of '*Wandel durch Annäherung*' (change through rapprochement), seemed to no longer believe in what had been the ultimate goal of Ostpolitik since the beginning, namely German unity; he had written as much in a 1988 book. As for Brandt, he had, in 1988, qualified as *Lebenslüge* (meaning a kind of 'existential lie') the idea of a German *reunification* (by contrast to that of a *unification*): see Timothy Garton-Ash, *In Europe's Name: Germany and the Divided Continent* (New York: Random House, 1993), p. 133 and p. 320.
173. On all this, see Garton-Ash, *In Europe's Name*, notably pp. 32ff., 112ff., and 446–447, as well as Zelikow and Rice, *Germany Unified*, p. 34. At the CDU congress in Wiesbaden in June 1988, some had suggested giving up the requirement of maintaining on the agenda the resolution of the German question – at least in terms of state unification – but Kohl imposed maintaining the traditional line.
174. TD Bonn 1449, 30 June 1989.
175. Vernon A. Walters, *Die Vereinigung war voraussehbar. Hinter den Kulissen eines entscheidenden Jahres* (Berlin: Siedler, 1994) p. 22ff. (General Walters, moreover, barely convinced his own authorities of the rightness of his predictions: see Zelikow and Rice, *Germany Unified*, pp. 35ff. and 393–393).
176. MAE, Sous-direction d'Europe orientale, note a.s. Relations franco-soviétiques, 8 September 1988.
177. MAE, note du directeur des Affaires politiques, B. Dufourcq, a.s. De l'Europe d'aujourd'hui à celle de demain, 20 February 1989, Secret, AD, DP, box 305.
178. Note de J. Blot, a.s. Visite de M. Gorbachev en France, 30 June 1989.
179. TD Moscou 4065, 2 July 1989, DSL Secret, AD, Europe 1986–1990, URSS, box 6685.
180. Meeting between Mitterrand and Gorbachev, 6 July 1989.
181. Meeting between Mitterrand and Bush, Kennebunkport, 21 May 1989; Bush and Scowcroft, *A World Transformed*, pp. 77–78.
182. Bush and Scowcroft, *A World Transformed*, p. 83. In Mainz, Bush had been content to ask that 'Berlin be next' (this was a reference to the fact that earlier in May the Hungarian government had symbolically undertaken cutting the barbed wire set up along the border with Austria: see chapter 2 of this volume , p. 86): see also Zelikow and Rice, *Germany Unified*, p. 31.
183 Zelikow and Rice, *Germany Unified*, p. 26ff. and 31; Bush and Scowcroft, *A World Trans-*

formed, p. 188; and Stephen F. Szabo, *The Diplomacy of German Unification*, New York, Saint Martin's Press, 1992, p. 13ff.
184. François Mitterrand, *De l'Allemagne, de la France*, Paris, Odile Jacob, 1996, p. 32.
185. See Gespräch des Bundeskanzlers Kohl mit Staatspräsident Mitterrand, Paris, 22. Juni 1989, *Deutsche Einheit*, pp. 305–310 (Kohl, on the other hand, evoked the 'German question' aspect of Gorbachev's visit with Bush, to whom he confided during a telephone conversation that the Soviet leader had reacted more moderately to his statements about the division of Germany than during his visit to Moscow in October 1988: see Telefongespräch des Bundeskanzlers Kohl mit Präsident Bush, 15. June 1989, *Deutsche Einheit*, pp. 300–301.)
186. Mitterrand and Gorbachev's joint press conference, 5 July 1989, *PEF*, July-August 1989, pp. 21–23. This statement grabbed the attention of the chancellor's entourage: see *Deustche Einheit*, pp. 345–356.
187. Interview to *Le Nouvel Observateur, The Independent, El Pais, La Repubblica* and *Süddeutsche Zeitung*, 27 July 1989, in *PEF*, July-August 1989, pp. 78–82; see Mitterrand's commentary, *De l'Allemagne*, pp. 32–33.
188. TD Bonn 117, 17 January 1989, DSL, AD, DP, box 281; MAE, Service des affaires stratégiques et du désarmement, note a.s. Consultations franco-britanniques (Chevening, 15–16 mai 1989), questions politico-militaires, 11 May 1989. The Bush team had a similar perception: Baker's entourage thought that the affirmation by the FRG of its interests and its sovereignty were a major new development that would weigh on the German-American relationship; see Szabo, *Diplomacy*, p. 11.
189. MAE, le chef du CAP, note, a.s. La relation franco-allemande, 30 April 1989, AN, 5AG4/CDM 33.
190. TD Bonn 1386–1387, DSL secret, 21 June 1989, AD, ASD 1985–1990, box 15.
191. MAE, le chef du CAP, note, a.s. La relation franco-allemande, 30 April 1989.
192. Conseil des ministres, 26 April 1989.
193. Dufourcq, note a.s. De l'Europe d'aujourd'hui à celle de demain, 20 February 1989, Secret, AD, DP, box 305. A number of developments that follow are based upon this document, which we find to be quite illustrative of the thinking in decision-making circles.
194. Allocution prononcée à l'occasion du 40e anniversaire du Conseil de l'Europe, 5 May 1989, *PEF*, May–June 1989, pp. 8–11.
195. 'The Eastern countries must make a step toward the conquest of individual liberties', he told Grosz, 'and the Western countries toward the conquest of collective social liberties': meeting between Mitterrand and Grosz, 18 November 1988, private papers.
196. 'Argumentaire' about Mitterrand's visit to Czechkoslavokia in December 1988, no date, private papers.
197. Dufourcq, note a.s. De l'Europe d'aujourd'hui à celle de demain, 20 February 1989.
198. 'Argumentaire' about Mitterrand's visit to Czechkoslavokia in December 1988.
199. See speech given for Willy Brandt's birthday, 20 January 1989. The French vision of the German problem since de Gaulle has been characterized by a prominent scholar as one of a Germany that would remain divided in a reunified Europe from the Atlantic to the Urals: see Garton-Ash, *In Europe's Name*, p. 24. Yet this is quite disputable: on the one hand, the general never ratified the definitive character of the division of Germany – on the contrary (see Prologue in this volume, p. xxii); on the other hand, by 1989, very few – including in Germany – still believed in the possibility of a 'state' unification in the foreseeable future.
200. Dufourcq, note a.s. De l'Europe d'aujourd'hui à celle de demain, 20 February 1989. Dufourq typically situated his reflection on 'l'Europe de demain' in a perspective of

'medium/long term' or 'from 10 to 20 years'. As for Mitterrand, he told Bush at Kennebunkport that the dislocation of the Soviet empire and the unification of Germany 'will not happen during the next ten years': see meeting between Mitterrand and Bush, Kennebunkport, 21 May 1989.
201. Mitterrand's interview to *Moscow News*, 1 June 1989, private papers.
202. See Conseil de défense, 20 July 1988, private papers.
203. Meeting between Mitterrand and Gorbachev, Moscow, 25 November 1988.
204. Still in February 1989, the Quai d'Orsay saw in the common home 'a concept with contours that are poorly defined but whose underlying long-term philosophy is quite clear': see Dufourcq, note a.s. De l'Europe d'aujourd'hui à celle de demain, 20 February 1989. As for Mitterrand, he told Gorbachev in July 1989: 'The most important part is to agree on what is to be put [in the common home]' but also 'on the way to proceed'; speech given by Mitterrand for a dinner given to Mikhaïl and Raïssa Gorbachev, 4 July 1989, private papers. On the common home, see Rey, 'Europe Is Our Common Home'.
205. Védrine, note pour le président de la République, 19 November 1988.
206. Dufourcq, note a.s. De l'Europe d'aujourd'hui à celle de demain, 20 February 1989.
207. Védrine, note pour le président de la République, 6 April 1989.
208. Dufourcq, note a.s. De l'Europe d'aujourd'hui à celle de demain, 20 February 1989.
209. Dossier de synthèse, a.s. Visite de M. Gorbatchev (4–6 juillet 1989), s.d.
210. Dufourcq, note a.s. De l'Europe d'aujourd'hui à celle de demain, 20 February 1989.
211. Dufourcq, note a.s. De l'Europe d'aujourd'hui à celle de demain, 20 February 1989.
212. MAE, La maison commune européenne: vues soviétiques et occidentales, 26 June 1989, AD, Europe, URSS 1986–1990, box 6685.
213. MAE, La coopération franco-allemande en matière de sécurité, 14 June 1989.
214. Dufourcq, note a.s. De l'Europe d'aujourd'hui à celle de demain, 20 February 1989.
215. Dufourcq, note a.s. De l'Europe d'aujourd'hui à celle de demain, 20 February 1989.

Chapter 2

THE RETURN OF THE GERMAN QUESTION
(August to Early November 1989)

If an end to the Yalta system appeared almost certain at the start of the summer of 1989, in a few weeks it became an inescapable reality in light of the acceleration of change in Eastern Europe. By the end of August, with the first postwar non-Communist government formed in Warsaw, the breadth of the upheaval was no longer in doubt: the Cold War – one of whose first stakes had been the fate of Poland – was well and truly over. That the USSR posed no obstacle to this decisive evolution was because Moscow, without renouncing a Soviet presence in Eastern Europe, still hoped to replace its former domination with a consensual influence. By the beginning of the autumn of 1989, the scenario of a gradual transition in Eastern Europe (the preferred scenario as seen from Paris) seemed quite realistic. Yet the effective renunciation by Moscow of the Brezhnev doctrine and the acceleration of democratization in the East would soon trigger a process that overturned this calculation. This was the crisis of the East German refugees coming into Hungary in the hope of crossing the border with the West. The crisis would be resolved after culminating in mid September, but it would have the effect of restoring the German question to major topicality.

While German reunification was still not on the diplomatic agenda, it came to the forefront of domestic debate in the Federal Republic and therefore injected itself among the preoccupations of Germany's partners – all

---

Notes for this section begin on page 105.

the more so because things were happening quickly in the GDR, where the refugee issue fed the protest movement that had appeared in the first months of 1989. By the start of October, Erich Honecker's regime was in desperate straits, increasingly contested domestically and less and less supported by a USSR now reluctant to endorse the GDR's obstinate refusal of any *perestroika*. Some days after Gorbachev's trip to East Berlin at the beginning of October for the fortieth anniversary of the state, Honecker was replaced by Egon Krenz. This was good news for Moscow, which could now hope for a stabilization of the East German situation. For a while Krenz did appear able to control events. As for the Bonn government, it remained cautious. Even if Helmut Kohl was no doubt already tempted to go farther, the German question was still formally part of a logic of rapprochement between the two German states. On the eve of the opening of the Berlin Wall – which of course nobody could predict – a paradoxical situation prevailed: although the question was now on everyone's mind, unification was not on the agenda, at least officially. By the start of the fall of 1989, French policy – like its partners' – appeared more and more split. On the one hand, the Mitterrandian vision of a gradual evolution seemed validated by the ongoing changes in Eastern Europe (including the GDR), perpetuating an unchanged attitude to German events: while recognizing the legitimate aspiration to unity, Mitterrand's diplomacy emphasized the necessary stability of a process that it envisaged taking a long time. On the other hand, though, questions were arising about the return of the German question: had not the moment come to update a discourse that might be caught short by the acceleration of events?

From Democratic Transition to the Refugee Crisis

It was in Warsaw that the decisive event of summer's end took place. After the electoral triumph of Solidarnosc on 4 and 18 June, the ability of the PUWP to maintain power appeared most uncertain.[1] The election of General Jaruzelski as president in July had helped reassure the Communists, but the formation of a government was delicate since Lech Walesa had excluded PUWP participation in it in advance. Then, once Solidarnosc had finally accepted the designation of Communists for the defense and the interior ministries and promised – after a warning from Moscow – that Poland's participation in the Warsaw Pact would not be called into question, on 20 August Jaruzelski turned toward one of Solidarnosc's historical leaders, Tadeusz Mazowiecki, for the post of prime minister. The first postwar government that was non-Communist in majority and direction was formed. Reassured by guarantees about keeping Poland in the Soviet bloc and key ministries in Communist hands, the Soviets accepted the new Polish government without major difficulty. No doubt Gorbachev still hoped that the changes in Poland might open the way to a renovated socialism – as was the case in Hungary, where power remained in the hands of reforming Communists.

At the end of the summer of 1989, it was the situation in Eastern Europe – and not the German question – that commanded attention, and some anxiety. The evolution playing out in Warsaw, noted Roland Dumas at the end of August, had a 'euphoric effect' on public opinion in the West, but it also carried 'risks of crisis'.[2] Westerners were nevertheless reassured by the Soviet attitude: the French embassy in the USSR in mid September judged that Gorbachev had remarkably reconciled support for the reformists in Warsaw and Budapest with maintenance of suitable relations with the conservatives in Prague and Berlin. If Solidarnosc's coming to power was a 'breach' in the bloc, the risk was being assumed by Moscow as the best chance for stabilizing the situation and assuring the 'permanence of Soviet preeminence'.[3] The Élysée was resolutely optimistic. Rejecting the 'ambient pessimism' that he attributed to proponents of the status quo, Hubert Védrine in a long note to Mitterrand on 13 September stressed that these 'quite extraordinary events' announced the 'gradual overcoming of Yalta and the emergence of a grand Europe' that would again hold 'the thread of its own history'. Refuting the idea of a fatally unstable transition, Védrine favored the 'hypothesis of a continuous and controlled evolution in the East' that would be 'the extension of what has been happening since 1985'. Banking on the 'CSCE provisions on the free circulation of goods and peoples', he reckoned that the 'regimes of Bucharest, East Berlin, Prague, and Sophia cannot resist eternally'. The president's adviser concluded: 'If one sees how Mr. Gorbachev maintains the course ... one ought to reflect before decreeing him incapable of leading the USSR ... toward a modern federation and transforming the Warsaw Pact into a classical military alliance allowing each member to choose its own domestic regime.'[4] Overall, far from being worrying, acceleration in the East seemed, this September of 1989, to validate Mitterrand's vision of the post-Yalta order.

It also confirmed, as a result, the main orientations of French policy. France 'should wish that M. Gorbachev succeeds' and at the same time 'have a policy of active presence' in the East, Dumas summarized.[5] This, the Quai d'Orsay noted, was what the Soviets were expecting: if they were thankful to the West 'for the restraint it showed' during the summer, they also understood 'that we are pronouncing in favor of changes resulting from dialogue and compromise'.[6] Védrine stressed that 'we have an essential interest in mutations in the East taking place in a controlled way': he was worried about 'the disastrous consequences' of the waiting game that he discerned among 'many Western leaders'. To the president, he suggested 'sweeping away hesitation' by giving the Europeans and Americans 'some signal of a very visible change of attitude'. This might take several forms: increasing French aid to Poland and Hungary but also to the USSR, monitoring effective progress in cooperation decided upon during the recent presidential visits to Czechoslovakia and Bulgaria, proclaiming close Franco-German cooperation on Eastern policy, inciting the Twelve to do 'much more' on the basis of the mandate given the European Commission during the Arche summit, writing to President Bush 'to fight conservative influences' in Washington, and finally, tackling these questions during the speech the president would give the following month to the European parliament in Strasbourg, as well as more immediately in French radio and television interviews.[7] To be sure, these recommendations echoed, if implicitly, the previously mentioned limitations of France's policy toward the East: the weakness of its effective presence in Eastern Europe despite the 'revival' of 1988–1989, and the failure of Franco-German cooperation in this domain. Later events were to confirm these insufficiencies. Yet the desire to encourage a movement that was thought amenable to being controlled did carry the day at this stage: 'History has been accelerating since our meeting in July and gives us important responsibilities', Mitterrand wrote to George Bush at the start of October.[8]

The Refugee Crisis

Meanwhile, the refugee crisis confirmed the extent of the upheavals induced by acceleration in the East.[9] At the start of May, the Budapest government led by the Gorbachevian Miklos Nemeth had symbolically undertaken to dismantle the 'Iron Curtain' by cutting the barbed wire along the border with Austria. The decision was without great practical bearing, since the great majority of Hungarians already had the ability to travel to Austria and thereby reach the West, and it changed nothing for the East Germans, who, under an old agreement between East Berlin and Budapest, were sent back to the GDR if they attempted to cross the border without an exit visa. In the following weeks, some of them would still try their chances via Hungary as well as via Czechoslovakia and Poland; stopped at the border, they took refuge in the FRG embassies in Budapest, Prague and Warsaw. This did not prevent a considerable number of East Germans from choosing Hungary as their summer vacation destination, in the hope of crossing the border there.

East Berlin now feared a hemorrhage analogous to the one preceding the construction of the Wall in the summer of 1961, especially since tens of thousands of legal departures had already taken place since the start of the year. Starting on 9 August, the Hungarian authorities ceased sending East

German nationals back to the GDR while continuing to prevent them from crossing their Western border; but the news spread that several hundreds of them had still managed to get across, and as a result the number of East Germans waiting at the Austro-Hungarian border grew throughout August. Then the leaders in Budapest took a historic decision: after secret discussions with Kohl and Hans-Dietrich Genscher at the Gymnich near Bonn on 25 August (during which Nemeth and Hungarian Foreign Affairs Minister Gyula Horn won the promise of West German economic support), they decided to open the border to East Germans, a decision that became effective on 10 September. Several tens of thousands of East German citizens thus passed to the West before the GDR prohibited trips to Hungary, which in turn led many other aspiring emigrants to go to Czechoslovakia and settle in the FRG embassy in Prague. They would finally be able to reach West Germany at the start of October, after Genscher's negotiations with East Berlin.

The crisis was, first of all, a revelation of the GDR situation. At the end of September, the French ambassador in East Berlin, Joëlle Timsit, described the 'psychological shock' induced in the GDR by the refugee affair, writing that the crisis was a symptom of a blocked society directed by an aged and sick head of state. In intellectual and Church circles this fed an effervescence illustrated by the peaceful weekly demonstrations in Leipzig. Yet Timsit thought that the situation did not seem truly 'prerevolutionary': the opposition was cut off from the population, and most especially, the GDR's 'three pillars' – ideology, the security force (Stasi) and the geo-strategic situation (Soviet military presence) – all remained stable.[10] This analysis, as we shall see, manifestly erred on the side of stability with regard to the country's future, yet it hardly differed from the one simultaneously formulated by American diplomacy, which expected the refugee crisis to have the positive effect of obliging the regime to engage in reforms without putting the very existence of the GDR into question.[11] International reactions confirmed this interpretation of the crisis as simply a symptom of the troubled East German situation, rather than something that was likely to destabilize the status quo. Washington was scarcely implicated: American diplomacy was above all activated by the wider problems of Eastern Europe and by Soviet-American relations (Eduard Shevardnadze was to be received by James Baker in Wyoming on 21 and 22 September).[12] The same was true of Soviet diplomacy: the USSR ostensibly stood aside from an affair that concerned primarily East Berlin, Bonn and Budapest, and in which it saw the possibility of catalyzing long-awaited reforms in the GDR – even if, as we shall see, Moscow was worried about consequences for the German question. Nikolai Portugalov, a leading 'Germanist' on the Central Committee of the CPSU, confirmed that the Hungarians had themselves taken the decision to open the border; 'Soviet leadership', he added, was not in a position 'to impose its views' on allies, which 'moreover would be contrary to the policy that the USSR has adopted'.[13]

Thus it was for Bonn that the crisis became a particular challenge. The FRG, in effect, had for years been managing the problem of *Übersiedler* (refugees) according to Ostpolitik 'norms', meaning by negotiating discreetly with East Berlin on individual cases while avoiding useless provocations and destabilization of the FRG-GDR relationship. Now the breadth of the refugee phenomenon made the limits of this approach apparent. Kohl and Genscher were in fact beginning to favor humanitarian objectives over inter-German relations, as illustrated by the agreement concluded with the Hungarian government at the end of August. Still, in this early autumn of 1989, the objective proclaimed by Bonn remained stabilization and reform of the GDR, as the director of political affairs of the Auswärtiges Amt, Dieter Kastrup, stressed during a meeting at the end of September in New York with his American, British and French homologues.[14] (It was at the same moment in New York that Genscher – with the help of Dumas who put pressure on the Czech Foreign Affairs Minister – obtained authorization for East German nationals present in the FRG embassy in Prague to go to the West, thus putting an end to the refugee affair.)[15]

The German Question "On the Agenda"?

In a few weeks this same affair would reopen a question that even two months earlier had appeared quite closed: 'The German question is once more on the agenda', declared Helmut Kohl on 22 August – a declaration that did not go unnoticed. For France as for the FRG's other partners, there was a new situation to be reckoned with. For decades the resolution of the German question had been postponed indefinitely by the West Germans themselves, but it now ceased being 'incantatory' and became a 'veritable political stake' for two reasons. First, Kohl exploited the emotion provoked in the Federal Republic by the images of the refugees. In a difficult position in his party and in public opinion, he seized the advantage he could take from the German question's return, if only by embarrassing the SPD, which was prisoner of its policy of rapprochement with an SED that was now discredited. Hence his declarations at the end of August were reiterated at the CDU congress in Bremen on 11 September.[16] Second and most especially, the refugee crisis posed the problem of the long-term future of the GDR for the first time since 1961. Even if the dominant feeling was that the crisis might be overcome if the country engaged in long overdue reforms, the French ambassador in East Berlin recognized that the episode 'obliges European states' – and in particular those who had rights and responsibilities with respect to Germany – 'to reflect on Germany's destiny'.[17] Even the Soviets, although they had no intention of 'abandoning the GDR', admitted that the crisis could only encourage the 'national aspirations on both sides of the border between the two German states'.[18]

The German problem, however, was not at this stage on the *diplomatic* agenda. The necessary conditions for that to happen were still far from having come together, especially on the Soviet side. Whereas the refugee crisis in itself did not much disturb Moscow, the same was not true of the return of the national debate that it provoked in the Federal Republic. From mid September on, Moscow's previously moderate tone began to harden with respect to the FRG, which was accused of wanting to use events to challenge the status quo settled on after the Second World War. Kohl's declarations in Bremen were particularly targeted: during his meeting with Baker in Wyoming, Shevardnadze deplored statements that reminded him of 'the 1930s', a judgment that in the coming months would become a Soviet leitmotif.[19] The head of MID told Dumas the same thing in New York on 25 September, denouncing the 'revanchist and even nationalist connotations' of Kohl's speech, which Moscow 'would not leave unanswered', for the USSR was attached to 'territorial realities'. Shevardnadze returned to the charge the next day, this time in public, in his speech to the United Nations Assembly. In short, the hardening was manifest: Moscow was clearly not ready to consider the prospect of German unity.[20] In this context, Westerners demonstrated restraint in their declarations, starting with the Americans. Questioned on 18 September in Montana, Bush did declare that he was 'not fearful' of unification, but this statement can only with difficulty be interpreted as marking an inflection of American policy.[21] This was confirmed by the meeting of the political directors of the four Western powers in New York a few days later: questioned by Kastrup on whether Baker (as he had declared in the press conference) had in effect spoken of the German question with Shevardnadze in Wyoming, the American representative, Raymond Seitz, responded in the negative, even mentioning a 'lapse' by the secretary of state; at this stage, the question was not 'on the agenda' of Western diplomats.[22]

The Germans themselves, moreover, now made evident their own caution. After his spectacular declarations at the end of August and beginning of September, Kohl, feeling that his Western partners were not ready for it, proved less inclined to pose 'the question that is burning on everyone's lips', noted the Quai d'Orsay.[23] The French ambassador in Bonn, Serge Boidevaix, noted that as early as mid September the chancellor and his supporters estimated 'that political exploitation of the situation is too risky', at least in those circumstances. Shevardnadze's declarations in New York and the Soviet hardening confirmed this inflexion: Boidevaix thought he was now witnessing a rapprochement between the CDU and the SPD over the necessary support for a policy of reform in the GDR. In short, domestic politics continued to influence the debate, but it now pushed in the direction of moderation. This was all the more so because Genscher, until then rather silent, began to speak out: in an interview published by *Der Spiegel* on 25 September, he rejected a concept of 'reunification' that he considered outmoded, and reasserted his attachment to the idea of rapprochement between the two German states thanks to the process of European construction and within the framework of a pan-European peace order. Rivalry between Kohl and Genscher would henceforth weigh heavily on the chain of events; for the moment, it led to moderate German positions. Boidevaix remarked in early October that the Germans were inclined to calm things down, with many of his interlocutors arguing that the debate on German unification was 'rather less' advanced in the FRG 'than in Washington, London or Paris.' Of course, there was some insincerity here: the French ambassador noted that 'the same people must admit that in Bonn and in the whole Federal Republic, they talk of nothing else'; and Boidevaix concluded that 'the long-term preoccupations are certainly very present' even if they remain 'unavowed'.[24] As autumn began, it appeared that each party – starting with those principally interested, the Germans – found an advantage in not saying things: this fact is important to understand the positions of everyone in this period.

The French attitude in this context remained in line with the preceding months: German unification was a legitimate objective but it was not at the moment timely. 'For a long time yet the Soviet Union will refuse reunification', Mitterrand declared in the Council of Ministers on 6 September – meanwhile adding that one must 'coldly envisage the possibility'.[25] 'Nothing allows us to think that the USSR – more than the Westerners – is ready to accept a reunification of the nineteenth-century type,' confirmed Védrine, for whom 'the maintenance of two German states' in a Europe 'where the obstacles to freedom have disappeared' might furnish a 'solution of durable transition'.[26] Faced with the return of the national debate in Germany, French diplomacy now proclaimed an attitude that was all the more serene because the question did not appear really topical. Thus, faced with Shevardnadze's diatribe against Kohl in New York, Dumas – who, we recall, was then helping solve the refugee crisis – defended the chancellor: one has to take into account the West German domestic political situation, he stressed, and not amalgamate it with the spirit of vengeance of the 1930s.[27] As for Mitterrand's public attitude in this period, it was characterized by discretion: only on 10 October did the French president comment officially on events, during a press conference held in Caracas. 'The problem of German reunification is not posed by the refugee crisis', he said, minimizing *ipso facto* its importance, 'but from the first day'. 'The fundamental facts' had not changed as a result of the crisis – even if it had 'become more topical', he added, recalling the legitimacy of the aspiration to unity of the German people but also the necessity of a democratic and peaceful process.[28] While this statement was in line with previous ones, a question was nevertheless already taking shape: would this discourse remain compatible with a possible acceleration of events?

The GDR Crisis and Honecker's Fall

By no means did the denouement of the refugee crisis at the end of September mark a halt to the dramatic evolutions in the East. On the contrary, the episode only fed the dynamics of contestation in the GDR: the opposition movement that had appeared in the preceding months was amplified in the first days of October.[29] In Berlin on the seventh and especially in Leipzig on the ninth, massive demonstrations marked an unprecedented challenge to the regime. Given the omnipresence of security forces, a bloody confrontation – like the one in Beijing a few months earlier – was feared. Yet leaders renounced a 'Chinese' solution that might have led to a bloodbath amid the festivities of the GDR's fortieth anniversary. Insistently invited to participate since the summer by the East German leader, Gorbachev hesitated: would that not risk sanctioning Honecker's immobility? But, fearing that his absence might be interpreted as a withdrawal of Soviet support and lead to a dangerous destabilization of the GDR, the Soviet leader went to East Berlin on 6 and 7 October. His attitude there was prudent: contrary to widespread opinion, his phrase about 'those who arrive late', whom life 'punishes', was not intended as a threat addressed to the SED leadership. Yet Gorbachev's visit made evident the extent to which the Soviet leaders had lost confidence in Honecker, who on 18 October was dismissed by the Politburo and replaced by Egon Krenz. Moscow may not have actively hatched Honecker's fall, but Gorbachev clearly welcomed it. Of course, Krenz incarnated continuity more than change (he had long been perceived as the possible heir to Honecker and remained identified with the regime's repressive policy), and Moscow would no doubt have preferred someone like Hans Modrow; still, the new Number One (who did obtain the support of the Soviet leaders and enjoyed a solid reputation as a tactician) might, at least initially, hope to succeed in holding the GDR together.[30] The new leader presented himself as an East German Gorbachev. Yet more than reforming, Krenz hoped to take the upper hand in the face of events that threatened to spin out of control. Asked about the significance of Krenz's nomination, Mitterrand was not mistaken: 'They're trying to control the movement … to try to master it', he correctly judged.[31]

That was indeed Moscow's goal. At the start of October, as the refugee crisis was winding down, a member of the French embassy in Moscow was told that the USSR thought a 'pause' necessary in the German issue.[32] Analyzing Gorbachev's speech in Berlin on 6 October, the Quai d'Orsay noted that 'Moscow's principal concern appears to be, in the long term, preserving the territorial status quo and geopolitical stability in Europe': if the Soviet chief had decided to press for reforms in the GDR and grant it some autonomy, it was above all 'in the hope of seeing political stability and economic efficiency strengthened in its principal partner in the Warsaw Pact.'[33] This analysis was corroborated a few days before Honecker's fall by Egon Bahr, who confided to Jean-Pierre Chevènement that Gorbachev had given an assurance that the Soviet army would not intervene in case of trouble and that he intended to push for reforms in the GDR.[34] In fact, the removal of the Honecker liability allowed Moscow to preserve the future, and his orderly replacement by Krenz was an overall success for Soviet leaders. Gorbachev, notes Hannes Adomeit, thus reached 'a major unspoken objective: the establishment of a reformist socialist system under a new leader'.[35] This was also how French diplomacy interpreted the end of the Honecker era: 'To avoid uncontrollable events, Gorbachev has contributed to pushing the GDR along the reform path', the Quai d'Orsay noted at the end of October.[36]

That East Berlin and Moscow were above all trying to resume control of events in the GDR and thereby master the dynamics of the German question was confirmed in the two or three weeks that followed, notably thanks to the meeting between Krenz and Gorbachev in Moscow on 1 November.[37] A large part of the meeting was devoted to the country's considerable economic problems as well as to the desirable political changes, suggesting that both parties believed in the possibility of a GDR reformed within the socialist framework with the help of the USSR. But what Krenz mostly wanted to find in Moscow was confirmation that the USSR would adhere to its traditional position concerning the existence of two German sates. Gorbachev did not fail to reassure his visitor: Moscow and East Berlin, he said, had on this subject a 'correct' line from which there was no reason to depart. Of course, he added – in line with his vision of a 'common home' – if the tendency to rapprochement between different economic, social and political systems was pursued for 'several decades', then 'perhaps' the question would be posed differently, but this was not a 'current political problem'. And, Gorbachev assured him, leaders like Thatcher, Mitterrand, Jaruzelski and Andreotti all shared the principle that the postwar situation must be preserved and considered it dangerous to pose the question of German unity. The United States too, at least until then, had adopted the same position, he added.[38] Overall, the

Krenz-Gorbachev meeting confirmed the orientation of Soviet policy: to be sure, the Quai d'Orsay thought it could not be excluded that 'the USSR is considering the possibility that progress in the rapprochement between the FRG and the GDR might make unavoidable the exercise of a right to self-determination that it today rejects'; yet Moscow clearly remained for the time being 'hostile to any modification of the postwar situation'.[39] This analysis was correct: for Moscow, Honecker's fall did not change (at least for now) the basic German situation.

The End of Ostpolitik?

The same was obviously not the case in Bonn. There the Berlin events could only feed the renascent debate on the national question, in the long term because the prospect of a democratized GDR ipso facto posed the question of the existence of a state whose identity rested on ideology alone, and in the short term because the future of inter-German relations raised obvious questions. Should one continue to support economically an exhausted GDR in the name of stability – which is what Krenz and Gorbachev were counting on – or, contrariwise, apply pressure to accelerate change in the direction of democracy and abandoning Communism? Honecker's fall certainly pushed Kohl – moved both by political considerations and his intuition of a historic moment for German unity – toward the second approach, at least deep down: without being able to speak of abandoning twenty years of Ostpolitik practice, this was indeed what was implicitly in play as of the end of October 1989.[40] After Honecker's fall, French diplomacy noted how much the GDR events strengthened the hand of the chancellor and his party. Threatened by the withering away of his power a few months earlier, he had effected a spectacular recovery thanks to a very favorable economic situation and also to 'the CDU's traditional discourse' on the German question, which was 'in phase with the dominant sentiment in public opinion'.[41] The French embassy in Bonn concurred: 'Events in East Germany have upset the federal political scene and currently ... Chancellor Kohl and his government appear to have benefited from a situation in which each gesture, each statement touches the Germans very deeply.'

Now clearly tempted by a more assertive policy toward unity, the chancellor, however, did not yet have complete freedom of action. Of course, noted the embassy, 'the Social Democrats are trying to make people forget the accusations of their having privileged contacts over recent years' with the SED, but they still stuck to the logic of Ostpolitik.[42] Meeting Gorbachev in Moscow on 17 October – the eve of Honecker's fall – Brandt still defended an approach that consisted of increased cooperation between the FRG and GDR and would allow the two German states to get closer to each other in the larger framework of an overall European rapprochement – an approach that Modrow would propose a few weeks later in the form of a 'contractual community' (*Vertragsgemeinschaft*).[43] Bahr, meanwhile, worried that destabilization of the GDR might jeopardize *perestroika*. Judging that unification was not imminent, he insisted on the idea of a 'rapprochement' between the two Germanys and prudently bet on the GDR's achievement of self-determination on the basis of what he described as East Germany's 'nascent identity'.[44] But even as the fathers of Ostpolitik thus remained faithful to its canons, it was most of all the attitudes expressed by Genscher, as Kohl's partner-adversary within the coalition, that inclined the chancellor to prudence. To be sure, Genscher judged that 'any policy that is founded on the existence of two German nations is doomed to failure,' as the Quai d'Orsay noted at the end of October. But his positions were clearly demarcated from Kohl's. For Genscher, the objective was 'unity between the Germans' and not unification in a state sense. Above all he wanted to avoid German policy contradicting European policy; he therefore wanted to make the rapprochement between the GDR and the FRG coincide with East-West rapprochement and the progressive emergence of a '*Gesamteuropa*'.[45] Kohl's willful approach to German unity was still far from being accepted across the German political field.

By the same token, Bonn's attitude remained cautious throughout the month of October, even after Honecker's fall – at least this was the message that West German diplomacy tried to give the Western allies, as suggested by statements from Rudolf Seiters (head of the Federal Chancellery and a close adviser to Kohl) during a breakfast with the American, British and French ambassadors on 24 October. Trying 'not to devalue' Krenz, Seiters, when asked what Bonn wanted from the West concerning the German question, replied clearly that 'we are not in the period of plans but in the period of processes'; the priority was to sustain the transition underway in Poland and Hungary 'so as to exercise an influence favorable to reforms' in the GDR.[46] Despite the rapid changes in East Berlin, Bonn's diplomats thus did not depart – at least, not officially – from a policy of gradual rapprochement with a GDR that was being encouraged to reform itself, an attitude explained by the need to observe the beginning of Krenz's tenure, but also by the domestic political situation in the FRG, described above, as well as a concern not to harm Gorbachev's position or disturb the Western allies. At the end of October, American diplomats in Bonn came to a similar realization: although the idea might be on everyone's mind, stated a telegram sent to Washington on 25 October, 'virtually no one believes reunification is the first order of business on the German-German agenda'.[47] In fact, if Kohl was indeed determined to press forward, the circumstances were not yet encouraging: the proclaimed priority remained democratization and reform of the GDR, as he confirmed to Krenz on 26 October.⁴⁸

Change in Washington

This attitude would change in the following weeks, especially under the influence of American policy, which until then had been marked by some caution. To be sure, Bush's commentary on 18 September had been interpreted by some in Bonn as support for the voluntarist position announced by Kohl at the end of August and beginning of September.⁴⁹ Yet during October, as the rhetoric had become more moderate in Bonn, the White House worried that American declarations might appear to exceed the intentions of the Germans themselves. Scowcroft asked Baker to use the word 'reconciliation' in preference to 'reunification' in a speech in New York on 16 October, and this semantic shift was interpreted by Kohl's entourage as marking an inflection in the direction of restraint.⁵⁰ After Honecker's fall, however, American discourse was newly modified toward more assertive support for Kohl's policy. The latter, during a telephone conversation with Bush on 23 October, had asserted his astonishment that questions were being raised in the United States and Europe about the solidity of the Western anchoring of an FRG suspected of being overly preoccupied with policy to the East so as to increase the chance for unity, and he had asked the U.S. president to pass along the message that change in the East was possible only thanks to Western solidarity.⁵¹ Bush delivered: in an interview published in the *New York Times* on 25 October, he declared that he did 'not share the concern that some European countries have about a reunified Germany', for the FRG's involvement in the Atlantic Alliance was 'unshakeable'.

To be sure, the import of this declaration should not be exaggerated; it merely restated the traditional U.S. position and called for caution. 'I don't think we ought to be out pushing the concept of reunification', Bush added, for this 'takes time' and requires 'prudent evolution'. Still, as the chancellor's entourage noted, the American president had responded rapidly to Kohl's request. As seen from Bonn, the episode thus confirmed the close and trusting relationship that existed between the two men, and this would evidently count increasingly in the weeks that followed.⁵² Also, the president's statement highlighted an aspect that would later prove determining: the importance of the Atlantic reliability of the Federal Republic in the eyes of the Americans, who would remain all the more serene about the prospect of German unity as it remained unambiguously inscribed within the NATO framework. This aspect did not go unnoticed by West German diplomacy, which was then beginning to foresee the solidity of

American support for unification as long as Bonn confirmed its Atlantic orientation.[53]

Right now, the consequences of this change in American policy appeared nevertheless limited: it was only to the extent that Kohl in the coming weeks would begin to 'capitalize' on Washington's support that its effects would be really felt. For the time being, French diplomacy noted that 'American support for the concept of reunification' was expressed with some 'precautions' and a concern to 'stagger the process over time'. Generally speaking, the Quai d'Orsay in October 1989 noted that the position of all the Western nations was to postpone the question of Germany unity and anticipate a protracted transition period. Thus Foreign Minister John Major indicated that the UK 'accepted the idea of reunification' but that 'much time would pass before it becomes concrete', while the Italian President of the Council Giulio Andreotti thought that the question 'was not current' and Spanish Prime Minister Felipe Gonzalez – although recognizing its inevitable character in the medium or long term – cautiously advanced the necessity of the prior strengthening of the European Community. If one adds the sober declarations of Genscher and the manifest determination of the Soviets to preserve the status quo, the overall picture, seen from the Quai, expressed a wait-and-see attitude with respect to the German issue. By this standard the French position that October was by no means more reserved than the rest.[54]

France and the German Question: 'Starting to Reflect'

In fact, seen from Paris, the changes in the GDR merely validated Mitterrand's approach over the past several months. Mitterrand's diplomacy in October 1989 stood by the hypothesis of a gradual rapprochement between the FRG and a democratized GDR that would open the way to an 'intermediate' situation, which would be more or less long-lasting, midway between the existing situation and unity properly speaking; this latter constituted, according to the Élysée, a 'scenario to which one should not be prisoner'.[55] Honecker's fall did not fundamentally alter this analysis: that very day, Védrine noted that 'the movement of rapprochement between the two Germanys appears inevitable' but its point of arrival 'is not set in advance', even if the result of 'state unity' was not to be excluded. Stressing that it was 'impossible to contest the legitimacy of aspirations to unity' to which the West had subscribed for forty years, he concluded that the movement should be 'monitored' and that the necessary synchronization should be assured between inter-German rapprochement, European construction and the pan-European process. This analysis evidently ascribed the resolution of the German question to the medium to long term and privileged the intermediate stages.[56] The same day, in the Council of Ministers, Mitterrand confirmed that the 'reunification of Germany is possible if the populations concerned require it,' adding that France would then want to watch over the 'democratic and peaceful' nature of the process. Yet the president scarcely believed in such an eventuality for the time being, for it would presuppose the USSR's acceptance of the GDR leaving the Eastern bloc.[57]

Still, against the backdrop of democratic transition in the GDR, French leaders could not ignore that the German question was well and truly back on the agenda; thus they wished now to discuss it with Moscow. With Dumas scheduled to go there in mid November, the Quai d'Orsay, in the aftermath of the fall of Honecker, was keen to discuss anew with Moscow a domain 'where Franco-Soviet cooperation could be useful'.[58] The message to be conveyed in Moscow was that France, historic partner of the FRG, could only 'reassert the rights of Germans to self-determination and to unity', but also that, like the USSR, it had 'a major interest in the stability at the heart of Europe being preserved'; the rapprochement between the two Germanys should therefore take place 'respecting the right of the four allied powers and in a framework of cooperation where the Franco-Soviet dialogue should have a prime place'.[59] The Soviets were no doubt interested: Gorbachev, the Kremlin let it be known, himself wished to bring up the issue with Dumas. Unsurprisingly, the French and Soviets in this autumn of 1989 were keen to renew their dialogue over the German question, a dialogue that had waned over the last few years, as we have seen.[60]

At the same time, the French and Germans seemed paradoxically less pressed to tackle the subject candidly together. In mid October, when Kohl asked to meet Mitterrand (whom he had not been able to see at the start of the month for health reasons), it was to discuss not the German question but other European subjects; these accompanied the menu of an informal dinner at the Élysée on 24 October. While the Quai d'Orsay did suggest profiting from the upcoming Franco-German summit to 'sound out' Bonn on the German question in order to avoid possible divergences arising later, both the Élysée and the Chancellery were keener to confine the discussion to European matters.[61] The Bonn summit on 2 November did give rise to an exchange on the German question, but Mitterrand and Kohl, while exchanging their analyses of events in the GDR, stuck to generalities. Progress in German unity was 'only possible within Europe', Kohl repeated; European construction brought closer the day 'when the division of Europe will be overcome' and Germany 'reunited', Mitterrand added. But the chancellor stressed that it would be 'absurd' to 'elaborate a plan [for the unity of] Germany' (*ein Deutschland-Plan*) since changes were so unforeseeable; he thus stuck to the line proclaimed by Bonn during the past weeks: the hour had come for reform in the GDR, not for unification.[62] In short, both sides hesitated to tackle head-on a question that was on everyone's lips. Kohl did not want to show his cards, even to Mitterrand, while the latter did not wish to give the question more urgency than he thought it merited.

Yet Mitterrand's policy had to recognize the renewed topicality of the German question, as shown by the French president's public declarations at the end of October and early November. Mitterrand was to speak before the European Parliament on 25 October in his capacity as president of the European Community. The Quai tried to make him bear on Community and Eastern European issues above all, but Mitterrand nevertheless did touch on the German question. Refuting the thesis that rapprochement between the two Germanys would lead the Federal Republic to be less interested in European construction, he asked: 'How could the German people be blamed for wanting to be together?'[63] Like Bush stressing West Germany's Atlantic fidelity in the *New York Times*, the president was thus responding to the preoccupation, expressed to him by the chancellor at the Elysée the previous day, with the 'gossip' that Bonn was turning away from the Community due to events in Eastern Europe.[64] If Mitterrand's speech in Strasbourg was a little less emphatic than Bush's, the logic of support for Kohl was quite the same. The Bonn summit the following week would be another occasion for Mitterrand to make things more precise. Asked by the press after the summit on 3 November whether 'he feared a possible reunification of Germany' ('listen closely to the President's reply, it is very important,' stressed Kohl), Mitterrand replied that 'what counts above all is the will and determination of the people', recalling the need for a 'democratic' and 'peaceful' process and mentioning in passing 'a certain form of intangibility' regarding the German-Polish border (the issue of the Oder-Neisse line was coming back to the foreground).[65] The president concluded: 'I am not afraid of reunification. I do not ask myself that kind of question as history advances. History is there. I take it as it is' – adding that France 'will adapt its policy accordingly'.[66] The statement did not mark a break with Mitterrand's preceding declarations, but both the place and the circumstance gave it a tone and clarity that the press did not fail to note.[67] The French president's declaration had evidently been agreed upon beforehand with the German chancellor.[68] Kohl, in the following days, would in fact publicly characterize as a 'great success' the fact that Mitterrand (after Bush) had thus spoken in a positive way of the 'possibility' of unification.[69] Even if (as we shall see) some people began to deplore the insufficiencies of the French discourse, at this stage it appeared in phase with German opinion, and in any case was also perceived as 'positive,' notably in Washington.[70]

European Imperatives

Seen from Paris, the acceleration of change in the GDR during October 1989 confirmed an idea that would henceforth condition French reaction to the return of the German question: Europe was the indispensable framework for its resolution. Mitterrand said so again publicly in Caracas on 10 October: the Community 'might bring a contribution, even a response, to the problems that would be created in case of German reunification'.[71] There is no 'alternative policy', he hammered at the Council of Ministers a week later: at best one might 'render the Community more attractive so that an eventually reunified Germany would prefer it to a policy of balancing between East and West'.[72] In his note of 18 October, Védrine summed things up: 'Everything remains manageable if this movement toward the end of the division of Germany does not advance more quickly than the construction of Europe and the general suppression of barriers between East and West.' Concretely this meant 'to force the pace of European construction and the deeper insertion of the FRG among the Twelve', 'to achieve monetary union in order to thwart a mark zone', to make the Community able to 'magnetize' Eastern Europe, and to seek a 'balance of forces at a low level' while maintaining existing alliances as guarantees of stability, 'during a rather long intermediate time'. All of French policy in the months to come was contained in this analysis, which reflected the Mitterrandian vision of recent years; a vision that, let us repeat, postulated that the resolution of the German question should be gradual, thus allowing for completing the European project in parallel: 'The question of comparative rhythms is essential', concluded Védrine.[73]

Still, the acceleration of events inevitably aroused a feeling of urgency in Paris with regard to Community affairs, a feeling fed by fear that the European project might be jeopardized by the end of the Cold War and German unification. Faced with upheavals in the East and an evolution in Germany that threatened to force European unification into the background, the stakes were clear: 'to eliminate the idea that the Community is outmoded by current events'. The immediate French priority in that regard remained of course the economic and monetary union, which was the Élysée's principal European preoccupation for the coming months and the stated goal of the French presidency in the second half of 1989, and it appeared more than ever necessary in order to contain German power. But the French were also aware of the importance of the political dimension of European construction, to which the Germans were particularly attached – and which could not be neglected if Paris wanted to obtain a green light for the EMU. Hence Guigou's suggestions for the Strasbourg speech: to stress that the single currency was indeed 'a decisive step toward a political Europe' and to show that the Community was able to provide the economic aid necessary for the countries of Central and Eastern Europe, and thus that it could have an 'Eastern policy'.[74] This last preoccupation responded to a dual concern: to counteract the nascent criticism about the shortcomings of EEC action in the East, and also to answer an increasingly insistent demand from Bonn, since Kohl was anxious (notably in order to justify his European policy to public opinion) to establish 'as close a link as possible between strengthening the Community and the policy toward countries of the East'.[75]

At the time, the French desire to respond to upheavals in the East primarily by reasserting European priorities did not appear to run up against major difficulties. Mitterrand and Kohl appeared in unison on this. The Élysée dinner on 24 October confirmed their agreement about the importance of a Community response to these challenges and the need to strengthen European construction.[76] The 54th Franco-German summit in Bonn on 2 and 3 November was the occasion for renewed assertions: by Kohl that he 'wanted the success of the Strasbourg summit precisely because of the evolution of events in Central and Eastern Europe', and by Mitterrand that for the same reasons, it was necessary 'to accelerate and reinforce Western European integration'.[77] Nevertheless, behind this mutual reaffirmation of European engagement, differences were taking shape that would be exposed in the following weeks. True, evolution in the German position on the EMU was judged encouraging at the Élysée; Kohl, his adviser Joachim Bitterlich let it be known in mid October, was now disposed to make the IGC begin in the second half of 1990 and finish in the second half of 1991. 'We should be able to have an agreement on the convening, the date and the overall agenda' of the IGC, concluded Mitterrand on 18 October.[78] In fact, on 2 November Kohl confirmed that he would be ready to launch the IGC at the end of 1990 and marked his wish to avoid any divergence between France and Germany on this subject. But behind this conciliatory statement – the misunderstandings of the spring seemed forgotten – one sensed reservations. Without hiding the political problems that this issue posed for him with the approach of the election, the chancellor indeed put the accent on still unresolved questions about the EMU, and he confirmed what his own European priorities were: setting up a policy of Community support for the processes of transition in Eastern Europe (notably Hungary and Poland), on which depended the success of the reformers; and beginning as rapidly as possible to reflect on the extension of the rights of the European Parliament – a red flag for

Paris – and beyond that on the future and ultimate purpose of the Community, in other words on the political union, the indispensable counterpart for Bonn of the Economic and Monetary Union.[79] With absolute priority to the EMU and distrust about institutional reforms put forth by one side, and persistent reservations about the single currency and the requirement to advance toward political Europe put forth by the other, the Franco-German perspectives on European construction in the autumn of 1989 were far from perfectly coinciding, as what followed would show.

The French were starting again to wonder about the European commitment of their German neighbor. Genscher's recent declarations, notably to *Der Spiegel*, were poorly received in the Quai d'Orsay. The German minister seemed to plead for a rapid enlargement of the Community to Eastern Europe while renouncing a security dimension to European construction, an approach that could only revive French fears of a German temptation to 'dilute' the building of Europe: 'the FRG seems to think that it has a greater role to play' between two blocs than 'in the thorough construction of a Western Europe', the Directorate of Strategic Affairs concluded.[80] True, the Élysée was less alarmist; Genscher's statements, it explained, had been badly interpreted.[81] Still, French policy was returning to its past doubts about a Genscherian policy in which the European Community 'would be only a moment in the constitution of a grand Europe'.[82] In short, in the autumn of 1989, against the backdrop of the return of the German question, Franco-German and European misunderstandings resurfaced. While Bonn put the idea of a common Franco-German Ostpolitik back on the table, the French poorly disguised their persistent distrust of this type of exercise.[83] As for the Germans, they deplored that 'a dialogue of the deaf' was occurring between Paris and Bonn about defense, which might 'cause the failure of a common policy' in this domain as well.[84] Acceleration of events in the East during October clearly began to loom over the bilateral relation, in particular over European issues.

"Is this not the time to review our discourse?"

It was in this context that some responsible for French diplomacy began to wonder if the approach and especially the French discourse on the German question could remain unchanged. At the origin of these speculations was the resentment spreading in the FRG about its Western allies, who were 'suspected and sometimes accused of preferring to keep the German and European status quo'.[85] Starting in mid September, Jean-Marie Guéhenno, the head of policy planning (CAP) at the Quai d'Orsay, wondered: 'Might we avoid the Franco-German relation being affected by such afterthoughts?' and 'Do we have to go farther than our traditional position?' Guéhenno thought so. True, he discarded 'clarification American-style', an allusion to 'increasingly clear declarations in favor of reunification' like those of Vernon Walters, the American ambassador in Bonn. He judged such positions counterproductive, liable to arouse Soviet toughening while offering an outmoded model for German unity, that of the traditional nation-state. But he also thought that the French position, although 'adapted to the situation', was not 'tenable over time', even if the Germans were for the time being satisfied by France's attitude (which, like the German attitude, was about avoiding a 'premature clarification'). Hence it was necessary to 'reformulate' this position by means of a 'solemn discourse on our vision of the German question' and of Europe, a discourse indispensable to 'appease tenacious fears nourished by the Germans with respect to us'. It would be a matter of strongly recalling 'the inalienable right of all Germans to self-determination and the desire of France to never be a historical obstacle to the realization of this legitimate aspiration'.[86] The question of the French 'discourse' on unification was posed.

Yet it would take nearly a month before Mitterrand expressed himself publicly again, in Caracas. As a result, in mid October the press began to speculate on the 'parsimony of French commentary': was this not a 'head-in-the-sand policy' in the face of the now 'ineluctable' German question? And did events justify limiting oneself to reminders of principles? asked Claire Tréan in *Le Monde*. Of course, she recognized that French leaders might take 'shelter' behind the 'Genscherian' approach that GDR reform and not unification was at issue. But for how long? Events showed that such an analysis eventually was 'simply not credible' – and yet, she noted that the French were 'only at the beginning of new thinking' and it was becoming urgent to 'lift the ambiguity'. Tréan concluded that 'the President of the Republic could not be content with incidentally reasserting the principle of reunification during a trip to Latin America while his entourage sticks to analyses that belong to an ostrich-like policy'.[87] At the Élysée these negative editorials aroused genuine surprise: Mitterrand's entourage thought he had long had 'a clear policy about the German question and changes in the East', so why change now? Yet the episode marked the start of an enduring misunderstanding between the Élysée and some print journalists, and it clearly showed the importance of the question of discourse in the management of the German question.[88]

This episode was echoed in the long memorandum that the head of the European Directorate at the Quai d'Orsay, Jacques Blot, devoted to the German question at the end of October, which appeared precisely to engage in this 'new reflection'.[89] The starting point of his analysis was a realization of the persistence of 'mutual suspicion': on the French side, of an FRG on the verge of drifting to the East to obtain unification; on the German side, of a France defending Germany's right to unity only because it was confident that the USSR 'would take charge of maintaining the status quo'. The German suspicion might be explained: France after the war had welcomed the division of Germany and the Germans remembered this. Even if things had moved on, the 'reasons for their suspicion' still had to be removed, for 'the GDR crisis was once again turning the German question into a contemporary issue and obliging us take a position'. Nevertheless, Blot added, 'it no longer suffices to say that we are favorable to free self-determination by the German people, we have to add that this is now a goal of French policy'– which, given the reality of Franco-German reconciliation and European construction signified 'taking responsibility for the German future as part of our own future'. In short, 'our language should move from the passive to the active.' 'Could it not be in Berlin, in the presence of the German President and Chancellor, that such a declaration might be made by the President of the Republic?' Blot noted that there was a strong expectation of such a speech in the FRG, where it was hoped that France would give its vision of the 'German future', as formerly de Gaulle had done.

In substance, Blot's analysis stuck to the Mitterrandian line about the need for a 'peaceful' and 'democratic' process. He stressed that the modes of the process 'cannot be left to German evaluation alone' even in the hypothesis (not to be excluded) of a crumbling of the GDR and a demand for joining the FRG; hence the respective roles of the two Germanys and the Four Powers in such a process had to be considered, for it was up to the two sovereign German states and the powers responsible 'to define the ways and means of an agreement' whose acceptance ultimately would remain up to the German people (the author was thus sketching what would become the '2 + 4' process). As for the European framework in which German unity would have to be achieved, ideally it should be the European Community, but without neglecting the greater European context. Hence European construction should be pursued 'in its totality' (including the political and military dimensions) while fostering the emergence in Central Europe of an ensemble that would have privileged relations with the Twelve while also keeping ties with the USSR, all within the framework of an institutionalized CSCE. And Blot suggested what might be 'the new formulation' of French policy, summarized as follows: France was favorable to self-determination while taking into account the existence of two German states, the inviolable character of the border with Poland, and the rights of the Four. It would not reject a priori any solution accepted by all parties, 'even reunification in the form of a single state entity' that would take its place in the context of the European Community. But 'except in case of a sudden dramatic evolution or a policy of *fait accompli*, such a solution does not appear realistic at this moment', he stressed, and it was not advocated either in the FRG or in the GDR. Hence, at the close of a 'peaceful settlement' that might be signed by the year 1995 (i.e. fifty years after the end of the war), the union of the two Germanys should take the form of a confederation, each of the two states keeping, if it wished, its social and institutional system as well as its international status and alliances. This confederation might be 'evolving' and lead in twenty or thirty years to a federal structure if the two states wished it and provided there was an agreement by the powers who were party to the peaceful settlement. At the same time the European Community would strengthen its cohesion without renouncing any of its potential, and the Helsinki process would be institutionalized.[90]

'This note has no other goal than to arouse reflection', concluded the head of the European directorate. Still, the memorandum is of great interest, for it expresses what was, only a few days before the fall of the Berlin Wall, the concept of the German question and the European future among those in charge of French diplomacy.[91] By embedding the gradual overcoming of the division of Germany in an overall recomposition of Europe, it echoed Élysée and Quai d'Orsay thinking at the end of October 1989, that is, at a moment when the German question was not yet formally on the diplomatic agenda and appeared to be a long-term matter. Yet because it anticipated a probable acceleration of events, the memorandum suggested a real inflection in French policy – at least in its presentation – while at the same time demonstrating what would soon appear as its principal shortcoming: the lack as yet of a strong discourse in France on the German question. Judging insufficient the simple recall of the legitimacy of the German aspiration to unity and the need to realize it amid political stability, it pleaded for a more daring approach that would lead to the solemn assertion of *active* French support for the goal of German unity, leading French diplomacy to make explicit the steps in the process that would make its achievement possible. However, in declaring in Bonn on 3 November that he was 'not afraid' of unification, Mitterrand, who stuck to a position balanced between acceptance of unity and the need for stability, showed that he had not yet chosen such an inflection. If his position remained in phase with events for the time being, the acceleration of the weeks that followed would disturb this balance.

Notes

1. The communist-led government coalition obtained 65 percent of the seats in the Sejm (the lower house), as agreed at the Round Table. The remaining 35 percent of seats were obtained as early as the first round by the opposition led by Solidarnosc, which otherwise obtained 92 of the 100 seats in the Senate (the upper house, for which the ballot was entirely free). The very low turnout during the second round made clear the plunging legitimacy of the communist rule. Above all, an unexpected event, the 'satellite' parties' disassociation from the PUWP, reduced to 38 percent the number of seats held by that party in the Sejm: see Lévesque, *1989*, p. 145ff.
2. Conseil des ministres, 30 August 1989, private papers.
3. TD Moscou 5673, 13 September 1989, Archives diplomatiques (AD), Europe, URSS 1986–1990, box 6650.
4. Hubert Védrine, note pour le président de la République, a.s. Évolution des pays de l'Est; conséquences pour l'Europe de l'Ouest et pour la France et relance de notre politique, 13 September 1989, private papers. (Jean-Louis Bianco, the secretary general of the Elysée, thought the note was 'interesting'.)
5. Conseil des ministres, 30 August 1989.
6. TD Moscou 5673, 13 September 1989.
7. Note pour le président de la République, a.s. Évolution des pays de l'Est, 13 September. Bianco approved these orientations, and Mitterrand particularly approved the last one.
8. Letter from Mitterrand to Bush, 5 October 1989, private papers.
9. On what follows, see Philip Zelikow and Condoleezza Rice, *Germany Unified and Europe Transformed : A Study in Statecraft*, Cambridge, Harvard University Press, 1995, p. 63ff.
10. TD Berlin 2504–2505, 22 September 1989, AD, Directeur politique (DP), 1988–1991, box 280.
11. See Zelikow and Rice, *Germany Unified*, p. 64 and p. 80.
12. See Zelikow and Rice, *Germany Unified*, p. 80 and p. 393.
13. TD Moscou 5933, 21 September 1989, AD, Europe, Allemagne 1986–1990, box 6125.
14. Réunion quadripartite des directeurs politiques, New York, 25 September 1989, compte-rendu de B. Dufourcq, secret, s.d., AD, DP 1986–1991, box 280.
15. Testimony in Richard Kiessler and Frank Elbe, *Ein runder Tisch mit scharfen Ecken. Der diplomatische Weg zur deutschen Einheit*, Nomos, Baden-Baden, 1993, p. 38.
16. MAE, CAP, note, a.s. Les Allemands de l'Ouest et la question allemande, 12 September 1989, Archives nationales (AN), 5AG4/CDM 33; TD Bonn 2106–2109, DSL, 10 October 1989, AD, DP 1988–1991, box 274.
17. TD Berlin 2504–2505, 22 September 1989.
18. TD Moscou 5933, 21 September 1989.
19. Zelikow and Rice, *Germany Unified*, pp. 73–74.
20. TD DFRA New York 1724, 25 September 1989, DSL Secret, AD, Europe, URSS 1986–1990, box 6674; TD Moscou 6083–6084, 2 October 1989, AD, Europe, Allemagne 1986–1990, box 6125.
21. See Zelikow and Rice, *Germany Unified*, p. 81.
22. Réunion quadripartite des directeurs politiques, New York, 25 September 1989, compte rendu de B. Dufourcq. As a matter of fact, the question had barely been discussed in Wyoming, where Baker was content with reminding Shevardnadze of the traditional Western position in support of the Germans' right to self-determination.
23. MAE, CAP, note, a.s. Les Allemands de l'Ouest et la question allemande, 12 September 1989.

24. TD Bonn 2106–2109, 10 October.
25. Conseil des ministres, 6 September, private papers.
26. Védrine, note pour le président de la République, a.s. Évolution des pays de l'Est, 13 September 1989. For the Élysée, the future of Eastern Europe was a more pressing subject, at this stage, than the German question: 'fear of reunification' prevails for some over the fear of 'chaos' in the East, which was a mistake, Bianco wrote in the previous note.
27. TD DFRA New York 1724, 25 September 1989.
28. Mitterrand's press conference in Caracas, 10 October 1989, MAE, *Politique étrangère de la France. Textes et documents* (PEF), September–October 1989, p. 120.
29. On this, see Hannes Adomeit, *Imperial Overstretch: Germany in Soviet Policy from Stalin to Gorbachev*, Baden-Baden, Nomos, 1998, p. 401ff.; and Zelikow and Rice, *Germany Unified*, p. 81ff.
30. The American ambassador in the FRG believed this: see Zelikow and Rice, *Germany Unified*, p. 86.
31. Press conference of Mitterrand and Mario Soares, 18 October 1989.
32. TD Moscou 6083–6084, 2 October 1989.
33. MAE, Direction d'Europe, sous-direction URSS, note a.s. La politique allemande de l'URSS, 19 October 1989, AD, Europe, Allemagne 1986–1990, box 6122.
34. Letter from Chèvenement to Mitterrand, 16 October 1989, private papers. Bahr thought Honecker would likely step down within two months but couldn't give the name of his successor with certainty.
35. Adomeit, *Imperial Overstretch*, p. 417. Anatoly Chernyaev, Gorbachev's adviser, thought that Gorbachev was hoping that, after Honecker, a '*perestroika*' would occur, bringing stabilization to the GDR; see Anatoly S. Chernyaev, *My Six Years with Gorbachev*, University Park, Pennsylvania University Press, 2000, p. 235. Gorbachev later recalled having believed for some time that Krenz was capable of reforming the FRG: see Mikhaïl Gorbatchev, *Mémoires*, Paris, Éditions du Rocher, 1997, p. 659.
36. MAE, Fiche, a.s. La vision soviétique de l'avenir de l'Europe: 'Maison commune' et 'Question allemande' [no date, end of October 1989], AD, Europe, URSS 1986–1990, box 6681.
37. The East German report is analyzed in Adomeit, *Imperial Overstretch*, pp. 420–430; and in Zelikow and Rice, *Germany Unified*, pp. 86–91.
38. Quotes taken from Adomeit, *Imperial Overstretch*, pp. 421–422. Gorbachev nevertheless noted in regard to the American attitude that 'some nuances' were expressed 'which still had to be examined', but his adviser Georgi Shakhnazarov minimized them by considering them to have been designed for the 'wider public'.
39. MAE, Fiche, a.s. Les relations entre l'URSS et la RFA, 9 November 1989, AD, Europe, URSS 1986–1990, box 6681; see also Fiche a.s. La vision soviétique de l'avenir de l'Europe, no date.
40. On this point, see Zelikow and Rice, *Germany Unified*, pp. 92–93. As for Kohl, he later confirmed that he had thought right away that there was 'no reason to give this regime [Krenz's] a time guarantee, no reason to stabilize it': Helmut Kohl, *Je voulais l'unité de l'Allemagne*, Paris, De Fallois, 1997, p. 93.
41. MAE, Sous-direction d'Europe centrale, note, a.s. 54e sommet franco-allemand. Bonn 2–3 novembre 1989, présentation générale, 23 October 1989, AD, Europe, RFA 1986–1990, box 6792.
42. TD Bonn 2211–2212, 25 October 1989, Europe, RFA 1986–1990, box 6792.
43. On this point, see Adomeit, *Imperial Overstretch*, pp. 422–423.
44. Letter from Chevènement to Mitterrand, 16 October 1989.

45. MAE, Sous-direction URSS, note à l'attention du directeur d'Europe, a.s. La 'question allemande' et l'avenir de l'Europe: vues de M. Genscher, 24 October 1989, AD, Europe, Allemagne 1986–1990, box 6119.
46. TD Bonn 2200, DSL, 24 October 1989, AD, DP 1986–1991, box 273; German verbatim in Gespräch des Bundesministers Seiters mit den Botschaften der drei Mächte, Bonn, 24. Oktober 1989, in *Deutsche Einheit. Sonderedition aus den Akten des Bundeskanzleramtes 1989/90*, Munich, R. Oldenburg, 1998, pp. 462–464.
47. Quoted by Zelikow and Rice, *Germany Unified*, p. 93.
48. Kohl, during a telephone conversation with the newly appointed East German premier, claimed to be ready to go through with cooperating with the GDR; see Telefongespräch des Bundeskanzlers Kohl mit Staatsratsvorsitzenden Krenz, 26. Oktober 1989, *Deutsche Einheit*, pp. 468–469; and Kohl, *Je voulais*, p. 96.
49. On this, Zelikow and Rice, *Germany Unified*, p. 93ff. and pp. 396–398.
50. A debate was then developing within the Bush administration – which was to some extent similar, as will be seen, to discussions being conducted in Paris – between the NSC staff, who were in favor of active support for Kohl's policy, and officials of the State Department, who were generally more cautious. The gap would become quite visible in the coming months (Scowcroft, until Honecker's fall, was himself 'skeptical' about the opportunity to support the goal of unification and therefore closer to the State Department than to his own associates): see George Bush and Brent Scowcroft, *A World Transformed*, New York, Vintage Books, 1998, pp. 188–189.
51. Zelikow and Rice, *Germany Unified*, pp. 93–94; for the German report, see Telefongespräch des Bundeskanzlers Kohl mit Präsident Bush, 23. Oktober 1989, *Deutsche Einheit*, pp. 459–460.
52. Vorlage des Ministerialdirektors Teltschik an Bundeskanzler Kohl, Bonn, 24. Oktober 1989, *Deutsche Einheit*, pp. 465–467 (Teltschik was made aware of Bush's declarations by agency dispatches on 24 October).
53. Responding to Bertrand Dufourcq, who questioned him on the American position after Bush's *New York Times* interview, Undersecretary of State Robert Kimmit emphasized the Atlantic reliability of the FRG to explain the absence of American concern with regard to a future unification: see Kiessler and Elbe, *Ein Runder Tisch*, pp. 56–57.
54. MAE, fiche, a.s. Attitude de nos principaux partenaires occidentaux à l'égard de la 'question allemande,' 30 October 1989, AD, Europe, URSS 1986–1990, box 6681.
55. Claire Tréan, 'La France, l'Allemagne et l'autruche,' *Le Monde*, 14 October 1989 (the author quoted remarks that Védrine had confided to her: see Hubert Védrine, note pour le président de la République, 16 October 1989, private papers).
56. Védrine, note a.s. Réflexions sur la question allemande, 18 October 1989, private papers. Védrine described the possible intermediate steps toward German unity as he saw them: 'freeing up of the circulation of people' and 'lightening of checks at the borders' between the two Germanys, 'removal of the wall', 'easy relations [between the citizens of East and West Germany] like [between] Austria and Hungary', 'situation [of FRG-GDR relations] like Benelux', 'confederation [between the FRG and the GDR]' and, finally, 'one [German] state'.
57. Conseil des ministres, 18 October 1989, private papers.
58. MAE, sous-direction URSS, note a.s. La politique allemande de l'URSS, 19 October 1989.
59. MAE, fiche, a.s. Les relations entre l'URSS et la RFA, 9 November 1989. The note suggested that Dumas could question Shevardnadze 'on the Soviet interpretation of the right to self-determination as it is mentioned in the German-Soviet declaration of June 1989'.

60. MAE, le sous-directeur d'URSS, note de synthèse, a.s. Visite de M. Dumas à Moscou (14 novembre), 9 November 1989, AD, Europe, URSS 1986–1990, box 6681.
61. Guigou, note pour le président de la République, Message de M. Bitterlich, collaborateur du chancelier Kohl pour les questions européennes, 13 October 1989, AN, 5AG4/6874; Dinner between Kohl and Mitterrand at the Élysée, 24 October 1989, Védrine's handwritten notes, private papers; MAE, Sous-direction URSS, note de synthèse, a.s. L'URSS, les évolutions en Europe et la 'question allemande', 25 October 1989, AD, Europe 1986–1990, RFA, box 6792; and Loïc Hennekinne, note pour le président de la République, Sommet franco-allemand de Bonn, 2 November 1989, AN, 5AG4/6874.
62. Deutsch-französische Konsultationen, Bonn, 2./3. November 1989, *Deutsche Einheit*, pp. 470–473.
63. Guigou, note pour le président de la République, Votre discours au parlement européen de Strasbourg, 19 October 1989, private papers; Mitterrand's speech before the European Parliament, 25 October 1989, *PEF*, September-October 1989, 175–183.
64. Dinner between Kohl and Mitterrand at the Élysée, 24 October 1989.
65. This position taken by Mitterrand on the German-Polish border (in line with the doctrine fixed by General de Gaulle in his press conference on 25 March 1959) was issued against a backdrop of a rising debate that would dominate the unification process in the coming weeks and months. One must recall that the Oder-Neisse problem was the result of the temporary nature of Poland's Western border as it had been established under the Potsdam agreements in 1945, its final fixing being postponed to a peace treaty that, of course, was never concluded. True, the FRG, through the 1970 Moscow and Warsaw treaties, had recognized the *inviolable* nature of the Oder-Neisse line and had made a commitment to not formulate any territorial claims under a peace settlement. However, according to West German legal doctrine, this recognition only involved the federal government and not a future united and sovereign Germany; the final border could only be fixed at the time of the final settlement of the German question. As a result, until unification the *Grenzfrage* (the border issue) would remain an important political stake, notably due to the weight within the CDU-CSU of the associations of refugees (*Vertriebene*), whose lasting hostility toward recognizing the Oder-Neisse line compounded the difficulties encountered by Kohl in this matter. In the autumn of 1989, this matter could only come to the forefront against the background of the return of the German question, for the perspective of unification raised ipso facto the question of the final settling of the border; on this question, see Timothy Garton-Ash, *In Europe's Name: Germany and the Divided Continent*, New York, Vintage Books, 1993, p. 216ff.
66. Mitterrand and Kohl, joint press conference, Bonn, 3 November 1989, *PEF*, November–December 1989, pp. 4–6.
67. Luc Rosenzweig and Claire Tréan, 'Écoutez bien la réponse du président', *Le Monde*, 6 November 1989.
68. The day after the fall of the Wall, Mitterrand congratulated himself on having made these remarks and thanked Kohl for having had in this regard an 'intuition': see Telefongespräch des Bundeskanzlers Kohl mit Staatspräsident Mitterrand, 11. November 1989, *Deutsche Einheit*, pp. 511–512.
69. See Tilo Schabert, *Wie Weltgeschichte gemacht wird. Frankreich und die deutsche Einheit*, Stuttgart, Klett-Cotta, 2002, p. 393.
70. Zelikow and Rice, *Germany Unified*, p. 95 and p. 400.
71. Mitterrand's press conference in Caracas, 10 October 1989.
72. Conseil des ministres, 18 October 1989.
73. Védrine, note a.s. Réflexions sur la question allemande, 18 octobre 1989.

74. Guigou, note pour le président de la République, Votre discours au parlement européen de Strasbourg, 19 October 1989.
75. Guigou, note pour le président de la République, Message de M. Bitterlich, 13 October 1989; see also Gilles Bresson, 'L'opposition met plein cap à l'Est,' *Libération*, 25 October 1989.
76. Dinner between Kohl and Mitterrand at the Élysée, 24 October 1989.
77. Deutsch–französische Konsultationen, Bonn, 2./3. November 1989, *Deutsche Einheit*, pp. 472–473.
78. Guigou, note pour le président de la République, Message de M. Bitterlich, 13 October 1989; and Conseil des ministres, 18 October 1989. Bonn formally confirmed on 30 October that the FRG would accept an initiation of the ICG in the second semester of 1990; see Guigou, note pour le président de la République, Votre entretien avec le chancelier Kohl lors du sommet franco-allemand, 1 November 1989, private papers.
79. Deutsch-französische Konsultationen, Bonn, 2./3. November 1989, *Deutsche Einheit*, pp. 470–473; during his meeting this same 2 November with French Prime Minister Michel Rocard, Kohl insisted even more on this last point and particularly on the prerogatives of the Parliament, and he was shown to be skeptical about the state of the Twelve's reflection on the EMU: *Deutsche Einheit*, pp. 474–476.
80. MAE, le directeur adjoint des affaires politiques, note pour M. Dufourcq, Extrait de la réunion des directeurs le 11 octobre, 11 October 1989, AD, DP 1988–1991, box 274; MAE, Service des affaires stratégiques et du désarmement, note, a. s. La France et le développement de l'Europe de la sécurité: éléments de réflexion, 24 October 1989, AD, DP 1988–1991, box 300.
81. Guigou, note pour le président de la République, Votre discours au parlement européen de Strasbourg, 19 October 1989.
82. MAE, Sous-direction URSS, note à l'attention du directeur d'Europe, a.s. La 'question allemande' et l'avenir de l'Europe: vues de M. Genscher, 24 October 1989.
83. The Auswärtiges Amt envisaging a meeting of the West German ambassadors in the East in mid October, Genscher suggested to Dumas that their French counterparts participate in it, but the French minister, upon reflection, doubted 'that the moment was very opportune': MAE, le directeur des affaires politiques, projet de note pour M. le président de la République, a.s. réunion conjointe des ambassadeurs de France et de République fédérale dans les pays de l'Est, 2 October 1989, AD, Europe, RFA 1986–1990, box 6782.
84. Guigou, note pour le président de la République, Message de M. Bitterlich, 13 October 1989.
85. MAE, CAP, Les Allemands de l'Ouest et la question allemande, 12 September 1989.
86. MAE, le chef du CAP, note a.s. La Question allemande, 12 septembre 1989 AN, 5AG4/CDM 33.
87. Claire Tréan, 'La France, l'Allemagne et l'autruche', *Le Monde*, 14 octobre 1989.
88. Védrine, note pour le président de la République, 16 October 1989; Védrine contested the remarks that Tréan attributed to him in her article (see here above, note 55) and thought she had 'isolated them from their context'.
89. MAE, le directeur d'Europe, Réflexions sur la question allemande, 30 October 1989, 61 p., AD, Europe, Allemagne 1986–1990, box 6119, also found in the presidential archives: AN 5AG4/CDM 33.
90. Blot proposed a 'tentative' calendar. 1989: France formally takes a position on German unity; 1990: exploratory talks are held, a Franco-German policy in Central Europe is designed, the international conference begins; 1990–1992: support is given to reforms

in the GDR, the European Union is accelerated, a 'flexible cooperation structure' is set up in Central Europe, the disarmament process continues; 1992–1995: the Helsinki conference takes place in 1992, the CSCE is institutionalized, a peace settlement with Germany is reached, a German confederation is created and referendums are held in the FRG and GDR; before that, no new membership in the Community is accepted, but relations between the latter, Eastern/Central European countries and the USSR are organized; finally, at the end of a period to be fixed (20–30 years), Germany may choose to go from confederate status to federal status, and a 'pan-European confederation' is created (this expression foretells the European confederation evoked by Mitterrand two months later).

91. Blot's note was situated in the continuity of Dufourcq's prospective note from February 1989 (see chapter 1 of this volume, p. 62), even if it went further in exploring the German question that in the meantime had fully resurfaced on the agenda.

Chapter 3

THE FALL OF THE WALL

(9–10 November–31 December 1989)

No episode remains more closely associated with the end of the Cold War and German unification than the fall of the Berlin Wall, which suddenly revealed the breadth of change and at the same time accelerated its rhythm. The events of the seven or eight weeks that followed, both in Germany and on the international level, succeeded each other very quickly; they conferred on the period an exceptional density that lasted until the end of the year as initiatives, meetings and international summits piled up upon one another. Among other things, there took place the informal summit of the Twelve at the Élysée (18 November), the presentation by Helmut Kohl of his plan for German unity (28 November), the American-Soviet summit in Malta (2–3 December), the NATO extraordinary summit in Brussels (4 December), the meeting between Mitterrand and Gorbachev in Kiev (6 December), the European Council in Strasbourg (8–9 December), the meeting of representatives of the four powers in Berlin (11 December), the meeting between Mitterrand and Bush in Saint-Martin (16 December), Kohl's visit to Dresden and his meeting with Modrow (19 December), and finally Mitterrand's trip to the GDR (20–22 December). Rarely has the international agenda been so full, and French diplomacy played its part.

But if it was a singularly dense period, it was also uncertain, complex, and in many respects contradictory. It was uncertain because the unpredictability of changes and the interplay of actors meant that nothing was

---

Notes for this section begin on page 149.

determined in advance. During these final weeks of 1989, the process underway became irreversible: still hypothetical on the eve of the Wall's fall, German unification had become a certainty by the end of the year. Yet the timetable and mode remained at this stage very indeterminate; more than ever, one must beware of analyzing policies or statements in light of subsequent certainties and instead try to establish their intrinsic logic at the time. This is all the more so because the period was complex and cannot be reduced to a linear progression. Following upon each other were times of acceleration (the fall of the Wall, the Ten Point Plan, Kohl's visit to Dresden) and times of deceleration, in particular after the various summits: a situation or ambience might therefore change totally in a few days, thereby falsifying the interpretations of facts that are badly situated in their context or else analyzed from the vantage point of hindsight, as is too often the case. But this was also a contradictory period, as these very events and changes belong to distinct and often antagonistic logics: a revolutionary logic of peoples – foremost the German people, who over a few weeks would be overwhelmed by the aspiration to unity; then a more contingent one of domestic politics, starting with the Federal Republic, where the national question quickly became a major stake; and finally, the conservative one of international diplomacy, where – beyond evident differences of approach in various capitals – there was a desire to frame and control the changes. Nor should it be forgotten that the attitudes of the various actors (starting with the USSR) were far from being perfectly coherent and reflected these same contradictions or dilemmas. French diplomacy of course did not escape this.

From the Fall of the Wall to the Élysée Summit

The event took place in the night from 9 to 10 November 1989 in a most unexpected way. Pressed by Bonn to soften the exit conditions for its citizens, the GDR regime that day had adopted measures whose effective scope was not clear but whose simple announcement led that very evening to a large number of East Berliners rushing to points along the length of the Wall in the hope of crossing it. The police left them free passage and during the night thousands of them rushed to the West; almost thirty years after its construction, the Berlin Wall 'fell' in front of the world's television cameras. None of the principal actors had anticipated the event or its suddenness, including Kohl.

As elsewhere, the surprise in Paris was complete: nobody imagined that the changes in the GDR could be so rapid. The first French reactions were prudent rather than reserved. Visiting Copenhagen, François Mitterrand referred to the situation on 10 November: 'These are happy events', he declared while repeating that he did not fear German unification, whose possibility seemed to him still quite remote.[1] This rather distanced tone – which he did not abandon in the following weeks and was reproached for – was not that remote from the one adopted the next day by George Bush.[2] In Paris, Prime Minister Michel Rocard was pleased that 'the German people are rediscovering their history and destiny', while Roland Dumas praised their 'patriotism' and 'wisdom'. Among politicians, it is true that some like Valéry Giscard d'Estaing did show their concern transparently: the event represents 'a gigantic question mark' because it raises the issue of German unity, said the former president.[3] As for public opinion, it appeared very positive from the start. A large majority of the French even expected a swift unification, believing it would not pose an obstacle to European construction.[4] The first reactions were thus illustrative of what they were to remain in the weeks and months to come: official declarations were controlled; political and media circles were divided and a portion of them reticent; and the French people were widely supportive of the prospect of German unification.[5] As the Germans analysed the respective attitudes of their principal Western partners, France typically occupied an intermediate place: the United States' attitude was seen as 'the most positive', that of France 'more reserved', and that of Great Britain 'clearly behind the two others', the Chancellery estimated on the faith of recent official declarations, noting that the French declarations – especially Mitterrand's on 3 November – sprang less from 'active support' (as in the American case) than from 'laissez-faire'.[6] Clearly the fall of the Wall crystallized previously diffuse and vague impressions in a lasting manner.

The first contacts after the event confirmed what lay behind public statements: the attitude of the French president in these crucial days (in line with his position for weeks) was to demonstrate understanding of what was happening in Germany, while being concerned about international consequences. Unsurprisingly, his first words directed at the Germans aimed to express his support. Kohl – who had interrupted a very important visit to Poland[7] to go back to Berlin and Bonn – did not manage to reach Mitterrand by telephone until 11 November. Remarking that the chancellor was 'living through moving hours', Mitterrand asked Kohl to express the French president's best wishes to the German people. Mitterrand was clearly pleased that he had taken a position on German unity on 3 November (a declaration that now appeared very timely), and he assured Kohl of his friendship. Kohl was concerned not to appear too eager. He described his personal impressions of Berlin's atmosphere as 'unimaginable', but assured Mitterrand that it was not a 'revolutionary' process that was taking place but an 'evolving' one: 'our goal is not to destabilize the situation', he insisted, promising to keep Mitterrand abreast of developments.[8]

In exchanges with Moscow, Mitterrand's policy was to appear reassuring – a posture he would maintain. From the start, the Soviet attitude in the face of the accelerating German events was characterized by a mixture of anxiety and detachment, thus expressing deep contradictions that would play a major role in subsequent events. At first, it was anxiety that prevailed. From the opening of the Wall, the MID spokesman warned that 'considerations on the reunification of Germany are an intellectual exercise that is not founded on reality'.[9] On 10 November, Gorbachev sent Mitterrand (as well as George Bush and Margaret Thatcher) an alarmist message. Mentioning a 'chaotic situation' with 'unpredictable consequences', he indicated having asked Kohl to take necessary measures to maintain order, denounced the 'voices raised in the FRG' that were challenging 'postwar reality' and 'the existence of two German states', and asked for a meeting of the Four Powers in Berlin.[10] When Gorbachev and Mitterrand talked on the telephone on 14 November, the Soviet leader, who in the meantime had received assurances from Kohl, proved calmer, but nevertheless he lambasted West German 'gesticulations' and deplored an 'artificial acceleration of events taking place there'. Mitterrand assured his interlocutor that 'the FRG would remain faithful to its commitments', and stated that 'one must take into account national aspirations, but not destroy equilibrium'. He proposed meeting Gorbachev in a third country 'for a two-hour conversation' after his anticipated meeting with Bush in Malta.[11] The message was well received: welcoming Dumas the same day for a long foreseen visit (the head of French diplomacy was thus the first Western official to go to Moscow after the fall of the Wall), Gorbachev was pleased that the French president understood 'that we must demonstrate a sense of responsibility'.[12] But while Paris – like Washington, and also Bonn – was reassuring Moscow, the French did not want to appear complacent: thus, in agreement with its partners, French diplomacy did not agree to the Soviet demand for a meeting of the representatives of the Four in Berlin, a question eluded during the telephone conversation on 14 November. Mitterrand's attitude was thus different from Thatcher's, who, in responding on 17 November to Gorbachev's message, had recognized that the speed of events 'carries in itself a risk of instability' and did not hesitate to say she was very attached to the quadripartite mechanism.[13]

'This Question is no Longer in the Foreground'

In any case, the first reactions from the principal actors quickly gave way to more reserved attitudes. Until the end of November there was a pause in events, with most capitals trying to calm things down, starting with

Moscow. While mechanically recalling that unification was not on the agenda, Soviet diplomacy thought that it had handled the Wall's fall adequately and could count on the support of Eastern countries disquieted by what was happening in Germany and ready to close ranks. If a certain nervousness persisted, the German question, as seen from the Soviet capital, appeared under control by mid November.[14] In fact, in the weeks following the Wall's fall, Gorbachev and his entourage still believed in the viability of a reformed GDR and consequently in the possibility of avoiding unification.[15] At first, this judgment was shared in the West. East German changes after the fall of the Wall credited the view that a reformed GDR could survive as a separate state: as the American ambassador in the GDR noted, it was human rights and democracy that dissidents were first and foremost demanding; as for self-determination, it would not necessarily lead to unification.[16] The appointment of Hans Modrow as Prime Minister on 13 November – Egon Krenz remaining head of state and of the Party – made this scenario credible. He was the 'right man' to apply a modern and democratic socialism, asserted the GDR ambassador to the general secretary of the Quai d'Orsay, adding that the issue of unification 'is not posed'.[17] Modrow's announcement on 17 November of an ambitious program of reforms and, most of all, of a proposal for a contractual community (*Vertragsgemeinschaft*) between the GDR and the FRG seemed to confirm this idea. Bonn's policy, moreover, remained cautious. True, Kohl stressed to the Bundestag on 16 November that aid to the GDR would depend on the reality of economic and political change – in other words, on the introduction of a market economy and free elections in the East – which in time might signify the end of the GDR. Yet on the occasion of this first parliamentary debate after the Wall came down, the chancellor insisted more on the priorities of the moment, i.e. freedom and reform of East Germany, than on unification. The French ambassador in Bonn noted that the apparent consensus between Kohl and Willy Brandt in this respect ought to reassure the Germans and their neighbors, even if the national question was now at the heart of the political debate.[18] In fact, appearing to be reassuring was indeed Kohl's objective: if objectively the Wall's fall could only advance the possibility of unification and his own determination to work for it, the chancellor's instructions continued to proclaim a reserved posture.[19] The same was true on the diplomatic level, where the Germans were trying to calm things: Genscher, passing through Washington on 20 November, tried to play down the question of unification, as the Americans noted. Washington, however, stuck to a cautious attitude of support for self-determination while being careful not to alarm the Soviets. Kohl and Bush, by telephone on 17 November, agreed on the advisability of maintaining this line; the latter repeated that he did not want to have 'the President of the United States posturing on the Berlin Wall'.[20]

It is not surprising in this context that the framework of the German question was not immediately modified, at least as seen from Paris. Of course, the fall of the Wall aroused concern among those responsible for French diplomacy: Bertrand Dufourcq, the Quai d'Orsay's political director, remembers that 'obviously the event took us by surprise' and that it inaugurated 'an uncertain phase'.[21] Jacques Blot, the head of the Quai's Europe directorate, recognized (in a much less calm analysis than his long memo of 30 October) that 'acceleration is prodigious' and mentioned the risk of 'rampant reunification'.[22] No doubt people at the Quai d'Orsay were worried about 'a reawakening of history'; the successive spurts of the following weeks would incontestably keep this worry alive, even if the key assumptions of France's German policy were not affected.[23] The Élysée was calmer. Quickly convinced that the fall of the Wall would not immediately upset the calendar, by 15 November Mitterrand thought that unification was no longer 'in the foreground', since the USSR could not accept it – as proved, he thought, by Gorbachev's 'non possumus' on 10 November.[24] As for the GDR, the Élysée observed that the dominant spirit there was for democratization and not for unification.[25] Mitterrand's associates wanted to interpret events as validating the French approach and discourse over the preceding weeks: the legitimacy of the aspiration to German unity, the necessity of a democratic and peaceful process – had not Mitterrand for months expressed this well-known position? Once the surprise had passed, Paris thus tried to re-situate the episode within the context of French policy. Asked by the press about why France was not 'more visible' after the fall of the Wall and why the French president did not take any 'initiative', Hubert Védrine referred back to the president's interview at the end of July as well as his statements in Bonn on 3 November.[26] Repeating Mitterrand's statement that the Berlin events were 'very happy and long awaited', his spokesman situated them in a continuous French policy, claiming that it represented a 'framework on the basis of which we are going to be able to work'.[27]

The Élysée Dinner

Yet Paris in the following days and weeks was keen to stress, above all, the need to frame German aspirations. This tendency was manifest during the first important international event after the fall of the Wall, the dinner at the Élysée on 18 November 1989. The idea of an informal meeting of the Twelve to 'discuss the situation' and 'close ranks' was suggested by Dufourcq to Dumas, who proposed it to Mitterrand on 12 November; the latter took the initiative the next day as current president of the European

Community.²⁸ The motivations were multiple: since the Élysée was criticized in the press for the absence of any strong reaction to the fall of the Wall, it wanted to reject any accusation of immobility; moreover (as we shall see), the meeting had the goal of preserving the Strasbourg summit three weeks later from the fallout of events in Eastern Europe. Finally, it aimed to deliver a message of moderation and to reassure those who were worried about how fast things were happening, especially Gorbachev.²⁹ Still, the question remained: what would the Twelve talk about, and would the German question be discussed? Paradoxically, the answer was negative: the rapid change of the situation in a few days, combined with Mitterrand's evident wish to calm things down, produced its effects. If the invitation made on 12 November was indeed the result of the fall of the Wall, the Élysée specified on 14 November that the German issue would be tackled 'only if someone wants to speak of it' but that 'it is not especially on the agenda'. And the next day, Mitterrand said he was glad that the Élysée meeting would not take place until 18 November: 'If we had met before, we would have spoken only of reunification.'³⁰ Little wanting to see the Twelve broach the subject, the Germans, moreover, did not insist on it for their own reasons and supported Mitterrand's wish for an open discussion that would not lead to a final communiqué.³¹

At the Élysée on the evening of 18 November, the French president opened the discussion by formulating four points: he thought that 'the democratization process in the East must be made irreversible' and declared himself for immediate aid to Hungary and Poland and 'perhaps' the GDR; he thought 'the question of borders' should 'not be raised'; he stressed that Gorbachev must not be 'destabilized'; and he proposed a study, to be conducted before the forthcoming Strasbourg conference, on how to increase the support and presence of the Community in Eastern Europe.³² Thus Mitterrand placed the debate on the terrain of change in Eastern Europe as a whole, mentioning the German question only indirectly. At the same time, he did not hide, at least implicitly, his preference for a cautious approach to the German question. His recommendation about borders, due to its ambiguity (was he talking about Oder-Neisse or all European borders, including that between the two Germanys?) could indeed be interpreted as signifying that German unification was not on the agenda, in his view.³³ Taking the floor, Kohl covered the GDR events in a speech almost forty-five minutes long. While reiterating the permanence of the FRG's commitment to Europe, he attributed current change to the solidity of the Atlantic Alliance, to the dynamics of the European Community, and to Gorbachev's policy. But while he supported 'respecting the will' of the East Germans (alluding to their right to self-determination), he deliberately abstained from speaking of unification, for he did not want to open with his eleven partners a discussion that might compromise his margin for maneuver.[34] In short, what was not said carried the evening; only Thatcher did not hesitate to openly tackle the question, without concealing her position: she was against 'any attempt to talk about either border changes or German reunification', which would hurt Gorbachev and 'also open up a Pandora's box of border claims right through Central Europe'.[35] At the end of the session, Kohl confided his impressions: 'Mitterrand, Gonzalez, Santer and Martens conducted themselves in a very friendly way', he told Teltschik, 'whereas Thatcher and Lubbers were particularly cold'.[36] The summit ended at midnight with Mitterrand's press conference. Asked about whether German unification had been mentioned, the French president responded in the negative: 'I know that this is a problem that occupies many minds, and that is perfectly legitimate, but it is a problem that was not on the agenda', he said, while recognizing that the consequences of current events on the balance of Europe were discussed 'by ricochet'.[37]

Mitterrand had a right to be content with the exercise. Not only had it allowed him to advance his Community priorities, but it appeared to confirm (undoubtedly also his objective) the now less urgent character of the German question, which Kohl's very attitude, in fact, seemed to accredit. At the same time, the informal summit allowed him to recall the need to frame the unification process internationally and to designate the Community as the privileged instrument to accomplish this. Reporting to the European Parliament on 22 November about the Elysée meeting in Kohl's presence, he stressed the need, beyond the 'profound emotion' of the moment, to 'take a little distance' from events so as to 'measure what separates dream from reality today'.[38] Writing to George Bush on the 24 November to inform him about how the summit went, he mentioned the structuring role of the Community and the need to sustain changes in the East 'without provoking a modification of strategic balances for which the Soviet Union is evidently not ready'.[39] And in the following days, he confided to the press his concerns inspired by the risk of instability in the East and the very difficult situation of the USSR. Warning against a return to territorial claims and national rivalries, he insisted (again recognizing the legitimacy of German unity) on the necessarily long duration of the process and the need to accelerate European integration.[40] In short, without hiding his apprehension about the uncontrolled consequences of current upheavals and his concern to protract German evolution over time, he tried to send a message of responsibility and to present the Twelve as a force for stability.

But at the same time, the Élysée meeting gave the impression of taking place on a level of unreality. Among the president's entourage, some wondered about the absence of the German question on the dinner menu: did it signify that the Europeans (especially the French and Germans) were unable to tackle this burning subject?[41] It is true that the tendency on all sides (including the German) was to avoid an open debate on unification. Kohl as much as Mitterrand had chosen to block the topic that evening – but for opposite reasons: for the former, it was a matter of preserving his options in the now obsessive German question, while the latter (like his European homologues) hoped that doing so would keep it under control. Yet this hope rested on what increasingly appeared a sham: the tendency of German leaders, headed by Kohl, to not acknowledge openly that their objective was now indeed unification. This was denounced by the chief editor of *Der Spiegel*, Rudolf Augstein, in a 20 November editorial that did not go unnoticed in Bonn and Paris: Bonn perhaps had a tactical interest in declaring that the Germans did not want unification, he argued, but the reality was otherwise and their partners should now confront reality.[42] If the fall of the Wall had not immediately dissipated the illusion – especially in Paris – that the German question could be postponed or at least treated in the long term, everyone really felt by the end of November that the moment of truth was approaching.

The Future of the Twelve and the Ten Point Plan

Upheavals in the East, European construction in the West: Mitterrand's diplomacy was caught after the fall of the Wall in a dialectic that would oscillate in the coming weeks between disquiet over instability and hope for integration. At first, the assessment in Paris of the impact of the Wall's fall on the pursuit of European construction was rather optimistic. Whereas numerous commentators increased their scepticism and judged that the Community project was now outmoded and condemned to an inevitable dilution, the Élysée was confident: didn't the Germans remain fundamentally attached to the European process?[43] Signals from Bonn were positive: Theo Waigel – scarcely enthusiastic, as we know, about the EMU – declared that 'developments in Eastern Europe would not have happened without European integration'.[44] In fact, it was less the attitude of the FRG that worried the president's entourage than the spreading idea that the Community, absorbed with its internal construction, might be 'unable to react in the face of events in the East'. Elisabeth Guigou wanted to challenge this idea. In her view (she had been insisting on this for weeks) this impression of powerlessness stemmed from the fact that it was not clear enough that the EMU would lead to political union, and that there existed a solution that embraced the Eastern countries other than their pure and simple membership. Hence, she said, one should envisage 'a radical reform' of institutions, make it the focus of the intergovernmental conference (IGC), and engage in 'systematic reflection' on relations of the Twelve with the East.[45]

The Élysée dinner was conceived as an answer to this latter preoccupation also: while responding to the 'media campaign' that (in his words) was pushing him to react on European terrain, for Mitterrand it was a matter of defining the position of the Twelve in their relations with the East and thus contributing to the political affirmation of the Community. But it was even more a matter of 'not encumbering' the coming summit in Strasbourg with the question of aid to the Eastern countries, which Bonn wanted to make the central issue of the summit. Indeed, in Mitterrand's view Strasbourg should above all launch the EMU, a move that aimed at no less than 'completing the European construction'.[46] In this sense, one might speak of diversion: Mitterrand's diplomacy accepted orienting the EEC more to the East (which was the focus of the Élysée dinner) in the hope of preserving the chances of a historic deepening of the Community in the West, to be decided upon in Strasbourg. Of course, the success of this diversion was partly offset by the fact that the Twelve at the Élysée had not tackled head-on the issue of German unity, which, against the backdrop of upheavals in the East, contributed to the impression that the issue had been deliberately ignored. This was contrary to the intended aim. Yet the result of the informal Élysée summit was not negligible: not only did the Twelve confirm their aid to Hungary and Poland and the decision to negotiate a commercial agreement with the GDR, but they also decided to study various important projects, including the opening to Eastern Europe of certain EC programs, the creation of a European foundation for vocational training, and especially the creation of a bank for Eastern Europe (the future EBRD), a recent idea suggested by Jacques Attali. Overall, then, the French president could consider the Twelve to have demonstrated the 'indissociable' character of changes in the East and integration in the West – and thereby contributed to preventing the dilution of the latter under the impact of the former.[47]

IGC: German Uncertainty

Yet the real priority in Paris remained the EMU. After the Élysée dinner, the president resumed his European tour with one central objective: to have the single currency launched in Strasbourg. Clearly, he thought it was more than ever indispensable, after the Wall's fall, to tie the FRG to a project that the French had long seen as a means of containing German power; the autumn's events and the prospect of a unified Germany that one day might perhaps be tempted to revive great-power aspirations only reinforced this determination.[48] In turn, the French president was manifestly eager to profit from the context to obtain advances with regard to the EMU despite the reservations Kohl had demonstrated for months. The existing circumstances would oblige the chancellor to give guarantees of his European credentials, Mitterrand felt; hence he had remarked to Dutch interlocutors on 20 November that, with a view to its unification, 'Germany will need to be considered as devoted to the European idea'.[49] Everything therefore conspired to make the coming Strasbourg summit a decisive test: Mitterrand repeated the same day at The Hague that he would indeed request in Strasbourg that the Twelve decide that the start of the IGC be set for the end of the year 1990.[50]

However, in a letter to Mitterrand dated 27 November, Kohl once more demurred. Casting doubt on the achievement of the economic convergences indispensable for the operation of the EMU, whether with regard to budgetary policy, tax harmonization, or the achievement of a single market, he proposed (this was the key point) a calendar in which *convening* the IGC would be put off until the European Council under the Italian presidency in December 1990. This meant postponing the political decision to launch the IGC by a year. Moreover, he expressed his desire to see the European Council in Strasbourg begin to debate the institutional reforms he thought necessary in the political domain, notably concerning the prerogatives of the European Parliament.[51] But these were unacceptable points to the French: for Paris, the technical dossier of the EMU was ready for implementation, since the report of the high-level working group under Guigou had been approved; the problem was rather how to maintain a political 'dynamic' until the start of the IGC. The idea of not convening it until a year later – and on the basis of a new examination of the dossier – therefore amounted in French eyes to an 'indefinite postponement'. As for reflection on institutional matters, Paris believed it should give way to the absolute priority of economic and monetary union.[52]

Kohl's letter – which indisputably marked a move backward – provoked concern in Paris, all the more so since the next day, in announcing to the Bundestag his Ten Point Plan, the chancellor proved unforthcoming about the future of European construction and silent on the stakes in Strasbourg. The conjunction of the letter of 27 November and the announcement on the next day was judged a matter of serious concern: did it signify that Kohl had decided to privilege German unification over European construction, contrary to what he had constantly asserted until then? Of course, in his public comments the French president did not reveal any particular concern; on 29 November in Athens, where he finished his tour of European capitals, Mitterrand stuck to reasserting his position: 'For myself, I think that it is fitting to fix this date right now.'[53] Behind the scenes, though, the reactions were sharp. Dumas thought the Germans 'were behaving with increasing arrogance' and that one had to be 'very firm' with them; he thought that it should be confirmed in no uncertain terms that in Strasbourg Mitterrand would pose the question of the IGC date and request that it open before the end of 1990. Finally, while he accepted the idea of an IGC on institutional questions that would take place *after* the conclusion of the EMU, Dumas judged it 'dangerous' to tackle these questions at Strasbourg; he feared (and Guigou rallied now to this viewpoint) that in the current circumstances, the opening of a debate on political union would make it still more difficult to agree on economic and monetary union. In total, Kohl's evasive attitude led to a confirmation of the Mitterrand line, if not its hardening. Not only did Paris intend to obtain the launch of the single currency in Strasbourg, but French leaders now refused (for the time being) to allow the EMU to overlap with any equivalent process of institutional reform.[54]

To be sure, the French were aware that domestic politics, with the German elections planned for the end of 1990, were the main explanation for Kohl's attitude.[55] Receiving Genscher on 30 November, Mitterrand and then Dumas verified that the German foreign minister did not have the same reservations as the Chancellor concerning the EMU. When Mitterrand asked whether German unification had not become a 'brake' for European construction and warned that slowing the process would be 'an open door to adventure,' Genscher responded that he shared the French concern 'on all points' and assured his interlocutors that he would work for a decision concerning the early convening of the IGC to be taken in Strasbourg.[56] But Genscher's proposal – which would not be the last time he proclaimed a position clearly nearer to views in Paris than those of Kohl – did not suffice to reassure French leaders, who were vexed about the 'electoralism' they ascribed to the chancellor and worried about the risk of seeing unification impose itself on German politics at the expense of European priorities. On 1 December, Mitterrand replied firmly to the Kohl letter. Sweeping aside technical objections, he confirmed that he would propose in Strasbourg that the Twelve decide that the opening of the IGC would take place before the end of 1990. Despite a semblance of concession – the IGC, he suggested, might really begin its substantive work at the start of 1991 and, once that was finished, the Twelve might tackle the question of institutional reforms with a view to realizing a European Union – Mitterrand kept his course. He was now resigned to engaging in arm-wrestling Kohl: it would be necessary in Strasbourg, he hammered out, to take 'decisions that unequivocally commit us [first] to the path of economic and monetary union'.[57]

28 November: Kohl Retakes the Initiative

The major event of the end of November 1989 remained the Ten Point Plan that Kohl presented to the Bundestag on 28 November.[58] For the chancellor, it was a matter of asserting control over a national debate that, in the absence of a strong position, risked escaping him at a time when he had decided to push ahead toward unity. Public opinion, in fact, remained undecided, and the debate in the Bundestag on 16 November had shown that politicians were divided over the long-term prospects. Meanwhile, Genscher incarnated an alternative policy at once more gradual and less oriented toward state unification, and his approach appeared to have the chance of winning over public opinion. At the same time, the GDR situation seemed quite uncertain: although pro-unity slogans ('*Wir sind ein Volk*') were now put forth by the opposition, Modrow's reform program and his proposal for a contractual community seemed to offer the regime a real chance to maintain itself, by the same token delaying the prospect for unification. Nor was an international rationale missing from Kohl's calculation. The American position seemed clear, and the assurance of Washington's active support was a decisive advantage for the chancellor. In a more surprising way, the Soviet attitude would seem to have also played a role, for while Moscow alternated between contradictory signals in the hope of arresting the process, Bonn chose to emphasize only the more positive aspects of the Soviet stance, to the point of reading into the Soviet position a sort of nihil obstat.[59] As for the Europeans, if most of the Community members preferred to maintain the German status quo for the time being (as confirmed at the Élysée dinner), Mitterrand had also expressed himself favorably in clear terms on 3 November. In any event, by taking the initiative, Kohl hoped to force a clarification of international positions as well as a dramatization of the national stakes.

This explains the Ten Point Plan's form and content. The form deliberately sought a surprise effect: the project was prepared in a few days by Kohl's closest collaborators without any member of the German government (starting with Genscher) being let in on the secret and without any foreign government being alerted in advance.[60] The content was a ten-point plan foreseeing successive stages that – at the end of a nonspecified period – would permit the achievement of German unity. These stages were: immediate humanitarian aid to the East Germans, cooperation over technology and the environment, etc., increased economic aid conditional on economic and social changes in the GDR, the establishment of a contractual community (like the one proposed by the Modrow government), creation of 'confederative structures' after free elections in the GDR, insertion of inter-German relations into the pan-European process, greater openness of the European Community to a democratized GDR and to other democratic countries of Eastern Europe, acceleration of the evolution of the CSCE, rapid progress on arms control, and finally the search for a European peace order conducive to the realization of the unity of the German people through the right to self-determination.[61] The Ten Point Plan demonstrated great political skill. While accepting the contractual community proposed by Modrow, Kohl intended to go well beyond simple cooperation between the two German states; while not denying the logic of 'small steps', he opted clearly for the prospect of unification; and while leaving the process vague in its timetable (Kohl was saying in private it would take five to ten years), he clearly made state unity the ultimate goal.[62]

The result was an incontestable success for the chancellor and a decisive impulsion toward German unity: until then an abstract idea, it was henceforward a concrete objective. For the citizens of the GDR, it now became a real option for the future, and in the FRG it became the center of national debate. Kohl had won his domestic politics bet and now found himself positioned to take charge of the movement and become the leader in the resolution of the German question, in which he would now set the tone. Genscher was forced to recognize this in congratulating him on his 'great speech'; as for the SPD, it was split and weakened, and gave Kohl's plan distant and conditional support. Finally and especially, at the international level, the Ten Point Plan irreversibly put German unity on the agenda by forcing the protagonists to take a position on it in the days and weeks to come. Two days later, Teltschik summarized the reactions in the principal capitals: 'totally positive' in Washington, clearly 'more critical' in London, 'less negative than at first sight' in Moscow. As for the French reactions, they were judged to be 'constructive'.[63]

French Reactions

Mitterrand at first displayed a certain detachment. Asked the next day about the Ten Point Plan, he declared that its content 'did not shock him at all'.[64] Of course, his entourage were displeased not to have been alerted in advance of Kohl's initiative and suspected him of having hidden his hand during the dinner of the Twelve on 18 November (wrongly, since the Ten Point initiative was conceived after that Élysée meeting). Élysée Chief of Staff Jean-Louis Bianco even saw this as a deliberate desire to leave Paris out.[65] By showing little respect for the forms of Franco-German cooperation, the procedure aroused Mitterrand's 'passing anger'.[66] Dumas, on 30 November, did not hide his concern from Genscher, who (holding himself at a distance from the chancellor) nevertheless loyally defended Kohl's initiative.[67] But the worry was most perceptible among politicians and in the media. The day of Kohl's speech, the Élysée press service was 'inundated with calls'. Had Mitterrand been informed of its content? Did the Ten Point Plan not ignore the interests of the Four Powers and those of the Twelve? Had it not been necessary to tackle the question at the Élysée on 18 November to obtain guarantees from Kohl? 'Let them talk', Mitterrand advised his spokesman.[68] Still, through its media impact the affair did contribute to the establishment of a certain distrust between Paris and Bonn after the end of November. Thus *Le Monde*'s correspondent in Bonn, Luc Rosenzweig, reproached Teltschik for the absence of a prior agreement with Paris. The latter justified himself: Mitterrand and Kohl had recently mentioned the German question and were in perfect understanding with one another. Besides, had it ever occurred to Mitterrand to consult another government before expressing himself on a question of national interest?[69] The Ten Point Plan, as we see, worked to reveal a misunderstanding that expressed defects in the Franco-German dialogue over recent weeks.

Yet more than the form, it was the content of the initiative that produced a powerful effect. More clearly than after the Wall's fall, French diplomacy was becoming aware of the irreversible character of the process: unity was now a German national priority, and there was consensus on this in the Federal Republic. 'The German question is today posed with an urgency all the greater in that the FRG's electoral deadlines now make it the central stake in domestic German politics', noted Jean-Marie Guéhenno, the head of the Quai planning staff, who clairvoyantly perceived that a rapid unification lay in the near future.[70] 'German policy is now clear', said Blot, summarizing Kohl's policy with a touch of pique: 'The hour of reunification has arrived, and we must facilitate its realization.'[71] Yet though the suddenness of the chancellor's initiative was surprising, and in certain respects destabilized the French, it did not change the principled position stated by Mitterrand's diplomacy: 'The desire for unity manifested by the German people is perfectly legitimate', it was stressed at the Quai d'Orsay after Kohl's speech, and 'no form of cooperation between the two German states can be excluded a priori'.[72] Mitterrand said as much: receiving South Korean President Roh Tae Woo on 30 November, he repeated that German unity 'is normal, legitimate' and that 'it goes in the direction of history'.[73] The same day he told Genscher that unification was to him 'an affair that cannot be stopped' and that France would stick by Germany.[74] The next day, Jacques Attali called Teltschik: at the Élysée, 'we can live' with the Ten Point Plan, indicated the president's special adviser.[75]

But if the Kohl plan included nothing in itself that was unacceptable, its omissions disturbed Paris, as they did Washington.[76] With Dumas and Mitterrand on 30 November, Genscher felt this: two days after Kohl's speech (and three days after the letter of the 27th), it was less the question of German unity than uncertainty over the future European policy of the FRG that worried the French, whom, as said above, he was trying to reassure. The weak European content of the Ten Points was indeed patent: while the chancellor had mentioned the EEC's capacity of attraction, he did not mention its political purpose, noted the Quai d'Orsay, where the usual questions about Bonn's intentions were being expressed. With the chancellor maintaining uncertainty about the EMU, French diplomacy feared, in the words of Blot, a German 'desertion' in Strasbourg.[77] As for the president, two days after Kohl's speech he again hammered the point that 'the hope for unification of Germany should not go in a direction opposite to the construction and unity of Europe'.[78] Beyond the European dimension, Paris also noted that the Ten Points, apart from those concerning the CSCE and disarmament, did not mention the international dimension of the process: 'Not a word about the Allies, not a word about neighbors, not a word about borders', said Blot indignantly – for him the message was clearly 'that unity is an affair for the Germans and them alone'. And so the Quai d'Orsay advanced more than ever the Mitterrand doctrine: unification was legitimate but it 'could only be done in a peaceful and democratic way' and only with the agreement 'of the two German states and the guarantor states of German status'.[79] Mitterrand did not say anything other than this: mentioning borders, alliances and the responsibilities of the Four, he simply insisted that the German approach must be 'responsible'.[80] On 30 November Genscher tried to be reassuring about this: the FRG, he said, rejected any 'isolated' venture; 'its destiny', he affirmed, 'is anchored in that of Europe'.[81] Still, the Quai d'Orsay appeared, at least for the moment, dismayed by this new acceleration of the German question, as Blot said in concluding a note with an alarmist tone: 'How to keep the initiative on the European scene?'[82] Now it was the risk of racing ahead that worried French leaders: events must not be rushed, Dumas stressed to Genscher on 30 November. Meanwhile, Mitterrand ominously expressed to Genscher his concern about a possible return to the 'Europe of 1913' (a formulation that would recur on his lips in the following weeks and months), and he declared the same day to his South Korean visitor that unification could not be done 'whenever' or 'in any manner' or ignore the rhythm of European transformations: 'if the rhythms are different, there is [the danger of] an accident', he explained, evoking the risk of a 'concern diffused throughout Europe and particularly strong in the USSR'. 'This is our problem', he concluded on a serious rather than anguished note: 'I hope it will be resolved.'[83] To frame the German process internationally and to control its rhythm to allow for the necessary European and international adaptations – this would be the stated priority of French diplomacy in the face of the acceleration following the Ten Point Plan.

From Malta to Strasbourg

Even if unification was presented as a long-term goal, the Kohl plan did place the German question on the international agenda: the issue found itself at the center of the major meetings of the following weeks. Yet while German unity became ipso facto a concrete prospect, most of the actors, including the French, tried to control the process by inserting it into multilateral diplomacy. Three important rendezvous in the first ten days of December 1989 testify to this: the Soviet-American summit in Malta (2 and 3 December), the NATO summit in Brussels (4 December) and the European summit in Strasbourg (8 and 9 December).

At a time when the Bush administration finally seemed disposed to engage in real dialogue and when Moscow was finally overcoming its initial worries about it, the Malta summit represented a test for Soviet-American relations. While the main items were the major bilateral issues such as disarmament or regional conflicts, the acceleration of events made the German question unavoidable. Of course, Gorbachev tried to minimize its urgency by asserting on the eve of Malta that it was not on the agenda. As for Bush, he tried to advance Soviet-American cooperation on the principal subjects, the German question being only one among them: his goal in this respect was to reassure Gorbachev, but without ratifying the idea of a lasting German status quo.[84] The Malta meetings marked an important stage in Soviet-American relations at a crucial moment for East-West relations. While Bush put forth his concern to respect Soviet interests by acting with moderation, Gorbachev assured his interlocutor that he accepted the American presence on the Old Continent and pleaded for gradual evolution in Europe: the end of the Cold War was now a reality in the relationship between the superpowers. As for the German question, it occupied only a limited place in Malta. Without seeming excessively worried, Gorbachev stuck to his position that the existence of two German states was a 'decision of history', and Bush insisted on the right of the Germans to self-determination while pledging caution.[85] The relative serenity of the exchanges and the limited importance granted the subject no doubt led the Americans to overestimate Moscow's toleration for German changes, and the Soviets to underestimate Washington's support for the unification process; but for the moment both parties could think they had rather close viewpoints on the German question, whose treatment, it seemed, would last a long while.[86] The joint press conference maintained this impression: while Gorbachev reiterated the proposition that he had formulated in Rome on 30 November about a CSCE summit that would confirm 'realities', Bush declared that the Helsinki process implied the 'notion of permanent borders',[87] a declaration that recalled Mitterrand's statements at the Élysée on 18 November and showed the existing ambiguity on this issue. Here too, the message was deliberate: after Malta, American diplomacy would confirm that the 'necessary stability' of the German question had been the subject of 'great insistence' on both sides.[88]

The Quai d'Orsay noted that Bush had insisted more on respect for borders than on the right to self-determination, and the Malta summit was mostly seen as a Soviet-American attempt to keep 'control' over changes and to sketch a framework of 'stability'. If French diplomacy allowed a predictable irritation to be perceived with respect to this Soviet-American 'condominium' logic, it noted with satisfaction that 'in a context of rapid and sometimes unpredictable mutations', the two great powers had tried to appear as guarantors of a 'stable transition'.[89]

The NATO summit in Brussels on 4 December was a logical follow-up to Malta. For Bush it was a matter of informing his homologues of the results of his meeting with Gorbachev. But the president had more ambitious goals that would guide American policy in the coming months: while the Americans, after the Ten Points, intended to support Kohl's policy, they were also trying to seize the helm and steer according to their own perspectives; to do so, they had decided to place the unification process within the Atlantic framework, a goal on its way to becoming a priority in Washington.[90] In Brussels, Bush indeed sketched his vision of the future of Europe and the alliance. Recalling that the West had never accepted the division of Europe, he designated the alliance as the privileged 'architecture' of 'peaceful change' and advanced the four 'principles' enunciated on 29 November by Baker: the exercise of self-determination should not lead to prejudging the final form of German unity; unification should take place in the context of Germany's maintained engagement within NATO and in the European Community; it should unfold peacefully and gradually; finally, regarding borders, it should respect the principles of the Helsinki final Act.[91] Kohl was satisfied. Referring to the Harmel Report of 1967 that defined the peacetime goals of NATO in detente, he stressed that there could be no peaceful settlement in Europe without a solution to the German question and that such a settlement must permit Germany to recover its unity. Defending his Ten Point Plan as a gradual and responsible approach – 'without a calendar', he underlined, but spread over a 'very long' period – he reiterated the FRG's European and Atlantic engagement.[92] The reactions to the chancellor's statements were mixed. Some seized the occasion to manifest their disquiet about the Ten Points; thus Andreotti (supported by Thatcher) expressed his 'preoccupation', which earned him a stinging response from Kohl: how would Italy act if it were divided along the Tiber? Mitterrand was calmer; noting that in Malta Bush had spoken of 'permanent borders', he insisted on the need to take into account Gorbachev's difficulties and to preserve the stabilizing framework of alliances. Mitterrand repeated that the emphasis on self-determination goes 'to the core of things' but that it must 'be democratic and peaceful'.[93]

Overall, the Brussels summit was an American success. Despite the reservations of some (starting with Thatcher), a consensus was taking shape within the alliance in favor of an approach consisting of sustaining the process while placing it in a stabilizing European and Atlantic framework.[94] The Germans were enthusiastic: the Brussels summit had not placed obstacles on the path to German unity, any more than the meeting in Paris on 18 November or in Malta the day before.[95] Paris was also satisfied: the alliance summit, after the Soviet-American meeting, had put the accent on the need to implement self-determination peacefully and gradually, and confirmed the necessity of a stable process.[96] At the Élysée, the reaffirmation on several occasions over a few days of the permanence of alliances (Gorbachev had said nothing else during the Warsaw Pact meeting in Moscow on 4 December) was seen as an indication that the German question would likely be put on hold, at least for some time. Védrine noted that 'reunification of Germany would involve ipso facto the dissolution of alliances'; inversely, he argued, this might lead one to think that their maintenance – which was desired on both sides – might postpone unification to the indefinite future.[97] In sum, Brussels, after Malta, confirmed in the West as in the East a sort of 'conservatism of blocs' and thus contributed to calming things, which appeared now to be the objective in Washington, just as in Paris. But the parallel stopped there, for while the United States privileged the Atlantic framework to manage the German process, France advocated more than ever the European framework, as was soon to be demonstrated.

Strasbourg, Act I: The IGC

By early December, a veritable test of wills between France and Germany was in the making over the decisions to take in Strasbourg. Analyzing Mitterrand's letter of 1 December in response to Kohl's of the 27 November, the Chancellery took note of the Élysée's rejection of the working calendar proposed by the chancellor and his demand to deal with institutional questions in parallel. Yet Joachim Bitterlich suggested to Kohl that he stick to his positions, and Bonn prepared for a test of strength.[98] The Élysée side was equally determined. Since Mitterrand expected to meet Kohl in Brussels in the margins of the NATO summit to unblock the situation, Guigou prepared a memorandum in which she stressed that the conditions posed by Bonn for the achievement of monetary union (convergence of economies, completing the single market) were already satisfied and that the German minister of finance was propagating 'false rumors' about the existence of divergences on the essential points, like the independence of the central bank, which in fact was accepted in Paris. As for the German demand that the question of political Europe be tackled immediately, Guigou stressed that completing the EMU would lead in any case to renovating the functioning of Community institutions; foreign policy could then be added and a definitive 'institutional hat' put on the whole European construction – all of which could be done before the year 2000. In total, she concluded, Kohl should 'understand that shifting the calendar presents the enormous risk of fraying the whole process' and that 'it is no longer only about the EMU that people would be wondering, but about Germany itself'. The Élysée was more than ever resolved to make the rallying of Germany to French priorities the test of the former's European involvement.[99]

The Brussels meeting between Mitterrand and Kohl did not take place, however, for reasons of agenda.[100] The two leaders' letters crossed the following day – an illustration of the temporarily difficult dialogue between the two men. On 5 December, Mitterrand wrote to Kohl (as to his other European partners) to expound the unfolding of the work of the council in Strasbourg, in which he wanted to grant a central place to the 'fundamental dossier' of the EMU. 'We should now pronounce on the date' of the IGC, he insisted, a decision 'henceforward perceived as the clearest proof that we could bring of our desire to take a new step in the Community'.[101] The same day, Kohl responded to Mitterrand's letter of 1 December: while stressing the need for a 'clear political signal' for the pursuit of European integration, he stuck to the 'working calendar' proposed on 27 November and, reiterating the need to enlarge the rights of Parliament and to tend toward political union, he evaded the IGC issue, advancing reasons of 'internal politics'.[102]

Kohl nevertheless perfectly measured the stakes in Strasbourg, as demonstrated by his conversation with Bush on 3 December in Brussels: without himself and Mitterrand, he said, 'there would be no advancing the Community process'. When the American president asked him if the French had (in his words) 'problems' with the Ten Point Plan, the chancellor responded in the negative and said he entirely shared Mitterrand's desire to see German unification remain inseparable from the process of European integration. Kohl affirmed to Bush his desire to 'move ahead' in Strasbourg.[103] The following days confirmed this intention, thereby putting an end to the tension over the IGC question. Shortly before the opening of the EC summit, the Chancellery let the Élysée know that Kohl was now ready to set the date for opening the IGC at the end of 1990. Thus the meeting opened on 8 December under good auspices, even if the climate, as we shall see, did not remain constantly good.[104] At lunch, Kohl gave his green light to the IGC, saying a clear timetable was required to demonstrate 'our desire to move ahead'.[105]

The success for the French presidency was on a par with the uncertainty that had prevailed until then: the EMU was now on track, and the risk of seeing the process of German unification challenge that of European integration was removed. 'The Germans understood that they could not both show excessive hurry (at least in the eyes of some) about the East and then put the brakes on the West', commented Mitterrand a few days later.[106] This was indeed the explanation of this turnaround: Kohl acknowledged the now manifest link existing between the European and German dossiers. To be sure, there was no formal 'bargaining' before Strasbourg, with Bonn – as has been alleged – reaffirming its European engagement by accepting an opening date for the IGC so as to obtain from its partners their consent for German unity.[107] Although implicit, the '*Junktim*' was nevertheless evident: Mitterrand and Kohl had too often repeated for years that European integration ought to be *the* response to the German question for it to be necessary for them to formulate a specific quid pro quo of any kind. In this sense, the Strasbourg outcome belonged to a historic logic – a logic that Paris had appeared to fear, during the run-up to Strasbourg, was being abandoned by Bonn. Of course, tactical politics did its work: confronted for months by its partner's hesitations over an issue that it considered essential to the future of European construction and hence to anchoring Germany in the Community, Mitterrand's diplomacy no doubt used the situation to force the German hand. As for Kohl, he understood that persisting with these same reservations would exact a considerable price for his major objective – German unity – at a moment when the latter was disturbing the Europeans, whereas giving way to Mitterrand would permit him to make progress on the unification question.

Strasbourg, Act II: The Political Declaration

The other great stake in Strasbourg was indeed the consent of the Twelve to the process of German unification. Although the Germans had renounced to obtain such consent on 18 November, they let it be known shortly before the summit – meanwhile, of course, the Ten Point plan had been announced – that this time they were expecting explicit support for the objective of German unity, in the form of a sentence that would appear in the political declaration to be devoted to changes in Eastern Europe. But this demand raised once more the issue of borders, with the eleven other capitals finding it difficult to mention unification without taking a clear position on the Oder-Neisse line. The political committee presided over by Dufourcq did not manage to find a language of compromise, with the German political director, Dieter Kastrup, digging in his heels on his position.[108] Thus the question of supporting German unity – contrary to the IGC issue that had been solved even before the meeting – would give rise to strong tension and even plunge the summit into a 'glacial' ambiance, in the words of Kohl.[109] A first incident occurred when, during lunch on 8 December, Thatcher mentioned again the need to keep 'current borders', producing a tense reply from the chancellor that recalled that the Ten Points referred to the CSCE: Kohl deplored the fact that under cover of the alleged permanence of the Oder-Neisse border, some people were trying to make the current border between the GDR and the FRG eternal. The tension diminished when Kohl confirmed his acceptance of convening the IGC.[110] But over dinner the same day, the climate deteriorated.[111] Thatcher, who did not conceal her hostility to the unification process, went once more on the offensive, supported by Andreotti and Lubbers; Kohl had to answer an interrogation worthy of a 'tribunal' and explain his Ten Point speech, for which he was reproached for accelerating the German issue. Mitterrand took shelter behind his role as president and did not intervene. The dueling was particularly lively over borders, on which Andreotti and Thatcher proved very hard; on this point, the French also expressed themselves through Dumas. Kohl, almost alone against everyone except Felipe Gonzalez, continued to be evasive on the issue of recognizing once and for all the Oder-Neisse line. Faced with this impasse, Mitterrand entrusted Dumas and Genscher with the job of finding a text of compromise with the help of their collaborators.

On 9 December, the twelve heads of state finally ratified the accord obtained by the ministers at the cost of long overnight negotiations. In their declaration on Central and Eastern Europe, they recognized that 'the German people will regain its unity through free self-determination', which ought 'to take place peacefully and democratically, in full respect of the relevant agreements and treaties and of all the principles defined by the Helsinki final Act', all 'in a context of dialogue and East-West cooperation' and 'within the perspective of European integration'.[112] True, one cannot speak here of a French success on a par with that achieved with regard to the EMU. Even if the green light given the day before by Kohl for the IGC had facilitated a compromise that might otherwise have failed, the affair had indeed almost led to a very serious crisis. Moreover, in the declaration, the Germans had been unwilling to go beyond recalling existing agreements (notably Helsinki), which did not suffice to establish the intangibility of the Oder-Neisse border. The issue was thus not really resolved and would continue to weigh in months to come.[113] Still, it was in Strasbourg that Mitterrand finally clarified his position on the border issue: 'the frontier between the FRG and the GDR is not comparable with the frontier between the GDR and Poland', he repeated in front of Kohl, after having underlined it to Gorbachev in Kiev. Thus ended the ambiguity of the preceding weeks: it was about the latter frontier between Germany and Poland, and not the former one between the two Germanys, that Mitterrand wanted to obtain definitive confirmation from Kohl.[114] Nevertheless, Paris could be satisfied with the result: while the Twelve had only recommitted themselves once again to the self-determination of the German people to which the West had been subscribing for decades within the Atlantic Alliance (as they had done in May at the Brussels summit), they had also specified 'the condition and framework for the process', not only by referring to Helsinki, but by situating it clearly 'within the perspective of European integration'.[115]

Overall, Strasbourg was a success for Mitterrand's diplomacy: Germany had reaffirmed its Community involvement and, in turn, the Twelve had clearly placed the German process within the European framework, a priority for Paris. Strasbourg (after Malta and Brussels) thus had a stabilizing effect: if Mitterrand, after the summit, reasserted his conviction that unification was 'inevitable' if the Germans wanted it, he also stressed that they 'cannot embark down this path without thinking of the reactions of the other European states', and he noted that in the FRG *'sangfroid* has returned'.[116] The Germans were satisfied with Strasbourg, too. True, Genscher was happier with the summit than Kohl – unsurprisingly, given their differences, especially over the border issue. For Genscher, Strasbourg confirmed that 'the strategy of Mitterrand and Dumas to link German unification and European integration' was well-founded; and it showed 'the fundamental difference in behavior between Mitterrand and Thatcher'.[117] But Kohl – despite difficult moments in Strasbourg – was also satisfied: had he not confided to Mitterrand on the morning of 9 December that he thought the projected conclusions of the presidency, which has been negotiated overnight, were 'successful'?[118] Even if he had to yield regarding the IGC and reduce his wishes for political Europe and institutional reforms, he could point to the green light he gave to the EMU – a gesture all the more significant, he stressed shortly afterward to Baker, in that it was given against German interests: it was, he explained, because Germany 'had need of friends'.[119] More importantly, Bonn had obtained for the first time from the European Community a declaration that used the terms of the letter on German unity appended to the Moscow Treaty of 1970, which, stressed Teltschik, represented a very great success for German diplomacy.[120] Even the Soviets were satisfied: Shevardnadze, in a letter to Dumas, was pleased 'that the Twelve had reaffirmed the rules emanating from the treaties and the Helsinki Final Act', which were 'fundamental for the maintenance of stability in Europe'.[121] Finally, Washington was pleased that the Strasbourg language on German unity was very close to the 'four principles' advocated by Bush in Brussels.[122]

At the end of two weeks of summits and meetings of all kinds, Bush and Mitterrand had the opportunity to review the situation on the occasion of their conversation on 16 December at Saint Martin, in the French West Indies – and to note the proximity of their viewpoints. If the Americans had the feeling that Mitterrand remained concerned by the changes going on, they also noted his general agreement with Bush concerning German unification, judged to be possible under the right conditions.[123] In fact, in his conversation with his American counterpart, the French president stuck to his reasoning that German unity was a 'perfectly natural' aspiration, posing only the problem of pace and mode. Concerned to avoid a 'phase lag' between European construction and unification, Mitterrand expressed apprehension about a statement from Ambassador Walters in favor of rapid unification, but Bush responded that this was not Washington's official position. For the rest, affirmed Mitterrand, France, 'undoubtedly the country closest to Germany', did not fear the eventuality of German unity in itself – unlike Great Britain, Belgium or the Netherlands, which were more worried, a fact that should be taken into account. He added: 'If there is an irrepressible push by the German population, we'll have to accept it.'[124] For the time being, Paris, like Washington, could conclude in mid December that it had contributed – each in its way – to framing, if not mastering, the process.

From Kiev to Berlin

Did France in this same period, as has been much alleged, try to oppose German unification? While sticking, in public declarations and during international meetings, to what had been his position for months – unification was legitimate but it should be framed internationally – did Mitterrand use another language in other circumstances, in particular with the Soviets, and did he try to make an alliance with them against German unity? Did he envisage using the 'rights and responsibilities' of the Four Powers to hinder the process? Finally and most especially, by paying a state visit to the GDR at the end of the year, did he want to pursue this same goal by trying to prolong indefinitely an East Germany that was already doomed? To answer these questions, we must linger over several events in December, foremost the meeting of Mitterrand with Gorbachev in Kiev on 6 December.

The initiative for the meeting came from the French side, going back to the telephone conversation between Mitterrand and Gorbachev on 14 November. The date was difficult to fix as the international agenda was so crowded. Shevardnadze, on 23 November, confirmed the date of 6 December with the French ambassador and added that the agenda was 'self-evident': the German problem, Eastern Europe, relations between the USSR and the Western world.[125] One objective for French diplomacy –

then chairing the EC – was to see to the elimination of any doubt that the Community would 'exist' and be strengthened after the Malta summit. Still, the principal motivation for France was clearly to discuss the German question bilaterally with the Soviets. To avoid destabilizing Gorbachev was for Mitterrand, as we know, a priority that the fall of the Wall had only reinforced; the trip to Kiev would be the occasion to reassert this concern, but also to know more about the state of mind of the Soviet leaders at a moment when they were sending contradictory signals.[126] The Quai d'Orsay was indeed starting to wonder if the USSR's hostility to German unity was likely to remain a constant.[127] Analysing the contradictions of Soviet policy, the French ambassador in Moscow, in an analysis transmitted to Paris before the Kiev meeting, posed the same question. Wondering why the USSR proclaimed such opposition to the prospect of German unity while it had accepted without batting an eyelid the liquidation of its Eastern Europe empire, Jean-Marie Mérillon of course invoked the historical and strategic givens specific to Germany that continued to weigh negatively on Soviet perceptions of that country. But he judged that this opposition also, and above all, resulted from the German problem being amalgamated with all Gorbachev's other difficulties (economic and social crisis, problem of nationalities, loss of Eastern Europe) so that Gorbachev was constrained to use this same German problem as a buffer to avoid 'general disintegration'. And Mérillon concluded with this lucid question: if he was today devoting all his energy to prevent German unity, 'was the Soviet Number One (whatever his current sincerity) perfectly credible' and 'must he not eventually, in a few months or a year, end up "compromising"?'[128] The picture of Soviet uncertainties and contradictions was thus vividly sketched, so it makes little sense to believe that Mitterrand went to Kiev with the idea of asking Gorbachev to aid him in opposing unification.[129] The reverse appears more probable: if Gorbachev had seemed calm in Malta several days earlier, the Soviets were now evidently worried, as was demonstrated on the eve of Kiev by the very harsh welcome for Genscher, who was then in Moscow, and on whom Gorbachev and Shevardnadze spent the anger inspired in them by the Ten Point Plan.[130] Clearly, Mitterrand intended to allay Soviet concerns over German unification, not play upon them.

While the Kiev meetings – which can be only partially reconstructed due to the paucity of firsthand documents – reflected common worries about the modes and pace of the process, they were therefore far from showing complete Franco-Soviet understanding about the German question.[131] What was actually said in Kiev? After Gorbachev recounted the Malta meetings, recalling the good personal relations he had established with Bush and the latter's responsible conduct (although Gorbachev complained of the American propensity to see the end of the Cold War as a victory for Western values), Mitterrand launched into a discussion of the German problem. The French president repeated his position: the unification of Germany, which he did not fear, was legitimate and could not be opposed; moreover, he stressed, the inter-German border was of a special kind since it separated a single people. Still, the process should unfold peacefully and democratically; it should neither challenge guaranteed borders (notably the Oder-Neisse line) nor upset European equilibriums; and it should not overtake the evolution in the East, the Community strengthening in the West, or the emergence of pan-European structures at the East-West level. German unity, in other words, could not occur without the completion of necessary European transformations. Recalling the importance of Franco-German friendship, Mitterrand said he had told the German leaders of his worries about Bonn's haste after the Ten Point Plan, and he stressed the necessity of contact between France and the USSR being maintained. Gorbachev said he shared Mitterrand's worries about Kohl's policy (the chancellor suffered from 'provincialism' and behaved 'like an elephant in a china shop', he said), and he reported the tenor of his meeting the day before with Genscher, without hiding the violent statements he had made to the German minister – to whom he had described Kohl's ten points as a 'diktat'. But for the rest, the Mitterrand-Gorbachev conversation did not result in any practical or political conclusion.[132]

The meeting between Dumas and Shevardnadze that took place in parallel (and for which we have precise and reliable minutes) confirms the preceding.[133] Forcefully relating details of Genscher's difficult visit, the Soviet foreign minister discussed the German problem in terms that denoted real anguish, but also obvious contradictions: thus he denounced German 'revanchistes' and spoke anew of a 'diktat', while conceding that Kohl 'does not want war' and that the 'question of reunification will necessarily arise one day or another'. It was incontestably the Soviet minister who tried to convince the French to oppose the German policy and not the reverse: 'You French have to clearly take a position and have the courage to say what you think', he said. But Dumas dodged: while he recognized that 'we must demonstrate vigilance' and that the Europeans 'must make their voices heard', he stressed above all that 'a certain tone would only stir up German touchiness'. Dumas reminded Shevardnadze of the French line that 'the German people have a right to self-determination' provided that it remains 'democratic and peaceful'. He did not take up Shevardnadze's demand for collaboration and for 'even closer' Franco-Soviet consultations.[134]

In short, while the French and Soviets proved equally concerned (a few days after the acceleration provoked by the Ten Point Plan) to moderate

German evolution, the Kiev conversations did not give rise in any way to a concerted policy to oppose unification, contrary to a widespread belief.[135] Such a policy would have been not only contrary to the line proclaimed for months by Mitterrand, but also hazardous due to Gorbachev's position, which the French president no doubt already perceived (despite Moscow's sometimes outrageous anti-German rhetoric) as not remaining eternally hostile to unification.[136] Of course, the meetings also showed agreement on the need and means to frame the process and notably the role of the CSCE – in Kiev Mitterrand accepted the Soviet proposal for a summit of thirty-five nations in 1990 – but for French diplomacy this could only be a Franco-Soviet and pan-European complement to a policy whose principal dimension remained Franco-German and Western European. Two days before Strasbourg, no doubt Mitterrand had already had confirmation of the German green light for the IGC, and one can scarcely imagine his taking the risk of exploding both the Franco-German couple and European construction in the hope of a hypothetical entente with the Soviets. In short, while Kiev was incontestably part of Mitterrand's plan to control the German question (which, although more assertive, was not so different from Bush's plan), nevertheless the idea of a French desire to overturn alliances, or to make a reverse alliance with the Soviets, quite simply does not stand up.[137] This, however, would not prevent the arousal of suspicion, notably among the Germans, who, being particularly sensitive about this, were tempted to see in the simple fact of the Kiev meeting a sign of collusion against them.[138]

The Meeting of the Four Ambassadors

Mentioned in Kiev, rights and responsibilities of the four occupying powers in Germany might have been the subject of possible concerted action between Paris and Moscow, thus confirming the hypothesis of a Franco-Soviet entente in the face of German unification – but this was not to be. The acceleration of events after the Ten Point Plan had led Moscow, at the suggestion of its ambassador to the GDR Vyacheslav Kochemassov, to reformulate a request for a meeting of the representatives of the Four Powers, a request first presented by Gorbachev on 10 November but on which the Western powers had not as yet acted.[139] On 8 December, MID confirmed to the Quai d'Orsay its wish to organize 'as soon as possible' in Berlin an 'exchange of views' among the Four 'about German affairs'.[140] The Soviet initiative in due form was put into effect the same day at the level of the minister-delegates in Berlin: the Soviet delegate asked for activation of the quadripartite mechanism over the question of Germany 'as a whole', while leaving the door open to an agenda limited to the problems of Berlin in case of Western reservations.[141] The intention was transparent: Moscow was trying to take the upper hand at a moment when the USSR was becoming aware that it 'had lost a great part of its leverage over German affairs'.[142] Paris was of course attentive to the Soviet initiative: the quadripartite rights and responsibilities had always been an important instrument of France's German policy, and, given the circumstances, French diplomacy was prone to use it – *not* (as has been asserted) to block the process, but to manage it.[143] Still, while Mitterrand and Dumas in this period did not refrain from recalling the importance they attached to the prerogatives of the Four, they were also quite conscious of the limits of this instrument, as shown by the Kiev conversations. Whereas before the Kiev meeting the Quai d'Orsay had envisaged discussing with the Soviets the possibility 'of a quadripartite consultation over developments in Berlin and in Germany as a whole', the question in Kiev was only touched on in general terms by Shevardnadze, without Dumas seizing the ball on the rebound.[144] The wait-and-see attitude was shared by the French and the Soviets, then, but the motivations were different on each side: while Moscow feared that the 'mechanism' of the Four might accelerate things, Paris was especially concerned not to antagonize Bonn. German diplomacy was indeed extremely reserved about, and even frankly hostile to, its activation: how could the Germans in 1989 accept that German affairs were being decided without them by the victors of 1945? As for the American administration, without being opposed, it was hardly enthusiastic – only British diplomats (or at least Downing Street) proved eager, as already signaled by Thatcher's letter to Gorbachev on 17 November.[145]

French diplomacy remained circumspect over this matter. After consulting its partners, the Quai d'Orsay on 9 December indicated to Boidevaix (who at the time chaired the group of three Western powers) that he might let Kochemassov know that Paris, London and Washington were disposed to a quadripartite meeting in the former building of the Control Council – a formal concession to Moscow – but only at the level of the Western minister-delegates in Berlin and the minister-counselor of the Soviet embassy; such a meeting, he should also make clear, would be limited to a discussion of Berlin questions and of the 'Allied initiative' on Berlin.[146] Meanwhile the matter was discussed in Strasbourg on the margins of the European Council. Meeting Mitterrand twice on 8 December, Thatcher had said she was favorable to a four-party meeting, but Mitterrand had eluded her by advancing the need to tackle the question directly with the Germans.[147] He did so with Kohl over breakfast the next day: even if he recognized that the subject was 'embarrassing', Mitterrand explained to the chancellor that 'he could not reject' Moscow's initiative, while assuring him that France would not take the lead in this business and that it would keep the German government informed about the discussions. He therefore suggested to Kohl maintaining close contact between Paris and Bonn over this matter.[148] Meanwhile Dumas was meeting with his British homologue Douglas Hurd as well as with Genscher, and he talked by telephone from Strasbourg with Baker. These consultations resulted on 10 December with the Western powers finally agreeing that the meeting, fixed for the next day, would be held at the level of the American, British and French ambassadors to Bonn and the Soviet ambassador to East Berlin.[149]

The meeting was closely prepared by the three Western ambassadors, who were concerned to coordinate their positions in advance. During the meeting at three, Boidevaix – who had previously met Jürgen Sudhoff, the secretary of state in the Auswärtiges Amt – clearly supported Bonn's demand that discussions should be restricted to issues concerning Berlin, so as not to give in to a Soviet maneuver that was evidently designed to enlarge the discussions to cover German affairs as a whole.[150] The meeting of the Four took place without any surprises. Although he had agreed to limit the debate to Berlin, the Soviet representative spoke at length on the need to maintain stability in Europe, his goal being evidently, noted Boidevaix, to 'show the press that the four ambassadors discussed the problems of Germany' as a whole. In addition, Kochemassov proposed that the four ambassadors meet regularly to make the arrangement lasting. Faced with that, the three Western representatives respected the 'script' they had agreed on, even if, noted Boidevaix (who, as far as he was concerned, took care to stick to Berlin questions) Walters, after much debate, nearly accepted a mention of the German question as a whole in the final communiqué (which required three-quarters of an hour of debate).[151] In total, the meeting of the four ambassadors brought nothing concrete, and the question of pursuing the exercise or not remained in suspense (it would resurface in January, to be solved by the establishment in February of the '2 + 4').[152] In this whole matter, French diplomacy at all levels demonstrated prudence in trying to avoid any side slipping, contrary to a widely held view.[153] But the real stakes were evidently symbolic: as Walters later summed it up, the scene at the Control Council gave an opportunity for 'the worst photo of the year' – the site and circumstances of the meeting indeed referred back to a totally different era, hence the very negative German reactions.[154] Hence also, (a few days after the trip to Kiev and the difficult debates of Strasbourg) the tendency emerged, notably in Bonn, to overinterpret the significance of the event and detect possible ulterior motives (notably in Paris) – a phenomenon aggravated by the press.[155]

The Trip to the GDR

Mitterrand's trip to the GDR ten days later was obviously not going to make things easier on that score. The trip was not at all impromptu: having come to France in January 1988, Honecker had invited Mitterrand to make a visit to the GDR in return. East Berlin figured among the destinations envisaged, starting in the fall of 1988, within the framework of the relaunch of France's policy to the East, but the trip kept being postponed: in addition to the usual scheduling problems, the East German regime remained closed to any reform, which made a French visit inopportune.[156] Discussed by Dumas and his East German homologue Oskar Fischer at the end of September 1989 in New York, the plan nevertheless took shape in mid October after Honecker's resignation, which removed one important political difficulty.[157] In that context (remember that the durability of the GDR was not in doubt at this stage), such a visit, for French diplomacy, was in fact tantamount to support for the democratic evolution in East Germany and was by no means seen as contradicting the reassertion of the right of Germans to self-determination.[158] The fall of the Wall a few days later confirmed this logic, and it led Mitterrand therefore to want to set the date as soon as possible: for the Élysée, the urgency of a presidential trip to the GDR (preferably before the end of the French presidency of the European Community) was merely a response to the acceleration of events in the East.[159] But the affair began to raise difficulties with Bonn from the moment of the official announcement, on 22 November, that Mitterrand's visit was scheduled for 20–22 December.[160] Although Kohl had never made an objection before, the French trip now posed a problem for him for domestic reasons: criticized for having let Mitterrand precede him to the GDR and thus be the first head of state to visit East Germany after the fall of the Wall, Kohl decided finally to go there himself on 19 December – before Mitterrand. Against the background of growing European uncertainties before Strasbourg, this scheduling issue (which testifies to the poor coordination between the Élysée and the Chancellery) was to give rise to a real misunderstanding, with certain of Kohl's circle expressing bitterness that was echoed in the press.[161]

The problem, however, went beyond a question of protocol. At the start of December, it was uncertainty about the future of the East German regime that put a question mark over the presidential trip. The Élysée was of course aware that events might rapidly sweep away the SED and its leaders. Krenz had to resign on 3 December, and it was believed that among the others 'only Modrow and a few individuals would linger'.[162] Sent to the GDR on a preparatory mission from 3 to 5 December, Caroline de Margerie mentioned in a memo of 6 December a 'curious impression of unreality' and concluded that nobody could predict what kind of state or regime the increasingly chaotic transition would lead to. On reading this memo, Mitterrand asked its author if she advised against the trip, which she did.[163] Yet the visit went ahead, with the president ignoring de Margerie's recommendation (which was motivated more by the uncertain practical conditions of the trip due to the regime's disorganization than by considerations of political opportunity).[164] Yet some, such as Guéhenno, did question the trip's very rationale: coming back from an eight-day trip to the GDR and FRG, the head of the CAP at the Quai d'Orsay was strengthened in his conviction that the process of the GDR's dissolution was irreversible and that the aspiration to unification would soon carry the day among East Germans. He noted particularly the fear among some representatives of the CDU – for whom relations with the GDR should remain a strictly German affair – that Mitterrand's trip would strengthen the East German regime, whatever that regime might have become by the time of the French visit. (Guéhenno noted that the SPD, by contrast, was favorable to contacts between the GDR and other countries of the Community.)[165] These fears were not without some justification: as far as they were concerned, East German leaders manifestly did consider that the trip and the possible signing of agreements with France on that occasion was a means for them to assert the GDR's vocation to remain a sovereign state.[166] Thus warned about the political stakes of his trip and the reservations it aroused in Bonn, Mitterrand tackled the question with Kohl in Strasbourg on 9 December. Stressing that he had no obvious reason to decline an invitation made by Honecker and renewed by Krenz, the president said he was still wondering about whether to go. Kohl, while advising caution, confirmed that Mitterrand had no reason to give up the trip.[167] Mitterrand evidently wanted to defuse the issue without going back on his decision, while Kohl (who deep inside himself no doubt scarcely approved of Mitterrand's initiative) could not ask him to give it up. The misunderstanding, unspoken, persisted.

So what idea did Mitterrand have of the future of the GDR, and why did he maintain his visit despite everything? This is a delicate question, and any anachronistic explanation must be avoided. Clearly, the French president, like any attentive observer, knew that the regime's days were numbered. But while the maintenance of a Communist state, even if reformed, was now unlikely over the long run, the temporary survival of a sovereign GDR, it must be stressed, was still not really in doubt at this stage. Kohl at this time was in fact talking of a unification process stretching over years and envisaging institutional relations between the two states (the confederative structures mentioned in the Ten Points) while expecting a trade and cooperation agreement between the EEC and the GDR. As for Baker, he chose to go to the GDR on 12 December (meeting Modrow in Potsdam) in order to precede the French president as well as assert Washington's support for reforms in East Germany.[168] True, some people were already lucidly predicting that the idea of an 'independent and democratic' state, as maintained by East German leaders and part of the West German opposition, was a 'chimera'.[169] But by mid December 1989, rare were those who had in effect buried the GDR. Clearly, Mitterrand's diplomacy privileged a progressive scenario, as did the French embassy in East Berlin, where it was observed that while the theme of unification was no longer 'taboo' in East Germany and people were starting to 'wonder about the reality of a particular path for the GDR', still many agreed 'that unification should not be done in haste'.[170] So without necessarily believing in the GDR's longevity come what may, Mitterrand no doubt thought that East Germany possessed a medium-term future, an estimation that was not aberrant at this stage. In these conditions – apart from personal factors that also played a role, such as the desire to see the situation for himself – the choice to maintain his visit was undeniably a political one. If it *cannot* be interpreted as a desire to oppose unification by betting on the survival of the GDR, it undeniably expressed Mitterrand's preference for a controlled process, which presupposed recognizing a GDR sovereignty that was at least transitory, if only until East German citizens had pronounced (democratically) on their national future. By the same token, it constituted a message intended for Bonn: German unification could not result from any fait accompli.

The sudden acceleration of events on the eve of Mitterrand's arrival, though, risked placing him in a dilemma. Kohl's visit to Dresden on 19 December had aroused scenes of jubilation; the chancellor later said that they had made him understand that unity was underway. In these conditions, the French president's trip would prove to be delicate. Still, his conversations with East German interlocutors, notably Modrow and President of the Council of State Manfred Gerlach, attest to Mitterrand's concern to maintain balance between affirming the right of Germans to self-determination and advocating the maintenance of the necessary international stability.[171] Repeating that he was not afraid of German unity, which was a historical goal and a legitimate process, Mitterrand stressed that its achievement must not abruptly challenge the European order, and that the desire of Germans (which remained unknown as far as he knew) should be expressed first. As soon as the German people had spoken democratically, he added, a process in stages that kept the situation under control might be put in place; for the rest, the European Community framework should remain the means of managing the German question, and the rights and responsibilities of the Four Powers should be advanced only within limits. Mitterrand did not express himself any differently in his public statements, particularly on 21 December to the students at Karl-Marx University in Leipzig, where he mentioned the need for free and democratic elections, asserting that France would accept German unity if the German people went in that direction.[172]

To be sure, East German leaders would choose to see in certain protocol statements made by Mitterrand, as well as in the economic and cultural agreements signed on the occasion of his visit, a confirmation of France's support for GDR sovereignty and of its confidence in the regime's durability.[173] But while Mitterrand did not hide his hostility to an overly rapid or uncontrolled unification, neither his statements nor his gestures could be interpreted as an attempt to oppose the unification process per se. The East German leaders, in fact, did not hide their difficult situation from him: the state was falling apart, and the demand for unity was being expressed with increasing force. Mitterrand recognized this growing aspiration when facing the press before leaving on 22 December, defending himself from being seen as wanting to slow the movement down: 'I am not among those who are putting on the brakes', he insisted.[174] And yet the symbolism of Mitterrand's absence alongside Kohl during the opening ceremony of the Brandenburg Gate on the evening of 22 December would durably (and negatively) influence perceptions of his visit. Although his possible presence had been discussed with Bonn, the president (after hesitating) thought he should not associate himself with what he saw as a German national celebration and thereby renounced the possibility of a strong image that might have compensated for the absence of a great speech from him on unity.[175] Still, in retrospect, although the visit to the GDR had arguably been an 'error' (as his closest entourage later admitted)[176] – or at least an inopportune act due to the wrong 'message' it might have expressed – it surely cannot be interpreted as an attempt on his part to hinder unification. Even if the extraordinarily fluid context of the moment, combined with the misunderstandings or silences between France and Germany, might have given credit to this idea, the trip was above all part of the Mitterrand initiative to seek a balance between the legitimacy of German self-determination and the need for European stabilization.[177]

German Unification and the New European Order

With the acceleration of the German question at the end of the autumn of 1989, the Quai d'Orsay in mid December observed 'the emergence of a debate on the future model of European security'. In fact, diplomatic events of the first half of December – in particular the Malta, Brussels and Strasbourg summits – posed the question of the future architecture of security, with each actor in the European game advancing his own preferences. Where did Paris stand? Unsurprisingly, it was the European Community that was considered more than ever the privileged framework within which to manage the post–Cold War situation, particularly since the Strasbourg outcome averted French fears of a disintegration and reaffirmed the future prospects for European construction. This was particularly true of the political and strategic dimension, which (once the EMU was on track) did not take long to return to the foreground of French preoccupations.[178] This was confirmed by French reactions to an American initiative that inaugurated one of the great debates of the post–Cold War years: that on the role of the Atlantic Alliance and its relationship to European construction. Indeed, eight days after the Brussels summit, Secretary of State Baker (on 12 December) delivered a speech in West Berlin that confirmed the priorities of post–Cold War American policy. Entitled 'A New Europe, a New Atlanticism', it was the veritable launch of a strategy whose goal was to reassert American leadership and the legitimacy of NATO against the background of the end of the Cold War and German unification. Baker advanced the three principal elements of the new European architecture that the United States was calling for. These were clearly expressed in an order of preference. First, NATO: while keeping its traditional role of defense, the secretary emphasized that it should increase its non-military role, notably over arms control but also in relations with the East. Next, the European Community: calling upon it to pursue its integration with the support of the United States, he added that it should establish with the U.S. 'institutional and consultative links that are clearly strengthened' and consequently, belong to a resolutely Atlantic perspective. Finally, the CSCE: charged with supervising the transition toward the post–Cold War era at the pan-European level, Baker said that it should be used to that effect in all its three dimensions, security, economy and human rights.[179]

The Berlin speech aroused mixed reactions. True, Paris noted that the vision of the German question expounded in the secretary of state's speech 'appears close to that expressed by French authorities' and confirmed in Strasbourg: reiterating the 'four principles', had not Baker stressed the gradual but also 'peaceful' and 'democratic' realization of unification?[180] On the other hand, the prospective part of the Berlin speech aroused distrust in Paris; the predominant role that the United States assigned NATO in the future European architecture, the Élysée noted, combined with the idea of an institutionalization of United States/Europe relations, highlighted their concern 'to halt their loss of influence in Europe' and their desire to 'make perennial their participation, even without a military presence, in European affairs'; this, the French believed, 'might be a problem for us' and lead to Franco-American differences.[181]

So the debate was launched: should European identity be affirmed in an independent way or develop within the Atlantic framework? At first, Mitterrand's closest advisers were tempted, out of European optimism, to respond favorably to Baker's initiative and – provided that its actual content would be acceptable – to his proposal for a treaty between the Community and the United States, in which Guigou and Védrine, after Strasbourg, wanted to see recognition by Washington of the pivotal role of the EEC. But Bianco contested this analysis: 'The Americans want to extend the Alliance to other subjects', he stressed; 'our interest is to assert Europe', which as yet still lacked a political dimension. Hence France must not allow NATO to 'monopolize the discussion on the political and military future' of the Old Continent.[182] This conclusion quickly prevailed in French analyses: the Baker proposal, it was argued, 'has the goal of confiding to the Atlantic Alliance – where the American preeminence is a given – the global mission of leading the evolution of Europe' in all its domains.[183] In short, the 'new Atlanticism' that the United States was trying to promote thanks to the end of the Cold War – paradoxically, the French believed, since in future the U.S. could only disengage from the Old Continent – was judged contrary to the necessary affirmation of a coherent and autonomous Europe. Such was the reasoning that would determine French policy in the coming months and years. To be sure, for the time being this issue did not give rise to Franco-American difficulties: even if Dumas had given a polite rejection the previous day, the 'Baker doctrine' did not seem to be a problem during Mitterrand's meeting with Bush at Saint Martin on 16 December.[184] Still, the French did measure the significance of the Berlin speech: 'At a moment when the contours of the future European order remain very uncertain and the Europeans themselves are wondering about them', the Quai d'Orsay noted that the Americans 'are staking out ground'.[185]

The Future of the Greater Europe

The acceleration of events in the East in the last weeks of 1989 led also to tackling in new terms the problem of organizing the 'greater Europe', which would be the other great debate of the post–Cold War years. These events indeed raised questions whose handling (notably the issue of borders) was related to the Helsinki process. Moreover, even if the Warsaw Pact remained, the end of Soviet domination would eventually pose the question of the geopolitical status of Eastern Europe and, by the same token, any future pan-European architecture. The CSCE, which Soviet diplomacy advanced in the autumn of 1989 as the framework within which to control change, was thus at the core of the debate – all the more so because in November Gorbachev had proposed the holding of a summit of the thirty-five member states during the year 1990. But if French diplomacy was from the start attached to the CSCE, it also wanted to keep it balanced: there could be no question of accepting a drift toward a collective security system that might challenge the alliance and especially the prospect of an independent strategic Europe. Hence, in Paris there was initially a rather reserved reaction to the proposal from the Soviet Number One.[186]

But Mitterrand decided otherwise: by saying in Kiev that he was favorable to a summit of the CSCE in 1990, he intended to show his interlocutor that the USSR would not be excluded from developments underway in Europe and that the Helsinki process might in effect contribute to framing the German question at the pan-European level.[187] His calculation was also long-term: following Kiev, the idea circulated through the Élysée staff that the CSCE ought to play a major role in the future European ordering and even enjoy a form of institutionalization – until then rejected by French diplomacy – by means of annual sessions, or even periodic summits.[188] In addition, with the two major powers sharing the same 'conservatism of blocs', as Malta had shown, the strengthening of the CSCE might help defuse the risk of the Community becoming corseted within the 'new Atlanticism' and hindered by the artificial maintenance of the two alliances. The Elysée was therefore ready to go farther down this path: 'You might in the coming days propose that the future summit of the 35 be the occasion to adopt a charter of Europe', suggested Védrine, for whom the CSCE, a 'global framework' that 'excluded nobody', ought to adopt an ambitious program for this event. The summit, he continued, might discuss 'the problem of borders; pursuit of the disarmament process in Europe; recognition of the role of the EEC in Europe; political, economic, and cultural cooperation between European states and organizations in Europe; eventual creation of institutions of the 35' – all of these leading to a 'rewritten and strengthened Final Act' that, under the name 'Charter', would govern the future of security and cooperation in Europe.[189] Védrine's idea was in fact to lead a year later to the Paris Charter signed at the CSCE summit in the French capital.

Still, the pan-European dimension of French policy remained to a large extent a function of its Community priority. The European revolutions of 1989 posed, as we have said, the question of the policy of the Twelve toward the East, hence the adoption in Strasbourg of a series of projects proposed by Mitterrand in preceding weeks, of which the most visible was for the future EBRD.[190] Of course, enlargement of the Community properly speaking was not on the agenda at the end of 1989, but the fall of the Wall and the end of Communism in the East – of which the Velvet Revolution in Prague and the fall of Ceausescu in Romania marked the final act – inevitably placed the question of the EC's openness to new democracies at the heart of the debate. The French, as already mentioned, were reticent about the idea of a new enlargement of the Community even before the upheavals of the summer and autumn. Now, with the changes under way, they began to be seriously concerned about the prospect: 'Reconciling European construction with the openness to the East is an imperative', noted the CAP, 'but [the EC] could not bear any enlargement until after its strengthening' and must therefore 'control its openness by offering satisfying alternative solutions to membership'.[191] The whole problematic of French policy in the coming months was enunciated here: how to give a Communitarian Europe a major role in the transformations in the East without taking the risk of a premature enlargement that might lead to the dilution of West European construction? How, in other words, to take charge of the organization of 'greater' Europe without giving up strengthening the 'smaller' one? Such was the background of the initiative launched to general surprise by Mitterrand on 31 December on the occasion of his New Year address to the French people. Although it should absolutely strengthen its structures, the Community, he said, had by its very existence 'powerfully contributed to the upsurge of the peoples of the East by serving as their reference point and pole of attraction'. The 'second stage', he added, ought to take the form of a 'European confederation in the real sense of the term, that would associate all the nation-states of our continent in a common and permanent organization of exchanges, peace, and security'. Intervening in the debate opening on the architecture of the greater Europe, Mitterrand thus launched what would become his grand project for the post–Cold War era.[192]

The Future of the German Question

To be sure, Mitterrand acknowledged in the same breath that the European future was full of questions: What would be the future of the alliances? At what pace should disarmament be pursued? What kind of cooperation must there be between East and West? Should frontiers remain intangible? What about reawakening nationalities? Finally and especially, 'in what form and under what conditions would the German people unite'?[193] In a European context of extreme fluidity, these questions were without any doubt shared by most of the actors. Nevertheless, the great question at year's end resided in the respective rhythms of the European and German changes. For Mitterrand's diplomacy, as we have said, the essential thing was to preserve a synchrony: German unification should accompany and not precede European transformation. At the end of 1989, this vision did not appear unrealistic, since the principal protagonists all proclaimed a desire to resolve the German question over time. This was true in Moscow, where the official line remained to oppose the very idea of German unification, or in any case to refuse to envisage it absent a profound evolution in European security.[194] And this appeared equally true in Washington: after Saint Martin, the French could legitimately feel that there existed between the two capitals an agreement to press moderation upon the Germans.[195] As for Bonn, Kohl himself said at the same time that he was 'doing everything so it does not go too quickly', adding 'I am trying to reduce the speed' of change.[196] His policy continued ostensibly to be one of *gradual* rapprochement between the FRG and the GDR, as suggested by the common declaration on 19 December in which Bonn and East Berlin said they were determined to place the relations between them in the context of Europe as a whole.[197]

Be that as it may, the hypothesis that the process of German unification might continue to be in sync with the transformation of Europe as a whole was indeed preferred by the Élysée at the end of 1989. This was witnessed by the favorable commentaries aroused in mid December by the official position on the German question adopted by the SPD (which was still divided and disoriented by the fall of the Wall) under the influence of Brandt, who had now clearly opted for unification. The Mitterrand advisers indeed saw in the SPD pronouncement a 'reasonable and balanced' document (which, they noted, 'coincided on many points with Chancellor Kohl's positions'). Bianco saw it as a 'good text' and Védrine noted that for Brandt's party 'the unification of Europe and the unification of the Germans were two closely linked things', and 'one could not be obtained to the detriment of the other'. For the rest, he remarked, the Social Democrats (who were close in this to Genscher) were developing an approach that was more gradual and more concerned about international repercussions than Kohl's. The SPD, stressed Védrine, was in favor of an unconditional recognition of the German-Polish border, and they saw German unification as more clearly a part of the European context than did the chancellor.[198] Mitterrand himself praised a document in which he discerned Brandt's influence: 'very remarkable on these questions, as he as been for a long time'.[199]

Mitterrand's interest in the SPD's approach is revealing: while confirming his acceptance of the goal of unification, such as Kohl had affirmed it in his Ten Point speech and from which the SPD plan did not fundamentally dissociate itself, it also reflected his preference for a controlled approach. Mitterrand, in other words, remained attached to the ideas of the founding father of Ostpolitik, which he judged not at all outmoded and which could be read in filigree in his own statements of 31 December. Of course, it remained to be seen whether the chain of events would be compatible with these same ideas. It must be repeated that while everyone saw that unification was now an irreversible process, nobody could predict the speed with which it would be realized some nine months later. At the end of 1989 Kohl himself was still counting in years. Yet without the principal actors being completely aware of it, a different outcome was in the cards. The break-up beginning in the GDR and the progression of an idea of unity that the East Germans saw less as a national imperative than as the solution to their concrete problems; the rising importance of this question in the domestic political debate in the Federal Republic; and Kohl's growing awareness (especially after his visit to Dresden) of the historic opportunity presented to him to become the 'Chancellor of unity'; the increasingly evident contradictions of Soviet diplomacy, no doubt henceforth incapable (politically as well as practically) of opposing the process of unification – all these could only lead to an acceleration of events that would escape the control of the statesmen involved.

Notes

1. Mitterrand press conference in Copenhagen, *Politique étrangère de la France. Textes et documents* (*PEF*), November-December 1989, p. 32.
2. On 9 November, the American president, in front of the press, claimed to be 'very happy' with the events and, when asked why he wasn't more enthusiastic, added that 'he was not the emotional type', which brought on –as for Mitterrand – criticism to which he responded repeatedly that he wasn't going to 'dance on the wall': see Philip Zelikow and Condoleezza Rice, *Germany Unified and Europe Transformed: A Study in Statecraft*, Cambridge, Harvard University Press, 1995, p. 105.
3. *Le Monde*, 12–13 November 1989. Organizing his defense facing his detractors some years later, Mitterrand did not miss noticing the former president's initial reactions, according to which he had lacked prudence by expressing himself in favor of German unity in Bonn on 3 November: see François Mitterrand, *De l'Allemagne, de la France*, Paris, Odile Jacob, 1996, pp. 55–57.
4. Survey quoted in Pierre Favier and Michel Martin-Roland, *La Décennie Mitterrand*, vol. 3, 'Les Défis', 1988-1991, Paris, Seuil, 1996, p. 182.
5. On the French attitudes and German perceptions in this period, see Ingo Kolboom, *Vom geteilten Deutschland zum Vereinten Deutschland. Deutschland-Bilder in Frankreich*, Bonn, DGAP/Europa Union Verlag, 1991, pp. 44–65; and Marie-Noëlle Brand Crémieux, *Les Français face à la réunification allemande, automne 1989–automne 1990*, Paris, L'Harmattan, 2004, p. 33ff.
6. Haltung der drei Westalliierten und der Sowjetunion zur deutschen Frage und zur Entwicklung in der DDR (17. November 1989), *Deutsche Einheit. Sonderedition aus den Akten des Bundeskanzleramtes 1989/90*, Munich, R. Oldenburg, 1998, pp. 546–547 (the writer of the memo underlined Mitterrand's expressions about the 'legitimate' nature of unification that he was 'not afraid of', but also his insistence on a 'long-term' process and his claim that French policy 'will adjust itself' to a unified Germany). Kohl would always distinguish between Mitterrand's personal vision, the sympathy of French public opinion, and the 'hesitations' of the political class, of which Giscard was in his eyes the most eminent incarnation: see Helmut Kohl, *Je voulais l'unité de l'Allemagne*, Paris, De Fallois, 1997, p. 127 and p. 131.
7. Kohl's visit to Warsaw was placed under the sign of reconciliation between the two countries and was largely dominated by the already very sensitive question of the German-Polish border, Prime Minister Tadeusz Mazowiecki having declared before-

hand that he hoped the visit would help clarify things. The SPD had introduced a declaration in the Bundestag that, quoting the terms of Genscher's speech at the United Nations on 27 September, said that 'the Poles had to know that their right to live within safe borders would not be questioned'. Voted in on 8 November by a large majority, this resolution – which went beyond what Kohl's party had accepted up until this point – was a step in the direction of the Poles, but another declaration adopted the same day by twenty-six CDU-CSU representatives, which recalled that no treaty had ratified the loss of Germany's 'Eastern territories', diminished its effect. At the end of Kohl's visit, the Poles believed that they had not received the reassurances that they had been expecting: see TD Bonn 2330 et 2347, 7 and 8 November 1989, and TD Varsovie 1693, 14 November 1989, AD, Europe, RFA 1986–1990, box 6772.
8. Telefongespräch des Bundeskanzlers Kohl mit Staatspräsident Mitterrand, 11 November 1989, *Deutsche Einheit*, p. 511.
9. TD Moscou 6721, 10 November 1989, AD, Europe, Allemagne 1986–1990, box 6125.
10. Oral message received on 10 November 1989 at 11:00 p.m., private papers.
11. Telephone conversation between Mitterrand and Gorbachev, detailed report by Loïc Hennekinne, 14 November 1989, private papers.
12. MAE, le directeur des Affaires politiques, Entretien entre M. Gorbatchev et M. Dumas le 14 novembre 1989, compte rendu de B. Dufourcq, 16 November 1989, AD, Directeur politique (DP) 1986–1991, box 284.
13. Message to Thatcher from Gorbachev, 17 November 1989, passed on to Mitterrand, private papers.
14. TD Moscou 6810 and 6858, 16 and 18 November 1989, AD, Europe, Allemagne 1986–1990, box 6125.
15. See Anatoly Chernyaev, *My Six Years with Gorbachev*, University Park, Pennsylvania University Press, 2000, p. 235.
16. Zelikow and Rice, *Germany Unified*, p. 104.
17. TD Diplomatie 23731, 14 November 1989, AD, Europe, Allemagne 1986–1990, box 6124.
18. TD Bonn 2413, 16 November 1989, AD, Europe, RFA 1986–1990, box 6772. By making a statement that would remain for posterity ('Jetzt wächst zusammen, was zusammengehört') on 10 November in Berlin in front of the Schöneberg Town Hall, Brandt had placed himself clearly in the perspective of unification (still rejected by a number of his SPD friends), thereby taking the upper hand in a party deeply divided on the German question: see Helga Haftendorn, *Deutsche Außenpolitik zwischen Selbstbeschränkung und Selbstbehauptung 1945–2000*, Stuttgart and Munich, Deutsche Verlags-Anstalt, p. 353 and note 16, p. 495. Despite Kohl's and Brandt's statements at the Bundestag on 16 November, which were meant to calm things, the tension was nonetheless palpable, as demonstrated by the violent argument that took place between the Berlin mayor, the SPD's Walter Momper, who was very reluctant about unification, accused the government of not sufficiently supporting Eastern reform, and spoke of 'the people of the GDR', and the CDU's Volker Rühe, who affirmed that East Germans would choose unification and denounced 'the historical error of social democracy' in that regard.
19. Horst Teltschik, *329 Tage. Innenansichten der Einigung*, Berlin, Siedler, p. 24 and 41.
20. Zelikow and Rice, *Germany Unified*, pp. 112–114. Receiving Kissinger at the White House on 13 November, Bush had confided that he didn't want to give the impression of 'pushing' unification and that he too would prefer a 'prudent evolution', Gorbachev not being able to accept 'losing' the FRG in his eyes: see Michael R. Beschloss and Strobe Talbott, *At the Highest Levels: The Inside History of the End of the Cold War*, Boston, Little & Brown, 1993, p. 138.

21. Bertrand Dufourcq, '2 + 4 ou la négociation atypique', *Politique étrangère* 2 (2000): 467–484.
22. MAE, Note du directeur d'Europe, Jacques Blot, Le réveil de l'histoire, 16 November 1989, Archives nationales (AN), 5AG4/7708.
23. Thus the GDR's ambassador was told three days after the fall of the Wall by the Quai that France 'would not be an obstacle to the German people's desire to unify' even if it did not intend to say 'yes to reunification tomorrow and no matter what the conditions': TD Diplomatie 23731, 14 November 1989.
24. Conseil des ministres, 15 November 1989, private papers.
25. Hubert Védrine, note pour le président de la République, 16 November 1989, private papers (Védrine quoted a French TV journalist, Dominique Bromberger, who, back from Berlin, observed that 'the reunification question [did] occupy people's minds' but that it was only 'obsessive for the Germans more than 65 years old'.)
26. Védrine, note pour le président de la République, 13 November 1989, private papers.
27. Védrine's interview with the French radio station RTL, 14 November 1989, *PEF*, November-December 1989, pp. 39–40.
28. Dufourcq, '2+4 '; Roland Dumas, *Le Fil et la pelote. Mémoires*, Paris, Plon, 1996, p. 339.
29. The 14 November conversation in Moscow between Dumas and Gorbachev showed that French diplomacy indeed sought, with the meeting at the Élysée, to reassure Moscow, and that the Soviets were receptive: Entretien entre M. Gorbatchev et M. Dumas le 14 novembre 1989, 16 November 1989.
30. Védrine's interview with RTL, 14 November 1989; Conseil des ministres, 15 November 1989.
31. On 16 November the Chancellery had nevertheless passed on to the Élysée the outline of a press release mentioning the Twelve's support for the democratization in the GDR and the establishing of a European peace order in which the Germans would be able to find their unity through self-determination (Bonn wished, with this minimum formula, to obtain a positive signal from the Twelve about German developments while avoiding a debate about unification that was not, from its point of view, within the competence of the Twelve): see Werner Weidenfeld, *Außenpolitik für die deutsche Einheit. Die Entscheidungsjahre 1989/90*, Stuttgart, DVA, 1998, p. 90 *ff*.
32. The only primary source available is Jean-Louis Bianco's report for Georgette Elgey, based upon Jacques Delors's testimony: see 'Dinner with the twelve heads of State and government on 18 November 1989' and Mitterrand's handwritten note passed on to Georgette Elgey, 'Notes pour ma conférence de presse du 18 novembre 1989', private papers; see also Margaret Thatcher, *The Downing Street Years*, New York, HarperCollins, 1993, pp. 793–794.
33. This ambiguity was no doubt voluntary. True, for Mitterrand it was chiefly the confirmation of the German-Polish border that was at stake in the German matter (the Oder-Neisse problem, barely some days after Kohl's visit to Poland, was, in fact, on the agenda), and it was this very precise point that was going to stay, in the coming months, at the top of France's priorities. Still, the formulation adopted by Mitterrand at the Élysée dinner (and which Kohl did not take notice of that evening) implicitly expressed a preference, if only for the time being, for a postponement of the debate on unification. This ambiguity was not typical of Mitterrand: Bush, as will be seen, would do the same at Malta two weeks later; as for Kohl, he would eventually lose patience at the mention of 'borders' in the plural, in which – aiming for Thatcher rather than Mitterrand, who would soon clarify things at Strasbourg – he noticed an implicit opposition to unification: see pp. 127–128 and 131–132.
34. Teltschik, *329 Tage*, p. 38.

35. Thatcher, *Downing Street Years*, p. 794. Discussion among Foreign Affairs ministers, assembled separately, was more open: they did broach the question of borders, in which Genscher (recalling his statement of 27 September and the Bundestag resolution of 8 November) did not hesitate to dissociate himself from Kohl: see Hans-Dietrich Genscher, *Erinnerungen* (Berlin: Siedler, 1995), p. 662ff.
36. Teltschik, *329 Tage*, p. 38.
37. Mitterrand's press conference after the informal summit of the Twelve, 18 November 1989, *PEF*, November–December 1989, p. 61.
38. Mitterrand's speech before the European Parliament, 22 November 1989, *PEF*, November–December 1989, p. 78.
39. Letter from Mitterrand to Bush, 24 November 1989, private papers.
40. Interviews with the *Wall Street Journal*, 22 November 1989, and with *Paris-Match*, 23 November 1989.
41. Personal interview.
42. 'Sagen was ist,' *Der Spiegel*, 20 November 1989; Bianco passed a translation of the article to the president with the note 'very important': AN, 5AG4/7708; see also Teltschik, *329 Tage*, p. 40.
43. Védrine, note pour le président de la République, 13 November 1989, private papers; Alain Minc was, here again, particularly targeted by the critiques of the presidential entourage.
44. Guigou, note pour le président de la République, Aides aux pays de l'Est. Derniers états des réflexions communuataires, 14 November 1989, private papers.
45. Guigou, note pour le président de la République, La Communauté européenne: quel équilibre entre son projet d'union politique et ses relations avec ses voisins d'Europe? 16 November 1989, private papers.
46. Conseil des ministres, 15 November 1989.
47. See Mitterrand's press conference after the informal summit of the Twelve, 18 November 1989, p. 58.
48. Favier and Martin-Roland, *La Décennie*, vol. 3, p. 201.
49. Meeting between Mitterrand and Ruud Lubbers, The Hague, 20 November 1989, Védrine's handwritten notes, private papers.
50. Mitterrand's press conference, The Hague, 20 November 1989, *PEF*, November–December 1989, p. 66.
51. Letter from Kohl to Mitterrand, 27 November 1989, and in attachment, 'Calendrier de travail pour les étapes ultérieures jusqu'en 1993,' AN, 5AG4/6903; see also the original German version in *Deutsche Einheit*, pp. 565–567.
52. MAE, le directeur des affaires économiques et financières, Pierre de Boissieu, note a.s. Suite des travaux sur l'Union économique et monétaire, 29 November 1989, AN, 5AG4/6903.
53. Mitterrand's press conference, Athens, 29 November 1989, *PEF*, November–December 1989, p. 107.
54. Guigou, note pour le président de la République, Votre entretien avec M. Genscher cet après-midi, 30 November 1989, private papers (as already mentioned, Guigou, over the previous weeks, had proved to be personally quite open to pressing German demands with regard to institutional aspects).
55. On Kohl's policy in this context, see Hans Stark, *Kohl, l'Allemagne et l'Europe. La politique européenne de la République fédérale 1982–1998*, Paris, L'Harmattan, 2004, p. 150 ff, and Stefan Fröhlich, *„Auf den Kanzler kommt es an': Helmut Kohl und die deutsche Außenpolitik*, Paderborn: Schöningh, 2001), p. 235ff.
56. Detailed report in Genscher, *Erinnerungen*, p. 676ff.; and TD Diplomatie 25193–25194, 4 December 1989, AD, Europe 1986–1990, RFA, box 6800.

57. Letter from Mitterrand to Kohl, 1 December 1989, AN, 5AG4/6926.
58. On the following, see the account of one of the main architects of the plan, Teltschik, *329 Tage*, p. 42ff. ; also see Weidenfeld, *Außenpolitik*, p. 97ff., and, for the American point of view, Zelikow and Rice, *Germany Unified*, p. 118ff.
59. Nikolai Portugalov, a Germany expert on the CPSU Central Committee, hinted to Teltschik on 21 November that the USSR would not be opposed to the setting up of a confederation between the FRG and a reformed GDR. Kohl's entourage chose to see this as a 'green light' from Moscow, no doubt overinterpreting the Soviets' message, as one can doubt that Portugalov wanted to go as far as Teltschik reported and that Moscow wanted to pass on such an important message through a respected but second-rank intermediary: see Zelikow and Rice, *Germany Unified*, p. 118. This whole affair illustrated a factor that Bonn would skillfully exploit in the coming months: confusion, even an increasing contradiction, within the Soviet leadership with regard to German affairs.
60. It could hardly be otherwise, since the German foreign minister himself was kept out of the loop. True, Kohl had given instructions to fax the transcript of his speech as well as a letter explaining the content to Bush at the same time that he would speak in the Bundestag on the morning of 28 November – i.e. in the middle of the night in Washington – but the message only arrived at the end of the day due to technical difficulties, well after the plan had been revealed by the media: see Zelikow and Rice, *Germany Unified*, pp. 121 and 408.
61. Text of the ten point program in TD Bonn 2507–2508, 28 November 1989, private papers, and MAE, *Documents d'actualité internationale (DAI)* 6 (15 March 1990): 106–108.
62. See Teltschik, *329 Tage*, p. 52.
63. Vorlage des Ministerialdirektors Teltschik an Bundeskanzler Kohl, Bonn, 30. November 1989, *Deutsche Einheit*, pp. 574–577.
64. Mitterrand's press conference, Athens, 29 November 1989, PEF, November–December 1989, p. 106.
65. Favier and Martin-Roland, *La Décennie*, vol. 3, pp. 189–190. Feelings, at the moment, were barely different at the White House: see Zelikow and Rice, *Germany Unified*, p. 408.
66. Personal interview.
67. Genscher, *Erinnerungen*, p. 676 ; and TD Diplomatie 25193–25194, 4 December 1989.
68. Védrine, note pour le président de la République, 28 November 1989 (with Mitterrand's handwritten annotation), private papers.
69. Teltschik, *329 Tage*, p. 61.
70. MAE, le chef du CAP, note pour le ministre d'État, a.s. L'Europe entre Malte et Strasbourg: quatre propositions, 29 November 1989, AD, Europe, Allemagne 1986–1990, box 6123. Guéhenno even envisaged a 'de facto reunification' within twelve months, with the FRG 'acquiring a decisive influence in all aspects of managing the East German state'. Guéhenno's analyses and those of his staff remained steadily clear-sighted in the next few weeks, notably on the evolution of Soviet policy and on the state of the GDR: see below notes 127 and 169. As for his proposals (accelerating disarmament, transforming alliances, affirming the political dimension of the EEC and achieving the EMU), they were not fundamentally divergent from Mitterrand's policies, but they were presented in a more proactive light: 'the acceleration of history' was 'replete with dangers', wrote Guéhenno, but 'it would be dangerous to want to slow it down'; it was a matter, he concluded, 'of changing the context of German reunification in order to make it both easier and more stable'. On the problem of anticipation and the contribution of the CAP in this period, see Samy Cohen, 'L'imprévision et l'imprévisible. Remarques sur le processus mitterrandien d'information et de décision,' in Samy Cohen, *Mitterrand et la sortie de la guerre froide*, Paris, Presses universitaires de France, 1998.

71. MAE, le directeur d'Europe, Réunification allemande et processus européen, 4 December 1989, AN, 5AG4/7708.
72. MAE, Fiche, a.s. Déclaration du chancelier Kohl (Bundestag, 28 novembre 1989), n.d., AD, Europe, URSS 1986–1990, box 6681.
73. Meeting between Mitterrand and Roh Tae Woo, 30 November 1989, private papers.
74. Genscher, *Erinnerungen*, p. 678. Speaking of this meeting, Genscher later recalled a Mitterrand who was 'not against reunification' and did not 'demonstrate being worried': quoted in Favier and Martin-Roland, *La Décennie*, vol. 3, p. 204.
75. Teltschik, *329 Tage*, p. 60.
76. The Americans above all deplored the absence of clear references to the question of borders and Germany's belonging to NATO: see George Bush and Brent Scowcroft, *A World Transformed*, New York, Vintage Books, 1999, pp. 196–197.
77. MAE, Service des affaires stratégiques et du désarmement (ASD), note de Philippe Guelluy, a.s. Programme en dix points du chancelier Kohl : implications stratégiques, 30 November 1989, AD, ASD 1985–1990, box 15; MAE, le directeur d'Europe, Réunification allemande et processus européen, 4 December 1989.
78. Meeting between Mitterrand and Roh, 30 November 1989.
79. MAE, le directeur d'Europe, Réunification allemande et processus européen, 4 December 1989; and MAE, Fiche, a.s. Déclaration du chancelier Kohl (Bundestag, 28 novembre 1989), n.d.
80. Meeting between Mitterrand and Roh, 30 November 1989.
81. TD Diplomatie 25193–25194, 4 December 1989.
82. MAE, le directeur d'Europe, Réunification allemande et processus européen, 4 December 1989.
83. Meeting between Mitterrand and Roh, 30 November 1989.
84. On the Soviets' state of mind at Malta, see Hannes Adomeit, *Imperial Overstretch: Germany in Soviet Policy from Stalin to Gorbachev*, Baden-Baden, Nomos, 1998, 446 ff.; on Bush's approach, see Zelikow and Rice, *Germany Unified*, p. 126ff. (in his letter of 28 November presenting his ten points, Kohl had asked Bush to be its defender before Gorbachev: see Schreiben des Bundeskanzlers Kohl an Präsident Bush, Bonn, 28. November 1989, *Deutsche Einheit*, pp. 567–573).
85. The Soviet detailed report of the meeting was published in the *Cold War International History Project Bulletin* 12/13 (fall-winter 2001): 229–241; see also Zelikow and Rice, *Germany Unified*, pp. 127–131.
86. See Beschloss and Talbott, *Highest Levels*, pp. 168–169. On the reasons for Gorbachev's moderate attitudes about the German question at Malta, see Adomeit, *Imperial Overstretch*, pp. 446–449.
87. This was not a very accurate statement, as noted by Zelikow and Rice, *Germany Unified*, p. 129.
88. TD Washington 3018, 3 December 1989, AD, ASD 1985–1990, box 133.
89. MAE, sous-direction URSS, note a.s. Le sommet américano-soviétique de Malte (2–3 décembre): bilan et perspectives, 5 December 1989, AN, 5AG4/CDM 38.
90. See Zelikow and Rice, *Germany Unified*, p. 126ff., and Robert L. Hutchings, *American Diplomacy and the End of the Cold War: An Insider's Account of U.S. Policy in Europe, 1989–1992*, Washington, DC, Woodrow Wilson Centre Press, 1997, p. 100. Despite the agreement that Bush and Kohl reached during a long meeting in Brussels, the U.S. president was clearly worried that German policy might get carried away: while expressing his support to Kohl, Bush emphasized the necessary moderation with Gorbachev; Kohl, while promising to stay cautious, told Bush that the movement would not be stopped: the process, he insisted, would take 'years', but the German question was like a 'ground-

The Fall of the Wall   155

swell': see Gespräch des Bundeskanzlers Kohl mit Präsident Bush, Laeken bei Brüssel, 3. Dezember 1989, *Deutsche Einheit*, pp. 600–609.
91. Zelikow and Rice, *Germany Unified*, p. 132ff.; Hutchings, *American Diplomacy*, pp. 105–106.
92. As proof of his plan's moderation, he underlined that he spoke of 'confederative structures' and not a 'confederation' (this was somewhat disingenuous: Bonn's preference for 'confederative structures' aimed to avoid formally recognizing the existence of two German states, which establishing a FRG-GDR confederation in the true sense of the term would have implied).
93. See the report of what precedes in TD REPAN 996–990, 4 December 1989, AD, ASD 1985–1990, box 215. Mitterrand remarked in regard to the borders that the 'treaties don't mention immobility nor intangibility, but inviolability, which isn't the same thing', thus showing that he was aware of this essential difference while leaning on Bush to legitimize his claim of a definitive recognition of the Oder-Neisse border.
94. Thatcher, *Downing Street Years*, pp. 795–796.
95. Teltschik, *329 Tage*, p. 67 (because it was an extraordinary NATO summit, no final communiqué was issued so there was no 'green light' to German unity, but the ministerial meeting on 14–15 December would issue a communiqué giving such a green light: see below, note 122).
96. *Le Monde*, 6 December 1989.
97. Védrine, note pour le président de la République, a.s. Sécurité de l'Europe après Malte et la réunion de l'OTAN, 6 December 1989, private papers.
98. Vorlage des Vortragenden Legationsrats I Bitterlich an Bundeskanzler Kohl, Bonn, 2./3. Dezember 1989, *Deutsche Einheit*, pp. 596–598.
99. Guigou, note pour le président de la République, Votre entretien avec le chancelier Kohl, lundi 4 décembre à Bruxelles, 3 December 1989, AN, 5AG4/7010.
100. This confirms a lack of communication between Mitterrand and Kohl, who in Brussels had found the time to meet Bush at length (Kohl was said to have 'snubbed' Mitterrand after the latter had allegedly done the same in Strasbourg on 22 November: see Favier and Martin-Roland, *La Décennie*, vol. 3, p. 204, and Weidenfeld, *Außenpolitik*, p. 144).
101. Letter from Mitterrand to Kohl, 5 December 1989, AN, 5AG4/6926.
102. Letter from Kohl to Mitterrand, 5 December 1989, AN, 5AG4/6926; and *Deutsche Einheit*, pp. 614–615.
103. Gespräch des Bundeskanzlers Kohl mit Präsident Bush, Laeken bei Brüssel, 3. Dezember 1989; Kohl repeated the following day during the NATO meeting that the FRG 'is ready to envision, in Strasbourg, bold measures as President Mitterrand wishes': TD REPAN 996–990, 4 December 1989.
104. Memories of the main actors are contradictory on this point. On the French side, Védrine wrote of a 'warm atmosphere': see Hubert Védrine, *Les Mondes de François Mitterrand. À l'Élysée 1981–1995*, Paris, Fayard, 1996, pp. 431–432; as for Mitterrand, he would later evoke 'a strained atmosphere': see Mitterrand, *De l'Allemagne*, p. 99 (it is likely that the 'atmosphere' was good when talking about the IGC, but that it deteriorated when the declaration on German unity was broached: see below, p. 131–133.)
105. Lunch on 8 December 1989, Strasbourg, Guigou's handwritten notes, private papers.
106. Conseil des ministres, 13 December 1989, private papers; Mitterrand would later downplay the consequences of a controversy that had set him against Kohl for several weeks and the doubts that he drew from it regarding his European commitment: Mitterrand, *De l'Allemagne*, p. 83–86.
107. Guigou confirms this: see Tilo Schabert, *Wie Weltgeschichte gemacht wird. Frankreich und die deutsche Einheit*, Stuttgart, Klett-Cotta, 2002, pp. 424–425. At the Quai d'Orsay, it was

feared that Strasbourg would give the impression of such bargaining: see Blot, note, Réunification allemande et processus européen, 4 December 1989.
108. Loïc Hennekinne, note pour le président de la République, Conseil européen. Déclarations politiques, 5 December 1989, AN, 5AG4/4160; Bertrand Dufourcq, '2+4'; and personal interview.
109. Kohl, *Je voulais*, p. 163; see also Bitterlich's concurrent testimony, 'In memoriam Werner Rouget: Frankreichs (und Europas) Weg nach Maastricht im Jahr der deutschen Einheit,' in Werner Rouget, *Schwierige Nachbarschaft am Rhein: Frankreich-Deutschland*, Bonn, Bouvier, 1998, p. 112 *ff*.
110. Lunch on 8 December 1989, Strasbourg, Guigou's handwritten notes. Evoking this exchange four days later with Baker, Kohl deplored that the mention of borders in the plural form maintained the confusion between the Oder-Neisse line and the intra-German border: see Gespräch des Bundeskanzlers Kohl mit Außenminister Baker, Berlin (West), 12. Dezember, 1989, *Deutsche Einheit*, pp. 636–641.
111. No detailed account of the dinner was found in the archives by the author, unlike Schabert, *Weltgeschichte*, p. 428–429, who quotes a report from Guigou; in addition, see Mitterrand, *De l'Allemagne*, p. 99; Dumas, *Le Fil*, p. 385; Dufourcq, '2+4'; Kohl, *Je voulais*, p. 163ff.; Genscher, *Erinnerungen*, p. 689ff.; Thatcher, *Downing Street Years*, p. 797 ; Favier and Martin-Roland, *La Décennie*, vol. 3, pp. 207–208; and Jean Lacouture and Patrick Rotman, *Mitterrand. Le Roman du pouvoir*, Paris, Seuil, 2000, pp. 215–216.
112. Conseil européen de Strasbourg, 8–9 December 1989, Conclusions de la présidence, *PEF*, November-December 1989, p. 140ff.
113. True, French diplomats highlighted, starting the day after Strasbourg, that the reference to the Helsinki principles implied 'the respect of borders and territorial integrity': see MAE, le ministre d'État, note pour Monsieur le président de la République, no date, private papers. The term 'respect', however, is not precise as it can cover the inviolability of borders (recognized by the above-mentioned agreements) as well as their intangibility (not recognized). Responding to journalists who observed that the border issue had not been dealt with in Strasbourg, Mitterrand nevertheless used this term again in an interview on 10 December: quoting the paragraph in question, he underlined that the final Helsinki Act 'includes the respect of borders': Mitterrand interview with Europe 1 and Antenne 2, 10 December 1989.
114. See breakfast meeting between Mitterrand and Kohl, Strasbourg, 9 December 1989, handwritten notes by Védrine, private papers. In the following days, the French insisted even more on the necessary recognition of the Oder-Neisse line, showing that they were not prepared to give up on this precise but essential point, as the coming weeks would confirm. Thus, reporting on the Strasbourg summit at the National Assembly on 12 December, Dumas insisted on the necessary recognition of the intangibility of Poland's western border. At a time when the chancellor wanted to avoid a divisive debate in Germany on this subject, Teltschik judged this position very severely, seeing in it the sign that France might want to 'slow down' developments in progress: Teltschik, *329 Tage*, p. 76.
115. MAE, le ministre d'État, note pour le président de la République, no date.
116. Conseil des ministres, 13 December 1989.
117. By requesting the recognition of the Oder-Neisse border, Mitterrand, according to Genscher, was not seeking to raise obstacles to unification but understood better than some German politicians the 'historical conditions' essential to its realization, while Thatcher, in his opinion, hesitated to recognize the inevitability of unification: Genscher, *Erinnerungen*, pp. 690–692.

118. Arbeitsfrühstuck des Bundeskanzlers Kohl mit Staatspräsident Mitterrand, Straßburg, 9. Dezember 1989, *Deutsche Einheit*, pp. 628–631.
119. As other proof, if necessary, of his tactical sense, Kohl added 'that he willingly gives France the glory of the success at Strasbourg' but that 'without him the deal would not have worked': Gespräch des Bundeskanzlers Kohl mit Außenminister Baker, Berlin (West), 12. Dezember 1989.
120. Teltschik, *329 Tage*, pp. 72–73.
121. TD Moscou 7293, DSL, 13 December 1989, AN, 5AG4/7708.
122. See Zelikow and Rice, *Germany Unified*, pp. 138 and 412, note 96. It must be emphasized that the communiqué of the NATO ministerial meeting in Brussels on 14–15 December repeated almost word for word the paragraph adopted at Strasbourg, that itself quoted the 1970 Brandt letter on German unity: see Teltschik, *329 Tage*, p. 81.
123. Though 'clearly very troubled' about German developments, in Saint Martin Mitterrand '[did] not project ... the alarm Thatcher recalled from the Strasbourg summit': see Zelikow and Rice, *Germany Unified*, p. 141.
124. Meeting between Mitterrand and Bush, Saint Martin, 16 December, Hennekinne's detailed report, private papers; see the corresponding American account in Zelikow and Rice, *Germany Unified*, pp. 141–142, as well as what Védrine reports about it: according to him, Bush affirmed 'we are not against reunification, but we are staying cautious' ('maybe he thought he would please Mitterrand by expressing himself in this way?', Védrine added); see Védrine, *Les Mondes*, p. 443.
125. Hennekinne, note pour le président de la République, Rencontre avec M. Gorbatchev, 16 November 1989, AN, 5AG4/CDM 33; TD Moscou 6921, 23 November 1989, private papers.
126. On Soviet attitude and contradictions in the period, see Adomeit, *Imperial Overstretch*, p. 441ff.
127. The CAP considered that, according to certain signs, unification was no longer a taboo in Moscow and that the Soviets might be willing to look for quid pro quos since they would not be able to hinder the German unification process in any case: see MAE, CAP, note, a.s. Réflexions sur l'URSS et la question allemande, AD, Europe, Allemagne 1986–1990, 30 November 1989, box 6123. As for the head of the Europe directorate, he suspected that Kohl could not have taken the risk of announcing his ten points 'without seeking some assurances in Moscow': see Blot, note, Réunification allemande et processus européen, 4 December 1989. These analyses were clear-sighted even if they clearly overestimated, on one hand, the degree of rationality of the USSR's German policy, and on the other, the degree of German-Soviet consultation at this stage.
128. TD Moscou 7079–7080, 4 December 1989, AD, Europe, URSS 1986–1990, box 6681.
129. The idea of an alleged attempt by Mitterrand, in Kiev, to lean on Gorbachev to block German unity appears very early in writings but it is not sustained by any credible evidence: see e.g. Stephen F. Szabo, *The Diplomacy of German Unification*, New York, Saint Martin's Press, 1992, p. 50, or Elizabeth Pond, *Beyond the Wall: Germany's Road to Unification*, Washington, The Brookings Institution Press, 1993, pp. 159–160. This notion is thereafter customarily repeated in a noncritical way and presented as fact in the literature: see typically Hutchings, *American Diplomacy*, p. 105 (Zelikow and Rice, *Germany Unified*, p. 137, are an exception).
130. See Genscher, *Erinnerungen*, p. 683ff.; and Adomeit, *Imperial Overstretch*, p. 449ff.
131. The meeting between Mitterrand and Gorbachev in Kiev does present us with a source problem. No detailed report was found in the French archives, with the exception of a 'debriefing' by Attali for Hennekinne and Védrine, private papers (this document

corresponds in part to the report published by Jacques Attali, *Verbatim*, vol. 3 (Paris: Fayard, 1995), pp. 360–367, whose original was not found) and of a note by Margerie pour le président de la République, Votre déplacement à Kiev le 6 décembre 1989, 23 January 1992, AN, 5AG4/CDM 33 (but this document was written ex post facto, at a time when Mitterrand was becoming concerned with the emerging negative narrative). The Soviet detailed report – of which a copy is to be found in the papers turned over by Zelikow and Rice to Stanford's Hoover Institution – is quoted by several authors in English or German translation, notably Zelikow and Rice, *Germany Unified*, p. 137; Adomeit, *Imperial Overstretch*, pp. 456 and 459–460; and above all Weidenfeld, *Außenpolitik*, p. 153–159 (but whereas Zelikow and Rice and Adomeit remain objective, Weidenfeld embellishes it with a number of subjective commentaries that distort the interpretation, moreover without Weidenfeld asking if the Soviet origin of the source might not be of a nature to form a bias, since the Soviets might have wanted to read more into Mitterrand's statements than there actually was). Weidenfeld also quotes the Soviet report (found in the same archival series) of a meeting between Attali and Gorbachev's adviser, Vadim Zagladin, in Kiev on the same day (see Weidenfeld, *Außenpolitik*, pp. 156–157). According to Zagladin, Attali declared that France 'does not want under any circumstances the reunification of Germany even as it understands that it is eventually inevitable', but – irrespective of the inherent contradiction that lies within this statement – one must here again question the authorized nature of Attali's quite extraordinary remarks (if they were indeed accurately reported by Zagladin), which are often quoted in support of the thesis of Mitterrand desiring to block unification, but seem rather to reflect Attali's personal concerns (on Attali's very poor credibility, see footnotes 10 and 11 in the prologue of the present book). Among the later recollections, one may quote Mitterrand, who reports Gorbachev's concerns but without the alarmist tone that Attali gives them at the end of the report that he later published in *Verbatim* ('help me prevent German reunification, otherwise I will be replaced by a military man'): see Mitterrand, *De l'Allemagne*, pp. 88–92; as for Gorbachev, he does not substantiate at all the notion that the French president asked him to hinder German reunification: see Mikhail Gorbatchev, *Mémoires*, Éditions du Rocher, 1997, p. 661. The summary that follows is based upon these various sources, from which we kept only what it was possible to cross-check.

132. According to accounts relying on the detailed Soviet report, Mitterrand, mentioning his upcoming visit to the GDR, suggested to Gorbachev – who was considering going there as well – that they carry out the voyage together. This intriguing suggestion (often cited in the literature as a clear sign of Mitterrand's alleged eagerness to block German unification, which in itself is a disputable interpretation) was not taken up by Gorbachev: Weidenfeld, *Außenpolitik*, p. 156; Zelikow and Rice, *Germany Unified*, p. 137. (Mitterrand's suggestion of a joint GDR visit does not appear in the French sources).

133. Ambassade de France en URSS, Note de Jean-Marie Mérillon, a.s. Compte rendu de l'entretien entre M. le ministre d'Etat et M. Shevardnadze à Kiev le 6 décembre 1989, 15 December 1989, 19 p., AD, Europe, URSS 1986–1990, box 6674.

134. Such was the 'language' that the Quai d'Orsay had suggested to Dumas before his meeting with Shevardnadze: see Fiche, a.s. Relations URSS-RDA, no date (dossier 'Entretiens de Kiev, 6 décembre 1989') AD, Europe 1986–1990, URSS, box 6681.

135. The Gorbachev-Mitterrand press conference in Kiev confirmed the same uneasiness towards the acceleration of German policy: Mitterrand warned that to 'push' the question of German unity could 'damage the changes that are taking place' and Gorbachev that 'no country in Europe could spare itself from taking action without taking European stability into account'. Meanwhile, it also highlighted what remained a fundamental difference: whereas Gorbachev recalled the historical 'reality' of the existence of 'two

German States that are sovereign', Mitterrand reiterated France's understanding for the 'aspirations' of the German people and referred to his 3 November declaration in Bonn: see Mitterrand and Gorbachev joint press conference, Kiev, 6 December 1989, *PEF*, November–December 1989, p. 134–140.
136. That is what he would maintain later: see Favier and Martin-Roland, *La Décennie*, vol. 3, p. 198; this account appears credible in the light of the Mérillon telegram cited above (in Strasbourg, Mitterrand moreover told Kohl that Gorbachev, in Kiev, did not 'react strongly' to the German question, and upon meeting the chancellor again in Latché on 4 January, he added that the Soviet proved to be anxious not of the process itself, but of its haste: see *Deutsche Einheit*, p. 630 and p. 685).
137. According to his adviser Andrei Grachev, it is more than likely Gorbachev who counted on Mitterrand to slow down the process: cited in Favier and Martin-Roland, *La Décennie*, vol. 3, p. 198. This is what Mitterrand would confirm to Bush in Saint Martin some days later: '[Gorbachev] wants us to help him to slow the movement. [He] is hostile to reunification. Not I. But I agree with him in saying that it should be slower': Védrine, *Les Mondes*, p. 489.
138. Teltschik noted that the French president, while summarizing his conversation with Gorbachev during his breakfast in Strasbourg with Kohl on 9 December, said nothing about the manner in which he himself had given his opinion on the German question while facing the Soviet leader; he thus implicitly revealed a suspicion toward Mitterrand: see Teltschik, *329 Tage*, p. 71.
139. See Wjatscheslaw Kotchemassow, *Meine letzte Mission. Fakten, Erinnerungen, Überlegungen* (Berlin: Dietz, 1994), p. 196ff. Meeting Boidevaix in West Berlin on 6 December, Kochemassov – like Shevarnadze with Dumas in Kiev the same day – intimated in thinly veiled terms that the USSR counted on cooperation with France to maintain the German status quo: TD Bonn 2579, 6 December 1989, AD, Europe, URSS, 1986–1990, box 6674.
140. Message oral de M. Chevardnadze remis le 8 décembre à 17 h 15, AD, Europe 1986–1990, URSS 6670.
141. TD Haus Berlin 318, 8 December 1989, AD, Europe, 1986–1990, Allemagne, box 6127.
142. The Soviets, however, hesitated before making the proposition, as some in Moscow feared that the quadripartite 'mechanism' could run the risk of playing itself out in the opposite direction of the one hoped for and accelerating the process by irreparably putting the German question on the diplomatic agenda: see TD Moscou 7203, 9 December 1989, AD, Europe, Allemagne 1986–1990, box 6125.
143. This point is essential: for French diplomacy, the quadripartite mechanism was an instrument to manage and *not* an instrument to deadlock German unification. The Quai had a very clear legal view of this matter. First, French diplomats noted that nothing in the various agreements of 1945 establishing the Four Powers' rights and responsibilities legally consecrated the division of Germany de jure, which was a de facto consequence of the Cold War and of Soviet policy: see MAE, sous-direction Europe centrale et nordique, Note a.s. La création de la RDA – aspects historiques et idéologiques, 23 October 1989, AD, Europe, Allemagne, 1986–1990, box 6119. In addition, the Quai did not lose sight of the fact that the Westerners, 'by exercising or by reserving for each occasion since 1945 their quadripartite rights and responsibilities', wanted to 'insure the maintenance of the principle of German unity': see MAE, Direction des affaires juridiques, note a.s. de l'Allemagne, 24 October 1989, AD, Europe, Allemagne 1986–1990, box 6119. Moreover, in his long note cited above, Blot mentioned that the Four 'had kept from their original rights a mandate to negotiate a German settlement' and already considered (this was the idea of the future '2 + 4') a negotiation between them and the two German states: MAE, le directeur d'Europe, Réflexions sur la question allemande, 30

October 1989, AD, Europe 1986–1990, Allemagne, box 6119 (see also chapter 2 in this volume, pp. 102–104). On these very important legal aspects, see also chapter 4, n. 42.
144. MAE, Fiche a.s. Relations URSS-RDA, Dossier d'entretiens de Kiev.
145. On the American attitude, Zelikow and Rice, *Germany United*, p. 139ff.; on that of Bonn, Weidenfeld, *Außenpolitik*, p. 179ff.
146. TD Diplomatie 25698, 9 December 1989, AD, Europe 1986–1990, Allemagne, box 6127. The 'allied initiative' was launched by Reagan in his speech in the ex-capital of the Reich in May 1987 and taken up by Bush two years later; following up on the 1971 agreement on Berlin, it aimed to adjust the quadripartite arrangements in order to improve the situation of Berliners: see Zelikow and Rice, *Germany United*, p. 379, n. 52.
147. See Favier and Martin-Roland, *La Décennie*, vol. 3, p. 207; a detailed report of Mitterrand's meeting with Thatcher was not found in the various French archives (Thatcher would later report that she found Mitterrand, that day, 'even more worried' than herself, an account that would feed the chronicle of Mitterrand's alleged anxieties towards German unification: see Thatcher, *Downing Street Years*, p. 796; but Thatcher's recollection needs to be handled with care: see below chapter 4, n. 9).
148. Breakfast meeting between Mitterrand and Kohl, 9 December 1989, Védrine's handwritten notes; and Arbeitsfrühstuck des Bundeskanzlers Kohl mit Staatspräsident Mitterrand, Straßbourg, 9. Dezember 1989 (Mitterrand told Kohl he thought that Moscow's approach was motivated by the situation of Soviet troops in the GDR. For the rest, he insisted, he had not yet considered the way in which it was necessary to behave in the quadripartite meetings, but he thought it was necessary to prepare for them together: how, for example, to react to a Soviet proposition to meet at the level of the four heads of state and government?).
149. TD Diplomatie 25703, 10 December 1989, AD, Europe, Allemagne, 1986–1990, box 6127.
150. After the three Western ambassadors' meeting, Boidevaix reported that his two colleagues, the British ambassador Christopher Mallaby and, especially, the American ambassador Vernon Walters, had shown themselves to be less concerned than he was to 'limit the debate' with Kochemassov, which would tend to nuance the American narrative of unwavering U.S. support of German diplomacy in this matter; see TD Bonn 2621, DSL, 11 December 1989, Europe, Allemagne, 1986–1990, box 6126, and note 151 below.
151. TD Bonn 2621, 11 December 1989 ; TD Bonn 2621, DSL, 11 December 1989, Europe, Allemagne, 1986–1990, box 6126 (Walters' rather inconsistent attitude is not reflected in the standard U.S. narrative – quite the contrary: see Zelikow and Rice, *Germany Unified*, p. 140.)
152. After the meeting, Boidevaix saw in the question of the permanence of the meetings 'a problem of political choice' and feared that 'if the experience continues, the group of the four ambassadors [will] be raised little by little by the Soviets to the rank of an organism having its word to say about Germany's destiny': see TD 2621, 11 December 1989. As a matter of fact, his colleague Mérillon noted from Moscow that two days after the meeting of the four ambassadors, the Soviets no longer presented it as centered on Berlin but insisted on its more general nature: see TD Moscou 7294, 13 December 1989, AD, Europe, Allemagne 1986–1990, box 6127.
153. See typically Zelikow and Rice, *Germany Unified*, pp. 139–141; Genscher's account is closer to the truth: see Genscher, *Erinnerungen*, p. 693ff.
154. The Germans made clear to the three other Westerners (during the meeting of the four political directors in the margins of the 14 December NATO ministerial meeting) their reluctance before the possible continuation of the exercise and their desire for information and close consultation: TD RPAN Bruxelles 1049, 14 December 1989.

155. The *Washington Post*'s Jim Hoagland typically reported that a French diplomat, commenting on the unpleasant character of the meeting for the Germans, had allegedly said that this was 'the point of holding it': see Zelikow and Rice, *Germany Unified*, p. 140 (the authors use this quote to substantiate the notion that the French allegedly supported the Soviet approach with regard to the four ambassadors' meeting, a very disputable assertion as seen above, pp. 137–139 and notes 150 and 151).
156. In addition, such a visit – a first – raised specific problems in the view of French diplomats: relations with the GDR, especially at the highest level, could obviously not be treated irrespective of relations with the FRG. For this reason the date of Honecker's visit to Paris, at Bonn's request, had been fixed *after* the East German leader had gone to the FRG in September 1987 (a visit, it is known, that was long postponed under the pressure of Moscow). Similarly, the Quai d'Orsay had recommended prudence before inviting Honecker to France for fear that Bonn would interpret the invitation as an international consecration of the regime (the French ambassador in East Berlin showing himself –without surprise – more favorable to such a visit): see Jean Musitelli, note pour le président de la République, Invitation de M. Honecker, 6 May 1987, private papers.
157. Hennekinne, note pour le président de la République, 26 October 1989, Visite en RDA, private papers.
158. This appeared clearly in Blot's above-mentioned long note; see Réflexions sur la question allemande, 30 October 1989, AD, Europe, 1986–1990, Allemagne, box 6119.
159. TD Berlin 3029, 13 November 1989 (handwritten note by Mitterrand), private papers.
160. As for the trip to Kiev, the announcement of the voyage in the GDR was therefore *not* a response to the 28 November Ten Point Plan, as many would later write, ignoring the chronology: see for example Pond, *Beyond the Wall*, p. 159.
161. When the French announced the date of Mitterrand's visit on 22 November, they probably thought, as had been initially planned, that Kohl would go to the GDR on 30 November: see TD Berlin 3035, 14 November 1989, DSL. But on the day after the announcement of Mitterrand's visit, the federal government spokesperson indicated that Kohl's visit would not take place before early 1990, while denying any disagreement with Paris about this and confirming that Mitterrand and Kohl had consulted each other regarding the French president's visit, which was 'also in the well-understood interest of the Germans': see TD Bonn 2459, 23 November 1989. Then the looming debate in the FRG led Kohl to schedule his own visit to the GDR on 19 December, a date that would be announced on 5 December: see TD Berlin 3186, 24 November 1989; TD Bonn 2488, 25 November 1989; TD Berlin 3214, 27 November 1989; and TD Berlin 3312, 5 December 1989, AD, Europe, Allemagne, 1986–1990, box 6120 (Teltschik would later assert that Mitterrand's visit had not previously been discussed with the Chancellery, which contradicts the above-mentioned declaration by the federal government spokesperson: see Teltschik, *329 Tage*, pp. 47 and 60.)
162. Hennekinne, note pour le président de la République, Evolutions en Europe centrale et orientale. Points de repères, 6 December 1989, AN, 5AG4/5098.
163. I did not come across this note in the various French archives, but its contents are quoted by Schabert, *Wie Weltgeschichte gemacht wird*, pp. 453–454; see also Favier and Martin-Roland, *La Décennie*, vol. 3, pp. 216–217.
164. Personal interview.
165. Védrine, note pour le président de la République, 6 December, 1989, private papers.
166. This was the message that GDR Minister of Foreign Trade Gerhard Beil passed on to Mitterrand via the intermediary of his counterpart Edith Cresson on 1 December: see Favier and Martin-Roland, *La Décennie*, vol. 3, p. 216.
167. Mitterrand denied having wanted to go to the GDR before Kohl and deplored the press

articles evoking a rivalry between them; not responding directly, Kohl rejoiced at being able to evoke these questions in early January in Latché: see Breakfast meeting between Mitterrand and Kohl, 9 December 1989, Védrine handwritten notes; and Arbeitsfrühstuck des Bundeskanzlers Kohl mit Staatspräsident Mitterrand, Straßbourg, 9. Dezember 1989.

168. Zelikow and Rice, *Germany Unified*, pp. 145–146; Vernon A. Walters, *Die Vereinigigung war vorraussehbar. Hinter den Kulissen eines entscheidenden Jahres*, Berlin, Siedler, 1994, pp. 65–66 (the Baker visit had given rise to a debate in Washington between those who feared a legitimization of the regime and a collision with Bonn and those who wanted to signal the American support for change – a debate similar to the one that unraveled at the same time in Paris, although a presidential trip and a ministerial visit are not equivalent from a symbolic political point of view).

169. See e.g. MAE, le chef du CAP, note pour le ministre d'Etat, a.s. L'Europe entre Malte et Strasbourg : quatre propositions, 29 November 1989. (Guéhenno and his colleagues also proposed, it has been said, a particularly lucid prospective of Soviet policy on the German question: see Cocquebert, note, a.s. Réflexions sur l'URSS et la question allemande, 30 November 1989.)

170. TD Berlin 3494, 16 December 1989, AD, Europe, 1986–1990, Allemagne, box 6120. It is likely that during this period Joëlle Timsit, the French ambassador to East Berlin, attached (not unlike her Western counterparts) an excessive importance to the institutional opposition and to intellectuals, most of whom were favorable to the maintenance of an East German state.

171. See meeting between Mitterrand and Gerlach, 20 December, handwritten notes by Hennekinne, private papers; see also excerpts of East German reports on the same talks and also of talks between Mitterrand and Modrow quoted from a document coming from the Potsdam archives, whose substance was authenticated by Attali and Védrine, in *Le Monde*, 4 May 1996. (There are no major discordances in content between the French and East German reports, but the latter, unsurprisingly, bring Mitterrand's reluctance vis-à-vis too rapid or uncontrolled a unification process more clearly to the surface.)

172. Rencontre de François Mitterrand avec les étudiants à l'université Karl Marx, Leipzig, 21 décembre 1989, *PEF*, November-December 1989, p. 210.

173. This is what came unsurprisingly out of the report of Minister of Foreign Affairs Oskar Fischer after Mitterrand's visit: underlining that it was the first official visit of a head of state of one of the three Western powers, it noted that the French president, even while declaring himself in favor of self-determination, had emphasized that the existence of the two German states should be respected and that he had 'expressed on several occasions his conviction that the GDR could find its political balance and reclaim a position of importance in Europe': see Bericht über den Staatenbesuch des Präsidenten der Französischen Republik, François Mitterrand, in der DDR von 20. bis 22. Dezember 1989, Bundesarchiv, Potsdam, I13-2886 C20 (a copy of this document was kindly passed on by Dr. Hans-Hermann Hertle, whom the author wishes to thank.)

174. Mitterrand press conference, Berlin, 22 December 1989, *PEF*, November–December 1989, p. 215.

175. We rely on this point on Favier and Martin-Roland, *La Décennie*, vol. 3, pp. 217–222; and personal interviews; see also Margerie, note pour le président de la République, Votre voyage en RDA les 20–22 décembre 1989, 23 January 1992, AN, 5AG4/CDM 33 (this document, of course, was written after the fact).

176. According to Guigou and Védrine: see Lacouture and Rotman, *Mitterrand*, p. 212 and Favier and Martin-Roland, *La Décennie*, vol. 3, p. 217; as for Mitterrand, he did not regret it: see Mitterrand, *De l'Allemagne*, pp. 101–117.

177. The contrast between Genscher's appreciation of the visit and Kohl's is in this regard meaningful: whereas the first gave credit to the French president for his trip to the GDR, the latter saw it as the departure point for the difficulties of his relations with Mitterrand: see Genscher, *Erinnerungen*, p. 705 and Kohl, *Je voulais*, p. 193.
178. Even if the Quai d'Orsay felt that for that moment 'the uncertainties were too significant to make it possible to see a glimmer of readable perspectives': MAE, ASD, note, a.s. Les evolutions à l'Est, la 'question allemande' et l'équilibre stratégique en Europe: élements de réflexion, 16 December 1989, AD, ASD 1985–1990, box 15.
179. On the Berlin speech, see Zelikow and Rice, *Germany Unified*, pp. 142–144.
180. SGDN, Note, Objet: le discours du secrétaire d'Etat américain J. Baker, 15 December 1989, private papers. In Paris it was also observed that Baker's vision inscribed itself in the logic of a maintenance of alliances as asserted in Malta and supported by the majority of European countries due to its stabilizing virtues. (In fact, Baker's comments in Berlin were perceived in the majority of European capitals – including Bonn – as a confirmation of the American desire to calm the situation: by hinting that a unified Germany needed to belong to NATO – a perspective that at the time was unanimously held to be unacceptable for Moscow – Washington, many believed, was in fact signalling its reluctance before German accelerations.)
181. Védrine, note pour le président de la République, a.s. Avenir des alliances. Evolution de l'Allemagne et position américaine, 13 December 1989, private papers.
182. Guigou and Védrine, note pour le président de la République, Propositions de M. Baker. Propositions de M. Gorbatchev, 14 December 1989, with handwritten comments by Bianco for Mitterrand, private papers.
183. SGDN, note, Le discours du secrétaire d'Etat américain J. Baker, 15 December 1989.
184. Meeting between Mitterrand and Bush, Saint Martin, 16 December; Zelikow and Rice, *Germany Unified*, pp. 141–142.
185. MAE, ASD, Note, a.s. Le 'nouvel atlantisme:' portée stratégique, 20 December 1989, AD, ASD 1985–1990, box 186.
186. Because it was made the day after the announcement of the Ten Point Plan in which the CSCE occupied center stage, some in the Quai d'Orsay saw in Gorbachev's proposition the sign of a possible German-Soviet understanding, Moscow accepting German unification in exchange for the implementation of a pan-European peace order – a worry all the more fierce, now that the Ten Point plan confirmed in Paris the impression that Bonn might be willing to give up the project of an independent politico-strategic Europe: see MAE, le directeur d'Europe, Réunification allemande et processus européen, 4 December 1989; see also MAE, ASD, note a.s. Programme en dix points du chancelier Kohl: implications stratégiques, 30 November 1989, AD, ASD 1985–1990, box 15. The Quai therefore counseled a 'wait and see' attitude in view of Gorbachev's initiative: see Fiche d'entretien, a.s. Proposition de M. Gorbatchev d'avancer Helsinki II à 1990, n.d., AN 5AG4/CDM 38.
187. This obviously does not mean that he shared the Soviet reading of Helsinki as involving a durable consecration of borders and in consequence of the German status quo: nothing in any documents suggests this interpretation (on this, see pp. 132 and 136).
188. Védrine, note pour le président de la République, a.s. Avenir des alliances. Evolution de l'Allemagne et position américaine, 13 December 1989.
189. Védrine, note pour le président de la République, a.s. Avenir de l'Europe, 15 December 1989.
190. In addition to the increase of EU aid to Hungary and Poland and the pursuit of the coordination of Western aid decided upon at the summit of the Arche, the French EC presidency – besides the creation of the EBRD – proposed in Strasbourg the creation

of a European foundation for vocational training, the opening of certain EC programs to Eastern European countries (Erasmus, Comett, Lingua) and the signature of trade agreements with the USSR and the GDR: see Margerie, note pour le président de la République, 'Conseil européen. Relations avec les pays de l'Est,' 6 December 1989, private papers.

191. MAE, CAP, note a.s. Construction européenne et bouleversements à l'Est, 29 November 1989, AD, Europe, Allemagne, 1986–1990, box 6123.
192. On the European Confederation, see chapter 7 of this volume, p. 347 and Frédéric Bozo, 'The Failure of A Grand Design: Mitterrand's European Confederation (1989–1991),' *Contemporary European History* 3, no. 17 (2008): 391–412. (In his long note dated 30 October 1989, Blot had advanced the idea of a 'pan-European confederation': see chapter 2, n. 90.)
193. Mitterrand's New Year Address, 31 December 1989, *PEF*, November–December 1989, pp. 227–228.
194. True, some in Gorbachev's entourage were beginning to hint informally that this official position might evolve under the constraint of realities, confirming the anticipations of the French embassy before the Kiev trip: see TD Moscou 7372, DSL Secret, 18 December 1989, AD, Europe, Allemagne, 1986–1990, box 6125; but Shevardnadze's speech to the European Parliament on 19 December – a curious mix of refusal and of conditionality, of old thinking and of opening – most of all reflected the growing contradictions of Moscow's Germany policy: see Adomeit, *Imperial Overstretch*, pp. 464–466.
195. This was confirmed by the French embassy in Washington, which cited a high-level American official, according to whom 'the French are more noisy and we are more diplomatic, but we all say the same thing': TD Washington 1172, 18 December 1989, AD, Europe, Communisme et Eurocommunisme 1986–1990, box 6097. Whereas the Americans may have argued that their policy in reality aimed to make unification acceptable by the USSR and the Europeans and thus to contribute to Bonn's objectives, Washington was in fact seeking to calm the situation: see Zelikow and Rice, *Germany Unified*, pp. 147–148.
196. Meeting between Mitterrand, Kohl and Jean-Pascal Delamuraz (president of the Swiss confederation at the time), 15 December 1989, detailed report by Hennekinne, private papers.
197. TD Berlin 3516, 19 December 1989, AD, Europe, Allemagne, 1986–1990, box 6120.
198. Védrine, note pour le président de la République, a.s. Analyse du communiqué de presse du SPD sur 'Les Allemands en Europe,' 14 December 1989, with handwritten notes by Bianco, private papers. (The document analyzed at the Elysée, entitled 'Deutsche in Europa', constituted the portion consecrated to the national question of the program that the SPD was about to debate some days later during its meeting in Berlin. See also above, n. 18.)
199. Conseil des ministres, 13 December 1989; three days later, he underlined that Weizsäcker and Brandt distinguished themselves from Kohl: Meeting between Mitterrand and Bush, Saint Martin, 16 December 1989.

Chapter 4

THE BREAKTHROUGH TOWARD GERMAN UNITY
(January-February 1990)

The question of German unity had reached the top of international preoccupations in the last weeks of 1989, but neither its process nor its pace was determined in advance. Yet everything changed quickly in the first weeks of 1990: the rapid degeneration of the GDR, whose economic decay had been underestimated, led to an irreversible quickening of the march to unity. By the end of January Mikhail Gorbachev was constrained to admit the now ineluctable nature of German unification. In endorsing the plan that Modrow had come to Moscow to present to him, he hoped that the process would be gradual, but he soon had to bow to the evidence, recognizing during Helmut Kohl's visit to Moscow on 9–10 February that unification would be rapid and would be primarily determined by the will of the Germans themselves. In this context, the two questions of the conditions under which unity might take place and the international framework for unification became the principal preoccupations in the major capitals. At the end of two weeks of intense negotiations that culminated in Ottawa on 13 February, a formula was specified: there would be a '2 + 4' process (the two German states plus the four guarantor powers), the purpose of which was precisely to discuss the external aspects of German unification.

Since in December French decision makers were still counting on a long-term process, they were – like others – caught short by the events of

---

Notes for this section begin on page 195.

January and early February. While it must be again emphasized that at no point did Paris challenge the legitimacy of German aspirations, François Mitterrand feared a policy of fait accompli from Bonn that would ignore the international situation. Perceiving a headlong rush on Kohl's part, the French president, concerned above all with the deteriorating situation in the USSR, once more insisted upon the requirement of international stability. But the Soviet green light changed the situation: once it had been accepted by Moscow, unification was now certain to occur over a relatively brief timetable. The adoption of the Ottawa formula was thus welcomed in Paris: whereas the German dynamic had previously seemed out of anyone's control, the 2 + 4 process (whose efficacy remained to be verified) allowed one to hope that the external aspects of unification would be the subject of negotiations that would take into account the interests of Germany's neighbors and international stability. The first weeks of 1990 were also marked by a return to fuller dialogue between Paris and Bonn. Faced with the acceleration of German unification, Kohl and Mitterrand shared a reaffirmation of the importance of the European framework. Of course, not all the difficulties were sorted out yet on that score, and not until March would there be a proper Franco-German initiative on the issue; but the elements of the new start that would culminate in the spring meetings of the Twelve in Dublin were already present by mid February. After stalling in December and January, the Franco-German dialectic was beginning to function anew.

The Crumbling of the German Democratic Republic

Decisive events took place in the course of January 1990. In the very first days of the year, with the two Germanys formally engaged in a scenario of gradual rapprochement, a reformed GDR still seemed a plausible hypothesis, at least as a transition. The Élysée noted that Kohl was speaking of a 'rapprochement that is taking form' through concrete measures, and the Quai d'Orsay observed that 'the new dimension of inter-German relations is daily becoming more concrete', prefiguring the 'contractual community' once imagined between the two Germanys.[1] But French decision makers poorly judged the real situation in East Germany. The GDR's future was in fact most uncertain, as Kohl clearly implied on 4 January during his meeting with Mitterrand at Latché, the president's house in southern France. To be sure, the chancellor still situated his policy in line with the Ten Point Plan: he wished to conclude a treaty on the contractual community between then and April, he confided to Mitterrand, so as to show the citizens of East Germany that things 'were moving', and he repeated that unification would take years because the two systems were so far apart. There would be a period of transition with confederative structures in place that would permit the two countries to cooperate while still belonging to two different blocs. Yet Kohl clarified for Mitterrand the actual state of the GDR, saying it was much worse than its leaders let on. If they did not quickly implement reforms to reestablish confidence, he stressed while wondering about their will or capacity to do so, the consequences would be catastrophic: the population's loss of patience meant an increased risk of a newly aggravated exodus to the West. In short, Kohl continued to proclaim his desire to advance step by step, but he hinted that everything would depend on the actual situation in the GDR, about which he did not conceal his pessimism. It seemed as if the chancellor wanted to prepare his interlocutor for a probable acceleration of events.[2]

Indeed this acceleration did take place shortly thereafter, due to the very rapid degradation of the situation in the East. Long overvalued in the West, the GDR's economy revealed itself as irremediably dilapidated; in addition, the regime proved incapable of taking the political situation in hand. Whole sections of the state ceased to function, and the lack of reforms by the Modrow government, combined with serious mistakes, among them the pseudo-dissolution of the Stasi, only increased the discontent. A vicious circle emerged in which the incapacity of the regime to implement indispensable reforms aggravated the situation still more, thereby reinforcing the attraction of unification to the population, just as Kohl had predicted during his visit to Dresden. At the same time the growing prospect of unity, which appeared to represent to East German citizens *the* solution to the country's problems (especially economic), made Modrow's reforming task still more difficult. This vicious circle was now reaching its breaking point: maintaining a viable GDR became increasingly chimerical when each day more than two thousand East Germans were choosing to go to the West and daily demonstrations proclaimed '*Deutschland einig Vaterland*'. By mid January, Kohl's entourage openly declared that the collapse of the GDR was possible. Horst Teltschik painted for Jean-Marie Guéhenno a very somber picture of the situation: the hemorrhage of East German citizens had worsened since Christmas, to the point that the state might 'crumble' before the first free elections, scheduled for 6 May, which would lead to a massive exodus with unpredictable consequences. The message was clear, as Guéhenno reported on 16 January: 'Everything leads the representatives of the Federal Chancellery to consider the evolution toward German unity as ineluctable and more rapid than initially foreseen.'[3]

The policy of gradual rapprochement between the two Germanys was simply no longer practicable: in effect, Kohl renounced it around mid January in favor of something that would quickly become a forced march toward unity.⁴ While Modrow was offering a treaty on 'cooperation and good neighborhood' between the FRG and the GDR, Kohl now refused to negotiate the content of the proposed 'contractual community' before elections were held in the East.⁵ Unwilling to compromise with a discredited regime, the chancellor wanted to talk only with a democratically elected East German government: this really was the end of the logic of Ostpolitik. At the same time Modrow realized how difficult it would be for him to hold on, and at the end of January East Berlin announced that the elections initially planned for May were advanced to 18 March. Bonn was pleased about this decision – which had been suggested by Kohl shortly before – for it hastened the necessary clarification of the GDR situation, even if this did not appear a priori to the advantage of his party. The CDU was historically less established in the East than was the SPD, which had possessed solid bastions there before the Nazi period. In any case, Kohl now thought that unification might be attained in one or two years, a scenario much more rapid than what he had been envisaging a few weeks previously.⁶

Mitterrand's Worries

While the December events, notably the summits of Malta, Brussels and Strasbourg, had by and large calmed things down after the Ten Point Plan, the January acceleration reawakened Paris' worries about the modalities and pace of the process. Mitterrand's principal contacts and meetings at the beginning of the year testify to this, starting with his meeting with Kohl in Latché. While his tone was grave, Mitterrand's language during the meeting remained in the pure line of what he had said for months: recognizing that unification was underway, he stressed that it was up to the Germans to decide, but he warned that they should take into account the international context, starting with the 'Russian problem'. This, he underlined, was inseparable from the 'German problem'. Warning of the risk of hardening in Moscow and even the fall of Gorbachev, whose fate, he insisted, now depended in large part on Kohl's policy, the French president now revealed on this score a pessimism clearly more marked than during their conversation in Strasbourg. He next emphasized the concerns of other European countries and the need to take into account the problem of timing of unification, and he enunciated his own main preoccupations: the future of European construction and military alliances, and the necessary confirmation of the German-Polish border. The French president's message once again was clear: unification was legitimate, but it had to avoid any forced march that might risk destabilizing the European and international environment.⁷

Kohl was nevertheless determined to act fast, further feeding Mitterrand's uneasiness, which was palpable during Margaret Thatcher's visit to the Élysée on 20 January. The conversation arose from shared disquiet, not over the prospect of German unity per se – which Mitterrand, unlike Thatcher, did not contest – but rather over the methods and consequences of the process. As often, the French president was keen to open up to the British prime minister. Deploring a certain brusqueness of the Germans, he summed up his discourse to them for Thatcher: 'You have the right to seek the self-determination of the German people, but I have the duty to take into account the preoccupations of the rest of Europe.' Bonn was 'pushing hard toward unification', he added, suggesting that the East German people, who were still only moderately attracted by the idea of unity, were being encouraged not only by the errors and discrediting of their own government, but also by pressure from the West Germans. Thatcher went farther, in a clearly anti-German register: mentioning 'German arrogance' several times, she denounced the FRG's economic stranglehold in Eastern Europe and was alarmed that a sudden questioning of established frontiers could risk fragmenting the Old Continent. She deplored the passivity of the great powers, which might seem to be giving a 'green light' to the Germans, and she wondered whether there were 'legitimate ways of slowing things down'. Yet the conversation made apparent a very substantial disagreement on the policy to follow: 'I will not say "no" to reunification; this would be stupid and unrealistic', Mitterrand declared, stressing that there was no effective way to put a brake on things and that 'nothing would be worse than raising objections, recalling treaties, but to no effect'. Mitterrand evoked the risk of arousing German 'anger' in reaction: 'We are somewhat with our backs to the wall', he concluded, although he accepted Thatcher's proposal to hold consultations between the two countries' ministers of foreign affairs and defense to examine possible options.[8]

Overall, while there was, to a degree, a shared uneasiness about Kohl's policy, the conversation pointed most of all to the fundamental difference in attitude between Mitterrand and Thatcher. By the same token, it confirmed the illusory character of the Franco-British entente that Thatcher had wished for in the face of German unity. She left disappointed: certain that Mitterrand shared her own prejudices without daring to express them, she had hoped, as she later wrote, to bring him to overcome 'his tendency to schizophrenia' and to envisage a strengthened cooperation so as 'to make use of all the means available to slow down reunification'. But she had to recognize that 'little or nothing in practical terms' came from the conversation. Persisting in her conviction that Mitterrand was not able to 'match private words with public deeds', she later conceded that he was nevertheless right 'that there was nothing we could do to halt German reunification'.[9] A few days later the French president would tell Italian President Francesco Cossiga that he had found the British prime minister 'very alarmed' and 'harder than other countries' with respect to Germany. The statements that he confided to his Italian counterpart confirmed Mitterrand's own attitude: unification in itself 'did not bother France', he said, provided that it did not arise from either a fait accompli or from unilateral action. The Germans, he added, should be asked to adopt a gradual and negotiated approach that would give German unity a 'less menacing' character, for the post-Yalta situation still carried a series of dangers: 'revival of nationalisms, national exasperation, the explosion of Europe'. Mitterrand particularly advanced his disquiet with regard to the USSR: if the Germans 'unify themselves without asking anybody's permission', he said, Gorbachev might not be able to resist but he was bound to 'get angry'; thus 'the Germans should be advised to be cautious'.[10] At the end of January 1990, it was more than ever Moscow's attitude that concerned Mitterrand's diplomacy.

Moscow's 'Yes'

But the Soviet attitude was fast changing in the early weeks of 1990, with Moscow in essence resigning itself to the inevitability of German unification.[11] In the first days of the year, the political counselor at the Moscow embassy, Michel Duclos, wrote a long analysis of Soviet policy on the German question. Duclos thought that 'the Soviets have no illusions' about the efficacy of any policy of attempted 'intimidation' that might be adopted by Moscow, and that they understood that 'respite' from any march toward unity 'would be at best provisional'. Still, he added, 'nobody knows what the Soviet leaders' dominant feelings might be'. Undoubtedly some of them were already convinced that 'reunification is only a matter of time', whereas others thought that on the contrary, it was not irreversible. Would Moscow adopt a 'blocking' strategy to prevent German unity, or would it prefer a 'bargaining' strategy to trade unification for a high price, such as an American withdrawal from Europe? Duclos concluded that the Soviets had a tactical interest in ostensibly proclaiming the first strategy in order to raise the stakes with a view to the second.[12]

Meanwhile, the Élysée was starting just then to concede that evidently the USSR could no longer prevent unification. Of course, as we have seen, Mitterrand continued to proclaim his worry about the consequences of German unity for Gorbachev and for *perestroika*, and this preoccupation would remain a constant until the end of the process. At Latché, though, he had found Kohl apparently confident about the possibility of reaching an agreement with the Soviet Number One: the chancellor had said that he hoped to meet him soon and was determined not to aggravate Soviet difficulties. Kohl told Mitterrand that he had some incentives to offer Gorbachev: significant economic aid to the USSR, he hoped, might facilitate things.[13] Kohl's optimistic statements (which were justified by what followed) could only encourage the reevaluation of the Soviet factor underway at the Élysée. 'Does Gorbachev have the means to prevent this reunification?' Mitterrand wondered during a Defense Council meeting on 16 January: '[T]hree months ago, the great Soviet power only had to frown and the whole world submitted, and now the Germans are beginning to think that the Russian threat no longer exists.'[14]

Contrary to what many people believed up to that time, the difficult situation in the USSR was now, paradoxically, playing in favor of German unity. That winter proved particularly harsh for Gorbachev as the considerable economic difficulties *perestroika* encountered were now compounded by serious distribution problems, and to the mix there was added a dramatic aggravation of the problem of nationalities. After violence in Georgia in December, the Baltic republics demanded independence at the start of the year, leading Gorbachev to make an urgent trip to Vilnius on 11 January. Although violence was avoided, the Baltic problem henceforth hampered his policy and even jeopardized the future of the Soviet Union. A few days later, nationalist agitation in Azerbaijan degenerated, leading to bloody repression in the streets of Baku. In this context, the German question, despite its international importance and potential to aggravate internal difficulties, was not a priority for Gorbachev. Soviet power was in fact divided on the subject, and the decision-making process only aggravated the contradictions of Moscow's policy, as illustrated by an important meeting held on 26 January in Gorbachev's office at the Central Committee. That day he gathered his main advisers to debate German policy, particularly the questions of which of the two Germanys, and which political forces within them, should now be privileged by Moscow as interlocutors. On the one hand, his top adviser for international policy, Anatoly Chernyaev, suggested a close link with the FRG and with Kohl, whom he thought a reliable partner, rather than with the GDR, over which Moscow had no longer any hold. On the other, Valentin Falin, head of the international department of the Central Committee and the principal 'Germanist' in the apparatus, supported by Alexander Yakovlev, advocated supporting the GDR and its leaders in order to resist West German pressure. Eduard Shevardnadze defended a position close to Chernyaev while recommending trying to moderate Bonn's policy in cooperation with London and Paris. Drawing conclusions from this debate, Gorbachev defined a line that borrowed from all sides concerning tactics but whose implicit strategic premise was to accept unity now as inevitable. The Soviet decision not to oppose German unity was thus taken outside the party's or state's formal bodies by an ad hoc committee that moreover debated the process rather than the deeper issue – a decision by default, in a way.[15]

Four days later, on 30 January, this green light was confirmed on the occasion of Modrow's visit to Moscow. The East German Number One, who was trying to regain control of events at home, arrived in Moscow with his own plan for German unification. While he now adopted the goal of unity that Kohl had proclaimed in November, he was also trying to postpone it and to preserve the existence of the GDR as long as possible. The Modrow Plan foresaw a gradual shift from the contractual community to a confederation and eventually to a federal state. In addition, the plan called for unification, to be accompanied by Germany's neutralization. During conversations between the two delegations, Gorbachev proved very favorable to the East German plan. Placing himself on the 'philosophical' terrain that he loved, he criticized Kohl's policy moderately, asserting that he would not accept a 'destabilization' of the GDR. Like Modrow, Gorbachev manifestly hoped that the elections of 18 March in the GDR, in which he was counting on an East German SPD success, would lead to a majority committed to a transition that was both gradual and in sync with European changes as a whole. Still, in endorsing the Modrow Plan, Gorbachev ipso facto accepted the prospect of unity: at the end of the Moscow meetings, the Soviet Number One recognized the existence of a dynamic that 'basically no one can any longer doubt'.[16]

In Bonn the news caused a sensation, while in East Berlin, where Modrow presented his plan the day after his return, it was recognized that the prospect of German unity was now quite real.[17] To be sure, the Soviets immediately tried to minimize the impact of the event, remaining steadfast in a schema that they fell back on repeatedly in the following months. In a letter sent to Mitterrand on 2 February, Gorbachev stressed the need to progress 'gently' and 'in stages'; mentioning the 'strong pressure' to which the GDR was subject, he warned against 'undue precipitation' and suggested maintaining 'close contacts between the USSR and France'.[18] Yet as the French embassy noted, the Soviets had in effect lifted 'objections that until shortly before had appeared to be insuperable'.[19] Obviously, Paris measured the impact of the event: the day after the Modrow-Gorbachev meeting, Dumas noted in the Council of Ministers that 'the Soviet Union, entrained by the movement taking place in Germany, admits the idea of reunification'. As for Mitterrand, the president thought that the latter was 'now a matter of fact' that should not be 'contradicted but supervised', and he held that 'the USSR no longer had either the psychological or political means to oppose anything at all'.[20]

It was henceforward clear that the acceleration of the process could not be stopped. Received on 1 February by Jean-Louis Bianco at the Élysée and by Dumas at the Quai d'Orsay, the mayor of West Berlin, Walter Momper, thought that, due to the crumbling of the East German regime and the rallying of all opposition parties to unification, 'everything is going to go quickly'. Momper thought it probable that shortly after the elections on 18 March there would be a referendum on German unity that would get a 'yes' vote of 80 to 90 percent.[21] At CAP, Guéhenno was convinced of the probability of a rapid unification: the 'decomposition of the GDR allows us to think that the question of unity will arise immediately after 18 March', whatever the results of the election.[22] Jacques Blot and Bertrand Dufourcq received confirmation from their German homologues. During a meeting in Bonn on 9 February, the German diplomats painted a somber picture of the GDR situation and announced the start of negotiations on unity between the two Germanys the day after the East German elections.[23] Aware of the real state of the GDR, Mitterrand's diplomacy at the start of February thus became fully convinced of the probability of a rapid scenario and of Kohl's determination to force the pace. The announcement on 6 February of his plan for economic and monetary unification of the two Germanys aimed to staunch the exodus to the West but was also clearly keyed to the 18 March elections, and it dissipated any remaining doubts. Unity would take place shortly, and it had every chance of taking the form of a takeover of the GDR by the FRG, not a merger. Still, there remained one uncertainty that concentrated everyone's preoccupations: would the process be framed internationally, or to the contrary, would it arise (as Mitterrand still feared) from a fait accompli? This was the question on which French diplomacy now focused.

The Path to Ottawa: Toward 2+4

The January acceleration acutely posed the question of external conditions for unification and hence the diplomatic framework within which it ought to take place. Faced with the growing dynamic of inter-German rapprochement, Moscow in mid January once again suggested the intervention of the four great powers. Arguing that they could not remain indifferent to negotiations between the two Germanys over the contractual community, Shevardnadze, in a message of 12 January addressed to his Western homologues, cited the need for four-party coordination that this time would bear not only on Berlin but on Germany as a whole. This Soviet demarche prompted consultations between the American, British and French ministers; Genscher, of course, wanted to be involved, and he expected the emergence of a 'common attitude'. The State Department, which had not forgotten Bonn's recriminations after the meeting of the four ambassadors in Berlin the month before, proposed rejecting the Soviet proposal while accepting an eventual discussion at a junior level on the Berlin issues alone.

As for Mitterrand, consulted by Dumas, he too judged that the Soviet demand was 'premature'.[24] Moscow's demarche was thus repulsed by the West, but the Soviets returned to the charge: in a note of 27 January sent to Washington, Moscow signaled the 'intensified activities' of the extreme right in the FRG as a reason for coordinated action against a 'neo-Fascist' danger induced by the rapprochement between the two German states. Surprised by an initiative that denoted the persistence of the old ways of thinking within the Muscovite bureaucracy, the Americans did not respond but did inform their partners.[25] The Soviets were also being insistent with the French; members of the Soviet embassy sounded out Mitterrand's advisers on the possibility of a four-party entente 'while there is still time' to demand 'much clearer commitments' from the Germans on the international conditions for unification.[26] But this had no tangible result.

Still, French leaders were hesitant. True, against the background of concern over German acceleration of the agenda Paris would have liked to be able to reactivate the four-party 'mechanism' in one way or another, as such a scheme would have the advantage of reassuring Moscow and sending a clear message to Bonn. Undoubtedly, deep down Mitterrand did not reject this recourse in the face of what he perceived as Kohl's dangerous hurry. When it was reported to him that the German press correspondents in Paris were wondering about the Élysée's reaction to the Soviet demands for four-party meetings and were observing that the quadripartite status was 'void', Mitterrand noted with some irritation that 'commitments made are only "void" after the agreement of those who made them'.[27] Yet the French president understood that intervention by the guarantor powers from which Bonn was excluded would be unacceptable to the Germans and would only dangerously alienate them. When Thatcher, during her visit to the Élysée on 20 January, defended the idea without any hesitation, Mitterrand asked: 'What purpose would be served by meetings of the Four' when the Germans have chosen a policy of 'fait accompli'? To 'maintain order in Berlin' and 'watch over the problem of reunification', retorted the British prime minister. 'That is judicial, legal', objected a skeptical Mitterrand, noting the risk of a very negative reaction from the Germans.

Mitterrand's diplomacy therefore stuck to a cautious position, all the more so in that Moscow shifted quickly on the German question after Modrow's visit. Still, the pure and simple exclusion of the guarantor powers from any role in the unification process, leaving Bonn total latitude, was not something that the French were ready to consider; such a formula would indeed have amounted to ratifying the 'fait accompli'. Of course, the German leaders saw no disadvantage in that; Bonn clearly would have preferred a process of '1 + 1'in which the FRG essentially managed unification with a GDR incapable of resisting West German pressure.[28] Even Genscher, it was remarked at the Quai d'Orsay, granted little place to the Four, as suggested by his important speech at Tutzing on 31 January, in which, trying to take the upper hand from Kohl, he presented his own vision of the process of unification, unsurprisingly stressing the CSCE and the pan-European process and downplaying the role of the Four occupying powers.[29]

But ignoring the rights and responsibilities of the guarantor powers was unacceptable to Moscow: had not Gorbachev restated that the two German states 'ought to take into account the interests of the four powers and of all European nations'?[30] He confirmed this in his letter to Mitterrand of 2 February, in which he thought it 'essential' that 'the maintenance of the rights and responsibilities of the Four Powers' be assured and suggested 'more active quadripartite consultations'. Nor did London envisage a process from which the Four would be purely and simply excluded, as confirmed by the firm statements of Thatcher at the Élysée on 20 January.[31] And while some in Washington, notably at the White House, were ready if necessary for the United States to renounce its prerogatives regarding Germany, the State Department thought it indispensable to implicate the Four in order to recognize a role for the USSR and to take into account the interests of the other European powers.[32] Therefore, somewhere between the impossible return to an exclusive role for the Four, recognized to be an anachronistic formula almost fifty years after the war's end, and the improbable renunciation by the great powers of all their prerogatives that ultimately guaranteed the international supervision of the unification process, it was necessary to find a compromise.

Inventing 2 + 4

Even if the formula was in the air in several capitals, it was American diplomacy that imposed it in early February. Rejecting both the idea of a simple negotiation between the two Germanys and the hypothesis of a solution defined by the Four, Dennis Ross and Robert Zoellick, two of the closest advisers to James Baker, proposed at the end of January a negotiation bringing together both the two German states and the Four Powers, a formula that thus was nicknamed '2 + 4'. Aware that the Germans could not accept the exercise unless it would lead unambiguously to unification, they imposed a triple condition: the two German states should participate wholly, the GDR representatives should emanate from a democratically elected government and, last but not least, the six participants must recognize that the end goal was indeed the realization of German unity. The secretary of state was immediately convinced that this formula was best able to respond to the Soviet problem: while giving Moscow a guarantee that its interests would be taken into account, it reduced the risk of a Soviet-caused stalemate and removed the equally dangerous prospect, feared by some in Washington, of direct negotiation between the USSR and Germany. The 2 + 4, in other words, corresponded best to American preoccupations and Western interests, and American diplomacy wanted to impose it. On 29 January, Baker, on the occasion of Douglas Hurd's passing through Washington, tried to convince the British of its advantages, which the Foreign Office (decidedly more amenable than Downing Street on the German question and now concerned to align itself with American diplomacy) seemed to accept without difficulty.[33]

French diplomacy was also quickly persuaded of the advantages of a solution that had been envisaged (among others) in Paris for some time. Blot, in his long analysis devoted to the German question, had proposed as early as October 1989 'that it is up to the two German states that are recognized as sovereign and to the four Allies to define the ways and means of an agreement'.[34] Mitterrand, in East Berlin on 22 December, had also mentioned such a possibility.[35] Therefore in the first weeks of 1990, French diplomacy was itself in search of a formula that preserved the prerogatives of the Four without alienating the Germans. In a note of 5 February, Hubert Védrine stressed that it was up to the Four Powers to grant the latter the formal recognition of their right to unification in exchange for a certain number of international commitments, which might be made 'in a conference of the Four and the two Germanys, hence six' or else blended 'into a larger ensemble', for example of thirty-five.[36] The next morning, Dumas, in Ireland for a meeting of the Twelve, met Baker, who was stopping at Shannon en route to Prague and Moscow. The American secretary of state had no trouble convincing his French homologue, though the latter suggested reversing the formula '2 + 4' into '4 + 2' (this apparently anodyne point would remain delicate, as we shall see) and indicated that he would propose the idea to President Mitterrand.[37] Returning to Paris, Dumas gathered a small group to reflect on the German question and submitted his conclusions to Mitterrand on 8 February through the intermediary of Védrine. The '4 + 2' formula, he thought, might permit 'drawing a line under the past' by ending the Four Powers' reserved rights but might also 'prepare the future' by tackling the consequences of German unity for European security. Still thinking it would be difficult to require it without provoking the anger of the Germans, and emphasizing that Baker shared the same approach, he reported that he had sounded out Genscher, who was ready 'to throw out a line' to the Four by mentioning such a formula in a forthcoming speech.[38]

Moscow was also rallying to Baker's proposal. The idea of six-party negotiations had been proposed during the meeting of 26 January by

Chernyaev and taken up by Gorbachev in his conclusions, but it encountered objections in MID. When Baker arrived in Moscow on 8 February, he realized the disarray of a Soviet diplomacy confronted with the acceleration of the process along with increasingly strong criticism from conservatives within the CPSU. Shevardnadze (visibly outstripped by events) defended the Modrow Plan and stuck to a rigid position that amounted to the Four alone meeting to discuss a peace treaty; when Baker tried to convince him of the better option of a six-way negotiation, the Soviet minister remained evasive. But Gorbachev, to the great surprise of the American, proved much more amenable on the German question in general and on the diplomatic process in particular. When Baker presented him with the 2 + 4 formula, Gorbachev admitted that the Soviet leaders had themselves envisaged six-party negotiations; of course he would prefer a 4 + 2 formula but he was not intransigent on this point. At the end of his visit, the secretary of state thought he had convinced the Kremlin to launch the diplomatic process comprising the Six and had contributed to preparing the ground for Kohl's visit two days later.[39]

It still remained to persuade the Germans, who more than ever were determined to deny the Four Powers the right to dispose on their own of Germany's fate.[40] Two days after the Tutzing speech, Baker wanted to profit from Genscher's visit to Washington on 2 February to try to convince him of the appropriateness of 2 + 4. Evidently concerned with the international environment, and no doubt also wishing to distinguish his approach from Kohl's, the German minister rallied to the formula personally, while insisting that the mechanism be indeed described as such, that is to say as 2 + 4: the German states being the primary ones concerned, Genscher insisted, there could be no question of calling it 4 + 2.[41] His personal consent, though, did not solve the question: not only did it not commit the German government as a whole, but it remained to specify the contours of the process. In fact, a week later on 9 February, the senior civil servants of the Quai d'Orsay, on the occasion of meetings with their homologues in the Auswärtiges Amt, realized how reserved German diplomacy remained. Indicating, as we have seen, that Bonn wanted to negotiate unification with Berlin immediately after the elections of 18 March, the German political director, Dieter Kastrup, presented a minimalist scheme in which the Four would effectively have only a token role: the FRG and the GDR would consult them 'formally' at the start of the process, then the agreement between the two states would be 'presented' to the CSCE, after which the Four would then simply surrender their rights and responsibilities.

For French diplomacy such a scenario was obviously inadequate, and it led to a 'very frank' discussion with the Germans. The representatives of the Quai, while rejecting the charge of 're-creating some tutelary power', placed themselves on legal ground, objecting that a number of problems, (starting with the recognition of the Polish border, which they put on top of the list), could not be resolved by the Germans alone. They cited the need for 'parallel' discussion with the Four that would lead to 'a series of arrangements forming a legal settlement' to which the powers would be party 'in order to put an end to the situation issuing from the War', and they stressed that it was up 'to German authorities to explain their opinion that this would be the normal way of proceeding'. While the idea of 2 + 4 made progress, its form as well as its substance was clearly not yet consensual. The political stakes were far from negligible, and they weighed in particular on Franco-German relations.[42]

From Moscow to Ottawa

This affair was nevertheless settled rapidly due to Gorbachev's definitive acceptance of the process. On 9 February, Kohl, accompanied by Genscher, arrived in Moscow. After having made him wait a long time – the chancellor had wanted to meet the Soviet Number One since the end of the year – Gorbachev had finally invited Kohl to come discuss the German question on the basis of the Modrow Plan, to which he had just given his own agreement.[43] Yet by the time of Kohl's arrival, the plan had already been overtaken by events, and the visit in effect would lead to a far more significant result. In the meantime, Washington had made the decisive choice of categorical support for the chancellor's policy. The Americans now believed that rapid unification, for which the essential condition, in the end, was maintaining Germany in NATO, would be the scenario most compatible with U.S. and Western interests, and they had decided to impose it in conjunction with the Germans.

The day after Baker's visit to Moscow, which preceded Kohl's by forty-eight hours, the White House wanted to send Kohl a message of full support, intended for him to receive before his conversations with the Soviet leaders. In a letter to Kohl on 9 February, Bush recognized that events were advancing faster than foreseen, but this just meant that 'our common goal for all these years of German unity will be realized sooner than we had hoped'. Recalling his wish to see Germany remain firmly within the Western alliance, he promised to oppose any attempt by Moscow to use the four-party mechanism to impose an outcome that suited it on the German negotiations.[44] This strong message was backed up by a letter from Baker, in which he divulged to the chancellor the substance of his conversations in Moscow, noting that Gorbachev was not 'locked-in' even if he had evident reservations about German unification, and that he might accept a 'sensible' approach, including in particular a 2 + 4 mechanism to deal with the international context. Thus Kohl and Genscher arrived in Moscow with important advantages: they were assured of Washington's support and informed about the state of mind of the Soviets.[45]

More than Modrow's visit barely ten days previously – during which the Soviets had accepted unification as a still-distant prospect – Kohl's appearance in Moscow marked a key moment in the resolution of the German question. Gorbachev proved ready now to confront German unity without any detour: 'I think there is no divergence in viewpoint between the Soviet Union, the FRG, and the GDR over unity', nor over the rights of Germans 'to aspire to it and decide on evolutions to come', Gorbachev solemnly declared during his tête-à-tête with Kohl on 10 February. About international conditions, the Soviet Number One also proved very open: the German people's choice should be made 'in the context of realities', he said, mentioning the German-Polish border and the question of alliances, without (as we shall see) making neutrality an absolute condition of Soviet consent. For the rest, while Kohl reiterated his categorical refusal of a conference among the Four alone, Gorbachev favorably mentioned Baker's proposal of a 2 + 4 conference and added, for the benefit of the German: 'Nothing [will take place] without you.'[46] The result of the Moscow conversations was sensational. Teltschik summed it up: 'It's the breakthrough! Gorbachev agrees to German unification' and does so without 'demanding a price' and 'without any threat' – 'What a meeting!'[47]

No doubt convinced of the probable collapse of the GDR, of which the chancellor painted a catastrophic picture, Gorbachev was thus led to give his consent to rapid unification.[48] This was the analysis by the French embassy in Moscow of this 'considerable' event, which signified that the USSR now considered unification to be 'ineluctable': faced with the deliquescence of the GDR and also with Bonn and Washington's 'vigorous offensive,' Gorbachev could only choose 'a realistic approach' and abandon for good the 'stalemating' strategy in favor of 'bargaining'.[49] The French embassy in Bonn echoed the analysis of the Auswärtiges Amt: Gorbachev had reacted pragmatically to the bleak description of the GDR and the risk of chaos portrayed by Kohl, who took his information from Modrow himself, whom he had met the previous week in Davos. Given that situation, Gorbachev recognized that it was now up to the Germans to decide the conditions and timetable of the process.[50] At the Élysée, the Moscow 'breakthrough' confirmed, more than Modrow's visit eight days before, that nothing could now stop rapid unification; in any case, as Mitterrand concluded to Andreotti two days later, 'the German problem no longer depends on Soviet good or ill will'. Implicitly, the French president recognized that his initial postulate was mistaken: far from Gorbachev's domestic difficulties leading him to resist unification, it was the opposite case that prevailed; the 'crumbling' of the Soviet state was benefiting the Germans.[51] Dumas's speech the next day to the Council of Ministers summed up the prevailing sentiment in Paris: 'Kohl plays skillfully on two registers. He paints the situation in the GDR in dramatic terms to his Western interlocutors. On the other hand, he portrays with optimism his relations with Gorbachev and the position taken by the USSR over reunification. Kohl wants to be the statesman who will have made German unity.'[52]

In these conditions, the question of the international framework was becoming an absolute priority. The day after the Moscow meetings, American diplomacy was determined to take advantage of the moment to impose the 2 + 4 formula: President Bush, 'applauding' the new flexibility of Soviet diplomacy, declared that the idea of 2 + 4 was 'making progress'.[53] An occasion quickly presented itself: on 12 and 13 February, the ministers of foreign affairs of the thirty-five countries of the CSCE gathered in Ottawa to discuss the 'Open Sky' initiative Bush planned to launch that spring to improve the verification of disarmament and to promote confidence and security-building measures. In fact the meeting turned out to be dominated by the German question and its international aspects. On the margins of the official meetings, Baker intensified his encounters with his homologues to arrive at an agreement formalizing the 2 + 4.[54] Despite last-minute uncertainty, which Kohl dissipated by confirming his agreement personally by telephone with Bush, the Germans' consent to the formula was given in Ottawa by Genscher.[55] That of the Soviets was confirmed by Shevardnadze, even if he appeared much more resigned to the inevitable acceleration of unification than truly enthusiastic about Baker's formula.[56] Paris and London having already agreed (as seen above), the only false note in Ottawa was the annoyance of European countries like Italy and the Netherlands, which, having been excluded from the process and learning of the agreement concluded among the Six, noisily deplored having been kept out.[57] On 13 February, the Six announced that they 'agreed that the foreign ministers of the FRG and the GDR would meet' those of France, the United Kingdom, the Soviet Union and the United States so as 'to discuss external aspects of the establishment of German unity, including the issues of security of the neighboring states', with 'preliminary discussions at the official level' to commence 'shortly'.[58] The 2 + 4 negotiations were born.

Paris was obviously satisfied. While he did not yet know of the Ottawa results, Mitterrand had indeed deplored to Andreotti that 'the German problem is escaping any cooperation' and for the moment was taking place as 'a fait accompli'.[59] The Ottawa agreement thus brought some comfort: it represented the assurance that a minimum of cooperation would take place on external aspects of the process and that the prerogatives of the Four Powers would not be ignored, which had not been certain until then.⁶⁰ Yet the result was not reached without difficulty: it had been necessary to force Kohl's hand, French leaders realized, now fearing that the compromise would remain only a hollow formula: one must 'very rapidly use the 2 + 4 formula', Dumas had said to Shevardnadze in Ottawa.⁶¹ Evoking two days later with his British colleague the 'real' risk of the Germans' 'playing down' the agreement since, as he stressed, they had only accepted the formula under joint pressure from the three Western powers, he stated: 'The Germans say 2 + 4 , I say 4 + 2', adding that if a 'tool' existed, it had now 'to be used'.⁶² In short, for Mitterrand's diplomacy the Ottawa result represented a point of departure rather than an end result. Still, while consecrating the presence of unification on the diplomatic agenda, the accord removed the previous weeks' uncertainty about a process imposed without cooperation. The time had come for a concrete discussion of the international conditions and foremost – in light of resumed dialogue between Paris and Bonn – the European conditions of unification.

From Latché to Paris: Resumption of the Franco-German Dialogue

Since the fall of the Wall and especially the Ten Point Plan, Franco-German relations, as we have seen, had been affected by the rapid sequence of events. The legitimacy of unification was by no means contested in Paris during the fall and winter, but the stress on the international conditions (the German-Polish border, European construction), as well as French trips to Kiev and then the GDR, had been *perceived* in the FRG as the expression of reservations, if not of a desire to hinder its movement. Inversely, the acceleration of events had led the French to wonder about the solidity of Bonn's European and international commitments. Starting in December 1989, the French and Germans were aware of the failings in their dialogue and of the risk of misunderstandings accumulating, especially since the media conveyed the impression of reciprocal sulking, with the leaders of the two countries said to have avoided each other several times. To counter this impression a meeting in Latché was scheduled for 4 January, which Kohl had been already looking forward to since Strasbourg on 9 December.⁶³ The chancellor had confided to Bush in early December that he was convinced that Mitterrand understood that it was not in France's interests to oppose unification, but he thought, as he would later say, that since the fall of the Wall the French president had been divided between sympathy for 'the revolutionary dimension' of events in the GDR and fear of the consequences of unification. In short, Kohl deplored that his good personal relations with Mitterrand were being 'put to the test', especially since the latter's visit to the GDR.[64] Without exaggerating the difficulties, people in Bonn were therefore aware of the importance of the Latché meeting, and Kohl intended to 'let no irritation appear' there and to demonstrate only 'mutual understanding and friendship'.[65]

At Strasbourg the conversation had mostly focused on the USSR and changes in the East. The meeting in Latché therefore was in effect for Kohl and Mitterrand the first occasion since the November Bonn summit (when the Wall was still up and they had scarcely got beyond the stage of generalities) to tackle the German question, and this time go to the heart of the matter.[66] In Latché, as has been said, the chancellor wanted manifestly to proclaim his determination to achieve unity while convincing his interlocutor of his sense of international responsibility. Kohl described the real situation of the GDR without hedging, and he did not hide his conviction that the East Germans aspired to unity. He admitted having a hard time understanding the doubts arising outside Germany: one might understand 'the fears of others', he granted, but 'a world was not constructed' on the basis of fears. Kohl conceded that the Germans must be attentive to their international environment: Adenauer's phrase that 'German problems cannot be resolved unless under a European roof' remained valid. It was thus essential to show that Germany did not advance alone and to preserve the Franco-German partnership so as to maintain the European dynamic; thus the chancellor proposed adopting a 'calendar' to tackle these points with Mitterrand. The latter replied in an ostensibly detached tone. At Latché his evident goal was to dissipate the misunderstandings about his attitude toward German unity properly speaking without minimizing his concerns over the process from an international viewpoint: 'Whether this pleases me or not, unification is for me a historical reality', which 'it would be unjust and stupid to oppose'; 'if I were German', he added, 'I would be for a unification as rapid as possible' – but, he granted, 'being French, I do not have the same passion for it'. And the president reminded the chancellor of the international stakes: the preservation of the 'Gorbachev experiment', the question of military alliances and, of course, the problem of the German-Polish border.

Rather cold at the start, the atmosphere warmed up during the meeting. After two months of intermittent communication, the two men were once again really speaking to each other. Concerning the 'atmospherics', Mitterrand complained of the treatment given him by the German newspapers; meanwhile, Kohl was concerned to avoid a divorce between the respective public opinions, hence he intended to give a speech in Paris two weeks later on Germany and Europe and suggested that Mitterrand agree to an interview on German television 'to manifest his sympathy' toward 'the march toward unity'. Concerning substance, Kohl and Mitterrand basically concurred with each other on the future of European construction, which they each saw as *the* only possible response to the challenge of unification. Yet they could hardly conceal that their current priorities were different: national for Germany, European and international for France. The two danced around the issue: while Mitterrand complained of the German press, Kohl subtly suggested a clarification of the French discourse.[67]

In short, the president and the chancellor were not yet really in tune with each other; hence a certain dissonance characterized the outcome of the Latché meeting. The German side described it as a 'key meeting' for Franco-German cooperation and the personal relation between Mitterrand and Kohl, which the latter was determined to consolidate. In the following days, this good impression was confirmed in Bonn, where, by contrast, governing circles were increasingly irritated by the negative attitude of Thatcher.[68] On the French side, the satisfaction was less pronounced. The meeting in Latché had not dissipated all the reservations about Kohl's policy, the haste of which was still a matter of concern for Mitterrand. Three days after Kohl's speech in Paris, the French president confided to Thatcher: 'I sent a kind word to Kohl ... but I did not send a representative to the lecture and I did not receive him. His statements could not involve me.'[69] As for the chancellor's suggestion of a statement from the president or interview aimed at German opinion, although reiterated by the Élysée spokesman a few days later it remained for the moment with no follow-up, so the question of the French 'discourse' or a grand speech from Mitterrand to the Germans remained open.[70] The acceleration of January clearly kept Mitterrand at some distance from Kohl and especially from his policy.

German Acceleration and European Imperatives

It was the 'breakthrough' obtained by the chancellor in Moscow in early February that changed the situation and led the Élysée in a few weeks to a much more constructive attitude, an evolution in which the European factor was determining. The now ineluctable character of unification provoked a sudden awareness in Paris of the challenges that this situation created for the Franco-German relation and consequently for European construction. Élisabeth Guigou played an essential role here at a time when Mitterrand was clearly still uncomfortable with Kohl's rapid unification policy. In a note of 2 February written for a visit to the Élysée by Jacques Delors, she began by sounding an alarm: 'On 3 November you accepted the idea of German unity', she wrote to Mitterrand, 'yet some declarations by French political leaders have completely blurred your message of understanding and are on the way to hurting the capital of trust acquired over the years'. She emphasized, however, that 'all those who want the Community to be strengthened subscribe from the start to your position' favorable to German unity.[71] Therefore, she wrote a few days later, '[i]f the Community is perceived by the Germans as hostile to their unification, we will lose along the whole line for we will not prevent reunification and we will have moreover ruined the Community future'. On the contrary, she continued, if the Community proves 'conducive to the rapprochement of the two Germanys, we will not prevent Germany becoming predominant (it already is) but at least we will have avoided it acting by itself in a totally autonomous manner'.[72] In short, she said, the choice was not between a unified Germany and a divided Germany, but between a united Germany embedded within the EEC or one entirely free in its movements. Guigou thereby formulated, at a key moment, the decisive argument that would bring Mitterrand in a few weeks to overcome his reserve about Bonn's policy and to refine along with Kohl the 'European response' to the challenge of German unity. Guigou's argument, it must be stressed, went in the direction of public opinion. In contrast to certain politicians and certain media, the French people were indeed very supportive of German unification if it took place in the context of the pursuit of European construction, and the president's entourage was perfectly well aware of this popular sentiment.[73]

The role of Delors, whose relations with the Chancellery were close, was also significant. Convinced of the inevitable nature of unification and the need to frame it within a strengthened European Community, the president of the European Commission mentioned on 17 January in Strasbourg the possibility of GDR membership in the EEC. This idea, favorably received in Bonn, was initially viewed with much less enthusiasm in the rest of the Community, where it was seen as a new German fait accompli.[74] Mitterrand told Thatcher (who considered it unacceptable) on 20 January that he thought Delors' declaration 'very imprudent', and Guigou, on the day of Delors's visit to the Élysée on 2 February, herself criticized the statement.[75] Still, the commission chairman's blunder served as a catalyst for Élysée thinking. Barely six days later, Guigou indeed sketched a line of reasoning that proved decisive in the evolution of the French position: if the GDR survived as a state, she wrote, the FRG would do everything possible to have it enter the Community and the consequences would be momentous. The GDR would have its own vote in the European Council, which it would add to that of the FRG, and it would receive a large share of structural funds. It might remain a member of the Warsaw Pact, which would be a problem for political Europe, and finally, the fact that it would be very difficult to not accept Austria into the Community as well meant there would eventually be three German states in the EC. The conclusion was evident: all in all, Guigou said, 'it was better [for France and Europe] for German unification to take place through absorption of the GDR by the FRG'.[76] The acceleration of events thus led in a few days to a significant change in Élysée thinking: not only was the formerly contested idea of an enlargement of the Community to East Germany now accepted, but, when everything was taken into account, a procedure of rapid and expeditious unification, meaning an integration of the GDR into the FRG – the formula favored by Kohl from the start – seemed the least bad option.[77] Clearly, the European stakes strongly influenced the French position on the German question: reservations about Kohl's 'haste' started to give way to constructive thinking about the European consequences of a unification judged now to be inevitable in a short time.

The march of German events, inversely, accelerated European thinking, bringing the Élysée to envisage seriously a parallel speeding up of Community construction. Delors, here again, was part of this change. He suggested in his speech in Strasbourg that the EMU should be accompanied by an institutional strengthening, which he envisaged on the model of a European 'federation' in which the Commission would play the role of executive, in line with German conceptions. He thus in effect relaunched the debate on political Europe. Commenting on this position for Mitterrand on 2 February, Guigou, without contesting the need for 'overall institutional revisions', took her distance from Delors's federalist conception by stressing the need to preserve the primacy of the European Council, which she thought ought to be recognized as the 'supreme organ' of the Community.[78] But some days later, she adopted the idea of a European relaunching: recognizing its urgency in order to 'frame the German situation', she suggested to Mitterrand 'a rapid initiative' toward political union. She wrote: 'The Community has an interest in inventing very quickly an institutional armature that would make the German situation banal' and would 'assure that Germany determines its orientations within the framework of the Community and not autonomously'. She put forward the decisive argument: 'Better for the European Union to be negotiated with a Germany still provisionally divided into two states and needing the Community, rather than with a reunified Germany that will no longer have need of anybody.' Her proposal was for a special European Council to meet as soon as possible and ask the ministers of foreign affairs for proposals to transform the Community into a political union, an initiative that ought to be prepared between Paris and Bonn. The intergovernmental conference on the EMU would then receive the mandate of reforming the Community institutions and coming up with an initiative aiming to constitute a European Union whose institutions would cap those of the Community.

If Guigou thus came back to a German idea that had caused misunderstandings before Strasbourg (i.e. coupling the march toward the EMU with that toward political union), she also tried to reposition such an initiative on the terrain of French conceptions of political Europe. These conceptions were much more intergovernmental than the German ones: while improving the 'democratic legitimacy of the system' (which for her did not mean just strengthening the Parliament), such an initiative ought, she stressed, to be primarily expressed through a strengthening of the role of the European Council, 'the only institution to have real legitimacy, to be visible to public opinion, to be able to realize unity between Community policy and foreign policy, to arbitrate the conflicts between Community institutions and define a strategy.'[79] Here was sketched in large part the program that would lead two years later to Maastricht.

Waiting for the Relaunching

These reflections echoed those of Kohl's entourage, which, against the background of the accelerated unification process, was perfectly aware of the importance of giving European partners proof of the continued commitment of the Federal Republic to Community construction. There was now more regular contact between the Élysée and the Chancellery.[80] Mitterrand and Kohl had arranged a fresh meeting for 15 February at the Élysée, and Guigou and Joachim Bitterlich – the chancellor's aide, very pro-European and with expert knowledge of France – met two days beforehand to prepare the meeting. The German's message was clear: the unification process would speed up after the elections of 18 March, and unity undoubtedly would be decided before the end of the year, which made 'the framing of Germany in the European process' necessary. While deploring the existence of 'many misunderstandings' and 'a reciprocal insufficiency of information', Bitterlich thought it 'indispensable to reflect on the common initiatives' for which Kohl was ready in several domains, whether on the European Community, security issues, pan-European structures or bilateral relations (Kohl's collaborator put back on the table the old idea of a Franco-German *Ostpolitik*). An initiative in the Community domain, he said, might be prepared together by the Élysée, the Chancellery, and the two foreign affairs ministers; it should focus not only on the EMU calendar but ought to 'give without delay the signal that the monetary union and the political union would be realized at the same time, i.e. by the end of 1992' (this, we recall, had been a key German request in the run up to Strasbourg).[81] Encouraged by her exchanges with Bitterlich, Guigou upped the ante in a new memo for Mitterrand the same day. German unification, she wrote, would no doubt accelerate after the elections of the 18 March in the GDR and perhaps culminate before those the FRG planned to hold in December. Now, Kohl was saying he wanted a Franco-German and European relaunch that would result in 'much more intense' bilateral relations and in 'the political union of Europe'. 'Why not take him at his word?' she asked. Guigou responded in advance to Mitterrand's objections: certainly Kohl had just proposed an economic and monetary union between the GDR and the FRG that testified once again to his desire to accelerate the march toward German unity at whatever cost, but this was in no way in contradiction with the EMU project adopted by the Twelve. True, Bonn still advanced an increased role for Parliament in a reform of European institutions, but they ought to be able to finally agree on a 'balanced' scheme in which the council, in which it was not certain that Bonn would demand an increase in voting weight in favor of a unified Germany, would play the key role.[82] At a decisive moment for German unification and for Franco-German relations, Guigou was virtually forcing the hand of Mitterrand to bring him to abandon his reservations about Kohl's speeded-up policy of unification and to envisage a broad reactivation of the Paris-Bonn relationship and of European construction.

Yet the situation was not quite ripe. The French and the Germans did not yet see eye to eye. To be sure, Mitterrand was convinced of the need to intensify European construction ('a local train', he said to Andreotti on 13 February), in response to German unification ('an express train'). But for the time being he stuck to his priority, the EMU (a priority that, as we know, was not shared by Bonn), even suggesting to Andreotti that he wanted to advance its calendar by bringing forward the date of the IGC. (This was an idea in the air in some capitals, as was Delors's proposal on 13 February for a special European summit that would meet as soon as possible after the GDR elections to examine the consequences of unification on the Community).[83] In short, Mitterrand still hesitated, in mid February 1990, to engage in the Franco-German and European relaunch as suggested by Bonn. Two sorts of obstacles explain the French president's attitude. First, his prior reservations about Kohl's policy were not entirely dissipated. Mitterrand thought that the project for the economic and monetary union between East and West Germany was, if not in contradiction with the EMU of the Twelve, at least consequential for the latter, so it should not be pushed without consultation, as Kohl was doing.[84] Second, his European priorities still did not match Kohl's. Mitterrand in mid February remained manifestly reticent about the idea of engaging in discussions right away on the institutional dimension, for he was apprehensive about Bonn trying to impose its own conceptions of the European Union, which were different from his own. What happened in Strasbourg was repeated: the French desire to accelerate the EMU process was answered by the German desire to tackle the institutional dimension, which resulted in an absence of any movement on either front for the time being.

The meeting between Kohl and Mitterrand at the Élysée on 15 February confirmed this. True, the two men fell over themselves to show European goodwill. Mitterrand, adopting Guigou's reasoning, confirmed his preference for an 'enlarged' Germany in the EEC rather than a 'thirteenth state'. He insisted that the impression be avoided that the EEC was marking time over German unification. There must be an intensification of European construction, he said, which meant implementing the EMU but also, he conceded, discussion of the prospect of political union. Kohl subscribed to the French president's statements: for him there was no alternative to cooperation between the two countries, and he intended to preserve the 'treasure' of thirty years of friendship between France and Germany by moving along with Mitterrand on this 'difficult path', notably by implementing what had been decided in Strasbourg, starting with the EMU. But while the two men agreed to approve the Delors proposal (taken up the following day by the Irish presidency of the EC) of an informal summit in Dublin in April to discuss the consequences of German unity, Mitterrand failed to convince Kohl, who pleaded his electoral constraints, to bring forward, if only symbolically, the date of the IGC on economic and monetary union.[85]

The dinner on 15 February nevertheless confirmed the reestablishment of a real dialogue that in Latché had still left something to be desired. Kohl found Mitterrand 'much more open and relaxed than a few weeks previously' and would later recall a 'very serious conversation'.[86] While Mitterrand had worried a month earlier about the former's haste, he now proved more understanding about an acceleration that he knew was irrepressible even if, he again stressed, he tackled the question not 'as a German patriot but as a French patriot'. 'The prospect of unification poses no problem for me as such', he repeated: 'I am not worried. It is a fact and has to be dealt with. I am not displeased by it.' Of course, he insisted, while unity per se was the problem of the Germans, its international consequences interested France. But most importantly Mitterrand and Kohl had renewed their previous relationship: not only had they recommenced speaking to each other, but they were listening to each other. If the Franco-German and European relaunch was still only in outline, the 'couple' was functioning once again.

Awaiting the 2 + 4

The relaunching of the European Community nevertheless remained in bare outline in mid February because international and security problems took precedence among the preoccupations of the capitals, including Paris.

Shortly after Modrow's visit to Moscow on 30 January, the Quai d'Orsay noted that the debate over the German question no longer concerned the principle of unification, but its mode.[87] With the future 2 + 4 being actively discussed, the international ramifications of German unity now lay at the heart of the process. At the Élysée, reflection on these aspects intensified in the first days of February; it was led by Védrine in parallel with Guigou's own reflection on the European aspects. The moment had come, Védrine wrote, to be specific about what Paris thought might be done to 'guarantee' the 'durably peaceful' nature of unification. The response was unsurprising, and would orient French policy in the coming months: apart from seeking new confirmation of German commitment to the Community process (which, in a sense, could in itself be considered a security guarantee), Védrine mentioned the clear recognition of the Oder-Neisse line, confirmation of the Federal Republic's renunciation of nuclear arms and, finally, the question of alliances, for which it was necessary to find 'a solution that does not dislocate the Atlantic Alliance nor provoke the USSR'.[88]

Three days later, he submitted to Mitterrand the conclusions of the working group gathered around Dumas to examine the international stakes of unification. They confirmed his personal analysis: the principal questions raised by German unity beyond its specifically European consequences concerned recognition of borders, the problem of alliances and the status of the FRG with respect to nuclear weapons. Those directing French diplomacy did not expect easy answers to any of these questions. Apart from the complexity of the problems at hand, they thought, one could anticipate an evasive attitude on Bonn's part, at least until the East German elections on 18 March. With the compromise on 2 + 4 still in limbo at the start of February, Mitterrand's main advisers continued to suspect the Germans of privileging a fait accompli policy. Thus the French thought it 'urgent' to pose 'precise questions' to Bonn. 'This will provoke a rustle in Franco-German relations, but it is inevitable anyway and there would be more disadvantages to doing nothing from here to 18 March', Dumas stressed, recommending making contact at the top level (president to chancellor) or else between the ministers of foreign affairs, so as to clarify things rapidly.[89]

The occasion for such an explanation came up quickly: the conversation of 15 February at the Élysée was indeed essentially devoted, apart from the European dossier, to the international and security aspects of German unification. The result meanwhile attained in Ottawa facilitated a discussion that the French had feared not being able to nail down with the Germans, who had previously seemed unwilling to be constrained. Far from avoiding troublesome subjects, the two men now had a long exchange expressing their shared concern to tackle problems in depth. Mitterrand enumerated to Kohl the principal international problems raised in his eyes by unification: the two men thus reviewed the question of Germany's status with respect to nuclear weapons, its position with regard to alliances and of course the problem of recognizing the Oder-Neisse border. The discussion made apparent the degree of sensitivity of these questions from the standpoint of Franco-German relations, prefiguring the debates of the coming weeks. The nuclear question scarcely seemed to pose a problem, and the chancellor confirmed to Mitterrand, who did not need to insist on this point, that united Germany would have the same obligations as the FRG and would thus renounce ABC weapons. The question of alliances appeared complex but manageable: 'we can find a solution,' Kohl assured Mitterrand when the latter said that he wanted to avoid destabilizing Gorbachev by seeming to threaten Soviet security. The Oder-Neisse border was unsurprisingly the most difficult subject, as shown by the chancellor's anger when the president insisted once more on the necessity of a clear recognition of it as a prior condition to unification.[90]

The non-nuclear status of Germany, its situation with respect to NATO, recognition of borders: as the international 'great bargaining' over Germany was about to begin following the adoption of the Ottawa mandate, the Élysée conversation did not resolve all these difficulties, but it had the merit of identifying them. Beyond the European problematic that was the clear priority, these same questions would be found, in this increasing order of priority, at the forefront of French preoccupations in the coming months.

Germany and the Alliance

Although it was not the prime French preoccupation, the situation of a unified Germany with respect to military alliances – in other words, NATO, since the Warsaw Pact was doomed – appeared from the start as the central question of the future international negotiation, since it conditioned both the status of the country and the future of European security. It had already been mentioned in the autumn, and Washington had early on posed the principle of maintaining a united Germany within NATO, but since then the issue had remained essentially theoretical. With unification now on the diplomatic agenda, it was now assuming a much more concrete dimension: hence the birth of a great debate that lasted until the start of the summer.[91] At the end of January, as the Bush administration, which was increasingly oriented to forthrightly supporting Kohl's policy, reflected on what would become the 2 + 4 process, the membership of a united Germany in NATO became the principal objective of American diplomacy, for it conditioned both the durability of the Atlantic defense system and the solidity of the Western anchoring of the future Germany.[92]

Yet acceptance by the Soviet Union of such a scheme seemed very improbable: if German unification was now judged inevitable in Moscow, throwing East Germany into the Western bloc appeared unacceptable for obvious political and strategic reasons. The Soviet refusal of a united Germany in NATO, it is true, was not yet expressed very vigorously at this stage: before Moscow gave its green light to German unity during Modrow's visit, the question of alliances was simply not in the foreground.[93] Yet the Modrow Plan, endorsed by Gorbachev, included the neutrality of united Germany, which made Védrine write the next day that 'circles close to NATO, who thought that the USSR would have such fear of a reunified and emancipated Germany that the Soviets would prefer to see it unified in NATO ... were mistaken'.[94] In short, it was no foregone conclusion that a solution to this problem might be found easily, given that the starting positions were so far apart.

True, the terms of a possible eventual compromise could be discerned early on. In his speech at Tutzing on 31 January, Genscher launched the idea that would finally prevail. The membership of united Germany in the alliance, he suggested, might go hand in hand with particular clauses governing the actual territory of the future ex-GDR: the speech tried to reassure the USSR that unification did not mean pure and simple displacement of the NATO defense system toward the East. Yet the concrete significance of such an arrangement, which would prove to be a key to the accord between Germany and the Soviets in July, was the subject over the following days of a sustained debate in Bonn and Washington alike. Genscher had remained evasive about the precise implications of such a formula: to what extent would the ex-GDR territory remain effectively covered by the defense guarantee of the Atlantic Alliance? What would be its concrete situation in relation to NATO's military organization? Would these arrangements be permanent or limited to the transition period during which Soviet forces might remain on ex-GDR territory before withdrawing? The stakes of this debate were important: the future security status of Germany and how solid its anchoring in the West would be, relations with the USSR and the question of what concessions could be envisaged to reassure Moscow, and of course, the future of the Atlantic Alliance and its long-term political and military viability all hung in the balance.[95] Thus while in mid winter the general terms of a possible solution appeared clearly – membership of united Germany in NATO with a particular status for former East German territory – the actual resolution of the problem was still far away.

True, Gorbachev did not adopt an intransigent position when confronted by Kohl on 10 February in Moscow, where the German chancellor categorically rejected the idea of German neutrality. On the other hand

Kohl assured Gorbachev that NATO territory would not be extended to the East.[96] The meeting, therefore, illustrated once more the openness personally shown by the Soviet Number One. Yet traditional Soviet diplomacy very quickly took the upper hand. According to the versions that MID diplomats gave of the Gorbachev-Kohl conversations intended for Paris as well as other Western capitals – squelching the optimism proclaimed in Bonn after Kohl's return – Soviet leaders had in effect 'categorically rejected' the idea of a united Germany remaining in the alliance, even with a specific arrangement for the former GDR; that hard line would remain unchanged in the coming months.[97] In addition, after Kohl's visit to Moscow, the American administration also hardened its position. Washington rapidly distanced itself from the Genscher formula: if the Americans were to accept the idea of 'special military status' for East German territory, this could not mean either neutralization or demilitarization of the Eastern part of united Germany; the latter, therefore, had to remain wholly in not only the alliance but also the integrated organization.[98] At the same time, the question was also becoming a major political stake in Bonn, where the coalition was divided: in publicly taking a stand against the Tutzing formula, which he judged too soft on Moscow, the CDU Minister of Defense, Gerhard Stoltenberg, unleashed a crisis with Genscher that was only settled on 19 February by arbitration imposed by Kohl in the form of a declaration signed by both ministers that was more favorable to Genscher.[99] This incident only increased Washington' concern. German public opinion on these subjects was volatile; moreover, on 19 February the SPD had signed a joint declaration with the East German SPD that stated that united Germany should not belong either to the Atlantic Alliance or to the Warsaw Pact. As a result, the Americans worried that the Bonn leaders might be in no hurry to defend a firm position faced with the Soviets, especially if Moscow might give the Germans a choice between NATO and unity, as many feared.[100]

In this context, as Kohl was getting ready to visit Camp David on 24 and 25 February, the Americans decided to make things clear with Bonn over the question of the German membership of the Atlantic Alliance. For the White House, the moment had come to clarify things: the Americans must now obtain a firm commitment from the chancellor on maintaining united Germany in NATO, in exchange for which Washington would support the unification process without any restriction. It was a decisive rendezvous: after the Ottawa accord and as the effective start of 2 + 4 negotiations approached, the Camp David meeting, in American eyes, was to definitively seal the understanding between Germany and the United States over the terms of German unification. At the end of the conversations, the goal was reached: while the Americans until then had dreaded a certain floating on the part of the Germans over the Atlantic question, Bush and Kohl agreed on the principle of maintaining all of united Germany in the alliance and in the integrated organization of NATO and on not challenging the Allied military presence on the territory of the current FRG, even if a 'special military status' (the formula was still quite vague) might be defined for the territory of the ex-GDR so as to appease Soviet fears.[101] Thus confirmed, the close German-American entente would from now on play a major role in the process of unification, particularly for security questions. The Soviets were not mistaken: after Camp David, Moscow let it be known that the USSR could not accept a Germany that would be an unrestricted member of the alliance.[102] Positions were fixed on both sides, and the great bargaining could begin.

Germany and NATO: The French Viewpoint

In this debate, French diplomacy, for the time being, found itself a spectator rather than an actor. The problem of the status of unified Germany did not represent as major a stake for France as it did for the U.S.: Mitterrand's priority, as we know, was much more European than Atlantic. Mitterrand was moreover convinced that the end of the Cold War would inevitably cast doubt on military blocs, which in his eyes downgraded the importance of the question: 'The system of alliances as it has functioned will be outmoded, outstripped in a few years', he declared to the Brazilian President Fernando Collor, who was in Paris on 6 February.[103] Nevertheless, Mitterrand's diplomacy was not totally disinterested in the subject: the debate that took shape at the start of February was closely followed in Paris, where a double concern would structure the French position in the coming months. On the one hand, the French evidently distrusted any sort of neutralization of Germany, which would lead to a challenge to its anchoring in NATO and beyond that to the whole Atlantic status quo; if this was not a leitmotif for Mitterrand, it was clear that from the start he excluded a hypothesis that had been opposed for decades by a French diplomacy quite as attached as its Western partners were to the Atlantic membership of the FRG.[104] On the other hand, at this stage Mitterrand's policy was to stress that German unification must not upset the East-West balance, and in this domain account should be taken of Soviet security interests: even if Moscow's green light to German unification showed the USSR's incapacity to block the process, Mitterrand thought that the Soviets could not accept a pure and simple integration of Germany into NATO and that it was more than ever indispensable to not antagonize Moscow. If Germany unified, he summed up on 15 February to Kohl, who was 'in total agreement' with his analysis, 'the Soviet withdrawal should not correspond to a Western advance'.[105] Unsurprisingly, the Élysée thus agreed to the Tutzing formula, without much bothering about its details: Mitterrand judged it 'judicious' (in unified Germany 'the lines of the Atlantic Alliance would remain where they are', he said) while his entourage saw it as a welcome 'de-fusing' of the issue.[106] The Quai d'Orsay recognized that Genscher's approach, even if it was far from bringing clear answers to all the questions, had the merit of making evident the unrealistic nature of a pure and simple integration of united Germany into NATO.[107]

Informed by the preceding twists in Soviet policy, the French, in any event, remained prudent. Nothing guaranteed that Moscow's attitude would not change over the question of the alliance as it had done over the question of German unity itself: Mitterrand as of the end of January did not exclude the possibility that Gorbachev in time would prefer to maintain Germany in the alliance rather than witness its 'autonomization'.[108] This hypothesis was indeed confirmed by the compromise formula sketched by Genscher and initially taken up by Baker at the start of February: 'The American and West German scheme has every chance of prevailing', wrote Védrine at the start of February, and it was not certain that the USSR could oppose it.[109] By the end of the month, some at the Quai d'Orsay took it as given that the Soviet requirement for a neutral Germany was only a negotiating position, behind which the USSR, banking on concessions on its military status, would end up accepting Germany remaining in NATO.[110] French leaders were convinced that the Germans would be prepared for such concessions if they were the price to be paid for unity: 'One cannot remove the suspicion that the priority they give to rapid reunification might lead them to accept very quickly not neutrality but a particular status in NATO', Admiral Jacques Lanxade, the president's military chief of staff, stated in mid February.[111]

More than distrust about the firmness of Bonn's Atlantic commitments (a distrust also detected in Washington, at least before the Camp David meeting), this analysis reflected the conviction that a unified and sovereign Germany would not accept for long the political and military constraints currently weighing on the FRG, whether integration in NATO or the foreign military presence on its soil. A few months later this conviction led the president to announce, to general surprise, the withdrawal of French forces from Germany after unification.[112] The future course of events gave the lie to this expectation, yet for the time being it fed in Paris an evident skepticism about the durability of the NATO status quo after German unification and led the French to question the pertinence of an American approach that bet everything on maintaining unified Germany within NATO, with the fewest restrictions possible. These doubts were summarized by the French representative to NATO, Gabriel Robin: 'The solidity of anchoring in the West that is expected from Germany's participation in NATO', he warned, 'cannot be superior to the solidity of NATO itself'.[113] In fact, the French were divided. On the one hand, everything led them to believe that NATO's integrated military structure would not survive the end of the Cold War and German unification. Either the USSR would obtain concessions effectively dismantling NATO, or unified Germany would seek its autonomy. Consequently the French 'model' would be validated, which might justify reaffirming now a position that challenged an 'integration' that France had been criticizing for years.[114] On the other hand, however, the French did not want to take the risk of precipitating the evolution of a more autonomous Germany, nor did Paris want to block American objectives. By all the evidence, this latter concern trumped the others, at least for the moment – hence the reserve observed in Paris, evidently wary of adopting the hypothesis of a status 'à la française' for united Germany in the alliance, for which the French could logically have been the advocates.[115] The following months confirmed French reserve over this issue, even if Mitterrand, as we shall see, would play a significant role in the 'great bargaining' that opened over the question of Germany belonging to the Atlantic Alliance.

Notes

1. Caroline de Margerie, note pour le président de la République, La situation en RDA, 3 January 1990, private papers; and MAE, Sous-direction d'Europe centrale et nordique, note a.s. Les relations interallemandes au seuil de l'année 1990, 3 January 1990, Archives diplomatiques (AD), Europe, Allemagne 1986–1990, box 6120.
2. Meeting between Mitterrand and Kohl, Latché, 4 January 1990, detailed report by Loïc Hennekinne; Gespräch des Bundeskanzlers Kohl mit Staatspräsident Mitterrand, Latché, 4. Januar 1990, in *Deutsche Einheit. Sonderedition aus den Akten des Bundeskanzleramtes 1989/90*, Munich, R. Oldenburg, 1998, pp. 682–690.
3. Horst Teltschik, *329 Tage. Innenansichten der Einigung*, Berlin, Siedler, 1991, p. 107; MAE, le chef du CAP, note a.s. Vers une accélération de la question allemande?, 16 January 1990, AD, Europe, Allemagne 1986–1990, box 6120.
4. On this, see Werner Weidenfeld, *Außenpolitik für die deutsche Einheit. Die Entscheidungsjahre 1989–1990*, Stuttgart, DVA, 1998, pp. 209–212; and Philip Zelikow and Condoleezza Rice, *Germany Unified and Europe Transformed: A Study in Statecraft*, Cambridge, Harvard University Press, 1995, pp. 158–159.
5. See Teltschik, *329 Tage*, pp. 109–110.
6. He did not admit it openly, however: whereas Jacques Attali bet him, during a telephone conversation on the morning of 30 January, that unity would be realized before the end of the year, Teltschik responded to him by bursting out into laughter: Teltschik, *329 Tage*, p. 118; see also Weidenfeld, *Außenpolitik*, p. 211.
7. Meeting between Mitterrand and Kohl, Latché, 4 January 1990; Gespräch des Bundeskanzlers Kohl mit Staatspräsident Mitterrand, Latché, 4. Januar 1990.

8. Meeting between Mitterrand and Thatcher, 20 January 1990, detailed report by Hennekinne, private papers. The agreed consultations did not result in anything tangible: see below, chapter 5, pp. 233–234.
9. Margaret Thatcher, *The Downing Street Years*, New York, HaperCollins, 1993, pp. 797–798. Thatcher's recollection agrees with the Elysée's detailed report on this particular meeting, but as a general rule she overestimated the community of thought between her and Mitterrand regarding Germany. Thatcher's anti-German preventions were flagrant: she wrote in her memoirs that while she did 'not believe in [the] collective guilt' of the Germans, she did 'believe in [their] national character', adding that Germany was 'by its very nature a destabilizing force rather than a stabilizing force in Europe': p. 791. Although complex and at times paradoxical, Mitterrand's personal feelings toward Germany were evidently very far from Thatcher's, and of course the French and British historical experiences with Germany differed fundamentally: by contrast with the British attitude, Franco-German reconciliation and European construction both largely conditioned French reactions to German unity in a positive way. True, Mitterrand (who seems to have entertained a certain fascination for the British prime minister) often appeared reluctant to contradict Thatcher head-on during their bilateral meetings, even when she used harsh words regarding the Germans, which could explain her ex post–tendency to enroll Mitterrand in her own germanophobia. But Thatcher's foreign minister, Douglas Hurd, understood very well that Mitterrand's apparent concurrence with Thatcher was 'just intellectual play' and that his actual policy was by no means to block German unification, a message he tried unsuccessfully to convey to Thatcher: see Douglas Hurd, *Memoirs* (London: Little and Brown, 2003), p. 383. As for Kohl, he notes in his own *Memoirs* that Thatcher 'seemed always to hear what she wanted to hear': Helmut Kohl, *Erinnerungen 1982-1990*, Munich, Droemer, p. 958.
10. Meeting between Mitterrand and Cossiga, 29 January 1990, detailed report by Hennekinne, private papers.
11. As said above, the permanence of Moscow's opposition to unification was already seen as doubtful in Paris at the end of November (see chapter 3 of this volume, p. 135). During a seminar in Moscow at the end of December, a representative of the Quai d'Orsay had, moreover, noticed the gap between the comments made by officials of the Soviet ministry of foreign affairs and the point of view of researchers (whether from the Institute for Europe, the Institute for the United States and Canada or the Institute for Global Economy and International Relations) for whom German unity was already a fact: MAE, note a.s. Entretiens à Moscou du sous-directeur des questions politiques à la direction des Nations unies (18–22 décembre 1989), 5 January 1990, AD, Europe, Allemagne 1986–1990, box 6125.
12. Michel Duclos, note a.s. Question allemande: perception soviétique, Moscou, 2 January 1990, AD, Série Affaires stratégiques et désarmement (ASD) 1985–1990, box 15.
13. Meeting between Mitterrand and Kohl, Latché, 4 January 1990; Gespräch des Bundeskanzlers Kohl mit Staatspräsident Mitterrand, Latché, 4. Januar 1990.
14. Conseil de défense du 16 janvier 1990, detailed report by Jean-Louis Bianco, private papers. Two days later on a trip to Hungary, Mitterrand wondered again before his interlocutors if the USSR still had the means to oppose the unification: see Meeting between Mitterrand and Reszö Nyers, 18 January 1990, private papers.
15. On this, see Hannes Adomeit, *Imperial Overstretch: Germany in Soviet Policy from Stalin to Gorbachev*, Baden-Baden, Nomos, 1998, p. 474ff.; see also Rice and Zelikow, *Germany Unified*, pp. 161–163; and Anatolii Cherniaev, 'Gorbachev and the Reunification of Germany: Personal Recollections,' in Gabriel Gorodetsky (ed.), *Soviet Foreign Policy 1917–1991: A Retrospective* (London: Frank Cass, 1994). Gorbachev on that day defined five

orientations: the creation of a group of six to negotiate the unification process (see below pp. 176–177); an orientation of Soviet policy in the direction of Kohl but without ignoring the SPD; the invitation of Modrow and Gregor Gysi, the new Number One of the ex-SED – rebaptized the PDS – to Moscow; the maintenance of a close collaboration with London and Paris; and the preparation of the withdrawal of Soviet forces from the GDR.
16. Adomeit, *Imperial Overstretch*, pp. 481–482; Rice and Zelikow, *Germany Unified*, pp. 163–164.
17. Teltschik, *329 Tage*, p. 120; TD Berlin 286, 31 January 1990, AD, Europe, Allemagne 1986–1990, box 6125.
18. Letter from Gorbachev to Mitterrand, 2 February 1990, private papers.
19. TD, Moscou 614, 2 February 1990, AD, Europe, Allemagne 1986–1990, box 6125.
20. Conseil des ministres, 31 janvier 1990, private papers.
21. Margerie, note pour le président de la République, Visite à Paris de M. Momper, maire de Berlin, 2 February 1990, AN, 5AG4 /7010.
22. In Momper's analysis, either the elections would produce 'a heteroclite coalition of intellectuals who seek to scheme' on the unity, and its procrastination would aggravate the exodus toward the FRG; or, which is more likely, the East German Parliament would decide 'without any hesitation for German unity:' see MAE, CAP, note a.s. Calendrier de l'unité allemande, 6 February 1990, AN, 5AG4/7010.
23. Before Bertrand Dufourcq and Jacques Blot, Dieter Kastrup emphasized that the number of daily departures toward the West was still around 2,000 and that the Modrow government faced the risk of collapse: see MAE, le directeur d'Europe, note pour le ministre d'Etat, a.s. Consultations du directeur des affaires politiques et du directeur d'Europe avec leurs homologues de RFA, 9 February 1990, secret, AN 5AG4 /7010.
24. Letter from Dumas to Mitterrand, 12 January 1990, AN 5AG4/CDM 36 (with handwritten annotation by Mitterrand); TD Bonn 125, 18 January 1990, secret, AD, Europe 1986–1990, Allemagne, box 6126; see also Zelikow and Rice, *Germany Unified*, pp. 154–156.
25. Zelikow and Rice, *Germany Unified*, p. 156.
26. Védrine, note pour le président de la République, 30 January 1990, private papers.
27. Védrine, note pour le président de la République (with annotation by Mitterrand), 23 January 1990, private papers.
28. See Weidenfeld, *Außenpolitik*, p. 223.
29. See Bertrand Dufourcq, '2 + 4 ou la négociation atypique'," *Politique étrangère*, n. 2/2000 pp. 467–484. The venue of Genscher's speech was obviously not neutral: in July 1963, Willy Brandt and Egon Bahr had sketched out their Ostpolitik at this small Bavarian town's Evangelical Academy.
30. Védrine, note pour le président de la République, 31 January 1990, private papers.
31. The Foreign Office was clearly less fixed on the German question than Downing Street: London diplomats emphasized the 'almost inevitable' character of the unification while minimizing the impact of Thatcher's reluctance, which was only about 'nuances in language' (in another remarkable understatement, the French ambassador noted nonetheless that Thatcher appeared 'to have less confidence than her Foreign Minister in the wisdom of the German people…'): see TD Londres pp. 166–168, 7 February 1990, AD, ASD 1985–1990, box 15.
32. On this, see Zelikow and Rice, *Germany Unified*, pp. 159–160 and 167ff.
33. Zelikow and Rice, *Germany Unified*, pp. 167–168 and p. 173. Some days later the Foreign Office confirmed to its interlocutors at the French embassy in London that a mechanism in which only the big powers would participate was not appropriate as it would alienate the Germans and give a blocking power to the Soviets: see TD Londres 166–167, 7 February 1990.

34. MAE, le directeur d'Europe, Réflexions sur la question allemande, 30 October 1989, AD, Europe, Allemagne 1986–1990, box 6119; on this memorandum, see chapter 2 in this volume, pp. 102–104; on France and the 2 + 4, see Dufourcq, '2 + 4'.
35. Evoking the unification, the French president had, that day, wished that the Four, who did not want to place the Germans under a regime of 'trusteeship' but who 'had things to say and to discuss on the international stage of European stability', would 'speak with the Germans': see Mitterrand's press conference upon completion of his state visit to the GDR, Berlin, 22 December 1989, MAE, *Politique étrangère de la France. Textes et documents (PEF)*, November–December 1989, p. 215.
36. Védrine, note pour le président de la République, 5 February 1990, National Archives (AN), 5AG4/CDM 33 (Védrine took up the same ideas in a note dated the 6 February in which he evoked 'a meeting of 6 (4 + 2)', AN 5AG4/7010).
37. See Zelikow and Rice, *Germany Unified*, p. 179; and Pierre Favier and Michel Martin-Roland, *La Décennie Mitterrand*, vol. 3, 'Les Défis,' Paris, Seuil, 1996, p. 233.
38. Védrine, note pour le président de la République, 8 February 1990, AN 5AG4/7010. It was probably this conversation with Genscher that, adding to the reflections led in Paris on the subject over the previous weeks and months, would later give Dumas and his entourage the feeling of having played a decisive role in the implementation of 2 + 4; see MAE, le directeur du cabinet du ministre d'Etat, note pour Hubert Védrine, 23 November 1991, AN, 5AG4/CDM 36 (the author of this note, Bernard Kessedjian, estimated retrospectively that 2 + 4 'was a French initiative', an assessment that – in addition to the problem of the order of the formula, i.e. 2 + 4 vs. 4 + 2 – appears to be exaggerated, even if it is true that the American initiative echoed, in many respects, the ideas raised in Paris).
39. On all this, see Zelikow and Rice, *Germany Unified*, pp. 180–185; and Adomeit, *Imperial Overstretch*, pp. 483–486. The acceptation of 2 + 4 by Moscow gave rise to a subsequent controversy between former Soviet officials. The 'old guard', namely Falin, later accused Gorbachev's entourage and in particular Shevardnadze of having discounted Soviet interests by accepting a 2 + 4 formula in Ottawa, whereas it was the 4 + 2 formula that ought to have been used to signify that it was up to the Four to fix the international framework of the unification *before* the two German states could decide it (according to Falin, Shevardnadze recognized having yielded to Genscher on this point): see Valentin Falin, *Politische Erinnerungen* (Munich: Droemer Knaur, 1993), p. 491; and, by the same author, *Konflikte im Kreml. Zur Vorgeschichte der deutschen Einheit und der Auflösung der Sowjetunion* (Munich: Karl Blessing Verlag, 1997), p. 162. Chernyaev, however, formally contested this version, assessing the order as having had no importance and holding that Gorbachev used the two formulas indifferently: see Adomeit, *Imperial Overstretch*, pp. 484–486. Be that as it may, the episode illustrates yet again Moscow's internal contradictions and their impact on Soviet politics.
40. See Aufzeichnung des Ministerialdirigenten Hartmann, Bonn, 29. Januar 1990, Deutschlandpolitik im gesamteuropäischen Rahmen nach den DDR-Wahlen im März 1990, *Deusche Einheit*, pp. 727–735. On this, see Hans-Dietrich Genscher, *Erinnerungen*, Berlin, Siedler, 1995, p. 709 ff; Richard Kiessler and Frank Elbe, *Ein runder Tisch mit scharfen Ecken. Der diplomatische Weg zur deutschen Einheit*, Nomos, Baden-Baden, 1993, p. 86ff.; and Frank Elbe, 'Resolving the International Aspects of German Unification: The "Two-plus-four" Process,' *German Yearbook of International Law* 36 (1993): 371–384.
41. Genscher even excluded, then, the name 'discussions at 6': see Frank Elbe, 'Resolving'.
42. MAE, directeur d'Europe, note pour le ministre d'Etat, a.s. Consultations du directeur des affaires politiques et du directeur d'Europe avec leurs homologues de RFA, 9 February 1990, secret. Shortly before this meeting, the Quai's Director of Legal Affairs

produced a detailed analysis of the quadripartite rights and responsibilities and the 'reserved' rights of the three Western powers. Recalling that the quadripartite rights concerning Berlin and Germany as a whole stemmed from the London Agreements of 14 November 1944 and the Berlin Declaration of 5 June 1945, he emphasized that the Three, while recognizing for the FRG 'the full authority of a sovereign state' in the Bonn and Paris Conventions of 1952 and 1954, had 'reserved' at the same time those rights, and that their persistence, from then on, did not in any way result from a concession of the FRG. He emphasized, in addition, that since the continuity of quadripartite rights had been recalled conjointly by the Four Powers on several occasions since the partition of Germany (in particular in the Berlin Agreement of 1971), the Four, despite their political and legal disagreements, 'were at least in agreement on the maintenance of reserved rights'. He recalled also that the three Western powers, as a result of the 1952 and 1954 agreements, had to 'consult the FRG on all questions pertaining to the exercise' of the reserved rights and that, of course, they had committed themselves to make a peace settlement and German unification their objective: see MAE, le directeur des affaires juridiques, note pour le Cabinet du ministre d'Etat, 'Droits réservés' alliés en Allemagne, 6 February 1990; and, also, note pour le ministre d'Etat, a.s. Droits réservés des Alliés en Allemagne, 7 February 1990, AD, ASD, 1985–1990, box 15; on all these aspects, see this volume, chapter 3, n. 143.
43. For Gorbachev, Kohl's invitation to Moscow was a logical follow-up to his meeting with Modrow: it was a question of discussing with the chancellor the 'rapprochement' between the two Germanys and the *Vertagsgemeinschaft* as 'steps toward a confederation of the two German states': see Schreiben des Generalsekretärs Gorbatschow an Bundeskanzler Kohl, 2. Februar 1990, *Deutsche Einheit*, pp. 748–749.
44. Schreiben des Präsidenten Bush an Bundeskanzler Kohl, 9. Februar 1990, *Deutsche Einheit*, pp. 784–785.
45. Schreiben des Außenministers Baker an Bundeskanzler Kohl, 10. Februar 1990, *Deutsche Einheit*, pp. 793–794; see also Zelikow and Rice, *Germany Unified*, pp. 185–188.
46. For the German detailed report of the extraordinary meeting between Kohl and Gorbachev (at which only Teltschik and Chernyaev participated in addition to the interpreters), see Gespräch des Bundeskanzlers Kohl mit Generalsekretär Gorbatschow, Moskau, 10. Februar 1990, *Deutsche Einheit*, pp. 795–807; see also Adomeit's analysis, *Imperial Overstretch*, pp. 486–491.
47. Teltschik, *329 Tage*, pp. 140–141. Teltschik, who said that Kohl 'brought back' to Germany the key to German unity that previously had lain in Moscow, was strongly criticized by Genscher and his entourage for a triumphalism that they judged somewhat reckless: the Genscher-Kohl rivalry was at its peak, and it was fueled by a persistent divergence over how international worries, especially Soviet ones, were to be taken into account.
48. See Mikhaïl Gorbatchev, *Mémoires*, Editions du Rocher, 1997, pp. 664–665; and Antoly S. Chernyaev, *My Six Years with Gorbatchev*, University Park, Pennsylvannia University Press, 2000, p. 264.
49. TD Moscou 888 and 894, 12 February 1990, AD, ASD 1985–1990, box 15.
50. TD Bonn 341–342, 12 February 1990, AD, ASD 1985–1990, box 15.
51. Meeting between Mitterrand and Andreotti, 13 February 1990, detailed report by Hennekinne, private papers.
52. Conseil des ministres, 14 February 1990.
53. TD Washington 396, 12 February 1990, AD, ASD 1985–1990, box 15.
54. On this, see Zelikow and Rice, *Germany Unified*, pp. 191–197 and, for the French point of view, Dufourcq, '2+4'.

55. From the outset, the White House was less convinced than the Department of State of the appropriateness of the 2 + 4 formula, fearing it might delay the unification process and grant a *droit de regard* to the USSR. The White House also feared that the arrangement had only been negotiated with Genscher but without Kohl's agreement. This explains how, during the Ottawa meeting, two telephone calls between the president and the chancellor were necessary to dispel the misunderstanding. While revealing a disagreement between the Department of State and the White House, the episode also confirmed the friction between the Chancellery and the Auswärtiges Amt and their divergence on the external aspects of the unification process, about which Genscher and his associates showed themselves more inclined to take account of the international environment than Kohl and his entourage, even if they eventually agreed on the 2 + 4 formula; see Weidenfeld, *Außenpolitik*, pp. 250–253.
56. This is what Dumas noticed during a meeting with Shevardnadze on the 12 February in Ottawa. Confirming the disarray of Soviet diplomacy, Shevardnadze confessed his 'powerlessness', regretting that the mechanism of the Four 'did not work'. The Soviet did not delude himself regarding the possibility of slowing down the process and considered 2 + 4 approach to be a lesser evil that could nonetheless be 'tried' even if it was clear that the important things would play out between the Germans and that it would quickly become 1 + 4: see the detailed report by Dufourcq, TD Diplomatie 3170, 14 February 1990, AD, ASD 1985–1990, box 15.
57. Expressing his frustration, the Italian minister Gianni De Michelis famously attracted a scathing response from Genscher: 'You are not part of the game.'
58. Communiqué of the Six, Ottawa, 13 February 1990; the sentence on 'the issues of security of the neighboring states' had been added in response to the pressing demand of Polish diplomacy, which wanted to see the question of the Oder-Neisse border taken into account: see Dufourcq, '2+4'.
59. Meeting between Mitterrand and Andreotti, 13 February 1990, detailed report by Hennekinne, private papers.
60. Personal interviews. French diplomacy probably shared the sentiment expressed in the Soviet MID at the same time: even if, as the Soviet director of Europe confided to the French Embassy in Moscow, it would have been preferable for things to have gone 'much more slowly and in a much more controlled manner', it was nonetheless considered an 'appreciable result' that the Germans had finally come to recognize the necessity of respecting the quadripartite responsibilities: TD Moscou 1022, 14 February 1990, AD, ASD 1985–1990, box 15.
61. TD Diplomatie 3170, 14 February 1990. Mitterrand would later recall that Kohl had 'yielded but with regret': see François Mitterrand, *De l'Allemagne, de la France*, Paris, Odile Jacob, 1996, p. 147; see also Hubert Védrine, *Les Mondes de François Mitterrand. A l'Elysée 1981–1995*, Paris, Fayard, 1996, p. 437.
62. Hurd subscribed for the most part to the remarks of his French colleague and recognized that it was necessary to 'create a pressure' and 'maintain strong the initiative taken in Ottawa': see Compte rendu, a.s. Entretiens du ministre d'Etat avec M. Douglas Hurd (Londres, 15 February 1990), AN 5AG4/AH 35. Wanting to prevent the Ottawa formula from becoming a dead letter, French diplomacy (see chapter 5 in this volume, pp. 209–210) would indeed insist in the following days and weeks on a rapid start to the talks. In addition, Dumas and Mitterrand would make it a point to evoke '4 + 2' rather than '2 + 4' in order to emphasize to the Germans that the role of the Four should not be forgotten: 'you say 2 + 4, we say 4 + 2', Mitterrand stated before Kohl at the Elysée on 15 February, provoking smiles around the table: see Mitterrand-Kohl dinner, 15 February 1990 at the Elysée, detailed report by Elisabeth Guigou, private papers (the German

detailed report does not mention this phrase: see Gespräch des Bundeskanzlers Kohl mit Staatspräsident Mitterrand, Paris, 15. Februar 1990, *Deutsche Einheit*, pp. 842–852).
63. Arbeitsfrühstuck des Bundeskanzlers mit Staatspräsident Mitterand, Straßbourg, 9. Dezember 1989, *Deutsche Einheit*, pp. 628– 631. Mitterrand and Kohl had 'missed' each other three times in the last weeks of 1989: in Strasbourg on 22 November, in Brussels on 4 December and in Berlin on 22 December. See chapter 3 of this volume, n. 100.
64. Gespräch des Bundeskanzlers Kohl mit Präsident Bush, Laeken bei Brüssel, 3. Dezember 1989, *Deutsche Einheit*, pp. 600–609; and Helmut Kohl, Kai Diekmann and Ralf Georg Reuth, *Je voulais l'unité de l'Allemagne*, Paris, de Fallois, 1997, pp. 165–166 and p. 193. Kohl (wrongly) judged that Mitterrand was at that time under the influence of Dumas, whom he believed to be hostile to unification (he believed this to be true of the Ministry of Foreign Affairs as a whole and of most of the Parisian political community). Kohl's negative appreciation regarding the role of Dumas was, it must be emphasized again, in sharp contrast with that of Genscher; see chapter 3 of this volume, p. 133. It may be explained by the proximity between the two foreign ministers – probably an aggravating factor in the eyes of Kohl – as well as by the tough stances taken by Dumas, in particular regarding the border question, as in Strasbourg in December or in Berlin in March. In regard to the alleged hostility of the Quai d'Orsay toward unification, it is quite possible that Kohl became convinced of it by reading the German press, which as a general rule had little sympathy for the Quai and for the 'French political community': see below, n. 67.
65. Teltschik, *329 Tage*, pp. 96–98. The author observed that whereas Mitterrand did not fear German unity, 'he indicated important obstacles to surpass'. Certainly, he continued, Kohl may have been 'upset' by some French declarations, namely those of Dumas, but there was not a 'serious irritation': should it come as a surprise that the French showed 'restraint', he asked, since numerous Germans from both sides themselves had 'difficulty' with German unity? And how could one demand from one's neighbors that they be 'more German than the Germans'?
66. Meeting between Mitterrand and Kohl, Latché, 4 January 1990; Gespräch des Bundeskanzlers Kohl mit Staatspräsident Mitterrand, Latché, 4. Januar 1990.
67. To the great displeasure of Kohl's entourage, on the same day of the talks in Latché the *Frankfurter Allgemeine Zeitung* published an article quoting a report written by the FRG embassy in Paris that rather negatively summarized French attitudes toward the German question. According to *FAZ*, the embassy, whose report was written before Christmas, estimated that 'the reservations of French political leaders' were 'larger and deeper than previously understood' in the two capitals, to the point that 'the question remain[ed] open to determine whether France would end up accompanying in a constructive manner an evolution that would lead to a reinforcement of the German position or whether one would look to stand in the middle of this evolution'. Noting the difference between the favorable attitude of public opinion and the doubts of the political community and the media as well as the temptation to slow things down that existed on the part of 'civil servants', the report concluded nonetheless that 'Mitterrand had as always the largest view' and that 'obviously convinced that unification would come', he 'hoped to contribute to orientate the process in an orderly way' and make it possible that 'the European unification process not be affected': cited in TD Bonn 35, 6 January 1990, AD, Europe, Allemagne 1986–1990, box 6124. Kohl's entourage reacted heatedly to the publication of the article on the same day of the Latché visit: see Teltschik, *329 Tage*, p. 98. Kohl himself, in Latché, minimized the affair by emphasizing that what newspapers wrote did not 'touch him' and that Mitterrand's stance was 'assimilated' in the German press, where everything was mixed together, to the attitude of the French political community as a whole.

68. Some days later, Kohl confided to his principal collaborators that 'everything depended [that] year on the support of the United States and France as well as cooperation with the USSR', and he declared himself 'ready to go as far as possible to meet Mitterrand and largely aid Gorbatchev': Teltschik, *329 Tage*, pp. 100 and 102. He then repeated to the American ambassador on 24 January that the evolutions underway depended on the friendship and confidence of the partners of the FRG, beginning with the United States and France: see Gespräch des Bundeskanzlers Kohl mit Botschafter Walters, Bonn, 24. Januar 1990, *Deutsche Einheit*, pp. 699–700; as for Thatcher, her interview in the *Wall Street Journal* dated 25 January, particularly virulent toward German policy, provoked anger in the Chancellery: Vorlage des Ministerialdirektors Teltschik an Bundeskanzler Kohl, Bonn, 25. Januar 1990, *Deutsche Einheit*, pp. 719–720; and Teltschik, *329 Tage*, p. 115.
69. Meeting between Mitterrand and Thatcher, 20 January 1990; see also Mitterrand's 17 January letter to Kohl and Kohl's 25 January response in *Deutsche Einheit*, pp. 694 and 718. The Chancellery was nevertheless happy with the lecture given by Kohl before the French Institute for International Relations on 17 January and with his favorable reception by the French press. (Kohl for the first time declared that no one in the FRG dreamed of putting the German-Polish border into question as a result of German unification, a statement welcomed in Paris: see Teltschik, *329 Tage*, p. 111.)
70. Védrine, note pour le président de la République, a.s. Suggestions d'actions vis-à-vis de l'opinion oust-allemande, 26 January 1990, private papers; evoking 'numerous critical if not hostile articles' in the German press especially from editorialists in whom he saw 'a mix of exaltation, bad faith but also a lack of information and true misunderstandings', Védrine suggested an interview with *Die Zeit* – a newspaper rather favorable to France – or, on the contrary, with *Die Welt* – very critical – or an interview with the major German newspaper editors (such as Kohl had done with French media), or also a speech delivered in the FRG 'on the future of relations between France and a reunified Germany'. Bianco strongly supported these 'excellent suggestions' that, in his opinion, were 'to be made quickly'; as for Mitterrand, he wrote 'discuss with me' on the note but did not conclude immediately.
71. Guigou, note pour le président de la République, Votre entretien-déjeuner avec Jacques Delors, le 2 février à 13 heures, 2 February 1990 ('very important', Bianco wrote on the note), AN 5AG4/7010.
72. Guigou, note pour le président de la République, L'unification européenne et la Communauté, 7 February 1990, AN 5AG4/AH 35.
73. Indeed, Bianco sent Mitterrand poll results that clearly showed that the French were still 'very largely favorable' to German unification and judged that far from being overtaken by the events in the East, European construction must be reinforced and completed by a political union of Twelve: see Marie-Ange Théobald, note pour Jean-Louis Bianco, 6 February 1990, 'Sondages relatifs à la réunification allemande et à l'Europe de l'Est et de l'Ouest,' AN, 5AG4/7010.
74. Guigou, note pour le président de la République, Compte rendu du conseil informel des ministres des Affaires étrangères de la Communauté à Dublin, samedi soir, 23 janvier 1990, AN 5AG4/7010; Vermerk des Vortragenden Legationsrats I Bitterlich und des Ministerialdirigenten Thiele, Bonn, 24. Januar 1990, Beziehungen EG-DDR, *Deutsche Einheit*, pp. 705–706; see also Favier and Martin-Roland, *La Décennie*, vol. 3, pp. 244–245.
75. Meeting between Mitterrand and Thatcher, 20 January 1990. Guigou presented the following alternatives: either the GDR would survive and its possible integration in the EEC should be examined according to the same criteria as the other candidates'; or it would be absorbed into the FRG following the collapse of the East German state and in-

tegrated ipso facto in the EEC: Note pour le président de la République, Votre entretien déjeuner avec Jacques Delors, 2 February 1990.
76. Guigou thought that in the case of an 'absorption' of the GDR, unified Germany could well ask for more votes in the council and a greater portion of the structural funds, but that the negotiation would be simpler than with a GDR that would have survived; in addition, 'the process would be more rapid, more simple and would not disturb during many years the development of the Community as would the negotiation for entry of an East-German state,' and it would be easier 'to discourage the other entry requests:' see Guigou, note pour le président de la République, L'unification européenne et la Communauté, 7 February 1990. Examining the voting rights in the European Council the following day, she reported that in 1957, the demographic differential between the FRG and France was 10 million, which had not prevented an equality of voting rights between Paris and Bonn in the treaty of Rome– implicitly suggesting that the difference of 17 million persons between France and a unified Germany would not necessarily give rise to a relative French loss of voting rights: Note pour le président de la République, Pondération des voix des Etats membres dans la Communauté européenne, 8 February 1990, AN 5AG4/AH 35.
77. It was at that moment that Kohl and his entourage chose a unification procedure in accordance with article 23 of the *Grundgesetz*, which allowed entry into the FRG of the Länder soon to be recreated in the GDR and presented the advantage of assuring the continuity of international engagements of the FRG (by contrast, the procedure under article 146 – preferred by the SPD, by East Berlin and by Moscow – entailed the gathering of a constitutive assembly, thus representing a much longer process and creating uncertainty with regard to the continuity of the FRG's international engagements: see chapter 5 of this volume, p. 214.
78. Guigou, note pour le président de la République, Votre entretien déjeuner avec Jacques Delors, le 2 février à 13 heures, 2 February 1990.
79. Guigou, note pour le président de la République, L'union politique de l'Europe, 6 February 1990, AN, 5AG4/AH 35.
80. When Kohl informed him by telephone on 5 February of his discussion with Modrow in Davos on the 3rd and of the latest developments in the GDR and announced to him his upcoming visit to Moscow, Mitterrand emphasized the importance of a narrow Franco-German entente and said he was very pleased with the absence of difficulties between them: Telefongespräch des Bundeskanzlers Kohl mit Staatspräsident Mitterrand, 5. Februar 1990, *Deutsche Einheit*, pp. 757–758. On Kohl's policies, see Hans Stark, *Kohl, L'Allemagne et l'Europe. La politique européenne de la République fédérale 1982–1998*, Paris, L'Harmattan, 2004, pp. 157ff.
81. Guigou, note pour le président de la République, Compte rendu de mon déjeuner avec Joachim Bitterlisch (sic), conseiller du chancelier Kohl, 13 February 1990, AN, 5AG4/7010.
82. Guigou, note pour le président de la Republique, Votre diner avec le Chancelier Kohl, jeudi 15 février, 13 February 1990, private papers. When the Kohl government had announced the monetary union project between the two Germanys some days before, Guigou had proved understanding: the decision, she wrote, was justified by the necessity to stabilize the situation in the GDR and the flow of refugees up until the elections: see Guigou, note pour le président de la République, Union économique et monétaire entre la RFA et la RDA, 7 February 1990, AN 5AG4/AH 35.
83. Meeting between Mitterrand and Andreotti, 13 February 1990, detailed report by Hennekinne; Guigou, note pour le président de la République, Déclarations de J. Delors au Parlement européen, 13 February 1990, private papers.

84. Conseil des ministres, 14 February 1990, private papers. Another sign of the persistence of a certain reserve toward the politics of Kohl was the agreement given by Mitterrand on 15 February to a visit to the Elysée, before the 18 March elections in the GDR, of the SPD leader Oskar Lafontaine, Kohl's future challenger in the December elections, who was vigorously opposed to a forced march toward unity: see Védrine, note pour le président de la République, 15 February 1990, private papers.
85. Mitterrand-Kohl Dinner, 15 February 1990; and Gespräch des Bundeskanzlers Kohl mit Staatspräsident Mitterrand, Paris, 15. Februar 1990, *Deutsche Einheit*, pp. 842–852.
86. Kohl, *Je voulais*, p. 248ff. On the French side, a 'long, dense, complete and nonetheless amicable' conversation is remembered: Védrine, *Les Mondes*, p. 490.
87. MAE, Service des Affaires stratégiques et du désarmement, note a.s. Processus de réunification allemande et alliances de sécurité. Hypothèses de réflexion, 7 February 1990, AD, ASD, 1985–1990, box 15.
88. Védrine, note pour le président de la République, 5 February 1990.
89. Védrine, note pour le président de la République, 8 February 1990.
90. F. Mitterrand / H. Kohl Dinner, 15 February 1990; and Gespräch des Bundeskanzlers Kohl mit Staatspräsident Mitterrand, Paris, 15. Februar 1990, *Deutsche Einheit*, pp. 842–852.
91. The most complete treatment of this question is found in Zelikow and Rice, *Germany Unified* (in this book, the question of the alliance – a priority for American diplomats – unsurprisingly occupies a central place throughout the analysis of the unification process); on the Soviet side, see Adomeit, *Imperial Overstretch*, p. 491ff.
92. See Zelikow and Rice, *Germany Unified*, pp. 165–172. By the end of January 1990, the authors conclude, the Bush administration had decided on a threefold policy facing the European upheavals: encouragement for a quick unification in the framework of NATO, setting up of a 2 + 4 process to negotiate its exterior aspects and maintenance of a significant number of American forces in Europe (hence the proposition, transmitted on 31 January by Bush to Gorbachev, to establish a ceiling of 195,000 men for the American and Soviet forces in Central Europe in the framework of the CFE negotiations, a number much reduced from the 275,000 advanced during the May 1989 initiative, but one with which the Americans hoped to stabilize their military presence in Europe).
93. See Adomeit, *Imperial Overstretch*, pp. 491–499. Gorbachev, the author notes, did not seize the opportunity of the 26 January meeting (see above, p. 171) to fix the Soviet position on this question: p. 478ff.
94. Védrine, note pour le président de la République, 31 January 1990, private papers.
95. The Tutzing 'formula' was in fact rather vague, for Genscher, in his speech, had contented himself with suggesting in general terms that there would not be an extension of NATO to the East and that the territory of the ex-GDR would not be incorporated into NATO or its military structures. Thus, his presentation did not respond to the precise question of the status of the territory of the ex-GDR in regards to article 5 of the Washington Treaty (would it be covered by the Atlantic defense clause or would it be neutralized, with all of the problems that this situation would pose for a united Germany?), nor the question of the military situation of this same territory (would it simply be exempt from any NATO military presence or purely and simply demilitarized, that is to say exempt from any German forces?). In private, however, Genscher showed himself more precise: he clearly envisaged the neutralization and the demilitarization of the territory of the ex-GDR: see Zelikow and Rice, *Germany Unified*, pp. 175–176, and Teltschik, *329 Tage*, p. 117 and p. 123; this seemed to be confirmed by Kastrup, who explained to Dufourcq and Blot on 9 February that a united Germany would remain in the alliance but that 'the zone of competency of the integrated organization would stop at the Elbe': MAE, Direction d'Europe, note pour le ministre d'Etat, 9 February 1990, a.s. Consulta-

tions du directeur des Affaires politiques et du directeur d'Europe avec ses homologues de RFA. The meaning of the Tutzing formula remained a source of debate for a long time, with Genscher's entourage contesting that he had envisaged a definitively demilitarized and neutralized East Germany, contrary to what certain people in Bonn and Washington reproached him for: see Zelikow and Rice, *Germany Unified*, pp. 427–428.

96. Indeed, while evoking a unified Germany outside of military blocs, Gorbachev showed understanding for the idea that neutrality was not acceptable for Germans and Westerners and insisted on the need to reflect on the matter: Gespräch des Bundeskanzlers Kohl mit Generalsekretär Gorbatschow, Moskau, 10. Februar 1990, *Deutsche Einheit*, pp. 795–807.
97. TD Moscou 1022, 14 February 1990, AD, ASD 1985–1990, box 15; see also Hennekinne, note pour le président de la République, 14 February 1990, private papers. In Ottawa the same day, Shevardnadze showed himself skeptical before Dumas regarding the belonging of a unified Germany to NATO, but without opposing it relentlessly, illustrating yet again the fuzziness of the Soviet line: 'Western politicians assumed that a unified Germany would remain in the framework of NATO', he emphasized, 'but how could they be so sure?' And, he asked: 'Was it known what this reunified giant would represent in the Atlantic Alliance in a few years from that point in time?' TD Diplomatie 3170, 14 February 1990.
98. American diplomacy had at first supported Genscher's formula, which Baker had approved during his passage in Washington in early February and which he had himself defended in Moscow some days later, ensuring that 'NATO's jurisdiction or forces would not move eastward'. Very quickly, however, the White House became worried about the concrete consequences of such a formula, which could mean that the territory of the ex-GDR would no longer be covered by the alliance, opening the way to its demilitarization pure and simple. As a result, NSC officials preferred evoking a 'special military status' for the ex-GDR, a language adopted by Baker as soon as he returned from Moscow and used by Bush in the letter he addressed to Kohl on 9 February. Visiting Bush on the 10th, the general secretary of NATO, Manfred Woerner, also insisted on the necessity of maintaining Germany in the alliance *and* in the integrated organization, and he emphasized that a special military status for the ex-GDR should not mean its neutralization or demilitarization. By mid February, the U.S. administration, keen to preserve NATO's status quo as much as possible, thus adopted a much more restrictive approach to possible arrangements concerning the ex-GDR: see Zelikow and Rice, *Germany Unified*, pp. 176–177, 180–184, 186–187 and 195–196.
99. On this, see Zelikow and Rice, *Germany Unified*, pp. 203–204. The French embassy in Bonn noted, however, that if the result of the arbitration of the chancellor 'was close to Genscher's theses', the communiqué 'does not totally close the door to a German military presence in the eastern part of reunified Germany': TD Bonn 422, 19 February 1990, AD, ASD 1985–1990, box 15.
100. A poll conducted on 15 February revealed that 58 percent of West Germans preferred a neutral Germany, and the Americans noted that officials in Bonn envisaged a dilution of alliances in a pan-European system or a withdrawal of a unified Germany from the integrated organization together with the withdrawal of Western nuclear weapons and conventional forces: Zelikow and Rice, *Germany Unified*, pp. 203–204.
101. Zelikow and Rice, *Germany Unified*, pp. 211–216; see also Gespräch des Bundeskanzlers Kohl mit Präsident Bush, Camp David, 24. Februar 1990 and 25. Februar in *Deutsche Einheit*, pp. 860–873 and 874–877.
102. TD Moscou 1321, 26 February 1990, AD, ASD 1985–1990, box 15; on 20 February in *Pravda*, Gorbachev had himself used tougher language, emphasizing the 'inadmissibil-

ity of the violation of the strategic military balance' between NATO and the Warsaw Pact: see TD Moscou 1180, 21 February 1990, AD, ASD 1985–1990, box 15.
103. Meeting between Mitterrand and Collor, 6 February 1990, private papers; see also Védrine's account, cited in Favier and Martin-Roland, *La Décennie*, vol. 3, pp. 234–235.
104. German neutralization 'was always desired by the USSR', and it 'was essential to not lend one's assistance to this tendency', he declared at the end of January: see meeting between Mitterrand and Lawrence Eagleburger, 29 January, private papers (the American diplomat had come to present the Bush administration's new disarmament initiative: see above, n. 92).
105. Mitterand-Kohl Dinner, 15 February 1990; Gespräch des Bundeskanzlers Kohl mit Staatspräsident Mitterrand, Paris, 15. Februar 1990.
106. Meeting between Mitterrand and Collor, 6 February 1990; Védrine, note pour le président de la République, 5 February 1990, private papers (from the Tutzing formula, Védrine took up the idea of a demilitarization of the territory of the ex-GDR, but not its neutralization).
107. MAE, Sous-direction des affaires stratégiques et des pactes, note a.s. Processus de réunification allemande et alliances de sécurité. Hypothèses de réflexion, 7 February 1990, AD, ASD 1985–1990, box 15
108. Conseil des ministres, 31 January 1990.
109. Védrine, note pour le président de la République, a.s. L'Allemagne et les alliances, 7 February 1990, private papers.
110. MAE, CAP, note de Nicole Gnesotto, 2 + 4: anticipation sur les positions soviétiques, 27 February 1990, AN 5AG4/CDM 36.
111. Amiral Jacques Lanxade, note pour M. le président de la République, Réunification allemande et coopération franco-allemande en matière de sécurité, 13 February 1990, private papers. Some days later, Lanxade brought up the subject again: the Germans were counting on the weakening of the USSR to impose a maximalist schema (Germany in the alliance, maintenance of the integrated organization and American forces, phased withdrawal of Soviet forces, the temporary demilitarization of the current GDR being their only concession), but it was probable that, if necessary, 'priority would be given by the German leaders without much hesitation to the unification and thus that a compromise would be accepted on matters relating to Germany's Alliance membership': Note pour M. le président de la République, Unification allemande et sécurité de l'Europe, 23 February 1990, AN, 5AG4/7010.
112. 'One can wonder', wrote Védrine, 'how much longer Germany will continue to accept concentrations of allied troops, military maneuvers, low altitude flights, short range nuclear weapons, etc. on its territory. Once united, Germany will affirm its sovereignty and autonomy, even while remaining in the Alliance': see Védrine, note pour le président de la République, a.s. Allemagne et alliances, 7 February 1990. As for Mitterrand, he declared himself convinced – despite Kohl's very strong denials – that foreign military presence in Germany would sooner or later be questioned after unification: see F. Mitterrand / H. Kohl dinner, 15 February 1990; and Gespräch des Bundeskanzlers Kohl mit Staatspräsident Mitterrand, Paris, 15 Februar 1990. On the announcement of the withdrawal of the French Forces in Germany at the London Summit, see chapter 6 in this volume, pp. 281–282.
113. TD REPAN 113–114, 13 February 1990, AD, ASD, 1985–1990, box 15.
114. This was the position defended by the Quai d'Orsay in a note dated the end of February, according to which 'we may wonder whether the moment has not come for a revision of the concept of military integration that we have contested in the past emphasizing its anachronistic character in relation to the evolution of East-West relations': see MAE,

Service des affaires stratégiques et du désarmement, note pour le directeur politique a.s. Réunification allemande/OTAN/sécurité éuropéenne, 20 February 1990, AD, ASD, 1985–1990, box 15.

115. Evoked here and there during February as a possible compromise, the hypothesis of a united Germany that would be non-integrated and exempt of stationed allied forces did not seem to be taken seriously in the French capital: not only had this hypothesis not been analyzed specifically, but it was judged that such an option would be difficult to accept by the main actors involved, including the USSR, for although this hypothesis would certainly lead to the withdrawal of Western forces from Germany – an old Soviet objective – it would also, at the same time, dangerously increase the autonomy of the Bundeswehr: see Lanxade, note pour le président de la République, Unification allemande et sécurité en Europe, 23 February 1990. At the Quai d'Orsay, it was emphasized that the French status in NATO was based on nuclear autonomy and that it was therefore not an option for Germany: see MAE, Service des affaires stratégiques et du désarmement, note pour le directeur des Affaires politiques a.s. L'unité allemande et l'Alliance atlantique: les options, 19 February 1990, AD, ASD 1985–1990, box 15. Bush, at any rate, excluded this option at Camp David in unequivocal terms: 'One France in the Alliance ... [is] enough for me', he responded to the chancellor, who had suggested the hypothesis: see Bush and Scowcroft, *A World Transformed*, pp. 252; and Gespräch des Bundeskanzlers Kohl mit Präsident Bush, Camp David, 24. Februar 1990, in *Deutsche Einheit*, pp. 860–873. Finally, whereas Gorbachev would put this hypothesis on the table during their meeting in Moscow on 25 May, Mitterrand would be careful not to encourage him: see chapter 5 in this volume, pp. 253–254.

Chapter 5

THE GREAT BARGAINING
(March–June 1990)

After the breakthrough registered in January and February, progress on the German question speeded up in the course of the following month: with the first meeting of the 2 + 4 at the level of political directors on 14 March, the diplomatic process was on track. A few days later, the result of the elections in East Germany powerfully strengthened the unification dynamic. With the last frictions between Paris and Bonn overcome, the diplomacy of François Mitterrand was now more comfortable with the accelerating German developments. True, the French position in the 2 + 4 was marked by a sometimes excessive formalism, at least at the beginning of the exercise, thereby fueling distorted perceptions of Mitterrand's alleged reservations over unification. Yet Paris's goal in these negotiations was clearly to contribute constructively to the solving of international problems raised by German unity. Its conception of the 'Ottawa exercise' (the 2 + 4, whose mandate had been adopted in the Canadian capital in February), halfway between the maximalist approach advanced in Moscow and the minimalist one privileged in Bonn and Washington, won out in the end.

During these months the French priority remained the German-Polish border problem, which for Paris needed to figure at the center of the international settlement concerning Germany unity. While the misunderstanding with Bonn on this subject faded after mid March, French diplomacy remained watchful. Even if the Élysée was now concerned to handle the

---

Notes for this section begin on page 258.

Germans carefully, French pressure no doubt contributed to making Helmut Kohl budge: by the end of spring, the resolution of the Oder-Neisse border problem had progressed considerably. At the same time, Paris and Bonn found a way to overcome the winter's difficulties. As of April, the Élysée and the Chancellery agreed on the principle of accelerating European integration with a view to achieving political union, a goal to which the Twelve would rally between the first European Council in Dublin at the end of April and the second one at the end of June. The Franco-German couple was off to a new start, returning to the intense bilateral cooperation that existed before the autumn of 1989. This was illustrated by the common attempt to contribute to resolving the crisis unleashed by the Lithuanian declaration of independence, as well as by Mitterrand's support for Kohl over economic aid to the USSR, which increasingly appeared as a key element of the East-West bargaining over Germany. As for the membership of united Germany in NATO – a principal stake of the bargaining – although it was not the top French priority, Mitterrand's diplomacy proved wholly in solidarity with his allies over this issue and paradoxically played an important role in convincing Gorbachev not to oppose it. This did not prevent the future of the Atlantic Alliance becoming again a bone of contention between France and the United States, however, thus announcing the return of the habitual transatlantic misunderstandings.

The 'Phony' Negotiation: French Diplomacy and the 2 + 4

Few diplomatic episodes have inspired so much analysis and commentary as the 2 + 4 negotiations over the external aspects of German unification. For the first time since the end of the Second World War, the great powers cooperated to deal with a problem that they had not been able to solve after 1945 but that the Cold War had frozen for a long while. Yet this peculiar negotiation was made interesting above all by its atypical and in certain respects paradoxical nature: its main goal, for the Western diplomats, was indeed to tackle the subject as little and as late as possible, to the point that it would serve increasingly as the clearinghouse of a grand bargaining process that was essentially taking place elsewhere. While French diplomacy did not have a preponderant part in this affair – except concerning the border question, treated below – it was fully engaged in it and played a more significant and constructive role than has so far been recognized.[1]

The adoption of the Ottawa mandate, as we have seen, was satisfying for Paris. Yet French leaders realized the gap between their desire to give substance to the coming negotiations and German hesitations: in effect it was only under strong pressure that West Germany had finally accepted the Ottawa 'formula'.² At the end of February and start of March, the French did not hide their impatience to put into effect the 'mechanism' and 'use the tool' as completely and as quickly as possible. At this stage, before negotiations, properly speaking, had begun, this concern to fully and rapidly apply the mandate involved procedural aspects. While the Germans and Americans insisted on the denomination '2 + 4', the French, led by Mitterrand and Roland Dumas, persisted in reversing the order, referring instead to '4 + 2' to stress the prerogatives of the Four – in particular over the border – and to put Germany on guard against any temptation to a fait accompli.³ This insistence would not last beyond the second half of March, though: not only did it not make much sense, but the French realized how much it annoyed the Germans, who were always touchy over this issue, especially since the Soviets – who were much more hardline than the French over the substance of the negotiations – themselves soon renounced this formal appellation.⁴ Bertrand Dufourcq soon agreed with his German homologue Dieter Kastrup on a compromise formula: one would henceforth speak of the 'group of Six' or the 'Ottawa group' in official documents relating to the negotiations.⁵ So even if it may, for a while, have fostered among the Germans the perception of a French reticence or frustration (in fact, Mitterrand and Dumas, in private, would continue to speak of '4 + 2'), this pique over the order of the formula remained inconsequential.⁶

The question of the schedule of the negotiations was more substantive: for Paris it was a matter of rapidly obtaining an effective start for talks to avoid the Ottawa mandate remaining a dead letter.⁷ French diplomacy therefore pleaded for an opening of the 2 + 4 without waiting for the elections on 18 March in the GDR, whereas the Germans wanted to deal only with a democratically elected East German government. As for the Americans, they were in favor of deferring the start of negotiations as long as possible to reduce the Soviet hold over the process by making the dynamic of internal German unification trump the international process.⁸ On the other hand, London and especially Moscow shared the French wish for a rapid start to negotiations and put pressure to that effect on West Germany. Finally, the Germans accepted that a first meeting of the Six would take place in Bonn on 14 March at the level of political directors.⁹

This first meeting (there would be a total of eight at that level and four more at the ministerial level) fixed a procedure in which political and especially symbolic stakes were very clear. Bonn was concerned to see meetings held on German soil, so the principle of alternating between Bonn and East Berlin was retained for political directors' meetings; the next one was to be held in East Berlin after the GDR elections. But the question remained open about the ministerial meetings, although it was decided that the first two of these (whose dates were not fixed) would definitely take place in the FRG and the GDR and that meetings would be presided over by each of the Six in turn. For the rest, the composition of the delegations was settled at the first meeting: beyond the ministers during ministerial meetings, the political directors would be accompanied by three aides throughout the exercise.[10]

On the French side, the 2 + 4 negotiations were the affair of the Quai d'Orsay. For this Mitterrand relied entirely on Dumas, with whom he was in complete agreement. The exercise was closely followed for him by Caroline de Margerie, but – except for the border issue and, less prominently, the issue of Germany renouncing ABC weapons – the Élysée intervened very little and was content with being kept informed. Margerie was in contact with Dufourcq, who regularly kept her abreast of the meetings of the Six. Dufourcq was thus the principal French negotiator of the 2 + 4: Dumas delegated it to him, satisfied with being briefed between ministerial meetings and with issuing occasional instructions. The proximity between Genscher and Dumas also allowed Dufourcq to hear his minister's views through his counterpart Kastrup, who was himself informed by Genscher – a very informal way of functioning, which was typical of Dumas's 'style'.[11]

Before tackling the negotiations, a final problem arose regarding both the substance and the procedure: to what extent should the Western countries coordinate their approaches to the 2 + 4? The question concerned first and foremost the 'quad' group (United States, France, Great Britain and West Germany): in order to assure maximum cohesion when face to face with the USSR, the Americans wanted systematic consultation leading to common positions before the six-way meetings.[12] Yet on instructions from the Élysée and Dumas, French diplomacy formally opposed this: Paris, unsurprisingly, refused any notion of a Western directorate and thought it counterproductive to give the Soviets the image of a 'bloc'. While recognizing that the positions of the four Western nations should often coincide, Paris accepted the principle of an exchange of information but objected to this being transformed into a 'preparatory Western organism'. Here again, this perhaps excessive formalism had hardly any consequences, since in substance French diplomacy demonstrated an undeniable Western solidarity during the whole exercise.[13]

The same type of difficulty appeared regarding NATO, with Washington wishing to give to the sixteen alliance members, with the support of Secretary General Manfred Wörner, a consultation role prior to the 2 + 4 meetings on the grounds that the negotiations would have an impact on the alliance. Apart from a concern to promote NATO's political role, the Americans thus wanted to 'hold' their allies while satisfying countries like

Italy and the Netherlands, which were not involved in the 2 + 4 and had been frustrated by the decisions being taken without them in Ottawa.[14] Here again, Paris – always sensitive about anything touching NATO's political role – would oppose what the Quai denounced (classically) as a 'drift' toward such a role.[15] Still, the French proved just as quickly concerned to prove their flexibility: arguing the risk 'of antagonizing our partners for a doubtful benefit', Dufourcq pleaded to Dumas 'not to push things too far', and Paris henceforth accepted the four Western nations' keeping the Sixteen regularly informed about the unfolding of the 2 + 4 – which would, in fact, happen without difficulty throughout the exercise.[16]

Positions Taken

After the first meeting of the political directors on 14 March, the positions of the principal actors in the negotiations could already be distinguished. It was confirmed that the FRG had a restrictive, even minimalist, approach: the 2 + 4 exercise – whose goal for Bonn was to assure the return to full sovereignty at the same time as to unity – would be limited to organizing the ending of quadripartite rights and responsibilities, with the Six engaging in *discussions* (not *decisions*) about the external aspects of unification. Issues of substance would be treated elsewhere, for example between the Germans and Polish over the border, and it could not be a question of Germany being assigned a special status or any kind of 'peace treaty' being imposed, a formula considered unacceptable more than four decades after the end of the war.[17] The Americans, meanwhile, took a position very close to Bonn's: to defer as long as possible the start of substantive discussions and limit the role of the Six to a strict minimum, notably over politico-military questions. For Washington this was the best way of attaining the principal goal, the maintenance without restriction of united Germany within NATO: by sustaining unconditionally Kohl's policy and by demonstrating complete Western cohesion, they could prevent Moscow from steering the process or 'bargaining over unification'.[18] The British – Margaret Thatcher having finally admitted the inevitable nature of German unification – shared the American objective to maintain Germany within NATO while also showing more concern, like the French, to see the Six play an assertive role on some issues like borders.

By contrast, the Soviets had an extensive, even maximalist approach to the exercise – a clear withdrawal from the openness demonstrated by Gorbachev when Kohl visited Moscow – regarding first the form of the talks, since they wanted to obtain a plain *peace treaty* that would close the accounts of 1945, and then the substance, Moscow's objective being to impose a limiting status on united Germany, in particular from a politico-military standpoint: confirmation of Germany's renunciation of ABC arms, but also its neutralization, demilitarization and denuclearization, all of which had to be attained thanks to a 'synchronization' between German unification and the transformation of European security. As seen from the Quai d'Orsay (as indeed from the other Western capitals), these requirements embodied the traditional aims of Soviet diplomacy since the 1950s: Moscow was trying to 'challenge Western security arrangements and foremost the Atlantic Alliance' and to 'advance its favorite themes' (collective security and the pan-European process) while imposing a transition period of several years, at the end of which the rights and responsibilities of the Four Guarantor Powers would finally be lifted.[19]

The French position resulted essentially from two orders of considerations that, to some extent, were contradictory. On the one hand, France wanted to assure that the German settlement took place in a context of stability, which implied bringing clear and definitive answers to the various questions relating to unification, starting with the problem of the border. This was to prevent any later challenges, and it took the form of an exacting, even rigorous approach to the 2 + 4 exercise, which might thereby lead to certain convergences between the French and Soviet positions. But on the other hand, France wanted to preserve the Franco-German relationship while refusing 'any neutralization of Germany or special military status' that might lead to a questioning of the Western security system or of the military potentialities of European construction, all of which would imply, inversely, a more restricted concept of the exercise and thus lie closer to the German and American attitude.[20] The latter considerations very quickly carried the day: although Mitterrand's diplomacy never lost sight of the former – notably concerning the procedure – the latter would determine the French position on the substance of solving the German question.

This was shown by the preliminary reflections made by the French foreign ministry during March. Reasoning that the Ottawa mandate encompassed 'all the external security conditions of the unification process', the Quai d'Orsay, at first, unsurprisingly proclaimed a rather extensive approach to negotiations. Far from constituting a simple complement to the process of unification, the 2 + 4 should definitively rule on questions relating to the quadripartite rights and responsibilities – starting with the Oder-Neisse border – and it should produce a veritable 'peace settlement'.[21] Yet the French diplomats were aware that they must not confer an overly general scope on such a settlement (the very notion of which was in fact vigorously rejected by the Germans), or else it would 'give the feeling that France is playing the game of the Soviets'. French diplomacy thus quickly agreed with its Western partners to limit the place given to politico-military questions in the 2 + 4, so as not to give Moscow leverage to impose on Germany a status that suited it; hence the necessity, advanced by Washington and accepted right away by Paris, of referring most of these questions to other bodies like the CFE or the CSCE.[22] In short, while Paris might seem to situate itself somewhere between Moscow and Bonn or Washington, the French position on an exercise whose stakes (apart from the border question) related foremost to Western security did in fact from the start respect the exigencies of solidarity with the allies.[23]

The Western Dynamic

The developments of the early spring would quickly confirm this. With the success in the GDR elections of 18 March of the 'Alliance for Germany' led by the CDU, which won 192 seats in the Volkskammer against 88 for the SPD (a triumph for Kohl), what little uncertainty remained about the rhythm or constitutional mode of the process was removed. It was now thought at the Chancellery that the six-party talks ought to finish in October or November, at the time of the CSCE summit, and that German unity might occur formally at the start of 1991: 'the rapid route' to unification was now 'a fact', Dumas recognized.[24] This was confirmed by the procedure adopted to conduct the talks. At this juncture, Kohl definitively chose article 23 of the Basic Law, a procedure that called for the direct adhesion to the FRG of the reconstituted Länder of the GDR, in preference to article 146, advanced by the Social Democrats, which implied convening a pan-German constituent assembly.[25] The impact of this choice on the international aspects of the process was considerable: the procedure in article 23 in fact amounted to the absorption of the GDR by the FRG, privileging the internal dynamic and limiting by the same token the intrusion of foreign powers in the process, whereas article 146 would have opened a long transition and consequently paved the way for international interferences. Perhaps even more importantly, the use of article 23 guaranteed the continuity of the FRG's international engagements, in particular concerning alliances, whereas article 146 would have led to renegotiating them – hence the Soviet insistence on article 146 and the Western preference for article 23.[26] This preference for article 23 was shared by French diplomacy, which, as we have already seen, favored it due to the guarantees of continuity it brought in the domain of European integration.[27]

As a result, the limits of the Franco-Soviet convergence over 2 + 4 now appeared very clearly. To be sure, before the beginning of negotiations in mid March, a certain proximity between Paris and Moscow had been perceptible: Dumas had proposed coming to discuss the 2 + 4 in Moscow to Shevardnadze, and the Soviets hoped to 'reach an entente' with the French on the international aspects of German unification, notably on security matters.[28] Yet barely three weeks later, the Quai d'Orsay noted that the Soviet conception of 2 + 4, which aimed to challenge the Atlantic status quo on account of German unification, was in fact very distant from the French one. If Mitterrand's diplomacy still supported the idea of a 'peace settlement', it was only to allow Moscow to 'save face', for the content of such a settlement as envisaged in Paris was really well short of Soviet requirements.[29] The conversations between Dumas and Shevardnadze on 30 March confirmed this: beyond the mutual satisfaction on seeing the 2 + 4 finally underway and despite the shared wish for close Franco-Soviet cooperation, the divergences were clearly more important, whether over the choice of article 23, which Dumas defended unambiguously, or over the Soviet idea of a 'synchronization' between German unification and the emergence of new security structures, which the French rejected for the reason that one should 'not overly enlarge the authority' of the Six. Politico-military questions, Dumas stressed, related to other bodies.[30] As of the end of March, it was clear that any convergences between France and the Soviets in the 2 + 4 process would be at best occasional.

This was all the more so because the acceleration of the process after the GDR elections played in favor of the West, whose approach was increasingly conditioned by the close understanding between Germany and the United States.[31] Aiming to thwart the Soviets and satisfy the Germans, the Americans were in effect determined to accelerate the process of unification while limiting the effective role of the 2 + 4, from which they had decided to exclude any politico-military questions as much as possible.[32] Thus the French position could only approach that of its partners even more. Not only did the Quai d'Orsay agree on the need to limit these questions in the six-party discussions, but French diplomats now mentioned only a 'final settlement' while stressing the need for a 'flexible' approach to the result of the 2 + 4. Emphasizing that France 'is in favor of rapid progress of the exercise', they argued that the 2 + 4 should not be conceived 'as an obstacle to the process of unification but on the contrary as a means of facilitating it', even if one must avoid giving the Soviets the feeling that one was 'putting a knife to their throat'.[33] In this context, the meeting of the four Western political directors on 10 April in Brussels showed an increased convergence. To be sure, a lively exchange did take place between French and Americans, who had distributed a document confirming their wish to reduce the scope of the 2 + 4 to a strict minimum; Dufourcq hammered that a renunciation by the Four of their prerogatives was inconceivable in the absence of a definite settlement of the border problem.[34] Meanwhile, agreement was almost complete over the security problems: the French – who recognized that 'any negotiation on the politico-military questions' would go in the direction of an unacceptable 'special status' for Germany – ratified without difficulty Robert Zoellick's suggestion that the treatment of security questions be sent to 'appropriate' bodies.[35]

By the end of April, as the negotiations had begun only at the staff level and talks were not yet beyond the procedural issues, the Americans and the Germans could be satisfied with the delaying tactics they had adopted. The dynamics of rapprochement between the two Germanys and the growing convergence between the Western powers were indeed producing effects: whereas the former, after the GDR elections, reduced the risk of the USSR using the 2 + 4 for purposes of blockage, the latter strengthened the German-American approach to the negotiations. In addition, Bonn and Washington could congratulate themselves on London's more constructive attitude: Thatcher, after meeting Kohl at the end of March and Bush in mid April in Bermuda, had finally acknowledged the inevitability of unification and now proved primarily concerned to preserve Western interests. The Americans had every reason to be satisfied with Paris's cooperative behavior as well. With the Franco-German misunderstandings overcome and Kohl and Mitterrand agreeing on a European initiative, Bush noted when he met Mitterrand at Key Largo on 19 April that there was no difficulty whatsoever between French and Americans over the 2 + 4.[36] In fact, at the end of April the French position was even closer to that of its partners: without excluding 'pro forma convergences' with Moscow occasionally so as to facilitate a compromise, the Quai d'Orsay thought it essential on substance to 'define a line that takes into account the need to preserve Western cohesion'.[37]

The Soviet Game

The Soviet position, for that matter, had scarcely changed. Despite some inflections or softening, the USSR at the end of April stuck to the approach proclaimed from the start: a maximalist conception of the scope of the 2 + 4 (even if Moscow no longer talked of a 'peace treaty'), the imposition on Germany of specific politico-military constraints, starting of course with nonmembership in NATO, and 'synchronization' between unification and the establishment of new pan-European security structures. Moreover, Moscow wanted to oppose the resort to article 23 – which it compared to nothing less than an 'Anschluss' – and instead privilege article 146 in the hope of slowing down the process.[38] True, on the occasion of a more open speech given by Shevardnadze in mid April, the Western nations could think that this position was likely to soften; rapidly, however, the 'hardliners' retook the ascendancy, although unofficially MID representatives made more nuanced statements. All this testified, against the background of deterioration in the domestic situation and the increasing precariousness of Gorbachev's power, to the confusion that dominated in Moscow when it came to diplomatic decision-making.[39] Yet Soviet immobility, combined with the slowness (desired by the West) with which the 2 + 4 negotiations took up substantive matters, was playing in favor of the Western powers: not only was the unification of the two Germanys becoming a de facto reality that Moscow had no means of opposing, but in delaying basic discussions on the international aspects – discussions that the Soviets, with their maximalist position, made vain in any event – the Western nations were in essence imposing their minimalist approach by default. During the second meeting of political directors of the 2 + 4 on 30 April, France noted that the USSR 'found itself isolated' and 'gave the paradoxical feeling of wanting to play for time while impotently witnessing the acceleration of concrete changes'.[40] On the eve of the first ministerial meeting of the 2 + 4, which finally took place in Bonn on 5 May, almost three months after the Ottawa mandate was adopted, the Western nations noted how the Soviets clung to their initial positions and wondered if they actually had the means to keep them or whether it was merely a matter for Moscow of 'saving face'.[41]

The ministerial meeting in Bonn confirmed this. Shevardnadze in his official speech stuck to a rigid approach of the 2 + 4 settlement and the necessary transformation of European security, combined with a warning against a united Germany's remaining in NATO, which the USSR continued to reject: 'On this point, we are not playing and we are not bluffing', he warned. Still, apart from the inscription into the 2 + 4 agenda of the establishment of 'appropriate security structures in Europe' conceded by the West (a casual way of mentioning the strengthening of the CSCE, suggested by Baker with Dumas's support), the Soviets received scarcely any guarantees that their worries would be taken into account in the negotiations. However, in Bonn Shevardnadze suddenly formulated a surprise proposal: to distinguish between the *internal* process of unification that might culminate quickly, and the *external* aspects that would be settled after a transition period of a few years during which the rights of the Four would be maintained. The suggestion confirmed that the USSR no longer had the means to oppose unification but was rather trying to give itself the leverage necessary to 'control' a unified Germany, which the West, starting with the Germans, evidently could not accept. Then the Soviet minister minimized the differences during the press conference following the meeting, so that the Westerners judged that its general tone had been 'largely positive'. The Americans and the British congratulated themselves that the Soviets, despite Shevardnadze's admonishments on this subject, had not *formally* challenged Germany's membership in NATO at this first ministerial meeting, while the Germans saw the idea of decoupling the external and internal aspects of the process as a de facto green light for attaining unity in the shortest time. The French also thought that in Bonn, the Six had progressed on several points in a direction 'in line with [their] general conception of the exercise', if only because it was now agreed that the settlement would be 'concluded by the necessary legal acts' and not 'in an informal and incidental way as initially desired by the FRG and the United States'.[42]

The day after the ministerial meeting in Bonn, though, uncertainty returned to affect first the form of 2 + 4 process – while it was now accepted that it would be a 'final settlement' containing legal obligations and that the lifting of the Four's rights and responsibilities would be conditional on this, the shape of the whole settlement remained to be defined – and then the sequence, for if the Soviet proposal to decouple the internal and external aspects might be interpreted as an admission of weakness, it also posed a formidable problem since it would consist of granting the USSR a durable *droit de regard* on Germany's status. But uncertainty was most dominant in the substance of the settlement, for the Quai d'Orsay noted that 'swords had not yet crossed' on basic questions. On the one hand the USSR, while advancing demands that it knew were unacceptable to the Western nations (such as Germany not belonging to NATO and development of new European security structures), remained vague, if not evasive, over its concrete requirements. On the other hand, the Western nations stuck to their approach of relegating major politico-military issues to other bodies, arguing that the Six did not have the authority to deal with them. In short, both sides were looking at the clock and playing a game of diplomatic hide-and-seek. And yet, 'the hour of truth' would eventually arrive: what would happen, the Quai d'Orsay wondered, if, when all the questions had been resolved from the Western standpoint, the USSR then opposed the conclusion of the settlement – thus blocking the lifting of Allied rights – for the reason that its own requirements had not been taken into account?[43]

The 2 + 4 at an Impasse?

The six weeks between the first ministerial meeting in Bonn on 5 May and the second in East Berlin on 22 June confirmed the uncertainty of these peculiar negotiations. While the Western nations had voluntarily delayed in engaging in them in order to limit the risk of seeing Moscow drawing benefits, by the end of the spring the situation was inverted: whereas unification of the two Germanys was rapidly becoming a reality, particularly in the economic domain, the objective of the FRG and its Western partners – Paris included – was now to conclude as rapidly as possible the 2 + 4 exercise so as to make unity coincide with sovereignty and prevent the USSR from having leverage over Germany's status.[44] While Genscher for a time gave the impression of accepting Shevardnadze's proposal of decoupling the external and internal aspects in the name of accommodating Soviet security interests, Kohl quickly imposed his line, close to Washington's: there was no question of allowing the USSR to gain control of a process that escaped it more and more, a reasoning fully shared in Paris.[45] The American administration held that the unification process must even be hastened and that the Soviets must be made to understand that the moment of truth of the negotiations was approaching, even if this meant offering them some compensation, which, as will be seen, Bonn and Washington were now actively contemplating. As for Kohl, he was determined to achieve German unity in the autumn so that the general elections planned for 2 December could be transformed into the first pan-German elections.[46] In fact, the chancellor's visit to Washington on 17 May confirmed the close understanding with the Americans over this double objective: maintaining Germany in NATO (Kohl reiterated his commitment made at Camp David) and a rapid conclusion to the unification process, whose external aspects would be settled *at the same time* as the internal aspects.[47]

Still, the Soviet unknown remained: would the USSR continue to wait and see, or would it block the negotiations? Between May and June, Moscow tried one and then the other tactic. The third meeting of the political directors of the 2 + 4 on 22 May in Bonn, under French presidency, resembled the preceding ones: sticking to their line, the Soviets behaved as if they felt the negotiations had not yet substantially begun, again showing a gap between the rather relaxed ambience and the ever incompatible nature of their basic positions with those of the West, at least on the politico-military aspects. Still, to the extent that these same aspects had been set aside during the talks, the French thought the meeting was positive. Even if the negotiations remained conditioned on solving politico-military issues, progress had occurred on the other questions, and the outline of the final settlement could be discerned on the basis of proposals submitted by Dufourcq after consultation with his partners. Dufourcq was pleased that the Western nations had thus succeeded in making 'the Soviets enter into the substance' and making them accept a calendar and a working program (it was understood that drafts should be submitted to the ministers at the East Berlin meeting a month later). He recognized, however, that 'it would be difficult to progress rapidly' on the fundamentals because the Soviets were continuing 'to play the clock'.[48] But time was not playing in Moscow's favor: despite some persistent differences, particularly over the sequence of the settlement, the West proved to have perfect cohesion and found itself thereby in a position of strength.[49]

The Western nations were also increasingly perplexed by the delaying tactic adopted by Moscow, and also by the vagueness, at times even incoherence, of the Soviet positions, which were rigid in official presentations but more flexible in unofficial contacts. Things happened, wrote Dufourcq, 'as if two kinds of diplomacies were superimposed, sometimes on the same day'.[50] Of course, the Quai noted at the end of May, Moscow's attitude and in particular the 'inertia' of its positions were a sign of weakness, but this same weakness might paradoxically have destabilizing effects, especially if it took the form of blocking negotiations.[51] In fact, the Soviets were becoming aware of the ineffectiveness of their approach and they realized that the dynamic of the negotiations were escaping them. In mid May the MID recalled Yuly Kvitsinski, until then ambassador to Bonn and foremost 'Germanist', to take things back in hand.[52] But if this change of personnel led to a greater coherence in Moscow's approach, it also led to a hardening of the official Soviet position. True, during the fourth meeting of the six political directors, on 9 June in Niederschönhausen (East Berlin), the Soviets proved more amenable, with the discussion mostly focusing on the border.[53] Still, they submitted an alternative outline for the final settlement (now in competition with the French one submitted on 22 May) that marked a clear hardening of their position, even a step backward: it was presented as a plain 'peace settlement' that prescribed a long transition period between unification and the lifting of quadripartite rights and responsibilities, and it included specific politico-military constraints for Germany as well as the transformation of alliances and the development of pan-European security structures.[54]

In these conditions, the following meeting of political directors in Bonn on 20 June was difficult and frustrating: the Soviets, who concentrated their efforts on politico-military issues that they wanted included in the 2 + 4, ran up against the Western refusal; they were now evidently trying to block things.[55] Two days later, on 22 June, the second ministerial meeting, held in East Berlin, confirmed the impasse. Shevardnadze developed proposals contained in a document prepared by Kvitsinski, which only hardened still more the preceding ones by pushing the maximalist concept: double membership of Germany in NATO and the Warsaw Pact, limitation of German forces to 200–250,000 men and establishment of a demilitarized zone in Germany while waiting for the dissolution of alliances, among other unacceptable demands. Although during informal exchanges Shevardnadze minimized the significance of his own proposals and agreed to pursue the 2 + 4 at a sustained rhythm, this was a cold shower for the West.[56]

Sidelining the 2 + 4?

By the end of June 1990, negotiations over the external aspects of German unification appeared well and truly blocked. Yet this was a trompe-l'oeil, for important things were in fact happening elsewhere. Indeed, it had become clear after the 22 June ministerial meeting that the 2 + 4 was not 'the place where most of the basic questions would be settled' and that the 'dynamic of negotiations' had moved beyond it: the main action was now situated in other bodies.[57] As a result, far from marking time, the process advanced more and more rapidly, if only because German unity was now almost complete in its internal aspects: 'The rhythm of unification never stops quickening', noted Mitterrand's diplomatic advisor on the eve of his meeting with Kohl on 22 June. Not only were the economic realities looming (the treaty on monetary union signed on 18 May was meant to go into effect 1 July), but political unification was accelerating, and it was now accepted that the procedure would finish before the end of October and permit pan-German elections to be held in early December. This acceleration could only produce a similar acceleration of the international process: the Germans wanted to conclude it in the autumn to avoid unity and sovereignty being out of sync and were supported in this by the Americans, who were more than ever determined to help Kohl as the West German elections approached. Moscow's capacity for obstruction now appeared much reduced: Loïc Hennekinne noted that 'the impression is prevailing that the Soviets will not be able to pose an obstacle to the rapid conclusion of the exercise'.[58]

In fact, as will be seen below, Gorbachev's attitude during his meeting with Bush in Washington at the beginning of June showed that the USSR could not oppose Western determination on the issue of united Germany's belonging to NATO exclusively. The stakes were now thus for Moscow 'to find by direct discussion with the various Western partners concerned' a formula 'that would allow presenting the Soviet retreat as something balanced by Western concessions'.[59] Even if the French diplomats in Moscow were wondering about the reasons for Shevardnadze's apparent hardening in Berlin on 22 June, they judged that there was scarcely any doubt that ultimately nothing much would remain of Moscow's demands in the final settlement; in fact, they believed, 'the concrete aspects of the final arrangement are already being discussed'.[60] Their colleagues at the Quai d'Orsay agreed: 'negotiation appears to be now going on in a bilateral way' between the Soviets and the Americans and between the Soviets and the Germans, they believed.[61] This is what was in fact happening: while the Americans discussed the NATO question with Moscow (on this more below), the French were beginning to understand that an even more important negotiation was perhaps now under way between Bonn and Moscow. After a new meeting between Shevardnadze and Genscher in Münster on 18 June (they had already met a week before in Brest-Litovsk, a symbolic site for German-Soviet reconciliation), Margerie noted that these '1 + 1' meetings were a 'parallel negotiation' to the Six and suggested that it was 'bilaterally' that 'a package' was being elaborated 'to enable the Soviet Union to consent to German unification', a 'package' in which German economic aid to the Soviet Union (until then a 'discrete part' of the German-Soviet negotiations) appeared as determining.[62] On the threshold of the summer of 1990, then, the 2 + 4 had become only a secondary stage; the essential action was situated elsewhere.

The Oder-Neisse Affair: 'The Cleansing Storm'

Apart from the European dimension – to which we shall return – the issue of the German-Polish border was the primary French preoccupation in the negotiations over the international aspects of unification. It is therefore suitable for us to return to an issue that was the direct cause of the final difficulties between Paris and Bonn in the spring of 1990.

It must be said that when the six-party negotiations began, Kohl's position on the border issue had scarcely changed despite numerous calls for clarification since autumn. Of course, the chancellor ceaselessly assured people in private that the Oder-Neisse line would not be called into question, but in public he still stuck to a legalistic attitude in line with the juridical doctrine fixed by Bonn thirty years earlier: only a united and sovereign Germany could definitively confirm its borders. In the face of growing pressure from the SPD opposition and from his coalition partners, starting with Genscher, and also the strong insistence of his international partners, led by Mitterrand, he was content to make calming declarations, as in his speech to the French Institute of International Relations on 17 January, when he said that no one in Germany was considering calling into question the current German-Polish border.[63] During February, his principal foreign interlocutors – Gorbachev on the 10th, Mitterrand on the 15th, Bush on the 24th – were able to detect that the chancellor remained close to his initial position. While trying to minimize the border problem and to assure them that united Germany would definitively recognize the Oder-Neisse line (which might be the subject of a treaty between the two countries, he conceded for the first time to Mitterrand, then to Bush), he continued to postpone the solution until after unification. Emphasizing the legal constraints, he denounced what he regarded as an exploitation of the theme by his opposition as elections approached and justified his attitude by citing his pedagogic concern: it was a matter of convincing the Germans (and foremost the associations of *Vertriebene*) of the need for a clear and definitive recognition of the Oder-Neisse line to confer incontestable legitimacy on it – which meant not rushing public opinion, he insisted.[64]

The French position was known: Mitterrand had ceaselessly insisted on it for months, in particular to Kohl, and he came back to it at Latché on 4 January and in Paris on 15 February. The French president affirmed his sympathy for the psychological and 'sentimental' dimension of the problem from the German point of view: he willingly recognized that the territories of the East had historically been most often German, and he testified to understanding the legal constraints by acknowledging that, legally, recognition of the border could only take place after unification. But he also said in no uncertain terms that it was necessary to confirm the Oder-Neisse border politically *before* unification and to guarantee it by a constraining juridical act *afterward*, which implied Kohl's taking a clear and definitive public position as rapidly as possible.[65] Mitterrand's approach was close to Genscher's and the SPD's, but this evidently was no solace for Kohl. It was no different in substance from that of his principal homologues, however; this was evidently true for Gorbachev, even if Soviet diplomacy was less concerned with the Oder-Neisse line than the NATO issue, and for Thatcher, even if she made less of this subject in the spring than she had done in the fall, and most importantly it was also true for Bush. In this affair, which it granted less priority, American diplomacy proved more concerned than the French to carefully handle Kohl and consequently it was less exacting on the modes of a solution, yet there was no difference between Paris and Washington on the need for a satisfying settlement, as Bush recognized at Key Largo.[66]

Although he often held forth on the historic indeterminacy of the German borders (as de Gaulle once had done), Mitterrand's attitude, however, was not motivated by fear of seeing the Germans effectively challenge the Oder-Neisse line in the future; he did not doubt Kohl's word over this. On the other hand, three series of considerations weighed in his reasoning and led him to disapprove of the chancellor's vacillation on this issue, which he attributed at the time to his 'electoralism'.[67] First, for him the problem of the German-Polish border had the value of a precedent: Mitterrand feared, as we have said, that a Europe liberated from Communism would succumb again to its nationalist or irredentist demons and head down the path of fragmentation, hence the need arose to consecrate the intangibility of borders that France, beyond the German-Polish case, even considered proposing as a general principle of the new European order.[68] Moreover, the settlement of the Oder-Neisse affair was for Mitterrand the touchstone of the way Germany would effect its unification. Would it steer the process by taking others' viewpoints into account, or would it do so via fait accompli and assertion of only the German viewpoint, which would risk arousing the lasting resentment of its neighbors or even challenge European stability?[69] Finally, from a more formal viewpoint, Mitterrand's diplomacy evidently considered that this question related specifically to the quadripartite rights and responsibilities – hence the French belief that a bilateral German-Polish negotiation over the border, which in itself was a necessity, nevertheless must be 'capped' by the 2 + 4. The Oder-Neisse question, in sum, was the most solid argument for requiring the Germans to engage in real negotiations over the international aspects of their unification, of which it was a central issue. Yet of course this requirement was seen by some as further proof, although without any grounds, of a French will to hamper the unification process.[70]

The Border on the Agenda

After Ottawa, the issue of the border came into the forefront of international preoccupations, and it was Warsaw, of course, that took the initiative. On 16 February, Prime Minister Tadeusz Mazowiecki summoned the French ambassador to share his worries, telling him that he 'was counting a lot on support' from Paris for the Polish position.[71] Mazowiecki explained in a letter to Mitterrand on the 20th that Warsaw was asking that the border be confirmed by a treaty that could only be signed and ratified by a united Germany, naturally, but that should be negotiated as quickly as possible with the two German states and initialed by them *before* unification; moreover, the Six (whose mandate mentioned the security of neighboring states) should deal with the border issue and dissipate any ambiguity over the Oder-Neisse line, knowing that Poland should be involved in this discussion.[72] The Polish request was brought by French diplomacy to the front line: in his speech of 1 March to the Berliner Pressekonferenz, Dumas, on Mitterrand's instructions, spoke the necessary 'truthful language' about the border, demonstrating that he could be critical of Kohl's attitude, even if he was also very positive about German unity and stressed that it was up to the Germans 'to choose its pace and mode'. Moreover, the speech was given in Genscher's ostensibly approving presence, which made the chancellor and his entourage strongly irritated at Dumas.[73]

Kohl, using the usual legal argument, categorically rejected the Polish idea of negotiating and initialing a treaty before unification; nevertheless, Dumas's statements, combined with pressure from Genscher and his own opposition, forced him to start to shift his position.[74] But not without detours and difficulties: in the following days Kohl took up the idea put forth at the end of December by the president of the Bundestag, Rita Süssmuth, which he had dismissed at the time: an identical *declaration* would be voted on by both the Bundestag and the East German Volkskammer after the GDR elections, which would certify that Germany, once unified, would definitively recognize the Oder-Neisse border by an international legal act. But Kohl declared at the same time that he wanted in return from the Poles a clear renunciation of any demand for reparations, as well as the granting of special status to the German minority in Poland, which caused a general international outcry and a serious crisis within his coalition.[75] This was nevertheless the position he presented during a telephone conversation on 5 March with Mitterrand, who was visibly skeptical about the chancellor's declared intention to clarify his attitude.[76]

But the next day, as a result of a difficult compromise with his political partners, Kohl's position changed again significantly: it was now understood that the government would shortly submit to the Bundestag a resolution calling for a joint declaration, to be voted in by the two German parliaments after the GDR elections, in which the inviolability of the Oder-Neisse border and the need to conclude a German-Polish treaty after unification would be reasserted, but with the link to the question of reparations and the German minority in Poland no longer being a precondition. That very day, the chancellor sent the draft of the resolution to Mitterrand and asked him to defend this approach during his coming meeting with the Polish leaders.[77] There was indisputable progress: from Warsaw to Washington via Paris, everyone was now pleased with the position adopted by Kohl, which was approaching Genscher's and ought therefore to calm the political debate in West Germany. At the same time, it was clear that it remained insufficient from the Polish government's viewpoint.[78] In fact, while Mitterrand was pleased with the evolution in the chancellor's attitude, which he saw as the result of his own insistence, he stressed the need to go farther on both the form and the substance. The Germans and Poles, he said, must now start to work on an international legal act to consecrate the border, and the subject must be discussed simultaneously in the framework of the six-party negotiations. Moreover, the draft resolution was imprecise since it did not explicitly mention the Oder-Neisse line and the term *inviolability* was used rather than the stronger *intangibility*.[79] Therefore, while the vote on the resolution in the Bundestag on 8 March was considered a success in Kohl's entourage, it was far from marking the endpoint of the affair from an international standpoint.[80]

The Return of the 'Little Entente'?

The ongoing status of the matter was demonstrated the day after the Bundestag vote by a visit by the Polish leaders to the Élysée at their own request. Mitterrand had decided to seize the opportunity of Jaruzelski and Mazowiecki's arrival to throw France's weight into the balance. Yet the French president was not prepared to go too far: he wanted to be 'useful' to Poland, he confided, but 'the Germans must be handled carefully', a preoccupation he would not forsake in the coming weeks.[81] Margerie's analysis, sent to him on the eve of the Polish visit, reflected this search for a balanced approach: recognizing that the Bundestag resolution marked progress (even if it remained short of Warsaw's demands), she noted that France had no reason to dissuade the Poles from trying to negotiate and initial a treaty with the Germans before unity, even if this request had little chance of succeeding due to Bonn's position. As for the Polish demand to participate in the six-party negotiations, it should be treated delicately due to the fact that the contours of the talks remained uncertain. She suggested using the following language with the Warsaw leaders: while understanding their worries and being favorable to the fact that they were trying to solve the issue with the Germans, France recognized that the border question should be tackled in the six-party negotiations and it was ready to seek with its partners 'a solution with which the Poles could be involved in one way or another'.[82] On this basis the Élysée, along with Dumas's office, prepared a carefully drafted statement that Mitterrand might make the following day during the Polish visit.[83]

The conversations on 9 March at the Élysée were characterized by gravity and even some anguish on the Polish side.[84] While Jaruzelski began by mentioning nothing less than 'a community of interest between Poland and France for the second time in the century', Mitterrand implicitly reminded his visitors of the limits of the Franco-Polish rapprochement, stressing that the French and the Germans had 'overcome the phenomenal disasters of war' and so had a 'special relation'. 'Whatever the form of unification', he warned, 'we are for it'. While his interlocutors wondered about ways of controlling the process of unification by imposing requirements 'at each stage', Mitterrand retorted that 'in no situation should you overplay your hand'. As for the essential subject of their conversation, the border, Mitterrand said France was 'determined to use every means at its disposal' to obtain a 'clear and precise recognition', without which 'it could not support the process of unification'. Yet he avoided endorsing all the Polish demands. While he recognized that the issue should be solved as much as possible between then and unification, he did not commit to the idea that a treaty ought to be effectively concluded or initialed *before* unity; and although he did not contest that the Four ought to be involved in the settlement, he 'asked for reflection' on the modes of Polish participation in the six-party conversations and was skeptical about the idea of a meeting of the group in Warsaw.

Overall, the president testified to sympathy for the Poles and showed himself ready to risk upsetting Bonn, but he was evidently concerned to mark certain limits. In fact, in the press conference that followed the meetings, his statements were calculated with a manifest concern to placate the Germans as much as possible and therefore remained overtly short of the Poles' demands. But these nuances would pass almost unperceived in Bonn: it was the strong signal given in Warsaw's direction and the criticism of a German position described as 'insufficient' that were noted across the Rhine.[85]

Mitterrand-Kohl: 'Cleansing Storm?'

In fact, Mitterrand's statements were interpreted in the Chancellery as the expression of pure and simple support for the Polish position. Teltschik cited an 'extraordinary' press conference in which Mitterrand had supposedly wholeheartedly found cause for the Poles; Kohl would even cite a resurrection of the 'little Entente' (an allusion to the complex system of French military alliances in Eastern Europe during the interwar period).[86] The episode gave rise to frank explanations on the occasion of a telephone call that the French president made to the chancellor on 14 March to give an account of the Polish leader's visit. Mitterrand informed Kohl that two points were agreed between Paris and Warsaw: first, the need to start immediate negotiations between Bonn and Warsaw that might be concluded after unification; and second, the presence of Poles at the 2 + 4, knowing that it was not a matter of transforming the six-party negotiations into seven-party ones. Visibly angry, Kohl replied with a long exposition: his position on the border could not be put into doubt after the Bundestag vote on the resolution on 8 March. The Poles, he said, were upping the ante for reasons of domestic politics without anyone taking into consideration his own domestic constraints; Paris, he deplored, was living 'on another planet'. Mitterrand replied with conciliatory statements: thanking Kohl for his explanations and showing understanding for his motivations, he emphasized that the press had misrepresented the tenor of the Franco-Polish conversations. Stressing that his position did not in fact exactly match that of the Poles, he said that this had contributed to poisoning the atmosphere. Minimizing in passing the political significance of his meeting the same day with the Social Democrat Oskar Lafontaine, Mitterrand said he was happy about his good relationship with Kohl despite their limited divergences.[87] Yet the next day, Teltschik gave the same message to Jacques Attali: the Germans were very astonished at the lack of trust evident in the Paris position, and Kohl's advisor added with a certain bluntness: 'France must make the Poles understand that they should not persist.'[88]

Nevertheless, the episode would be quickly put behind them. While minimizing the impact of Mitterrand's position on his own attitude, Kohl would later speak about the 14 March conversation as a 'cleansing storm'.[89] Yet the French pressure was clearly not without effect on the chancellor, who was well and truly constrained, as his entourage suggested in the days following the Poles' visit to Paris, to make a new effort.[90] Though he had opposed the holding of a seven-party meeting in Warsaw, which

Mitterrand was not in fact demanding despite their discussion of it, Kohl had, during the telephone conversation on 14 March, admitted that a form of Polish participation in the 2 + 4 over the Oder-Neisse issue would be 'logical'.[91] The same day, the political directors of the Six, meeting in Bonn for the first time, agreed to include borders in the subjects to treat and especially agreed to Poland's participating in debates concerning the Oder-Neisse issue.[92] Although Teltschik dryly warned the French the next day that it was still 'out of the question' for the Four to 'stand guarantee' for a German-Polish treaty, a formula Bonn considered humiliating, there had indeed been progress concerning the role of the 2 + 4 in the settlement of the problem, a role that the Germans now admitted. But they also began to budge on another point Mitterrand had raised: the need to start German-Polish negotiations now.

This time, it seems it was Bush who obtained Kohl's commitment, thanks to an astonishing misunderstanding. When the U.S. president had called him on 20 March before receiving Mazowiecki at the White House the next day, Kohl, wanting to show goodwill, had confided that he was disposed to make an agreement with Warsaw on the content of a *letter* by which the Bonn government would transmit and endorse the resolution by the two German parliaments once it had been voted in. But Bush, having understood that the chancellor was ready to discuss with the Poles the text of the *treaty* itself, had presented this hypothesis the next day to Mazowiecki personally, in the hope of mediating between Bonn and Warsaw. Then, realizing after the fact that he had gone beyond Kohl's intentions, Bush, during a new conversation with Kohl on 23 March, obtained (not without strong insistence) a new concession from the chancellor: the latter suggested that he might agree in advance with Mazowiecki on the content of the *resolution* by the two German parliaments, which would be taken up in the treaty that would be negotiated later. Though Kohl continued to refuse to open formal negotiations over the treaty before unification, once more there was therefore progress, which the Americans attributed to themselves; they thought they had 'ironed out' the border issue. But in reality the progress redounded just as much to Mitterrand, without whose insistence Kohl would undoubtedly not have budged, as to Bush, who indeed would not go beyond this somewhat involuntary pressure on the chancellor.[93]

The Border at the 2 + 4

Although it was not yet completely solved, by the end of March the problem of the border ceased to occupy the foreground or to weigh on Franco-German relations. Receiving the Bavarian minister-president Max Streibl (who admitted not understanding Kohl's attitude over Oder-Neisse) at the Élysée on 28 March, Mitterrand did not linger over the issue, which he mentioned only 'for the record'.⁹⁴ He intended to remain vigilant, though: while recognizing a 'very positive' change by the Germans over this, he confided to Dutch Prime Minister Ruud Lubbers at the start of April that he wanted to see the Germans 'engage in a more formal way' and start negotiations with the Poles 'without delay'.⁹⁵ He mentioned the question in passing to Kohl during the Franco-German summit in Paris on 25 April, stressing that 'as for the Oder-Neisse border, it is important that it be clear', but he hurried to add that he understood 'what this represents on the emotional and sentimental plane'.⁹⁶ A few days later, with Thatcher (to whom he had vented a few months earlier over Kohl's attitude), he stressed that after much hesitation the chancellor had finally publicly committed himself, which marked progress: 'I admit there is a German legal problem, but one can make declarations of intention', he summarized, confirming that the problem was on its way to being resolved.⁹⁷

In fact, the question of the border did not disappear, but it became the concern of diplomatic staffs, who treated it as one of the principal subjects within the 2 + 4 framework. Still, West German diplomats dragged their feet over making the advances, to which Kohl had consented in March, more concrete.⁹⁸ Dufourcq took the measure of German hesitations during a conversation with Kastrup at the start of April: while confirming the scheme for an identical resolution from the two German parliaments, Kastrup confirmed that Bonn wished to begin tackling the question soon with the Poles, but he let it be understood that the Six should take it up only later. If they were now ready to engage in bilateral negotiations that they had formerly rejected, the Germans manifestly intended to delay as much as possible the intervention of the Four and reduce them to 'taking note' of a German-Polish agreement.⁹⁹ But Paris remained concerned about the role of the guarantor powers, as much for legal as for political reasons. The border question was part of their reserved rights, and its settlement therefore implied their participation. Too, the role of the Four and the threat of a 'guarantee' on their part acted as a prod to force Bonn to engage more vigorously with Warsaw.¹⁰⁰ Seen from Paris, the German attitude was judged to be retreating from the results of the 2 + 4 meeting of 14 March, for it risked voiding the role of the Six in the Oder-Neisse question entirely.¹⁰¹ This is why French diplomacy contested the American conception that the Four might abandon their rights without exercising them: while Paris recognized that 'the essence of the negotiation' on the border would unfold between Germans and Poles, the Quai d'Orsay wished for a 'sequence' in the 2 + 4 settlement that would make its effective conclusion contingent on resolution of the Oder-Neisse problem.¹⁰²

In these conditions, throughout April Paris maintained pressure on Bonn to clarify the modes of Polish participation in the work of the 2 + 4 on the border, in line with what had been decided on 14 March.[103] This insistence paid off: during the meeting of the 2 + 4 political directors on 30 April in East Berlin, it was understood that the six ministers would decide, on 5 May during the first ministerial session of the 2 + 4 in Bonn, on the modes of involving the Poles; moreover, the two German delegations announced they would go to Warsaw on 3 May to launch bilateral consultations.[104] Unsurprisingly, it was to the border that Dumas devoted his speech on 5 May: happy over the beginning of German-Polish conversations and recognizing that the affair would be solved in part bilaterally, he nevertheless stressed the role of the Six and insisted that the modes of Polish participation be fixed.[105] At the end of the ministerial meeting, the French were satisfied: not only had the Germans and Poles begun to negotiate bilaterally, but agreement had been reached among the Six on the need for a settlement including the necessary legal acts, in particular concerning the border, and the modes of involving Poland had been made precise. The Poles would be invited to participate in the third ministerial meeting planned for Paris in July, as well as the meeting of political directors that would precede it.[106]

The Germans Budge; the Poles Up the Ante

Henceforth, for French diplomacy the border question was a matter of attentive follow-up rather than urgent preoccupation. Paris wanted to make sure that the dossier was progressing according to the dual approach it favored: the bilateral path that should produce a German-Polish treaty, and the 2 + 4 process that should lead to 'consecrating' the whole thing.[107] Of course, the Germans remained very sensitive about the issue and opposed any formula that smacked of a constraint, notably on the part of the Four: they were trying, noted Mitterrand, 'to acquire the status of a great sovereign nation with no particular restrictions'.[108] Still, an important advance was recorded on the occasion of the meeting of the six political directors in Bonn on 22 May under French presidency. Paris, we recall, on that day submitted an outline for the final settlement that included certain legal instruments relative to borders and stipulated that the Six would acknowledge the German-Polish treaty as well as the constitutional reforms that Germany would have to accomplish to prevent any risk of irredentist claims, starting with the suppression of article 23 of the Basic Law. More importantly, Bonn enunciated five principles meant to lead to a definitive solution: a German-Polish treaty would be concluded concerning the border; unified Germany would be composed of the territories of the FRG, GDR and Berlin; it would not formulate any territorial claims; its constitution would be amended as a consequence; and finally, the four powers would acknowledge these principles. This package was welcomed by the five partners of the FRG, although the French, British and Soviets underscored that the Four ought not only to *acknowledge* the said principles but also *consecrate* the definitive character of the German borders. In total, even if the modes of a legally binding solution remained to be clarified, Paris considered an important step forward to have been taken.[109]

Instead it was the Polish viewpoint that now concerned the French, because as Bonn became more open, Warsaw began to stiffen its position. Some days after the first German-Polish meeting on 3 May and the 2 + 4 ministerial meeting of 5 May, Polish Minister for Foreign Affairs Krzysztof Skubiszewski confided to the French ambassador that while Warsaw continued to defend the idea of negotiations prior to unification, 'realism' demanded 'flexibility'. It would be difficult to obtain an initialed treaty in due form before German unity, so the essential thing was to go as far as possible in that direction to 'nail down' negotiations, he said.[110] Still, consultations that took place in mid May at the Quai d'Orsay at Warsaw's request revealed that the Poles were not satisfied with the German offers. Reporting that the first German-Polish meeting on 3 May had been difficult, Polish diplomats were most demanding on the content of the settlement: it should include an actual legal recognition of the Oder-Neisse line and not a simple guarantee of its inviolability, should entail modifications not only of the Basic Law but of other internal West German norms (e.g. relating to the definition of citizenship), and should establish conditions for the definitive lifting of quadripartite prerogatives. The French, while confirming their attachment to a legally unequivocal settlement at 2 + 4, were cautious: Dufourcq stuck to expressing 'the hope that the Poles and Germans manage to elaborate a satisfactory solution' and that the Six 'will have only to introduce it into the final settlement'.[111] The same view arose during Mazowiecki's latest visit to the Élysée on 28 May: faced with the Polish prime minister, who, while pleased that his country was invited to the ministerial meeting in Paris in July, regretted that the German-Polish conversations had scarcely produced results, Mitterrand was noncommittal. Noting that 'the German postulate has not changed' over the impossibility of concluding a treaty before unity and stressing 'the evolution' represented by the prospect of a resolution by the two parliaments, he recognized that it would be necessary 'for the Germans to be more forthcoming'. But remarking that Bush did not want to harm Kohl and that French pressure 'was annoying' to the chancellor, he stressed that it 'would be excessive to ask them for a completed process before unification'. Mitterrand concluded that 'the Germans have to go farther for everything to be prepared diplomatically before unification. We will see if that is done' – but he added: 'You keep asking for more.'[112] Evidently Mitterrand, now more worried about the risk of Polish overbidding than about German inertia, was concerned not to collide with Bonn's susceptibilities.

The month of June confirmed the softening of Bonn's position. Even if German diplomacy remained focused on preserving the forms and not appearing to cede to pressure, there was progress within the 2 + 4. Given the insistence of Paris, London and Moscow that the articulation between the German-Polish negotiations and the six-party negotiations be clearly delineated and that the role of the Four be affirmed in the settlement, the Germans accepted a compromise suggested by Paris during the meeting of political directors in East Berlin on 9 June. The limitation of the territory of a united Germany to the Federal Republic, the GDR and Berlin, and its conclusion of a treaty with Poland, would both be posed as principles by the Six in the final settlement. The two other principles advanced by Bonn on 22 May, renunciation of any territorial claim and modification of the Basic Law, would be contained in German declarations of intent. Finally the Four, hereby formally exercising their rights and responsibilities, would acknowledge these commitments by declaring (as the French had suggested on 22 May) that their application would establish the definitive character of the border.[113] They were now very close to what would be the final settlement concerning the border.

The evolution of the German position was also manifest in Kohl's declarations, which finally broke with the previous ambiguities in his public statements. In a speech at Harvard on 7 June, the chancellor pronounced the word 'intangible' about the Oder-Neisse border for the first time in public: until then he had used the notion of 'inviolability'.[114] In effect, the chancellor understood that the moment had come to clarify his position definitively. Recognizing that the question was still painful for some, he declared before the CDU on 11 June that 'there will not be German unity without recognition of the Oder-Neisse border'. Two days later, stressing that all West Germany's partners without exception were requiring it, he warned: 'Whoever refuses the Bundestag resolution on the recognition of the Oder-Neisse border should tell me how [else] he intends to achieve unity.'[115] And on 21 June, in a declaration to the Bundestag that he considered one of the most important of his political life, Kohl repeated these arguments: 'Either we confirm the existing border, or else we are gambling on our chance of reaching German unity.'[116] The same day, the Bundestag and the Volkskammer each voted to accept the expected resolution, which marked German commitment to concluding a treaty with Poland and resolving the question definitively.[117] Now, as the second 2 + 4 ministerial meeting in East Berlin ran into an impasse over politico-military questions, the border solution was clearly progressing. Genscher on this occasion informed his homologues that the German government was endorsing the joint resolution and would now transmit it to the Polish government. Dumas saluted 'an important act' that would allow the Oder-

Neisse border issue to be settled in a definitive way, and he suggested that the German-Polish treaty be prepared without delay.[118] At the end of June, French diplomacy judged that the border 'dossier' 'was now ripe to be settled once and for all'.[119] Henceforth the main French preoccupation was to do everything to assure the success of the ministerial meeting with Polish participation in Paris on 17 July.

From the Franco-German Misunderstandings to European Relaunch

Franco-German tension over the Oder-Neisse border during the first half of March 1990 was the final episode of misunderstandings between Paris and Bonn. While the premises of a rapprochement had appeared in early February, the turning point really came a month later. Several factors contribute to explaining it, starting with the East German elections on 18 March. To be sure, Mitterrand did not wait for this date to be persuaded of the probability of a scenario of rapid unification. The Élysée, as we have seen, was convinced as of the first days of February that the acceleration was irrepressible and that the path of article 23 was preferable from a Community standpoint. Contrary to what has been written, Mitterrand had not banked on a victory by the SPD, which was hostile to a rapid process and favored article 146, in the hope of things slowing down.[120] Still, the vote did have consequences for French policy, since one of Mitterrand's two requirements, the 'democratic' unfolding of unification, was now fulfilled. Kohl's and the CDU's electoral success on 18 March could only lead Mitterrand to proclaim unreserved support, as when on the next day he said: 'Good luck to Germany.'[121] Paradoxically, Mitterrand's adoption of a more enthusiastic public discourse coincided in this early spring of 1990 with the opposite phenomenon in the French press and media, where one witnessed a recrudescence of questions, even anguish, about German unification as it was about to be realized, as well as rising criticism of the French policy of the preceding months, which was characterized by some people as lacking anticipation and by others as excessively passive. The Élysée was aware of a phenomenon that once more arose from a deficit of 'communication' from Mitterrand over the German question in 1989–1990.[122] On the other hand, despite a slight slippage since the autumn, public opinion remained unequivocally favorable to German unity and to European unification, which the Élysée never lost sight of.[123]

The patent absence of any credible substitute for the relation with Bonn was another significant factor in the Franco-German rapprochement at the end of winter 1990. This was evident with respect to Franco-British relations. From the start on 20 January, when Thatcher had suggested to Mitterrand an entente between Paris and London to deal with German unification, the limits of this idea were apparent. Mitterrand did not share Thatcher's visceral distrust of the Germans, nor her wish to brake if not impede unification.[124] Despite the French president's acceptance in principle of close bilateral consultation, that consultation would scarcely go beyond the recognition of convergences over the 2 + 4. At the foreign ministers' meeting on 15 February, the Franco-British rapprochement ran up against the role of European construction: while Dumas had mentioned the hypothesis of its acceleration to frame German unity, Douglas Hurd did not hide his skepticism. The Iron Lady had dropped a lapidary sentence on this subject at a dinner at the French embassy in London in mid March: 'It is not European construction that will tie Germany [to Europe]; it is [rather] Germany that will dominate European construction.'[125] Mitterrand's diplomacy could not seriously consider a Franco-British entente that for Thatcher would translate into a pure and simple alignment not only with her anti-German feelings, which even the Foreign Office considered embarrassing, but on her anti-European ideas. In any case, in April Thatcher began to resign herself to the inevitability of unification. After her meeting with Bush in Bermuda on 10 April, she placed herself in Bush's wake and henceforth proclaimed the goal of preserving NATO at all costs.[126] Since meanwhile the limits of convergence with Moscow were clearly appearing and (as we shall see) relations with Washington were again subject to the eternal transatlantic misunderstandings, it was perfectly clear that there was no possible alternative to the Franco-German relation and to European construction. In fact, such alternatives were never seriously envisaged in Paris in the first place.

The last factor in the revived entente between Paris and Bonn was that the Oder-Neisse affair had in the end acted as a catalyst for rapprochement. In truth, at no time had Franco-German tension over the border issue really threatened the bilateral relationship: Kohl knew perfectly well that he would eventually have to yield, and Mitterrand was at pains to handle his German partner carefully: 'Franco-German relations are good' despite 'unimportant nervous crises', he said to Lafontaine on 14 March.[127] In short, the episode left scarcely any trace; better still, it contributed to hastening the Franco-German and European revival that until mid March was just a working hypothesis. There were two complementary reasons for this. The first was that for both Kohl and Mitterrand, the border question was highly emblematic of the need for the European project. While Kohl referred systematically to Franco-German reconciliation as a model for German-Polish reconciliation, Mitterrand constantly insisted on the ability of European construction to overcome national antagonisms and to 'attenuate the rigor of borders'. The Oder-Neisse affair, in other words, acted to reveal the European imperative against the backdrop of the end of the Cold War and of German unification.[128] The second, more tactical, reason was summarized by Mitterrand during a conversation with the Portuguese premier on 23 March: 'To correct the impression given by the debate over the Oder-Neisse border, the Germans will have to prove to be good European partners.'[129] In short, as had been the case prior to Strasbourg, the 'Junktim' Germany-Europe would function fully: Kohl had decided to give European pledges, and Mitterrand was persuaded to seize the opportunity.

European Relaunch: Kohl's New Offer

In the first half of February, when the Chancellery had hinted at Kohl's willingness to take the initiative in Europe, Mitterrand, as we have seen, had not followed up on the idea (strongly supported by Élisabeth Guigou) of a Franco-German joint initiative. The Élysée dinner on 15 February, in spite of the good atmosphere, had not resulted in any concrete advance. Kohl rejected advancing the date of the IGC concerning monetary union, and Mitterrand was not open to an institutional reform of the EC. When the latter received Lafontaine on 14 March – the very day of his 'stormy' conversation with Kohl over the Oder-Neisse affair – things had hardly moved. While regretting that there had been no 'progress' over these past months, the French president was resigned: 'Everyone knows that German unity will go more quickly' and that 'we will not advance on European unity before the end of the year', the former being an 'objective brake' on the latter. His priorities remained unchanged, however: he wanted to accelerate the economic and monetary union.[130] But Kohl was still not disposed to accept this scenario. Disappointed at not obtaining any advance in the realm of institutional reforms in Strasbourg, he wrote to Delors on 13 March that he envisaged putting such reforms back on the table.[131] On the occasion of conversations between Teltschik and Attali on 15 March in the presence of Bitterlich and Guigou, the Germans reiterated their proposal for an initiative on political union. Kohl, they indicated, judged it necessary thereby to 'disarm the distrust over German unification' but also to 'get the EMU better accepted in the Federal Republic'. (The Germans suggested in passing that the chancellor might in that case accept advancing the start of the IGC to September or October since it was no longer at the center of electoral debate there, but there was no follow-up). Bonn's scheme, Guigou reported to Mitterrand after the meeting, would be the following: teams at the Élysée and the Chancellery would, in close liaison with Dumas and Genscher, refine a joint proposal for institutional reform; then the two countries would submit it to the extraordinary meeting in Dublin at the end of April, proposing that the European Council set a calendar and a procedure. Guigou stressed that the idea of political union 'was ripening' in many capitals, where it was hoped that Paris and Bonn would move things along, and she promised to give Mitterrand precise proposals the following week. The president, following very favorable advice from Jean-Louis Bianco, this time did ask her to 'work on this hypothesis'.[132]

Reiterating her thoughts from the preceding months, Guigou submitted her ideas to Mitterrand on 20 March. Calculating that the EMU was 'necessarily the occasion of a review of all the institutions' (the German thesis), she stressed that such a reform should not have the 'principal goal' of strengthening Parliament nor of enhancing the European Commission, in favor of which an imbalance had appeared in the past several years, to the detriment of the council. She believed a 'solution from above' could be found by 'bypassing the actual Community thanks to the creation of a veritable European Union' that would recognize the preeminent role of the council, with a 'Congress' linking the existing Parliament to a second chamber issuing from the national parliaments. Since 'the whole system' would thus be 'capped' by the council and the congress, the commission and its president could be given 'increased management powers', and the Parliament could get 'a real right of amendment'. In the event of agreement with Bonn on this basis, Guigou suggested a Franco-German initiative to obtain the agreement of the Twelve in Dublin to advance the IGC on the EMU to September and to launch preparatory work immediately for an IGC on the European Union.[133] As we see, the terms of the 'deal' that would lead to Maastricht were clearly laid out: recognition by the French of the need for an ambitious institutional reform, and acceptance by the Germans of the preeminence of the intergovernmental logic.

In the following days Mitterrand became gradually convinced of the opportunity for a formal and concerted initiative with Bonn. He was still reflecting aloud with his Portuguese counterpart on 23 March: while he no longer seemed as worried as in the previous months about the EMU being endangered by the opening of an uncertain institutional debate, he nevertheless wondered about the modes of an eventual discussion of institutions, and without being opposed to growth in the role of Parliament, he stressed that any reform ought to lead above all to increasing the role of the European Council ('the Commission is not the government of Europe'). Still, he marked the need to deepen thinking: 'I intend to prepare a memo before Dublin to clarify French ideas', he confided, without mentioning a possible Franco-German initiative.[134] In fact, the movement toward political union mentioned by Delors in January was already launched: in a memorandum transmitted to the other governments of the Twelve on

22 March and inspired by the president of the European Commission, the Belgian government suggested convening an IGC specifically on institutional questions or, failing that, instructing the IGC already convened at the Strasbourg summit to deal with these questions.[135]

The next day Guigou transmitted another important element to Mitterrand, who was preparing a television broadcast in which he would tackle the theme of Europe: Genscher, she reported, had declared (and Kohl's advisors confirmed) that unified Germany would not ask for an increase in the number of its commissioners or European deputies nor, even more importantly, a reweighting of Council votes. This, we remember, had been Guigou's key argument six weeks earlier in favor of unification by 'absorption' of the GDR.[136] Now it seemed as if Mitterrand, due to Kohl's growing insistence, was convinced of the need to seize the occasion to advance together in the direction of political Europe. Trying on 25 March to dissipate any idea of a 'quarrel' with Bonn and to exorcise French fears over Germany, Mitterrand said that Germany 'was solidly anchored to European policy' and that he 'would demonstrate that with Kohl in the coming weeks'. Three days later on 28 March, Kohl took a further step: welcoming Irish Prime Minister Charley Haughey in Bonn, he suggested that the Twelve in Dublin on 28 April call for an IGC devoted to political union. The next day, Mitterrand gave his agreement to this idea.[137]

From Dublin I to Dublin II

In the three weeks that followed, the consent given by Mitterrand to the principle of a political relaunch would result in a proper Franco-German initiative. To be sure, the Élysée remained worried about becoming entrained in an institutional reform whose content would be marked with the seal of German conceptions and consequently distanced from French ideas. Thus the first days of April saw a rather clear gap between Paris, where it was insisted that the major orientations of a relaunch be determined prior to such an initiative, and Bonn, where the quick announcement of a common approach was desired and the French were suspected of dragging their feet and not wanting the Germans to run the show. The Germans, Guigou confirmed after a new meeting in Bonn on 2 April, were 'extremely desirous of developing a joint initiative' that would allow asserting the 'urgency' of a political Europe, but they did not want to announce the content of an institutional reform at Dublin.[138] So how to move forward? Guigou suggested proceeding in stages to Mitterrand: Dumas would soon have a full discussion with Genscher to try to quickly obtain indications about the German ideas, and if this was conclusive, then in Dublin the foreign ministers might be asked to start to reflect with a view to reporting to the European Council at the end of June (which should also take place in the Irish capital).[139] On 5 April, she reported after a new conversation with Bitterlich that Kohl 'desires in any case to make a proposal on European union in Dublin', so that it would be 'very clear that German unification is being done within the European framework' and that he could not be reproached for holding up European construction. The message was clearly that Kohl would prefer a Franco-German initiative but that he would go forward with the idea whatever happened. Guigou thought a compromise possible: if the chancellor wanted to give a signal about political union at Dublin I (where at least the prospect of an IGC would be mentioned), he might be content for the Twelve to ask the foreign ministers for a report on political union to be presented at Dublin II in late June.[140]

It was finally on this plan that agreement between the Élysée and the Chancellery was reached in the following days. On 11 April, Attali called Teltschik to give the Élysée's 'green light' to the joint initiative.[141] This took the form of a letter from both Mitterrand and Kohl addressed to the acting president of the Community (Haughey) on 19 April. The two leaders asked that the European Council at Dublin I decide that the preparatory work of the IGC on the EMU be accelerated – this was still the French preoccupation – and that the Twelve decide at the same time to launch preparatory work for an IGC on political union. The foreign ministers would be charged with establishing a first report for Dublin II, knowing that the two intergovernmental conferences would meet in parallel, with the goal that both the EMU and political union would go into effect on 1 January 1993 after ratification by the national parliaments. In substance, the Mitterrand-Kohl letter remained evasive: the objective of political union would be to 'strengthen the democratic legitimacy of the Union', to make its institutions 'more effective', to assure the 'coherence of its actions' in the economic and political domains and, finally, 'to define and apply a common foreign and security policy'.[142]

Evidently the Franco-German initiative was at the confluence of two logics: Mitterrand's concern to confirm the economic and monetary union, through which he hoped to frame the power of the new Germany, and Kohl's desire to legitimate unification thanks to a revival of political Europe. In fact, the letter's vagueness about the latter mirrored an agreement that was still minimal, containing unresolved differences reflecting the German wish for an institutional reform favorable to Parliament and to the Commission on the one hand, as expressed by the notions of legitimacy and efficiency, and the French wish to preserve the intergovernmental logic. Hence the French insisted on 'coherence' that only the Council could assure and on a common foreign policy that could only emanate from the latter. The French and Germans had nevertheless clearly launched a dynamic that would culminate twenty months later: 'European unity and German unity are being made together, this has always been the European dream', noted Kohl during the Franco-German summit on 25 April, adding: 'But we have to do this together', to which Mitterrand replied: 'I am available.'[143] The extraordinary European Council in Dublin on 28 April concluded favorably. On the one hand, it confirmed the inscription of unification within the European framework: as expected, the Twelve ratified the modes of the gradual integration of the territory of the GDR into the Community (not as a thirteenth state but as a consequence of the forthcoming unification of the two Germanys) without a modification of treaties. On the other hand, it confirmed the placing on the agenda of the revival desired by Paris and Bonn: even if they deferred a final decision on convening an IGC on political union to Dublin II, the Twelve rallied to the objective put forward by Mitterrand and Kohl in their letter of 19 April – the establishment of a European Union on 1 January 1993.[144]

The three months that separated the two European Councils in Dublin confirmed this dynamic and further specified the contours of the relaunch, on which French diplomacy wanted to imprint its seal. Returning from Parknasilla (Ireland), where the foreign ministers of the Twelve had met on 19 and 20 May, Dumas reported to Mitterrand that the meeting 'enabled an important step toward the political union sketched by the Franco-German initiative' and that the idea of an IGC was 'practically enacted'. On substance, Dumas noted a certain number of more or less widely shared ideas: the need for an increased role for the national parliaments in order to strengthen the legitimacy of Community institutions; the fact, recognized by the majority of the Twelve but also by Delors himself, that the Council must remain the keystone of the Union; the idea that a foreign and security policy could only be defined gradually; the importance of assuring the unity and cohesion of the process by coordinating Community developments and those related to political cooperation: all these elements, Dumas underlined, clearly ran in the direction of French theses.[145] Encouraged by these convergences, the Élysée insisted that Dublin II not only ratify the holding of an IGC on political union but also reflect on its substance. Reflection ought especially to bear on the common foreign and security policy mentioned in the Mitterrand-Kohl letter, which presented, from the French standpoint, the advantages of advancing the role of the Council and framing that of the Commission: 'Only the European Council', stressed Guigou, 'can take the lead in this domain'.[146] The Kohl-Mitterrand meeting of 22 June in the Rhine village of Assmannshausen on the eve of Dublin confirmed their desire to go forward with the European dossier.[147] More importantly, the European Council held on 25 and 26 June in the Irish capital reflected the restored power of the Franco-

German engine once the disagreements of the last months had dissipated: as foreseen, the Twelve decided there on the simultaneous holding of the IGC on the EMU and of another IGC on political union, the first to open on 13 and the second on 14 December in Rome under Italian presidency. The European summit was also the occasion for the French president to explain his ideas, anticipating the debate that would dominate the next eighteen months: 'the federal purpose' of European construction, the importance of 'multiplying common positions with a view to a foreign and security policy that would gradually assert itself' and the need to preserve the engine role of the European Council – all these orientations would ultimately win in Maastricht.[148]

A Franco-German Ostpolitik?

The renewal of Franco-German ties not only resulted in European revival, but also translated after April into close cooperation on two decisive issues from the standpoint of relations with Moscow, and at a key time for the process of German unification: the Lithuanian crisis and economic aid to the USSR. The first, which had been brewing for weeks, burst into the open on 11 March when the parliament in Vilnius formally declared the republic's independence. From the start, the crisis sparked vivid worries in the West. Pushed by hardliners, the Kremlin adopted a policy of intimidation that might lead to confrontation, for the Lithuanians were determined to go all the way in their drive for independence. In short, the crisis threatened the pursuit of *perestroika*. It particularly worried Washington, for while the Bush administration could not appear to oppose Lithuanian independence without provoking strong reactions in public opinion and in Congress, it also wanted to treat Gorbachev carefully; hence it wished to see a dialogue between Moscow and Vilnius.[149] This was also the concern of Mitterrand's diplomacy, which more than ever was preoccupied with the fate of the Soviet Number One. While Paris did not contest the right of the Baltic republics to self-determination – France had never recognized their annexation – the French stressed the need for a 'negotiated process', which alone was capable of producing 'pacific' change.[150] But it was perhaps Bonn that was most disturbed: in the event of Moscow's hardening, escalation might dangerously complicate (if not compromise) the unification process. Calming things down was thus an absolute priority for German diplomacy.[151]

The lead came from the French, who broached the issue with the Americans at Key Largo on 19 April. While Gorbachev decreed an embargo against Lithuania on the same day, Mitterrand pleaded with Bush in favor of a measured reaction to the Kremlin's hardening. 'Let us not require of Gorbachev what we would not require of the dictator who would succeed him', declared the French president, for whom the Lithuanians 'had proved to be in an unfortunate hurry', adding that 'if they are fanatics, this will end in blood'.[152] Talking in parallel with Baker, Dumas suggested a Franco-German initiative asking the Lithuanians to place their declaration of independence on hold so as to allow a negotiated process with Moscow, an approach that received encouragement from the Americans.[153] The initiative – which the Chancellery saw as a concrete example of the 'common Ostpolitik' it had long been proposing – was refined on 25 and 26 April at the Franco-German summit in Paris, during which Kohl and Mitterrand agreed on the need to avoid a provocation of Moscow that might produce a chain reaction.[154] In a letter of 26 April addressed to the president of the Supreme Council of Lithuania, Vytautas Landsbergis, the two men, while recognizing the legitimacy of the right to self-determination, suggested to him 'suspending for a time the effects of the decisions' taken by the Vilnius parliament so as to facilitate the opening of negotiations with Moscow that might lead to a 'solution acceptable to all'.[155] Whereas he had not responded favorably to a preceding missive from the French president encouraging him to show restraint, Landsbergis this time proved more constructive: in his response to the Franco-German letter on 2 May, he said he was ready to consider a possible suspension of the effects of the declaration of independence.[156] While the crisis was not completely defused, French diplomacy was optimistic: calls by the American administration and the Franco-German initiative had obliged the two parties to accept dialogue.[157] In fact, Lithuanian Prime Minister Kazimiera Prunskiene, whom Kohl received on 11 May, proved open to dialogue, an attitude that the chancellor attributed to the close Franco-German cooperation over this issue.[158] Tension dissipated at the end of June, when, the Vilnius parliament having voted a moratorium on independence, Moscow announced the lifting of the blockade it had decided two months previously. Paris and Bonn's initiative, in collaboration with Washington, had contributed to removing a dangerous obstacle on the road to German unification.

As spring ended, the question of economic aid to the USSR would also give rise to close cooperation between the two countries. Kohl, as seen above, was persuaded early on that assistance to the USSR would be a decisive factor for the resolution of the German question: in January, Bonn had granted food aid, a gesture that had contributed to calming Soviet leaders after the Ten Point Plan. The question became central after the start of May, when the Soviets formally requested economic and financial assistance from West Germany. Teltschik's secret trip to Moscow on 14 May, accompanied by the chairmen of Deutsche Bank and Dresdner Bank, had made it possible to start negotiations between the two countries. Of course, Kohl's envoy did not hide that, from the German viewpoint, granting aid of this magnitude (the Soviets were speaking of DM 20 billion in credits) ought to be part of a comprehensive 'package' in which the solution of the German problem figured: in other words, in exchange for West German goodwill, Bonn was expecting Moscow to make concessions on 'hard' points such as the participation of united Germany in NATO. This was the start of a grand bargaining process that would bear fruit two months later, and in which German economic aid, Teltschik would later write, would be the 'catalyst.'

In the weeks that followed, the Germans approached their Western partners in the hope of involving them in a policy of massive aid to the USSR. Informed in May of German-Soviet contacts, the Americans, however, were hesitant to participate in this effort: the Bush administration found it hard to imagine consenting to significant economic assistance to the USSR, given that it was not engaging in decisive reforms and the Lithuanian crisis had not yet been peacefully defused.[159] As for the French, they had suspected the existence of negotiations of an economic and financial nature between Bonn and Moscow for some time, but were not really apprised of them until mid June.[160] In a letter addressed to Mitterrand and his other partners on 18 May, Kohl made himself the advocate of Gorbachev's request for Western aid in the form of long-term credits. Stressing the importance of such assistance for the future of *perestroika*, he asked the French president for his support for the Soviet demand, which he promised to present to the European Council in Dublin, and he revealed the existence of discussions on loans to be granted by German banks (and guaranteed by the German government), for which he expected in return 'a constructive attitude' from Moscow on pending questions linked to German unification, in particular membership in NATO. On the eve of the Assmannshausen meeting on 22 June, where the chancellor intended to tackle the question with the president, Guigou brought further details: Kohl wished that the West's desire to support the USSR be confirmed in Dublin at the end of June by the Twelve, then in Houston at the start of July by the G7, and that this be done 'without making Gorbachev lose face', since he had not presented his request for aid publicly. For the rest, the chancellor wondered how to win over those who, like Thatcher, were opposed to such aid, and in what framework (the G7, EEC, etc.) to grant this assistance.[161]

The Élysée was open to Kohl's request: not only was it preferable not to let the Germans act alone in this affair, but the chancellor's initiative echoed Mitterrand's insistence on Western aid for *perestroika*. The very day after Kohl's letter, in an interview in *Le Monde,* the French president said he was ready to propose 'financial, commercial, and technical aid' to the

USSR during the Dublin and Houston summits. Responding to the surprise of the Germans, who saw him appropriating their own proposal, the French made it clear that Mitterrand had given this interview *before* receiving the chancellor's letter; the two men had quite simply had the same idea at the same moment.[162] Whatever the case, at Dublin on 25–26 June Mitterrand defended Kohl's request that the Twelve provide support for a vast financial aid program for the USSR. Although Thatcher's opposition to aid that she considered ill-advised from an economic standpoint limited the effective impact of the decision (the European Commission was only charged with studying the issue of credits to the USSR), the essential thing from the German standpoint was that the Twelve, in making this issue a major theme in Dublin, had given a favorable signal to Gorbachev, for which the Chancellery was grateful to Mitterrand.[163] The relationship between France and Germany was once again fully in play.

The Great Game: German Unification and the Atlantic Alliance

The question of the Atlantic Alliance dominated current events until the summer of 1990. There was a dual debate: How could the USSR be made to accept German membership in NATO? And, reciprocally, what would be the long-term consequences of German unification and the end of the Cold War on the alliance, European security and the Euro-American relationship? There was a dialectical relationship between these two issues: the future status of Germany in the alliance was bound to deeply influence the evolution of NATO; inversely, the transformation of the Atlantic Alliance quickly appeared as a key item in East-West bargaining, for it represented a currency of exchange to obtain the Soviet green light for maintaining united Germany within NATO. French diplomacy was split: Paris announced complete solidarity over Germany's future NATO membership, but the evolution of the alliance itself quickly became a bone of contention in relations between Paris and Washington, prefiguring the difficult debates of the post–Cold War decade.

When 2 + 4 negotiations started, positions had not changed. On the German side, Kohl reaffirmed on 8 March to the North Atlantic Council the line agreed with Bush at Camp David: Germany should remain a full member of NATO. Proving confident about the result of the 'poker game that was starting' (in his terms) with the USSR, he knew he could count on American support; Washington recognized, as did Bonn, the need to take Moscow's worries into account and accept specific arrangements for the territory of the former GDR.[164] But Soviet diplomacy stuck to the intransigent position announced since mid February: on the occasion of a new visit by Modrow to Moscow on 6 March, then in an interview with *Pravda* on the 7th, Gorbachev declared that a unified Germany's membership in NATO was categorically excluded. Of course, Moscow leaders recognized that the situation would change if the alliances were transformed into 'political' organizations thanks to the emergence of pan-European security structures. But this old slogan of Soviet diplomacy found no support in the West, which rejected any idea of 'synchronization' between German unification and the pan-European process. As we have seen, the Dumas-Shevardnadze meetings at the end of March showed the distance separating Moscow from Paris, despite the French concern to take Soviet interests into account.[165] At the 2 + 4, for example, the French and their Western partners quickly agreed to avoid discussions of the politico-military status of Germany that would risk playing the Soviet game. Generally speaking, Paris rejected anything that might lead to a form of neutralization, as Mitterrand stressed again on 14 March to Lafontaine, who was personally hostile to the pure and simple maintenance of united Germany within NATO and the recourse to article 23, the two of which were linked.[166]

Despite the impasse since the start of the six-party talks on the issue of German membership in NATO, the Élysée nevertheless continued to think that things remained unsettled, for two main reasons. The first was that the Soviet refusal was considered to be tactical: Moscow's intransigent declarations, according to Lanxade, were a way of 'raising the stakes'.[167] Védrine repeated that it was 'probable' that the Soviets would end up accepting a unified Germany remaining in NATO and that their attitude of refusal was not their 'last word': not only, he argued, could they not oblige the FRG to *leave* NATO – even by blocking the 2 + 4 or by entrenching themselves in East Germany at the risk of a showdown – but they would probably end up preferring that a united Germany continue to be 'framed' by the alliance.[168] In short, the French were convinced that Soviet opposition might be overcome, given some concessions. The second reason was that, seen from Paris, Moscow should obtain these concessions without too many difficulties. The French, as already mentioned, doubted the Germans' resolve to maintain the NATO apparatus after unification at all costs. While the great East-West bargaining was about to take place, Paris was skeptical: 'One wonders', the Quai noted, if Atlantic 'activism' will remain 'a priority of German diplomacy'.[169] The French underlined the bad image of NATO in West German public opinion and splits among its politicians, with a rather strong current in the SPD as well as the FDP in favor of a collective security system that would take the place of military blocs.[170] Thus since the start of the spring the most likely scenario as seen from Paris was a double agreement: by the Soviets to maintain Germany in the alliance, and by the Germans to transform NATO (or at least German participation in it) in a way acceptable to the Soviet Union.

French Skepticism, American Disquiet

As a result, French worries now concerned the future of the alliance, which was becoming the stake in a great transatlantic debate between France and the United States in particular, a debate that went on for the next year and a half. Mitterrand's point of departure was the conviction that Germany, once unified and rid of Soviet forces, would no longer accept an Allied military presence on its soil. His conviction was fed by the growing hostility of German public opinion to that military presence over several years, which certainly could only be exacerbated by unification and the return to complete sovereignty. Mitterrand, as we have seen, had mentioned several times to Kohl the prospect of a repatriation of French forces from Germany, and he considered a withdrawal of all Western forces as probable in time (even if he thought that an American military presence – which he did not challenge – might remain elsewhere in Europe).[171] In short, the French began with the hypothesis that the Atlantic status quo was fated to face profound challenges after the end of the Cold War and German unification, due to an inevitable American disengagement from Europe. At the Quai d'Orsay, as at the Élysée, it seemed evident that in a few years 'only a few American troops will remain in Europe' and that the integrated organization would become 'loose'.[172]

But how to maintain a credible Western defense, a minimum of Euro-American coupling, and the necessary politico-military framing of Germany – all objectives to which the French remained attached? French thinking on all these issues was, unsurprisingly, oriented to an affirmation of the Western European dimension, conceived as the natural compensation for a probable American withdrawal: 'If we think it is dangerous for us to let NATO become a loose organization and to let Germany become autonomous without NATO being replaced with something else', Védrine analyzed, 'we have to propose … that Europe be equipped with a common defense and security policy' that would be 'the logical complement of the march of the Community toward political Europe'.[173] This was only the very start of a careful approach. For years, Mitterrand's thinking about European defense had been prudent: one had to avoid not only arousing the opposition of the United States and its closest allies, he believed, but also being led onto dangerous ground, like that of sharing nuclear decisions, which the Germans were suspected of wanting.[174] Thus the French president was cautious: 'One has to begin asking whether European defense can be organized', he conceded to his Portuguese counterpart on 23 March, adding skeptically, 'But against whom?'[175] Still, under the circumstances of spring 1990, the debate over the emergence of European defense and its compatibility with maintaining NATO could not help being rekindled, once more setting Paris and Washington at odds.

French skepticism about maintaining the NATO status quo was matched by serious U.S. worry over the same subject. But this would lead the Americans to opposite political conclusions: in the first months of 1990, fear of a possible challenge to the American presence in Europe nourished among Washington leaders a conviction that everything should be done to avoid such a withdrawal, which would lead to the United States' inevitable return to isolationism.[176] Brent Scowcroft put it plainly to Attali, who had come to meet him at the beginning of March at the White House: the United States was worried to see its presence and role in Europe lose their justification in the absence of an enemy, all the more so because the administration was facing 'very strong isolationist pressure' in Congress, which might lead to a withdrawal of American forces if the Germans demanded it. Bush's adviser added that the Americans felt 'concerned' by the possible recurrence of political instability in Europe, which 'had led them twice into war', and they wanted consequently to create a 'political framework' that would 'justify a military presence despite the absence of an enemy'. The best way of doing so, said Scowcroft, was to use NATO. Attali relayed this conversation to Mitterrand the next day, transmitting as well the White House proposal for a working visit by the French president to the United States. Curiously, he took from his exchange with Scowcroft the impression of a 'disoriented' United States that seemed to him 'without strategy or even tactics.'[177]

This impression scarcely lasted, however. True, the French in the following weeks detected the persistence of American disquiet. At the start of April Ambassador Jacques Andréani summarized the dominant feeling among the highest U.S. officials: 'As good as they may be, the changes in Europe risk resulting in a challenge to our presence on this continent', whose maintenance was still 'essential'.[178] Lanxade made the same observation a few days later: 'The disquiet is considerable at all levels over the possibility of maintaining American troops in Germany', he wrote. That West German public opinion had become so unfavorable to this, he added, could only aggravate the risk of isolationist reaction in the United States. Yet Mitterrand's military chief of staff also detected what now appeared to be *the* response of Washington to this challenge: the desire to use NATO to justify maintaining the American presence in Europe and consequently (given the diminution of the Soviet threat) the determination of American diplomacy to 'compensate for the inevitable reduction of the military role of the Alliance by an increase in its political function'. This, he underlined, created in Washington 'a very strong frustration with French diplomacy, which it reproaches for an overly systematic opposition to any initiative in favor of the Alliance'.[179]

New Transatlantic Misunderstandings

French anticipation of an inevitable withdrawal of the United States, for which the assertion of a political and strategic Europe was meant to compensate, thus ran into American determination to do everything to avoid such a withdrawal, including the invention of new justifications for NATO. As the meeting between Mitterrand and Bush in Key Largo on 19 April was approaching, the traditional misunderstanding between Paris and Washington resurfaced. In February/March, the French had observed a return in force of the idea, formulated by Baker on 12 December in Berlin and then defended by Wörner, of the necessary 'politicization' of the alliance and an assertion of its 'new' missions.[180] In early April, the Élysée noted that the United States 'had successfully managed these last weeks a taking in hand' of the alliance by advancing its political role. Attempted discussion of 'out of area' and other subjects (terrorism, drugs), the desire to coordinate the work of the 2 + 4 and that of the Sixteen, and the effort to institutionalize a dialogue between Eastern countries and the alliance were the principal elements of the American offensive over NATO, according to Paris, which essentially consisted of seeking an 'alternative vocation' to collective defense in accordance with the Harmel Report of 1967.[181]

By the same token, it was noted, Washington now manifested a growing anxiety about French policy, always little amenable on all these subjects. Worse, the Americans were tempted to think that the French were now systematically obstructing their efforts to maintain NATO and their presence in Europe, to the point of putting words in their mouths: 'France, it is heard in Washington, is preventing the strengthening of the alliance; does she favor our departure from Europe?'[182] The Élysée was worried about this tendency. While there was no longer 'major contention' with Washington over formerly litigious problems (for example, the relation between NATO and the 2 + 4, on which there had been a compromise in March), American diplomats 'suspect France in advance of not being favorable to NATO's new missions'; therefore the essential question, concluded Védrine, was to know 'how far Bush and Baker want to extend these new missions'.[183]

French diplomacy was not really surprised by this renewal of former frostiness. As Andréani noted: '[T]he quarrels they make for us today over the respective place of NATO and European cooperation in Western consultation, over "out of area," and over the coordinating role of the Alliance – all go back twenty years ... The novelty is simply that today the Americans believe their presence in Europe is threatened and they have decided to defend by attacking.' Instead of 'imagining transformations that would allow a redefinition of the transatlantic tie by taking into account the abasement of the Soviet Union and the political emergence of Western Europe', he wrote, 'they have chosen to keep NATO as it is and to push enlarging its justification by finding it new tasks'.[184] Gabriel Robin concurred: 'the difference in philosophy' between Paris and Washington is 'profound' and it is 'inevitable' that the Americans 'find us in their way'.[185] In short, the French understood that the end of the Cold War was bound to revive a fundamental misunderstanding whose stake was the respective futures of the American presence in Europe and of the political (and in time, military) affirmation of the Europe of Twelve. Hence they wondered about how to react. On 9 April, Mitterrand gathered his principal advisers to discuss these difficulties, which he, too, considered inevitable: 'I understand that they themselves do not know well what they want because they feel that Europe is escaping them ... we can't do anything about that.' The president concluded: 'there is evidently no question of reintegrating into the integrated command [and] we must be firm about what is essential, what technicians call *out of area* and *out of subject*,' but for the rest, 'there is no reason to make ourselves unduly disagreeable'.[186] In fact, Lanxade stressed the same day, France had nothing to gain by letting 'tension' develop with the United States over NATO, since the alliance 'can only change very deeply and have its weight reduced ineluctably, to the benefit of the Community and of the CSCE'.[187]

Strong in this conviction – anchored in the traditional French reading of the end of the Cold War – the Élysée thus wished to calm things with Washington, but without reversing itself. A 'global' opposition to American projects would be 'untenable', Védrine thought, but the absence of French reservations would signify a green light to the American-led 'new Atlanticism'. Hence the line he suggested in anticipation of the Key Largo meeting: telling Bush 'that the American proposals are interesting but need to be made more precise', and suggesting for this purpose a true debate, in which the French would fully participate, on the future of the alliance, which might conclude with an Atlantic summit a year from now.[188] Reassuring the United States about maintaining their presence in Europe without ceding on the enlargement of NATO's missions, and bringing them to recognize European aspirations while being ready to debate the evolution of the alliance: such was Mitterrand's approach in the hope of pacifying relations with the Americans and preserving Europe's future at a crucial moment for transatlantic relations.

The Key Largo Meeting

The summit was carefully prepared in Washington, where much was expected from it. Relations between the two presidents had stayed excellent since Kennebunkport, and the American leaders hoped that the Florida meeting would make Mitterrand sensitive to their worries about keeping the U.S. presence in Europe after the Cold War.[189] In a long letter sent to him on 17 April to prepare for their meeting, Bush stressed the 'crucial importance' of Franco-American relations for European stability and reiterated his personal regard for the French president: 'There is today no European leader whom I respect more than you.' Then he got to the kernel: 'The most important message I wish to send is that I am convinced that the United States should remain deeply engaged in Europe and within the Atlantic Alliance and that they will remain so.' He added that 'the Atlantic Alliance is an essential element for the future of Europe' and did not conceal his worry: 'If NATO is left with only a narrow military function, its importance and the support it has among Western peoples is bound to diminish as the Soviet military threat attenuates', by the same token sapping U.S. involvement in Europe; hence its 'strengthened political role' must be recognized.[190] American thinking could not be more clearly stated, and it would inevitably clash with French thinking.

Yet the Key Largo summit was 'pleasant and non-confrontational'.[191] The problems of the moment – German unification, relations with the USSR – gave rise to only short exchanges, so easily did the French and Americans agree on these subjects. The main part of the conversation concerned the long-term future of the transatlantic relation. Both sides were trying to prove conciliatory. Mitterrand made many assurances that French policy did not aim to exclude the United States from Europe: 'France is your ally, a loyal ally', he assured. Meanwhile Bush tried to dissipate the idea, mentioned in the press in preceding weeks, that the United States wished France to return to the NATO fold: 'We do not have the intention of making you come back to the integrated command', stressed Baker. On the problem of the future role of the alliance, though, the positions remained far apart: Bush repeated that in order to permit maintaining American engagement on the Old Continent, NATO must be able 'to extend its field of competence' to all the problems that might affect Europe. Meanwhile Mitterrand rejected any enlargement of the alliance's scope and merely observed that from his viewpoint, 'anything that touches European security and equilibrium is political'.[192]

To be sure, after their conversation the two men agreed on the need to reflect on the adaptation of the alliance and on the idea (suggested by Mitterrand) of an Atlantic summit to do so before the end of the year. Yet they had far from identical views on the long-term evolution of the transatlantic relation. On the American side, worries were not soothed after Key Largo: 'The thrust of Mitterrand's remarks was to keep NATO confined to its traditional role – defense against a massive Soviet attack on Western

Europe', which was 'precisely what we did not want, and would surely result in the atrophy of the Alliance', noted Scowcroft, who was now 'even more convinced that the U.S. and France had significantly differing views of the future of Europe and our role in it.'[193] The French side thought the meeting 'had gone to the bottom of things' but also insisted on the limits of a possible evolution of the alliance in the direction desired by the Americans: 'Our policy', stressed Dumas to Wörner on 24 April, 'is to act in such a way that Europe exists more and more', which, he insisted, was by no means incompatible with keeping NATO.[194] 'The Americans have the perfect right to participate in the new European equilibrium' in which 'they are involved anyway, since their armies are in Europe and they are in the Alliance', Mitterrand hammered to Kohl at the Franco-German defense and security council on 26 April, 'but the objective of this alliance should not be exceeded'.[195] The debate was only beginning.

Transforming NATO, Persuading the USSR

The debate quickly rebounded due to the acceleration that the Americans imposed on NATO's adaptation. In this spring of 1990, the Bush administration thought the moment had come to secure the Soviet leaders' consent to maintaining united Germany in the Western alliance by proclaiming a transformation of the alliance that would persuade them it no longer represented a threat.[196] Barely a few days after Key Largo, the Americans shared their desire for a NATO summit no longer at the end of the year, but at the end of June or beginning of July, so as to open as rapidly as possible 'perspectives which might make unified Germany belonging to NATO acceptable for the USSR'.[197] This abrupt American rallying to the idea – which had kicked around for some time in Brussels – of an Atlantic summit in the near future upset French diplomacy: while Paris, as Mitterrand had told Bush in Key Largo, wished to give some time to the assessment of the alliance's future, Washington's rush carried the risk of seeing the review exercise proposed by Mitterrand 'preempted'. A summit brought forward to the summer in the name of the need to persuade Moscow of the change in NATO might indeed ratify moves contested by Paris, starting with the 'politicization' of the alliance.[198]

In a message of 2 May, Bush confirmed to Mitterrand his wish for a summit at the end of June or start of July so as to demonstrate quickly the alliance's capacity for adaptation to new circumstances. Although he referred to the Key Largo conversations and suggested (evidently to coat the pill) that this summit would be the occasion to launch reflection that might culminate on the occasion of another summit at the end of the year, he did not hide that it was now a matter of promoting the future 'political' role of the alliance so as to convince Moscow of its profound transformation and more generally of the West's good intentions. Bush announced in passing his decision to give up FOTL (the successor to the *Lance* short-range missile) and his wish to see SNF negotiations open soon – options categorically excluded a few months previously – as well as his intention to see the Sixteen define 'common allied objectives' for the CSCE summit at the end of the year, thus confirming the inflection of American diplomacy in favor of the latter.[199] Mitterrand's diplomacy could only take note of this acceleration: while maintaining its reservations about the politicization of NATO and stressing that this could only be the beginning of reflection on the alliance's future, Paris nevertheless accepted the principle of a summit at the start of July in London. Mitterrand told Thatcher that 'Germany within NATO may be less worrying for the Russians' and acknowledged that 'we must play on that'.[200]

The month of May saw the Americans intensify their efforts to persuade the Soviets, but success at this stage appeared less than assured. Behind counterproposals that were hardly credible, such as the 'non-total' belonging of Germany to NATO or its double membership in the Atlantic Alliance and in the Warsaw Pact, Soviet leaders did not give up any ground. Passing through Moscow at the end of April, the chief of the French general staff, General Maurice Schmitt, found his interlocutors 'very cool' and even 'aggressive' on the German problem.[201] During the first ministerial meeting of the Six in Bonn on 5 May, Shevardnadze, as mentioned above, was particularly hard on the question of NATO membership for Germany, categorically rejecting it. Still, the French noted certain encouraging signs coming from Moscow, where the acceleration of preparations for the CSCE summit, the abandoning of the modernization of the *Lance* missile and the announcement of the coming alliance summit were favorably welcomed.[202] Washington now thought the real stake was to offer compensations in order to persuade Moscow. As a result, the U.S. attitude was increasingly forthcoming with regard to the CSCE.

But most importantly, Washington wished to 'have the effort of persuasion bear on NATO': the alliance had to become both less militarized and nuclearized (hence the recent Bush initiative on SNF) and more open to the East (hence Wörner's trips around Eastern Europe). Kohl, who had come to Washington on 17 May accompanied by Genscher and Stoltenberg, entirely approved of these moves.[203] In Moscow the next day, Baker tried to convince the Soviet leaders of the rightness of this approach, laying out nine 'points' designed to persuade them to accept united Germany's membership in NATO. Elaborated by Zoellick, this incentive 'package' called for: (1) new conventional negotiations that, once the CFE was concluded, would limit troop levels in Central Europe, including those of the future Bundeswehr; (2) acceleration of the opening of SNF negotiations; (3) reaffirmation by Germany of its commitment not to possess ABC weapons; (4) nondeployment of NATO forces in the territory of the ex-GDR during the transitional period; (5) definition of a substantial period of transition to allow the withdrawal of Soviet forces from the GDR; (6) reexamination of NATO strategy that would lead to a radical transformation of its conventional and nuclear posture; (7) settlement of the German border problem; (8) strengthening of the CSCE structures; (9) establishment of economic relations between united Germany and the USSR that took Soviet interests into account. But for the time being, the Americans' effort to persuade Moscow were in vain: not only did the Soviets stick to their requirement of specific military restrictions being imposed on united Germany within the framework of the Six, but they seemed to redouble their opposition (including Gorbachev's) to its staying in the alliance, a scenario they presented as strategically and historically inconceivable.[204]

25 May: Mitterrand in Moscow

A week after Baker, it was Mitterrand's turn to go to the Soviet capital, where he was expected on 25 May. His visit came at a key moment, since Gorbachev was himself expected in Washington on 30 May. In a letter to Mitterrand of the 22nd, Bush recounted Baker's visit to Moscow: without mentioning the 'nine points' (of which the French were not informed at this stage), the U.S. president was worried about the Soviet tenseness on the German question and the NATO problem, which he attributed to Gorbachev's bad domestic situation and the showdown with Lithuania. These developments might 'cast a shadow' on the coming American-Soviet summit. Bush concluded: 'I will be most appreciative of any advice or counsel that you are able to share with me after your visit to Moscow.'[205] On the eve of Mitterrand's departure for Moscow, the Élysée gave great attention to the U.S. president's message, which confirmed both the risk of the Soviets blocking the 2 + 4 process and the determination of the Bush administration to do everything to keep Germany within NATO: 'We have had an indication', signaled Védrine to Mitterrand, 'that the Americans are very attentive to what might be said on this question of keeping the alliance intact during your conversations Friday in Moscow'.[206]

The French president thus arrived in the Soviet capital perfectly aware of the stakes of the German-NATO issue, which would in fact dominate the conversations. Gorbachev proved particularly virulent in the face of what he regarded as a forcible German-American imposition of German unification within NATO, a scenario that he categorically rejected. Moscow, he declared, wanted a demilitarized Germany. German unification and the overcoming of blocs had to be synchronized and the USSR would keep its forces in the GDR as long as Germany was in NATO, he added.

Confronted with Gorbachev's diatribe, Mitterrand chose frankness, and even a certain brutality: not hiding his own unease about the forced march imposed by Kohl with American support ('we both would have preferred that reunification occur more slowly', Gorbachev would later recall), the French president placed himself on the terrain of 'realities'. 'I do not see how to forbid unified Germany from choosing its alliances as agreed in Helsinki', he warned at the start, adding: 'You cannot prevent unified Germany from belonging to NATO', if only because the FRG, which was already in the alliance, was getting ready to 'swallow' the GDR; 'airy words', he hammered, 'are useless' given the Germans' and the Americans' determination to impose this solution. Certainly, he concluded, the USSR might harden its position, but at the risk of a general destabilization of Europe; France, meanwhile, could not isolate itself from its allies, starting with the United States. The French president judged 'preposterous' the scheme, put forward by Soviet diplomacy, of Germany's simultaneous membership in both alliances. As for Gorbachev's suggestion of a 'French-style situation' (Germany in the 'political' alliance but not in the 'military' alliance), he said he saw no disadvantages but he clearly refrained from encouraging his interlocutor in this direction.[207] Overall, Mitterrand's statements reflected his state of mind: while he hinted that he did not attach the same priority to this issue as his closest allies and did not share their desire to impose their scheme at all costs, he also objected to any idea of abandoning solidarity with them, thus making Gorbachev understand that there was no credible alternative to German membership in NATO in the current situation. At the same time it must be said that he was not fully informed about Baker's nine points and Washington's willingness to give compensations to Moscow, which explains the severe tone he adopted about American policy.

The French president drew a discouraging conclusion from his conversations in Moscow: Gorbachev's hostility to the presence of unified Germany in NATO 'appears to be neither a feint nor a tactic', he wrote to George Bush on 28 May. While stressing that he had told the Soviet Number One that it 'was not reasonable to dream of another solution', Mitterrand concluded that Gorbachev 'has scarcely any margin of maneuver' and that the tight calendar envisaged by Kohl for an international settlement on Germany risked encountering 'serious obstacles'.[208] In fact, the French president was being excessively pessimistic, for Moscow drew a 'very positive' view of his visit, retaining a 'triple message': Mitterrand's 'firmness' on membership of Germany in the alliance, about which Gorbachev's entourage indicated that he was 'struck by the clearness of the analysis' put forward by the French president, but also his 'openness' to Soviet security worries, as well as his 'call for dialogue and imagination.'

As a result, the Kremlin promised that the Soviet Number One would go to Washington 'with a spirit of compromise'.[209] It must therefore be acknowledged, as Gorbachev recognized later and his adviser Anatoly Chernyaev confirmed, that Mitterrand, by the solidity of his position and arguments, had well and truly convinced Gorbachev on 25 May of the futility of the Soviet opposition to keeping united Germany in NATO. No doubt the French president's persuasive force resulted from the fact that the leader of the least 'pro-NATO' Western country was placing himself alongside the United States and the FRG, thus removing any hope Gorbachev had of reaching his ends, and thus he contributed to the important Soviet concession that the Americans would receive the following week.[210]

The Washington Summit

In Washington on 31 May, the first day of the Bush-Gorbachev summit, Gorbachev clearly began to shift his position. While the conversation had begun rather badly – the Soviet Number One at first stuck to his usual theses, such as Germany belonging to both alliances – Bush asked him if he agreed to recognize that any country had the right, as the Helsinki final Act said, to belong to the alliance of its choice. Mitterrand had posed this question a week earlier in Moscow. Yes, replied Gorbachev, provoking consternation among some members of his delegation. Marshall Akhromeyev and Valentin Falin made their disapproval evident. The Americans were surprised, but they soon obtained confirmation of this concession during the press conference on 3 June in the form of a declaration agreed in advance with the Soviets.[211]

This was a turning point; Gorbachev now stopped systematically opposing a united Germany remaining in NATO. But the episode was arguably not the final breakthrough that the Americans later claimed, overlooking Mitterrand's role a week earlier.[212] Whereas Gorbachev lifted his opposition, one could not really speak of his complete acceptance: for him, free choice of alliances still did not imply that Germany necessarily had to choose to remain wholly in NATO.[213] Recounting the episode to his Western partners, Bush in fact refrained from overestimating the impact of Gorbachev's concession; Kohl, in whom Bush confided, at first scarcely paid any attention to it, choosing after the Washington summit to insist on the need to succeed at the forthcoming NATO summit in London.[214] American diplomacy in the following days stuck to this low profile: during the 'quad' meeting of political directors in London on 5 June, Zoellick confined himself to indicating that the Soviets in Washington had said only that they were 'interested' in the idea of starting from the principle of free choice of alliances, and he suggested that the West should concentrate on the 'nine points', about which the allies were now informed. On

7 June, during the NATO ministerial meeting in Turnberry (Scotland), Baker was equally careful: in Washington the Soviet position had still appeared to him to be 'in gestation', hence 'major importance' was accorded to the Atlantic summit to show them that their preoccupations were taken into account.[215]

The few weeks that followed were marked by indeterminacy. In the discussions that followed with the Americans (the Baker-Shevardnadze meeting in Copenhagen on 5 June) and especially with the Germans (Genscher and Shevardnadze in Brest-Litovsk and in Münster on 11 and 18 June), the Soviets did show some progress on politico-military questions. They seemed now to accept the idea that the troop level of the future Bundeswehr might be fixed within the framework of future conventional negotiations, with the CFE taking note of a German declaration that would then be taken up in the 2 + 4.[216] But they were still far from formal acquiescence to united German membership in NATO – hence the impasse we have seen in the 2 + 4, where progress remained hostage in mid June to politico-military issues. Gorbachev, recounting his conversations with Bush on 12 June to the Supreme Soviet, reasserted the importance of new collective security structures going beyond existing alliances. In short, it now appeared probable to the French diplomats in Moscow that the Soviets were leaning toward acceptance, but were not there yet.[217] Receiving East German Prime Minister Lothar de Maizière at the Élysée on 18 June, Mitterrand summarized his feelings: 'Gorbachev told me he did not agree with this plan [united Germany in the alliance without extension of the NATO military apparatus over to the GDR], but he may be obliged to accept it.' 'The water is still cloudy in the bottle', concluded the French president, who said he was 'totally in agreement' with the idea put forward by de Maizière of a greater role for the CSCE 'to reassure the USSR' and 'not give the impression of a victory of the West over the East'.[218] It was clear at this stage that the Soviet leaders were expecting a lot from the West: hence the blocking of the 2 + 4, where, noted Dufourcq, '[T]hey visibly intend to make no concession at all before ... the Alliance summit.'[219] Accomplishing a sufficiently deep transformation of the alliance to make German membership in NATO acceptable to the USSR was precisely what the Western countries, led by the Americans, wanted to get down to at the London summit.

The Atlantic Dynamic

Now a dual dynamic was at work in the alliance: the plan to transform NATO, on which the Bush administration was working so as to preserve the Atlantic institution and long-term American presence in Europe – an objective vigorously reasserted in the U.S. president's speech at the University of Oklahoma on 4 May – was combined with a more tactical goal, to achieve a renovated NATO freed from attributes of the Cold War that could facilitate the German settlement. Both objectives moved in the direction of a 'politicized' alliance taken in hand by Washington: hence the renewal of the Franco-American disagreement that would culminate in London in July. The French may have shared the U.S. concern to 'prove to the USSR that its interests were well taken into account', but the Quai d'Orsay expressed its 'reservations' about Washington's approach. The Americans, the Quai's strategic directorate thought, were losing sight of the fact that alliance evolution must first respond to the 'central question', which was 'what places the Americans and Europeans respectively want to occupy in the future Alliance'.[220] For French diplomacy, the goal of the ministerial meeting at Turnberry in Scotland (7–8 June) was thus to assure that the renovation of the alliance proposed by Mitterrand in Key Largo was not reduced simply to measures to reassure the USSR that would surely be adopted in London. Proceeding 'haphazardly' was unacceptable: the French said there must be 'overall reflection' that should lead to adapting NATO in all its aspects, including its internal equilibrium, which should result in a new summit a year from now. But while Paris obtained the mention of the importance of such reflection in the communiqué adopted at Turnberry, the French had no illusions: 'The long term view of our principal partners on the future of the Alliance differs profoundly from ours', wrote Robin, who remarked the day after the ministerial meeting that 'none of our European allies has judged it opportune to stress that the Alliance of the future ought to have a more European character'.[221] This was confirmed by Franco-American consultations that took place at the Quai d'Orsay on 15 June, when Undersecretary of State Reginald Bartholomew insisted on the politicization of the alliance and its new strategy, meaning precisely the two dimensions of the renovation privileged by Washington. Conversely, Bartholomew was skeptical about the idea of Europeanization of NATO, since only the French, according to him, were using this 'language'.[222]

Things hurried along two weeks before the London summit. In a letter of 21 June to Mitterrand, Bush unveiled his intentions at the approach of a meeting that he judged one of 'the most important in the history of the Alliance'. The draft declaration that he submitted to Mitterrand as well as to Kohl, Thatcher, Andreotti and Wörner, he insisted, must be brief, stripped of bureaucratic language, and written to be read by the general public. The draft declaration included: an invitation to Gorbachev to come address the alliance, a proposal to the USSR and other Eastern countries to open liaison missions to NATO, a call for the intensification of conventional disarmament, the abandonment of the concept of 'forward defense' and the accent placed on multinational corps so as to strengthen the legitimacy of the forces stationed in West Germany, a revision of the strategy in the direction of nuclear weapons as 'last resort' and an institutional strengthening of the CSCE with the creation of a secretariat and a conflict prevention center.[223] All these ideas, some of which were indeed quite spectacular, represented the fruit of several weeks of interagency work in Washington, with the goal of resulting in a text up to the dual stakes of transforming the Atlantic Alliance and securing Soviet acceptance of a united Germany in NATO.[224]

Bush's letter confirmed French fears. 'The Americans show their game clearly', commented the head of the strategic directorate at the Quai d'Orsay: under cover 'of facilitating USSR acceptance of unified Germany in NATO', the London summit was for them the occasion to 'reassert their vision of the Alliance', all by a 'last minute move' aimed at getting their own orientations adopted. Philippe Guelluy, the head of the directorate, rejected both the idea of accrediting the representatives of the Eastern countries in NATO, a beacon measure of the American program to 'politicize' the alliance, and the idea of setting up multinational units, which, he said, would 'marginalize us *a priori*' while leading to 'an excess of military integration'.[225] At the Élysée, Lanxade made a similar assessment: Bush's propositions, which essentially went in the direction of an increase in NATO's political role and toward a strengthening of military integration, did not open 'any European perspective with respect to security', and they contained 'the germ of a strong divergence with Washington about the future architecture of Europe', which could only 'incite us to remain in our current situation vis-à-vis the integrated organization'. In short, commented the president's military chief of staff, 'although we might have thought that our partners would choose changes allowing our rapprochement, we now ought to give up this hope for a while'. However, Lanxade recommended avoiding very strong opposition. 'It is almost inevitable', he said, that things would evolve 'due to American military disengagement and the consolidation of the European political union'; it was better, for the time being, to be content with correcting in the declaration the points 'that appear important to us', such as obtaining a mention of the 'European prospects' of the alliance and recalling that France was not concerned by what related to military 'integration'.[226] Defense Minister Jean-Pierre Chevènement was much more incisive. Denouncing 'a text of German-American compromise that, under a formulation designed to reassure the Soviets, strengthens the integrated command and American leadership' and especially 'aims to postpone the threshold of nuclear deterrence to a hazy horizon' by proclaiming a doctrine of 'last resort contrary to the French deterrence doctrine', Chevènement thought it 'absolutely necessary to hold France outside this declaration'. It was useless, he said, to try to 'avoid a clash' with the Americans; French interests were too much at stake in this affair.[227]

As the London summit approached, Mitterrand's diplomacy thus found itself in a quandary that went back to the habitual French dilemmas. On the one hand, the American program of 'renovating' NATO as it was sketched was seen in Paris as disputable. Reassertion of military integration, continuation on the path of new missions for the alliance and reassertion of the logic of flexible response: all went against the French vision of the alliance's future after the Cold War, which hypothesized a probable American disengagement, at least in the long term. On the other hand, Paris could only share the American will to give the USSR as much proof as possible of the transformation of NATO to obtain its consent over the German question, and more generally to help overcome the East-West confrontation. For the time being, it was the latter rationale that counted in French reactions: 'On many points your ideas are like mine', Mitterrand wrote to Bush on 29 June: 'I entirely approve of your general approach aiming to strengthen the defensive character of the Atlantic Alliance, to preserve the security of its members, and to promote a balanced and verifiable disarmament by "extending the hand of friendship" to the countries of Eastern Europe ... NATO, in adapting itself, may play a very useful role in this evolution. Your draft declaration is very exactly in this spirit.' At the most, the French president confined himself to formulating a few 'observations'. He wanted to reassert French military non-integration (even if, Mitterrand specified, France remained available for reflection on the future of the alliance as mentioned in Key Largo) and the logic of deterrence that underpinned the French nuclear strategy. He also wished not to prejudge the measures for strengthening the CSCE before the Paris summit and wanted to reiterate his preference for an institutionalization of the CSCE rather than institutionalized contact between NATO and the Warsaw Pact. Still, during the approach of the London summit, which would be decisive for the German question and the future of the alliance, Mitterrand kept very quiet about his reluctance.[228] For Paris, as for its partners, the success of the 'great bargaining' was indeed the priority.

Notes

1. These 'paradoxes of an atypical negotiation' were well recounted by France's main negotiator at the 2 + 4: see Bertrand Dufourcq, '2 + 4 ou la négociation atypique,' *Politique étrangère*, n. 2/2000, p. 467–484.

2. Roland Dumas repeated this on 9 March at the Elysée during a visit by Polish leaders who came to address the border problem: 'In this entire Ottawa affair, the Germans dragged their feet. Genscher hesitated during an hour in Ottawa and he telephoned three times to Kohl. All of the pressure of the three Westerners was necessary for them to accept': see meeting between Mitterrand, Jaruzelski, Mazowiecki and Skubiszewski, 9 March 1990, handwritten notes by Caroline de Margerie, AN 5AG4/CDM 34. On the Polish leaders' visit, see pp. 225–227.
3. See chapter 4 of this volume, p. 176 and 181. Dumas came back to it on 9 March: the Germans 'wanted to invite the four others themselves. We settled by having the Six issue the invitation': meeting between Mitterrand, Jaruzelski et al., 9 March 1990.
4. Reporting on the Genscher-Shevardnadze talks in Windhoek (Namibia) on 22 March, Kastrup emphasized to Boidevaix that the Soviets had 'definitely said "2 + 4"': TD Bonn 778, 28 March 1990, Archives diplomatiques (AD), série Affaires stratégiques et désarmement (ASD) 1985–1990, box 16. As for Shevardnadze, he explained to Dumas at the end of March that the inversion of the formula was the result of 'German manipulations', while adding that 'the appellation had no importance': see TD Moscou 2501–2502, 30 March 1990, AD, ASD 1985–1990, box 16. (Shevardnadze was later criticized by the 'hard-liners' for having yielded to Bonn on this: see above, chapter 4, note 39.)
5. Dufourcq, '2 + 4'. Although the letter of the Ottawa mandate was not very explicit, it was nonetheless closer to the 2 + 4 notion than the 4 + 2 approach, for it stated that 'the foreign ministers of the FRG and the GDR would meet the foreign ministers' of France, the United Kingdom, the USSR and the United States.
6. Personal interviews. Mitterrand's collaborators, aware of his touchiness on this point, would nonetheless often continue to refer, internally, to '4 + 2' and, on some documents, '2 + 4' was crossed out and replaced by '4 + 2': see e.g. Ministère de la Défense, Note de Marc Perrin de Brichambaut pour le ministre, 26 March 1990, private papers.
7. The Quai wanted 'a quick pace' to 'avoid stalemate' but wanted to avoid 'haste': see MAE, note de la sous-direction des affaires stratégiques et des pactes (ASP) pour le directeur des affaires politiques, a.s. Quad du 13 mars 1990, ordre du jour commenté (questions de sécurité), 12 March 1990, AD, ASD 1985–1990, box 16.
8. TD Washington 508 and 510, 23 and 24 February 1990, AD, ASD 1985–1990, box 15. This point was brought up with Kohl during his visit to Camp David: see Philip Zelikow and Condoleezza Rice, *Germany Unified and Europe Transformed: A Study in Statecraft*, Cambridge, Harvard University Press, 1995, p. 209.
9. TD Diplomatie 4335, 5 March 1990; TD Moscou 1532 and 1624, 3 and 6 March 1990, AD, ASD 1985–1990, box 16; Caroline de Margerie, handwritten note, 'Q. allemande (B. Dufourcq) HV 6 mars 1990,' AN 5AG4/CDM 36.
10. Detailed account in TD Diplomatie 5300–5302, 16 March 1990, AD, ASD 1985–1990, box 16. The political directors of the Six met alternatively in Bonn and East Berlin on 14 March, 30 April, 22 May, 9 June, 20 June, 4 July, 19 July and 6–7 September, and the ministers met in Bonn (5 May), East Berlin (22 June), Paris (17 July) and Moscow (11–12 September). The delegations were led, at the civil servant level, by Dufourcq (France), Dieter Kastrup (FRG), Robert Zoellick (United States), John Weston (United Kingdom), Anatoly Adamishin then Yuly Kvitsinski (USSR) and Hans Misselwitz (GDR). Dufourcq was assisted by Denis Gauer (Europe directorate), Thierry Dana (strategic affairs) and Marie-Reine d'Haussy (legal affairs). Among the members of other delegations were: Peter Hartmann (Chancellery) and Frank Elbe (Auswärtiges Amt) for the FRG and Raymond Seitz (Department of State) as well as Robert Blackwill and Condoleezza Rice (NSC) for the United States; see Dufourcq, '2 + 4'.
11. Personal interviews; see also Dufourcq, '2 + 4'. The Ministry of Defense had only a late and limited role in the decision-making process as a result of the exclusion, desired by

Western powers, of politico-military questions in the 2 + 4. With the talks largely underway, Jean-Pierre Chevènement asked that his ministry be informed of the 2 + 4, which was accepted by Dumas: see letter from Chevènement to Dumas, 31 May 1990, AD, ASD 1985–1990, box 16. (Chevènement would intervene in particular in the question of a united Germany's renunciation of ABC arms: see chapter 6, note 13.)
12. The 'quad', an informal framework of cooperation between France, the FRG, the United States and the United Kingdom, had been established during the second Berlin crisis in 1959 to associate the FRG with the decisions of the three Western powers with regard to Germany before spreading later to all strategic questions concerning the Western alliance.
13. MAE, le directeur des affaires politiques, Quad du 13 mars à la Celle-Saint-Cloud, compte rendu de Bertrand Dufourcq, secret, 16 March 1990, AN 5AG4/CDM 36; see Margerie, 'Q. allemande,' 6 March 1990; Dufourcq, '2 + 4'; and personal interviews.
14. TD RPAN Bruxelles 165, 174–177, 184 and 190, 6, 9, 13 and 14 March 1990, AD, ASD 1985–1990, box 16.
15. MAE, le directeur des affaires politiques, Quad du 13 mars à la Celle-Saint-Cloud, 16 March 1990, AN 5AG4/CDM 36. Dufourcq asked the French representative to NATO, Gabriel Robin, 'to put Wörner on guard'; see TD RPAN Bruxelles, 15 March 1990, AD, ASD 1985–1990, box 16.
16. MAE, le directeur des affaires politiques, note pour le ministre d'Etat, articulation entre le mécanisme à Six et l'Alliance atlantique, 19 March 1990, AD, ASD 1985–1990, box 16; and Dufourcq, '2 + 4'.
17. 'For Bonn', the Quai summarized, 'it is essentially up to the two German states to reach an agreement before submitting decisions to the Six, who would then take note of it': MAE, ASP, note, a.s. Ordre du jour pour les reunions des 'Six.' Positions de nos partenaires et premières conclusions du groupe, 20 March 1990, AD, ASD 1985–1990, box 16. (Another motive of Bonn's refusal of a peace treaty was, of course, that it could lead some to raise the question of possible reparations; see Dufourcq, '2 + 4'.)
18. MAE, ASP, Positions de nos partenaires, 20 March 1990. The White House was skeptical about the actual impact of the 2 + 4: the process was 'vague, fuzzy and will not work. Germany will decide alone on everything', Brent Scowcroft confided to Jacques Attali: Jacques Attali, note pour Monsieur le Président, sur mon déjeuner avec le général Scowcroft à la Maison Blanche le jeudi 8 mars 1990, 9 March 1990, private papers.
19. MAE, ASP, Positions de nos partenaires, 20 March 1990.
20. Dufourcq, '2 + 4'; see also TD Diplomatie 18803, 18806 and 18812, 17 September 1990, private papers.
21. MAE, ASD, note pour le directeur des affaires politiques, a.s. Rencontres à deux plus quatre sur l'unification allemande: aspects relatifs à la sécurité, 16 February 1990, AD, ASD 1985–1990, box 15.
22. MAE, ASP, note pour le directeur des affaires politiques, a.s. Quad du 13 mars 1990. Ordre du jour commenté (questions de sécurité); and note a.s. Ordre du jour pour les réunions à Six, 20 March 1990, AD, ASD 1985–1990, box 16. The latter note suggested that the 'peace settlement' might take the form of a 'final act' defining 'some major political principles' (restoration of sovereignty and of unity, inscription in the European and pan-European process, etc.) to which the necessary legal acts would be annexed, in particular concerning the German-Polish border. As for politico-military questions, they would mainly be treated in the CFE (if conventional) or in a possible negotiation on the SNF (if nuclear) as well as in the CSCE, where the future pan-European architecture could be sketched out.
23. The initial American perception, however, was that French diplomacy, close here to the

Soviets', took an overly extensive approach to the mandate, in particular on politico-military questions. Such was the feeling in Washington after the Quad meeting that took place on the eve of the 14 March meeting of the Six: see Zelikow and Rice, *Germany Unified*, p. 227. This is not confirmed in the French detailed report: see MAE, le directeur des affaires politiques, Quad du 13 mars à la Celle-Saint-Cloud, 16 March 1990, AN 5AG4/CDM 36 (American perceptions of France's position in this preliminary phase were possibly influenced negatively by its objections on the subject of Western cooperation that dominated the 13 March discussion).
24. Dumas interview with the French radio station RFI, 19 March 1990, MAE, *Politique étrangère de la France. Textes et documents (PEF)*, March–April 1990, p. 33; see also TD Bonn 664, 20 March 1990, AD, ASD 1985–1990, box 16.
25. TD Bonn 513, 559 and 683, 2, 7 and 21 March 1990, AD, ASD 1985–1990, box 16; see also chapter 4, note 77. Paris noted, early in March, that Genscher, sensitive to the Soviet reluctances, showed reservations toward article 23 but would quickly rally to it: see Margerie, 'Q. allemande,' 6 March 1990.
26. Article 146 was more favorable to Soviet plans because, due to the complexity of the constitutional procedure, it organized a very gradual process of unification and thus offered better chances to arrive at a neutralization of Germany thanks to the renegotiation of its international commitments; as for article 23, it was regarded as nothing less than 'revanchist' by the Soviets in that it permitted the takeover of the GDR by the FRG: see TD Berlin 119, 12 March 1990, and TD Moscou 1913, 14 March 1990, AD, ASD 1985–1990, box 16.
27. MAE, service des affaires stratégiques et du désarmement, note a.s. Unification allemande-Questions de sécurité, 7 March 1990, AD, ASD 1985–1990, box 16. The French clearly preferred article 23, even if they advanced the EC argument more than the NATO argument: see e.g. Meeting between Mitterrand and Max Streibl (minister-president of Bavaria), 28 March 1990, AN 5AG4/CDM 33.
28. TD Diplomatie 4335, 5 March 1990, and TD Moscou 1905, 14 March 1990, AD, ASD 1985–1990, box 16.
29. MAE, ASP, note pour le cabinet du ministre, a.s. Entretien avec M. Chevardnadze (Moscou 30 mars 1990). Groupe à Six, 28 March 1990, AD, ASD 1985–1990, box 16.
30. TD Moscou 2501–2502, 30 March 1990, AD, ASD 1985–1990, box 16; detailed report of the same meeting by Eric Danon in MAE, Cabinet du ministre d'Etat, Entretien du ministre d'Etat avec M. Chevardnadze (Moscou 30 mars 1990), 31 March 1991, AN 5AG4/CDM 36. Dumas however recognized, as the Soviets emphasized, that article 23 raised the problem of its subsequent possible application to other German populations and that the Germans should be asked to abrogate it after unification.
31. The visit of Genscher to Washington in early April confirmed this understanding: see TD Bonn 871, 4 April 1990, AD, ASD 1985–1990, box 16.
32. There was a 'German-American convergence', the Quai noted, on limiting the scope of 2 + 4 and accelerating the dynamic of unification in order to attain the American objective of Germany's maintenance in NATO: MAE, service des affaires stratégiques, note de Philippe Guelluy a.s. Prochain sommet américano-soviétique, 10 April 1990, AD, ASD 1985–1990, box 16; and TD Washington 820–921, DSL, 28 March 1990; TD Diplomatie 6986–6987, 5 April 1990; and TD Washington 884, 5 April 1990, AD, ASD 1985–1990, box 16.
33. MAE, ASP, note pour le directeur des affaires politiques a.s. Quad du 10 avril: travaux du groupe des Six et questions de sécurité, 5 April 1990, AD, ASD 1985–1990, box 16.
34. It was suggested in the American document that the Four might terminate their rights on Germany without exercising them previously: see Draft Preparatory Paper: Options

for a Settlement on Germany, secret, n.d., AN 5AG4/CDM 36; see also MAE, note de B. Dufourcq pour la direction juridique et la direction d'Europe, a.s. Formes d'un règlement de la question allemande, AD, ASD 1985–1990, 11 April 1990, box 16; and MAE, Direction d'Europe, note pour le directeur des affaires politiques a.s., Commentaires sur le document de réflexion américain, 17 April 1990, AN 5AG4 / CDM 36.

35. MAE, le directeur des affaires politiques, compte rendu du Quad du 10 avril (Bruxelles), 12 April 1990, AN 5AG4/CDM 36. Details of Zoellick's suggestion were as follows: Bundeswehr troop limits, desired by the Soviets, would be negotiated in the CFE; the question of SNF, whose withdrawal from the territory of West Germany they also desired, would be treated via negotiation with NATO; the prohibition of ABC weapons would be the subject of a German unilateral declaration; the transitory politico-military status of the GDR territory could be raised in the 2 + 4; finally, Germany's NATO membership should obviously remain a matter for Germany and the allies to decide. These suggestions to a large extent reflected French views (see above, note 22); Dufourcq suggested nonetheless that it would be necessary for the Six, in a general-purpose political document, to evoke certain aspects pertaining to the politico-military context, if only to give the semblance of compensation to the Soviets.

36. Zelikow and Rice, *Germany United,* p. 232ff. In a letter sent to Mitterrand shortly before Key Largo, Bush exposed in detail the American 2 + 4 approach (exclusion of politico-military issues, necessary Western cooperation before meetings of the Six, a limited mandate and the need to reestablish sovereignty at the same time as German unity, vigilance toward Soviet intentions); the Elysée had no objections: see Letter from Bush to Mitterrand, 17 April 1990, and Loïc Hennekinne, note pour le président de la République, Message du président Bush, 18 April 1990, private papers. In Key Largo, in fact, the 2 + 4 was hardly discussed, for there was no disagreement between Bush and Mitterrand: see pp. 248–250.

37. Regarding the form of the settlement, the French position, much like the British one, remained at that stage in between the German-American position and that of the Soviets. For Paris, the aim was to obtain 'a set of documents of various natures' that would be concluded *after* unification (due to the need to obtain, on specific points such as the border, the commitment of a united Germany) and would allow the 'lifting in block' of the rights and responsibilities of the Four. In terms of the contents of the settlement however, the French position was closer to that of Bonn and Washington than that of Moscow, since the Quai d'Orsay felt that any arrangement conferring a special politico-military status on Germany had to be ruled out: see MAE, ASP, note a.s. Travaux du groupe d'Ottawa: formes possibles d'un règlement definitif, 26 April 1990, AD, ASD 1985–1990, box 16. Based on this position, which it believed was a balanced one, Paris hoped to be able to broker a compromise between the Six: on the form, by introducing the notion of a 'final settlement' halfway between the Soviet demand for a 'peace settlement' (Moscow had stopped talking about a 'peace treaty') and the German refusal of any such formula, and on the contents by suggesting that the 'politico-military context' of unification might be evoked in political, nonbinding terms in the final settlement, in order to give a façade of satisfaction to the Soviets by mentioning, in particular, the pan-European process, but without making a true concession to them on the military status of Germany nor the future of European security: MAE, le directeur des affaires politiques, note pour le cabinet du ministre d'Etat, à l'attention de M. Kessedjan, a.s. Prochaine réunion des directeurs politiques du groupe des Six (30 avril). Points en suspens, 27 April 1990, AD, ASD 1985–1990, box 16 (Dumas's chief of staff agreed to these suggestions).

38. TD Moscou 2662 and 3225–26, 6 and 26 April and TD Bonn 1043, 21 April 1990, AD, ASD 1985–1990, box 16.

39. See Zelikow and Rice, *Germany Unified*, p. 240ff., and Hannes Adomeit, *Imperial Overstretch: Germany in Soviet Policy from Stalin to Gorbachev*, Baden-Baden, Nomos Verlag, 1998, p. 502ff.; see also Dufourcq, '2 + 4'.
40. Detailed report of the second meeting of the six political directors in East Berlin on 30 April in TD Berlin 1172–1173, 1 May 1990, AD, ASD 1985–1990, box 16. The meeting, which focused on the agenda of the 2 + 4 talks, was indecisive: the Soviet request that the 'synchronization' between German unification and the transformation of European security be inscribed in the agenda of the 2 + 4 was blocked by the Western powers. A compromise nonetheless was reached on the notion of a 'final settlement under international law' and the termination of rights and responsibilities of the four powers'. French diplomacy was satisfied by this formulation, which, while avoiding the notion of a treaty or a peace settlement to which Bonn was opposed, specified that the settlement would be 'final' and would include obligations under international law: see MAE, Sous-direction d'Europe centrale et nordique, note a.s. Groupe d'Ottawa: 'Règlement final de droit international,' AD, ASD 1985–1990, box 16.
41. Bonn thought that the Soviets' objective was indeed face saving and that Moscow 'was no longer able to master the game'. For the rest, the Quai observed the day before the ministerial meeting in Bonn that the Westerners displayed identical positions, on security issues in particular, even as they had 'different sensitivities on the modalities'. The Americans and Germans were ready to abandon the rights and responsibilities of the Four at the end of a minimal procedure, whereas the French and British had a 'more orthodox' reading of these rights and, without agreeing to Soviet demands, insisted on a 'true legal settlement', a position that would have its way during the 2 + 4 meeting of 30 April, when the notion of a 'final settlement under international law' was accepted: see MAE, ASP, note a.s. Etat d'avancement des travaux du groupe d'Ottawa, 2 May 1990, AD, ASD 1985–1990, box 16.
42. TD Diplomatie 8907, 7 May 1990, AD, ASD 1985–1990; and MAE, le directeur des affaires politiques, compte rendu, a.s. Première session ministérielle du groupe des Six, Bonn (5 mai 1990), 17 May 1990, AN 5AG4/CDM 36. In addition to the border issue, whose discussion he wanted to prioritize, Dumas's speech aimed to place emphasis on the need to treat 'with care and definitively' the external consequences of German unification, which implied 'lifting the rights and responsibilities at the same time as concluding a settlement under international law', and to defend the Western position on the politico-military issues: no imposed 'special status' on Germany, the liberty to remain in the Atlantic Alliance and referral to competent authorities to allow the consideration of 'the security interests of all'; see Schéma d'intervention générale, 5 May 1990, AD, ASD 1985–1990. During the session, Dumas, together with Baker, defended a compromise leading to a place on the agenda for the negotiations on 'politico-military questions, having in mind approaches of appropriate security structures in Europe'.
43. MAE, ASP, note pour le directeur des affaires politiques, a.s. Travaux du groupe des Six: le point après la première réunion ministérielle, 10 May 1990, AD, ASD 1985–1990, box 16. The same uncertainty was expressed in Bonn. Detailing the results of the Bonn ministerial meeting on 8 May at NATO, Kastrup said it was difficult to predict when the 2 + 4 would be concluded, all the more so because Moscow now spoke of a transition period of two to three, if not five years, during which the quadripartite rights would remain in vigor beyond Germany's 'internal' unification. The Soviets emphasized that Shevardnadze's proposition to decouple internal and external aspects meant a green light for unity but also aimed to make the Germans understand 'that Moscow still had a card to play on the international stage': see TD RPAN Bruxelles 374–375, 8 May 1990 and TD Moscou 3577, 7 May 1990, AD, ASD 1985–1990, box 16.

44. MAE, service des affaires stratégiques et du désarmement, note de Ph. Guelluy pour le directeur politique, 14 May 1990, AD, ASD 1985–1990, box 16.
45. See TD Bonn 1219, 10 May 1990; Letter from Baker to Dumas, 15 May 1990 and MAE, ASP, note pour le cabinet du ministre d'Etat (s/c du directeur des affaires politiques), 16 May 1990, AD, ASD 1985–1990, box 16. See also Zelikow and Rice, *Germany Unified*, pp. 251–253. According to the German press, France and Great Britain welcomed the Soviet decoupling idea because it would allow them to keep their rights pertaining to Germany for some years. Yet these commentaries were without foundation: even from the Quai's point of view the question of the 'sequence' remained problematic, and after the Bonn meeting French diplomacy believed that it 'would be necessary to go quickly and avoid the Soviet trap of a discrepancy' between internal and external unification; see TD Bonn 1185, 7 May 1990, and note de Ph. Guelluy, 14 May 1990, a.s. Prochain sommet américano-soviétique, 10 April 1990, AD, ASD, 1985–1990, box 16.
46. TD Bonn 1219, 10 May 1990; and Zelikow and Rice, *Germany United*, p. 254ff.
47. TD Washington 1273, 18 May 1990, AD, ASD 1985–1990, box 16.
48. TD Diplomatie 10225–10227, 23 May 1990; and MAE, le directeur des affaires politiques, note pour le ministre d'Etat, a.s. réunion du groupe des Six (Bonn le 22 mai), 24 May 1990, AD, ASD 1985–1990, box 16. The schema proposed by the French included a preamble followed by a certain number of legal elements (borders, Berlin, lifting of rights and responsibilities of the Four); in addition the Six would have to take note of the German-Polish treaty and the modifications to the German constitution (see above, note 30). As for the calendar, the Americans' insistence on a conclusion of the exercise before the end of the year prompted no remarks from the Soviet delegation.
49. The French and in a lesser way the British held on to the idea that the final settlement, which would be refined by the Six, would, in order to assure a complete 'legal security,' be signed by the five upon completion by a unified Germany of the acts provided for in the settlement, in particular the conclusion of a German-Polish border treaty. This would imply a discrepancy of several weeks between the unification and lifting of the quadripartite rights, its duration depending on the rapidity with which the Germans would accomplish the necessary acts. As for the Germans and the Americans, they desired a definitive signing by the Six, their argument being that the sequence advocated by the French, even if limited in time, would introduce the same type of 'discrepancy' between the internal and external aspects of unification that the Soviets sought: see MAE, le directeur des affaires politiques, note pour le ministre d'Etat, a.s. réunion du groupe des Six (Bonn le 22 mai), 24 May 1990. The debate continued, without being concluded, during a 5 June 'Quad,' with Kastrup refuting the French schema, which he judged contrary to the idea that Germany would recover its sovereignty and its unity at the same time: MAE, le directeur des affaires politiques, compte rendu a.s. Quad du 5 juin: question allemande, 11 juin 1990, AD, ASD, 1985–1990, box 17.
50. See Dufourcq, '2 + 4', and TD Moscou 3828, 17 May 1990, AD, ASD, 1985–1990, box 16.
51. MAE, ASP, note a. s. L'hypothèque soviétique sur la conclusion de l'exercice à six: conséquences d'un blocage, 28 May 1990, AD, ASD 1985–1990, box 16.
52. Kvitsinski was at that point 'the soul' of the Soviet propositions, said Kastrup upon his return from Moscow at the beginning of June: see MAE, le directeur des affaires politiques, compte rendu, a. s. Quad du 5 juin: question allemande, 11 juin 1990, AD, ASD 1985–1990, box 17.
53. TD Diplomatie 11451–53, 11 June 1990, AN, 5AG4/CDM 36.
54. Règlement de paix définitif concernant l'Allemagne fondé sur le droit international (document cadre), proposition soviétique du 9 juin 1990; and MAE, ASP, note pour le directeur des affaires politiques, a.s. travaux du groupe des Six: schéma soviétique de règlement definitif, 18 June 1990, AD, ASD 1985–1990, box 17.

55. British detailed report to NATO in TD RPAN 502, 21 June 1990 and MAE, le directeur des affaires politiques, note pour le ministre d'Etat, a.s. Réunion du groupe d'Ottawa (Bonn 20 juin), 21 June 1990, AD, ASD 1985–1990, box 17.
56. Dufourcq, '2 + 4'; see also MAE, note du sous-directeur d'Europe centrale et nordique pour le directeur des affaires politiques, a.s. Négociation des '4 + 2 (sic)'. Analyse du projet soviétique de règlement remis pendant la réunion ministérielle du 22 juin; MAE, ASP, brief a.s. Réunion ministérielle du groupe d'Ottawa (22 juin 1990). Eléments de langage pour le sommet européen, 23 June 1990; and American detailed report to NATO of the ministerial meeting in TD RPAN 508–509, 25 juin 1990, AD, ASD 1985–1990, box 17.
57. Dufourcq, '2 + 4'.
58. Henekinne, Notes pour le president de la République, Entretiens avec le chancelier Kohl. Unification de l'Allemagne, 20 June 1990, and Situation politique en Allemagne, 21 June 1990, AN, 5AG4/CDM 33.
59. Ambassade de France à Moscou, note a.s. L'URSS, l'Allemagne et les Alliances, 18 June 1990, private papers.
60. TD Moscou 4528, 26 June 1990, AD, ASD 1985–1990, box 17.
61. MAE, ASP, note opérationnelle, 21 June 1990, a.s. Session ministérielle du groupe des Six (Berlin, 22 juin 1990), AD, ASD 1985–1990, box 17.
62. Caroline de Margerie, Note pour le président de la République, Négociations germano-soviétiques et prochains sommets (OTAN-CSCE), 21 June 1990, AN, 5AG4/CDM 33.
63. Kohl stated that the Germans did not intend to start a border dispute that would menace the peace order in Europe, and (taking up Genscher's formula at the UN in September 1989, which itself had been taken up in the resolution voted on by the Bundestag on 8 November) he said that the 'Poles should have the certainty to live in recognized borders'; see chapter 3, note 7, and Werner Weidenfeld, *Außenpolitik für die deutsche Einheit. Die Entscheidungsjahre1989/1990,* Stuttgart, DVA, 1998, p. 479ff. On the legal and political implications related to recognition of the Oder-Neisse border, see above, chapter 2, note 65.
64. Gespräch des Bundeskanzlers Kohl mit Generalsekretär Gorbatschow, Moskau, 10. Februar 1990; Gespräch des Bundeskanzlers Kohl mit Staatspräsident Mitterrand, Paris, 15 Februar 1990; and Gespräch des Bundeskanzlers Kohl mit Präsident Bush, Camp David, 24. Februar 1990, in *Deutsche Einheit. Sonderedition aus den Akten des Bundeskanzleramtes 1989/90,* Munich, R. Oldenburg, 1998, p. 795–807, 842–852 and 860–873.
65. Meeting between Mitterrand and Kohl, Latché, 4 January 1990, detailed report by Hennekinne; Mitterrand-Kohl Dinner, 15 February 1990 at the Elysée, detailed report by Elisabeth Guigou, private papers.
66. 'We are in agreement on the Polish border,' Bush declared: see Mitterrand-Bush lunch, Key Largo, 19 April 1990; on the American point of view, see Zelikow and Rice, *Germany Unified,* p. 217 ff (characteristically, Zelikow and Rice only consecrate a few pages – not always precise – to the subject, which they clearly consider secondary).
67. Personal interviews.
68. Of course, the Helsinki final Act did not consecrate the intangibility but the inviolability of borders, and it recognized the possibility of 'peaceful change' of these. Yet against the backdrop of the looming Oder-Neisse debate and the rise of other territorial claims, Dumas wrote to Mitterrand: 'I allow myself to draw your attention to the more general problem of borders in Europe, a theme that, if we are not careful, could rapidly poison the whole process taking place: eastern border of Poland, eastern border of a unified Germany, Soviet-Romanian borders, Hungarian-Romanian borders, etc. without mentioning the situation in the USSR and the (more than likely close) perspective of unilateral declarations of independence of the Baltic states.' This, he said, raised the need

to 'maintain in the general approach to the German problem, as for the whole of the European problem, two principles: intangibility of borders (which marked the limits to the principle of self-determination); an international legal guarantee and a multilateral mechanism for negotiation'; see Dumas, note pour Monsieur le président de la République, n.d., a.s. La Pologne et les frontières allemandes, n.d. [early March 1990], private papers.

69. Chevènement summarized the problem: to admit that German unification could take place without a confirmation of the Polish border (or the reaffirmation of Germany's renunciation of ABC arms) would be 'an implicit recognition of the superiority of the right to self-determination of Germans over the right to security and peace of Europeans': see Chevènement, note à l'attention de Monsieur le président de la République, 23 February 1990, private papers. (Chevènement, who did not share Mitterrand's trust in the Bonn leaders, did not hesitate to wonder whether the Germans 'exclude forever an attempt to recover the lost provinces' and 'become a nuclear power'.)

70. The idea that the French used the border issue to complicate or slow German unification is advanced e.g. (without the author providing any serious evidence) by Robert L. Hutchings, *American Diplomacy and the End of the Cold War: An Insider's Account of US Policy in Europe 1989–1992*, Washington, Woodrow Wilson Center Press, 1997, p. 115–116 and 387.

71. TD Varsovie 335–336, 17 February 1990, AD, ASD 1985–1990, box 15.

72. Letter from Mazowiecki to Mitterrand, 20 February 1990, AN, 5AG4/CDM 34. The same letter was addressed to the three other guarantor powers. These demands were made public two days later by Mazowiecki during a press conference: see TD Varsovie 379, 22 February 1990, AD, ASD 1985–1990, box 15.

73. Speech made by Dumas at the Berliner Pressekonferenz, 1 March 1990, PEF, February–March 1990, p. 3. See also Roland Dumas, *Le Fil et la Pelote. Mémoires*, Paris, Plon, 1996, p. 342; François Mitterrand, *De l'Allemagne, de la France*, Paris, Odile Jacob, 1996, p. 153; Kohl, *Je voulais*, p. 261; and Horst Teltschik, *329 Tage. Innenansichten der Einigung*, Berlin, Siedler, 1991, p. 164–165. On Kohl's judgment concerning Dumas, see chapter 4, note 64.

74. TD Bonn 508, 1 March 1990, AD, ASD 1985–1990, box 16; Teltschik, *329 Tage*, p. 165.

75. On all this, details in Weidenfeld, *Außenpolitik*, p. 487ff.

76. Kohl emphasized that it would be legally impossible to go beyond such a declaration by the two German parliaments before unity, and he defended the connection established with the reparations and the rights of the German minority by domestic considerations, in particular the danger of the far right taking up the border issue; hence, he said, the Poles must make some concessions. Mitterrand answered that whereas he understood the chancellor's motivations, from a political point of view a 'clear declaration of intention would be welcome'. Kohl said that he intended to make such a declaration after the adoption of the resolutions by the two parliaments, perhaps on the occasion of a debate in the Bundestag. Mitterrand concluded by saying that he 'would reflect' on this and inform Kohl after his meeting with the Poles: see Telefongespräch des Bundeskanzlers Kohl mit Staatspräsident Mitterrand, 5. März 1990, *Deutsche Einheit*, p. 909–912.

77. Message from Kohl to Mitterrand, 6 March 1990, AN 5AG4/CDM 34; the draft resolution prepared by the Chancellery included the substance of the declaration to be adopted by the two German parliaments: right of the Poles to 'live in secure borders', reaffirmation of the 'inviolability of the borders of Poland' and need for settlement of the question by a 'treaty concluded between a government of Germany as a whole and the Polish government' (the question of the reparations and of the German minority was only mentioned for the record and without a constraining connection); see text of the draft resolution in *Deutsche Einheit*, p. 913.

78. TD Bonn 577, 7 March 1990; TD Varsovie 464, 7 March 1990; and TD Washington 658, 13 March 1990, AD, ASD 1985–1990, box 16. The Polish government was happy with the abandonment of the link with the reparations, in which it saw a German climb-down, but emphasized that a declaration by the two parliaments remained insufficient and that Poland should be invited to participate in the 2 + 4.
79. Conseil des ministres, 7 March 1990, private papers. On this important distinction, see note 68 and note 114.
80. Teltschik, *329 Tage*, p. 169; TD Bonn 8 March 1990, AD, ASD 1985–1990, box 16.
81. Margerie, handwritten annotations, 'Président, 7 mars,' AN 5AG4/CDM 34 (the author wrote inadvertently: 'It is important to be useful to *France* but while accommodating the *Germans*'). Dumas was less worried than Mitterrand by the idea of irritating Bonn: noting that Genscher was unable to force Kohl to clarify his position, he went as far as to suggest that France 'might engage itself unilaterally' in favor of the intangibility of the border, a 'prelude to a possible assistance agreement' (an agreement that he nonetheless recognized as being 'premature' to bring up): Dumas, note pour Monsieur le président de la République, La Pologne et les frontières allemandes, [n.d., early March 1990]. The note was probably written before the resolution project drawn up on 6 March by the coalition in Bonn; see Dumas, *Le Fil*, p. 343).
82. Margerie, Note pour le président de la République, La frontière Oder-Neisse, 8 mars 1990, AN, 5AG4/7010.
83. Védrine, note pour le président de la République, 9 mars 1990, AN, 5AG4/CDM 34; Mitterrand made changes in the proposed statement to accommodate Bonn, adding: 'Germany is our friend, we are allies and associates'; he also replaced 'the negotiation of [the German-Polish treaty] must be initiated without delay' with '[France] wishes that the negotiation be initiated without delay'.
84. Meeting between Mitterrand, Jaruzelski et al., 9 March 1990.
85. Mitterrand-Jaruzelski-Mazowiecki-Rocard joint press conference, *PEF*, March–April 1990, p.14–21. A careful reading of Mitterrand's remarks confirms his willingness to make a prudent statement (see above, note 83). After recalling the reality of Franco-German reconciliation and friendship, he declared that France regarded the Oder-Neisse border as 'intangible', that Poland 'must be associated' with the work of the Six concerning it (knowing that 'Poland was not a member of the Six, it's clear,') and that it was up to the Four 'to give their opinion on this matter, one could even say to give their guarantee to this international act'. He added that he 'desired' that a legal act be negotiated as soon as possible between Bonn and Warsaw, specifying: 'It is a matter of making sure that the debate on the border be resolved, I did not say validated, promulgated but resolved before unification'. As for Mazowiecki, he reiterated the Polish position and the demand that a German-Polish treaty on the border be initialed *before* unification with the participation of the Four Powers.
86. Teltschik distorted Mitterrand's position, reporting that he had endorsed Mazowiecki's position entirely, including the need for a treaty signed before unification, which did not in fact correspond to Mitterrand's careful words: Teltschik, *329 Tage*, p. 171; Kohl, *Je voulais*, p. 269.
87. Telefongespräch des Bundeskanzlers Kohl mit Staatspräsident Mitterrand, 14. März 1990, *Deutsche Einheit*, p. 943–947; and Mitterrand-Kohl telephone conversation, 14 March 1990, AN, 5AG4/CDM 33. The question of the border was evoked with Oskar Lafontaine, who declared that Mitterrand's position on the Oder-Neisse line was the same as that of the SPD. As for Mitterrand, he repeated: 'What I said to Jaruzelski, I said ten times to Kohl and to Genscher. There is no Franco-Polish alliance … Oder-Neisse: recognize it. Negotiate [a treaty] now with the Poles … You will ratify it after

the unification', adding: 'That needs to be settled between Germans and Poles and the 4 will give their guarantee': meeting between Mitterrand and Lafontaine, 14 March 1990, detailed report by Margerie, AN 5AG4/CDM 34.
88. Lunch meeting between Attali and Teltschik, 15 March 1990, AN, 5AG4/CDM 33.
89. Kohl, *Je voulais*, p. 271. Kohl, in his memoirs, writes that Mitterrand 'had simply poorly appreciated the real situation' – not recognizing the plain fact that Mitterrand's position had forced him to loosen his own.
90. See Vorlage des Ministerialdirigenten Hartmann an Bundeskanzler Kohl, Bonn, 13. März 1990, Polnische Westgrenze, *Deutsche Einheit*, p. 937–941.
91. Telefongespräch des Bundeskanzlers Kohl mit Staatspräsident Mitterrand, 14. März 1990, and Mitterrand-Kohl telephone conversation, 14 March 1990.
92. TD Diplomatie 5300–5302, 16 March 1990. Dufourcq was vocal on the question of the border on 14 March; the previous day, during the meeting of the 'quad', he suggested that the Six travel to Warsaw, but Kastrup refused categorically: MAE, le directeur des affaires politiques, Quad du 13 mars à la Celle-Saint-Cloud, compte rendu de Bertrand Dufourcq, secret, 16 March 1990. (Mitterrand was probably informed of this exchange, which would explain why, the following day, he avoided reviving the idea of a meeting at 6 + 1 in Warsaw on the occasion of his telephone conversation with the chancellor.)
93. The German sources do not reflect this episode, except that they note the fact that Kohl, in his conversation with Bush on 20 March, in effect evoked only the possibility of Bonn agreeing with Warsaw on the contents of a letter endorsing the future resolution: see Telefongespräch des Bundeskanzlers Kohl mit Präsident Bush, 20. März 1990, *Deutsche Einheit*, p. 961–963; and Kohl, *Je voulais*, p. 280; as for the German detailed report of the conversation on the 23 March, it is not available. On the American side, see George Bush and Brent Scowcroft, *A World Transformed*, New York, Vintage, 1998, p. 260–262, and a more detailed account in Zelikow and Rice's *Germany Unified*, p. 219–222 (Rice and Zelikow quote Teltschik, although his diary is silent on this episode). If it was Bush who harvested this new German concession, Mitterrand had unquestionably paved the way: it was shortly after his meeting with the Polish leaders on 9 March that the Chancellery began to rally to the idea that it was necessary to start negotiating with Warsaw (even if Kohl did not mention this to Mitterrand on the 14th): see Vorlage des Ministerialdirigenten Hartmann an Bundeskanzler Kohl, Bonn, 13. März 1990, Polnische Westgrenze.
94. Meeting between Mitterrand and Streibl, 28 March 1990, detailed report by Margerie AN 5AG4/CDM 33.
95. Meeting between Mitterrand, Lubbers, Van Den Broek and Dumas, 3 April 1990, private papers.
96. Meeting between Mitterrand and Kohl, 25 April 1990, private papers.
97. Meeting between Mitterrand and Thatcher, 4 May 1990, private papers.
98. This led the Poles to remain insistent with Paris: TD Varsovie 6018, 26 March 1990, AD, ASD 1985–1990, box 16.
99. TD Diplomatie 6986–6987, 5 April 1990, AD, ASD 1985–1990, box 16. Kohl's entourage felt that it was preferable to engage themselves rapidly on the path of a negotiation with Warsaw rather than take the risk of seeing themselves subjected to the imposition of a 'guarantee' by the Four on the Oder-Neisse border, which would be humiliating since it would reflect a lack of confidence towards Germany: see Vorlage des Ministerialdirigenten Hartmann an Bundeskanzler Kohl, Bonn, 13. März 1990, Polnische Westgrenze, *Deutsche Einheit*, p. 937–941.
100. MAE, Direction des affaires juridiques, note pour le directeur des affaires politiques, 9 April 1990, a.s. Frontière Oder-Neisse, AN, 5AG4/CDM 34: basing itself on the texts adopted since 1945 (see also chapter 2, note 65, chapter 3, note 43 and chapter 4, note 42)

the Quai's legal consultants felt that the 'intervention of the four Allies in the settlement of the question of borders ... was indispensable legally since the border issue pertained to their reserved rights'. The French, like the British as well as the U.S. Department of State, were thus in disagreement with the idea defended by the White House according to which the resort to article 23 of the *Grundgesetz* would ipso facto settle the Oder-Neisse problem, since a unified Germany would inherit the obligations of the FRG and GDR, which both recognized the borders: see Zelikow and Rice, *Germany Unified*, p. 222 and p. 435 note 55.

101. MAE, ASP, note pour le directeur des affaires politiques a.s. Quad du 10 avril: travaux du groupe des Six et questions de sécurité, 5 April 1990.
102. MAE, note de B. Dufourcq pour la direction juridique et la direction d'Europe, a.s. Formes d'un règlement de la question allemande, 11 April 1990, box 16.
103. MAE, le directeur des affaires politiques, note pour le cabinet du ministre d'État, à l'attention de M. Kessedjian, a.s. Prochaine réunion des directeurs politiques du groupe des Six (30 avril). Points en suspens, 27 April 1990.
104. TD Berlin 1172–1173, 1 May 1990. Warsaw kept putting pressure on Paris: see Letter from Skubiszewski to Dumas, 30 April in TD Varsovie 850, 1 May 1990, AD, ASD 1985–1990, box 16.
105. Schéma d'intervention générale, Bonn, 5 mai 1990. Dumas emphasized in addition the need to 'clearly mark the geographical framework in which German unity would be realized: the Federal Republic, the Democratic Republic of Germany and Berlin', and specified that in the six-party settlement it would probably be necessary to make reference to the German-Polish treaty as well as the abolition of article 23 of the *Grundgesetz* (on this point, see note 30).
106. TD Diplomatie 8907, 7 May 1990.
107. MAE, ASP, note pour le directeur des affaires politiques, a.s. Travaux du groupe des Six: le point après la première réunion ministérielle.
108. Conseil des ministres, 9 May 1990, private papers.
109. TD Diplomatie 10225–10227, 23 May 1990; MAE, le directeur des affaires politiques, note pour le ministre d'Etat, a.s. réunion du groupe des Six (Bonn le 22 mai), 24 May 1990; and Dufourcq, '2 + 4.'
110. TD Warsaw 893, 8 May 1990, AD, ASD 1985–1990, box 16.
111. TD Diplomatie 9638, 16 May 1990, AN 5AG4/CDM 34. The Polish delegation was led by the deputy director for Europe. One week later, Skubiszewski confirmed to the French ambassador that Warsaw, failing a properly initialed treaty, still hoped that the text of such a treaty could be finalized before unification, whereas Bonn only agreed to work with Warsaw to arrange the text of the resolution of the Bundestag. See TD Varsovie 1027, 23 March 1990.
112. Meeting between Mitterrand and Mazowiecki, 28 May 1990, private papers. It is true that the German-Polish conversations during the month of May were difficult: whereas the Auswärtiges Amt wanted to be forthcoming, the Chancellery showed itself very reluctant and refused any discussion on the future treaty; it was ready to evoke only the declarations of the Bundestag and of the Volkskammer: see Weidenfeld, *Außenpolitik*, p. 494ff.
113. TD Diplomatie 11451–53, 11 June 1990; Dufourcq, '2 + 4.'
114. TD Bonn 1503, 8 June 1990, AN, 5AG4/ CDM 34. It was nonetheless the *inviolability* of the German-Polish border that was mentioned in the resolution that was passed by the Bundestag and the Volkskammer on 21 June, as in the one passed by the Bundestag on 8 March (and it would be the same in the German-Polish treaty that would be signed on 14 November). It would have been difficult for the Germans to accept that these

declarations or instruments referred expressively to the *intangibility* of the Oder-Neisse line: the inviolability of borders was alone recognized as an international principle in the Helsinki final Act, and so an affirmation of the intangibility of the German-Polish border would have marked a singularization of Germany. It remains that the intangibility of the Oder-Neisse border, in these acts and in particular in the 2 + 4 treaty, was implicitly recognized: it was deduced from Germany's recognition of the 'existing' German-Polish border and from the affirmation that it would never in the future bring up any territorial claims.

115. Teltschik, *329 Tage*, p. 264 and 271.
116. TD Bonn 1632–1634, 21 June 1990, AD, ASD 1985–1990, box 17.
117. The resolution, the French embassy noted, went further than the one of 8 November, which simply proclaimed the rights of the Poles to live within secure borders, and it did not take up again the text from 8 March that still mentioned Poland's renunciation of reparations (but, as seen above, without making it a condition). For the rest, it confirmed the inviolability of the border (and not its intangibility: see above, note 114), Germany's renunciation of all territorial claims, and its desire to definitively confirm the border by an international treaty: see TD Bonn 1617, 19 June 1990, AD, ASD 1985–1990, box 17.
118. TD Diplomatie 12716–12719, DSL, 25 June 1990, private papers. The French thus continued to put pressure on the Germans to engage them to enter into the treaty negotiations as soon as possible. It is true that two days earlier, Kastrup had confided to Dufourcq that Bonn was no longer opposed to the idea of beginning the negotiation of certain elements of the treaty before unification: see MAE, le directeur des affaires politiques, note pour le ministre d'Etat, a.s. réunion du groupe d'Ottawa (Bonn 20 June), 21 June 1990.
119. Dufourcq, '2 + 4'.
120. Although, several weeks before the elections in the GDR, an SPD victory seemed most possible, Mitterrand did not expect the unification process to be put into question as a result: 'A majority in the GDR will likely declare favorable to unity on 19 March', he confided to Giulio Andreotti on 13 February, adding that even if one could expect a 'prudent approach' from the SPD, he did not see 'what could prevent reunification': see Meeting between Mitterrand and Andreotti, 13 February, private papers. As for Guigou and Védrine, they even thought that a SPD victory in the East would probably lead Kohl to want still to accelerate the movement: see Guigou, note pour le président de la République, Votre dîner avec le chancelier Kohl jeudi 15 février, 13 February 1990; and Guigou and Védrine, note pour le président de la République, 15 February 1990, private papers. Finally, when he received Lafontaine at the Elysée a few days before elections in the GDR whose result now appeared very uncertain, Mitterrand did not endorse Lafontaine's preference for a slow unification process under article 146: see Meeting between Mitterrand and Lafontaine, 14 March 1990.
121. Mitterrand added to it 'his personal congratulations' to Kohl on 20 March: see Message for Kohl, Tuesday 20 March 1990, private papers.
122. See Védrine, note pour le service de presse, 12 March 1990; and note pour le président de la République, a.s. État d'esprit dans les médias à propos de l'Allemagne, 23 March 1990, private papers. See also Pierre Favier and Michel Martin-Roland, *La Décennie Mitterrand*, vol. 3, 'Les Défis,' (1988–1991), Paris, Le Seuil, 1996, p. 242–243; and Hubert Védrine, *Les Mondes de François Mitterrand. À l'Élysée 1981–1995*, p. 454–455.
123. See Marie-Ange Théobald, note, La réunification allemande, les conséquences des événements en Europe de l'Est et l'opinion publique. Actualisation de ma note du 6 février, 3 May 1990, AN, 5AG4/7010; on the evolution of French public opinion from the fall of 1989 to the spring of 1990, see Marie-Noëlle Brand Crémieux, *Les Français face à la réunification allemande, automne 1989-automne 1990*, Paris, L'Harmattan, 2004, p. 33–49.

124. See Margaret Thatcher, *The Downing Street Years*, New York, Harper-Collins, 1993, p. 798; and François Mitterrand, *De l'Allemagne, de la France*, Paris, Odile Jacob, 1996, p. 43; also see chapter 4 of this volume, pp. 168–170 and, esp. note 9.
125. Meeting between Dumas and Hurd, 15 February 1990, AN, 5AG4/AH 35. The meeting between the two defense ministers on 21 February, on the other hand, did not run up against any European obstacle, Franco-British military collaboration being a pragmatic affair; yet it did not open onto the perspective of an extended cooperation: see Le ministre de la Défense, note à l'attention de Monsieur le président de la République, 23 February 1990, private papers; see also TD Londres 370–372, DSL Secret, 13 mars 1990, AD, ASD 1985–1990, box 16.
126. TD Londres 428–429, 21 March 1990, AD, ASD 1985–1990, box 16.
127. Meeting between Mitterrand and Lafontaine, 14 March, 1990.
128. Mitterrand-Kohl Dinner at the Elysée, 15 February 1990. Kohl, for instance, evoked Franco-German reconciliation as a model for German-Polish reconciliation in his speech to the Bundestag before the vote on the resolution on the border on 21 June: see TD Bonn 1632–1634, 21 June 1990.
129. Meeting between Mitterrand and Cavaco Silva, 23 March 1990, detailed report by Loïc Hennekinne, private papers.
130. Meeting between Mitterrand and Lafontaine, 14 March 1990.
131. Schreiben des Bundeskanzlers Kohl an Präsident Delors, 13. März 1990, *Deutsche Einheit*, p. 935–936; for an analysis of Kohl's policy in this context, see Hans Stark, *Kohl, l'Allemagne et l'Europe. La politique européenne de la République fédérale 1982–1998*, Paris, L'Harmattan, 2004, p. 157ff.
132. Guigou, note pour le président de la République, Entretien avec les collaborateurs du chancelier Kohl, MM. Horst Teltschik et Joachim Bitterlich. Conseil européen de Dublin, 15 March 1990, AN, 5AG4/CDM 33.
133. Guigou, note pour le président de la République, Quel pourrait être le contenu d'une initiative sur l'Union politique de l'Europe?, 20 March 1990, private papers.
134. Meeting between Mitterrand and Cavaco Silva, 23 March 1990.
135. Guigou, note pour le président de la République, Aide mémoire du gouvernement belge sur les perspectives de l'Union politique, 23 March 1990, private papers.
136. Guigou, note pour le président de la République, Votre émission sur TF1. Unification allemande et Communauté européenne. Derniers éléments, 23 March 1990, private papers; see chapter 4, note 76.
137. *Le Monde*, 27, 30, and 31 March 1990.
138. Guigou, note pour le président de la République, Entretien à Bonn, le 2 avril, avec M. Teltschik et M. Bitterlich. Union politique, AN, 5AG4/7009; see also Vorlage des Ministerialdirektors Teltschik an Bundeskanzler Kohl, Bonn, 3. April 1990, Vorbereitung Sonder-ER Dublin, 28. April 1990, *Deutsche Einheit*, p. 1004–1007.
139. Guigou, note pour le président de la République, Initiative franco-allemande à Dublin, 4 avril 1990, AN, 5AG4/7009.
140. Guigou, note pour le président de la République, Conversation téléphonique avec M. Bitterlich, 5 April 1990, AN, 5AG4/7009 ; see also Vorlage des Vortragenden Legationsrats I Bitterlich an Ministerialdirektor Teltschik, Bonn, 6. April 1990, Vorbereitung Sonder-ER Dublin, 28. April 1990, Bonn, 6. April 1990, *Deutsche Einheit*, p. 1010–1011.
141. Teltschik, *329 Tage*, p. 195.
142. Message from Mitterrand and Kohl to Haughey, 19 April 1990, *PEF*, March–April 1990, p. 76.
143. Meeting between Mitterrand and Kohl, 25 April 1990, private papers.

144. See Guigou, notes pour le président de la République, La communauté et l'unification allemande; Union politique; and Conseil européen de Dublin, 27 April 1990, private papers; and Favier and Martin-Roland, *La Décennie*, vol. 3, p. 245-246.
145. Ministère des Affaires étrangères, le ministre d'État, note pour Monsieur le président de la République, n.d., private papers; *Le Monde*, 22 May 1990.
146. Guigou, note pour le président de la République, Votre rencontre avec le chancelier Kohl le 22 juin. Préparation du Conseil européen de Dublin. Union politique, 21 June 1990, AN, 5AG4 CDM 33; see also Guigou, Note pour le président de la République, Votre entretien avec M. Haughey, le 8 juin à 18 h 45, 8 June 1990, private papers.
147. Entretiens FM-H. Kohl à Assmanhausen (*sic*), handwritten notes by Hennekinne, 22 juin 1990, private papers; Gespräche des Bundeskanzlers Kohl mit Staatspräsident Mitterrand, Assmannshausen und auf dem Rhein, 22. Juni 1990, *Deutsche Einheit*, p. 1247-1249; Teltschik, *329 Tage*, p. 283-284; Kohl, *Je voulais*, p. 333ff.
148. Intervention du président de la République au Conseil européen de Dublin (25 et 26 juin 1990) sur l'union politique (extraits), 6 July 1990, private papers; *Le Monde*, 28 June 1990.
149. On this, see Bush and Scowcroft, *A World Transformed*, p. 215ff.
150. MAE, Fiche a.s. Situation des pays baltes: position française, confidentiel, 14 March 1990; and MAE, communiqué diffusé le 12 mars 1990, AD, série Europe 1986-1990, URSS, box 6681. Legally, Paris adopted the same position as Washington: having never recognized its annexation, it did not need to recognize the independence of Lithuania; yet Paris did not at that point wish to establish formal diplomatic relations with Vilnius because Lithuania did not fully exercise its sovereignty over its territory: see Michael R. Beschloss and Strobe Talbott, *At the Highest Levels: The Inside Story of the End of the Cold War*, Boston, Little & Brown, 1993, p. 194.
151. See e.g. Vorlage des Ministerialdirektors Teltschik an Bundeskanzler Kohl, Bonn, 29. März 1990, Lage in Litauen, *Deutsche Einheit*, p. 987-988; Weidenfeld, *Außenpolitik*, p. 349; Kohl, *Je voulais*, p. 294.
152. Mitterrand-Bush Lunch, 19 April 1990, Key Largo, private papers.
153. Dumas, *Le Fil*, p. 396ff.; and Zelikow and Rice, *Germany Unified*, p. 257.
154. Meeting between Mitterrand and Kohl, 25 April 1990; 55. Deutsch-französische Konsultationen, Paris, 26. April 1990, *Deutsche Einheit*, p. 1056-1059; Teltschik, *329 Tage*, p. 209.
155. Letter from Kohl and Mitterrand to Landsbergis, 26 April 1990, private papers.
156. Letter from Landsbergis to Mitterrand, 2 May 1990, AD, Europe 1985-1990, URSS, box 6682. In his letter dated 19 April 1990, Mitterrand had advised a negotiation process with Moscow, but Landesbergis in his response dated the 24th continued to demand the immediate recognition of Lithuania: see letter from Mitterrand to Landsbergis, 19 April 1990, and letter from Landsbergis to Mitterrand, 24 April 1990, AD, Europe 1985-1990, URSS, box 6682.
157. TD Moscou 3556, 4 May 1990, AD, Europe 1985-1990, URSS, box 6681.
158. Letter from Kohl to Mitterrand, 15 May 1990, AD, Europe 1985-1990, URSS, box 6682.
159. At the most, Bush, during Gorbachev's visit at the end of May and the beginning of June, agreed that the G7, whose next summit would be held in Houston in July, might examine the possibility for a multilateral program of aid to the USSR, including substantial credits: see Zelikow and Rice, *Germany Unified*, p. 271 *ff.*
160. In a note dated 12 June, Margerie was still reduced to conjectures regarding a possible negotiation between Soviets and Germans on an economical and financial 'package' destined to facilitate the acceptation of German unification by Moscow. Despite German denials (Genscher denied that the FRG was in the process of 'buying' the unifica-

tion from the Soviets), this note reflected remaining French interrogations with regard to a possible German-Soviet entente: outlining an implicit (and quite daring) parallel with the Ribbentrop-Molotov pact of 1939, Margerie wrote that a 'secret protocol would bear today ... not on the distribution of influence zones in Central Europe but on the amount of German credits injected in the Soviet economy': see Margerie, note pour le secrétaire général, Etats-Unis et RFA,12 June 1990.

161. Letter from Kohl to Mitterrand, 18 June 1990, private papers, and Guigou, note pour le président de la République, Votre rencontre avec le chancelier Kohl. Aide à l'Union soviétique, 21 June 1990, AN, 5AG4/CDM 33. See also Teltschik, *329 Tage*, p. 274.
162. *Le Monde*, 20 June 1990; Teltschik, *329 Tage*, p. 279 and 283.
163. *Le Monde*, 28 June 1990; Teltschik, *329 Tage*, p. 287; see also Zelikow and Rice, *Germany Unified*, p. 325–326.
164. TD RPAN Bruxelles 174–177 and 184, 9 and 13 March 1990; MAE, ASP, note, a.s. Aspects externes de l'unification de l'Allemagne, 15 mars 1990, AD, ASD 1985–1990, box 16.
165. TD Moscou 1628, 1648, 2422 and 2501–2502, 7, 29 and 30 March 1990, AD, ASD 1985–1990, box 16.
166. Meeting between Mitterrand and Lafontaine, 14 March 1990; telephone conversation between Mitterrand and Kohl, 14 March. Teltschik emphasized the following day that those who favored article 146 were equally for Germany's exit from NATO: Attali- Teltschik Lunch, 15 March 1990.
167. Lanxade, note pour le président de la République, Appartenance de l'Allemagne unifiée à l'Alliance atlantique: position soviétique, 23 March 1990, private papers.
168. Védrine, note pour le président de la République, a.s. Que va devenir l'OTAN?, 23 March 1990, and note a.s. Quels sont les objectifs de nos principaux interlocuteurs sur les alliances et la sécurité?, 3 April 1990, private papers.
169. MAE, ASP, note a.s. L'unification allemande et l'Alliance atlantique: aspects techniques, 28 février 1990, AD, ASD 1985–1990, box 16.
170. MAE, ASP, note, a.s. L'unification allemande, l'URSS et le pacte de Varsovie, 1 March 1990, AD, ASD 1985–1990, box 16.
171. See Meeting between Mitterrand and Cavaco Silva, 23 March 1990, and Lanxade, note pour le secrétaire général, 10 April 1990, private papers: Lanxade sent to Mitterrand the position of one of Kohl's close collaborators, the former defense minister Rupert Scholz, in favor of a withdrawal of all nuclear arms and foreign conventional forces from Germany; annotation by Mitterrand: 'Interesting, keep.' On this point, see chapters 4 and 6 of this volume, p. 194 and pp. 281–282.
172. Védrine, note pour le président de la République, a.s. Entretien avec M. Lafontaine. Avenir de l'Alliance et position allemande, 14 March 1990, private papers; see also MAE, ASP, note a.s. L'unification allemande et les forces stationnées occidentales, 5 March 1990, AD, ASD 1985–1990, box 16.
173. Védrine, note pour le président de la République, a.s. Que va devenir l'OTAN?, 23 March 1990; and Lanxade, note, Appartenance de l'Allemagne unie à l'Alliance atlantique: position soviétique, 23 March 1990 ; Quai reflections are reflected in MAE, ASD, Schéma a.s. Evolutions en Europe. Enjeux et perspectives, Contribution pour réunion chez HV, 17 March 1990, AD, série Directeur politique (DP) 1986–1991, box 300.
174. MAE, ASD, Schéma a.s. Évolutions en Europe. Enjeux et perspectives, 17 March 1990.
175. Meeting between Mitterrand and Cavaco Silva.
176. On Washington's point of view at the beginning of 1990, see Bush and Scowcroft, *A World Transformed*, p. 230ff:
177. Attali, note pour Monsieur le Président, sur mon déjeuner avec le général Scowcroft à la Maison Blanche le jeudi 8 mars 1990, 9 March 1990, private papers.

178. TD Washington 891–892, 5 avril 1990, AD, ASD 1985–1990, box 130 *bis*.
179. Lanxade, note pour Monsieur le président de la République, Sécurité en Europe: position américaine, 9 April 1990, private papers.
180. TD RPAN 237–238, 27 March 1990, AD, ASD 1985–1990, box 130 *bis*.
181. Védrine, note a.s. Quels sont les objectifs de nos principaux interlocuteurs sur les alliances et la sécurité?, 3 avril 1990; TD Washington 956, 12 April 1990; and MAE, ASP, note, Rencontre du président de la République avec le président Bush (Key Largo 19/4/1990), n.d., AD, ASD 1985–1990, box 130 *bis*.
182. Védrine, note pour le président de la République, a.s. Relations franco-américaines, 4 April 1990, private papers; TD Washington 891–892, 5 April 1990.
183. Védrine, note pour le président de la République, a.s. différends franco-américains, 11 April 1990, private papers.
184. TD Washington 891–892, 5 April 1990, AD.
185. TD RPAN 275–276, 10 April 1990, AD, ASD 195–1990, box 130 *bis*.
186. Detailed report from Bianco to Georgette Elgey, 23 April 1990, private papers.
187. Lanxade, note pour Monsieur le président de la République, Sécurité en Europe: position américaine, 9 April 1990.
188. Védrine, note pour le président de la République, a.s. Votre rencontre avec le président Bush; le rôle de l'OTAN, 11 April 1990, private papers; see also Guigou, note pour le président de la République, Relations entre les États-Unis et la Communauté européenne. Sur quoi pourrait porter un accord entre la Communauté et les États-Unis?, 11 April 1990, private papers.
189. Bush and Scowcroft, *A World Transformed*, p. 266.
190. Letter from Bush to Mitterrand, 17 April 1990 (French translation) and Hennekinne, note pour le président de la République, Message du president Bush, 18 April 1990, private papers.
191. Bush and Scowcroft, *A World Transformed*, p. 267.
192. Meeting between Mitterrand and Bush, 19 April 1990, Key Largo; Bush and Scowcroft, *A World Transformed*, p. 267–268.
193. Bush and Scowcroft, *A World Transformed*, p. 268.
194. TD RPAN 342–344, 26 April 1990, AD, ASD 1985–1990, box 130 *bis*.
195. MAE, le directeur des affaires politiques, Conseil de défense et de sécurité franco-allemand, 3e session, Paris, le 26 avril 1990, compte rendu de B. Dufourcq, 27 April 1990, private papers.
196. See Bush and Scowcroft, *A World Transformed*, p. 268; and Zelikow and Rice, *Germany Unified*, p. 237–240.
197. TD RPAN 322, 23 April 1990, AD, ASD 1985–1990, box 16.
198. MAE, ASD, note pour le cabinet du ministre d'État, a.s. Sommet(s) de l'Alliance, 27 April 1990, AD, ASD 1985–1990, box 133 (at Key Largo, Bush did not seem to clearly warn Mitterrand of his intention to speed up NATO's calendar, contrary to what Zelikow and Rice suggest in *Germany Unified*, p. 240).
199. Message from Bush to Mitterrand, 2 May 1990, AD, ASD 1985–1990, box 217; see also MAE, ASD, note pour le cabinet du ministre d'État, a.s. Sommet de l'Alliance atlantique, lettre du président Bush au président de la République, 3 May 1990, AD, ASD 1985–1990, box 133; the author notes: 'We must now specify ... whether we consider that the possibility of a summit in June-July meets our position in Key Largo or whether we wish a later event to consecrate the result of reflections.'
200. Meeting between Mitterrand and Thatcher, 4 May 1990; see also Mitterrand's speech during the spring session of the North Atlantic Assembly, 11 May 1990, *PEF*, May–June 1990, p. 27–28.

201. TD Moscou 3225–3226, 26 April 1990, and 3546, 4 May 1990, AD, ASD 1985–1990, box 16.
202. TD Moscou 3577, 7 May 1990, AD, ASD 1985–1990, box 16.
203. TD Washington 1151, 1204 and 1273, 8, 11 and 18 May 1990, AD, ASD 1985–1990, box 16.
204. Zelikow and Rice, *Germany Unified*, p. 262–266.
205. Letter from Bush to Mitterrand, 22 May 1990, private papers.
206. Védrine, note pour le président de la République, 23 May 1990, private papers. The Quai d'Orsay was also cognizant of the necessity to display a firm position in Moscow: it believed that France should reject 'any idea of a special status, which would be destabilizing' and that 'the only rule should be that of respect for the principle of sovereignty (see the Helsinki Final Act of and the UN Charter);' and the note suggested that Mitterrand's visit could be the occasion to ask the Soviets 'which guarantees they desire to soften their position on Germany's membership in NATO:' MAE, Sous-direction URSS, Schéma d'entretien, Visite officielle de travail du président de la République à Moscou (25 mai 1990), 21 May 1990, AD, Europe 1986–1990, box 6682.
207. See Meeting between Mitterrand and Gorbachev, Moscow, 25 May 1990, detailed report by Védrine, private papers; detailed report by Gorbachev in Michail Gorbatschow, *Wie es war. Die deutsche Wiedervereinigung*, Munich, Econ, 2000, p. 131ff.; and Attali, handwritten notes, private papers. The latter document illustrates the extremely poor reliability of Attali's book, so flagrant are the discrepancies between the transcript published in the book and the original document written by Attali himself: whereas in that document it was Gorbachev who suggested a situation 'à la française' for Germany in NATO, in the transcript of the meeting as published in the book it was Mitterrand who made the suggestion: see Jacques Attali, *Verbatim III, 1988–1991*, Paris, Fayard, 1995, p. 496ff. (Some commentators have relied on this very unreliable source to denounce Mitterrand's alleged 'duplicity' in the question of the membership of Germany in NATO, whereas in fact Mitterrand seems to have been the first to convince Gorbachev of the unavoidable character of a unified Germany in NATO.)
208. Letter from Mitterrand to Bush, 28 May 1990, private papers. Since he was probably not informed of Baker's nine points of the previous week, Mitterrand interestingly reported to Bush that he had told Gorbachev that 'the Westerners would certainly not refuse to clarify the guarantees that he would be in the right to expect for the security of his country', and he continued: 'I think that we must seek to defuse Mr. Gorbachev's worries. I will offer to you as well as to our partners propositions when we meet', suggesting that he himself was reflecting on assurances similar to those offered by Baker. Indeed, in a note dated 1 June, Védrine and Lanxade, noting the ongoing impasse over Germany's NATO membership (the Elysée evidently did not know that Gorbachev had made an important concession in Washington the previous day), suggested to Mitterrand that France, before the NATO summit that should kick off the reflection on the future of the alliance, make propositions 'to facilitate the search for a compromise … on the security questions and on the insertion of the USSR in the world economy'. Without knowing that the Americans and the Germans had been working on this since mid May – in security and economic terms respectively – the Elysée thus also envisaged a 'package' destined to obtain Moscow's green light on Germany's NATO membership; see Védrine and Lanxade, note pour le president de la République, 1 June 1990, private papers.
209. TD Moscou 4097, 1 June 1990, AD, Europe 1986–1990, URSS, box 6682.
210. Gorbatschow, *Wie es war*, p. 135–136. This important point was confirmed to the author by Anatoly Chernyaev during a conference organized by the Norwegian Nobel Institute in Oslo-Lysebu, 17–19 June 2002; see also Marie-Pierre Rey, 'Europe is Our Com-

mon Home: A Study of Gorbachev's Diplomatic Concept,', *Cold War History*, vol. 4, n° 2 (01/2004), p. 33–65; and Dufourcq, '2 + 4'.
211. Zelikow and Rice, *Germany Unified*, p. 275ff.; Gorbatchev, *Mémoires*, p. 136ff.; and Adomeit, *Imperial Overstretch*, p. 518ff.
212. See typically Zelikow and Rice, *Germany United*, p. 270–271. Beyond these authors' natural tendency to highlight the Bush administration's successes, their biased treatment of Mitterrand's role is not surprising: not only had Mitterrand, in his letter to Bush dated 28 May, emphasized Gorbachev's intransigence in this matter (again, Mitterrand did not seem to realize that he had in fact convinced him, in Moscow, of the inevitability of a unified Germany's membership in NATO), but it could after all appear paradoxical to the Americans that it was the French president who had reached this result.
213. The Soviet Number One would later minimize the concession made to Washington, preferring to speak of a 'compromise': see Gorbatchev, *Mémoires*, p. 669.
214. Adomeit, *Imperial Overstretch*, p. 520ff.; and Zelikow and Rice, *Germany Unified*, p. 280–282.
215. MAE, le directeur des affaires politiques, compte rendu, a.s. Quad du 5 juin: question allemande, 11 June 1990; and TD RPAN 451–459, 11 June 1990, AN, 5AG4/CDM 8.
216. See Zelikow and Rice, *Germany Unified*, p. 283–303; TD Bonn 1528–30, 12 June 1990; and TD RPAN 487, 19 June 1990, AD, ASD 1985–1990, box 17. This solution was from the beginning preferred by the French and by their partners: see above, note 22. On the question of conventional disarmament in connection with German unification, see MAE, sous-direction du désarmement, note de Gilles Andréani, Le traité FCE et les évolutions politiques en Europe, 8 March 1990; TD Diplomatie 6305–6306, Dufourcq, 29 March 1990, secret DSL, AD, ASD 1985–1990, box 16; and personal interviews. Refusal to 'singularise' Germany by putting limits on its forces through the 2 + 4, the need to conclude rapidly a CFE treaty (whose objective was to reduce the risks of surprise attack rather than to limit German forces, and which should thus not be blocked in the name of German unification), launching of a 'FCE 1 *bis*' negotiation to manage the transition from 23 to 22: in total, the feeling at the Quai d'Orsay was that French diplomacy, 'which had constantly sought to reduce the Alliance to Alliance aspect of the [CFE] negotiation' had thus contributed to the solution of an important aspect of the German question.
217. The French embassy in Moscow, in mid June, wagered on a progressive Soviet acceptance of united Germany's NATO membership: Gorbachev, in discussions with Mitterrand and Bush, had realized the firmness of the Western powers in this matter and their desire to refrain from exploiting the situation and take consideration of Soviet interests – hence the importance of the upcoming London summit to convince Moscow: TD Moscou 4363–4364, 18 June 1990, AD, ASD 1985–1990, box 17, and Ambassade de France à Moscou, note, a.s. L'URSS, l'Allemagne et les Alliances, 18 June 1990, private papers.
218. Meeting between Mitterrand and de Maizière, 18 June 1990, private papers. Reporting two days later to Baker on his conversation at the Élysée, de Maizière emphasized that Mitterrand had not insisted on Germany's NATO membership and showed himself more interested in the role of the CSCE. Asked by Baker whether Mitterrand thought that the CSCE should be substituted for NATO, de Maizière, however, said that the French president did not go that far: see Zelikow and Rice, *Germany Unified*, p. 294.
219. MAE, le directeur des affaires politiques, note pour le ministre d'État, a.s. Réunion du groupe d'Ottawa (Bonn 20 juin), 21 June 1990.
220. MAE, ASP, note a.s. L'hypothèque soviétique sur la conclusion de l'exercice à six: conséquences d'un blocage, 28 May 1990.

221. MAE, ASP, note a.s. Session ministérielle du Conseil atlantique (Turnberry, 7–8 juin 1990), Présentation générale, 31 May 1990; TD RPAN 466, 13 June 190, AD, ASD 1985–1990, box 17; and TD RPAN 445–448, AD, ASD 1985–1990, box 130 *bis*.
222. TD Diplomatie 12097, 19 juin 1990, AD, ASD 1985–1990, box 130 *bis*.
223. Letter from Bush to Mitterrand, 21 June 1990, AD, ASD 1985–1990, box 217.
224. On the genesis of the London declaration and the preparation for the NATO summit, see Zelikow and Rice, *Germany Unified*, p. 303ff.
225. MAE, ASD, note de Philippe Guelluy, a.s. Lettre du président Bush, 22 June 1990, AD, ASD 1985–1990, box 217. Note that the author of this note believed that the nuclear aspects of the draft declaration were altogether acceptable and that the notion of weapons of 'last resort' was close to the French point of view – a surprising stance in view of the remarks that Mitterrand would make two weeks later in London (see chapter 6 of this volume, p. 281).
226. Lanxade, note à l'attention de Monsieur le secrétaire général, 25 juin 1990, Sommet de l'OTAN, 25 June 1990, private papers.
227. Letter from Chevènement to Mitterrand, 26 June 1990, private papers. The main fear held by Chevènement was that the 'last resort' strategy would lead to a quickened denuclearization of Europe. This trend, he believed, would likely be encouraged by a Germany that he deemed 'ready for everything' to buy its unity, while the Americans would be 'at the tow of the German public opinion which was always hostile towards foreign nuclear arms'. Chevènement's analysis reflected his own personal anxieties: it was essential in his opinion to defend the French nuclear posture, in order 'to maintain the role and the rank of France in Europe at the 2000 horizon between the military superpower (the USSR) and the economical power (Germany) whereas the maritime power (the U.S.) would retire across the oceans'. The maintenance of France's deterrence posture, he said, was indispensable so that it could continue to 'exist as a third European power'.
228. Teletyped message from Mitterrand to Bush, 29 June 1990, very secret, private papers; see Zelikow and Rice, *Germany United*, p. 319–320.

Chapter 6

FROM LONDON TO PARIS

(Summer and Autumn 1990)

It was at the start of the summer of 1990 that the real breakthrough to German unity took place. The Atlantic summit in London on 5 and 6 July was a preamble: by adopting a declaration that expressed their intention to transform NATO and to move beyond the logic of confrontation, the Allies gave the Soviet Union a strong signal that they hoped would induce Moscow to accept the maintenance of united Germany within NATO. The bet was won. At the end of decisive conversations in Moscow and in the Caucasus on the 15 and 16 July, during which the great bargaining was concluded between the Germans and the Soviets, Helmut Kohl and Hans-Dietrich Genscher obtained satisfaction in exchange for specific political and military arrangements involving the territory of the future ex-GDR and for considerable German economic and financial aid to the USSR. The Caucasus breakthrough put an end to the impasse in which the 2 + 4 negotiation had found itself since the end of the spring: the ministerial meeting in Paris on 17 July saw the lifting of the Soviet veto on the NATO question and resulted in a compromise with the Poles on the border issue, now practically resolved. With the intra-German process gathering speed in the background (the treaty on political union was signed between the GDR and the FRG at the end of August and the date of unification was fixed for 3 October), it remained only to put finishing touches on the final settlement. After an ultimate, suspenseful diplomatic round that lasted

---

Notes for this section begin on page 300.

until a few hours before the signing of the document, it took place as foreseen on 12 September in Moscow. The Four having previously suspended their rights and responsibilities, on 3 October Germany recovered both unity and complete sovereignty.

For French diplomacy it was time for an assessment. With the winter's difficulties forgotten, the Quai d'Orsay thought the outcome positive overall: despite initial misgivings, Paris had essentially attained its objectives in the negotiation on the international aspects of German unity and had contributed constructively to the elaboration of the final settlement. In this context, the diplomacy of François Mitterrand wanted to make the CSCE summit in Paris from 19 to 21 November 1990 an event that would mark the end of the Cold War. The summit's success, however, remained symbolic: the German question was already solved, and the Gulf crisis (Iraq had invaded Kuwait on 2 August) now dominated international events. The page of Yalta was quickly turned. The priority for French diplomacy was henceforth to work for the establishment of a new European 'architecture' in line with its ideas.

From the London Summit to the Caucasus Breakthrough

American determination to obtain a decisive result on 5 and 6 July in London was confirmed in the days preceding the summit. Only on 29 June did Washington transmit to the other capitals the proposed declaration that had been confidentially sent on the 21st to Bonn, London, Paris and Rome. American diplomacy gave the allies only a brief time to react: Washington was opposed to the NAC permanent representatives in Brussels examining the American proposal, which was only to be discussed in London by the ministers of foreign affairs themselves. This procedure – expeditious, to say the least – aimed to make sure the Sixteen endorsed it with a minimum of amendments that might distort the American text.[1] Paris could merely take note of Washington's 'forcing' and its refusal to take account of the French view. Noting the 'gradual erosion of the idea of a global review of the problems of the Alliance' since Key Largo and stressing that the American approach did not leave 'any opening to a specific role for Western Europe in defense matters', Ambassador Jacques Andréani deplored the fact that short-term preoccupations were thus trumping 'the need to fundamentally rethink the Alliance's structure and equilibriums'.[2] As for Admiral Jacques Lanxade, who had gone to the White House to discuss these matters on 29 June, he came back convinced of the 'hasty and often contradictory' nature of the American proposals, which he saw merely as 'a somewhat pathetic attempt to safeguard the American presence in Europe'.[3]

In this context, French diplomacy was divided between the temptation to voice its disagreements and a wish to soften the sharp edges, knowing that the primary stake of the summit was to obtain a Soviet *nihil obstat* about keeping Germany in NATO. The Élysée sifted the American draft to distinguish between those articles of the declaration that posed no problem from the French standpoint since they corresponded to the 'general orientation' defended by Paris, those that should produce the customary mention of 'concerned allies' to allow France implicitly to demarcate its position and, finally, those where French officials should try to obtain a rewrite.[4] Lanxade's mission to Washington allowed him, as the president's military chief of staff, to explain the Élysée's reaction to the American proposals. While he did not minimize the reservations that some of them aroused in Paris – the creation of new multinational forces, the notion of nuclear weapons as weapons of 'last resort' or the passages that in effect preempted the results of the coming Paris summit of the CSCE – he tried, following the nonconfrontational line decreed by the Élysée, to give a constructive twist to French objections. The White House received the objections 'without irritation', he reported, since the Americans were trying to avoid exposing a Franco-American fracture over NATO.[5]

The London Summit

Still, the summit underscored the French dilemma. In London, Mitterrand started out by being amenable: in his first contribution on 5 July, he said he was pleased with the planned American declaration, of whose 'spirit he approved'. Stressing that this was a 'crucial' moment and that the alliance must adapt to the new situation, he recognized that the document 'went largely in that direction'. While recalling France's particular position, he confirmed that it 'would participate in any reflection [aimed at] adapting the Alliance to the exigencies of times to come', and he expressed the wish that 'another summit of the same type might in due course draw the conclusions that events would impose'. In short, while endorsing the American wish to give Moscow a signal of change, the French president emphasized without acrimony that London did not mark the culmination of the alliance's adaptation and that France remained available for the forward-looking reflection mentioned in Key Largo.[6]

Yet examination of the declaration by the ministers of foreign affairs later that same day led to a sharp French hardening. The exercise lasted until after midnight and proved very laborious, since James Baker had decided not to yield on anything.[7] As a result, the next day Mitterrand proved more critical about a document that French diplomacy had not managed to inflect much at all. While he recognized that this 'audacious and courageous' text marked 'an innovation, an opening toward the former adversaries', he now stressed his reservations. Repeating that his country held to 'being outside the integrated command' and that all the articles of the declaration dealing with the latter 'do not concern France', he criticized (as, in fact, did Margaret Thatcher) the notion of nuclear weapons to be used only as a last resort as contrary to the very idea of deterrence.[8] This presentation was considered disappointing by the Americans, who – while understanding French frustration at the 'bulldozer' tactics of their diplomacy – noted that Mitterrand took his distance from the entire text. The 'London declaration on a transformed North Atlantic Alliance' nevertheless appeared to be a great success for Washington. By proclaiming a transformation of the alliance and holding out a hand to their former enemies, the Western nations, under American impetus, had essentially 'delivered' the commitments advanced in Baker's 'nine points'.[9]

The impression of French bad humor resulted especially from the closing press conference, during which Mitterrand, publicly expressing his criticism of the London declaration, announced to general surprise that 'logic' would demand that French forces withdraw from Germany after unification. Of course this hypothesis had been envisaged for many months by Mitterrand, who had often told Kohl of his conviction that German public opinion would not accept a foreign military presence for long. (The German chancellor had constantly refuted this, protesting his wish to see the FFA maintained). Thus Mitterrand's announcement arose foremost from the new dynamic of Franco-German relations that was being set up in the context of German unification.[10] But at the time it could be interpreted only as a manifestation of French disarray in the wake of the Atlantic summit. Indeed, one of the high points of the summit lay in the plan to establish multinational units so as to prevent the risk of rejection of foreign forces by German opinion. Seen from Paris, however, this showed how much the idea of a European defense (which from the French standpoint might have offered a solution to the problem of the legitimacy of foreign forces in Germany) had been neglected in London, aggravating Mitterrand's irritation at European security being taken in hand by the Atlantic Alliance, as was perceptible since the spring.

Thus, even if French officials were attached after the fact to minimizing what were presented as simple 'reflections', the announcement of the eventual withdrawal of the FFA disturbed the Americans, who were worried by a French withdrawal's possible impact on their own forces. Such a withdrawal might, Washington feared, accredit the idea of a symmetry between the Soviet pullout from the GDR and a Western withdrawal from the FRG. This worry the French did not bother to quell: 'Perhaps this will incite [the Americans] to take our position more into consideration when they deal with the future military status of Germany', commented the French ambassador in Washington, confirming implicitly that Mitterrand's London announcement, more than simply whim, had purposely signified French dissatisfaction with the results of the NATO summit.[11] This dissatisfaction was summarized in Gabriel Robin's assessment of the summit: of course the Americans had been successful, to the extent that the declaration adopted was very close to their initial plan and that it tended to make NATO nothing less than 'the center of the recomposition of Europe' – in particular due to the proposal made to the countries of Eastern Europe to establish diplomatic links with it, but also because of the suggestions concerning the future of the CSCE. And yet, the French NATO permanent representative continued, if the United States had proved that they 'controlled NATO' by imposing a predetermined result in the name of short-term considerations, they had not demonstrated that they knew 'where they wanted to lead it'. France, he concluded, constrained as it was to 'stand outside' due to Washington's 'barely concealed indifference' to its viewpoint, could only see this result as a 'lost opportunity'.[12] The London summit thus confirmed existing misunderstandings between France and the United States.

Moscow's Green Light

After London, though, it was less the future of the alliance than the Soviet attitude to Germany's NATO membership that was at the heart of speculations. Since Gorbachev's abandonment of an attitude of pure and simple refusal during his meeting with Bush a month earlier, official Soviet diplomacy had scarcely given any actual signs of changing, as shown by the ministerial meeting of the 2 + 4 in East Berlin on 22 June. The meeting of political directors on 4 July, which also took place in East Berlin, saw no substantial progress on politico-military questions, with one important exception: agreement over the German renunciation of ABC weapons, reached at the insistent demand of French diplomats, for whom this had been a major goal on the same level as recognition of the Oder-Neisse border, as we know. The agreement was reached despite the reservations of West German diplomats, who were more than ever concerned to present this renunciation (which of course was not disputed in itself) as the result of a German sovereign decision. The compromise formula, adopted on 4 July and modeled on the Paris agreements of 1954, stipulated that the two German states would declare that unified Germany renounced ABC weapons; note would then be taken of this commitment in the framework of the 2 + 4 settlement.[13] The meeting on 4 July also ruled that the question of the German troop level would be dealt with within the framework of the CFE, so some progress was also made on this now central point in Soviet preoccupations. (As their July 15 visit to Moscow approached, Kohl and Genscher tried to agree on the level of military troops that united Germany was ready to have fixed within the CFE, giving rise to a difficult debate within the governing coalition.[14])

Yet the Western nations remained uncertain about Moscow's attitude to Germany's belonging to NATO, as suggested by their exchanges during a 'quad' meeting after the London NATO summit on 6 July. Whereas Baker hoped to obtain Moscow's agreement thanks to the positive effect of the London declaration – the Soviets could not say 'that NATO had done nothing', he noted – and to the limits put on the Bundeswehr troops, Genscher, supported by Dumas, stressed the importance of the economic and financial portion of the 'package' that was being put together in order to convince the Soviets. Hence, hammered both the German and the Frenchman, a positive signal was needed at the coming G7 summit: 'Can we answer "no" to Soviet demands?' asked Dumas of the reluctant American and Briton, adding: 'A "yes" in London, a "no" in Houston – this would be incomprehensible.'[15] (The Houston summit on 9–11 July later confirmed Washington and London's hesitation to commit to a program of aid to the USSR. Kohl and Mitterrand scarcely obtained more than that the Seven would take up the suggestion, adopted by the Twelve in Dublin two weeks earlier, of a *study* of the needs of the Soviet economy, to be conducted by the IMF before the end of the year.[16]) In short, although the Western nations could think they had done the maximum to convince Moscow to accept maintaining Germany in NATO, nothing was yet gained on the eve of Kohl's departure for Moscow in mid July. It would be 'unreasonable' to believe that one might 'impose everything' on the USSR, stressed Kvitsinski to the French ambassador, advancing the view that very strong 'internal pressure' was weighing on the Soviet leaders.[17] In fact, opening on 2 July, the 28th Congress of the CPSU was the theater of an offensive by conservatives who concentrated especially on the foreign policy of Gorbachev and Eduard Shevardnadze, who were accused of having 'lost' Eastern Europe. As the meeting of 2 + 4 in Paris approached, the Quai d'Orsay – while recognizing the tactical element in the Soviet position – did not exclude a dead end occurring there, which 'would mark the failure of the policy of the United States and the FRG, both of which for six months had been conceiving all their diplomatic actions in line with the goal of obtaining Soviet acceptance of united Germany within NATO'.[18]

Ultimately, this fear was not warranted, however: Kohl and Genscher's visit to the USSR on 15 and 16 July resulted in the definitive breakthrough toward unity. Three days before, Bonn learned that Gorbachev was inviting the German leaders to travel to the province of Stavropol, his homeland, after a first round of meetings in Moscow. While the Chancellery wanted to avoid exaggerating hopes of success, it saw the confirmation of the invitation (which until then had been just a possibility) as a good omen.¹⁹ Meanwhile, of course, Gorbachev had won the upper hand against his adversaries in the CPSU Congress: reelected general secretary on 10 July, his domestic position seemed more solid than ever. Understanding that any other option was unrealistic and taking into account the gestures from the West, in particular the London declaration, he had now decided to solve once and for all the question of German membership in NATO, even if this meant overlooking strong reservations, including within his own entourage.²⁰

From the start, Kohl and Gorbachev placed their Moscow tête-à-tête on 15 July in historic perspective. After a long evocation of the past, in particular the Second World War, which both had experienced as young men, and of the future cooperation between the two countries, Gorbachev tackled the 'current' questions. The Soviet Number One squarely formulated his position in four points: united Germany would be made up of the territories of the FRG, the GDR and Berlin; it would renounce ABC weapons; NATO military structures would not be extended to the former GDR territory and the Soviet military presence there would be the subject of a transitional agreement; and finally, the rights of the Four Powers would be lifted. At this point, the chancellor demanded to hear confirmation that Germany would obtain its full sovereignty *at the moment of unity* and that it would be free to remain a member of the alliance. 'That goes without saying', replied Gorbachev, who added that de jure the question of German NATO membership was 'clear'. Kohl calmly registered this declaration. If the rest of the discussion showed that things were less clear de facto – the concrete meaning of the principle of the non-extension of NATO structures to the former GDR indeed gave rise to an inconclusive exchange – he described the conversation, when the meeting was enlarged to both delegations, as 'extraordinarily good and constructive'.²¹ Teltschik thought that the essential thing was henceforward settled at the end of this first meeting: 'Gorbachev accepts that Germany remains a NATO member', he rejoiced. As for the Soviet renunciation of the transitory upkeep of the rights of the Four from the day of unification, it constituted for him a 'second surprise': 'What a sensation!' he concluded. 'We did not expect such concessions.'²²

The meeting the next day in the Caucasus was a suspenseful finale. To be sure, the agreement converged without difficulty on a figure of 370,000 for the Bundeswehr troops and on the principle of two treaties over Soviet forces – one on the conditions of their transitional stay and withdrawal, the other on financial compensation. Yet the modes of united Germany belonging to the alliance and in particular the status of the territory of the ex-GDR were the tough items of the negotiation. While Gorbachev and Shevardnadze, evidently wanting to save face, tried to exclude any advancement of NATO military structures in the ex-GDR not only *during* but *after* the period of three or four years during which Soviet forces would remain stationed there, Kohl and Genscher, manifestly attentive to not wander away from the position agreed with Washington, flatly opposed such a formula by advancing the sovereignty of united Germany as well as the validity of the Atlantic guarantee for all of German territory. Although difficult, a compromise on this key point came at the end of long exchanges. There would be no extension of NATO structures *during* the transition period so that only non-integrated German forces might be present in the ex-GDR in that period. There would further be no introduction of foreign forces or nuclear weapons in this same territory *after* the Soviet withdrawal, although German forces present in the East might then be integrated into NATO.[23] The formalization of the compromise on this precise but critical point would still cause difficulty in the coming weeks and was not publicly unveiled that day, but it essentially put an end to six months of uncertainty about this key issue in the 'great bargaining', thus permitting a happy conclusion to the German-Soviet summit.[24] In fact, some hours later during the joint press conference in the locality of Zhelednovosk, Kohl summed up in eight points – previously agreed with Gorbachev – the tenor of the agreements, provoking the surprise of journalists and governments across the world.[25]

'You've Done Very Well'

It was from the press reports that Germany's partners became aware of the agreements: even had they wished to do so (which may be doubted), the move to the Caucasus did not technically allow the Germans to keep the Western capitals informed in real time about the negotiations. (The first American reaction, betraying evident surprise, was in fact interpreted by the press as a sign that Washington had not been informed by Bonn, or even as the expression of dissatisfaction about the result attained in the Caucasus, an interpretation that U.S. diplomacy went out of its way to correct by pointing out the conformity of the result with its own expectations.) So it was only upon his return that Kohl communicated to his partners the results of his trip to the USSR. The visit, he wrote soberly to Mitterrand, marked 'an advance toward German unity'; the chancellor then summarized the accord reached in the Caucasus and thanked the French president for his support as well as that of his other Western partners.[26] As for Genscher, he informed his three Western colleagues on the morning of 17 July in Paris during the 'quad' meeting that was being held just before the ministerial session of the 2 + 4. Invited by Dumas to speak, he expressed 'the gratitude' of the Federal Republic for the assistance that its three allies had brought to the process. 'We have attained our objective', he said. He then commented on the points of agreement reached in the Caucasus and responded to questions and requests for clarification from Baker and Douglas Hurd. While Baker was not excessively enthusiastic, perhaps reflecting disappointment about restrictions on NATO forces in the ex-GDR, Hurd, in a gesture of fair play, said: 'You've done very well.' Genscher remained modest: 'It was evident that the Soviets wanted to settle everything', he said, emphasizing that the results of the London summit had played a big role. 'It must be recognized that many had doubts about the possibility of unified Germany in NATO', he added, concluding: 'I am convinced that the solution we have arrived at is good for all of Europe.'[27] The rest of the day confirmed the unblocking of the politico-military issues within the 2 + 4, which the Quai d'Orsay thought were now 'practically solved': the ministerial meeting in Paris in effect 'ratified the lifting of the Soviet veto on the realization of German unity within NATO'.[28] The next day, Dumas related this result to the French Council of Ministers: 'Germany is not triumphant', he affirmed, but 'it obtained the essence of its demands', that is to say, the belonging to the Atlantic Alliance of a unified Germany and the lifting of the rights of the Four. This result conformed to the goals of France, Mitterrand noted, emphasizing that French diplomacy had from the start asserted the 'necessity' of keeping Germany in the alliance while stressing 'that NATO should not profit from circumstances to advance its military arrangements'.[29]

From Unblocking the 2 + 4 to the Final Settlement

The Caucasus meeting did not solve everything, however. As the Paris meeting approached, French diplomacy remained particularly concerned about the border issue, which it had turned into a priority. While Paris had judged it 'ripe' to be solved at the end of June, last-minute difficulties at the beginning of July tempered this optimism. During the 2 + 4 meeting of political directors in East Berlin on 4 July – to which Warsaw had been invited to send a representative to help prepare the Paris ministerial meeting – Warsaw's representative, Jerzy Sulek, raised three objections that revealed the persistence of Polish distrust toward German intentions. Noting that the plan refined by the Six made no explicit reference to the '*peace* settlement' mentioned by the Potsdam agreement (as we recall, agreement had been reached within the 2 + 4 on the notion of '*final* settlement'), he worried that this lacuna might open the way to later disputes, since the texts of 1945 referred expressly to the conclusion of such a peace settlement in order to definitively fix the borders. In addition, he reiterated the

Polish requirement of a modification not only of the Basic Law but also of certain German legislation, notably regarding citizenship. Finally, he put forward the need to condition the final lifting of the quadripartite rights on the entry into force of the future bilateral German-Polish treaty.[30]

In Berlin, Sulek did receive assurance from his six interlocutors that there was 'no doubt' about the definitive character of the settlement, but the German representative put an absolute veto on the demand for modifying internal legislation, which, Kastrup hammered, infringed upon German sovereignty. Moreover, Kastrup repeated that Bonn did not intend before unity to go beyond the Bundestag and Volkskammer resolutions of 21 June. Despite French and Soviet support on the last point raised by the Pole (conditionality of the lifting of quadripartite rights on the entry into force of the bilateral treaty), which met Parisian concerns about the still-open question of the 'sequence' of the settlement, the Polish delegation essentially went back to Warsaw empty-handed.[31] Two days later in London, Genscher repeated to his three Western colleagues that a demand that tied the lifting of the Four's rights to the entry into force of the bilateral treaty, which Dumas defended while Hurd insisted on the need to 'reassure' the Poles, was 'unacceptable' to West Germany, since it would amount to making united Germany's sovereignty conditional on the signature of a treaty that the Poles themselves might refuse to conclude – in which case the lifting of rights and responsibilities would also be blocked, and the settlement would collapse. The German representative could only deplore Warsaw's intransigence.[32]

French diplomacy fretted about this impasse as the ministerial meeting in Paris approached: it would be 'regrettable', the Quai said, 'to let the Poles leave Paris without having found a satisfactory solution to their problem'.[33] Thus Bertrand Dufourcq visited Warsaw on 12 July to try to overcome these difficulties. Meanwhile, Bonn had shown a little more flexibility. Reporting the tenor of conversations between the four Western nations in Houston a few days before, Dufourcq was thus in a position to sketch to Skubiszewski the following scheme: the German-Polish treaty would deal exclusively with the border issue and would use the content of the resolutions of 21 June; more importantly, it would be refined and signed *immediately* after unification, so that it could be submitted for ratification by the parliament of united Germany 'at the same time' as the 2 + 4 settlement. The Polish foreign minister proved more open to this presentation than his staff: although he reiterated the observations formulated on 4 July in Berlin, he no longer made their acceptance by Bonn a precondition for his agreement.[34] This reaction was registered with satisfaction in Paris, where it was thought that such a scheme was 'no doubt the best that the Poles could obtain from the Germans', even if it did not bring them the 'total legal security' that the subordination of the lifting of the quadripartite rights to the bilateral treaty would do, a formula definitely unacceptable to Bonn.[35] On the eve of the Paris ministerial meeting, the worry remained nevertheless palpable at the Élysée, where it was noted that 'the French are the only ones to speak with both parties and to try for solutions'. 'If tomorrow the question was not solved on these bases', warned Caroline de Margerie, the German pressure 'will be even greater for France to stop making itself the advocate of Poland. Already isolated, we risk being gradually accused of putting useless obstacles in the way of unification'.[36]

These fears were quickly banished. In Paris on the morning of 17 July, Genscher informed his Western colleagues that Bonn was disposed to make a gesture in Warsaw's direction. While he repeated that Germany could not accept its sovereignty depending on the border treaty, he confirmed that the Federal Republic was ready to commit to concluding the treaty very quickly on the bases of the German parliamentary resolutions. Despite pressure from Hurd, Baker and Dumas, who all wanted the final settlement and the bilateral treaty to be concluded concomitantly, Genscher, while admitting that the two processes would unfold 'closely together', stuck to a twofold procedure: 'first sovereignty, then we sign and ratify' the treaty with Warsaw, the German minister reiterated, insisting that he was at the end of his concessions and that German opinion would not accept any more: 'We do not like being treated as partners in whom there is no confidence.' But if the issue of the 'sequence' thus remained open despite the insistence of his partners, Genscher advanced a supplementary concession: he indicated that he was ready, in order to respond to the Polish objection concerning the absence of explicit mention of a 'peace settlement', to affirm in the six-party settlement that confirmation of the definitive character of the border was 'an essential contribution to the peace order in Europe'. And he promised to inform Skubiszewski about this concession before the session of the ministerial meeting in the afternoon, in which the Polish minister had been invited to participate.[37]

The meeting now unfolded in a satisfactory manner. Skubiszewski acknowledged the German advances, in particular that the resolutions of the two parliaments 'create a climate very favorable to the elaboration of a treaty between the two countries'. Genscher solemnly repeated that the treaty would be signed and ratified in 'the shortest possible' interval after unification, and he proposed, as previously agreed with Skubiszewski, a formulation mentioning the contribution of the border settlement to the peace order in Europe. Since the Pole now proved satisfied with the German declarations, Dumas proposed consigning these points to the minutes of the meeting, which was accepted by the participants. French diplomacy could thus conclude that thanks in particular to the goodwill of the Polish minister, 'the general agreement reached on the way to solving the border problem marks decisive progress in the work of the group'. Dumas was moreover pleased that 'the solution of this central question' of the exercise 'was found in Paris': combined with the advance registered over the politico-military issues after the meeting in the Caucasus, the Quai d'Orsay rejoiced that this success enabled everyone to 'conclude that the principal political problems linked to the external aspects of unification are now solved'.[38] Welcomed at the Élysée the next day, Skubiszewski thanked Mitterrand for French support and was happy that 'yesterday's results are good'. Yes, the president commented, 'the Germans resisted' because they had not wanted 'to tackle the problem now', but Germany was henceforth 'committed before the world to recognizing the border'.[39] The same day in the Council of Ministers, Mitterrand came back to the affair: 'There was a certain opposition in views between France and the FRG', and while it had been 'stifled', the controversy 'had been no less stiff'; yet, he concluded, 'it must be recognized that [France] was right'.[40]

Toward the Final Settlement

The lifting of the Soviet veto over the NATO question and then the agreement on the border put an end to the impasse in which the 2 + 4 had languished for several weeks. Referring to this double advance on 17 July, Dumas suggested that the six political directors translate it into legal terms by starting now to draft the final settlement. At the end of the Paris meeting, the French director hoped that this 'clerk's role' devolved on the group of Six would be facilitated by the existence of a 'sketch' of the final settlement that Paris had proposed on 22 May, in agreement with its Western partners. But there was still a lot of work to do to transcribe into it the decisions already agreed to by the Six, those taken in other forums, and the last compromises still to be negotiated with Moscow. 'This will not necessarily be easy', noted Dufourcq after the ministerial meeting, emphasizing 'that the calendar demands completion before 19 November', the date of the CSCE summit in Paris during which the results of the 2 + 4 work were to be presented to the 35 (Bonn at this stage envisaged signing the final settlement in January 1991 in Germany).[41] But things in the end went much faster than planned. On 19 July, a new meeting of the political directors of the 2 + 4 in Bonn enabled an advance on the elaboration of the settlement: each participant promised to supply a draft of a part of the text by 15 August, with the French delegation taking charge of the passage devoted to the borders.[42] In the first days of August, Bonn thought that it might be possible to conclude the 2 + 4 process at the ministerial meeting in Moscow on 12 September, with unification occurring in its wake;

the Genscher-Shevardnadze meetings in Moscow on 16 and 17 August allowed the Germans to note the Soviets' agreement to such a deadline. On 23 August, the Volkskammer decided to fix the accession of the GDR to the FRG for 3 October, on the basis of article 23 of the Basic Law. (The chancellor meanwhile tried to bring the date of the general elections forward, from 2 December to 14 October, but he ran up against the SPD's refusal.[43]) The treaty between the FRG and the GDR on political unification, negotiated since July, was finally signed on 31 August. It now remained only to conclude the negotiations on the external aspects of unification.

The Germans and Soviets had steamed ahead at the same time to conclude the various bilateral agreements on which Kohl and Gorbachev had shaken hands in the Caucasus. These had to be turned into no fewer than four treaties: a general political one was devoted to bilateral relations, and three others dealt respectively with the stationing and withdrawal of Soviet forces, the transitional financial arrangement for these forces and finally the commercial obligations inherited by united Germany from the GDR.[44] The exercise was delicate. For Bonn it was primarily a matter of reassuring its Western partners – starting with Paris – who were openly worried about the scope of the agreements in preparation between Bonn and Moscow, in which they feared an eastward 'drift' by the new Germany. 'The essential goal', assured the Auswärtiges Amt, 'was to allow Mr. Gorbachev to be able to show that German unity represents a gain for the USSR' and that 'its interests, especially economic, are not harmed'.[45] But it was also, and more importantly, a matter of punctually concluding negotiations whose economic and financial stakes were considerable and which Moscow, in the very last days of August, appeared to challenge at the last moment by requiring from Bonn a supplementary economic effort, in particular the financing of the repatriation of Soviet forces. It was therefore not until 10 September that Kohl and Gorbachev, after two telephone conversations, reached a definitive understanding on the 'price' of unification, thus lifting the remaining obstacle to concluding the international settlement.[46]

The settlement was now practically ready, the central question of 'sequence' having been settled in August. As we have seen, this issue had proved problematic due to the contradiction between the desire of the Germans, supported at first by the Americans, to see the return of unity coincide with the recovery of full sovereignty, which presupposed concluding the Six's exercise before 3 October, and the necessary 'legal security', which implied, inversely, making the lifting of quadripartite rights and responsibilities contingent on the completion of the expected acts of united Germany – in particular concerning the border, as France maintained.[47] The agreement on this last point, reached in Paris on 17 July, left the problem intact in its entirety, since Bonn wanted to negotiate and sign the treaty with Warsaw only *after* unification and the lifting of quadripartite tutelage. How then could the Four, once the final settlement was signed, 'indicate that they still manifested an interest in the border treaty'? Hurd had objected, while Baker wondered if there might be a means 'of doing it [everything] all at the same time: unification, the final settlement, and the treaty'.[48] It was in the following weeks that a compromise managing these two viewpoints was proposed by the British: the final settlement, of which one article would include the *termination* of rights and responsibilities, would be signed by the Six before unification, but it would be specified that the settlement would only enter into force upon ratification by the Five after unification, which would maintain a lever to put possible pressure on Germany if it reneged on the border question. Meanwhile the Four, once the six-party settlement was signed, would declare their *suspension* of the exercise of their rights from the day of unification, which would allow Germany to recover its sovereignty immediately and thereby to fulfill the acts mentioned in the settlement in full sovereignty. This solution, to which French diplomacy rallied without difficulty, had been ratified during the meeting of political directors in East Berlin from 4 to 7 September. At this stage, the essential part of the settlement was thus finalized; now, thought the Quai d'Orsay, 'except for a last minute surprise, agreement should be obtained in Moscow'.[49]

The final days of the 2 + 4 negotiations would nevertheless face remaining difficulties. As might be expected, these bore on politico-military issues and especially the status of the territory of the ex-GDR, about which the Caucasus compromise, as seen above, retained some ambiguities. To be sure, the Berlin meeting at the start of September solved most of the problems that still remained in the writing of the settlement, notably concerning the limitations on the German military, whether in terms of ABC or of conventional weapons. With regard to the former, the two German states made the planned declarations of renunciation at the NPT review conference in Geneva on 22 August, and the corresponding text was adopted in the form of a clause in the final settlement. With regard to the latter, Genscher and de Maizière having, as agreed, declared at the CFE conference in Vienna on 30 August that united Germany would reduce its troops to 370,000 men in three or four years, Moscow obtained the mention in the settlement that the Soviet withdrawal would take place 'in liaison' with this reduction. Yet at the end of the Berlin meeting – less than a week from the ministerial meeting in Moscow – the West was worried that the Soviets would try to up the stakes by adding formulae that went beyond what had been agreed and might 'by successive nudges' create restrictions to Germany's belonging to Western defense by imposing 'a special and diminished military status' upon it.[50]

In fact, not only did the Soviets now demand mention of a strict conditionality between Soviet withdrawal and the reduction of German military strength – a mention evidently unacceptable for the Western powers, who refused to go beyond the 'liaison' between the two as conceded in Berlin – but they wanted to forbid any deployment of dual-capacity weapons in the former GDR, which would have drastically limited the future deployment of the Bundeswehr. In addition, they required that foreign forces be not only banned from being *stationed* there, as agreed in the Caucasus, but also from any *crossing* of the former inter-German border, which would have deprived NATO of any possibility of performing maneuvers or exercises with the Bundeswehr there. All these measures were considered unacceptable in Washington, London and (somewhat less categorically) in Paris, for 'they aim[ed] at a quasi-demilitarization of East German territory'.[51] French diplomacy, however, did not want to sound dramatic: it should be possible, Dumas's entourage thought, to find a compromise that preserved both Western interests and the possibility for Moscow to 'save face'.[52] The Quai thought on the eve of the Moscow meeting that the main risk would be 'that the Germans and Soviets agree with each other' on compromises that 'would pose a problem for the British and Americans', the latter having asked insistently that the Germans 'make no supplementary concession' before the meeting of the Western powers planned for just before the ministerial meeting of the 2 + 4.[53]

There was a certain foresight in the Quai's analysis: the will of the Germans to conclude, combined with the distrust of the British and behind them, the Americans, indeed led to a last-minute 'psychodrama'.[54] Whereas the six political directors who gathered in the Soviet capital on 11 September found a mutually satisfactory formula (inspired by the CFE negotiations) over dual-capacity weapons, they ran up against the problem of non-German forces being forbidden to cross the prior inter-German border, as the Soviets required. To be sure, Kastrup and Yuly Kvitsinski drafted a compromise by which the final settlement would mention that foreign forces would not be either stationed or deployed in the former East Germany, with an appended protocol signed by the six ministers specifying that it would be up to the German government to apply this measure in a 'reasonable and responsible' manner, 'taking account of the security interests of each'. But British insistence on obtaining explicit stipulation that the ban on deployment would not prevent NATO exercises (at least those with a scope inferior to 'grand maneuvers') – a detail that the Soviets categorically rejected – led to an impasse that roused fears that the ministerial meeting would fail, since the Soviet delegation had indicated that the next day's session would not take place as planned unless there was agreement.[55] After a series of discreet meetings led in the middle of the night by Genscher, the affair was finally resolved at the French embassy the next morning, thanks to a 'little push' from Dumas, who at Genscher's request put pressure on Hurd and Baker to accept the compromise of the night before.[56] This last episode had the 'most remarkable character,' noted the Quai d'Orsay with some amusement, of 'opposing the Americans and especially the British to the Germans more than to the Soviets themselves'.[57]

Once these last hiccups were overcome, the closing ceremony could take place at the end of the morning of 12 September, with each minister saluting the event in his fashion by infusing it with his own particular perspective. Genscher thanked the participants at length and particularly stressed the roles of Bush, Gorbachev and Mitterrand. Dumas stressed the contribution of German unification to European integration and insisted on Franco-German cooperation. De Maizère insisted on the specific responsibilities of Germany in the establishment of peace. Baker stressed that Germany was unifying in peace and freedom as a member of the Atlantic Alliance and of the European Community. Hurd took up the same themes and was pleased the process culminated in Moscow since the USSR had held the key to the solution. Shevardnadze's sober conclusion mentioned the mutation of the European context by insisting on the CSCE process, the transformation of relations between NATO and the Warsaw Pact, and the establishment of new European structures. All these speeches underlined that although German unification closed the chapter of the Cold War, it opened at the same time a new phase whose stakes were the setting up of a new European order – for which there existed competing visions, as we shall see. In the meantime, noted the main French negotiator, the Ottawa exercise finished 'in a particularly relaxed atmosphere'.[58]

Germany Unified, Europe Reconciled

The signing on 12 September 1990 in Moscow of a 'treaty on the final settlement with respect to Germany' put an end to a provisional situation that had lasted forty-five years. In Paris as in other capitals, it was time for stocktaking. Recapitulating the successive stages of the 2 + 4, Dufourcq recalled that things had not been a priori smooth. The Ottawa mandate was not very explicit, and the positions of the main protagonists were far removed from each other. Whereas the first ministerial meeting in Bonn on 5 May had allowed the goal to be clarified, resulting in a 'final settlement of international law', and had marked some progress on the border issue, the uncertainty over politico-military questions had persisted until the Stravropol meeting. Only the lifting of the Soviet veto over German membership in NATO had enabled the elaboration of the final document, even if negotiations were pursued until the last minute. Overall, though, concluded Dufourcq, the treaty went 'clearly beyond' what had been imagined at the start of the exercise: the final settlement did not 'contain all the clauses' and did 'not carry the name', but it contained 'certain essential aspects' of the peace treaty mentioned in the 1945 documents. 'It is through what is not said', he concluded, 'that the agreement of 12 September really puts an end to the period opened in 1945', and the FRG had shown skill in its ability 'to manage to draw a line under the past without referring to it'.[59]

The Federal Republic was evidently the major winner. 'Involved in the negotiations and in the signing of the treaty through the representatives of its two states', the German people, stressed Dufourcq, would recover its sovereignty 'from the realization of its state unity'. Germany 'finds its place again in the concert of nations without any discrimination being any longer imposed on it'.[60] The French negotiator would underline this success ten years after the events by emphasizing the roles of Kohl and Genscher, who, despite the tensions that opposed them to each other within the coalition, knew how to conduct the process 'by imprinting their own rhythm on it'. In comparison, he continued, Soviet diplomacy had appeared 'often at a loss, without any real strategy, fixated on positions disconnected from events'.[61] Moscow earned a mixed report: on the one hand, it had obtained only 'window dressing' satisfaction for the intransigent positions it had proclaimed at the start over politico-military issues, while on the other hand the USSR got 'enormous economic and financial aid from Germany', vital for pursuing *perestroika* but giving 'the lackluster impression of an acquiescence that was bought'. 'The principal motor of change', he summed up, had been the crumbling of the 'USSR's capacity to prevent anything'.

For Washington, on the other hand, the overview appeared indisputably positive to the French negotiator: 'The United States attained their goal', which was to maintain unified Germany within NATO, and the Americans 'appeared as the most faithful supporters of Chancellor Kohl'. True, in the final phase the Americans had been led 'to oppose the Germans as too open to Soviet demands', and the negotiations to elaborate a new legal basis for the stationing of Western forces in the FRG, begun in the summer, 'allowed [them] to glimpse that sovereign Germany would not necessarily be a grateful and docile partner'.[62] Overall, though, the United States, 'in taking a number of initiatives, in leading a perfectly coordinated diplomacy and in bringing constant support to the Chancellor's efforts,' had acquired 'a durable capital of sympathy' while engaging in a transformation of the Atlantic Alliance that opened 'new avenues at the moment when it was losing its enemy of forty years'. In comparison with the United States, Dufourcq went on, the overview appeared more 'mitigated' for Great Britain, even if, 'once the first reservations of Margaret Thatcher were overcome, the British negotiators had fully played the game and contributed, thanks to their diplomatic skill, to finding compromise solutions'.[63]

So what was the Quai's final assessment of its own, i.e. France's, performance? Reflecting the dominant sentiment in Paris – now that the difficulties of the autumn and winter were forgotten – the French negotiator considered it positive overall. French diplomacy, he thought after the signing of the final settlement, 'had obtained satisfaction on the points it considered essential', in particular the legal nature and structure of the final settlement, the Oder-Neisse question, and the renunciation by Germany of ABC weapons, and it might congratulate itself on the fact that 'no politico-military constraint that might block future European evolution' and give the USSR a 'right of oversight' or 'control' over European defense projects had been imposed on Germany.[64] And while the result had been attained at the price 'of a certain tension' over the border issue, Dufourcq later would stress that the Germans ultimately recognized that French pressure had 'hastened' the solution of the Oder-Neisse problem. Most of all, 'the process of unification had been accompanied by a relaunch of Franco-German cooperation' that eventually led to the Maastricht Treaty, a satisfying result that the former director of political affairs would attribute in good part to the quality of personal relations between Genscher and Dumas.[65]

To be sure, some questions remained: beyond the 2 + 4 – which had been only the diplomatic accompaniment to Germany's return to unity and sovereignty – what would be the choices and aspirations of a Germany 'new in its territorial composition' and 'freed from all the past obstacles to its policy'? The French diplomat responded with prudent optimism: 'One might think that after having obtained the reunification whose key was in Moscow', Germany would give top priority to European integration: '[I]t is still in this framework that its principal economic interests and best prospects for the future remain.'[66] This judgment no doubt reflected French leaders' state of mind on the threshold of German unification: if the extraordinary events of the last twelve months had not dissipated all the old 'German uncertainties' of French diplomacy, France was, at the same time, more than ever aware of the irreplaceable character of Franco-German relations and of the need to affirm European perspectives in order to overcome these uncertainties.

France-Germany: New Departure and Old Debates

These same questions were perceptible on the occasion of the diplomatic meetings at the start of the autumn of 1990. Despite the growing importance already assumed by the Gulf crisis – an event that would rapidly come to symbolize the end of the Cold War almost as much as did German unification – the new fact of German unity still dominated the international agenda. The Munich summit of 17 and 18 September presented a suitable opportunity to size up French-German relations. The two capitals wanted to seize the occasion of their fifty-sixth consultations since the Franco-German treaty of 1963 to close a chapter whose moments had sometimes been delicate. Paris was aware that this last summit before unification 'was of decisive importance for the future' and that 'anodyne results' might be interpreted as indicating a 'fading' of the bilateral relationship. Bonn worried about press commentaries and reflections among French politicians on the theme of the end of the privileged relationship, and therefore it hoped to place the event under the sign of continuity and strengthening of Franco-German relations. The Chancellery suggested the adoption in Munich of a joint declaration, a draft of which it sent a week before the summit to the Élysée, where it was well received.[67] In Munich Mitterrand proved concerned 'to make his irritation of the last months forgotten'; such was at least the memory that Kohl, refraining from any negative commentary, retained of the 'eloquence' with which the French president paid homage to Franco-German relations and went on to stress how much the French 'had the feeling of having accompanied their German friends and neighbors on the road' to unity. As for the Germans, they were keen to pass along the message that nothing was changed in the privileged relations between the two countries.[68] The common declaration saluted 'the achievement of unity' obtained by the German people 'alongside and thanks to the explicit support of its allies and friends, France especially' and stressed that this event was opening up to both countries 'new possibilities of cooperation in all domains'.[69]

Yet if the Munich conversations simultaneously marked a sort of return to normality and a new start, they also demonstrated the persistence of old debates that unification had only revived, in the forefront of which was the question of relations with the USSR. The Germans and Soviets had just initialed in Moscow the 'grand' treaty that would be formally signed in Bonn by Gorbachev and Kohl on 9 November, and that made Paris worry about a possible German drift to the East.[70] The subject was frankly tackled by Genscher and Dumas in Munich: the former repeated that the treaty aimed essentially to facilitate acceptance of German unification by Soviet opinion, whereas the latter 'much regretted' that on this occasion the French and Germans had not defined a 'Community approach' to relations with the USSR.[71] This conversation recalled the debates of 1988–1989 over a 'common Ostpolitk'; Teltschik was happy that the French had finally agreed to place it as a goal in the Munich declaration, whereas the

French deplored how little the Germans cared for bilateral consultation over policy toward Eastern Europe.[72] Combined with other subjects tackled at Munich, including the future of the FFA and various aspects of the restart of the process of European unification, the episode illustrated the questions that Paris still had, on the eve of German unification, about the future international choices of the 'new' Germany.

German unification had also its effects on Franco-Soviet relations. With relations with Germany occupying a growing place in their foreign policy, the Soviets were keen to diversify their options: 'Whatever the developments with Germany, the Soviet-French factor will remain the decisive factor', Shevardnadze stressed to Mitterrand on 18 July. The French were ready to come back to a close relation that had been eclipsed for almost two years by the spectacular rapprochement between Bonn and Moscow: 'With Germany at the center of Europe, its neighbors need a basis for an entente', the French president had replied.[73] At the end of July, Gorbachev proposed meeting Mitterrand before the CSCE summit and signing on this occasion a 'treaty of cooperation and friendship', an idea that French leaders welcomed, as confirmed by Dumas's trip to Moscow on 26–27 August.[74] Quickly, though, doubts began to surface in Paris: against the background of wide-ranging German-Soviet negotiations, might not such an initiative, while making evident the imbalance in means between France and the FRG, give credit to the idea of French competition with Bonn, thereby ruining the chances of a common European policy toward Eastern Europe?[75] Moreover the French were concerned – as Dumas confided to Genscher in Munich – that the Franco-Soviet treaty might 'give the impression that we are shifting to an "alliance de revers"' against greater Germany.[76] The Élysée and the Quai d'Orsay were hesitant in the face of the risk that France 'might have the air of running behind the Germans' or that the treaty proposed by Moscow brought nothing 'really striking' to appeal to public opinion. The Russians and Germans no doubt both had an interest in such a treaty, but, concluded Bianco, 'the more I think about it, the less I see [our interests] reflected there'.[77] But things were too far advanced, and the 'treaty of entente and cooperation' between France and the USSR was signed during Gorbachev's visit to Paris and Rambouillet on 28–29 October 1990. Yet this visit would be dominated by the Gulf crisis: unification had already passed to the background.[78]

The Paris Summit

Meanwhile, different initiatives were put forth to complete the German unification process after the signing of the 2 + 4: approval of the treaty between West and East Germany by the Bundestag and the Volkskammer on 20 September; the exit of the GDR from the Warsaw Pact on 24 September;

suspension by the guarantor powers, in the margins of the CSCE ministerial meeting in New York on 1–2 October, of their rights and responsibilities as of the day of unification; accomplishing of unity on 3 October by the accession of the GDR to the FRG; ratification of the 2 + 4 treaty by the Bundestag on 5 October and by the U.S. Senate on the 10th (Great Britain, France and the USSR would do the same respectively in November, January and March); and finally, on 14 November, the German-Polish treaty on the border, which was initialed in Warsaw. In this context, the CSCE summit in Paris on 19–21 November, initially conceived as playing a major role in the process, appeared as the last formality of a German unification that had already happened. Yet French diplomacy did attach a certain importance to this formality: Paris insisted, symbolically, on being the site where the end of the Cold War would be consecrated.

Mitterrand's diplomacy had played a significant role in launching the process leading up to the CSCE summit in the final weeks of 1989. In Kiev, we remember, the French president had taken up the idea, advanced by Gorbachev a few days previously in Rome, of a meeting of the heads of state and government of the 35. In the context of late 1989, a strengthened CSCE seemed to Paris to be a desirable forum for the organization of European security beyond blocs and an appropriate framework for management of the process of German unification, both of which, it was thought, would take place over a long period.[79] But with the rapid acceleration of the German question in the course of January, it became apparent that the Helsinki process would advance more slowly than unification; moreover, Paris was now taking care – as will be seen – that an overly vigorous affirmation of the CSCE did not kill off the idea of a European 'confederation', which Mitterrand had launched on 31 December and about which the Élysée was starting to think seriously.[80] The launch of the 2 + 4 negotiations could only lead to confining the 35 to a subsidiary role in the settlement of the German question: the Westerners, as we have seen, wanted to avoid tackling politico-military questions head-on in the settlement and rejected any idea of 'synchronization' between it and the setting up of pan-European security structures.[81] Meanwhile, Washington consented to the holding of a CSCE summit before the end of the year, and in the course of the spring the 35 had chosen Paris over Vienna to organize it. But with the German process still accelerating, it became clear by spring's end that the summit of the 35 would do little more than 'acknowledge' German unification.[82] This did not mean that the CSCE had no role in the 'great bargaining', for the prospect of its institutional reinforcement would indeed largely contribute to making the Soviets accept maintaining Germany in NATO, as we have seen, and it was in the framework of CFE negotiations – themselves an integral part of the CSCE – that the limitations on the Bundeswehr took place. But it was essentially a matter of accompanying a process that culminated before the Paris summit.

Hence the French felt frustration as that summit approached: had not the NATO summit in London preempted the results of the Paris summit by announcing the institutional strengthening of the CSCE? In addition, the London summit had opened the way to a dynamic of the political affirmation of the Atlantic Alliance in the direction of the East that might result in competition with the CSCE. Mitterrand's diplomacy nevertheless sought during the summer to find a central place for the Paris summit: 'The international conference that is most important is not the NATO summit', Mitterrand asserted, still manifestly in a state of irritation caused by the London summit: 'it is the future meeting of the CSCE' that prevailed, and the president underlined that 'this meeting will take place in Paris, according to the lines of France's foreign policy'.[83] This was perhaps saying too much. To be sure, the diplomats of the host country did have a pivotal role in the preparation of this first summit of the 35 since Helsinki in 1975, and the French conceptions of the future of the CSCE would be revealed as rather close to the point of equilibrium among the 35. Nevertheless, from the start the task proved 'complex and charged'.[84] If France stuck to its traditionally balanced and gradual approach to the CSCE, Pierre Morel – the diplomat close to the Élysée designated by Dumas to head up the French delegation to the summit preparatory committee that met in Vienna starting in July – would have to stand firmly to thwart the 'drifts' that the Quai d'Orsay feared on the part of the Soviets but also the Germans, in particular in the direction of collective or cooperative security and its corollary, 'institutional proliferation'.[85]

At stake for Paris in these circumstances was the attainment of a summit that consecrated the end of the division of Germany and of the Cold War in the French capital, without leading to results unacceptable for European security. So it was above all visibility that French diplomacy sought, in particular in the writing of the final document: Paris wished for 'a text reflecting clearly the exceptional historical significance of the moment,' knowing that the summit 'was not a CSCE conference similar to those that [had] preceded it' and that the document it produced should not 'miss a historic chance'.[86] This desire for a notable event appeared through the French concern to swing world attention to the Paris summit: while the Germans and Americans wished to foreground the results of the ministerial meeting of the 35 in New York on 1–2 October – the eve of German unity – the French obtained Bonn's understanding: 'In New York the results of the 2 + 4 negotiations will be presented', Genscher indicated to Dumas in Munich, 'but this will not put the Paris summit in the shadows'. Satisfied, the Frenchman rejoiced: 'The Paris summit will be a great moment.'[87]

The event, in fact, did not pass without notice. With the signing of the treaty on conventional forces in Europe, the adoption of a 'Charter of Paris for a New Europe' that announced 'an era of democracy, peace and unity' and saluted German unity, and the institutionalization of the Helsinki process, Paris could be pleased that in bringing European leaders together for the first time to 'organize the new Europe', it had hosted 'an exceptional event' whose 'importance escapes nobody'.[88] And yet, as Védrine later recognized, this was not 'the event of the century's end' that Mitterrand and Dumas had been expecting. The reason was that 'everything had already been resolved' in a bilateral fashion or in the 2 + 4: the 'end of Yalta' had been proclaimed without much surprise in Paris, for it was 'a fact that has already been accepted for quite a while'.[89] With the page of the Cold War now turned, it was instead the stakes of the new European 'architecture' that mattered.

Notes

1. TD Washington 1691, 1 July 1990, and MAE, sous-direction des affaires stratégiques et des pactes (ASP), note a.s. Projet américain de déclaration pour le sommet atlantique du 5 juillet, 2 July 1990, Archives diplomatiques (AD), série Affaires stratégiques et désarmement (ASD) 1985–1990, box 217; Hubert Védrine, note pour le président de la République, a.s. préparation du sommet de l'OTAN, 29 June 1990, and Note pour le président de la République, a.s. préparation du sommet de l'OTAN, 2 July 1990, private papers; see also Philip Zelikow and Condoleezza Rice, *Germany Unified and Europe Transformed: A Study in Statecraft*, Cambridge, Harvard University Press, 1995, p. 314ff.
2. TD Washington 1691, 1 July 1990.
3. Amiral Jacques Lanxade, note à l'attention du président de la République, Sommet de l'OTAN – Entretiens à Washington, 2 July 1990, private papers; see also TD Washington 1691, 1 July 1990.
4. Védrine, note pour le président de la République, 29 June 1990, a.s. préparation du sommet de l'OTAN, 29 June 1990 (Védrine in particular felt that the two paragraphs concerning the CSCE 'overly prejudged' the results of the Paris summit – results that the Elysée did not want NATO to preempt).
5. Lanxade, note à l'attention du président de la République, Sommet de l'OTAN – Entretiens à Washington, 2 July 1990.
6. TD RPAN 550, 9 July 1990, AD, ASD 1985–1990, box 217.
7. James Baker boasted of having obtained the adoption of a fundamentally intact declaration and kept the memory of a Roland Dumas who was opposed to 'almost everything' (the French minister showed himself particularly reluctant to embrace the idea that Eastern European countries name ambassadors to NATO): see James A. Baker III (with Thomas M. DeFrank), *The Politics of Diplomacy: Revolution, War and Peace 1989–1992*, New York, Putnam, 1995, pp. 258–259; and Zelikow and Rice, *Germany Unified*, pp. 322–323.

8. TD RPAN 555, 9 July 1990.
9. See Zelikow and Rice, *Germany Unified*, p. 323. The London declaration included: an invitation to Gorbachev to speak before NATO; an offer to the USSR and to the Eastern European countries to establish 'regular diplomatic liaison' with the alliance; the proposition of a new CFE negotiation that would include discussing troop ceilings; the creation of NATO multinational corps and the abandonment of 'forward defense'; decreasing the number of NATO's nuclear weapons and adopting a strategy of 'last resort' as well as opening a negotiation about SNF as soon as CFE was over; the proposition of an institutionalization of the CSCE to be adopted by the Paris summit: see Declaration of London concerning a Renovated North Atlantic Alliance, http://www.nato.int/docu/
10. Questioned the day after London by his counterpart Gerhard Stoltenberg, Jean-Pierre Chevènement specified: 'the President thinks that a diminution of our [military] presence [in Germany] is inevitable' and that 'it would be better that we announce it ourselves before the pressure of opinion makes itself felt': see Ministère de la Défense, compte rendu des entretiens entre les ministres français et allemand de la Défense (Ammerschwihr, 7 juillet 1990), 9 July 1990, AN, 5AG4/CDM 33. The question would later be addressed during the Franco-German consultations in Munich on 17 and 18 September, but Mitterrand stood by his argumentation and Kohl by his: see Meeting between Mitterrand and Kohl, Munich, 17 September 1990, private papers. Mitterrand's London statement was far from being without effect: manifestly worried, the Germans made it known to the French in late July that they wished to bring up the question of the French forces in Germany and, beyond that, the future of Franco-German defense cooperation: see Lanxade, note à l'attention de M. le président de la République, cooperation francoallemande en matière de defense, 31 July 1990, private papers. Even if it revealed in part Mitterrand's bad mood in London, the French threat of withdrawal of the FFA had the effect of making Germans aware of the stakes of maintaining military cooperation with the French, which would contribute to its relaunching (the decision taken in the following months to create a Franco-German corps would as a matter of fact lead to the postponement of the withdrawal of the French forces in Germany: see chapter 7 in this volume, p. 321 and 343.)
11. TD Washington 1780, 13 July 1990, AD, ASD 1985–1990, box 17: in Washington on 13 July, Elisabeth Guigou emphasized that Mitterrand's statement in London was a matter of reflection and not a decision; asked about the same subject by the American chargé d'affaires in Paris, Bertrand Dufourcq confirmed that there was no decision but only an 'analysis of the situation': MAE, sous-direction du désarmement, note pour le cabinet du ministre d'Etat, a.s. Retrait des forces françaises d'Allemagne, 18 July 1990, AD, ASD 1985–1990, box 217. U.S. reactions were nevertheless most skeptical regarding the French attitude in this affair: see Zelikow and Rice, *Germany Unified*, pp. 323–324 (the authors speak of an 'erratic' announcement).
12. TD RPAN 558, 10 July 1990, AD, ASD 1985–1990, box 217.
13. While Dieter Kastrup on 4 July insisted that Germany had to formulate this sovereign renunciation without the intervention of the Four, Dufourcq was alone– without American or British support and with only very moderate support from the Soviets, despite their position having been very firm up to that point – in asking that the final settlement make explicit reference to it. His aim was to grant 'a supplementary political value' to a renunciation that in any case was ensured from the legal point of view, since unified Germany inherited the legal commitments made by the FRG in 1954 under the Paris Agreements and in 1968 under the NPT: see TD Londres 1159–1160, 5 July 1990; and Caroline de Margerie, note pour le président de la République, Négociations 4 + 2 (sic):

la renonciation de l'Allemagne aux armes ABC et les frontières, 5 July 1990, private papers. Despite the difficulties encountered in this dossier due to German susceptibilities and American reluctance – both more formal than substantial – the ABC question, in comparison with the other French priority in the German settlement – the Oder-Neisse line – proved to be much less salient and controversial (one recalls that it had not posed a problem during the important 15 February conversation in which Kohl had assured Mitterrand that a unified Germany would inherit the obligations of the FRG in this respect: see chapter 4 of this volume, p. 190). In fact, the matter was addressed in the negotiation rather belatedly: Dumas having insisted during the 'quad' meeting in Turnberry in early June on the necessity to provide for a mention of the German ABC renunciation in the final settlement, Baker had at that point objected that it was important to avoid giving satisfaction to the Soviet demand that politico-military questions be discussed. Knowing that there was in fact agreement on substance between the Six, Dumas had then contented himself with the need for such a mention being taken note of by the Six, the moment when it would be formally introduced to the 2 + 4 remaining open for now. However, with the Berlin 2 + 4 meeting of 4 July approaching, the Quai d'Orsay believed that the moment had come to definitively clarify this point. Aware that the FRG was unlikely to accept that the final settlement stipulate that Germany would not produce ABC weapons, French diplomats advanced the formula of a unilateral German engagement that the Six would then take note of, a formula that was in effect adopted in Berlin on 4 July on the insistence of Paris (the problem would be definitively settled in early September: see below, note 50); on this, MAE, ASD, note a.s. Statut nucléaire de l'Allemagne, 28 May 1990, AD, ASD 1985–1990, box 16; TD Diplomatie 11451–11453, 11 June 1990, private papers; MAE, ASD, note pour le directeur politique, a.s. Confirmation par l'Allemagne de son engagement à ne pas fabriquer d'armes ABC, 2 July 1990, AD, ASD 1985–1990, box 17. (Chevènement, in mid June, showed himself extremely worried about the hypothesis that Germany would avoid all engagements regarding ABC weapons, evoking even the risk of a nuclear Germany that 'in ten years' would be tempted to 'get along with the Russians' or, inversely, to 'roll them back in their steppe' [sic]; he therefore asked Mitterrand in 'the interest of the future stability of Europe and peace' to demand, if possible in agreement with Thatcher, a clear commitment on the part of the Germans. Chevènement's very harsh language reflected his typical obsessions toward Germany, and likely also a lack of information on the negotiation actually being conducted at the time (the Quai d'Orsay was in fact quite vigilant on this dossier). Still, Mitterrand, in reaction to Chevènement's letter, asked Dumas to follow closely the affair: see letter from Chevènement to Mitterrand, 19 June 1990, private papers, annotations by Mitterrand).

14. TD Bonn 1796, 4 July 1990, AD, ASD 1985–1990, box 17; see also Zelikow and Rice, *Germany Unified*, pp. 319. Genscher, anxious to reassure Moscow, recommended 350,000 men, Kohl and Stoltenberg 400,000; the compromise was made at 370,000 (Kohl, in the Caucasus, obtained Gorbachev's agreement to this figure by arguing that going below this limit would mechanically bring about the abolition of the conscription).
15. Réunion ministérielle du Quad (Londres, 6 juillet 1990), AN, 5AG4/CDM 36.
16. Like the Twelve, the Seven thus brought only *political* support to Kohl's desire to display Western readiness to help Gorbachev out of his economic difficulties. As a result, the FRG alone supported the bulk of economic aid to the USSR in the form of short-term credits negotiated between Bonn and Moscow in May-June to the total of DM 5 billion (not counting the agreements that were made later during the summer, in particular regarding the financial compensation for the maintenance and then withdrawal of Soviet forces in the GDR: see Zelikow and Rice, *Germany United*, pp. 321–327).

17. TD Moscou 4838, 12 July 1990, AD, ASD 1985–1990, box 17.
18. MAE, ASP, note a.s. Session ministérielle du groupe des Six (Paris, 17 juillet 1990), séance du matin, AD, ASD 1985–1990, box 17.
19. Horst Teltschik, *329 Tage. Innenansichten der Einigung*, Berlin, Siedler, 1991, p. 310.
20. See Zelikow and Rice, *Germany Unified*, p. 332; and Hannes Adomeit, *Imperial Overstretch: Germany in Soviet Policy from Stalin to Gorbachev*, Baden-Baden, Nomos, 1998, p. 517ff. On the eve of the arrival of the Germans, Valentin Falin attempted to bring Gorbachev to defend a minimum position by addressing an 'energetic memorandum' to him: there should be no German participation in the NATO military structure – as in France's case – and, 'minimum minimorum', no stationing of nuclear arms on the entire German territory. Gorbachev responded: 'I will do what I can, but I fear that the train has already left.' Valentin Falin, *Politische Erinnerungen*, Munich, Droemer Knaur, 1993, pp. 393–394.
21. Gespräch des Bundeskanzlers Kohl mit Präsident Gorbatschow, Moskau, 15. Juli 1990, *Deutsche Einheit. Sonderedition aus den Akten des Bundeskanzleramtes 1989/90*, Munich, Oldenburg, 1998, pp. 1340–1348; and Delegationsgespräch des Bundeskanzlers Kohl mit Präsident Gorbatschow, 15. Juli 1990, *Deutsche Einheit*, pp. 1352–1355.
22. Teltschik, *329 Tage*, pp. 323–324; Anatoly Chernyaev, who attended (as did Teltschik) the first Gorbachev-Kohl meeting on 15 July, also estimated that the essential was acquired that day: see Anatoly S. Chernyaev, *My Six Years with Gorbachev*, University Park, Pennsylvania University Press, 2000, p. 282.
23. See Gespräch des Bundeskanzlers Kohl mit Präsident Gorbatschow im erweiterten Kreis, Archys/Bezirk Stavropol, 16. Juli 1990, *Deutsche Einheit*, pp. 1355–1367.
24. It was indeed a compromise. Of course, the Germans would emphasize the concessions made by Moscow: the Soviets had finally accepted that the German forces in the ex-GDR would be integrated in NATO after the withdrawal of the Soviet troops. This German emphasis on a Soviet retreat was not false: Gorbachev and Shevardnadze had indeed tried, at first, to obtain from Kohl and Genscher a complete and definitive 'de-NATO-ization' of the territory of the ex-GDR that would have taken the form of a ban on German forces in the ex-GDR being integrated into NATO even after the departure of the Soviet troops. Emphasizing Soviet concessions evidently allowed Kohl to highlight his worry in this final bargaining to preserve the interests of NATO and to respond to those in the alliance who suspected him of being ready to sacrifice these interests to obtain unification (see Teltschik, *329 Tage*, p. 338; Helmut Kohl, *Je voulais l'unité de l'Allemagne*, Paris, De Fallois, 1997, pp. 354–355 and p. 363; and Pierre Favier and Michel Martin-Roland, *La Décennie Mitterrand*, vol. 3, 'Les Défis', Paris, Seuil, 1996, p. 259). But a close reading of the detailed report of the conversations also sheds light on an important *German* concession: faced with the oft-reiterated insistence of Gorbachev and Shevardnadze, Kohl agreed in fact expressly that neither *foreign* forces nor nuclear arms would be stationed in the ex-GDR after the Soviet withdrawal – a detail Kohl avoided publicly mentioning that day in his press conference, although he did specify it later to his Western partners (see below, notes 25 and 26). Can Kohl's hesitation to make this concession and reveal it publicly be explained by his reluctance to antagonize the Americans, who would probably have preferred the preservation of the possibility of a presence of non-German forces in the East? It is likely. Be that as it may, the result obtained in the Caucasus can be situated somewhere between the Genscher-Stoltenberg compromise imposed by Kohl in February and the formula refined by Kohl and Bush some days later in Camp David (see chapter 4 of this volume, p. 193): true, the Germans did not formally accept the definitive non-extension of NATO structures to the East, but, practically, the stationing ban on foreign forces in the ex-GDR came close to it.

25. The eight points were: a united Germany comprised of the FRG, the GDR and Berlin; abrogation of the rights of the Four at the moment of unity; the right of a unified and sovereign Germany to choose its alliances; the conclusion of a treaty between a united Germany and the USSR for the withdrawal of its troops from the GDR in three or four years; non-extension of NATO structures and non-integration of German forces in the ex-GDR during the period in question; maintenance of American, British and French forces in Berlin as long as Soviet forces remained in the ex-GDR; reduction of forces of a united Germany to 370,000 men in three or four years in the framework of the CFE; renunciation of ABC arms and confirmation of the participation of a united Germany in the NPT: see AFP dispatch, private papers (the point concerning the non-introduction of foreign forces or nuclear arms in the territory of the ex-GDR after the Soviet withdrawal was not mentioned: see above, note 24, and below, note 26).
26. Letter from Kohl to Mitterrand, AN 5AG4/CDM 33; and *Deutsche Einheit*, pp. 1374–1376 (contrary to the eight points presented during the press conference in the Caucasus, Kohl specified that 'no foreign troops or nuclear arms should be deployed' in the ex-GDR: see above, notes 24 and 25).
27. Compte-rendu de la réunion du Quad (Paris, 17 juillet 1990), AN, 5AG4/CDM 36. Baker, who showed himself markedly less positive about Genscher's account than did Douglas Hurd and Dumas, questioned him on whether the interdiction of the presence of foreign troops in the territory of ex-GDR after the Soviet withdrawal would apply 'only in times of peace or also in times of war' – a rather nonsensical question (quickly swept away by Genscher) that confirmed a certain American mistrust towards the Stavropol compromise, a mistrust that was confirmed later.
28. TD Diplomatie 14436, 18 July 1990, AD, ASD 1985–1990, box 17; see also Bertrand Durfourcq, '2 + 4 ou la négociation atypique', *Politique étrangère*, No 2/2000 p. 467–484.
29. Conseil des ministres, 18 July 1990, private papers.
30. This request marked a hardening, because Warsaw had previously abandoned its initial requirement to see the treaty negotiated and initialed before the unification. It can be explained by the worry that grew in Poland over the idea circulating again in CSU circles in early July (namely by Theo Waigel, who raised his voice in this sense) that the bilateral treaty should not only deal with the border but also with the rights of the German minority in Poland. This was an unacceptable idea for the Poles, who feared that the treaty on the border would be postponed, if not abandoned, without a remaining means to pressure Bonn once the quadripartite rights were lifted: see Werner Weidenfeld, *Außenpolitik für die deutsche Einheit. Die Entscheidungsjahre1989/1990*, Stuttgart, DVA, 1998, p. 500.
31. TD Londres 1159–1160, 5 July 1990; and Caroline de Margerie, note pour le président de la République, Négociations 4 + 2 (*sic*): la renonciation de l'Allemagne aux armes ABC et les frontières, Londres, 5 July 1990, private papers.
32. Réunion ministérielle du Quad (Londres, 6 July 1990), AN, 5AG4/CDM 36.
33. MAE, ASP, note de présentation générale, a.s. Groupe des Six. Session ministérielle de Paris (17 juillet 1990), 10 July, AD, ASD 1985–1990, box 17.
34. TD Diplomatie 13906, 13 July 1990, DSL, AN, 5AG4/CDM 34; see also Dufourcq, '2 + 4'. The schema presented by Dufourcq reflected a clarification of Bonn's position since it excluded any idea of a treaty in which the settlement of the border would be linked to other questions – such as that of the German minority in Poland – and it included a very short delay for its conclusion (this offer was confirmed by Kohl in a letter to Mazowiecki dated 13 July: see Weidenfeld, *Außenpolitik*, p. 502; and Schreiben des Bundeskanzlers Kohl an Ministerpräsident Mazowiecki, Bonn, 13. Juli 10, *Deutsche Einheit*, pp. 1339–1340).

35. MAE, Sous-direction d'Europe centrale et nordique, note opérationnelle, a.s. Session ministérielle du groupe des Six avec participation du ministre polonais (Paris, 17 juillet), 13 July 1990, AD, ASD 1985–1990, box 17.
36. Margerie, note de pour le président de la République, La réunion ministérielle des 4 + 2 du mardi 17 juillet et la question des frontières, 16 July 1990, private papers. (Margerie underestimated the Germans' availability to clarify their position and the new flexibility noticed in Warsaw by Dufourcq.)
37. Compte-rendu de la réunion du Quad (Paris, 17 July 1990), AN, 5AG4/CDM36.
38. TD Diplomatie 14436–14438, DSL, 18 July 1990 and TD Diplomatie 14491, DSL, 21 July 1990, AD, ASD 1985–1990, box 17.
39. Meeting between Mitterrand and Skubiszewski, 18 July 1990, detailed report by Margerie, private papers.
40. Conseil des ministres, 18 July 1990, private papers.
41. TD Diplomatie 14436–14438, DSL, 18 July 1990, AD, ASD 1985–1990, box 17; Dufourcq, '2 + 4', pp. 467–484; and Compte-rendu de la réunion du Quad (Paris, 17 juillet 1990).
42. MAE, le sous-directeur d'Europe centrale et nordique, note pour la direction des affaires juridiques, a.s. Aspects extérieurs et unification allemande, 23 July 1990; and TD Diplomatie 14542, 23 July 1990, AD, ASD, 1985–1990, box 17.
43. TD Bonn 2090, 9 August 1990 and 2178, 20 August 1990, AD, ASD 1985–1990, box 17; compte-rendu des entretiens des quatre directeurs politiques à Londres, 23 August 1990, secret, AN, 5AG4/CDM 36.
44. TD Bonn 2178, 20 August 1990, AD, ASD 1985–1990, box 17.
45. MAE, Direction d'Europe, compte-rendu de la rencontre des directeurs français et allemands le 30 août 1990 à Bonn, 3 September 1990, AD, ASD 1985–1990, box 17. (Responding that day to Kastrup's explanations, Dufourcq did not hide a certain worry in regard to what might be perceived as a German *Alleingang* in the direction of the USSR, a worry that also expressed itself at the Elysée, where the fear was that Bonn might avoid any Franco-German or EC coordination in its relations with the East: see Védrine, note pour le président de la République, 25 July 1990, 5AG4/7010.)
46. On this, see Zelikow and Rice, *Germany Unified*, pp. 347–352; and Teltschik, *329 Tage*, p. 352ff.
47. See chapter 5, note 49.
48. Compte-rendu de la réunion du Quad (Paris, 17 juillet 1990).
49. TD Berlin 2058, 7 September 1990, AD, ASD 1985–1990, box 17. The Quai found this sequence acceptable provided that 'it be very clear that the definitive settlement would not enter into force until after ratification by all of the party states': MAE, note pour la direction juridique, a.s. Suspension et levée des droits et responsabilités quadripartites sur l'Allemagne, 1 August 1990, AD, ASD 1985–1990, box 17; see also MAE, ASP, note a.s. État des travaux du groupe des Six: visite du ministre d'État à Moscou (25 août 1990), AN, 5AG4/CDM 36; and TD Moscou 5278, 5367 and 5409, 10, 17 and 22 August 1990; TD Bonn 2178, 20 August 1990; TD Berlin 2058–2059, 7 September 1990, AD, ASD 1985–1990, box 17; and Dufourcq, '2 + 4'.
50. TD Berlin 2058–2059, 7 September 1990, AD, ASD 1985–1990, box 17. It should be noted that the French in Berlin obtained the Germans' word that the definitive settlement would mention that a united Germany would be bound 'in particular' by the NPT. For Paris, this amounted to an implicit reference to the commitment taken in the framework of the WEU during the Paris Agreements of 1954, a commitment that French diplomacy continued to judge valid and would have liked to see explicitly reaffirmed in the Six's settlement, while Bonn refused up to that point to make any reference to it, even implicitly, as Kastrup had again indicated bluntly to Dufourcq and John Weston some days

before: see compte-rendu des entretiens des quatre directeurs politiques à Londres, 23 August 1990, secret; see also note 13 above.
51. MAE, ASP, note a.s. Règlement définitif concernant l'Allemagne: points susceptibles de discussion à la session ministérielle de Moscou, 10 September 1990, AD, ASD 1985–1990, box 17. If Kohl remained firm with Moscow on the question of dual-capacity weapons, he was on the other hand not ready to yield to the Americans on the non-crossing question, estimating that the clause on the non-stationing of foreign forces in the GDR implied that allied maneuvers (for which he judged there was enough space in the FRG) were excluded: see Vorlage des Vortragenden Legationsrat I Kaestner an Ministerialdirektor Teltschik, Bonn, 7. September 1990, *Deutsche Einheit*, p. 1531; and Teltschik, *329 Tage*, p. 361.
52. See MAE, Cabinet, note pour le ministre d'Etat a.s. Dernières difficultés de la négociation '4 + 2' [sic], 9 September 1990, AN 5AG/CDM 36. (The author of the note deplored that the 'Stavropol compromise, negotiated between Kohl and Gorbachev without consultation of the Allies, forbid all foreign stationing in ex-GDR after the period of transition' and estimated that an 'ideal' outcome would have been 'to be able to station, after the transition period, even in limited number, non-integrated European contingents such as the Franco-German brigade'. Without displaying the same bitter disappointment as the Americans and the British showed toward the Stavropol compromise, the French, therefore, did not have a fundamentally different interpretation of it, judging that the Germans had indeed made excessive concessions – yet the French dissatisfaction, predictably, bore on its European rather than on its Atlantic ramifications.)
53. MAE, ASP, note de présentation générale, a.s. Session ministérielle du groupe des Six à Moscou (12 septembre 1990), 10 September 1990, AD, ASD 1985–1990, box 17. (The Americans showed themselves especially insistent on the non-crossing question. On 8 September Scowcroft emphasized to Uwe Kaestner, a close associate of Kohl, that such a clause could put into question a united Germany's membership in NATO, a remark that Kaestner took note of 'without comment': Vorlage des Vortragenden Legationsrat I Kaestner an Ministerialdirektor Teltschik, Bonn, 10. September 1990, *Deutsche Einheit*, p. 1538.)
54. The expression comes from Dufourcq, '2 + 4', pp. 467–484; see also TD Diplomatie 18448–49, DSL, 13 September 1990, AD, ASD 1985–1990, box 17. The affair is related in detail by Zelikow and Rice, *Germany Unified*, pp. 359–360.
55. The problem was essentially of a political nature, for in substance there was agreement among the Western powers that the banning of foreign force deployments in the ex-GDR should be interpreted as allowing maneuvers of only limited scope (less than 13,000 men, the ceiling provided for by the Stockholm agreements).The quarrel between the Germans and the British – the Americans being in fact on the same wavelength as the latter, even if they did not put themselves forward – thus rested on the need, or lack of it, to specify it explicitly at the risk of antagonizing the Soviets. In this context, the insistence of London could only be considered with severity by the Germans, tempted to see in it a Downing Street maneuver or, at least, the mark of an obvious defiance toward the German propensity to compromise with Moscow: see Zelikow and Rice, *Germany Unified*, pp. 362 and 477; and MAE, note pour le ministre d'Etat a.s. Dernières difficultés de la négociation '4 + 2' [sic], 9 September 1990.
56. Dufourcq, '2 + 4'; and Roland Dumas, *Le Fil et la Pelote. Mémoires*, Paris, Plon, 1996, pp. 343–344.
57. MAE, note de Bertrand Dufourcq, a.s. Traité portant règlement définitif concernant l'Allemagne: les étapes de sa conception, 2 October, AD, ASD 1985–1990, box 17.
58. Dufourcq in TD Diplomatie 18848–18849, DSL, 13 September 1990.

59. MAE, note de Bertrand Dufourcq, a.s. Traité portant règlement définitif concernant l'Allemagne: les étapes de sa conception, 2 October 1990; see also MAE, note a.s. Traité portant règlement définitif concernant l'Allemagne: exégèse du texte, 2 October 1990, AD, ASD 1985–1990, box 17.
60. TD Diplomatie 18803, 18806 and 18812, 17 September 1989, private papers.
61. Dufourcq, '2 + 4'. The French embassy in Moscow offered a slightly different analysis: if German unification marked 'the end of an era' and coincided with 'the profound internal crisis of the USSR', Jean-Marie Mérillon reported that the assessment of the German settlement was positive in Moscow despite a minority of critics, including Falin, who criticized Gorbachev and Shevardnadze for a lack of firmness. In fact, Mérillon judged, 'the sometimes puzzling stances of Soviet diplomacy during negotiations retrospectively inscribe themselves in a rather logical curve of coherent bargaining', and the Soviet officials obtained 'lots' from Bonn in respect to the 'weakness of their deal to start out with': TD Moscou 5658, 10 September 1990, AD, ASD 1985–1990, box 17.
62. TD 18803, 18806 and 18812, 17 September 1989. Because the 23 October 1954 convention on the presence of foreign forces on the territory of the FRG expired after unification, it was necessary to replace it with a new legal basis for the maintenance of these forces. But whereas the Americans and British wanted a simple renewal of the existing agreements, the Germans, emphasizing legal and political reasons (in particular the position of the Green Party and the SPD), wanted to renegotiate the contents, to the great displeasure of Washington and London, Paris showing itself – without surprise, given Mitterrand's position – more relaxed. Bonn finally accepted, under pressure from Washington, essentially to prolong the 1954 agreements: see Zelikow and Rice, *Germany Unified*, pp. 353–355; and MAE, ASP, note, Projet de déclaration allemande sur la présence et le statut des forces étrangères sur le territoire de la RFA, 2 August 1990; note a.s. Forces stationnées en RFA: renouvellement du fondement politique et juridique, 3 August 1990; note pour le directeur des affaires juridiques, a.s. De l'échange de lettres sur la présence des FFA, 24 September 1990; and TD Bonn 2116 and 2203, 14 and 23 August 1990, AD, ASD 1985–1990, box 17. The French ambassador in Washington reported that a united Germany promised to be, for the United States, a more difficult partner: recalling that the Americans, after having attempted to calm the game after the fall of the Wall, had then left it to Kohl to determine 'the rhythm and the modalities of unification' once it was clear that Bonn would commit itself to preserve NATO, Jacques Andréani concluded that 'the principal objective of Washington, i.e. membership in NATO, had been obtained, but at the price of developments that could later diminish its impact': TD Washington 2199, 13 September 1990, AD, ASD 1985–1990, box 17.
63. Dufourcq, '2 + 4'.
64. TD Diplomatie 18803, 18806 and 18812, 17 September 1998.
65. Dufourcq, '2 + 4'.
66. TD Diplomatie 18803, 18806 and 18812, 17 September 1989.
67. MAE, CAP, note de Pierre Buhler, a.s. Le stationnement des forces allemandes en France: propositions pour une alternative, 10 September 1990, AD, ASD 1985–1990, box 17; MAE, compte-rendu de l'entretien entre M. Tremeau et M. Ischinger (10 August 1990), AD, Europe, RFA 1986–1990, box 6782; Védrine, note pour le président de la République, 10 September 1990, private papers.
68. Kohl, *Je voulais*, pp. 393–393; and Teltschik, *329 Tage*, pp. 368–369. The latter reports – also without making comments – the extent to which Mitterrand held on to emphasizing that France had clearly supported the objective of German unity without restriction.

69. Déclaration commune de M. le président de la République et du chancelier fédéral de la République fédérale d'Allemagne, Munich, 17 and 18 September 1990, MAE, *Politique étrangère de la France, (PEF)*, September-October 1990, pp. 70–72.
70. Three days before the German-Soviet treaty was signed in Moscow on 13 September – the day after the 2 + 4 conclusion – three of Mitterrand's closest advisers, supported by Jean-Louis Bianco, who judged the 'German drift' as 'very preoccupying', co-signed an alarmist note in which they underlined that the draft German-Soviet treaty included a commitment to mutual non-aggression that was 'written in ambiguous terms' with regard to the Atlantic commitments of the FRG and they denounced 'a hard blow for the project of a European political union', to which, they noted, no reference was made in the treaty. All of that, they warned, 'will have the effect of a bomb'. The authors therefore recommended a French intervention (Bianco suggested a 'severe warning' from Dumas to Genscher) in order to persuade the Germans to inscribe in the treaty a 'Community clause' (in other words, a reference to the competencies of the Community as well as the objective of the European Union) and advised that its conclusion not be announced until after the 18 September Franco-German summit: see Guigou, Védrine and Loïc Hennekinne, note pour le président de la République, Projet de traité germano-soviétique, 10 September 1990, private papers. The same day, having received from the Chancellery the Franco-German declaration project in which Paris and Bonn committed to leading common policies to the East (one of Bonn's old preoccupations), Védrine suggested that Dumas, who was set to meet Genscher in Moscow at the signing of the 2 + 4, take advantage of the meeting to ask that the commitment apply, precisely, to the German-Soviet treaty in preparation: Védrine, note pour le président de la République, 10 September 1990, private papers. But this was to no avail: the treaty was 'negotiated at great speed and without taking into account French demands', Margerie noted a few days later; see Margerie, note pour le président de la République, Thèmes du sommet: questions internationales, questions communautaires, sujets bilatéraux, 14 September 1990, private papers.
71. Genscher responded: 'I considered your Community objections in my speech during the signing and I will say it again next Thursday in the Bundestag': see Meeting between Dumas and Genscher, Munich, 17 September 1990, private papers.
72. The idea of common policy to the East, Teltschik noted, was a 'proposition that the Chancellor had made publicly two years earlier without a reaction from the French government': see Teltschik, *329 Tage*, p. 369; see chapter 1 of this volume, pp. 49–51.
73. Meeting between Mitterrand and Shevardnadze, 18 July 1990, detailed report by Margerie, private papers.
74. Message from Dumas to Mitterrand, 26 July 1990, private papers; and TD Moscou 5472–5474, 27 August 1990, AD, Europe, URSS 1986–1990, box 6681.
75. Védrine, note pour le président de la République, 25 July 1990.
76. Meeting between Dumas and Genscher, Munich, 17 September 1990.
77. Bianco, note pour monsieur le Président, Traité franco-soviétique, 21 September 1990, private papers. Bianco noted that the Soviets had committed themselves to ensuring that the Franco-Soviet treaty would intervene before the German-Soviet treaty, which had not been the case. He also emphasized 'unacceptable clauses', in particular the non-aggression commitment that he judged contrary to NATO (he deplored that the Germans had accepted similar clauses in the German-Soviet treaty). These clauses would later be rejected by Paris during the remainder of the negotiation, without Moscow insisting that they be upheld: see MAE, Direction d'Europe, note pour le ministre d'Etat, a.s. Traité franco-soviétique, 17 October 1990, AD, Europe, URSS 1986–1990, box 6670.

78. Meeting between Mitterrand and Gorbachev, Paris, 28 October 1990; Meeting between Mitterrand and Gorbachev, Rambouillet, 29 October 1990, detailed reports by Hennekinne, private papers.
79. See chapter 3 of this volume, p. 137 and pp. 145–147.
80. Hubert Védrine, note a.s. La sécurité européenne: l'avenir des alliances; la CSCE et le sommet à 35; la confédération, 29 January 1990, private papers.
81. See MAE, Direction d'Europe, Cellule CSCE, note pour le cabinet du ministre d'Etat, a.s. Sommet des chefs d'Etat et de gouvernement en 1990, 27 March 1990, AD, ASD 1985–1990, sous-direction des questions multilatérales (QM), box 12.
82. Hennekinne, note pour le président de la République, Les Etats-Unis et la CSCE, 18 April 1990, private papers; MAE, le ministre d'Etat, note à l'attention de Monsieur le président de la République, 18 June 1990, private papers. Dumas assigned two other objectives to the Paris summit: 'seal the agreement on conventional disarmament' and 'trace the perspectives of tomorrow's Europe'.
83. Conseil des ministres, 18 July 1990, private papers. Mitterrand used the same terms before Shevardnadze the same day: see Meeting between Mitterrand and Shevardnadze, 18 July 1990.
84. MAE, Direction Europe, cellule CSCE, note a.s. Comité préparatoire au sommet du sommet de Paris de la CSCE. Projet d'instructions pour la délégation française, 2 July 1990, AD, ASD 1985–1990, QM, box 14.
85. TD Vienne 525–529, 27 July 1990, and TD Vienne 6 August 1990, AD, ASD 1985–1990, box 14.
86. TD Vienne 643, 6 September 1990, AD, ASD 1985–1990, QM, box 14.
87. Meeting between Dumas and Genscher, Munich, 17 September 1990.
88. TD Diplomatie 24745 and 25469, 22 November and 4 December 1990, AD, ASD 1985–1990, QM, box 12.
89. Hubert Védrine, *Les Mondes de François Mitterrand. A l'Elysée 1981–1995*, Paris, Fayard, 1996, p. 500.

Chapter 7

FRENCH DIPLOMACY AND THE NEW EUROPEAN ARCHITECTURE (1990–1991)

If discussion about European architecture throughout 1990 had remained tightly dependent on the process of German unification, the completion of the latter in October was not an endpoint. From the autumn of 1990 to the autumn of 1991, the European agenda was dominated by a great debate on the organization of the Old Continent after the Cold War. Each of the main actors in the European game tackled this debate with its own expectations, presuppositions and preferences. A dynamic of institutional competition set in, fed by rival priorities over the three principal dimensions to which European architecture pertained: the Western European dimension, the Atlantic dimension, and finally the pan-European dimension.

For French diplomacy the Western European dimension had been and remained primary. Beyond the fluctuations of the autumn and winter of 1989–1990, unification confirmed the irreplaceable character of the Franco-German relationship. Though it had briefly revived French uncertainties about Germany, it had also demonstrated after the spring of 1990 that only the strengthening of cooperation between the two countries would allow them to get beyond their divergences thanks to the dynamic of European unification. Hence the necessary pursuit of that Franco-German dialectic remained the central postulate of a French diplomacy for which European

---

Notes for this section begin on page 361.

construction was more than ever a categorical imperative. But this European priority was also motivated by French appreciation of the future role of the United States in Europe. Faithful to the Gaullist vision, Mitterrandian diplomacy anticipated, as we know, that an American withdrawal from the Old Continent was inevitable after the Cold War. While the French remained attached to maintaining a form of U.S. guarantee in Europe, the priority they gave to the pursuit of European construction was largely justified by the need to complement such a withdrawal with the affirmation of a European entity capable of influencing future international affairs and eventually assuring its own security. Finally, changes in Eastern Europe also appeared to justify France's European ambitions. While worrying about the risks of fragmentation caused by the post-Communist meltdown and fearing the consequences of such chains of events on European stability – this was the source of François Mitterrand's fear of 'a return to 1913' – French diplomacy tried to prevent these risks by supporting the pursuit of reform in the USSR, fostering the transition of Eastern Europe and privileging a logic of pan-European cooperation. The French aim was to encourage the recomposition of the entire Old Continent, now liberated from the tutelage of the superpowers – a recomposition in which the European Community would of course play the motor role.

The principal French objectives in the great debate over European architecture in 1990–1991 followed logically. The first objective was to bring about the culmination of the Community relaunch of the spring of 1990 by putting the EMU firmly on track and launching the project of political union, whose main expression should be the establishment of a common foreign and security policy and then eventually the creation of a European defense. Opened in December 1990, the two Community intergovernmental conferences remained France's absolute priority over the following months. France's next and corollary objective was to work for the restructuring of the Atlantic Alliance as a function of the political and strategic emergence of Europe, which implied a profound transformation of NATO. In the autumn of 1990 even the Americans seemed ready to put such a change on the agenda, and it became the subject of discreet but close conversations between Paris and Washington in late 1990 and early 1991. France's final objective was to put in place an institution charged with reorganizing the Old Continent as a whole along the lines of a 'European' Europe, in which the Community would constitute for Eastern Europe the necessary yeast of prosperity and stability. It was a matter of making the idea of a 'European Confederation' (launched by Mitterrand on 31 December 1989) result in an actual plan, which the French president tried to promote actively starting in the autumn of 1990.

The international and strategic context in which French diplomacy wanted to attain these objectives was in very rapid evolution. The euphoria at the end of the Cold War (still present at the time of the Paris summit in November 1990) gave way with hardly any transition in a few months to uncertainty about the post–Cold War situation. Starting on 2 August, the Gulf crisis culminated in the first weeks of 1991 in operation 'Desert Storm', while the second semester of 1991 was to be marked by the breakup of Yugoslavia in the summer and then the dissolution of the USSR in the autumn. All these developments weighed on the discussion of European architecture throughout 1991 and interfered with Mitterrand's designs, for French expectations were to a large extent being thwarted by the major tendencies that were now taking shape, not least the powerful American reinvolvement in European affairs, which was felt starting in the spring of 1991. Combined with the decomposition of Yugoslavia and the accelerated end of the USSR, this factor weighed heavily in the months and years to come, and was to have a lasting effect on the post–Cold War European landscape as it appeared at the end of 1991.

From Rome to Maastricht

Once the page was turned on unification at the end of summer 1990, the priority went to consolidation of the European relaunch sponsored by France and Germany, which had to be transformed in a decisive step toward the European Union. 'Nothing is settled in advance', warned Mitterrand, more than ever conscious that the pursuit of European construction was 'a difficult task'.[1] One question dominated everyone's mind: now united and sovereign, would Germany maintain its European engagement? The answer was not long in coming. The Munich Franco-German Summit on 17–18 September was marked by the German chancellor's vigorous pro-European reassurances, and it gave rise to a common declaration reaffirming that 'the two countries will continue to be the motor of European construction', their objective being the establishment of 'European union as the solid basis for the unity of Europe as a whole'.[2] The fifteen months that followed confirmed this. Despite inevitable difficulties – reflecting the European and Atlantic dilemmas of the new Germany in an international environment in rapid transformation – the Franco-German dynamic won out, and it was this that would assure the success of Maastricht at the end of 1991.

The French goal in this autumn of 1990 was double: to advance in parallel toward economic and monetary union and toward political union, both being the subject of an intergovernmental conference planned for mid December. The EMU, which remained for Paris a prime objective, now seemed on track. Even if the Élysée still noticed hesitations in German economic and financial circles, the Eleven (Great Britain stood apart) were in agreement on the essential things, in particular the independence of the future European Central Bank, which Bonn made a condition and to which Mitterrand had rallied.[3] Of course, some important questions remained, notably over the content of the second phase of the EMU and the schedule for passing to the third phase (this point would remain at the forefront of French preoccupations, since Paris wanted to avoid a second phase that was constraining in terms of monetary policy but of indeterminate duration: for France it was a matter of obtaining assurance that the single currency would be established in a 'reasonable time period').[4] Still, this issue, which a year previously (in the run-up to Strasbourg) had caused a Franco-German showdown, was now on the right path.

So it was political union that would essentially mobilize French diplomacy until the end of 1991. Previously promoted mostly by Bonn, which wished above all to strengthen the powers of the Commission and of the European Parliament, it had become a priority for Paris, too, in the wake of the relaunch of the spring of 1990. Since then, the French had been trying to orient the debates according to their own perspectives. While recognizing the 'federal purpose' of political union and accepting the strengthening of the *acquis communautaire*, French diplomacy tried above all to preserve the prerogatives of states and to privilege the goal of a common foreign and security policy. These aims came together through French advocacy of a determining role for the European Council.[5] This tendency was confirmed in the autumn: although the Élysée defended itself against the accusation of wanting to rewrite 'a Fouchet plan founded on intergovernmental cooperation', French ambitions did not fit within the integrationist logic either. 'If one wants to put into effect a common foreign and security policy,' insisted Élisabeth Guigou, 'only the European Council can give a strong impetus'.[6] The French priority was thus to put in place a CFSP 'that might later extend to defense' and to consecrate the 'motor role' of the council, which alone held 'the necessary legitimacy and decision-making capacity', while strengthening the existing institutions (parliament, commission, and council) and 'preserving the existing equilibrium' among them.[7]

As the ICG approached, Mitterrand's diplomacy tried to 'frame' the exercise as much as possible, by means of the confirmation of the Paris-Bonn understanding. In Munich on 17 September, Dumas suggested to Genscher that they come up quickly with a new Franco-German text that would specify the content of the future common foreign policy beyond the Mitterrand-Kohl letter of 19 April, the terms of which remained vague.[8]

True, there still remained at the start of autumn an 'uncertainty' about Bonn's intentions. The French in particular wondered whether the Germans would follow them on this terrain – the intergovernmental and foreign policy – which was not what they had traditionally favored with respect to European construction. 'Nobody knows what the Germans want to do,' noted the diplomat Pierre de Boissieu, who would be the French representative to the IGC on political union.⁹ Still, in the following days the Quai d'Orsay and the Auswärtiges Amt managed to agree on a text approved by Genscher and Dumas. While acknowledging some German preoccupations over the role of the European Parliament, it largely reflected French ideas and might therefore serve as a basis for a joint initiative.¹⁰ French and German diplomacies thus rediscovered their capacity to lead others along: '7 to 8 delegations', thought de Boissieu on the eve of the European Council in Rome on 27–28 October, were 'ranged alongside the Franco-German tandem' so as to 'construct a veritable political union with a true common foreign and security policy'. The role of France and Germany, he concluded, 'will be central'.¹¹

Between the Élysée and the Chancellery indeed, a dynamic was established that was to result a year later in Maastricht. As the launch of the IGC approached, Mitterrand and Kohl retook the initiative in the form of a new letter on political union addressed on 6 December to the acting EC president Giulio Andreotti. Mentioning a widening of the competences of the Community in the areas of environment, health and social policy, the letter proposed as well the entry into the European field of some issues of justice and policing. These would become the so-called third pillar of the project. The French and Germans also proposed strengthening the democratic legitimacy of the Union through the creation of a European citizenship, the growth in powers of the European Parliament and an augmented role for national parliaments. But most importantly, they wanted to strengthen the Union's effectiveness by reaffirming the role of the council, and to introduce a common foreign and security policy with the council as the decision making body. Having a vocation to extend to 'all domains', the CFSP would result in a 'veritable common security policy, which would eventually lead to a common defense'; this would occur through a 'clear organic relation' between the political union and a WEU rendered 'more operational' and intended 'to be part eventually of the political union, elaborating on its behalf the common security policy'.¹² This blueprint became the center of debate in the months to come. The Kohl-Mitterrand proposals were far-reaching, particularly over foreign and security policy, where they echoed the French ambition to reach real European autonomy. They also expressed, Paris thought, a 'spectacular evolution' in Bonn's hitherto cautious position in that realm, an evolution that French diplomacy attributed above all to the personal will of the chancellor.[13] This analysis was correct: Kohl would resolutely steer the European course throughout 1991 and prove the most solid partner in this domain (Genscher, by contrast, would be more withdrawn over European matters and especially concerned to preserve the transatlantic link while promoting the CSCE).

For the time being, the Kohl-Mitterrand proposals regarding political union and the CFSP were welcomed warmly even if they aroused from the start two types of objections: those of partisans of an even more 'integrated' Europe, including the Commission in Brussels and the Dutch, both of whom disliked any promotion of the prerogatives of the European Council, and of the British, who rejected the very idea of a European Community that would tend to deal with defense. And of course, behind the British one discerned in the background the equally reluctant Americans.[14] So the French and Germans did not have all their ideas taken up in the 'framework' of the IGC on political union adopted by the Twelve at the European Council in Rome on 14–15 December, but this relative disappointment led them to want to increase their cooperation even more: 'Our collaborators should work closely together' for the IGC, stressed Kohl the day of its opening.[15]

The Franco-German dynamic did persevere in the following months, notably regarding the CFSP. On 4 February the French and Germans presented to the ICG, whose work was actually beginning, proposals that took up elements of the Kohl-Mitterrand letter of 6 December. Recalling that the CFSP should 'eventually open the prospect of a common European defense', they reiterated the idea of a 'clear organic link' between the political union and the WEU, which would, in addition, constitute 'the channel of cooperation' between the former and NATO.[16] As spring began, the Élysée was satisfied with the cooperation of Bonn. Seen from Paris, the context was promising. The Gulf War, in which Europe as such had been absent, was ending, and Kuwait was liberated on 27 February. The French and British had participated separately, but despite this the French thought that the crisis might lead Europeans to become aware of their collective international responsibilities.[17] With Paris and Bonn recalling the Franco-German objectives in a joint communiqué on 22 March, a new meeting of the Twelve at the level of foreign affairs ministers on 26 March made apparent a growing convergence on political union.[18] The work had 'progressed well', especially regarding the CFSP, thought the Élysée in mid April, happy that the Luxemburg presidency had now decided to get involved in writing the future treaty on political union.[19] Caroline de Margerie – who at the Élysée took in hand the dossier after the nomination of Guigou as Minister for European Affairs in the autumn – wrote enthusiastically to Mitterrand that the draft treaty 'responds to the goals that you fixed with Chancellor Kohl in your joint letter of 6 December 1990'.[20]

European Oppositions and Atlantic Obstacles

Still, this dynamic was to get mired down in the spring of 1991 due to two closely linked obstacles. The first resulted from growing opposition within the Twelve, led by Great Britain. John Major, who had succeeded Margaret Thatcher in November 1990 and intended to reintroduce his country into the European game – he spoke of placing Great Britain once more 'at the very heart of Europe' – by this very fact posed a serious problem for French diplomacy. It was no longer possible to count on Great Britain's self-exclusion from the process.[21] Mitterrand gauged this situation during a conversation with the new British prime minister at the Élysée in mid January. While the ultimate goals of the two countries remained distant – London held itself outside the EMU and gave only lip service to the CFSP, rejecting the prospect of a European defense that would challenge the primacy of the Atlantic Alliance – common points also existed, starting with the same distrust of an excessive strengthening of existing Community institutions and a shared desire to maintain the prerogatives of the national governments, especially over foreign and defense policy. But this carried the risk of seeing Great Britain complicate the situation by playing upon tactical rapprochements: 'Europe was used to British opposition and to making its plans without her', stressed Mitterrand that day, adding, despite Major's European protestations: 'Your approach is not really more reassuring, for it is more clever.'[22] As London no less cleverly emphasized some of its own convergences with Bonn, especially over the importance of the transatlantic tie, and overshadowed its differences with Germany, which were in the main institutional, Paris wondered in the spring of 1991 whether British diplomacy was trying to approach the Franco-German couple in order to 'sabotage it' or on the contrary 'to insert itself into it'.[23] For the French president, the answer was soon no longer in doubt: Major, while tackling the European problem 'intelligently', had 'weakened the others' determination', he stressed to German President Richard von Weizsäcker, adding: '[W]ith Mrs Thatcher, it was easier to deal. I will miss her.'[24]

But the British were not the only worry for Mitterrand's diplomacy that spring. Among the Twelve, the Netherlands was increasingly becoming a determined opponent of the French vision of the political union and the CFSP, and especially of its eventual extension into defense matters. This was on the one hand because, like the Brussels Commission, the Dutch stuck to an integrationist conception of political Europe that Paris rejected, and on the other hand because like the British, they advocated the primacy of the Atlantic Alliance and refused the very possibility of a European defense. 'How can you be against it?' Mitterrand asked Prime Minister Ruud Lubbers in mid May, pointing out the need to inscribe in the future treaty if only 'one sentence about the prospect' of a common European defense.[25] If one adds the Irish opposition (due to its neutrality) and the Danish hesitations (due to Atlanticist scruples), the dynamic, heretofore favorable to French ideas about political union, appeared fragile faced with both the partisans of integrationist Europe and the staunch supporters of the Atlantic Alliance.

The second obstacle was related: the U.S. influence – or intrusion – on the European process, which was now inseparable from the Atlantic problematic. Starting in the autumn of 1990, the European relaunch aroused Washington's concerns, reviving old U.S. dilemmas about European construction: might the Community transform itself into an economic and political bloc that would exclude the Americans?[26] These worries appeared clearly on the occasion of the negotiations over the declaration on relations between the United States and the European Community, the idea for which, advanced by Washington, went back to James Baker's speech in Berlin on 12 December 1989. For American diplomacy, it was a matter of effecting a new institutionalization of transatlantic ties beyond what already existed in the political and military domain covered by the Alliance, while reaffirming the central character of the latter. Yet unsurprisingly, the exercise ran up against the usual French reticence, motivated by fear of seeing the still-fragile European identity diluted in an Atlantic ensemble. In essence, Paris feared that 'prior consultations' or 'overly frequent and regular' meetings between the United States and the Community would mortgage the autonomy of the latter by making it an obligation for the Twelve to coordinate with Washington before any important decision. Hence there emerged last-minute difficulties before the signing of the Declaration – during what turned out to be a very discreet ceremony on the margins of the Paris summit of the CSCE at the end of November – a scenario that recalled in attenuated manner the vagaries of the 'year of Europe' in 1973–1974 and heralded a return to transatlantic misunderstandings.[27]

But American worries especially pertained to the politico-military realm. In the wake of the Kohl-Mitterrand letter of 6 December, the U.S. leaders feared that the Franco-German initiatives might lead to a separate European military entity competing with NATO. The Americans were particularly worried about a WEU subordinated to a European political union or even in time absorbed into it, since for them Europe's military arm must remain an appendage of NATO. As the IGC on political union and the post–Cold War adaptation of the alliance progressed in parallel, the future of the WEU and its position in relation to the Europe of the Twelve and to NATO thus became the pivot of the European and Atlantic debate.²⁸ These worries continued into the first weeks of 1991, as witnessed by the warning the Americans gave the Europeans on the eve of the ministerial meeting of the WEU on 22 February. This took the form of a memorandum signed, in Baker's absence, by the Undersecretary of State Reginald Bartholomew, in which the U.S. warned the Europeans against any impulse to establish their own military entity.²⁹ Clearly the objective was to weigh into the debate among Europeans; in Washington, the French ambassador confirmed a 'stiffening' of the U.S. position on the question.³⁰ In Paris, the U.S. move, at any rate, was interpreted as aiming to prevent 'any potential development of the political union' in the name of maintaining a NATO monopoly over Western defense, an attitude that worried the Élysée, where it was thought that priority should go to 'preserving the future by not renouncing in advance in the treaty of political union any ambition in this domain' and to 'making the United States accept it'.³¹

This affair was quite important for Mitterrand. Not only was the French president convinced of the need to proclaim the prospect of a European defense, without which the Community would always remain unfinished, but he judged this requirement justified by his anticipation (which he did not hide) of the inevitability of American disengagement from Europe, at least in the long term, for which the Europeans should prepare. At the same time, Mitterrand was persuaded that the United States would find the prospect of a European defense acceptable, provided it preserved their interests. In this spring of 1991, he did not spare his efforts to try to convince his U.S. counterpart by advancing a moderate and pragmatic approach. Betting on the White House's openness – compared to the State Department – and on his excellent relations with George Bush, he seized the occasion of their meeting in Martinique on 14 March to try to move things along. As in Key Largo a year previously, the meeting was cordial. Beyond the recurrent difficulties between the two diplomatic establishments, the Gulf War had just ended and confirmed the mutual personal trust between the two presidents, permitting an open dialogue.³² Regretting that American diplomacy had, with the Bartholomew memorandum, given the impression 'of being overly fearful of European unity', Mitterrand tried to be reassuring: European defense was only a long-term 'virtuality', whereas NATO was a durable 'reality'; so, he added, 'it is a scholastic dispute' about whether to chose one or the other, for 'NATO and the embryo of European defense should coexist'. The French president assured his partner that 'if this hope [of increased European autonomy] must be at the cost of a rupture or a serious clash with the United States, then it is not worth it'. Protesting that he did not remember the tenor of the Bartholomew missive, and thus separating himself from his own diplomacy, Bush was sympathetic: 'I believe that we are not so far apart', he told Mitterrand. Still, the discussion did not dissipate the basic difficulty: justifying his hope that Europe would gradually 'acquire the means to defend itself' by a probable American withdrawal ('where will NATO be in twenty years?'), Mitterrand probably only confirmed Washington's worry about a French policy that the Americans had a tendency to see as a self-fulfilling prophecy. Inversely, by stressing, as Robert Zoellick did, that 'NATO should remain the principal guarantor of security', the Americans implicitly acknowledged their reservations about Europe acquiring its autonomy in the military domain.[33] The whole Franco-American disagreement – already perceptible in outline a year earlier in Key Largo – was here being newly but quietly expressed.

In the coming months Mitterrand, for his part, stuck to his line of argument: 'There is a reality – NATO – which will fade; and there is a virtuality – European defense – which will strengthen', he repeated shortly afterward to von Weizsäcker, adding: '[W]e don't have to choose today and not for years. The Europeans who say "right away, a common defense" are speaking nonsense. So are the Americans who reject it in principle.'[34] But this pragmatism had no great effect in Washington, where the tension about European projects was evident, especially in the State Department. True, American diplomacy did try to soften things: at the beginning of April Baker spoke in a more nuanced way about the prospect of a European defense; still, he primarily reasserted the centrality of the Atlantic Alliance.[35] Meanwhile in that spring of 1991, the evolutions within NATO (and in particular, as we shall see, the reform of the integrated military structure) confirmed the United States' wish, as relayed by Great Britain, to constrict European ambitions. Thus in the decision, announced in May, to create a rapid reaction force (RRF) under British command, the Élysée saw a desire to frame any European security and defense identity as tightly as possible or even nip a future European defense in the bud. 'The United States wants to prevent Europe from constituting the embryo of a common defense of the Union', Mitterrand lamented on 12 June, evoking 'a major American offensive'.[36]

All this obviously had an effect on the Franco-German pairing. On 10 May, Baker and Genscher signed a joint declaration that left little place for a Western European identity, with NATO remaining the 'forum of agreement on all policies with an impact on the commitment to security and defense of its members'. A few days later, Kohl's visit to the United States confirmed that Bonn could not ignore the American factor and that Germany, which had been severely criticized in the United States for its absence from the Gulf crisis, remained torn between European ambition and U.S. allegiance.[37] At the same time, as we shall see, Bonn proved scarcely cooperative over the issue of the European Confederation, a priority in Paris during the run-up to the Prague meeting that was supposed to launch it.³⁸ To be sure, the Germans were not renouncing the objectives of the CFSP and continued to endorse the prospect of a common defense, even if the French observed that they were 'not in a hurry' to define the specifics.³⁹ But the French and Germans sharply diverged over NATO, with Bonn accepting the RRF project. During the Franco-German summit in Lille on 29–30 May, Mitterrand regretted that 'French and German reactions are not the same', concluding pessimistically: 'There is no European defense.'⁴⁰ In fact, at the end of the first semester of 1991, the dynamic over CFSP seemed to have collapsed. As the European Council in Luxemburg approached on 28–29 June, Paris and Bonn were not able to agree over a new joint letter or even over a simple text that might serve as a basis for statements by Kohl and Mitterrand. 'The Germans want to give something to Europe and something also to the Atlantic Alliance', was the summary at the Élysée, where it was realized how much the Atlantic situation continued to influence German policy.⁴¹

More generally, it was the European relaunch that appeared to be left hanging. While the Luxemburg presidency had accomplished, from the French standpoint, excellent work that Paris wanted to see enacted by the Twelve during the coming council in Luxemburg, the Élysée observed 'a certain floating in Bonn', the Chancellery having resolved that it would be simply a transitional council, with the risk of seeing the Dutch presidency that would take over on 1 July undo the work of the Luxemburg presidency.⁴² By the same token, differences now threatened to take the upper hand in the Community, including between French and Germans. These were not simply over the nature of the proposed political union (the 'communitarian' versus 'intergovernmental' character of CFSP, mention of an eventual common defense, the role of the European Parliament, etc.) but also the economic and monetary union (duration of the second phase and conditions of transition to the third).⁴³ As the Luxemburg council approached, Mitterrand realized all the 'difficulties', which he attributed to the 'multiplicity of games everyone was playing', including Kohl, whom he judged 'evasive by nature', making West Germany an 'unpredictable, flighty partner'.⁴⁴ Paris perceived the risk that the fabric woven over the last fifteen months would be undone: Kohl 'always reasons first as a tactician', stressed Guigou, and 'only the threat of a crisis with France' might – as had happened in December 1989 in Strasbourg – stop his 'tergiversations'. 'He must not be allowed to continue to dither over his commitments', she concluded, recommending firmness to Mitterrand.⁴⁵

The Relaunch within the Relaunch

The following weeks, however, exonerated Kohl and relieved the French suspicions. In the summer of 1991, Kohl took the necessary steps to revive the Franco-German motor over the European defense issue, effecting with Mitterrand a veritable 'relaunch within the relaunch'. At the summit in Lille on 30 May, Kohl had proposed a meeting to delve into defense, a suggestion that Mitterrand (although disappointed with how European and Atlantic affairs were evolving) had accepted.[46] Faced with the latter's skepticism ('what was decided in NATO is serious for Europe and for Franco-German relations', Mitterrand stressed), Kohl a month later had come back to the issue: 'I do not share your pessimism', he insisted, stressing that 'a political union without defense policy is unimaginable'. He proposed that the Élysée and the Chancellery prepare a new initiative: 'As German Chancellor, I cannot accept that the paths of France and Germany diverge', Kohl hammered.[47] These good intentions were confirmed in the course of July. Margerie and Pierre Morel (who replaced Loïc Hennekinne as Mitterrand's diplomatic advisor) summarized the Chancellery's ideas as presented by their homologues Joachim Bitterlich and Peter Hartmann: the CFSP would extend to all security matters and would aim at a common defense policy, while a more operational WEU would implement decisions of the European Council and at the same time play the role of the alliance's European pillar. Finally, they suggested adding to this institutional schema a relaunch of bilateral military cooperation through a reinforcement of the Franco-German brigade that might – the Germans hoped – justify maintaining the FFA. All these ideas won the Élysée's approval. Margerie judged the institutional proposals to be essentially in line with the French vision: if they were adopted, 'we will be in a very good position to resume negotiations on this chapter of the treaty', she wrote. As for the proposed Franco-German brigade, it was similar to an idea advanced in June by General Christian Quesnot, who had just replaced Admiral Jacques Lanxade as Mitterrand's military chief of staff: to study a 'Franco-German army corps within a European perspective'.[48]

Yet Washington's reservations remained. Mitterrand was able to measure them during a conversation with Bush at Rambouillet on 14 July.[49] So when the president and the chancellor met as planned at Bad Wiessee in Bavaria on 23 July to discuss these matters, the U.S. factor was very present. Taking up the outline elaborated the previous weeks between Bonn and Paris, Kohl said he was determined to make progress and suggested that he and Mitterrand endeavor to overcome Washington's reservations by explaining themselves directly to Bush. Mitterrand went into a long exposition in which he did not hide his doubts: the ongoing military reform of NATO threatened to enclose the Europeans within a structure 'completely dependent on a Washington that would stifle any notion of European defense', an evolution that he judged 'anti-historical', given the inevitable nature of the eventual American disengagement. The hostility of Great Britain, the Netherlands, and 'a few others', he continued, showed there did not really exist any European spirit with regard to defense. But this discouraging introduction was mainly intended to clarify things. Repeating his conviction that 'political construction of Europe is not to be conceived without military construction', Mitterrand in fact endorsed Kohl's voluntarist approach: 'If you are in this frame of mind', he told him, 'I am interested'. The French president approved in passing the idea of an enlargement of the Franco-German brigade that might justify maintaining the FFA and equilibrate the military reform of NATO. Overall, the conversation in Bad Wiessee revealed a real convergence, with Kohl proclaiming his own doubts about the future of American policy with respect to Europe ('we are not at their behest') and advancing his European convictions: 'If we do not act now, things will be lost in the sand', he stated firmly, adding that 'we two have a personal relationship that will not recur for a long time'.[50] The same shared skepticism about the future of U.S. engagement on the Old Continent and conviction of European imperatives: these were the factors that in the summer of 1991 explained the relaunch of the Franco-German dynamic that proved in the end to be decisive.

After Bad Wiessee, the common initiative followed its course despite growing differences between Paris and Bonn – to which we shall return – over Yugoslavia. At the end of August, the Élysée and the Chancellery refined proposals pertaining to the political union (preparing the passage of the treaty over the CFSP) and the WEU (preparing in parallel a declaration by WEU member states).[51] In mid September, Védrine, who replaced Jean-Louis Bianco as general secretary of the Élysée, was able to present to Mitterrand the result of this work, underlining that this Franco-German relaunch (three months before Maastricht) 'would have resounding effects'.[52] In Bonn on 18 September, the two leaders registered their agreement on the terms of the initiative, with the French president's only reservation bearing on Kohl's proposal that the two go together to meet the U.S. president to present their project. While he recognized the opportunity to inform the Americans, Mitterrand feared that such a trip would give credit to the idea of a 'delegation of power' granted by Washington. Thus it was decided that the approach would be made by Védrine and Hartmann to Scowcroft, with the principal European capitals being informed subsequently.[53]

The Paris-Bonn rapprochement in this autumn of 1991 bore not only on the CFSP: the French also persuaded the Germans to reject the planned treaty on political union prepared by the Dutch presidency, which the Élysée thought both too 'communitarian' in its structure and too lacking in ambition with respect to the CFSP. This led in turn, to Paris's satisfaction, to the Twelve taking up the plan of the Luxemburg presidency instead.[54] One year after unification, the Franco-German relaunch was taking place on the basis of a desire to reaffirm the friendship between the two countries. The important visit of Mitterrand to the 'new Länder' from 18 to 20 September bore witness to this: it had 'an important symbolic aspect' and aimed to make the 'different appreciations' that had existed at the start of the unification process be finally forgotten, but it was first and foremost about reaffirming France's place as Germany's major political partner and the importance of its effort at economic and cultural investment in the former GDR.[55] By the same token, a tangible sign of the consolidation of the Franco-German tandem was the uncertainty that was now manifest in London. Evidently preoccupied after the Bad Wiessee meeting, Major wrote to Mitterrand at the start of August to discuss CFSP and defense, saying he was 'convinced that for the IGC on political union to have a satisfactory outcome in this domain, it should be on a basis agreed between us'.[56] This initiative reflected London's growing isolation in relation to Paris and Bonn: the Europe of defense as it was being sketched was Franco-German, not Franco-British. (British isolation was confirmed at the end of September by the abandonment of the Dutch project for political union, preferred by London, despite its communitarian orientation, because of its minimalist aspirations with respect to the CFSP.[57])

At the start of October, Bonn and Paris had still to inform their partners of their initiative before making it public. Hartmann and Védrine were received by Scowcroft in the White House on 4 October. Without communicating the exact text, they summarized for him the main points and stressed that Paris and Bonn wished to avoid any misunderstanding with Washington. Scowcroft's reaction was encouraging: congratulating them on the 'general spirit' of the Franco-German move, he insisted, predictably, on the role of the WEU, which the Americans hoped to see evolve into a 'hinge' between the Atlantic Alliance and the Twelve rather than remain the instrument only of the latter. Returning to Paris, Védrine called the American reaction 'as positive as possible', although he noted with some regret the continued U.S. 'wish to lock everything into NATO'. Hence he insisted on the need for the Franco-German initiative to be advanced quickly to avoid losing 'precious time' as Maastricht approached, lest counterproposals multiply once the content of the Franco-German plan became known. Such counterproposals, he believed, would not fail to appear if – in accordance with the wishes of Bonn, which was more concerned than ever to treat Washington carefully – one waited until the alliance summit at the start of November to launch the plan.[58] In fact, things now accelerated: on 4 October, Douglas Hurd and Gianni De Michelis made public a joint initiative on the CFSP and defense whose tone was clearly Atlanticist – the WEU playing the role of NATO's European pillar in line with British theses – which constituted a counter-shot to the initiative from Bonn and Paris.[59]

But the London and Rome move only reinforced the German will to accept French arguments about the need to accelerate the calendar of their own joint proposal: announced to the British as well as to the Dutch and Spanish – the latter were very close to the French and Germans on this issue – the Franco-German initiative resulted in a new joint letter from Mitterrand and Kohl addressed on 14 October to President of the European Council Ruud Lubbers, to which were attached the various proposed drafts elaborated since the summer. Published on the 15th, the letter also mentioned in fine – the Élysée had had to battle with the Chancellery over this – the strengthening of bilateral military cooperation with a view to creating the 'kernel of a European corps that might include the forces of other WEU member states'.[60] As we will see, this short announcement, by hinting at the possible establishment of a genuinely European military structure that would be the outcome of Franco-German cooperation, quickly revived transatlantic misunderstandings.[61] For the time being, however, with Maastricht two months away, Paris and Bonn spectacularly again took the upper hand in the European debate.

Difficulties in the Autumn

Now the other Europeans had to be convinced. The Franco-German move was rather welcomed among the Twelve, including those usually less forthcoming. Informed by Védrine, Lubbers reacted encouragingly.[62] The Italians kept a low profile.[63] Overall, the Mitterrand-Kohl letter had the expected effect, less than two months from the conclusion of the IGC, of reframing the debate on political union and its spearhead, the CFSP. London had hoped before the Mitterrand-Kohl letter to influence Paris and Bonn's initiative by means of a discussion among French, Germans, Italians and British (hence the Hurd–De Michelis move), but it now found itself isolated.[64] Thus the Franco-German initiative caused a British hardening: stressing that London accepted that the European Union have a 'defense' dimension in the long term, on condition that 'the links of Europe with North America be preserved', Major did not disguise his reservations about the joint initiative, starting with the close link between the political union and the WEU and the eventual establishment of European forces that might compete with NATO. 'The idea that one must subordinate the WEU to the European Council or that we could give the political union a defense policy that might not be totally compatible with our engagements in NATO', warned the British Prime Minister, 'is simply not negotiable.'[65] Great Britain posed more than ever as guardian of the Atlantic dogma.

In this context, the U.S. reaction weighed heavily. The Americans were split between resigned acceptance and proclaimed distrust. On the one hand, once the details of the Franco-German initiative were known, the

White House, in line with the attitude adopted by Scowcroft, was careful not to react negatively to the institutional proposals concerning the CFSP and common defense, which were the kernel of the Paris and Bonn plan. Although they did not hide their hope that between then and Maastricht the dynamic of the Twelve would inflect those proposals from Paris and Bonn in a more Atlantic direction – especially over the positioning of the WEU in relation to the alliance – U.S. leaders did not intend to intervene (at least openly) in a debate that clearly concerned the Europeans.[66] On the other hand, the White House did openly worry about the plan for the Franco-German corps, which revived U.S. concern over the emergence of any military structure competing with NATO; this aspect weighed heavily as the alliance's Rome summit approached.[67] (Despite a revival of Franco-American tension over other subjects, that summit, as we will see, nevertheless produced a favorable result from the standpoint of European ambitions in matters of security and defense, with the Sixteen recognizing their legitimacy to act autonomously in this sphere. This was much to the satisfaction of the Élysée, where there was now more confidence about the success of the Franco-German initiative: it had been welcomed, and the NATO summit 'went well'; the Paris-Bonn entente was complete, Margerie wrote in mid November.[68])

The Return of the Greater Germany?

As Maastricht approached, the Franco-German relationship was nevertheless harshly tested over two very different issues, both of which cast light on the temptations of national assertion by the 'new' Germany in an international context in rapid evolution and increasingly dominated by the Yugoslav crisis. The first concerned the demand to increase German representation in the European Parliament to reflect the larger population after unification, a demand that was badly received in Paris, which wanted to preserve the balance between the large countries. (In addition, the preceding year Bonn had promised to not demand modification of the treaties on this point – a commitment, as we have seen, that had contributed to pacifying French worries about the consequences of unification.[69]) 'I sympathize with the German preoccupation', Mitterrand declared to Kohl on 14 November, 'but this would be a grave departure from the spirit of the original treaties that relied on parity'. And the president put his partner on guard against the risk of 'awakening anti-European sentiments': 'Everywhere one will tell me that we have now gone to a German Europe', he warned, implicitly deploring a challenge to a fundamental aspect of the Franco-German entente.[70] The affair threatened to result in an actual showdown as the summit of the Twelve approached, but it was set aside by Kohl and Mitterrand a few days before Maastricht, thus preserving the summit from negative fallout and illustrating once again the two partners' capacity to dispense with their divergences in the interests of their common objectives.[71]

The second issue was far more explosive: it concerned the Franco-German differences over the Yugoslav crisis, now in the foreground of international concerns. After brewing for months, the crisis became an open conflict after the proclamation of Slovenian and Croatian independence at the end of June 1991.[72] From the start, Europe was divided. While Germany proclaimed its sympathy for the self-determination of the Yugoslav republics, other European countries, led by France and Great Britain, tried to control the process. Paris thought in essence that the independence of Croatia and Slovenia, like German unification previously, should remain compatible with the requirements of European stability. The test appeared formidable for the Franco-German couple: not only did the differences between Paris and Bonn threaten to break the European dynamic whose priority was precisely the establishment of a common foreign and security policy, but the risk existed (at least as Paris perceived it) of seeing the same differences aggravate a local conflict that might, as a result, exceed the control of anyone. The implicit threat was to pit the European powers against each other, thus marking the 'return to 1913' that had haunted Mitterrand since the autumn of 1989: it was 'the breakup of Europe' that was at issue, he stressed to Kohl even before the first shots were fired in Yugoslavia.[73]

True, at the start of the conflict Paris and Bonn still agreed to try to maintain a form of voluntary association between the republics: this was the mission of the European 'troika' sent there during the Luxemburg EC summit. But the vainness of this hope soon appeared during the summer, against the background of the deterioration of the situation on the ground, posing ipso facto the issue of whether to recognize Slovenia and Croatia – in favor of which Germany was building up pressure. By the same token, the risk of a German *'Alleingang'* that would split the Community apart became more threatening.[74] As a peace conference opened in the Hague at the start of September at the initiative of the Twelve, Mitterrand's diplomacy adopted a dual approach: to dissuade German diplomacy from *unilateral* recognition of the republics, and to seek a compromise on the parameters of a *concerted* and conditional recognition (covering borders and the rights of minorities) that alone might guarantee a peaceful process: 'Self-determination, yes', declared the French president in Berlin on 19 September, 'but wild self-determination ... no'.[75] The day before in Bonn, Mitterrand and Kohl – without hiding their differences, which were now amplified by the media distortions (as previously over unification) – said they were determined to try to set these differences aside so as to not compromise a European project judged all the more important now that war had returned to Europe. 'For me, the priority is Maastricht' Kohl stated, adding that without European unification, 'we will never manage to leave our past behind us'.[76]

Two months later, with open warfare raging in Croatia, this attempt at rapprochement reached its limits. Under pressure from Genscher, who was very active on this issue, German diplomacy was more and more tempted to abandon the common European position, and although in September Kohl had promised to Mitterrand to avoid an *Alleingang*, he now appeared less determined to resist the temptation of immediate and unconditional recognition, for which public opinion and his partner-adversary Genscher were pushing.[77] Despite warnings from the Élysée about a decision that risked splitting the Twelve even as it aggravated and extended the conflict in Bosnia-Herzegovina and prevented a political solution, the Chancellery confirmed at the start of December that Kohl, for reasons of 'political credibility', would have to recognize Slovenia and Croatia before Christmas.[78] The Yugoslav affair, Védrine wrote, risked becoming a serious apple of discord in Maastricht: whatever the Twelve decided there about political union, he warned, might a few days later be 'reduced to nothing' by such a decision. So the secretary-general of the Élysée suggested elaborating a 'doctrine' applicable to all situations of 'dis-unification' like that in Yugoslavia, a doctrine that would aim to reconcile the right to self-determination and the requirements of international stability, as had occurred with the German unification process, and that might serve as the basis for a Franco-German compromise.[79] These efforts were in vain: as the summit approached, differences between the two countries turned into a dialogue of the deaf. 'I am not against the principle' of recognitions, stressed Mitterrand, 'but they should be combined with international guarantees'. 'How can we not move?' retorted Kohl, evoking the 'enormous' problem of German domestic politics.

Yet once again, the realization of their disagreement was what made the two men agree, essentially deciding that the Yugoslav issue should be left aside in Maastricht so that the European summit might not fail on its account.[80] In this compromise it was Paris that conceded the most: despite their conviction that the policy advocated by Bonn was wrong, French leaders had given up opposing it directly at this stage. Their attitude amounted to choosing the lesser evil: 'the breakup of Yugoslavia is a tragedy, but that of the Community would be a catastrophe', Dumas summarized a few days after Maastricht.[81] Bonn unilaterally recognized Slovenia and Croatia on 23 December 1991, and Germany was followed on 15 January 1992 by the eleven other member states, with France finally having chosen not to oppose these recognitions. This decision would weigh heavily later on: much more than the difficulties of 1989–1990, the Yugoslav crisis placed the Franco-German couple in the coming months on the verge of rupture and threatened the pursuit of European unification. For the time being, however, the essential thing seemed preserved: the setting aside of the Yugoslavia problem suppressed the last real obstacle that might still block the road to Maastricht.

The Success of Maastricht

This road was now clear. Worried at the start of the Dutch presidency, French leaders were now more confident: while the EMU negotiations progressed, the abandonment of the Dutch project at the end of September and the return to the project worked out by the Luxemburg presidency (which Paris preferred for its structure of three separate 'pillars') augured well.[82] This optimism was confirmed on the eve of the Franco-German summit in mid November, in particular over political union, for which the foreign affairs ministers of the Twelve had produced a draft treaty that suited both Paris and Bonn. Now the objectives of French diplomacy for the coming weeks were clear: to get adopted at Maastricht a text 'very close' to this draft, especially in its structure; to confirm the understanding with Germany over the CFSP and common defense; and to temper Bonn's requirements concerning the European Parliament while obtaining its support over social and industrial policy, two other important priorities of Mitterrand's diplomacy.[83] This program seemed within reach thanks to the solidity of the relationship between Mitterrand and Kohl, who had mentioned on 14 November 'an exceptional Franco-German constellation' while affirming his wish for the 'German train to take the irreversible direction of Europe'.[84] A corollary of the solidity of this tandem was the growing isolation of Great Britain. While some months earlier Major had appeared able to disturb the European game, at the end of the year he was begging that London not be left by the wayside, drawing an understanding but firm answer from Mitterrand: 'We ought to help you, but not by abandoning the reason that unites us.'[85] True, on the eve of the summit the battle was not yet won, but faced with probable difficulties – the British exception, Dutch uncertainty, objections of all sorts – the two principal partners were determined to lead in a fight that Mitterrand described as 'decisive': 'We have to go in there and keep the ball rolling for forty-eight hours', Kohl said.[86] This is precisely what they did in Maastricht on 9 and 10 December, isolating Britain and neutralizing a Dutch presidency that was manifestly tempted to play London's game, and thus assuring the success of the summit. It concluded in the small hours of 11 December with an agreement on the draft treaty, which was to be signed after its final refinement on 7 February 1992.[87]

The essential thing for Paris was the EMU, the priority objective of French policy for the past three years. At the end of almost one year of the IGC, the Élysée on the eve of the summit thought the conditions were ripe to 'make Maastricht a great success with regard to the economic and monetary union'. Mitterrand and Kohl agreed to reject the clause granting the general right of exemption demanded by London, and the possibility of opting out of the treaty was conceded to Great Britain alone. In addition, before the summit the finance ministers had refined a mechanism for shifting to the third phase that was designed to prevent any obstacle. So the only remaining question in Maastricht was the possible buffer date for adopting the single currency, which Mitterrand keenly wished to obtain in order to make the EMU irreversible.[88] The close Franco-German agreement now fully bore fruit. Mitterrand, having discreetly prepared the ground with Kohl (but also with Andreotti), and playing on surprise effect, obtained in Maastricht what he had hoped for: 1 January 1999 would figure in the treaty as the limit date for the passage to the third phase, which meant that the countries that fulfilled the corresponding criteria would then adopt the single currency without new discussion. He thus carried off a success whose effect, Major later recognized, had been 'to transform a future option into an immediate commitment'.[89]

The second French priority, concerning political union and in particular the CFSP, was also attained in Maastricht. As Mitterrand recognized before the summit, in this domain 'things were more fluid, the text more complicated and more confused', but the French president accepted this: 'We are not going to build a foreign policy all at once.'[90] In fact, the formula that was finally retained bore the marks of the compromises that had to be made: the treaty specified that the CFSP 'shall include all questions relating to the security of the Union, including the eventual framing of a common defense policy, which might in time lead to a common defense' (article J.4), a convoluted wording that deferred the possibility of a European defense to a distant future. As for the WEU, it was certainly recognized to be 'an integral part of the European Union', but its activity should remain complementary to that of NATO, a language that reflected the delicate balance between the 'European' conceptions of Paris and Bonn and the more 'Atlanticist' ones of London, Lisbon, The Hague or even Rome. Yet for Paris the essential thing was achieved: as Mitterrand and Kohl had suggested in April 1990 and then reaffirmed in December 1990 and October 1991, the treaty proclaimed the ambition to have a common foreign and security policy and envisaged the possibility of a European defense, the 'Ariane's thread' that the French and Germans had sought for more than ten years.[91] In addition, the CFSP decision-making process remained intergovernmental – authority in this realm resided exclusively in the European Council, which ruled essentially unanimously – obviously reflecting French conceptions. (Mitterrand's diplomacy had only to shelter behind British intransigence over this issue.) In a more general way, the French could congratulate themselves on the institutional dimension of the Maastricht result, which belonged to what had been conceived from the start in Paris: the structure of the treaty, with its three 'pillars' (the EC pillar including the EMU, the political union with the CFSP, and home affairs and justice), responded to the French concern to avoid the CFSP becoming a Community affair, while assuring the overall coherence of the union thanks to the European Council's preeminent role. Moreover, the growth in powers of the European Parliament desired by the Germans was to take place within certain limits, Bonn having revised downward its requirements in this respect before the summit. (At Maastricht the Germans also accepted, under British pressure, that the word 'federal' be suppressed, obtaining in return that a new IGC would convene five years after the signing of the treaty so as to revise it in a more federal direction.)[92]

Of course, Mitterrand in turn had to make concessions, with respect to industrial policy, for example, over which France obtained only a commitment in principle whose real scope was limited by the rule of unanimity. (This concession was necessary to obtain progress on the social chapter that was considered the more important question in Paris.) Overall, however, the result of the Maastricht summit was incontestably in line with French ambitions, whether over the EMU or political union. True, the single European currency had been won at the cost of the victory of German concepts (independence of the central bank, criteria of convergence, etc.), but had not French diplomacy, as seen earlier, been resigned to these from the start? As for political union, it had necessitated concessions in the direction of Bonn's more federalist ideas, especially with regard to the role of the European Parliament, but the final result was nearer to French ideas, constituting in many respects the outcome of the process launched thirty years before by the Fouchet Plan. This outcome had not been blocked by the fall of the Berlin Wall, but rather made more dynamic as a result of it: Maastricht in this sense was indeed the Franco-German response to German unity. 'I am entirely in agreement with you that our close and trusting personal cooperation has contributed decisively to the success of Maastricht', wrote Kohl on 15 December in response to a message from Mitterrand the previous day.[93] Mitterrand echoed this appreciation on television the same day: 'It is one of the most important events of this past half century', he stated, adding: '[I]t is a moment that prepares for the following century.'[94] Whatever the fragility of this result – which the aggravation of the Yugoslav crisis quickly made evident – Maastricht was, for Mitterrand's diplomacy, the longed-for outcome of the great European debate. The rest, starting with the Atlantic problematic, was seen as more secondary.

France and NATO: The Missed Rendezvous?

Bush and Mitterrand, we recall, had agreed in Key Largo in April 1990 that the events of 1989–1990 would have consequences for the future of the Atlantic Alliance and that this matter should be openly debated. But far from the objective study of the issues envisaged, the French had observed at the London summit a 'nailing down' of the Atlantic debate in the name of the more urgent concern to convince the USSR to accept keeping united Germany within NATO, which led to French disappointment in the outcome of the summit. Yet barely had the Atlantic euphoria subsided after London than the White House started to worry about Mitterrand's reservations, leading to a little-known episode of Franco-American rapprochement in the following months. Faced with a NATO future that appeared quite uncertain once the Cold War was behind it, Washington indeed wished to resume the dialogue with Paris over the alliance. In mid July, Lanxade and Robert Blackwill, Scowcroft's assistant for European affairs at the NSC, agreed on the necessity of a deeper bilateral dialogue.[95] At the same time, the American representative to NATO, Robert Taft, approached his French homologue Gabriel Robin. Stressing that Washington remained favorable to an overall reflection on the alliance's future as envisaged by Bush and Mitterrand at Key Largo, he suggested that this review be conducted within the framework of the Atlantic Council, in parallel with the reexamination of the NATO strategy decided in London (from which Paris had dissociated itself), with the understanding that the results might be ratified during a new summit in 1991. The Frenchman saw this as a sign of Washington's discomfort after the July summit: the French abstention, he commented, bothered the Americans, who wanted unanimity and who might be well disposed to make concessions to pry France out of its 'waiting game'.[96] At the start of September, Taft reiterated his proposal: while the Fifteen might pursue the review of NATO's strategy within the framework of a group presided over by the Briton Michael Legge, which France was welcome to join if it wished, the Sixteen including France would tackle the future of the alliance in larger political terms under the direct authority of the Atlantic Council.[97] This desire for dialogue was confirmed the next month on the occasion of a visit by Lanxade and Margerie to Washington, where they noted the increasing doubts of their hosts: the waning perception of any Soviet threat, the evolution of a Germany now united and sovereign, the probable reductions in U.S. forces in Europe and the emergence of a European security and defense identity all aroused in the White House 'real perplexity' about the possibility of maintaining the Atlantic status quo for any length of time. Hence, thought Mitterrand's two advisors, the U.S. leaders' wish to deepen discussions with France, which they saw as holding 'certain keys to the future organization of security in Europe' – a realization probably owing something to Mitterrand's announcement in London of the withdrawal of the FFA. Scowcroft and his assistant David Gompert, moreover, were anxious to clarify the strategic concept of 'last resort' that had aroused Mitterrand's criticism in London: they insisted it was not a matter of giving up deterrence, but of giving it a more political presentation so as to reassure the Soviets and facilitate keeping nuclear weapons in Germany. Overall, the two Frenchmen got the impression of a real openness on the part of the Americans and concluded that perhaps there was an opportunity for rapprochement, particularly over the question of compatibility between a 'renovated Atlantic Alliance' and the 'gradual construction of a more European defense structure'.[98] This impression was accurate: in the autumn of 1990 the White House did indeed consider that the relation with France was determining for the future of the Atlantic Alliance – hence its wish for close discussions with the Élysée.[99]

These overtures could not leave Paris indifferent. French leaders, as we know, were persuaded that the long-term future of the transatlantic relationship needed the assertion of Europe, and that the latter presupposed the acceptance by the United States of a profound transformation of NATO: hence the inclination to dialogue with Washington. In the autumn of 1990, this took place at several levels, first between the White House and the Élysée: with the misunderstandings over nuclear doctrine quickly dissipated, Lanxade was able to probe NATO problems (in particular, the future of military integration) during regular meetings with Scowcroft and his staff, especially Gompert and his assistant Philip Zelikow. Though these talks were probably given more significance on the U.S. side than on the French side – the Élysée military chief of staff had no specific mandate from Mitterrand to negotiate over these questions – the meetings benefited from the quality of Lanxade's contacts in Washington and enabled better cooperation between the Élysée and the White House, which the Iraq crisis confirmed.[100] But the dialogue was also renewed at Evère (NATO headquarters), where Robin responded positively to Taft's initiatives: he judged it difficult to participate in the work of the Legge group but thought it possible and desirable to contribute to the Sixteen's thinking about the future of the alliance, which French diplomacy had repeatedly called for and which it might thus influence favorably. Following instructions from Paris, the French representative announced in mid

September that his delegation would take part in the debate on the future of the alliance, in particular the brainstorming sessions that would take place in the Atlantic Council starting the following month.[101] Last but not least, at the same time the French, U.S., German and British representatives (Robin, Taft, Hans-Friedrich von Ploetz and Sir Michael Alexander), who met regularly in 'quad' at NATO headquarters, decided they would devote their meetings to the same subject. It was in fact within this exclusive and confidential four-party framework that the most substantial debate took place and the most significant convergences occurred over the next few weeks and months.[102]

Convergences at NATO

Launched effectively at the start of October, the reflection of the Sixteen quickly became rather disappointing to the French. True, the key subjects were broached in brainstorming sessions: the fundamental objectives of the Atlantic Alliance, the transatlantic link, relations between NATO and the European Community as well as with the WEU, relations with Eastern Europe and the USSR, the future role of military forces and new 'challenges' to the alliance.[103] Yet Paris thought at the end of several weeks that the exercise would result in nothing tangible, since the participants stuck to 'conventional' views: while deploring that their partners were trying to justify maintaining the alliance by giving it inappropriate 'new tasks' such as dialogue with Eastern countries, the French realized that the debate would bring no answer to questions raised about the proper role of the Europeans in the Atlantic ensemble. Worse, they noted that the Legge exercise was meanwhile outstripping its mandate to reexamine only NATO's strategy; meanwhile the Fifteen were in fact tackling all the problems of European security in the absence of France.[104] Seen from Paris, the reflection on the alliance's future – whether by Fifteen or Sixteen – seemed to have begun badly in the autumn of 1990.

Things went better in the meetings between the four ambassadors, however, which quickly led to unexpected convergences on the heart of the problem, i.e. the future of the integrated military organization. At the instigation of Taft, the four-way conversations tackled these questions in mid October. As the opening of the IGC on political union approached, the U.S. representative was concerned to know about European plans with respect to the CFSP and defense, aware that those could not be without consequence for NATO as the WEU drew closer to the EU political union.[105] In the following days, the conversation turned to WEU-NATO relations, concerning which Alexander explained British ideas. These leaned toward making the WEU the European pillar of NATO, which, he suggested, might take place by giving 'dual hats' (WEU and NATO) to the permanent representatives. Taft proving to be quite open in this discussion, Robin pushed the argument: they should also apply the principle of dual hatting to the NATO Military Committee (the body where the national chiefs of staff of member states were represented) in order for the WEU to have its own planning capability, and they should especially reflect on the consequences of the foregoing on the integrated military organization.[106] Progressively, the Frenchman led his three colleagues to recognize that 'NATO structures [are] at the heart of the problem' and that the erection of a European defense pillar would necessarily imply that NATO 'give some space' to the Europeans – an argument that Taft admitted by stressing that even if the Pentagon was hesitant about the idea of a European command structure, there was no definite policy about this in Washington at this stage.[107]

By mid November, the conversations had clearly progressed: when Robin drafted a 'non-paper' that aimed to start the debate on the reform of the military organization by showing to what extent the existing one was 'outmoded' in the new strategic context, his colleagues did not refute his analysis. Better still, the American representative was sympathetic to the French idea of increasing the prerogatives of NATO's Military Committee (especially with regard to planning) at the expense of SHAPE, an overture that led Robin to conclude that the conversations had entered a new phase.[108] The four ambassadors now plunged ahead in the hope that their ministers would validate their labor on the occasion of the next ministerial meeting: hence they decided to present their respective capitals with a synthesis, a document drafted by the Briton on which they agreed at the end of November.[109] This document reflected the real progress of the preceding weeks' conversations. After having recalled the fundamental character of the Atlantic Alliance, it stressed that 'in the years to come, the Europeans will have to assume more responsibility for their own defense,' which would lead them to develop a 'specific' role that might be translated into independent action 'if and when such action is judged appropriate.' The WEU would constitute 'for the time being' the suitable forum for this role, whose affirmation would go hand-in-hand with the 'major changes' to be brought to the NATO organization so as to adapt it to the new context: 'slimmer and less rigid structures,' 'more mobile and flexible forces,' and eventually the transfer of certain responsibilities from the major commands to the Military Committee.[110] Having submitted this text to Washington, Taft reported at the start of December that the reaction was good, the dominant feeling being that one must explore paths thus opened; he thought there was no principled objection foreseeable from the United States, where there was full awareness of the need to 'revise' NATO structures.[111]

With the confirmation of the American opening, Robin pushed ahead and made himself the advocate of a policy actively betting on the emergence of a real European pillar within NATO. Of course, he recognized that France could ignore the 'overture' made by Washington and privilege (within the framework of the IGC) the affirmation of a defense and security dimension within the European Union, while sticking to its own particular status within NATO. But he stressed that this would risk Washington's blocking the emergence of a real European defense pillar, and by the same token allow the alliance's to slip down a bad slope – for lack of a Europeanization that was indispensable for its long-term preservation. As the December 1990 ministerial meeting loomed, Robin resolutely defended the approach of the past several weeks. Considering that 'the emergence of a European defense pillar, the normalization of France's status within the Alliance, and the adaptation of the NATO structure' were 'three facets of the same problem', he advised 'accepting the American offer' of a complete overhaul. Of course, he admitted, this approach required making a decision: 'Pending the outcome of the Atlantic debate, one must either freeze the work of the Twelve on the defense chapter or agree for the Twelve to refer this back to the WEU, but in any case avoid interference that could only complicate things'; it was indeed essential 'not to give the Americans the impression that we are pursuing two strategies at the same time', and it was urgent to formulate quickly French proposals for reforming the military organization, without which the allies would go ahead and ignore Paris.[112] The French representative insisted that European defense would remain 'a Platonic idea' as long as the integrated military organization did not evolve, which should take place through the questioning of SHAPE's preeminence. 'The enterprise, no doubt, will appear as redoubtable as the fortress that must be taken', he conceded, 'but never have the circumstances been as propitious as now'.[113] Almost a quarter-century after the French withdrawal, Robin was indeed wagering on a radical transformation of NATO and on the affirmation of the European dimension within the Atlantic Alliance, with the corollary of a 'normalization' of France's status.

The Limits of Rapprochement

Yet the wager was made at a bad time, for the following weeks highlighted the limits of both sides. On the French side, at the end of 1990, Parisian leaders (in contrast with Robin) were manifestly doubtful about the scope and reality of the U.S. overtures. Seen from the Quai, the four-way exercise was actually 'leveling off': whereas it had allowed the heart of things – the future of integration – to be tackled, the Quai's directorate of strategic affairs thought that apart from the rebalancing between SHAPE and the

Military Committee, the ideas in the British synthesis document on the reform of the military structure still reflected mostly 'Atlantic' ideas. Thus it would be premature to envisage institutional arrangements like the WEU-NATO 'double hatting', for in the absence of a well established European defense – meaning, autonomous in relation to the alliance – such a reform would be 'superficial,' if not 'counterproductive'. Paris thought (inversely to Robin's reasoning) that the debates between the Twelve and within the alliance should be carried on *pari passu*, for it was up to the Europeans to 'decide from the perspective of their political union, the way they intended to integrate the defense dimension into European construction'.[114] The prospect of a European defense, in other words, was the priority and could only be decided upon by the Europeans, who should not confine themselves a priori to asserting a European dimension within the Atlantic Alliance. This was also the opinion at the Élysée, where the Evère exercise was followed from a distance and where it was thought, moreover, that a real transformation of NATO was unlikely in the absence of the prior political affirmation of Europe. As seen from Paris, in other words, any Atlantic prospect was secondary in relation to the CFSP and the prospect of European defense – and all the more so because the Élysée was getting ready to launch a new initiative with Bonn in the form of the common letter of 6 December, as we have seen.[115] In short, Paris had already firmly chosen to wager everything on the IGC, ipso facto according limited significance to the debates internal to the alliance.[116]

At the same time, the limits of the U.S. overture were appearing. Zelikow confided to a member of the French embassy in mid November that while the United States supported the idea of a European pillar, the latter should not 'marginalize' NATO to the point of making it an 'empty shell'. He added that the Americans had no objection to the strengthening of political cooperation among Europeans, but that any defense dimension they attempted should be clearly situated within the Atlantic Alliance, according to the British schema.[117] Thus on the eve of the ministerial meeting of December 1990, the limits of the Franco-American rapprochement had become clear. Dufourcq, on the occasion of a 'quad' meeting of political directors on 4 December, thought the work conducted by the four ambassadors in Evère was 'encouraging', but he also stressed that the Twelve must advance in parallel on political union and warned that 'for France to engage in a renovation of the Alliance, there must be a modification of its current structures' that went well beyond the affirmation of a European group in its midst. His American homologue, Raymond Seitz, in reply reiterated Washington's interest in a European pillar emerging but warned against any idea of independent structures that would risk 'emptying NATO of its substance and therefore losing the justification for the

American presence in Europe', which is what would happen if the WEU were under the authority of the European Council rather than NATO.[118] But this was precisely the heart of the initiative of 6 December: Paris and Bonn advanced the need for a 'clear organic link' between the WEU and political union – hence the rather negative reaction from Washington, astonished at such a proposal, which came at a time when Evère was studying a close relation between the WEU and NATO.[119] As Robin had feared, the discussion about to open at the IGC now threatened to collide with what had been happening for a few weeks within the alliance. As 1990 drew to a close, the French representative remained favorable to pursuing the exercise started two months earlier: 'The present occasion, if not seized now, is unlikely to occur again for a long time', he underlined. Still, while recommending that Paris clarify that its objective was 'real military autonomy and a profound reform of the integrated structure', he did not conceal that 'our partners will likely ask for symmetric guarantees'.[120] This implicitly recognized that the rapprochement had reached its limits.

The first weeks of 1991 in effect exposed these limits more sharply. As the four ambassadors went into details, the Frenchman was brought to realize that the notion the Americans and British had of a European pillar was narrow, to say the least, since they reserved a quasi-monopoly for NATO and granted the WEU only a subsidiary military role.[121] Moreover, while they accepted the idea of a WEU Military Committee and military staff, it remained to be seen, Robin recognized, whether the committee would have its own planning capacity and its staff be equipped with a real European chain of command. Finally and especially, the French representative stressed that the Americans and British were ruling out eventual European forces being permanently distinct from Atlantic forces. According to the British representative, it could only be a matter of forces 'separable' but 'not separate' from the integrated military structure. Without excluding later changes that might eventually bring Paris to make 'some movement', Robin thus had to acknowledge that these conceptions fell short of the French ideas (according to these conceptions, the European pillar outside NATO 'would barely begin' and the European pillar in NATO would 'remain to be built', he summarized). Under such conditions, he recognized, there could hardly be a call for an 'agonizing reappraisal' of France's relations with NATO.[122] The Quai was even more categorical: the office of strategic affairs noted the 'particularly restrictive' character of the U.S. and British positions and concluded that 'such an approach, fearful and suspicious about the European dimension', was not 'of a kind to respond to the actual stakes'.[123] In short, French leaders now held that a European pillar within NATO, of which London made itself the champion with Washington's support, was but a chimera, and the Élysée was convinced that British activism concerning the WEU aimed above all to 'preserve the essential characteristics of NATO'.[124] Implicitly stressing his scant interest in NATO discussions, Mitterrand said the same thing to Major in mid January 1991: 'If the WEU has the function of being an appendage of NATO, there is no reason to fabricate a supplementary organization.'[125]

In this context, the Bartholomew memorandum at the end of February – even if, as seen above, it aimed primarily to influence the debates of the Twelve and within the WEU – had an inevitable effect on the discussions within NATO. In Paris, the approach was interpreted as another illustration of Washington's rejection of a profound reform of the NATO structure and as a confirmation of the need for France (as long as a real European perspective was not clearly visible) to avoid making substantial concessions that would not be paid back in kind.[126] Before the meeting between Mitterrand and Bush in mid March in Martinique, the Quai d'Orsay believed that even if the conversations of the four ambassadors had been 'interesting', no 'clear vision of the future of the renovated Atlantic Alliance' had emerged. In addition, the office of strategic affairs noted that the military organs of NATO (SHAPE, the Military Committee) were already beginning a restructuring 'that leaves scarcely any room for the Europeans'. In these conditions, Franco-American convergence about a major transformation of NATO appeared little more than hypothetical, and the Quai thought the meeting in Martinique should, above all, help 'clarify misunderstandings' by making the Americans understand that a security identity constituted an 'inseparable' element of European construction, even if its assertion should 'be gradual and articulated with the Atlantic military arrangements'.[127] The same attitude prevailed at the Élysée, where as the Bush-Mitterrand talks approached, it was thought that 'the essential issue' at this stage was not NATO reform, but rather 'the American attitude to a possible and future foreign and security policy common to the Twelve'.[128]

The Martinique meeting confirmed this analysis: it showed the absence of real convergence between the Americans and the French on the transformation of NATO military structures. The subject was not even brought up: it was clear that Washington refused to question the NATO status quo and France refused to question the need for European defense autonomy.[129] As already mentioned, the summit also showed the limits of American tolerance with regard to French objectives over European defense, even if they had been tactfully explained by Mitterrand. Overall, Martinique thus marked the failure of the Franco-American rapprochement anticipated in the autumn of 1990. With the departure of Lanxade, who was shortly afterward named chief of staff of the French armed forces, the conversations between the Élysée and the White House faded away. Meanwhile, the four-way exercise at NATO became lost in the sands during the spring, 'nobody having', Robin regretted, 'either new ideas or further instructions'.[130] Both sides had been genuinely willing to talk at the end of 1990 and start of 1991, but this was not sufficient to overcome their mutual reservations. In Paris, despite the openness of Lanxade and Robin, neither the Élysée nor the Quai was inclined to engage in a transformation of the alliance that was judged hypothetical and implied giving up the priority of the CFSP and European defense and abandoning the particular status of France within NATO. This was all the more so because Washington was suspected of wanting to maintain artificially its Atlantic leadership despite a U.S. disengagement that Paris considered inevitable in the long run, which would lead to a questioning of NATO in any case.

At the same time, in Washington, despite a certain opening in Bush's entourage, the military, supported by Secretary of Defense Dick Cheney, were not ready – against the background of the Gulf crisis – to rearrange NATO's military structure, while the State Department under Baker did not conceal its hostility to the French plans for a politico-strategic Europe. This hostility was fed by the traditional fear of seeing NATO emptied of its substance and the presence of the United States in Europe questioned, thus nourishing American isolationism, but also by a newer worry characteristic of the post–Cold War era: might the European Union be able eventually to take decisions of a kind to affect U.S. interests, for example by implicating the United States despite itself in a European crisis? The failure of the Franco-American rapprochement thus merely reflected a basic difference of views on the future of European and Atlantic security after the Cold War.[131]

France-NATO: Return to 'Normal'

In the spring of 1991, the tendency was therefore to reaffirm the usual pattern of French relations with NATO: 'There is no question', said Dumas a few days after the Martinique meeting, 'of rejoining either surreptitiously or openly' the integrated organization.[132] In fact, France's position in the Atlantic Alliance had been validated in the eyes of French leaders by the experience of the Iraq crisis. As the Quai d'Orsay thought: 'The Gulf War has shown that the French position of refusing to place itself under the integrated command in peacetime in no way harms the efficacy of common defense.'[133]

While a French 'normalization' with respect to NATO was excluded, French leaders still realized the limits of a position of pure and simple immobility: as Lanxade and Védrine had stressed before Martinique, the risk was 'seeing NATO be reformed without us' and consequently 'blocking the path for a long time to any European defense ambition' while putting the brake on the dynamic of political union. France could not maintain its reservations about NATO without validating the distrust of its partners.[134] This analysis led Paris to make a limited movement in the alliance's direction: the very day after the Martinique meeting, France announced its intention to participate in the alliance's strategic rethinking. Since the Legge working group of the Fifteen had departed from its initial mandate (the future of flexible response and forward defense) and its discussions now embraced all the security problems and their consequences for the evolution of the alliance, France could no longer stand apart, it was emphasized.[135] Even if Paris insisted that its decision by no means challenged its own particular status within the alliance, the Fifteen were pleased and disposed to take the French willingness to join into account. 'We have the possibility of having a certain number of our ideas approved', said Robin with satisfaction, wanting to intervene rapidly in the discussion to avoid it getting stuck in the 'usual stereotypes'.[136] This French gesture in the direction of the alliance was obviously tactical: it was a matter of 'avoiding the current thinking within the Atlantic Council (whether in the 'brainstorming' sessions or in the Legge working group) leading to restrictive conclusions that would preempt the results of the Twelve's thinking'.[137] Yet although limited, the overture paid off: the NATO ministerial meeting in Copenhagen on 6–7 June ended with a final communiqué that to Paris's satisfaction saluted 'efforts aiming to strengthen the security dimension of the European integration process' and recognized the importance of progress by the Twelve toward political union, acknowledging that it was up to them to 'decide on the necessary arrangements to express a foreign and security policy and a defense role' and that procedures should be defined to assure 'the necessary transparency and complementarity' between the Atlantic Alliance and the European Union.[138] The French approach seemed validated, at least in part: at the cost of limited rapprochement and of selective participation in the process of NATO adaptation, Paris got the alliance to pledge not to impede its European ambitions.

But this tactic also rapidly encountered its limits, which reflected NATO's military realities – over which Paris had no hold. If the French had been able, since the autumn of 1990, to have their say on the political part of the alliance's adaptation (brainstorming in the Atlantic Council, the four-way exercise) and, starting in the spring of 1991, on its strategic part (the Legge group), they were from the start still excluded from the military dimension that pertained to the NATO integrated bodies. After the London summit, it was in this domain that thinking advanced fastest, if only for the precise reason that France was not implicated in it, leaving the field free for its 'integrated' allies to take action without it.[139] At the end of November, Robin noted the rapid progress of thinking at SHAPE and in the Military Committee. The SACEUR, General John Galvin, had already presented his thoughts about the restructuring of integrated forces and commands: as advocated by London, the new proposals put the accent on mobility, multinationality and force projection capacity, and they envisaged the creation of a NATO rapid intervention force.[140] The review process ended at the end of May 1991 at the meeting of the Defense Planning Committee, during which the fifteen 'integrated' countries adopted a new force structure spearheaded by the RRF, a projection-capable rapid reaction force of 70,000 troops composed of European contingents under British command and answerable to SACEUR.[141]

This result, as seen above, was badly received in Paris: in effect, it sealed off the military reform of NATO before the strategic and political rethinking had ended – engendering, in French eyes, a problem of 'method' with serious consequences.[142] Moreover, this result preempted the rethinking process in two ways. First, the characteristics of the RRF, which was presented as contributing to the defense of the 'flanks' of the alliance, nevertheless implicitly suggested a future 'out of area' role for NATO, which was by no means a matter of consensus and hindered the future out of area missions that the French thought belonged to the future European security and defense identity. Secondly, the presentation of the RRF as a European force appeared to be a sham due to its operational dependence on American military means and its status as an integrated force – a sham destined, as seen from Paris, to prevent a real European defense prospect from emerging.[143] The RRF, summarized Quesnot, 'might well constitute the secular Anglo-Saxon arm of a renovated and expansionist NATO in its attributes and its geographic reach', thus putting a brake (despite the Copenhagen compromise) on 'the emergence of a European security and defense identity'.[144] This analysis was not false: despite the denials of those who conceived it, the restructuring of the integrated forces (whose military logic Paris did not contest) indeed aimed 'to give NATO's military structures a central role' in order to preserve their rationale and make possible in practice new NATO missions, all to the detriment of possible European structures.[145]

The U.S. willingness to restore its grip over NATO was felt not only in the military dimension, but also in the political one, as witnessed by the growing impulse of American diplomacy in the spring of 1991 to extend the alliance's influence toward the East by playing on the theme of its 'politicization' – a theme introduced, as we saw, at the London summit in the hope of convincing the USSR to accept maintaining united Germany within NATO, and in the longer term preserving the alliance's role and the U.S. military presence in Europe. True, the idea of a role for NATO out of area, advanced during the Gulf crisis after August 1990, rapidly proved unsustainable, with Paris consistently opposing it by pointing to the letter of the treaty and the counterproductiveness of implicating the Atlantic Alliance in the Middle East.[146] If the question had not disappeared totally from the Atlantic debate during the year 1991 (the RRF reintroduced it surreptitiously), the prospect was clearly premature, as Mitterrand said in no uncertain terms to Bush in Martinique, rejecting the idea of 'extending the authority [of NATO] over the planet'.[147] But it went differently for the alliance's political role, which, as Robin noted at the end of 1990, had become a 'major axis for the renovation of NATO', producing, he wrote, a 'foggy discourse on a new NATO charged with assuring the stability of Europe and facing new challenges'.[148] As Robin's remarks made clear, French diplomacy remained most reticent about an orientation that it considered was likely to maintain artificially the Atlantic status quo in the short and medium term, while implying a dangerous dilution of the alliance in the long term.

Under pressure from Washington, the question nevertheless came back to the fore in the spring, and therefore Paris had to stake out very clear limits: the functions of the alliance should not be extended to all the problems of security in Europe. As for relations with the countries of Eastern Europe, they should not lead to 'recuperating' for the benefit of NATO the procedures adopted within the CSCE, nor prevent the European Community and the WEU from playing their roles.[149] To no avail: the United States, noted the Quai d'Orsay, was trying, by means of multiplying liaison and cooperation programs with former members of the Warsaw Pact, to 'make NATO the central element in the future pan-European security architecture'.[150] In this context, Baker's speech in Berlin on 18 June 1991 (eighteen months after the one he gave shortly after the fall of the Wall), in which he mentioned 'an Atlantic Community from Vancouver to Vladivostok', could only confirm the dominant feeling in Paris: American diplomacy was conducting a campaign to try to take in hand the future of the Old Continent's security under the hegemony of the Atlantic Alliance.[151]

Combined with the alliance's 'politicization', the military reform of NATO was thus bound to collide with French objectives. Faced with what Mitterrand felt was a veritable 'offensive' to perpetuate U.S. control over Europe at a time when it was in fact withdrawing, maintaining the French 'difference' in the alliance was more important than ever. True, Franco-American relations at the highest level were not affected by this situation. (An irony of the era was that they could be distinguished from relations between the Quai d'Orsay and the State Department, whose two heads were notoriously at loggerheads.) Although it had been four months since the Martinique meeting and the climate was now 'less good', in the summer of 1991 the Élysée noted the White House's concern to keep close contact with it over European and Atlantic questions.¹⁵² But this did not prevent the French president from expressing himself as clearly as possible to his American homologue during their meeting in Rambouillet on 14 July: not concealing his skepticism about the transformation of NATO and in particular about the creation of the RRF, he reaffirmed in plain terms that he did not intend to renounce a French 'decision-making autonomy' inherited from General de Gaulle.¹⁵³

The Rome Summit

The Atlantic agenda was now dominated by the preparations for the Rome summit on 7–8 November.¹⁵⁴ In this context, everybody was interested in calming things down. The White House wanted to avoid reproducing the London scenario by keeping close contact with the Élysée to prevent misunderstandings and 'to capitalize on the good understanding between the two Presidents'.¹⁵⁵ Meanwhile, the main objective for Mitterrand's diplomacy was to avoid Rome becoming an obstacle along the path to Maastricht. The French president combined strategic firmness ('I cannot accept that Rome forbids Maastricht adopting the principle of a common defense', Mitterrand stressed to Felipe Gonzalez) and tactical flexibility ('if the Americans maintain the language of Copenhagen', he added, 'it is a little bit fictional, but not too harmful').¹⁵⁶

But the Franco-German initiative of 15 October complicated things anew. Although Paris and Bonn had been able to defuse U.S. opposition to the initiative and bring U.S. leaders to accept its institutional aspects in terms of the CFSP and defense as well as EU-WEU relations, the Americans were still very reserved about its military aspects, in particular, the plan for a Franco-German corps. Here the Americans thought that they had been poorly informed, if not misled, beforehand by the Germans and the French, which led to a sharp reaction. True, Washington understood that the goal was to justify maintaining the FFA by establishing a bilateral framework for the French military presence in Germany, a goal to which the Americans could only subscribe, but the idea that the Franco-German corps was the embryo of a veritable military structure that would be affirmed within the WEU reawakened, particularly in the Pentagon, the fear of a redundant military structure that might in time compete with NATO. This was all the more so because the first commentaries on the Franco-German initiative were focused on this very proposal, which had been added at the last minute and was described in the press as tending to create nothing less than a 'European army'.¹⁵⁷

In short, the eternal debate over the compatibility between European autonomy and maintaining the existing role of NATO was again underway, and it threatened to compromise the Atlantic Alliance summit. In a letter of 23 October to Mitterrand, Bush worried that this developing controversy over the Franco-German corps might lead to 'serious divisions' within the alliance, and he stressed that 'it made it difficult for the Americans to support the European security and defense identity'.[158] These worries were relayed a few days later at the NATO headquarters. Taft proved particularly virulent in his criticism of the Franco-German corps, which he presented as an attack on NATO's integrated command, leading von Ploetz and Robin to reply in turn that the Franco-German initiative was on all counts compatible with the Atlantic Alliance.[159] In the following days, Paris made every effort to reassure Washington: without renouncing their ambitions, the French pointed out that the Americans had not been taken by surprise, that the main goal of the Franco-German corps was to assure maintaining the FFA and that the October 15 initiative primarily concerned the drafting of the Maastricht Treaty rather than the language on European military structures.[160] Mitterrand replied to Bush by reaffirming 'the importance that France gives the Alliance;' while he recognized that the plan for a Franco-German corps might be interpreted badly by some, he stressed that 'any fear of "duplication" or "substitution" was without foundation'.[161] Although the quarrel over the European corps had only begun (it would poison transatlantic relations throughout 1992), these efforts worked for the time being: on a mission to Washington on 4 November to bring Scowcroft up to date a few days before Rome, Morel and Quesnot reported that American leaders were 'noting our effort at compatibility and transparency', and the two advisors concluded that 'the Franco-German initiative is accepted', even if 'it calls in return for various signals of reassurance about the permanence of the Alliance'.[162]

Thus the Rome summit took place without too much drama, at least concerning the issue of European identity. While the latter was the subject of tense discussion, the French were satisfied with the result. Taking up the language adopted in Copenhagen, the declaration by the sixteen heads of state and governments recognized that 'the development of a security identity and the role of Europe with regard to defense' would strengthen the efficacy of the alliance and constitute 'an important foundation for the renovation' of the latter, with 'these two positive processes strengthening each other'.[163] Moreover, French diplomacy thought it had managed to influence the content of the new strategic concept after having joined the discussions in March. Paris was able to endorse it except for a few paragraphs concerning the integrated military structures, in which reference was made to 'concerned allies', thereby implicitly dissociating France from those paragraphs.[164] Of course, the fundamental debate was not resolved: 'If Western Europe intends to create an organization of security outside the Alliance, tell me so now', Bush stated in the Rome session.[165] The conversation between the American president and the French president on the margins of the Rome summit confirmed this. 'We think [that a European security identity] is in the interests of Europe and of the United States', conceded Bush, 'but I do not want to do anything to feed isolationism'. 'One has to avoid a self-fulfilling prophecy', added Baker. Mitterrand was acquiescent: 'History will decide. No problem', he replied philosophically after having once more explained his doubts about the capacity of future American presidents to maintain a presence on the Old Continent and his conviction that consequently Europe must organize its own defense. For the Frenchman, the essential thing was accomplished: the alliance summit had not shut off the long-term prospect of a Europe of security and defense. Rome would not be an obstacle on the road to Maastricht.

So it was on a different score that the Rome summit gave rise to difficulties that yet again led to the affirmation of a dissident French position. The issue was once more the 'politicization' of the alliance in general and in particular its role toward Eastern Europe and the USSR. In the autumn of 1991, the dramatic events of the summer, including the failed coup in Moscow and the disintegration of the USSR (touched on in the conclusion to this volume), could only strengthen a tendency perceptible since the spring. As the Rome summit approached, Washington wanted to make the institutionalization of relations with the countries of Central and Eastern Europe, which were themselves now very insistent about their relations with NATO, a major subject of the summit, despite French objections.[166] In this context, in the autumn of 1991 the Élysée tried for a balance: on the one hand, noted Védrine, it was difficult to oppose those countries' desire for rapprochement, which was supported by the United States, but on the other, one had to prevent NATO from 'obtaining a monopoly on the problems of security in Europe'.[167] As Rome approached, the French position (relative openness over relations with Eastern countries, combined with insistence on the development in parallel of the CSCE) was rather welcomed in Washington.[168] Manifestly, the Élysée also wanted to avoid a quarrel with the United States on this point in order to 'concentrate on the essential', namely Washington's acceptance of the prospect of European defense.[169] So without departing from its basic reservations about the alliance's politicization, the Élysée pragmatically acquiesced to a package of measures the allies would discuss with the 'Nine', meaning the former Warsaw Pact members and the three Baltic republics, on the occasion of the upcoming ministerial session at the end of December. The December meeting would in fact ratify the creation of a 'North Atlantic Cooperation Council' (NACC), combining the Sixteen and the Nine.[170]

But a quarrel nevertheless could not be avoided in Rome. It crystallized over the draft declaration on the evolution of the situation in the USSR that Washington, acting on an idea from Baker, submitted to the allies three days before the summit. Its purpose was to define 'criteria for the use of protagonists in the institutional debate between the center and the [Soviet] republics' after the Moscow coup attempt, whether over human rights, democracy, respect for international commitments made by the USSR or the devolution of the Soviet nuclear arsenal (which was the most sensitive issue with Soviet decomposition in the background).[171] If the Élysée was not fundamentally in disagreement with the substance of the text, in particular its political and strategic aspects, Mitterrand unsurprisingly voiced reservations about both the procedure and the tone. He regretted that the Baker document was submitted barely forty-eight hours before the summit, and he observed that 'it is not up to NATO to define all the aspects of Soviet policy', disapproving particularly of admonitions in the document about adopting a market economy and Western values.[172] Thus the London scenario was replayed: on the first day, debates on the strategic concept and on relations with the East unfolded without problem, but the clash took place on the second day, when the French obtained virtually no amendment of the draft declaration, which was fiercely defended by Baker. Mitterrand took exception to the declaration in the plenary session, making gibes at a text 'falling from heaven at the last minute' and 'its preaching tone'.[173] After the summit, the president summarized for the press his viewpoint on NATO's evolution and its 'new political mission', which he stressed 'needs to be clarified': 'The Alliance is good', he recognized, 'but it is not the Holy Alliance'.[174]

As in London the previous year, the incident, although motivated by a specific issue, illustrated a more general French malaise about the evolution of the Atlantic Alliance: far from being limited to its role as last resort against an otherwise diminishing threat, as the French had anticipated, the alliance, under the leadership of a United States resolved to remain a 'European power', was emerging in the immediate post–Cold War period as the pivot of European security. (Among other undesirable effects this tendency contained an explicit threat to Mitterrand's plan for a European Confederation, as will be seen in the following paragraph.) While Mitterrand's diplomacy had to accommodate itself to some extent to this evolution, it did lead to a durable maintenance of the French 'difference' within the Atlantic ensemble: at the Rome summit, Mitterrand unmistakably reaffirmed the thirty-year logic of relations between France and NATO, simultaneously advancing 'military and strategic solidarity' while staying 'outside the integrated command', and refusing an enlargement of the geographic field and missions of the alliance.[175] In this sense, overall the year 1991 had been one of missed rendezvous.

The Failure of the European Confederation

The year 1991 would also feature a lost opportunity: the idea of a European Confederation was launched on 31 December 1989, and its failure was consummated eighteen months later. 'This idea, launched too early and without preparation, was still-born', Védrine summarized in his memoirs, where he passes over the subject rapidly.[176] Although the project, as seen above, had been announced by Mitterrand on the occasion of his address to the French people on New Year's Eve 1990 to the great surprise of his entourage, the astonishment had more to do with the choice of moment and language. The president had not consulted his advisers beforehand, and the notion of a confederation appeared somewhat ill-defined and rather vague. Still, the idea was in line with the preoccupations of Mitterrand's diplomacy for the past months and even years, which the acceleration of autumn 1989 had brought to the fore.[177] First and foremost, the purpose was to preserve the Community from the risk of dilution that would be implied by a premature enlargement, while offering all the new democracies of Central and Eastern Europe, whose membership in the EEC was considered out of the question for the time being, a European perspective that would contribute to their stability. It was also a matter of fostering the reemergence of a 'greater Europe' that would be reconciled and freed of its dependence on the United States and the Soviet Union, while assuring the latter an anchoring in Europe. The confederation, in other words, was inseparable from the Western European priority of French diplomacy and, as a corollary, of its pan-European preoccupations, which remained in line with the Gaullist concept of a Europe 'from the Atlantic to the Urals'. It was in this double direction that Mitterrand's collaborators turned in their first commentaries on the plan. Because it amounted to an 'alternative to EC membership', for which the Élysée had been seeking a formula since the new candidates (notably Austria) had applied at the start of 1989, 'the Confederation offers a chance to avoid the dilution of the Community', said Guigou, stressing that it would also have 'the immense advantage of making visible the possibility of intermediate formulas between EC membership and the current situation'. With regard to the role of the superpowers, Guigou distinguished between the proposal's political and military aspects, in which she underlined that 'it is not possible to exclude the United States', and 'economic, technological, and ecological domains', in which it would be suitable to 'hold the U.S. at a distance'. As for the Soviet Union, it could not integrate itself in these latter aspects for a long time, but its involvement in the confederation project was vital to assure its adherence to the changes underway in Europe.[178] Far from marking a new orientation, the idea of a confederation thus belonged to an already well-established train of thought.

However, from the start the confederation posed more questions than it provided answers. Having received many reactions from journalists, diplomats and other French and foreign personalities, Védrine reported on 8 January 1990 that while the idea was 'unanimously understood and approved', it also raised questions: why include from the start a USSR still far from having achieved its democratic cast? And why exclude the United States, which had decided to remain a European power at all costs, and thus risk a confrontation with Washington? What would be the powers of the confederation, and how would it function? More importantly, how would it interact with existing organizations, starting with the Community, which was already engaged in a policy of active cooperation with the countries of the East, and with the CSCE, which was particularly designed to deal with security and in which the United States and Canada participated?[179] These questions would constantly crop up during the following eighteen months and inhibit the plan's progress.

In fact, very early on, those responsible for French diplomacy were sensitive to the difficulties of the project, which meant it became for the most part defined in negative terms. Enumerating the potential problems, Guigou stressed that it would 'be dangerous to fix too quickly the structures of the Confederation' and above all that it would be necessary quickly to discern 'what we should *not* do'. 'After an evaluation of the pitfalls to be avoided', she argued, 'it will be easier to find positive proposals about what it is possible to do'.[180] The Quai d'Orsay was just as cautious, if not frankly skeptical. Hazarding an exegesis of Mitterrand's proposal, the director of political affairs, Dufourcq, noted the traps: "There are many questions to be explored, not with a view to taking public positions, but for ourselves: unless we want to risk being attacked on all sides, it seems we have no interest in being too precise too soon about what we mean by a Confederation', he emphasized, knowing, however, that one had to be clear enough about the project in the hope 'that the coming international events do not in any way compromise our project, but instead foster it'.[181] As we see, French diplomacy was aware of its rather narrow margin of maneuver and consequently of the need for a cautious approach.

Mitterrand had decided to advance nevertheless. In the first months of 1990, he promoted his idea, notably with the leaders of the countries of Central and Eastern Europe. During his visit to Hungary in mid January, which had been scheduled as part of the relaunch of the Eastern policy dating back to 1988, he underlined that the European Community could not 'extend itself indefinitely to all countries' and stressed to Mathias Szuros, then the interim Hungarian head of state, that 'the other countries of Europe need to establish an organic contact with Western Europe, as we also have to do with Eastern Europe'.[182] He made the same defense and illustration of his idea to the Polish leaders who came to the Élysée on 9 March. Although the discussion, as we have seen, centered on the German question and the Oder-Neisse problem, Mitterrand took the opportunity to mention his desire for, once the 'structures of the Twelve' were strengthened, a 'Confederation that would be endowed with a permanent structure'.[183] And ten days later with Vaclav Havel, now president of Czechoslovakia, Mitterrand clearly declared, while pleading in favor of Eastern Europe's adopting a 'synthesis' between the market economy and socialism (undoubtedly a conviction that partly motivated his plan), that 'you cannot enter the EEC now, for it has very strict rules and there are prior candidates', hence evoking a need to create the European Confederation. 'We are close in our thinking', Havel answered.[184]

In the spring of 1990, things were going well. 'Your project for a European Confederation has been well received in the countries of Central and Eastern Europe', Margerie said in a note to Mitterrand at the start of April. Yet the context in the coming months did not lend itself to the successful launch of the plan: the Western European agenda was largely devoted to the Community recasting pushed by Paris and Bonn, the German unity question focused the international agenda until the end of the summer and the pan-European agenda was dominated by the CSCE summit until the autumn. The latter, as we have seen, could only interfere with the confederation plan: while the confederation was distinct from the CSCE 'in both its composition and its political aim', the Paris summit 'has taken over the whole year's calendar', noted Margerie, concluding that 'it would instead be in 1991' that the confederation project might be launched successfully.[185] For all these reasons, it was only in the autumn of 1990 that things started to move, a delay that, along with the rapid changes in the East taking place in the background, no doubt contributed to stalling the project. Whatever the case, Mitterrand seized the opportunity of a visit to Czechoslovakia in mid September to propose to Havel holding in 1991 in Prague the 'Assises' (the inaugural meeting) of the confederation, gathering together persons from the political world and civil society of Europe as a whole in order to initiate the project (Mitterrand was thinking along the lines of the Hague Congress of 1948, in which he had participated and which was a model for him).[186] He was more than ever persuaded of the need for it once the page was turned on German unification in the fall of 1990: the confederation, he told a dozen personalities gathered at the Élysée to discuss the future of European architecture on the eve of the CSCE summit, was about 'averting the risks of dislocating the continent'.[187]

The Prefiguration of the Confederation

To design the confederation and launch the process that would result in the Assises, Mitterrand designated a diplomat familiar to the Élysée, now a member of the Conseil d'Etat, Jean Musitelli.[188] Starting at the end of 1990, Musitelli led the study for the proposed concrete content of the plan at the Quai d'Orsay, where he was named advisor to Dumas while also reporting to the Élysée; he would be helped by a young diplomat named Roland Galharague. Their study quickly took an interministerial direction due to the technical nature of the subjects treated. The base of the confederation would indeed consist of concrete cooperation between the European Community and Eastern Europe, hence the role of the SGCI (the French government's interministerial coordinating committee on European affairs) in trying to identify priority areas. They also used outside experts like the geographer Michel Foucher, an academic who had done work at the Elysée. On the political level, Guigou, now minister for European affairs, was of course personally involved in the process.[189] In parallel, Musitelli kept in liaison with the Czechs to prepare the Assises. At the end of January 1991, he went to Prague for initial discussions, which enabled him to present the state of French thinking and to outline the main features of the meeting, scheduled for mid June in the Czech capital. Reporting on his mission to Dumas, he said he found the Czechs 'very receptive to our proposals' and 'manifestly flattered to co-sponsor with France an operation of this scope ... The mechanics of preparing the *Assises* are thus launched on the basis of very close Franco-Czech cooperation, about which we can congratulate ourselves'.[190]

Yet when the substantive thinking started in the last weeks of 1990, things were scarcely more advanced than after Mitterrand's announcement of his idea almost a year before. In confiding the mission to Musitelli, the president had given him no particular instructions, and so first Musitelli had to establish a sort of 'doctrine' for the confederation.[191] His method was to rely on Mitterrand's and Dumas's declarations and use them 'to trace the contours' of the project: the confederation would be an 'organization of a legal nature' that 'would not imply transfers of sovereignty', but whose purpose would be 'the coordination of national policies in certain areas', and it would be 'lightly structured'. It would be open to all European democratic countries that respected the rule of law – but without this criterion being too strictly applied, the objective being precisely to 'strengthen the democratic evolution across the whole Continent' (the USSR, in other words, should not be a priori excluded). The confederation's powers would be both political, including consultation and coordination among member states, and technical, with various fields of cooperation being 'identified and gradually developed', such as the environment, energy and transportation, all of 'variable geometry,' meaning that some areas would not necessarily be open to all participating countries.[192]

Things went quickly in the first weeks of 1991. By the end of January, those responsible for French diplomacy had a working calendar until the Prague Assises and an overall concept of what the confederation might be.[193] 'Offering Europeans a framework in which to discuss among themselves, on perfectly equal footing, the affairs that concern them', in order to 'bind' Central and Eastern European countries to Western Europe, to help them fight against their centrifugal tendencies and to create 'a zone of European prosperity': these were the goals of a project that Mitterrand's diplomacy intended to inscribe within a 'rather loose' institutional structure, in contrast with the Community, but nevertheless as part of an 'ambitious' political concept and at the same time as stemming 'from concrete achievements.'[194] Overall, while nourishing the political ambition to organize a 'Greater Europe' that would be a 'European Europe', it was a matter of 'creating bridges' between East and West in the principal sectors of activity, which would amount, in some fashion, to 'piloting a policy of territorial planning at the level of the Continent'.[195]

While working on the 'supply', French leaders did not lose sight of the 'demand'. From the start of their thinking about the Confederation program at the end of 1990, the Quai d'Orsay wanted to know the reactions of all European countries, which the French embassies were asked to collect.[196] By this means, the promoters of the project were from the start aware of the questions that the confederation might raise – which they had in fact anticipated a year earlier. As privileged partners of French diplomacy in this affair, the Czechs themselves put forward their own questions, echoing those posed in Eastern Europe. While they had 'no reservation about the validity and urgency of the Confederation', reported Musitelli on his return from Prague at the end of January 1991, 'they wonder about future relations with the United States, about the place that the USSR will occupy, and about the Confederation's intersection with the Community'.[197] These, in fact, were the three obstacles that the project would encounter in the coming months.

At the start of 1991, however, these issues did not appear crippling, and conceivers of the confederation tried to answer them with targeted lines of argument. First, on U.S. non-participation: the French stressed that the project was in line with U.S. objectives to offer a Western anchor and prevent the crumbling of Central and Eastern European countries after the disintegration of the Communist bloc. It was a legitimate ambition: the European Community, they argued, needed to be able to organize the European space as the United States was trying to do in its own zone with Canada and Mexico. In any case, the confederation project did not challenge the U.S.'s 'fundamental' contribution to European security, which would remain assured by the Atlantic Alliance as well as by the CSCE.[198] Then on Soviet participation: inclusion of the USSR in the project, they argued, was necessary: to exclude it would provoke its 'keen resentment', whereas to include it would attenuate the risks of implosion that would otherwise mark its probable breakup. This was also a legitimate objective: while the USSR was not yet a democratic state, its belonging to Europe was the best way to foster its democratization, and Soviet participation would not pose a serious risk for European equilibrium. Furthermore, its inclusion in the economic realms would be under a variable geometry, corresponding to the state of its economic evolution, and in any case, the U.S. presence in security bodies would continue to counterbalance Soviet military power in Europe.

As for the European Community, French leaders tried to forestall the objection – no doubt the most serious – that the confederation was conceived either as a 'substitute' or an 'ante-chamber' for membership in the EC. Itself founded on the basis of 'extremely constraining' economic lines and currently engaged in a 'profound recasting' with the ongoing IGCs, the European Community, they insisted, 'could not respond immediately' to the needs of the countries of Central and Eastern Europe. While waiting for their eventual integration among its member states, the confederation was therefore 'a pan-European pragmatic response founded on an ambitious political objective', namely to 'group together right now on an equal footing all the European countries' thanks to 'concrete cooperation' developed in a 'flexible institutional form'.[199] Finally, French leaders answered the objection that the confederation would be redundant in relation to the existing pan-European institutions, notably the Council of Europe and especially the CSCE: the Quai d'Orsay stressed that the CSCE, as an interstate institution whose vocation related mostly to security, would not be in competition with a confederation that primarily responded to a need for cooperation by means of concrete projects conducted in variable geometry in accordance with a rationale of 'solidarity'.[200]

The Difficult Spring of the Confederation

By integrating these lines of argument into their project, the promoters of the confederation hoped to defuse incipient objections. In the spring of 1991, the moment of truth was approaching as the project entered its 'diplomatic' phase. While preparing for the Prague Assises, French diplomacy wanted to start discussion with other governments: this was the goal of a memorandum sent by Dumas in mid April to all his European homologues. This ten-page document summarized French thinking. The confederation, it explained, would respond to a 'historic necessity': to assemble a Europe 'finding itself again', thanks to the end of the Cold War, around 'concrete achievements', allowing it to weave 'a de facto solidarity' (recalling the vocabulary of the Schuman plan declaration establishing the Coal and Steel Community of 1950) and 'to escape the risk of atomization and insularity. The confederation, it added, would have to 'find its place in the constellation of European organizations' alongside the European Community, which should be strengthened but to which the confederation was not an 'alternative', the CSCE, whose role would 'be in no way effaced' and the Council of Europe, as well as the EBRD and the 'Pleiades of bodies' that, like Eureka or the European Environmental Agency, were 'so many designated partners of the future Confederation'.

Combining from its start 'the maximum efficiency with the minimum of bureaucratic structures', its functioning would be situated at three levels, whose coherence would be guaranteed by a network of personal representatives of the heads of state and governments. At the level of 'political coordination', the heads of state and government would meet in alternation with the CSCE summit, with meetings of foreign affairs ministers held in between, to decide policy. At the level of 'operational decision-making', relevant ministers of the concerned countries would define concrete actions as a function of policy directives. Finally, at the level of 'project management', the implementation of plans would be effected by existing bodies or entrusted to ad hoc ones as the case may be. These projects would be propelled and supervised according to a 'pragmatic method' privileging domains of intervention like energy, the environment, transportation, the circulation of people and the cultural dimension. The document concluded on an optimistic note: 'The confederal spirit already exists, even before being embodied in political structures. It is only a matter of encouraging the movement.'[201]

Yet things would prove more difficult in practice. As the French became more specific about their ideas, the questions gave way to real reservations. Now the Czechs made their worry quite apparent. Sensitive to objections that might harm the plan, Havel, the French ambassador in Prague reported as early as February, 'hesitates to commit his credibility' to an enterprise 'that might risk his being blamed by his other partners'.[202] The malaise was confirmed in the following weeks, with the Czechs proposing to invite some American and Canadian figures to the Assises – an idea that a priori did not please the French – and stressing that 'it would be difficult in Prague to accept that the USSR be part of discussions while the United States was excluded'.[203] This question of whom to invite to the Prague inaugural meeting, which related to the issue of the contours of the future confederation, was in the foreground of conversations between Mitterrand and Havel at the Élysée on 23 March: 'The presence of the USSR bothers the Czechs', stressed Margerie, with Havel being 'very insistent' about an eventual U.S. participation in the Assises.²⁰⁴ In fact, the conversation displayed a much less close understanding than that reached during Mitterrand's visit to Prague six months previously. While taking into account his interlocutor's worries, the French president reiterated his arguments in favor of the confederation: membership in the Community, he repeated, 'would take time'. But the Czech did not conceal his reservations: the confederation, he said, must not lead to making the Central and Eastern European countries 'second rank' countries, nor 'harm existing institutions'. And Havel explained his worries over the future of the United States' presence in Europe to Mitterrand, who finally dropped his objection to U.S. participation in the Assises.²⁰⁵ Prague's reaction to the project was 'more reserved than a year ago', the Czech press confirmed after the meeting.²⁰⁶

The Czech attitude, in fact, was in unison with the current state of mind in most Central and Eastern European countries. With the exclusion of the United States and the participation of the USSR – the latter causing fear due to both its mass and its probable disintegration – coming on top of the worry about the confederation serving as a brake on Community membership and the risk of duplicating other European organizations, these and all the 'list of objections being expressed and the questions raised' now appeared very clearly.²⁰⁷ As the spring of 1991 started, Mitterrand's diplomacy had to bow to the evidence, as Dumas summarized at the end of March to the French ambassadors to Central and Eastern Europe gathered at the Quai d'Orsay: one had gone 'from the stage of questions to one of suspicions, then to one of fear'; hence a need to explain things.²⁰⁸ This realization took place against the mixed result of the restart of French policy initiatives to the East decreed in 1988: in this sense, the confederation's difficulties marked the limits of French influence in Central and Eastern Europe despite the efforts of the past three years.²⁰⁹ More fundamentally, it was a reflection of the profound transformation of the Eastern bloc's political, strategic and also psychological situation eighteen months after the revolutions of the autumn of 1989. There was a paradox: while the Warsaw Pact was moribund (its military structure was dissolved in February and the Pact was officially ended on 1 July 1991), the USSR no longer appeared menacing; meanwhile the process of conventional disarmament should also reassure Central and Eastern European countries. Yet Védrine noted that these countries still felt a 'diffuse sentiment of insecurity' that pushed some of them toward Western institutions, starting with the Atlantic Alliance. Mitterrand's advisor judged that 'much more than a need for protections against hypothetical threats', this movement expressed 'an impatient desire to integrate into Europe and the Western world'. This movement was clear among the Czechoslovaks and the Poles, who were asking for close relations with NATO, where Havel had been received at the end of March. The Atlantic organization, Védrine noted, was tempted to encourage the rapprochement of the former Soviet bloc countries, under American pressure.[210] If these new tendencies did not invalidate the project from the viewpoint of its French creators – if only because the confederation did not relate to security in their eyes – they did constitute an obstacle whose size the French had underestimated. Indeed, this strong demand for Western institutions, against the background of a security vacuum (real or imagined), could only bring these countries to hesitate over anything that might delay their membership in (or, from their standpoint, their return to) the West. The confederation would pay the cost of this quick evolution of the mentality in Central and Eastern Europe.

Another difficulty was a deficit in the Franco-German entente over this issue. True, Kohl had endorsed the idea of the confederation in his conversations with Mitterrand, and the declaration adopted at the Munich summit (17–18 September 1990) noted their joint determination to act in this direction.[211] Moreover, when Mitterrand's diplomacy launched into the project in 1991, Bonn said it was disposed to bilateral cooperation and Dufourcq agreed with Kastrup on the idea of designating a German equivalent to Musitelli.[212] Even if the Germans strongly insisted on the need to avoid any 'transatlantic exclusion' and echoed U.S. concerns in this respect, the presentation by Musitelli of the French blueprint in Bonn on 5 March was rather well received, with the Auswärtiges Amt even proposing setting up a Franco-German working group to plan the Assises.[213] Yet this cooperation would not see the light of day, a factor that counted for a lot in the failure of the plan some weeks later. Taking the risk of 'vexing' the Germans and seeing them show a visible 'tepidness', the French were in fact scarcely inclined to associate them closely with the launch of the plan: Paris feared that the confederation, as formerly the common Franco-German Ostpolitik that had not been followed up, would be transformed into a simple French 'endorsement' of German ambitions in Central and Eastern Europe.[214]

German 'tepidness' became still more apparent in the following weeks, with Bonn expressing 'questions' and even 'worries', as Margerie signaled at the end of April.[215] The meeting between the French and German ambassadors to Central and Eastern Europe on 16 and 17 May 1991 in Weimar demonstrated these German reservations, which were particularly clear on Genscher's part. Bonn diplomacy no longer concealed its lack of enthusiasm about a project that less and less satisfied Central and Eastern European countries, starting with Poland, Hungary and Czechoslovakia. Instead, the Germans now openly supported their wish to belong as soon as possible to the Community itself, and Bonn noted as well that the project more and more displeased the United States. In addition, the confederation competed with Bonn's own pan-European ambitions, in which Genscher clearly privileged the CSCE, whose ministers of foreign affairs were to meet in Berlin barely a few days after the Prague Assises, a meeting that he wanted to make a success. As a corollary, Germany remained loyal to the Atlantic Alliance, for which Genscher envisaged, with Baker, a greater political role toward Central and Eastern Europe, as advanced in their joint declaration adopted on 10 May.[216] Before the Lille summit, the Élysée could not help realizing that a 'serious difference' existed between France and Germany over the European Confederation. Mitterrand's diplomatic advisor deplored German 'demagoguery' with respect to Central and Eastern European countries, whom they left hoping for rapid membership in the Community, while giving the French the 'spoiler role'. All this, Morel noted, made the objective of a common policy toward the East difficult to attain.[217] At the end of spring 1991, as already seen, this 'serious difference' fed French doubts about the solidity of the FRG's Western European commitment in its entirety.

The U.S. factor was obviously also present in the background of difficulties the French encountered over the Confederation affair in the spring of 1991. Because it excluded the United States, the project was fatally perceived by the Americans as contrary to their staunch determination to preserve their engagement in Europe after the Cold War. Since the first weeks of 1990, the Élysée had expected an American campaign to turn the new Eastern European democracies away from the project.[218] This fear was realized a year later when the plan was really launched: recognizing that 'the plan for a European Confederation can only *a priori* indispose the United States', the Quai d'Orsay noted that Washington 'had already manifested its bad humor by decrying the project to certain countries of Eastern Europe'.[219] Of course, the French objected that American participation in European security would not be questioned despite the United States' non-participation in the confederation, since the project did not concern security problems *stricto sensu*, but this objection, as seen from Washington, was unacceptable. Unsurprisingly, the Americans let it be known that they would not accept 'being used by the Europeans for security and held apart from other domains'.[220] The confederation, therefore, did not escape that 'American offensive on a grand scale' that Mitterrand had denounced in mid June: against the background of the great debate on the respective future roles of the European Union and the Atlantic Alliance in the Old Continent's security, the Americans saw the planned confederation as emblematic of a vision that tended to exclude them. It was in this context that Baker, as we have seen, pronounced his second Berlin speech on 18 June 1991, a speech that could only be interpreted by the French as a counterblast to the very idea of a confederation: it expressed, thought the Quai d'Orsay, a 'propensity towards global Atlantic hegemony' and a 'certain incapacity' to 'take the European fact into account'.[221] Ultimately only Moscow in the spring of 1991 actively supported the confederation project, one key objective of which was to preserve the European anchoring of the USSR – and its support was explained by the growing perception among the Soviet leaders of the urgency of getting external aid to enable reform in the USSR to succeed.[222]

The Prague Fiasco

As the Assises approached, French diplomacy was perfectly aware of the problems: the reactions were 'nuanced as a whole' but 'in some cases marked by some perplexity, if not skepticism', as the European office directorate at the Quai d'Orsay summarized the situation on the eve of the Prague meeting, with some understatement. There was a more pronounced interest in the confederation at the 'periphery' (the USSR and Balkans) than at the 'center' (Poland, Hungary, Czechoslovakia), French diplomats observed.[223] Deprived of real support in the West and afflicted by growing doubts that tempered interest in the East, was the confederation condemned in advance? More than ever convinced of its necessity, Mitterrand by no means gave up the idea, at least in the long term: 'We have to work on it keenly', he declared to the Hungarian Prime Minister Joszef Antall, advancing the risk of splintering due to reawakened nationalisms: 'We now live in an "explosive" Europe.'[224] The Élysée hoped the project would take off after the Prague meeting, hence suggestions were made by the entourage about announcements that Mitterrand might make in his speech. He might propose a new initiative in the sphere of civil society, perhaps the creation of a 'pan-European movement' – again a reference to 1948 and the 'European movement' created after the Hague Congress – or deliver a 'report on the state of Europe'. Or he might make a move toward governments, transmitting to them the results and proposals from the Assises, and inviting concerned ministers to make a quick study of concrete projects, or calling for yet another summit to really 'unleash' the confederal process.[225] But the Quai d'Orsay was more skeptical than ever about what could be expected from the Assises, even if they hoped to give the exercise 'high political visibility'.[226] In any case, the French leaders were aware that the future of the confederation would depend largely on the turn it took in Prague.

Mitterrand himself paradoxically contributed to the failure of the process. The very day the Assises opened, he gave an interview to Radio-France Internationale in which he did not conceal his deepest thoughts: while he fully recognized the vocation of the new democracies to one day enter the European Community ('I could not ask for more'), he stressed the danger, in the event of rapid enlargement, of seeing the Community transformed into a simple free trade zone, even as he repeated that the countries concerned were incapable of entering for the time being. The French president pleaded for a confederation in which they would feel 'at ease to discuss their interests with the countries of the West' as an 'intermediate' phase that might 'last decades and decades'. A blunder? Though he later acknowledged 'perhaps having put things a little crudely', Mitterrand defended himself by saying that his statement 'corresponded to reality'. But at the very least it was (as Musitelli would later concede) 'an unfortunate declaration' and it had an impact on the unfolding of the meeting, as shown by the speech Havel gave that very day to the 150 participants.[227]

The Czech president developed a prospective analysis that the Quai d'Orsay – choosing to emphasize the positive – judged 'very close to our views', at the end of which he stated that a confederated Europe with at least 'embryonic' institutions was 'reasonable, desirable, and even probable'. Yet he also somewhat dismissively characterized Mitterrand's project as 'a futurological vision', concluding that the confederation should in no way distend the transatlantic tie nor become a brake on, or a substitute for, the membership of the countries of Central and Eastern Europe in the European Community. As for the work of the participants, the Quai thought it was of 'a high standard' and demonstrated the urgency of the problems to be treated at a pan-European level in various domains of activity (energy, communication, environment, migrations, culture), but it also made apparent the weak attraction of the idea of institutionalizing the European Confederation. The Germans and Anglo-Saxons, French diplomats noted, thought the existing institutions were sufficient, and a majority of the other participants went no farther than the idea of a slender coordinating body to be headquartered in Prague. At the end of the Assises, the balance sheet for French diplomacy was thus mixed: it had certainly been the 'occasion for a fruitful debate' that had demonstrated the validity of the project, but it was now up to governments to 'materialize the unanimous hope in an eventual integration of our continent, whatever the denomination one gives to this project'.[228] This balance sheet was assimilated by Mitterrand on 14 June in a speech that was very low-key, giving the confederation a minimalist definition: 'What interests me is the content and I am even ready for that content to remain without a name,' he declared, recognizing that 'if, after a certain time, as brief as possible, all the democratic countries of Europe were able to belong to the Community and if the members of the Community were able to accept that too, then the problem would be solved.'[229]

The failure of the confederation did not appear evident immediately after the Assises. French diplomacy was at first tempted to focus on the positive aspects of the operation despite a skeptical press: 'We have to profit from the momentum to carry on the work', Musitelli reiterated a few days after Prague.[230] But Mitterrand had few illusions: while the debates had indisputably confirmed the functional necessity of the confederation, they had also illuminated the organic difficulties: the Assises had 'worked very well' on concrete subjects of cooperation because they were about 'precise things', he stressed to the Irish prime minister a few days later, but 'when one talks of institutions, the law professors take over ... and then!' he lamented, while recognizing at least implicitly that the chance of seeing the confederation emerge as an organization, even if minimally, was low. This verdict was quickly becoming inescapable. In the first days of July, Musitelli had to acknowledge that while the Assises had 'measured, lifesize, the impact of our ideas', they had also illuminated the obstacles, particularly the 'weakness of our support'. Only the USSR, Czechoslovakia and Poland, he noted, had mentioned the confederation during the CSCE meeting in Berlin a few days after Prague, and 'indifference' if not 'hostility' to the project was being relayed by the 'obstinate silence' of others: only fifteen countries had replied to the memorandum. More importantly, there was a 'mobilization of adversaries' of the project. Not content with launching the idea of a 'Euro-Atlantic community', the United States, he noted, was putting pressure on the countries of the East to 'keep quiet' about their support, while in Berlin the majority of participants had pronounced in favor of simply strengthening the second basket of the CSCE, which is 'the best way of emptying the Confederation of any substantive content'. Musitelli concluded that time was short if one wanted to 'capitalize' on the Prague achievement, all the more so since the Assises had not led to any 'framework' or 'working calendar'. Thus he proposed a rapid launch of 'practical actions', i.e. to pursue the strategy in the direction of civil society and to bring up concrete projects so as to engage in intergovernmental work while 'circumventing political obstacles', which implied avoiding giving the confederation an institutional 'visibility' 'that would make it from the start a stake in insoluble political and diplomatic conflicts'. He stressed that one had to put in place 'confederal coordination', for example in the form of a 'club of delegates for the Confederation' that might meet in Paris in the autumn to examine the 'follow-up' to Prague, which would enable 'occupying the terrain until the end of the year'.[231]

But even this modest program was not to succeed. Putting the accent on concrete aspects of the program, as suggested by the Quai d'Orsay so as to give 'visibility' to following up the confederal process, while 'leaving aside questions of principle' quickly led to an impasse. It became clear that 'numerous relevant projects' were already underway without it being possible to 'label them' a posteriori as part of the confederation.[232] More importantly, the prospect of even an embryonic institutionalization of the confederation appeared to be blocked. The Czechoslovakian attitude was typical: favorable at the end of the Assises to the installation in their capital of a very slight structure in the form of a 'center' or 'small secretariat' designed to assure the follow-up to the project – as Havel proposed to Mitterrand in a letter of 30 June – the Czechs retracted the offer shortly thereafter. Whereas by way of explanation they advanced their financial constraints and the fact that they already had to support the cost of a permanent secretariat of the CSCE whose creation had been decided at the Paris summit in November 1990, their wish now not to be in the front line was evident; the French ambassador in Prague noted that they clearly did not want to be implicated in a project that annoyed the Americans and divided the Europeans.[233] 'The Americans are conducting a campaign against the Confederation', Mitterrand said to Romanian Prime Minister Petre Roman, 'and the Czechs do not want to oppose them'.[234]

On 19 August he wrote a letter in reply to Havel's, underlining his worry about leaving the many ideas and proposals debated in Prague as a 'dead letter' and suggesting an informal meeting in the autumn of 'delegates' to the confederation that governments would designate. But evidently he had no illusions. On the same day, the attempted coup in Moscow (see the conclusion to this volume) placed the last nail in the coffin of the confederation. The climate changed radically, Musitelli later remembered: 'Everything stopped [then]. From then on the absolute priority was given to Maastricht and the Confederation was written off.'[235] A few weeks later, the Élysée had the feeling of a 'return of interest' in the project, but nothing came of it. Henceforward, French leaders saw the political need to 'grant each country of Central and Eastern Europe the right to belong to the Community when the time came' and observed that these countries were ready 'to live as "candidates"'. This amounted to admitting, if only implicitly, that the very concept of the confederation was outmoded – or at least that it would boil down to managing the transition of the new democracies to membership in the Community – a membership whose lengthy delay had been the goal from the start.[236]

In the autumn of 1991, the European Confederation was clinically dead. In many respects this was a foreseeable collapse: from the start, as we saw, its promoters were aware of its intrinsic difficulties. As these became apparent over months, they had brought the actors to deploy an inventive diplomacy but also to reduce the ambitions of the project. Therefore, the reasons for the collapse of the project were due less to diplomatic 'errors' properly speaking (even if there were some, like Mitterrand's interview on 12 June) than to the nonrealization – patent in the middle of 1991 – of the expectations that had initially motivated it. First, concerning the evolution in European security: far from the serene transition to democracy and prosperity that could still be hoped for a year previously, there was an accelerated return to instability, even the risk of breakup to the East, which the confederation was meant to prevent. Then there was the role of the superpowers in the European system: instead of the anticipated withdrawal of the United States after the Cold War, there was a strong U.S. reengagement on the Old Continent, and instead of the stabilization desired for a USSR that was supposed to remain a major element in the European equilibrium, there was a precipitate Soviet crumbling. And finally, there were the political choices and diplomatic orientations of the countries of Central and Eastern Europe: instead of the search for a sort of third ideological and geopolitical way after the failure of Communism, these countries felt the irresistible attraction exercised by Western institutions, starting with the European Community and the Atlantic Alliance, and they desired (encouraged by some with a degree of demagoguery) to get close to these institutions as quickly as possible, instead of finding themselves waiting in a fragile and uncertain pan-European organization.

As the summits of Rome and Maastricht approached, with the dislocation of the USSR and the start of war in Yugoslavia in the background, these realities definitively condemned a project whose content – East-West cooperation to effect the reunification of the continent – had been scarcely disputed, but whose container, a new pan-European institution, no longer appeared essential. It was instead flatly rejected. In this sense, what was demonstrated more than the collapse of the project itself was the partial – and at least temporary – failure of Mitterrand's vision of the European order to which it belonged, a vision much in line with the Gaullist one of a 'European' Europe. French diplomacy rapidly turned the page on the failure of the confederation, which the success of Maastricht at the end of the year would somewhat attenuate, confirming France's Western European priority. But this failure would nevertheless give credence – no doubt unjustly – to the image of a policy that had not been able to react adequately when faced with the acceleration of events in Central and Eastern Europe. This is an image that Mitterrand's attitude during the last months of the USSR – from the attempted coup in Moscow in August to the implosion of the Soviet Union in December – also abetted.

Notes

1. Speech delivered during the formal session of the Czechoslovak Federal Assembly, Prague, 13 September 1990.
2. Elisabeth Guigou, note pour le président de la République, Votre entretien avec le chancelier Kohl. Questions européennes, 17 September 1990; Meeting between Mitterrand

and Kohl, Munich, 17 September 1990; and Déclaration commune de M. le président de la République française et du chancelier fédéral de la République fédérale d'Allemagne, M. Helmut Kohl, à l'occasion des 56è consultations franco-allemandes, Munich, 17 et 18 septembre 1990, MAE, *Politique étrangère de la France. Textes et documents, (PEF)*, September–October 1990, pp. 70–72.

3. Guigou, note pour le président de la République, Votre entretien avec le chancelier Kohl. Questions européennes, 17 September 1990. On this point, see chapter 1 of this volume, p. 53.
4. Isabelle Bouillot, note pour Jean-Louis Bianco, Union économique et monétaire, 8 October 1990; and MAE, Pierre de Boissieu, note a.s. Conseil européen de Rome: UEM, 23 October 1990, private papers: 'We will not accept to make considerable "convergence" efforts to prepare ourselves … for the precarious or the eternal.'
5. See chapter 5 of this volume, p. 237ff.
6. Guigou, note pour le président de la République, Votre entretien avec le chancelier Kohl. Questions européennes, 17 September 1990.
7. For the rest, the Elysée conceded, measures in favor of a 'Europe of citizens' could be envisaged, a Spanish idea that Paris supported in order to rally Madrid to French conceptions: see Caroline de Margerie, note pour le président de la République, Conseil européen de Rome-Union politique, 26 October 1990; and schéma d'intervention, 26 October 1990, private papers.
8. Meeting between Mitterrand and Kohl, Munich, 17 September 1990; Meeting between Dumas and Genscher, Munich, 17 September 1990, private papers.
9. MAE, le directeur des affaires économiques et financières, note a.s. Union politique: réunion des ministres des Affaires étrangères à Asolo, 27 September 1990, private papers. On German European policies of the period, see Hans Stark, *Kohl, l'Allemagne et l'Europe. La Politique européenne de la République fédérale 1982–1998*, Paris, L'Harmattan, 2004, p. 179ff.
10. Guigou, note pour le président de la République, Union politique: préparation d'un document franco-allemand, 1 October 1990; and Margerie, note pour le président de la République, Union politique: préparation d'un document franco-allemand, 15 October 1990, private papers.
11. MAE, le directeur des affaires économiques et financières, note de Pierre de Boissieu, a.s. Conseil européen: Union politique: état des lieux, 24 October 1990, private papers.
12. Message commun du président de la République et du chancelier Kohl au président Andreotti sur l'union politique (Paris et Bonn, 6 décembre 1990), MAE, *PEF*, November–December 1990, pp. 90–91.
13. TD Bonn 3308, 18 December 1990, Archives diplomatiques (AD), série Affaires stratégiques et désarmement (ASD), 1985–1990, box 130 bis; and Margerie, note pour le président de la République, Entretien avec J. Bitterlich, 25 January 1991, AN, 5AG4/7009.
14. Margerie and Hubert Védrine, note pour le président de la République, a.s. Réactions à l'initiative que vous avez prise avec le chancelier Kohl sur l'Union politique, 10 December 1990, private papers ('up until now there has not been an American reaction', they noted, 'but we think that it would be desirable that between now and the opening of the IGC on the political union Roland Dumas enter into contact with Mr. Baker to explain to him what we have in mind regarding perspectives of a European defense and tell him again that all of this is compatible with the American desire to maintain NATO by adapting it'.)
15. Breakfast meeting between Mitterrand and Kohl, Rome, 15 December 1990, AN, 5AG4/CDM 33: 'Nothing remains of our letter' on the CFSP, Mitterrand lamented (indeed, the Twelve, in their recommendations to IGC negotiators, did not take up the key formula

of a 'clear organic relationship' between the political union and the WEU: see Conclusions de la présidence, Rome, 14 and 15 December 1990, in MAE, *PEF*, November–December 1990, pp. 113–121).
16. Margerie, note pour le président de la République, Entretien avec J. Bitterlich, 25 January 1991; Margerie and Védrine, note pour le président de la République, a.s. Suite de votre initiative de décembre avec le chancelier Kohl sur l'Union politique, 31 January 1991; and proposition franco-allemande sur la politique de sécurité commune, Bruxelles, 4 February 1991, private papers.
17. Margerie, note a.s. Votre entretien avec le chancelier Kohl. Union politique et union économique et monétaire, 15 February 1991; Margerie, note a.s. Votre entretien avec le président von Weizsäcker (jeudi 21 mars à 13h). Questions européennes, 21 March 1991, AN, 5AGA/CDM 33; Meeting between Mitterrand and Claudio Martelli, 19 February1991; Meeting between Dumas and Genscher, 21 March 1991, private papers.
18. Communiqué conjoint franco-allemand, Paris, Bonn, 22 mars 1991, *PEF*, March–April 1991, p. 66; *Le Monde*, 28 March 1991.
19. Margerie and Védrine, note a.s. Union politique-Politique étrangère et de sécurité commune, 12 April 1991, private papers.
20. Margerie, note pour le président de la République, Votre entretien avec le chancelier Kohl: Conférences sur l'Union politique et sur l'Union économique et monétaire, 24 April 1991, private papers.
21. On all this, see John Major, *The Autobiography*, London, Harper & Collins, 1999, p. 264ff.
22. Lunch Meeting between Mitterrand and Major, 14 January 1991, private papers.
23. Margerie, note pour le président de la République, Relations germano-britanniques-Questions européennes-Entretiens entre MM. Kohl et Major du 11 mars, 18 March 1990, private papers. (During the first months of the year, London also clouded the issue of EMU by emphasizing the concept of a '*common* currency', an idea that could obviously seduce those who wished to slow if not foil the adoption of a *single* currency; hence Mitterrand's reluctance: see Réunion sur le projet français de traité sur l'union économique et monétaire chez le président de la République le 26 janvier 1991, private papers.)
24. Lunch meeting between Mitterrand and von Weizsäcker, 21 March 1991, AN 5AG4/CDM 33.
25. Lunch meeting between Mitterrand and Lubbers, 16 May 1991; Hubert Védrine, note pour le président de la République, a.s. Déjeuner avec M. Lubbers, 16 May 1991, private papers.
26. On all this, see Robert L. Hutchings, *American Diplomacy and the End of the Cold War: An Insider's Account of U.S. Policy in Europe, 1989–1992*, Washington, Woodrow Wilson Center Press, 1997, p. 158ff.
27. Letter from Baker to Dumas, 26 October 1990; MAE, fiche, a.s. Déclaration sur les relations CE-Etats-Unis, 7 November 1990; TD Diplomatie 26416, 15 December 1990; and MAE, le directeur des affaires politiques, note de B. Dufourcq pour B. Kessedjian, a.s. Message Baker à propos de la déclaration euro-américaine, 24 December 1990, AD, série Directeur politique (DP), box 289.
28. TD Washington 2915, 6 December 1990, AD, ASD 1985–1990, box 130 bis.
29. On all this, see Hutchings, *American Diplomacy*, p. 273ff.
30. TD Washington 458, 20 February 1991, AD, ASD 1991–1994, OTAN 5.0. If the effects of this approach were perhaps stronger than intended by Bartholomew and his assistant, James Dobbins, it nonetheless did reflect the staunch rejection of European projects by the State Department bureaucracy, by contrast with a seemingly more forthcoming White House; personal interview.

31. Védrine and Admiral Jacques Lanxade, note pour le président, 11 March 1991, private papers.
32. The meetings began with an assessment of the Gulf crisis. As Mitterrand evoked a 'euphoric period of friendship between our two countries' in the wake of the crisis, Bush expressed his 'satisfaction' and thanked him for this 'total camaraderie'. 'I told you from the beginning that we would be with you', emphasized Mitterrand, regretting in passing that 'later on, some doubted France's position' – an allusion to the suspicions that certain French gestures had sparked in Washington, particularly in the Department of State, especially Mitterrand's last ditch-effort in January to find a pacific solution just a few days away from the ultimatum: see Meeting between Mitterrand and Bush, Martinique, 14 March 1991, private papers. If he deplored that the 'bureaucracies' did complicate things, Bush would later confirm this judgment: 'At our level ... François was always there and we always stood together': George Bush and Brent Scowcroft, *A World Transformed*, New York, Vintage 1998, p. 339. These difficulties between 'bureaucracies' are confirmed by Baker, who in his memoirs does not dissimulate the poor quality of the relations between the Department of State and the Quai d'Orsay and his personal relations with Dumas in this period: see James A. Baker III and Thomas M. DeFrank, *The Politics of Diplomacy: Revolution, War and Peace 1989–1992*, New York, Putnam, 1995, namely p. 314ff.
33. Meeting between Mitterrand and Bush, Martinique, 14 March 1991, second part, private papers.
34. Meeting between Mitterrand and von Weizsäcker, 21 March 1991, AN 5AG4/CDM 33; Mitterrand-Andreotti Dinner, Friday 22 March 1991, 8 p.m., private papers; Meeting between Mitterrand and Lubbers, 16 May 1991, private papers.
35. MAE, sous-direction Amérique du Nord, note, a.s. entretien de M. le président de la République avec M. Richard Cheney, secrétaire à la défense des Etats-Unis (lundi 27 mai 1991 a 17h), 24 May 1991, private papers.
36. Conseil des ministres, 12 June 1991, private papers.
37. TD Bonn 1123, 13 May 1991; and TD Washington 1234, 22 May 1991, private papers; details in Hutchings, *American Diplomacy*, p. 289ff.
38. Note pour le président de la République, Votre entretien avec le chancelier Kohl: la Confédération, 28 May 1991, private papers.
39. TD Bonn 1202, 16 May 1991, private papers.
40. Meeting between Mitterrand and Kohl, Lille, 29 May 1991, AN 5AG4/CDM 33.
41. Note pour le président de la République, Vos entretiens avec le chancelier Kohl et M. Santer (mardi 25 juin à 9h et à 11h), 24 June 1991, private papers.
42. Note pour le président de la République, Entretien à la Chancellerie à Bonn, vendredi 17 mai 1991, 22 May 1991, AN, 5AG3/CDM 33; and Note pour le président de la République, Votre entretien avec le chancelier Kohl: les CIG sur l'union politique et sur l'union économique et monétaire, 28 May 1991, private papers.
43. Note pour le président de la République, Préparation du Conseil européen de Luxembourg, Réunion du mercredi 19, à l'issue du Conseil des ministres, 18 June 1991, private papers.
44. Conseil restreint de préparation au Conseil européen de Luxembourg, mercredi 19 June, 11h30, private papers.
45. Le ministre délégué chargé des affaires européennes, Elisabeth Guigou, Note pour le président de la République, Votre entretien avec le chancelier Kohl le 25 juin, 24 June 1991, private papers.
46. Breakfast meeting between Mitterrand and Kohl, Lille, 30 May 1991, AN, 5AG4/CDM 33.

47. Breakfast meeting between Mitterrand and Kohl, 25 June 1991, AN, 5AG4/CDM 33.
48. Margerie, note pour le président de la République, Traité d'union politique. Politique étrangère et de sécurité commune, 19 July 1991 (it should be noted that the Elysée had a small divergence with Bonn's institutional proposals: Védrine judged the German project to transfer the WEU council to Brussels in order to facilitate consultations with NATO 'not urgent', which reflected a French conception of European autonomy from NATO that was more ambitious than the German one); see also Pierre Morel, note pour le président de la République, Sécurité de l'Europe: propositions allemandes (rencontre avec le chancelier Kohl le 23 juillet), 20 July 1991, private papers. The idea of what in autumn would become the European army corps seems to have simultaneously appeared in Bonn and Paris, but with distinct motivations: to legitimize the maintenance of the French forces in Germany on the German side, and to respond to NATO's military reform on the French side, where the Franco-German corps was presented by its author as a 'counter-proposition' to the RRF: see général Quesnot, note à l'attention de M. le président de la République (sous couvert de M. le Secrétaire général), Projet d'un nouveau dispositif militaire de l'OTAN et conséquences sur l'émergence d'une identité européenne de sécurité et de défense, 11 June 1991, private papers. On the European corps, see Jean-Yves Haine, *L'Eurocorps et les identités européennes de défense. Du gage franco-allemand à la promesse européenne*, Documents du C2SD, no. 33, Paris, 2001.
49. Once the French president had one more time exposed his desire to implement an 'embryo' of a European defense that would not be harmful to NATO, his American counterpart did not hide his preventions: 'If Europe had another solution outside of NATO, U.S. public opinion would immediately withdraw its support of NATO and our maintenance in Europe': meeting between Mitterrand and Bush, Rambouillet, 14 July 1991, private papers.
50. Meeting between Mitterrand and Kohl, Bad Wiessee, 23 July 1991, private papers.
51. Morel, Compte rendu de la réunion du 24 août 1991 avec les collaborateurs du chancelier Kohl, 30 August 1991, AN 5AG4/CDM 33.
52. Védrine, note pour le président de la République, 18 September 1991, private papers.
53. Meeting between Mitterrand and Kohl, Bonn, 18 September 1991, AN, 5AG4/CDM 33.
54. Margerie, note pour le président de la République, Votre entretien avec le chancelier Kohl. Le traité d'union politique, 18 September 1991, private papers; *Le Monde*, 2 October 1991.
55. MAE, Direction d'Europe, note a.s. Visite du président de la République en RFA. Note de synthèse, 12 September 1991, private papers. The visit was considered a success: see *Le Monde*, 22–23 September 1991.
56. Letter from Major to Mitterrand, 1 August 1991, private papers. (At the summit of Dunkerque on 24 June, Mitterrand had not hidden the importance of Franco-British divergences on the political union and in particular on the CFSP: see Meeting between Mitterrand and Major, Dunkerque, Monday 24 June 1991, private papers.)
57. Margerie, note pour le président de la République, Votre entretien avec M. Major (mercredi 11 septembre à 19h), 10 September 1991, private papers.
58. Védrine, note pour le président de la République, 7 October 1991, private papers.
59. Anglo-Italian Declaration on security and defense in Europe, 4 October 1991, private papers. The text marked progress because it confirmed 'the perspective of a common defense policy' that the British had refused up to that point and recognized that the WEU, as a 'defense component of the Union', should 'take into account' the decisions of the European Council in the area of the CFSP. For the rest, however, the Atlantic tonality prevailed in the declaration, the WEU staying equidistant between the Union and the Alliance and the latter remaining 'the essential venue for the adoption of policies having an incidence on defense and security commitments'.

60. Védrine, handwritten note, 10 October 1991; Caroline de Margerie, handwritten note, 11 October 1991; Letter from Mitterrand and Kohl to Ruud Lubbers, 14 October 1991, private papers.
61. Wanted by Margerie, this announcement suggested that the French conception of a European force that would be a response to NATO military restructuring imposed itself over the German conception of a bi-national unit aiming to legitimize the maintenance of French forces in Germany. Indeed, whereas Paris and Bonn had theretofore discussed the possibility of a 'Franco-German corps destined to intervene primarily' in Central Europe 'in the NATO framework', a defense ministry official remarked, 'the five lines in the 14 October letter have upset this straightforward concept': 'it is now necessary to envisage a NATO role *and* a WEU role', the latter implying the possibility of a purely European action. See Ministère de la Défense, cabinet du ministre, note de Jean-Claude Mallet pour M. le ministre, Initiative franco-allemande, 25 October 1991, private papers.
62. Védrine, note pour le président de la République, 16 October 1991, private papers.
63. The Italian attitude was rather unclear: whereas De Michelis, who had co-signed the text with Hurd, believed that a 'convergence' existed between the two documents (see *Le Monde*, 18 October 1991), Andreotti did not dissimulate to Mitterrand his reservations while distancing himself from the Anglo-Italian initiative of which he said he had been informed at a very late time: see Meeting between Mitterrand and Andreotti, Viterbo, 17 October 1991, AN, 5AG4/CDM 33.
64. See Meeting between Dumas, Hurd, Pierre Joxe [French defense minister] and Tom King [UK defense minister], 13 October 1991, private papers.
65. Letter from Major to Mitterrand, 23 October 1991, private papers.
66. Letter from Scowcroft to Védrine, 14 October 1991, private papers.
67. On these aspects, see pp. 343–344.
68. Margerie, note pour le président de la République, Votre entretien avec le chancelier Kohl: les conférences gouvernementales, 14 November 1991, private papers.
69. Margerie, note pour le président de la République, Représentation allemande au parlement européen, 10 October 1991; and Philippe Bastelica, note pour le président de la République, Sommet franco-allemand de Bonn (14 et 15 novembre1991). Parlement européen, 14 November 1991, private papers. See also chapters 4 and 5 in this volume, pp. 184–185 and n. 76 and chapter 5, p. 237.
70. Meeting between Mitterrand and Kohl, Bonn, 14 November 1991, first part, AN 5AG4/CDM 33.
71. Meeting between Mitterrand and Kohl, Bonn, 14 November 1991, first part; Margerie, note pour le président de la République, Conseil européen de Maastricht. Demandes allemandes, 21 November 1991, private papers; see also Pierre Favier and Michel Martin-Roland, *La Décennie Mitterrand*, vol. 4, 'Les Déchirements', Paris, Seuil, 1999, pp. 217 and 231. It was finally during the European Council of Edinburgh (11–12 December 1992) that a Franco-German compromise was found in a package also concerning the question – very important for Paris – of the headquarters of the European Parliament: augmentation of eighteen members of Parliament for the FRG and six members of Parliament for the three other 'big' EC powers and confirmation of Strasbourg as headquarters of the European Parliament. (The question would return to the forefront at the end of the 1990s, at that time concerning the new balancing of votes in the European Council demanded by Germany.)
72. The Yugoslav crisis is beyond the scope of this book and of itself justifies a work consecrated to French policy, which remains controversial. In the absence to this day of a true historical work, see Favier and Martin-Roland, *La Décennie*, vol. 4, pp. 183–198 and pp. 234–247.

73. Meeting between Mitterrand and Kohl, Lille, 29 May 1991.
74. Meeting between Mitterrand and Kohl, 25 June 1991; Morel, note pour le président de la République, 8 July 1991; and MAE, direction d'Europe, note a.s. La RFA et la crise yougoslave, 11 September 1991, private papers.
75. Discours prononcé par François Mitterrand à l'invitation de la Berliner Pressekonferenz, Berlin, 19 September 1991, *PEF*, September–October 1991, pp. 54–58; see also Pierre Morel, note pour le président de la République, Votre déjeuner du mercredi 18 avec le chancelier Kohl: Yougoslavie, 18 September 1991, private papers.
76. Meeting between Mitterrand and Kohl, Bonn, 18 September 1991. As he had done eighteen months earlier, Mitterrand complained to Kohl of caricatures in the German press in which 'the FRG is for Croatia, France for Serbia', after which he added: '[W]ith that, we end up in 1914 again.'
77. Morel, note pour le président de la République, Sommet franco-allemand: Yougoslavie, 14 November 1991, private papers.
78. Morel, note pour le président de la République, Dîner avec le chancelier Kohl: Yougoslavie, 3 December 1991, private papers.
79. Védrine, note pour le président de la République, a.s. Votre dîner avec le chancelier Kohl—Yougoslavie, 3 December 1991, private papers. Védrine's proposition was characteristic of the reading by the Elysée of the Yugoslav problem and German policy. Noting that the Germans had finally accepted that their unification be orchestrated with international conditions guaranteeing – according to Mitterrand's formula – its 'democratic and pacific' character thanks in particular to the 2 + 4 formula, it was now a matter of convincing Bonn to fix a 'doctrine' applicable to situations of 'dis-unification': in essence, these would also be considered legitimate as long as they intervened democratically and pacifically (no resort to violence, respect for the Helsinki agreements and the Paris charter, minority rights, arbitration in issues of borders).
80. Meeting between Mitterrand and Kohl, 3 December 1991; Mitterrand-Kohl Dinner, Tuesday 3 December 1991, private papers.
81. In a note to Mitterrand dated 14 December: see Favier and Martin-Roland, *La Décennie*, vol. 4, p. 244. (During his 3 December meeting with Kohl, Mitterrand, while keeping his arguments against a quick and unconditional recognition, only idly suggested that France would not follow Germany on that track. Kohl thanked him some days later after the Maastricht summit for his 'understanding' toward Bonn's position in this affair: see Letter from Kohl to Mitterrand, 15 December 1991, private papers.)
82. Margerie, notes pour le président de la République, La conférence intergouvernementale sur l'union politique: premiers mois de la présidence néerlandaise, 15 October 1991; and Conférence intergouvernementale sur l'UEM: point des travaux, 16 October 1991, private papers (the three pillars were, respectively, the Community pillar, the CFSP pillar and the Police and Judicial Cooperation pillar).
83. Margerie, note pour le président de la République, Votre entretien avec le chancelier Kohl: les conférences intergouvernementales, 14 November 1991, private papers.
84. Meeting between Mitterrand and Kohl, Bonn, 14 November 1991.
85. Mitterrand-Major Lunch, London, Monday 2 December 1991, private papers.
86. Meeting between Mitterrand and Kohl, 3 December 1991. See de Boissieu's analysis of the positions of other delegations: MAE, le directeur des affaires économiques et financières, brief, a.s. Positions des délégations, 25 November 1991, private papers.
87. For a detailed account of the 'end game' in Maastricht, see Favier and Martin-Roland, *La Décennie*, vol. 4, p. 227ff.
88. Margerie and Guillaume Hannezo, note pour monsieur le président, Union économique et monétaire. Projet de traité résultant des discussions entre ministres des Finan-

ces, 5 December; see also Margerie, note pour le président de la République. Questions européennes: vos entretiens avec MM. Lubbers, Kohl et Andreotti lors du sommet de l'OTAN, 6 November 1991, private papers.
89. Major, *The Autobiography*, p. 283.
90. Meeting between Mitterrand and Austrian Chancelor Franz Vranitzky, 3 December 1991, private papers.
91. Hubert Védrine, *Les Mondes de François Mitterrand. A l'Elysée 1981–1995*, Paris, Fayard, 1997, p. 475.
92. Margerie, note pour le président de la République, Conseil européen de Maastricht, 7 December 1991, private papers; see also Favier and Martin-Roland, *La Décennie*, vol. 4, p. 231.
93. Letter from Kohl to Mitterrand, 15 December 1991, private papers.
94. Interview accordée par François Mitterrand à TF1, dimanche 15 décembre 1991, *PEF*, November–December 1991, pp. 151–158.
95. See Hutchings, *American Diplomacy*, p. 274ff.; and Philip Zelikow and Condoleezza Rice, *Germany Unified and Europe Transformed: A Study in Statecraft*, Cambridge, Harvard University Press, 1995, pp. 466–467.
96. TD RPAN 578 and 581, 17 July 1990, AD, ASD, 1985–1990, box 130 bis.
97. TD RPAN 734, 11 September 1990, AD, ASD 1985–1990, box 130 bis: Taft proposed that the Sixteen work on the basis of paragraph 19 of the London declaration, which tasked the council with 'supervising' the work on 'the adaptation of the Alliance to new circumstances'; as for the Fifteen, they would work on the basis of paragraph 20, which provided for the elaboration of a 'new allied military strategy' in the conventional and nuclear domain.
98. Margerie and Lanxade, note à l'attention de Monsieur le président de la République, Entretiens à Washington sur la sécurité en Europe, 20 October 1990, private papers.
99. Replacing Robert Blackwill at the NSC in the beginning of August 1990, David Gompert was told by his authorities that it was important to treat two related problems, the future of NATO and France's role. He received from Scowcroft a 'general mandate' to discuss the 'basic problems' with Lanxade; personal interviews.
100. Hutchings, *American Diplomacy*, p. 274. While recognizing that Mitterrand was not involved at this stage, Hutchings, himself then a member of the NSC, describes the Lanxade-Scowcroft-Gompert-Zelikow meetings as 'exploratory discussions', but this characterization goes beyond the Elysée's intentions. Lanxade saw the talks essentially as an improvement of the dialogue that he had led with his White House interlocutors on these questions since his arrival at the Elysée in 1989: personal interviews; see also Zelikow and Rice, *Germany Unified*, pp. 466–467.
101. TD RPAN 734, 11 September 1990 and RPAN 764, 18 September 1990, AD, ASD 1985–1990, box 130 bis.
102. TD RPAN 867, 19 October 1990, AD, ASD 1985–1990, box 133. This affair has remained little-known due to the discretion desired by its protagonists; see the allusive remarks of Gabriel Robin, 'To the Editor', *Survival* 38, no. 2 (summer 1996): 188–189.
103. Manfred Wörner, note aux représentants permanents, Bilan général des séances de brassage d'idées au Conseil, confidential OTAN, 12 December 1990; TD RPAN 931–932 and 959–960, 9 and 19 November 1990, AD, ASD 1985–1990, box 130 bis; and TD RPAN 825–828, 848–849, 888–890 and 1003–1005, 8, 16, 29 October and 3 December 1990, AD, ASD 1985–1990, box 130 bis.
104. MAE, service des affaires stratégiques et du désarmement, Note pour le directeur des affaires politiques, a.s. Visite de M. Gompert. Revue stratégique de l'Alliance, 2 November 1990, AD, ASD 1985–1990, box 133.

105. TD RPAN 857, 17 October 1990, AD, ASD 1985–1990, box 133.
106. TD RPAN 867–868, 19 October 1990, AD, ASD 1985–1990, box 133.
107. TD RPAN 894, 30 October 1990, AD, ASD 1985–1990, box 133; and TD RPAN 920–921, DSL, 8 November 1990, AD, DP, box 300.
108. TD RPAN 963, 17 November 1990, AD, ASD 1985–1990, box 133. A preponderant role of the military committee in relation to SHAPE, in particular in the area of planning, was a longtime French claim (in the early days of NATO, the military committee, in fact, had been originally devised as a body by which the Atlantic Council would assure its tutelage on the organization and the military commands).
109. TD Bruxelles 985, 27 November 1990, AD, DP, box 300.
110. 'The European Security and Defense Identity and NATO,' synthesis document written by the permanent British representative, 28 November 1990, AD, DP, box 300.
111. Taft reported that in Washington a transfer of certain responsibilities from the military commands towards the NATO Military Committee was envisaged as a possibility and that it was recognized that a future European entity might operate both inside and outside the alliance: TD RPAN 1007–1008, 3 December 1990, AD, ASD 1985–1990, box 133. On a visit to Washington some days before, Marc Perrin de Brichambaut, Jean-Pierre Chevènement's diplomatic adviser, had also obtained the impression of an American opening to the work of the four and the idea of a European pillar in NATO: TD Washington 2829, 27 November 1990, AD, DP, box 300.
112. TD RPAN 974–975, 20 November 1990, AD, ASD 1985–1990, box 133.
113. TD RPAN 1021–1022, 4 December 1990, AD, ASD 1985–1990, box 133.
114. MAE, sous-direction des affaires stratégiques et des pactes, Note pour le directeur des affaires politiques, a.s. Réunion des directeurs politiques le 4 décembre, 3 December 1990, AD, ASD 1985–1990, box 133. The note estimated in particular that the mention in the British document of the possibility of a European operation 'if and when such action is deemed appropriate' would establish the preeminence of the alliance. Moreover, the affirmed principle of a defense that must remain 'collective' and associate European as well as U.S. forces reflected the preference of the 'integrated' allies and their desire to 'dilute European cooperation in a larger Western entity'. In a note for Dumas some days later, the tone was even more negative: 'Behind an apparent opening, London and Washington are looking to recuperate the European idea in a very Atlanticist perspective.' MAE, services des affaires stratégiques et du désarmement, note pour le ministre d'Etat, a.s. Rencontre des quatre ministres occidentaux en marge du prochain Conseil atlantique (Bruxelles 17 décembre), 15 December 1990, AD, ASD 1985–1990, box 218.
115. Personal interviews. The Elysée was obviously informed of the four-party exercise: see MAE, le directeur des affaires politiques, handwritten note from Dufourcq for Védrine, 30 November 1990 (Dufourcq transmitted to Védrine the British synthesis document), AD, DP, box 300. Yet the Elysée's limited interest in the conversations in Evère is verified by the quasi-absence of notes consecrated to this subject in its archives.
116. The approach led by Robin – as he probably sensed, as shown by his earlier recommendation to 'freeze the work of the Twelve' on defense – was thus essentially counter-cyclical. The French delegation at NATO in the autumn of 1990 clearly lacked precise information on the Franco-German initiative being discussed at the time: see TD RPAN 857, 17 October 1990, AD, ASD 1985–1990, box 133. It can thus be supposed that Robin was all the more committed to the four-party conversations because he did not know the detail of the Franco-German initiative that came to fruition on 6 December and that the Quai d'Orsay and the Elysée allowed him to lead what they essentially perceived as an exploratory conversation (rather than a negotiation) to see what Washington was ready to concede on NATO. As a result, it is quite possible, as Robin worried, that this

maneuver was perceived by the Americans as part of a French double game on NATO and European defense, even if it is very unlikely that this could of itself explain the failure of the rapprochement, whose causes were in fact more structural.

117. TD Washington 2747, 14 November 1990, AD, ASD 1985–1990, box 130 bis.
118. MAE, Compte rendu a.s. Réunion des quatre directeurs politiques: rénovation de l'Alliance atlantique et sécurité européenne, no date, AD, ASD 1985–1990, box 133.
119. TD Washington 2915, 6 December 1990, AD, ASD 1985–1990, box 218.
120. TD RPAN 1063–1064, 13 December 1990, AD, ASD 1985–1990, box 218.
121. London and Washington wanted to reserve for NATO the monopole of collective defense, but their refusal to recognize that collective defense would only concern a possible Soviet threat (implicitly giving credit, against the backdrop of the Gulf crisis, to the notion of a NATO defense role out of area) meant that the WEU would be de facto limited to a rather modest security role, one that of course would be out of area: see TD RPAN 87, 24 January 1991, AD, DP, box 300.
122. TD RPAN 70, 21 January 1991, AD, ASD 1991–1994, OTAN 5.0; TD RPAN 87, 24 January 1991, AD, DP, box 300 (the idea of 'separable but not separate' forces was taken up again at the Brussels summit in January 1994).
123. MAE, ASD, note pour le directeur politique, a.s. Réunion des directeurs politiques, Bruxelles, 24 janvier 1991. Evolution de l'Alliance, 22 January 1991, AD, ASD 1991–1994, OTAN 5.0.
124. Margerie, note pour le président de la République, Votre entretien avec M. Major (lundi 14 janvier 12h30). Questions européennes, 14 January 1991, private papers.
125. Meeting between Mitterrand and Major, 14 January 1991.
126. MAE, sous-direction des affaires stratégiques et des pactes, note, Réunion affaires étrangères-défense du 28 février, 1 March 1991, AD, DP, box 304.
127. MAE, ASD, note pour le cabinet du ministre d'Etat, à l'attention de M. Danon, a.s. Rencontre du président de la République et du président Bush. Projets européens de sécurité et évolution de l'Alliance atlantique, 8 March 1991, AD, ASD 1991–1994, OTAN 5.0.
128. Védrine and Lanxade, note pour le président de la République, 11 March 1991, private papers.
129. Meeting between Mitterrand and Bush, Martinique, 14 March 1991, second part.
130. TD RPAN 275 and 455, 20 March and 14 May 1991, AD, ASD 1991–1994, OTAN 5.0.
131. Robin would later write that the attempt failed 'not because Washington rejected it but because Paris was not ready for it', assessing the integrated military structure as doomed and preferring to bet on the emergence of a European identity, hence the French refusal to sacrifice France's 'special status': see Robin, 'To the Editor'. Meanwhile Hutchings recognizes the existence of an American reluctance as well: see Hutchings, *American Diplomacy*, p. 275; and personal interviews. (It should be noted that the work of the four ambassadors would find an extension in the rapprochement attempt between France and NATO – fruitless in the end – led by Jacques Chirac in 1995–1996: see Frédéric Bozo, *La France et l'Alliance atlantique depuis la fin de la guerre froide. Le modèle gaullien en question (1989–1999)* (Paris: Cahier du Centre d'études d'histoire de la défense, No.17, 2001.)
132. Cited in Claire Tréan, 'La relation de la France à l'OTAN n'est pas modifiée,' *Le Monde*, 23 March 1991.
133. MAE, ASD, note a.s. Entretien du secrétaire américain à la Défense avec le président de la République: projets européens de sécurité et évolution de l'Alliance atlantique, 22 May 1991, ASD 1991–1995, OTAN 5.0. (Indeed, the nature of the French military participation in 'Desert Storm' and, in particular, the operational procedures that were used were a transposition of agreements existing between France and NATO: see on this point Bozo, *La France et l'Alliance atlantique*, pp. 24–25.)
134. Védrine and Lanxade, note pour le président de la République, 11 March 1991.

135. *Le Monde*, 17–18 and 23 March 1991: interestingly, the French decision was, at first, largely interpreted as the sign of a major change of policy toward NATO, which it was not – on the contrary, even, given that it was taken in the context of an acknowledgment in Paris of the unlikelihood of an overhaul of the alliance.
136. TD RPAN 263–264, 18 March 1991, private papers; Mitterrand was favorable to it: 'We should hurry up, write and deposit our propositions', he instructed Morel.
137. MAE, ASD, note, a.s. Entretien du secrétaire américain à la Défense avec le président de la République: projets européens de sécurité et évolution de l'Alliance atlantique, 22 May 1991.
138. Final Communiqué of the ministerial session of the North Atlantic Council, Copenhagen, 6–7 June 1991.
139. On all this, see Kori Schake, 'NATO after the Cold War 1991–1995: Institutional Competition and the Collapse of the French Alternative', *Contemporary European History* 7, no. 3 (1998): 379–407.
140. TD RPAN 974–975, 20 November 1990, and MAE, sous-direction ASP, note a.s. Réflexions de SACEUR sur la restructuration des forces du commandement allié en Europe, AD, ASD 1985–1990, box 133. For the rest, NATO forces in Central Europe would include four to five multinational army corps stationed in the Western part of the FRG, and one German national army corps stationed in the ex-GDR, all supported by a rapid reinforcement capacity.
141. Details can be found in Bozo, *La France et l'OTAN. De la guerre froide au nouvel ordre européen* (Paris: Masson, 1991), p. 181ff.
142. 'MM. Dumas et Joxe critiquent la réforme de l'OTAN', *Le Monde*, 6 June 1991.
143. Védrine, note pour le président de la République, 6 June 1991, private papers.
144. Quesnot, note à l'attention de M. le président de la République, Projet d'un nouveau dispositif militaire de l'OTAN, 11 June 1991.
145. See Schake, 'NATO after the Cold War'. Of course, the British defended themselves from accusations of such intentions: hence Major assured Mitterrand that the RRF only reflected a technical reorganization of NATO forces and that it had no out of area attributions: see Meeting between Mitterrand and Major, 24 June 1991. The British ambassador in Paris reiterated that it was not a matter of 'pulling the carpet from under the feet' of Europe because London separately proposed the creation of a rapid reaction force of the WEU earmarked for 'out of area': Letter from Ewen Ferguson to Védrine, 10 July 1991, private papers.
146. In effect, in the Gulf crisis, NATO only played a role limited to consultations between members and the preparation of the possible defense of Turkey: see MAE, ASP, fiche, a.s. Nouveaux défis pour la sécurité de l'Alliance, 13 December 1990, AD, ASD 1985–1990, box 218 (two extraordinary ministerial sessions consecrated to the Iraqi crisis were held on 10 August and 10 September). The 'temptation to headlong rush out of area has its limits', the French noted with satisfaction at the end of 1990, since a large number of the allies were not disposed to it: TD RPAN 1063–1064, 13 December 1990, AD, ASD 1985–1990, box 218.
147. Meeting between Mitterrand and Bush, Martinique, 14 March 1991, second part.
148. TD RPAN 1063–1064, 13 December 1990, AD, ASD 1985–1990, box 218.
149. Morel, note pour le président de la République, Votre entretien avec M. Cheney (lundi 27 mai à 17h), 27 May 1991, private papers.
150. MAE, ASD, note, a.s. Entretien du secrétaire américain à la défense avec le président de la République: projets européens de sécurité et évolution de l'Alliance atlantique, 22 May 1991.
151. MAE, ASD, note a.s. Discours du secrétaire d'Etat américain sur 'l'architecture euroatlantique.' Analyse liminaire des aspects stratégiques, 20 June 1991.

152. Morel, note pour le président de la République, Votre entretien avec le président Bush, dimanche à 16h30: note générale, 13 juillet 1991, private papers (Mitterrand's diplomatic adviser distinguished between Baker's attitude, marked by a certain 'hubris', and that of Bush, more open at least from a declaratory point of view).
153. Meeting between Mitterrand and Bush, Rambouillet, 14 July 1991.
154. TD RPAN 654–655, 28 June 1991, AD, ASD 1991–1994, OTAN 5.0.
155. Scowcroft Message to Védrine, Secret, no date [late September/early October 1991], private papers (Scowcroft specified that Washington wanted contacts with London and Bonn as well).
156. Meeting between Mitterrand and Gonzalez, Madrid, 25 October 1991, private papers.
157. TD Washington 2284 and 2303, 18 and 23 October 1991, private papers; Hutchings, *American Diplomacy*, p. 281. Védrine and Hartmann, it seems, had brought up the project of the Franco-German corps with Scowcroft on 4 October, but presenting it as aiming to legitimize the maintenance of a French division in the FRG and to facilitate through this France-NATO relations, which pleased Washington. But the Americans then felt cheated upon reading the Mitterrand-Kohl letter of 15 October, for the mention of a Franco-German corps as the embryo of a military cooperation within the WEU reflected, in their view, the objective of an autonomous European military structure, a perspective that was judged unacceptable since it would compete with the NATO integrated military organization and, worse, possibly take away from it the German division concerned. U.S. resentment seems to have been especially strong (in particular in the Department of State and with the military) toward the Germans, who were seen as having betrayed the confidence that had been built between Bonn and Washington at the time of German unification: see Schake, 'NATO after the Cold War'; Hutchings, *American Diplomacy*, p. 281; and personal interviews. Yet Hartmann and Védrine likely had not deliberately dissimulated this aspect to Scowcroft on 4 October: the decision to include the Franco-German army corps in the 15 October initiative was indeed taken shortly before its release, i.e. after their visit to Washington, and it was forced upon the Chancellery by the Elysée: see p. 324.
158. Letter from Bush to Mitterrand, 23 October 1991, private papers: highlighting that Washington had up to that point abstained from any public criticism of the Franco-German initiative despite 'serious reservations', he asked Mitterrand to confirm that it was not about considering a 'substitute for the Alliance, even long-term'.
159. TD Bruxelles 1114–1118, 28 October 1991, private papers.
160. TD Washington 2302, 22 October 1991, private papers.
161. Letter from Mitterrand to Bush, no date (late October 1991), private papers.
162. Morel and Quesnot, note pour le président de la République, Préparation du sommet de Rome. Compte rendu des entretiens de Washington (lundi 4 novembre), 5 November 1991, private papers.
163. NATO, Rome Declaration on peace and cooperation, Rome, 7–8 November 1991, http://www.nato.int/docu/comm.htm.
164. The document recognized implicitly that the Franco-German corps would contribute to the reinforcement of the Atlantic Alliance: see Quesnot, note à l'attention de Monsieur le président de la République, Sommet de Rome les 7 et 8 novembre 1991. Concept stratégique de l'Alliance et réforme des structures de commandements, 6 November 1991; and Morel, note pour le président de la République, Sommet de l'Alliance atlantique à Rome (7–8 November 1991), note générale, 6 November 1991, private papers. Paragraphe 52 of the strategic concept recognized (after Bonn's suggestion) the role of the 'integrated and multinational European structures as they continue their development in the context of a European defense identity that would take shape': see 'The new stra-

tegic concept of the Alliance', Rome 7 November 1991, available at http://www.nato .int/doc/comm.htm.
165. Cited in Hutchings, *American Diplomacy*, pp. 281–282.
166. TD RPAN 981, 4 October 1991, AD, ASD 1991–1994, 572; MAE, ASD, note, L'Alliance et ses relations avec l'Europe centrale et orientale, 25 October 1991, AD, ASD 1991–1994, OTAN 511 (since spring 1991, the leaders of Poland, Hungary and Czechoslovakia had one after another gone to NATO to plead in favor of the alliance's consideration of their security problems).
167. Védrine, handwritten note, no date [late October–early November 1991], private papers. It should be noted that Mitterrand already did not exclude an eventual adhesion of the countries of Eastern and Central Europe to the Atlantic Alliance: 'If they ask for it, it is important to consider it', he recognized before Cheney while underlining that 'any membership attempt should be the subject of a parallel negotiation with the Soviets. The CSCE broke the block to block approach. It should not be encouraged again': Quesnot, note à l'attention de Monsieur le secrétaire général, Entretien du président de la République avec M. Cheney le 27 mai 1991 en présence de MM. Dumas et Joxe, 28 May 1991, private papers.
168. Morel and Quesnot, note pour le président de la République, Préparation du sommet de Rome. Compte rendu des entretiens de Washington (lundi 4 novembre), 5 November 1991.
169. Védrine, handwritten note, no date [late October-early November 1991], private papers.
170. Morel, note pour le président de la République, Sommet de l'Alliance atlantique à Rome (7–8 novembre 1991), note générale, 6 November 1991, private papers.
171. Morel and Quesnot, note pour le président de la République, Préparation du sommet de Rome. Compte rendu des entretiens de Washington (lundi 4 novembre), 5 November 1991.
172. Morel, note pour le président de la République s/c de M. Hubert Védrine, Déclaration sur l'évolution de la situation en URSS, (with handwritten annotations by Mitterrand), no date, private papers; and Morel, note pour le président de la République, Sommet de l'Alliance atlantique à Rome (7–8 November 1991), note générale, 6 November 1991.
173. Morel, note de pour le président de la République s/c de M. Hubert Védrine, Intervention du président de la République sur le projet de déclaration sur l'URSS, Rome, 8 November 1991, private papers.
174. Mitterrand, handwritten note, Les 9 points de la France à la réunion de Rome de l'OTAN, no date, private papers.
175. Mitterrand, handwritten note, Les 9 points de la France à la réunion de Rome de l'OTAN, no date.
176. Védrine, *Les Mondes*, pp. 448–449. On this affair, see Frédéric Bozo, 'The Failure of A Grand Design': Mitterrand's European Confederation (1989–1991),' *Contemporary European History*, N°17, 3 (2008), pp. 391–412.
177. See chapter 1 and chapter 3 of this volume, pp. 62ff and 145ff.
178. Guigou, note pour le président de la République, Quelques réflexions sur la Confédération européenne et son articulation avec la Communauté, 11 January 1990, private papers; see also Quelques réflexions sur l'organisation future de l'Europe, [no signature, but clearly authored by Guigou], no date [early January 1990], private papers.
179. Védrine, note pour le président de la République, a.s. Confédération européenne, 8 January 1990, private papers.
180. Guigou, Quelques réflexions sur l'organisation future de l'Europe, n. d.
181. MAE, le directeur des affaires politiques, note, a.s. de la Confédération européenne et des questions qu'elle pose, 4 janvier 1990, private papers. As for the Quai's director of

legal affairs, evidently perplexed, he could only state that in international law, the term 'confederation' refers to 'a loose and imprecise formula of association between States': 'the pavilion of "confederation" is susceptible to cover a variety of merchandise', Jean-Pierre Puissochet noted, concluding that it is 'difficult to do anything other than ask questions': MAE, le directeur des affaires juridiques, note pour le ministre d'Etat, a.s. Premières réflexions sur la notion de confédération européenne, 7 February 1990, private papers.
182. Meeting between Mitterrand and Szuros, 18 January 1990, private papers.
183. Meeting between Mitterrand, Jaruzelski, Mazowiecki and Skubiszewski, 9 March 1990, handwritten notes by Margerie, AN 5AG3/CDM 34; on the discussion regarding the Oder-Neisse border on the same day, see chapter 5 of this volume, pp. 225–227.
184. Meeting between Mitterrand and Havel, 19 March 1990, detailed report by Loïc Hennekinne, private papers.
185. Margerie, note pour le président de la République, Confédération européenne, 3 April 1990, private papers. On the preparation of the Paris summit, see chapter 6 of this volume, p. 297ff.
186. Pierre Favier and Michel Martin-Roland, *La Décennie Mitterrand*, vol. 3, 'Les Défis (1988–1991),' Paris, Seuil, 1996, pp. 172–172.
187. TD Diplomatie 23614, 12 November 1990, AD, ASD 1991–1994, sous-direction des questions multilatérales (QM), box 13; and *Le Monde*, 10 November 1990.
188. Letter from Mitterrand to Havel, 21 December 1990; and TD Prague 45, 11 January 1991, private papers.
189. MAE, le conseiller auprès du ministre d'Etat, note de Jean Musitelli pour le directeur de cabinet du ministre d'Etat, a.s. Confédération. Organisation, 9 January 1991, private papers. The SGCI asked the various French ministries to list the domains in which a cooperation could be envisaged between the countries and Central Europe and those of Western Europe, in order, 'thanks to concrete propositions, to define the foundation of what could one day constitute a "European confederation"': see Premier ministre, SGCI, note, 'Confédération:' relevé de conclusions, 25 January 1991, private papers.
190. TD Prague 99, 25 January 1991; MAE, le conseiller auprès du ministre d'Etat, note de Jean Musitelli pour le ministre d'Etat, a.s. Assises de la Confédération européenne, 28 January 1991, private papers.
191. Favier and Martin-Roland, *La Décennie*, vol. 4, p. 173.
192. Such were the conclusions of a meeting organized on 17 December 1990 by the head of the Europe directorate, Jacques Blot, and Musitelli: see MAE, Direction d'Europe (CSCE), note a.s. Réunion du groupe de réflexion sur les Assises de la Confédération, 24 December 1990, AD, ASD 1991-1994, QM, box 20. Shortly before, the Quai's planning staff had produced a series of notes proposing an outline of the confederation and its various aspects: see in particular MAE, CAP, note a.s. La confédération européenne, 13 December 1990 and Note a.s. La confédération européenne: une esquisse, 13 December 1990, private papers.
193. MAE, le conseiller auprès du ministre d'Etat, note a.s. Confédération. Calendrier prévisionnel (premier semestre 1991), 31 January 1991, private papers.
194. MAE, Direction des affaires économiques et financières, note a.s. Confédération, 24 January 1991, private papers.
195. Favier and Martin-Roland, *La Décennie*, vol. 4, p. 173.
196. TD Diplomatie 691, 20 December 1991, AD, ASD 1991–1994, QM, box 20; and MAE, Direction d'Europe, note a.s. Réunion du groupe de réflexion sur les Assises de la Confédération, 24 December 1990.
197. MAE, le conseiller auprès du ministre d'Etat, note de Jean Musitelli pour le ministre d'Etat, a.s. Assises de la Confédération européenne, 28 January 1991.

198. MAE, CAP, note pour le cabinet du ministre d'Etat (à l'attention de M. Musitelli), a.s. La confédération européenne et les Etats-Unis: projet d'argumentaire, 1 March 1991, private papers.
199. MAE, Direction des affaires économiques et financières, note a.s. Confédération et Communauté: projet d'argumentaire, 26 February 1991, private papers.
200. MAE, Direction d'Europe, note de Roland Galharague, a.s. Confédération et CSCE. Contribution à la réflexion, 27 February 1991, AD, ASD 1991–1994, QM, box 20. (In a note written some months earlier, the deputy director of the Quai's planning staff, Pierre Buhler, suggested that the CSCE would remain 'the essentially interstate forum for Euro-Atlantic security' that it had been successfully over the past fifteen years, whereas the confederation would have the mission to reactivate Europe's 'capillarity' by defining 'integrated policies for the whole of the continent' according to a transnational logic, thereby decoupling the security aspects from the economic and human aspects, which up to that point had been treated together in the Helsinki process (of course the United States, as we shall see, refused precisely to accept such decoupling): MAE, CAP, note a.s. La CSCE est-elle encore nécessaire?, 25 September 1990, AD, ASD 1991–1994, QM, box 20.) As for the Council of Europe, the promoters of the confederation estimated that its 'activis' was not a problem: the Council of Europe 'cannot be the Confederation', whose aim was political, but on the other hand, the Confederation 'could valorize the work' of the Council of Europe: MAE, le conseiller auprès du ministre d'Etat, note de Jean Musitelli pour le ministre des Affaires européennes, Comité des ministres du Conseil de l'Europe à Madrid. Confédération, 20 February 1991, private papers.
201. Letter from Dumas to his European counterparts, no date. (mid April), with the memorandum attached, AD, ASD 1991-1994, QM, box 20 (a project had been written by Galharague: see projet de mémorandum, AD, ASD 1991-1994, QM, box 20.)
202. TD Prague 116, 1 February 1991, private papers.
203. TD Prague 201, 22 February 1991, private papers.
204. Margerie, note pour le président de la République, Déjeuner du samedi 23 mars avec M. Havel: Confédération européenne, 23 March 1991, private papers. Margerie feared that the presence of Americans in the conference, even as simple observers, would 'irreversibly' lead to the participation of the United States in the confederation: in 1948 the Congress of the Hague, she highlighted, did not have one American associate. She agreed with Musitelli, who was reluctant to 'redo the CSCE' and proposed a compromise formula: invite as observers Americans who are members of organizations such as the EBRD: MAE, le conseiller auprès du ministre d'Etat, note pour le ministre d'Etat, a.s. Assises de Prague. Personnalités à inviter, 7 March 1991, private papers.
205. Lunch meeting between Mitterrand and Havel, Saturday 23 March 1991, private papers.
206. Agence France-Press Dispatch, Prague, 25 March 1991, private papers.
207. MAE, le conseiller auprès du ministre d'Etat, note a.s. Confédération. Etat des lieux, 21 March 1991; and Note a.s. Projet de confédération européenne: réaction des autres pays européens, no date, private papers.
208. MAE, Direction d'Europe, note de compte rendu, a.s. Conférence des ambassadeurs en Europe centrale et orientale, Paris, 25–26 March 1991. Première séance du travail: Confédération européenne, 25 March 1991), AD, ASD 1991–1994, QM, box 20.
209. MAE, Direction d'Europe, note de compte rendu, a.s. Conférence des ambassadeurs en Europe centrale et orientale, Paris, 25–26 mars 1991. Compte rendu de la deuxième séance de travail: bilan et perspective de la relance à l'Est; et compte rendu de la quatrième séance de travail consacrée aux questions économiques (matinée du 26 mars 1991), AD, ASD 1991–1994, QM, box 20.
210. Védrine, note pour le président de la République, a.s. Problèmes de sécurité en Europe centrale et orientale, Paris, 26 March 1991, private papers.

211. Déclaration commune à l'occasion des 56e consultations franco-allemandes les 17 et 18 septembre 1990. See also the detailed reports of the Latché and Paris meetings on 4 January 1990 and 15 February 1991 in *Deutsche Einheit. Sonderedition aus den Akten des Bundeskanzleramtes 1989/1990*, Munich, Oldenburg, 1998, pp. 687 and 849–850.
212. TD Diplomatie 11 janvier 1991, AD, ASD 1991–1994, QM, box 20. (The diplomat designated by the Auswärtiges Amt was Wilhelm Höynck.)
213. TD Bonn 555 and 573, 5 and 6 March 1991, AD, ASD 1991–1994, QM, box 20.
214. Favier and Martin-Roland, *La Décennie*, vol. 4, p. 173.
215. Margerie, note pour le président de la République, Votre entretien avec le chancelier Kohl. Confédération, 24 April 1991, private papers.
216. TD Bonn 1202, 16 May 1991, private papers.
217. Morel, note pour le président de la République, 57e sommet franco-allemand (mercredi 29 et jeudi 30 mai). Note de présentation générale, 29 May 1991, private papers.
218. TD Washington 25, 5 January 1990, AD, ASD 1991–1994, QM, box 20; Hubert Védrine, note pour le président de la République, 7 February 1990, private papers.
219. MAE, CAP, note de Pierre Buhler, a.s. La Confédération européenne et les Etats-Unis, 27 February 1991, AD, ASD 1991–1994, QM, box 20.
220. The message was relayed to the French by the Germans: see TD Bonn 555, 5 March 1991.
221. MAE, ASD, note a.s. Discours du secrétaire d'Etat américain sur 'l'architecture euro-atlantique.' Analyse liminaire des aspects stratégiques, 20 June 1991, AD, ASD 1991–1994, 572; see Favier and Martin-Roland, *La Décennie*, vol. 4, pp. 169–170; Hutchings, *American Diplomacy*, p. 162ff.; see also above p. 342.
222. TD Moscou 2652, 6 June 1991, AD, ASD 1991–1994, QM, box 20.
223. MAE, Direction d'Europe, note a.s. Réactions en Europe au projet de Confédération, 10 June 1991, AD, ASD 1991–1994, QM, box 20.
224. Meeting between Mitterrand and Antall, 21 May 1991, private papers.
225. Morel, note for Védrine, 11 June 1991, a.s. Mode d'emploi des suites des Assises de la Confédération, 11 June 1991, private papers.
226. MAE, Direction d'Europe, note de Roland Galharague, a.s. Confédération européenne: hypothèses de suivi des Assises, 11 June 1991, AD, ASD 1991–1994, QM, box 20.
227. Favier and Martin-Roland, *La Décennie*, vol. 4, pp. 175–176.
228. TD Diplomatie 12836–12847, 17 June 1991, AD, ASD 1991–1994, QM, box 20.
229. Allocation prononcée à l'occasion de la séance de clôture des Assises de la Confédération européenne, Prague, 14 June 1991.
230. TD Diplomatie 13055–13056, 18 June 1991, AD, ASD 1991–1994, QM, box 20.
231. MAE, le conseiller auprès du ministre d'Etat, note de Jean Musitelli, Confédération: l'après Prague, 2 July 1991, AD, ASD 1991–1994, QM, box 20.
232. MAE, note a.s. Confédération européenne. Compte rendu de la réunion interministérielle du 18 juillet 1991, private papers.
233. TD Prague 734, 11 July 1991, AD, ASD 1991–1994, QM, box 20; and Letter from Havel to Mitterrand, 30 June 1991, private papers.
234. Meeting between Mitterrand and Roman, 19 July 1991, detailed report by Morel, private papers.
235. Favier and Martin-Roland, *La Décennie*, vol. 4, pp. 176–177.
236. Morel, note pour le président de la République, Entretien avec le président Havel: Confédération européenne (mardi 1er octobre à 11h), 1 October 1991, private papers. (Morel suggested the creation of a 'Confederal European space', which would aim to 'multilateralize' the relations between the countries in Eastern and Central Europe and the Community, rather than an 'addition of bilateral accords'.)

Conclusion

MITTERRAND AND THE END OF THE USSR

As the 28th Congress of the CPSU in July had illustrated, the summer of 1990 marked the apogee of the 'Gorbachev moment'. By the autumn, his power was insufficient to impose the necessary changes on the country, and he appeared increasingly challenged in the context of growing and glaring problems.[1] First, there were the economic difficulties: the success of reforms in this domain was an essential condition of the future of *perestroika*, and their failure instead only aggravated the problems, leading Gorbachev to increase demands for financial help that the West considered with growing skepticism. Then there were the political difficulties: the 28th Congress had confirmed Mikhail Gorbachev's personal power but also saw the rise of the conservatives against the background of the aggravation of centrifugal and nationalist tendencies among the republics, with Russian President Boris Yeltsin appearing increasingly as a rival to Gorbachev.[2] There was thus a momentum toward crisis that in the final weeks of 1990 took the form of a temptation to return to authoritarianism. Gorbachev demanded and obtained stronger powers in the hope of imposing his reforms, while at the same time he tried to make an alliance with Communist Party hardliners in the hope of neutralizing them. This 'rightward' shift was denounced by Eduard Shevardnadze in December, when he resigned his post as minister of foreign affairs, sounding the alarm about the danger of a 'dictatorship.'

At the end of 1990, the gravity of the situation left no doubt: the Soviet Union, the Élysée judged, was on the way to 'disintegration' due to the

---

Notes for this section begin on page 384.

impulses to independence in its republics, and this process was 'aggravated by the crisis of power in the state' and the marginalization of the CPSU, as well as by the rivalry between Yeltsin and Gorbachev, which entailed 'paralysis and the absence of decision' and might lead to an authoritarian takeover. Moreover, the analysis went on, the USSR was plunged into a 'dramatic economic and social crisis' that risked deepening, since 'it was becoming difficult in these circumstances to believe in the success of new reforms'. The Elysée diplomat Jean Lévy concluded that 'without a miracle accompanied by massive international aid', the USSR 'will not be able to undertake economic reform and democratic construction at the same time'.[3]

Still, Mitterrand remained more than ever persuaded of the need to support Gorbachev. While he recognized that 'one has to wonder about his chances of lasting', his reasoning was simple: 'There is no proof that he has lost', he confided to Romanian Prime Minister Petre Roman at the end of January 1991: 'Gorbachev, who is an intelligent and sensible man, is better than any Marshal who will flatter nationalism and drown protest in blood.'[4] The deterioration of the situation in the Baltic republics – where Soviet security forces took control in the first days of 1991, leading to a bloody repression in Lithuania for which Gorbachev would always deny responsibility – did not change Mitterrand's analysis. Even if he recognized the legitimacy of the aspirations to self-determination and condemned the use of force by Moscow, Mitterrand remained convinced of the need not to aggravate Gorbachev's domestic difficulties by supporting independence movements that were precipitate and non-negotiated. French leaders were sensitive to Gorbachev's argument that 'it would be an unpardonable historic error' for the West 'to turn away from the Soviet Union' and to put *perestroika* in danger when it had reached a 'crucial stage'.[5] Even if he had to face strong domestic criticism after the events in the Baltic republics, the U.S. president's attitude over this issue, and more generally with respect to Gorbachev, did not differ from that of his French homologue, as confirmed by their dialogue when they met in Martinique in mid March 1991: 'They want us to skirt around Gorbachev. I do not agree', said George Bush. 'I don't agree either', answered Mitterrand. 'I don't know what his chances are, but I do not want to reduce them.'[6]

The spring of 1991 seemed to bring an amelioration. Measuring the danger of an extremist drift, Gorbachev turned again to the democrats and tried to get closer to Yeltsin. Strengthened by the positive result of the referendum of 17 March, he began a process to elaborate a new Union treaty, giving more sovereignty to the republics while starting negotiations with the Balts. In this less strained political context, the question of economic reforms and Western support moved once more to the foreground. This raised the issue of Gorbachev's invitation to London, where the summit of the Seven was to take place in mid July. The possibility of inviting Gorbachev had been projected after the Houston summit, and the French were favorable toward it. It was a matter of showing the support of the Western powers by aiding Gorbachev's reforms, a line that Kohl and Mitterrand continued to defend together, notably in the face of strong U.S. reservations about financial support that the Americans considered ineffective in the absence of radical changes in the Soviet economy.[7] Despite the paltry concrete results obtained in London – where he was finally invited to meet the Seven after their summit – Gorbachev thanked the French president for his support: 'France had the clearest position', he told Mitterrand.[8]

The Attempted Coup of August 1991

If the London meeting allowed the Soviet Number One to cut a good figure on the international scene by posing as a recognized interlocutor of the major Western powers, it could not conceal the persistent gravity of his domestic situation. At this start of summer 1991, Gorbachev in effect appeared to be marginalized in his own country, notably in contrast to Yeltsin. Elected president of the Russian Federation in June by universal suffrage, the latter now enjoyed a democratic legitimacy that Gorbachev lacked. Even if Gorbachev still performed certain regal functions such as setting the 'great politico-military options' of the nation and 'setting its foreign policy', Paris clearly perceived that the Soviet Number One now had only 'theoretical' power'; sooner or later, the Quai d'Orsay thought, the changes under way would lead 'ineluctably' to his departure, voluntary or not.[9] For his part, Mitterrand still refused to consider that the Gorbachev era was over, but he was fully aware of his extremely fragile position; the Élysée, therefore, was not surprised by the events in Moscow on 19–21 August.[10]

Early on the morning of 19 August, Paris and other capitals received the news of Gorbachev being deposed while on vacation in the Crimea by a 'state committee' composed of Vice President Gennady Yanaev and Prime Minister Valentin Pavlov. From start, the president and his entourage were torn between certainty that the attempted coup d'état could only fail eventually (Mitterrand saw it as a 'last convulsion') and the necessary prudence in the face of events that were unpredictable in the short term. This state of mind, it must be noted, was shared by the principal Western leaders, starting with the Americans.[11] The contacts established in the middle of that day confirmed this dilemma, in particular the telephone conversation between Mitterrand and Bush: suggesting that the West react by advancing 'principles' and 'criteria' that should prevail in relations with the USSR, the French president stressed that the coup d'état 'might fail' and that he did not believe in its success over time, while recognizing that 'the intermediate period might be very dangerous'. The U.S. president said he agreed with this analysis and was concerned to avoid 'declaring anything that might bring grist to the mill of those who want us to begin re-arming right away'.[12] In the following hours, the official French reactions remained guarded, even at the risk of seeming to accommodate the coup plotters. In a communiqué published at the end of the day, Mitterrand declared that he attached 'a high price' to 'the life and freedom' of Gorbachev and Yeltsin (who was surrounded in the Russian Parliament building) being 'guaranteed', and he warned that 'the new leaders of Moscow will be judged by their actions'. Then the president spoke live on television at 8:00 P.M.: while wondering about the chances of success of a 'change running against the current' that might 'interrupt' but not 'arrest the movement', he read a letter from Yanaev, who curiously justified the use of force by citing the need to pursue Gorbachev's domestic reforms as well as his international policy. Mitterrand denied accepting these assurances 'at face value', but he nevertheless spoke of 'the new leaders' in the USSR and did not spontaneously condemn the putsch. It was only when the explicit question of his doing so was posed that he answered, manifestly surprised: 'Of course! How can you ask this question?'[13]

The next day, Mitterrand found himself in a difficult position, for meanwhile the tone had hardened among his Western partners – especially Bush, whose initial commentary had appeared just as prudent as Mitterrand's.[14] Hence the Élysée's concern to adjust its tone, especially since it began to look as if the coup d'état might in effect be rapidly aborted, due to its internal dissensions but also due to action taken by Yeltsin, who now incarnated democratic legitimacy in the face of the putsch. On the morning of 20 August, the Élysée issued a new communiqué in which Mitterrand lamented the impossibility of reaching Gorbachev by telephone and stressed 'the urgency of coming back to democratic practices'; meanwhile Roland Dumas in The Hague signed a declaration by the Twelve that 'firmly' condemned the coup d'état. In the afternoon, Russian Minister of Foreign Affairs Andrei Kozyrev, passing through Paris, was received by Secretary General of the Élysée Hubert Védrine and then by Dumas.[15] After a confused evening and a tense night in Moscow, the failure of the coup d'état was patent by the morning of 21 August. Everything ended in the afternoon with the arrest of the putsch leaders and Gorbachev's return to Moscow at the end of the day. Meanwhile, Mitterrand was able to establish communication with Yeltsin, still under siege, and assure him that France 'supports [his] fight'.[16] The next day Mitterrand was finally able to speak with Gorbachev, who, responding to the French president's regret at not having been able to reach him in Crimea during the three days of the putsch, declared that he had 'learned of your clear position, firm as always' and said he was 'grateful' for this 'powerful support'.[17]

Mitterrand's attitude was nevertheless criticized, for example by former President Valéry Giscard d'Estaing, who on the evening of 20 August said he was 'struck by the initial weakness of a certain number of Western leaders'.[18] What can be said with hindsight? Mitterrand himself would later recognize having been maladroit on television on the evening of 19 August: by reading (granted, with an ironic tone) Yanaev's letter, by not explicitly condemning the putsch except in answer to a journalist's question and by mentioning the 'new leaders', he may have given the impression of giving them sanction. Yet although the form of this unfortunate appearance was characteristic of his personal style – he would later invoke the need for 'sang-froid' – this does not explain everything. Mitterrand, in his first reactions – like most Western partners, starting with George Bush – incontestably made the debatable choice of prudence over disapproval, for two reasons at least: the desire not to upset French public opinion, and the concern not to burn bridges with Soviet 'leaders' who might perhaps have to be dealt with for a while and on whom depended the personal fate of Gorbachev, which was a major concern for him.[19]

But beyond that, the episode was revealing of Mitterrand's vision of the future of the USSR. Mitterrand did *not* deliberately abandon Gorbachev, but it is probable that the paradoxical assurances that the putsch leaders gave of their desire to pursue Gorbachev's policies, in particular his foreign policy, encouraged Mitterrand to take a wait-and-see attitude, given his fatalism with respect to a weakened Gorbachev's political future. Behind this attitude, there was a double fear: that of a return to a Cold War situation, which an overly brutal Western reaction could have provoked, and that of an uncontrolled breakup of the USSR, which was looming even before the putsch. Did Mitterrand, with this attitude, deliberately 'hold out a pole' to the 'new leaders', as Pierre Favier and Michel Martin-Roland think? This may be debated; once again, Mitterrand's attitude (irrespective of the time lag between Washington and Paris) was not fundamentally different from Bush's. Be that as it may, it is probable that his initial reactions were influenced by his conviction of the need to 'solve the major dilemma of the Soviet Union,' to wit, 'pursuing economic and political reforms while avoiding the dislocation of the empire'.[20]

The Breakup of the USSR

Yet the putsch and its failure further aggravated this dilemma to the point of making it insurmountable. Revealing a disintegration that was henceforward irreversible, the episode acted as a catalyst toward the evolution underway and ultimately led in barely four months to the end of the Soviet Union. After the putsch, the personal position of Gorbachev appeared irremediably damaged: while the Soviet Number One on his return from Crimea acted as if the event had been only a quickly closed parenthesis, and declared that he would continue his reform policy, his weak position was now obvious, in particular vis-à-vis Yeltsin, who seemed to be the real winner and who profited from the situation to assert his power and to advocate a real break with the Soviet system. Yeltsin was further able to do this because the failed coup d'état definitively discredited the CPSU, whose preeminence its authors claimed to be restoring. With Yeltsin having suspended the party's activities on Russian territory, on 24 August Gorbachev resigned from his post as its secretary general and dissolved its Central Committee, keeping only his functions as president of the USSR.

But events had badly damaged the Soviet Union, now weakened by the rise of the republics, starting with Russia itself, which had appeared as the real counterpower to the putsch. Ukraine proclaimed its independence on 24 August, and at the end of the month the three Baltic republics finally obtained the establishment of diplomatic relations from various European countries – including France, which had never recognized their annexation – thereby winning final recognition of their independence.[21] In an analysis written at the end of August, the French ambassador in Moscow, Bertrand Dufourcq, predicted the probable death of the Soviet Union under the impact of the self-assertion of the republics begun in Ukraine. He did note that some people 'are betting on the maintenance of a center' to 'create a counterweight that would moderate Russian power', but he wondered if Gorbachev had 'the will' to play this role and 'whether he still had the means to do so'.[22]

French diplomacy at the end of summer 1991 was fully aware of the situation in what many were already calling 'the ex-USSR'. Yet Mitterrand's policy consisted of doing nothing that might help precipitate an uncontrolled breakup, the risk of which was now looming large. Mitterrand spoke to the Canadian leader Jean Chrétien at the start of September about 'the fall of the Soviet Empire' under 'its own weight', but, mentioning the risk of disintegration in Yugoslavia, he hurried to state that one had 'to avoid Europe falling into a thousand pieces'.[23] The next day, during a press conference at the Élysée, he asserted his preference for maintaining 'a sufficiently united central body' that might continue to represent a 'solid pole' in Northeastern Europe. But the French president nevertheless pointed out security imperatives to observe if disintegration did occur: nuclear safety must be maintained (the fate of Soviet weapons was becoming a major preoccupation), conventional disarmament treaties must be taken up and implemented by the states succeeding the USSR, and conflicts among the republics must be settled and new ones prevented.²⁴ The stakes at this stage were no longer to keep a dying USSR together but to preserve a minimal community among republics, starting with Russia, Ukraine and Byelorussia.

In the weeks that followed, Mitterrand kept up a systematic attitude of support for Gorbachev, on whom he placed his hopes of seeing the maintenance of an entity able to prevent the risk of uncontrolled disintegration. To Boris Pankin, the new Soviet minister of foreign affairs, he stressed his 'wish to see [Gorbachev] dominate the difficulties [that were] before him, notably of establishing a solid structure among the Republics'.²⁵ This attitude led him to make various gestures of consideration to Gorbachev, who was invited to stop in Latché on 30 October on the way back from Madrid, where he had participated in the launch of the conference on the Middle East. Gorbachev said he was determined to create 'a [new] Union of sovereign states' that could function as a substitute for the moribund USSR as the second 'pillar' of Europe, the other pillar being the European Community. Mitterrand answered that he was convinced of the need for this union to be 'strong'.²⁶ The attitude of the U.S. president, it must be added, was no different. After Madrid, where Bush and Gorbachev had met, the White House line remained unchanged, Brent Scowcroft summing it up as follows: 'We should do nothing that causes Gorbachev any harm' even if the latter incarnated no more than 'the ghost of the center'.²⁷ A few days later, in the margins of the NATO summit in Rome, Mitterrand and Bush noted the proximity of their views. While the former appeared more worried about the consequences of the disintegration of the USSR – 'the future war is there', he said about the Ukraine – the latter spoke plainly about maintaining a federal entity: 'There has to be something resembling a union. There has to be a strong and coherent power.'²⁸

The following weeks showed the French and the Americans that this was only a pious wish. In an interview with the Indian Prime Minister Narasimha Rao at the end of November, Mitterrand recognized that the crumbling of the USSR and of its empire – which he said could be foreseen, though the rapidity with which it occurred was perhaps unexpected – had already 'changed the face of the world'. Mentioning the disintegration of Yugoslavia – 'the list is not closed', he said – he did not conceal his disquiet over the emergence of a 'Europe of ethnicities': 'The former empires of Europe, German, Russian, Austro-Hungarian, Turkish, would be today unbearable, but they had prevented the explosion of rival nationalities.' He concluded: 'I was against the system of the USSR but I am not overjoyed about its disappearance.'²⁹ On 8 December, the disappearance was finally consummated: Yeltsin and his Ukrainian and Belarussian colleagues met near Minsk to 'register' that the USSR no longer existed 'as a subject of international law and geopolitical reality'. They proclaimed in its place a Community of Independent States (CIS). Until the end, Mitterrand hoped against hope that a coherent entity would remain in one form or another. Still, it was mostly out of personal respect for Gorbachev that he assured the latter, during a telephone conversation on 14 December, that 'the position of France' is that 'there is only a single country, of which you incarnate the existence'. But Gorbachev admitted that the USSR 'was falling to pieces' and that his role was now limited to trying to make the process keep a 'constitutional form' and not end in 'chaos', while Mitterrand recognized that the issue of the international recognition of the former Soviet republics was arising: '[P]ressure was increasingly strong.'[30]

The next day, Mitterrand and Bush could only acknowledge the definitive death of the USSR and the political demise of Gorbachev: 'I do not think that he will be around long', the French president declared while saluting the Soviet Number One's final efforts to maintain a minimum of cohesion among the republics: 'Gorbachev wants to remain in history as the one who liberated his people from tyranny and who tried to federate the remains of this immense empire, but I don't think he can exercise real power.'[31] Ten days later, on 25 December, Gorbachev effectively quit his functions as president of the USSR, while on the roofs of the Kremlin the Russian flag was raised in place of the Soviet flag. 'The Soviet Union collapsed by itself and has lost its empire, effacing the traces of both Stalin and Peter the Great', Mitterrand declared in his end-of-year wishes to the French people on 31 December. Then, evoking 'the terrible images of the combat among the peoples of Yugoslavia' and the risk of 'contagion' that it carried, the president stressed the importance of the other major event of this end of 1991, the agreement reached at Maastricht: 'In the Europe that is being made, there is a grand design capable of creating enthusiasm, of gathering people together, and justifying hope.'[32]

Notes

1. Antatoly Chernyaev wrote that it was at the end of the summer of 1990 that these necessary changes ought to have been decided upon, which would have meant recognizing that the *perestroika* 'was a revolution that implied the transformation of the existing order': see Anatoly S. Chernyaev, *My Six Years with Gorbachev* (University Park: Pennsylvania University Press, 2000), p. 293ff.
2. Reporting on a meeting in Moscow between Prime Minister Valentin Pavlov and former French Prime Minister Raymond Barre alongside European company heads, one

of Mitterrand's closest advisers, Anne Lauvergeon, related 'the profound intellectual and organization disarray of the USSR': the absence of a clear vision of the future of the Union, vague character of the economic reform program, diffused feelings of irresponsibility, etc.: Anne Lauvergeon, note pour le président de la République, Situation en USSR, 7 November 1990, private papers.
3. Jean Lévy, note pour le président de la République, Situation intérieure de l'URSS: anomie et entropie, 13 December 1990, private papers.
4. Meeting between Mitterrand and Petre Roman on Wednesday 30 January 1991, 10 A.M., private papers.
5. Letter from Gorbachev to Mitterrand, 5 February 1991; Roland Dumas judged the letter 'full of good sense' and estimated that 'it confirmed to us that our choices were good': Roland Dumas, handwritten note, 6 February 1991, private papers. (Mitterrand had written to Gorbachev to express his 'strong concern' after the events in Vilnius and emphasize that their effect on European opinions could only be 'strongly negative'; recalling that France had never recognized the annexation of the Baltic states and that they were bound to 'restore [their] sovereignty', he recognized nonetheless that this evolution should happen by 'dialogue' with Moscow and by considering 'legitimate political, economical and security imperatives': letter from Mitterrand to Gorbachev, 17 January 1991, private papers.)
6. Meeting between Mitterrand and Bush, Martinique, 14 March 1991, second part, private papers. The line of the White House – even after the Gulf War, during which Washington had been particularly attentive to the need to preserve its relationship with the Kremlin – remained at that point clearly that of personal support of Gorbachev and to his policy of preservation of the Soviet Union, whose stability was regarded as relevant to U.S. 'national interest': see Michael R. Beschloss and Strobe Talbott, *At the Highest Levels: The Inside Story of the End of the Cold War* (Boston: Little & Brown, 1993), p. 345ff.
7. See Letter from Kohl to Mitterrand, 22 May 1991; Meeting between Mitterrand and Kohl, Lille, 29 May 1991, private papers. Extending an invitation to Gorbachev, in the eyes of the Elysée, offered another advantage, especially if it marked the beginning of a 'progressive enlargement' of the G7: to make it possible to 'loosen the American grip' in the group, an objective of Mitterrand's diplomacy since 1981: see Hubert Védrine, note pour le président de la République, 13 May 1991, private papers.
8. Meeting between Mitterrand and Gorbachev, London, 17 July 1991, with handwritten notes by Pierre Morel, private papers. The issue of support for the USSR was a very political one. Because of the lack of clarity of the Soviet reform projects, even the countries that were most favorable to granting Moscow such support – the FRG and France – indeed showed themselves reluctant to engage financially. As a result, Gorbachev only obtained a status of special associate for the USSR in the IMF and World Bank, whereas Moscow had hoped for status as member in its own right.
9. MAE, fiche, Avenir de M. Gorbatchev, 10 July 1991, private papers.
10. It is not possible here to recount the detail of the events of these three days; for a precise narration, see Favier, Pierre, and Michel Martin-Roland, *La Décennie Mitterrand*, vol. 4, 'Les Déchirements', 1991–1995 (Paris: Seuil, 1999) p. 47ff.
11. On the U.S. side of the affair, see Beschloss and Talbott, *At the Highest Levels*, p. 421ff.
12. Telephone conversation between Mitterrand and Bush, 19 August 1991 at 12:55 P.M., private papers. Called by Mitterrand a few minutes later, John Major and Helmut Kohl shared this point of view: see Telephone conversation between Mitterrand and Kohl, 19 August 1991; and Telephone conversation between Mitterrand and Major, 19 August 1991 at 12:30 P.M., private papers. It should be noted that none of the three leaders, during these contacts, evoked the urgency of an explicit condemnation of the coup d'État.

13. Cited in Favier and Martin-Roland, *La Décennie*, vol. 4, pp. 55–57; see letter from Yanaev to Mitterrand, private papers (the letter was handed to Védrine by the Soviet ambassador Yuri Dubinin on 19 August a little after 7:00 P.M.).
14. Speaking to the press in Maine on 19 August at 8:00 A.M. local time (2:00 P.M. in Paris, i.e. a little after his telephone conversation with Mitterrand), Bush said that he hoped that the USSR would satisfy its international obligations and praised Gorbachev; still, refusing to worry the opinion, he refrained from explicitly denouncing the putsch, which he only characterized – according to a formula suggested by Brent Scowcroft – as 'extraconstitutional'. Then, seeing that his early reaction raised critical voices, he began to adopt a new approach on the evening of that same day in the White House's press room (thus during the night, Paris time, and *after* Mitterrand's televised 8:00 P.M. speech): he now spoke of an 'anti-constitutional' and 'illegitimate' action: see Beschloss and Talbott, *At the Highest Levels*, p. 429–433. (Favier and Martin-Roland shed an inexact light on this point in *La Décennie*, vol. 4, p. 57: in fact, only Major had explicitly condemned the putsch as anti-constitutional *before* Mitterrand's televised speech on 19 August; neither Bush nor Kohl had at that point done that.)
15. See Favier and Martin-Roland, *La Décennie*, vol. 4, p. 61ff: Dumas had made an office available to Kozyrev, and it was agreed that, in case of the physical elimination of Yeltsin or Gorbachev – a scenario that could not be excluded – Kozyrev would be invited to form a government in exile in Paris. In a meeting with Mitterrand after the coup d'état had failed, the Russian minister thanked the president for '[this] quite extraordinary welcome' and declared that 'we will remember how France supported us': see Meeting between Mitterrand and Kozyrev, 22 August 1991, private papers.
16. Telephone conversation between Mitterrand and Yeltsin, 21 August 1991, private papers. In a letter addressed to Mitterrand the following day, Yeltsin thanked him for his 'solicitude' toward Russia: see Message from Yeltsin to Mitterrand, 22 August 1991, private papers. Yeltsin had up to that point been treated with some distance by French leaders who were concerned – as were the Americans – not to disturb Gorbachev. In April 1991, after having been poorly received by the European Parliament (where the French Socialist Jean-Pierre Cot had called him a 'dictator'), he had nonetheless been briefly introduced in the office of Mitterrand while he was being officially received by the general secretary of the Elysée. After the putsch he became an irreplaceable interlocutor, and Mitterrand invited him to France: see Telephone conversation between Mitterrand and Yeltsin, 23 August 1991, private papers
17. Telephone conversation between Mitterrand and Gorbachev, 22 August 1991, private papers.
18. Valéry Giscard d'Estaing especially criticized Mitterrand's reading of the letter of Yanaev. This was payback time for Giscard, who had long resented being called Brezhnev's 'little telegrapher' by Mitterrand after his meeting with the Soviet leader in 1980: see Favier and Martin-Roland, *La Décennie*, vol. 4, p. 64.
19. Concern for Gorbachev clearly led Mitterrand to exercise prudence when dealing with the leaders of the coup d'état. Hence Mitterrand's communiqué dated the end of 19 August emphasized Gorbachev's 'life and liberty' rather than condemning the putsch, as his staff had suggested: 'things should not be mixed together', he said, 'for the life of Gorbachev and Yeltsin is in question. Of course, the coup must be condemned; I will do that tonight on television': see Favier and Martin-Roland, *La Décennie*, vol. 4, p. 55. To Gorbachev, who on 22 August told Mitterrand that those who took part in the putsch 'were capable of everything to present [him] as a ruin', Mitterrand would confide, 'I feared so', thus explaining to Gorbachev the tone of his communiqué: Telephone conversation between Mitterrand and Gorbachev, 22 August 1991.

20. Favier and Martin-Roland, *La Décennie*, vol. 4, p. 68–69. The image of Mitterrand's attitude toward the putsch would be further tarnished by a somewhat convoluted episode: in a book published two months later and entitled *Le Putsch* in its French version, Gorbachev wrote that he regretted that Mitterrand (unlike Bush) had not called him in the Crimea before publicly denying this affirmation during his visit to Latché in late October (discussed later in this chapter). It seems that this affair resulted from unauthorized corrections made by some of Gorbachev's aides on the original manuscript: see Favier and Martin-Roland, *La Décennie*, vol. 4, p. 70–72, and Andreï Gratchev, *L'Histoire vraie de la fin de l'URSS. Le naufrage de Gorbatchev*, Monaco, Editions du Rocher, 1992, p. 132–134.
21. Worried about offending Gorbachev, Bush would wait for 2 September to do likewise – which he would later be criticized for – whereas Moscow would recognize the Baltic independences on 6 September.
22. Cited by Favier and Martin-Roland, *La Décennie*, vol. 4, p. 73–74.
23. Meeting between Mitterrand and Chrétien, 10 September 1990, private papers.
24. Mitterrand's press conference, 11 September 1991, MAE, *PEF*, September–October 1991, p. 27.
25. 'I am not one of those who seek the dismantling' of the union, he added: '[I]t's a factor of imbalance.' See Meeting between Mitterrand and Boris Pankin, 25 October 1991, private papers. 'You are considered in Moscow as the champion of this trend so useful for our country', Yuri Dobinin had told Mitterrand some days before: see Meeting between Mitterrand and Dobinin, 3 October 1991, private papers.
26. Meeting between Mitterrand and Gorbachev, 30 October 1991, private papers; detailed Soviet report in Gratchev, *L'Histoire vraie*, p. 124.
27. Beschloss and Talbott, *At the Highest Levels*, p. 447. The White House's analysis after the failed coup d'État and during the autumn was very close to the one that was made at the Elysée: in the absence of ties between republics, namely from an economical and military point of view, the risk would be atomization and ethnic conflicts; in addition, beyond his personal feelings for Gorbachev, Bush felt that the maintenance of a central government was essential to assure the control of the Soviet nuclear arsenal: see Beschloss and Talbott, *At the Highest Levels*, p. 443–445.
28. Meeting between Mitterrand and Bush, 8 November 1991, private papers.
29. Meeting between Mitterrand and Rao, 26 November, private papers.
30. Telephone conversation between Mitterrand and Gorbachev, 14 December, private papers.
31. Telephone conversation between Mitterrand and Bush, 15 December 1991, private papers.
32. Mitterrand's New Year Address, 31 December 1991, *PEF*, November–December 1991, p. 177.

Epilogue

TWENTY YEARS AFTER

As François Mitterrand hinted on 31 December 1991, the two principal events of the end of that year – the Maastricht Treaty and the dissolution of the USSR, against the background of open warfare in Yugoslavia – marked the end of the historic sequence opened by the upheavals of 1989. But their near simultaneity also illustrated the ambivalence of the new period that was beginning, the hopes it inspired as well as the fears that it legitimately aroused. So how, at the end of the great debate on European architecture of 1990–1991, did an assessment of Mitterrandian policy look? Moreover, did the post–Cold War structures of Europe, as they would be effectively put in place in the coming years, correspond to his conceptions and his aspirations? And in the longer term, to what extent were France's goals for post-Yalta attained, insofar as one can judge twenty years later?

The answer, at the end of 1991, was nuanced. The assessment was positive in the Western European dimension thanks to the result achieved at Maastricht, which testified a posteriori that the Franco-German pair had been able to absorb the shock of unification. The European relaunch desired by Mitterrand and Kohl in the spring of 1990 had aimed to rise above the difficulties of the autumn, and its successful outcome twenty months later confirmed this approach. Despite the increased weight of France's partner across the Rhine, the Paris-Bonn relationship remained the structural axis of European construction. Far from renouncing European integration – an outcome the French, fearing a sort of 'German Gaullism', had dreaded for a while – a now united and fully sovereign Germany remained fundamentally attached to it. Far from becoming obsolete due to the end of the Cold War and German unification – as the Cassandras had predicted after the fall of the Wall – European construction appeared assured of keeping a central place in the post-Yalta landscape in accordance with the French vision.

On the other hand, the assessment at the end of 1991 was less favorable concerning the transatlantic dimension: heir to the Gaullist vision – in which the end of the Cold War and the disappearance of the Soviet threat would ipso facto entail the United States' inevitable disengagement from Europe, over time – the Mitterrandian scenario for post-Yalta was contradicted, at least for the time being. Capitalizing on German unification and then the Gulf War, Washington vigorously reestablished its Atlantic leadership and started in 1991 to lay the bases for an alliance adapted to the post–Cold War situation via a rationale enlarged to 'new missions' of security. Instead of a rebalancing that favored a Western Europe called to become a strategic actor in itself, there followed an unexpected reaffirmation of the established Atlantic order, and as a corollary, a still limited assertion of European ambitions about security and defense. There also followed, quite logically, the confirmation (at least provisionally) of France's position of aloofness within the alliance.

But it was in the pan-European dimension that the balance sheet of French policy was most unfavorable in 1991. The failure of the European Confederation, patent since the summer of that year, marked the limits of the Mitterrandian project for the post–Cold War period at the level of the continent, a project here again derived from the Gaullist grand design of a Europe from the Atlantic to the Urals, freed of the tutelage of the superpowers. According to Mitterrand's vision, the countries of the East would progressively rediscover their European vocation while a Europe of the Twelve would become the principal pillar of stability and prosperity throughout the European continent. But contradicting the realization of that vision in the immediate aftermath of the Cold War were the new democracies' attraction to the Western model and their desire to take their places as quickly as possible in European and Atlantic institutions, the maintenance and even reaffirmation of American influence in Europe and, simultaneously, the weakening (then crumbling) of the Soviet counterweight.

The years that followed – roughly the 1990s – confirmed this situation and contributed by the same token to tarnishing the balance sheet of Mitterrand's diplomacy faced with European upheavals at the end of the 1980s. Indeed, during the post–Cold War period – i.e. roughly the final decade of the century – there emerged and were confirmed tendencies largely in contradiction with French calculations and hopes of the years 1989–1991. By 1992, the worsening of the Yugoslav conflict and the outbreak of bloody war in Bosnia-Herzegovina were already justifying Mitterrand's fears of a 'return to 1913' (or 1914), a historical reference whose pertinence was symbolically confirmed by the French president's visit to Sarajevo on 28 June of that year (on that very day in 1914, the Archduke of Austria was assassinated in Sarajevo, thus provoking the first World War). Far from the reconciled and pacific Europe of which Mitterrand had made himself the advocate, and which the European Confederation might have helped build, it was a Europe of fragmentation and nationalisms that was taking shape, at least in the southeast and to a lesser extent in the center-east of the Old Continent. Very soon, the risks of a return to 'the Europe of Sarajevo' materialized, especially with regard to the future of the EC: barely was the ink dry on the Maastricht Treaty than France and Germany (the latter appearing more and more tempted to assert its own interests as a function of its new power and rediscovered sovereignty) broke over the conflict in the ex-Yugoslavia. With the two countries diverging dangerously in this matter, some people feared nothing less than a breakup of the European Union.

Although this worst-case scenario was finally avoided, the European Union appeared powerless faced with the tragedy playing out in its own backyard. Lacking the means and especially the political cohesion and will, the Twelve failed to reestablish peace in this first post–Cold War European conflict. It was the very rationale of European construction and its vocation as pivot of stability of the Old Continent that appeared to be in question, thus challenging the main premise of French policy in the post–Cold War era. At the same time, the internal dynamic of European construction was stalled: the difficult process of ratifying the Maastricht Treaty (especially in France, where the 'yes' barely carried during the referendum of September 1992), the difficulties of economic and monetary integration of the Twelve and the priority given to enlargement over deepening (marked by the three new memberships in 1995 of Austria, Finland and Sweden, and by launching a process in the direction of the former Communist countries) combined to produce, during the first half of the 1990s, a swing away of the Community pendulum.

As a result, there took place a re-Atlanticization of European security to a degree unprecedented since the origins of the Cold War. Far from the French anticipation of an American withdrawal from Europe due to the disappearance of the Soviet threat, the Balkan conflicts, combined with European internal divisions and impotence, would in effect lead the United States to a grand demonstration of the indispensable nature of its role in the stability of the Old Continent after the Cold War. Despite initial hesitations, the U.S. intervention in the conflict in Bosnia-Herzegovina in the summer of 1995, and its key role in the settlement imposed in Dayton in the autumn, marked a turning point whose significance would be confirmed at the time of the Kosovo crisis in 1998–1999. By pointing to the central place of NATO in the reestablishment and maintenance of peace, by confirming the pertinence of its new security missions and by opening the way to the eastward enlargement of the alliance, into which three former members of the Warsaw Pact (Hungary, Poland, the Czech Republic) made their entry in the spring of 1999, these events consecrated the durability of the American involvement on the Old Continent even as they revealed the fragility of the European Union's political and strategic ambitions. A decade after the end of the Cold War, the Mitterrandian concept of Europe's future seemed far removed from the realities, whereas the role and place of France in post-Yalta Europe remained out of reach of the ambitions that had underlain Mitterrand's diplomacy at the time of the 1989–1991 'revolutions'.

Twenty years afterward, has the moment not come to revisit the end of the Cold War and to reconsider the assessment of French policy in the light of more recent events? By closing a historic sequence characterized (for want of anything better) as 'the post–Cold War era', and by stressing, ten years after the fact, the real final point of 'Yalta', the events of 11 September 2001 and their impact have indeed entailed upheavals that in many respects validate what the main French expectations had then been. This is particularly true regarding the role of the United States in Europe. Already perceptible at the end of the 1990s with the redefinition of its strategic priorities, the U.S. tendency toward disengagement from the Old Continent was reinforced by the attacks on New York and Washington. By declaring war against global terrorism, which soon was erected into a new paradigm of international relations, Washington ipso facto ratified the end of the European priority in its grand strategy. Of course, the manifestations of the U.S. presence in Europe – starting with NATO itself – have not disappeared and might still last for years, but they have arguably become of lesser significance. Even if the awareness of the strategic revolution represented by the U.S. retreat from Europe requires time (especially on the part of Europeans), this fact, which was at the center of Mitterrandian calculations for the post–Cold War era, today appears as a central reality for the future of the Old Continent.

To this is added the new assertiveness of the European Union. If Maastricht was almost immediately followed by a weakening of the political dynamic of European construction, the 1990s were nevertheless marked by the silent and steady pursuit and deepening of integration. These changes are today reaching maturity. The implementation of the EMU and the launching of the euro, the assertion of the CSFP and the establishment of a European security and defense policy (ESDP), the adoption of a constitutional treaty and, after its rejection by France and the Netherlands in

2005, of a new 'simplified' treaty (whose future, however, depends on its ratification by Ireland): in a decade and a half all these landmarks have transformed the virtual features of Maastricht into economic, political and strategic realities. Even though some of these realities remain embryonic, in particular in the politico-military realm, they are beginning to give substance to the ambition of a 'European power' (*Europe puissance*) that France had advocated for several decades. To be sure, the Franco-German pair, as a result of the enlargement of the European Union to twenty-seven members, has lost the ability to mechanically lead that it had possessed in 'smaller Europe', before the fall of the Wall. But twenty years after a German unification that, it was feared, might crack the balance and the privileged partnership that had been established between them, France and Germany remain indispensable partners without which there can be no leadership of the European Union.

Finally, combined with progressive American disengagement, the rise in power of the European Union can only change the situation at the pan-European level, for it is the EU that now appears the principal pivot of stability and prosperity on the Old Continent. Its expansion to include twelve more countries of Central, Eastern and Mediterranean Europe in 2004–2007 is in this respect a major factor. While Southeastern Europe awaits planned membership, the prospect of an extension of the EU to all the Old Continent is today a realistic perspective, as is a Europe that has definitively overcome the divisions of the Cold War. This prospect can only strengthen the EU's preponderant role in European security: contrary to the situation at the start of the 1990s when the Yugoslav crisis broke out, it now derives mainly from the responsibility of Europeans themselves; inversely, this new reality can only contribute to the U.S. tendency to disengage from the Old Continent. Overall, the Europe of the post–Cold War era, as it is establishing itself at the dawn of the twenty-first century, is perhaps not so removed from what had been the French vision at the time of the decisive events studied in this book. One can at least guess that some of the changes underway today would not have been possible except thanks to the decisions and directions taken twenty years ago. It is also by the standard of this long duration that one can appreciate what has been done.

Paris, June 2008

Chronology

1988

January
22: 25th anniversary of the Elysée Treaty and signing of additional protocols

February
28: Hans-Dietrich Genscher's memorandum on the EMU is adopted by the Twelve

March
2–3: NATO summit in Brussels

May
8: François Mitterrand is reelected president of France

June
27–28: European summit in Hanover
28–1 July: 19th Conference of the CPSU

September
15–17: Roland Dumas visits Czechoslovakia

October
10–12: Eduard Shevardnadze visits Paris
24–27: Helmut Kohl visits Moscow

November
8: George Bush is elected president of the United States
17–19: Hungarian Prime Minister Karoly Grosz visits France
25–26 Mitterrand visits the USSR

December
7: Mikhail Gorbachev delivers a speech before the United Nations General Assembly
8–9: Mitterrand visits Czechoslovakia

1989

January
18–19: Mitterrand visits Bulgaria
20: Bush enters office

February
6: round table talks between the Polish government and Solidarnosc begin
10–11: the HWSP's central committee adopts the principle of a multi-party system in Hungary
15: the withdrawal of Soviet forces from Afghanistan is complete

March
6: negotiations on Conventional Forces in Europe (CFE) begin

April
5: round table talks in Warsaw conclude
24: first meeting of the Franco-German Defense and Security Council in Paris
27: Kohl's declaration on disarmament before the Bundestag

May
2: Hungarian Prime Minister Miklos Nemeth undertakes the symbolic dismantling of the Iron Curtain along the Austro-Hungarian border
20–21: Bush and Mitterrand meet in Kennebunkport, Maine.
30–31: NATO summit in Brussels
31: Bush delivers speech in Mainz

June
4: repression in Beijing's Tiananmen Square; first ballot of elections in Poland
12–15: Gorbachev visits the FRG
14–16: Mitterrand visits Poland
18: Solidarnosc triumphs during the second ballot of elections in Poland
26–27: European summit is held in Madrid

July
1: French presidency of the European Community begins
4–6: Gorbachev visits France
6: Gorbachev delivers speech before the Council of Europe in Strasbourg
9–12: Bush visits Poland and Hungary
14–16: summit of the Seven at the Arch at La Défense
19: General Wojciech Jaruzelski is elected president of Poland

August
9: Hungarian authorities stop repatriating East German nationals attempting to cross the border with Austria
20–24: Tadeusz Mazowiecki forms a non-Communist government in Poland
22: Kohl declares that 'the German question is again on the agenda'
25: Kohl and Genscher meet with Nemeth and Gyula Horn at Gymnich

September
10: Hungarian authorities open the border with Austria to East Germans
21–22: Shevardnadze and James Baker meet in Wyoming

October
6–7: Gorbachev visits the GDR; 40th anniversary of the East German state
18: deposition of Erich Honecker, replaced by Egon Krenz, at the head of the Socialist Unity Party (SED)
24: Kohl and Mitterrand informally dine at the Elysée

November
1: Krenz visits Moscow
2–3: 54th Franco-German summit in Bonn
3: joint Mitterrand-Kohl press conference in Bonn
9–10: fall of the Berlin Wall
9–14: Kohl visits Poland (the visit is interrupted by the fall of the Berlin Wall)
13: Hans Modrow is named prime minister of the GDR
14: telephone conversation between Mitterrand and Gorbachev
17: Modrow proposes a 'contractual community' (*Vertragsgemeinschaft*) between the FRG and the GDR
18: informal summit and dinner of the Twelve is held at the Elysée
24: beginning of the 'Velvet Revolution' in Czechoslovakia
28: Kohl proposes a Ten Point Plan for German unity
29: 'four principles' are expressed by Baker

30: Gorbachev, in Rome, proposes a CSCE summit in 1990; Genscher meets Mitterrand and Dumas in Paris

December
1–2: Bush-Gorbachev summit in Malta
3: Bush and Kohl meet in Brussels; Krenz and the entire politburo of the SED resign
4: extraordinary NATO summit is held in Brussels
5: Genscher meets Gorbachev and Shevardnadze in Moscow
6: Gorbachev and Mitterrand meet in Kiev
8–9: European summit in Strasbourg
11: representatives of the Four Powers meet in Berlin
12: Baker delivers speech in West Berlin
16: Bush and Mitterrand meet in Saint Martin
19: Kohl visits the GDR and meets with Modrow in Dresden
20–22: Mitterrand visits the GDR
22: opening ceremony of the Brandenburg Gate
22–25: fall of the Ceausescu regime in Romania
29: Vaclav Havel is elected president of the Czechoslovakian parliament
31: Mitterrand announces his European Confederation plan

1990

January
4: Kohl and Mitterrand meet in Latché
11: Gorbachev, in Vilnius, attempts to block the Baltic declaration of independence
17: Jacques Delors, in Strasbourg, discusses the hypothesis of membership of the GDR in the EEC
18–19: Mitterrand visits Hungary
20: Mitterrand and Margaret Thatcher meet at the Elysée
26: Gorbachev convenes a restricted meeting of his advisers to discuss the German problem
30: Modrow meets Gorbachev in Moscow
31: Genscher delivers speech in Tutzing

February
6: Kohl announces his plans for an economic and monetary union between the FRG and the GDR; Dumas and Baker meet in Shannon
7: Baker visits Moscow

9–10: Genscher and Kohl meet Gorbachev in Moscow
12–13: "Open Sky" conference in Ottawa
13: agreement in Ottawa on the terms of the 2 + 4 negotiation
15: Kohl and Mitterrand dine informally at the Elysée
24–25: Bush and Kohl meet at Camp David

March
1: Dumas delivers speech at the *Berliner Pressekonferenz*
6: Modrow visits Moscow again
8: the Bundestag votes a resolution on the Oder-Neisse border
9: Polish leaders visit the Elysée
11: Lithuania declares independence
14: first meeting of political directors at 2 + 4 is held in Bonn; Oskar Lafontaine visits the Elysée
18: success of the 'Alliance for Germany' in the GDR elections
19: Havel and Mitterrand meet at the Elysée
21: Mazowiecki meets Bush in Washington
30: Shevardnadze and Dumas meet in Moscow

April
10: Bush and Thatcher meet in Bermuda
13: Gorbachev threatens Lithuania with an embargo
19: Bush and Mitterrand meet in Key Largo; Kohl and Mitterrand write a letter on political union to the acting president of the European Community
25–26: 55th Franco-German summit at the Elysée
26: Kohl and Mitterrand write to Lithuanian president Vitautas Landsbergis
28: summit of the Twelve in Dublin (I)
30: meeting of political directors at 2 + 4 is held in East Berlin

May
5: first ministerial meeting at 2 + 4 is held in Bonn
14: Horst Teltschik secretly visits Moscow
17: Kohl visits Washington
18: Baker visits Moscow
22: meeting of political directors at 2 + 4 is held in Bonn
25: Mitterrand visits Moscow
28: Mazowiecki meets Mitterrand at the Elysée
31–2 June: Bush-Gorbachev summit is held in Washington and at Camp David

June
7: Kohl, at Harvard, expresses the inviolability of the Oder-Neisse border
9: meeting of political directors at 2 + 4 in East Berlin
11: Shevardnadze and Genscher meet in Brest-Litovsk
18: Shevardnadze and Genscher meet in Munster; East German Prime Minister Lothar de Maizière is received by Mitterrand at the Elysée
20: meeting of political directors at 2 + 4 is held in Bonn
21: the Bundestag and the Volkskammer pass the resolution on the Oder-Neisse border
22: ministerial meeting at 2 + 4 is held in East Berlin; Kohl and Mitterrand meet in Assmannshausen
25–26: summit of the Twelve in Dublin (II)

July
1: coming into force of the economic and monetary union between the GDR and the FRG
2–15: 28th Congress of the CPSU
4: meeting of political directors at 2 + 4 is held in East Berlin
5–6: NATO summit in London
9–11: summit of the Seven is held in Houston
15–16: Gorbachev and Kohl meet in Moscow and in the Caucasus
17: ministerial meeting at 2 + 4 is held in Paris
19: meeting of political directors at 2 + 4 is held in Bonn

August
2: Iraq invades Kuwait
16–17: Shevardnadze and Genscher meet in Moscow
26–27: Dumas visits Moscow
31: treaty on political unification is signed by the FRG and the GDR

September
4–7: meeting of political directors at 2 + 4 is held in East Berlin
11–12: ministerial meeting at 2 + 4 is held in Moscow; treaty on the final settlement with respect to Germany is signed
13–14: Mitterrand visits Czechoslovakia
17–18: 56th Franco-German summit is held in Munich

October
1–2: meeting of the ministers of the CSCE in New York
3: Germany is unified
28–29: Gorbachev and Mitterrand meet in Paris and Rambouillet.

November
9: German-Soviet treaty is signed in Bonn
14: German-Polish treaty is signed in Warsaw
19–21: CSCE summit and signing of the CFE treaty in Paris

December
6: Kohl and Mitterrand write a letter on political union to Giulio Andreotti
14–15: European summit is held in Rome; the IGCs are launched
20: Shevardnadze resigns

1991

January
13: bloody repression occurs in Lithuania
14: John Major and Mitterrand meet at the Elysée

February
22: Bartholomew-Dobbins memorandum is circulated
25: dissolution of military structures of the Warsaw Pact
27: liberation of Kuwait

March
14: Mitterrand and Bush meet in Martinique
17: referendum held in the USSR on the future of the Soviet Union
23: Havel and Mitterrand meet at the Elysée

May
10: Baker and Genscher issue a common declaration
29–30: 57th Franco-German summit in Lille

June
6–7: NATO ministerial meeting in Copenhagen
12–14: Assises of the European Confederation in Prague
18: Baker mentions in Berlin an "Atlantic community from Vancouver to Vladivostok"
27: the Yugoslav army intervenes in Slovenia
28–29: European summit in Luxembourg

July
14: Bush and Mitterrand meet in Rambouillet

15–17: summit of the Seven in London in presence of Gorbachev
23: Kohl and Mitterrand meet in Bad-Wiessee
30–31: Bush-Gorbachev summit in Moscow

August
19–21: putsch in Moscow
24: Ukraine declares its independence
27: France and the Baltic States reestablish diplomatic relations

September
2: the United States recognizes the independence of the Baltic states
7: the conference on Yugoslavia opens at The Hague
18–20: Mitterrand visits the new Länder of the FRG

October
4: Anglo-Italian initiative on the CFSP
14: Kohl and Mitterrand write to Ruud Lubbers
30: Gorbachev and Mitterrand meet in Latché

November
7–8: NATO summit in Rome
14–15: 58th Franco-German summit is held in Bonn

December
8: Russia, Ukraine and Byelorussia "take note" of the end of the USSR
9–10: European summit is held in Maastricht
23: the FRG recognizes Croatia and Slovenia
25: Gorbachev resigns and the USSR dissolves

Sources

Archival Collections

1. Archives nationales (Paris):

Archives de la présidence de la République, fonds François Mitterrand (5AG4), boxes 2317, 2627, 4066, 4160, 4329, 4406, 5098, 6523, 6874, 6903, 6905, 6926, 7009, 7010, 7708, 11385, 11437, 11441, AH 35/1, CD 222, CD 226, CD 266, CD 414, CDM 8, CDM 33/1, CDM 34/5, CDM 35/2, CDM 36/2, CDM 38/3, CDM 48, EG 170, EG 181, EG 203.

2. Archives diplomatiques (Ministère des affaires étrangères, Quai d'Orsay, Paris):

Affaires stratégiques et de désarmement (ASD), série Affaires stratégiques 1985–1990, boxes 12–17, 130, 130 bis, 132–135, 185, 186, 194, 214–220.

Affaires stratégiques et de désarmement, série Affaires stratégiques 1991–1994, OTAN 5.0, 511, 572 et 59.

Affaires stratégiques et de désarmement, série Questions multilatérales (QM) 1991–1994, boxes 11–15, 18, 20, 25.

Direction Europe, série Allemagne 1986–1990, boxes 6119–6130.

Direction Europe, série RFA 1986–1990, boxes 6769–6772, 6776, 6782–6800.

Direction Europe, série URSS 1986–1990, boxes 5694, 6649, 6650, 6670, 6671, 6673–6685.

Direction Europe, série communisme et eurocommunisme 1986–1990, boxes 6092, 6095–6097.

Série Directeur politique (DP), 1986–1991, boxes 260–263, 273–275, 278, 280–284, 286–289, 291–317.

3. Private papers:

Personal papers of several former advisers to François Mitterrand.

Published Primary Sources

Hanns Jürgen Küsters and Daniel Hofmann, eds., *Deutsche Einheit. Sonderedition aus den Akten des Bundeskanzleramtes 1989/90*. Munich: R. Oldenburg, 1998.

Public Documents

Ministère des affaires étrangères, *Politique étrangère de la France* (PEF), textes et documents.

Ministère des affaires étrangères, *Documents d'actualité internationale* (*DAI*).

Politique et société. La France des années Mitterrand 1981–1995. CD-ROM. Paris: La Documentation française, 1996.

Memoirs and Diaries

Attali, Jacques. *Verbatim*, vols. 1–3. Paris: Fayard, 1993 and 1995.

Baker, James A., III, and Thomas M. DeFrank. *The Politics of Diplomacy: Revolution, War and Peace 1989–1992*. New York: Putnam, 1995.

Bitterlich, Joachim. 'In Memoriam Werner Rouget. Frankreichs (und Europas) Weg nach Maastricht im Jahr der deutschen Einheit', in Werner Rouget, *Schwierige Nachbarschaft am Rhein. Frankreich-Deutschland*. Bonn: Bouvier, 1998.

Bush, George, and Brent Scowcroft. *A World Transformed*. New York: Vintage Books, 1999.

Carle, Françoise. *Les Archives du Président*. Monaco : Editions du Rocher, 1998.

Chernyaev, Anatoly S. *My Six Years with Gorbachev*. University Park: Pennsylvania University Press, 2000.

Cherniaev, Anatolii. 'Gorbachev and the Reunification of Germany: Personal Recollections', in Gabriel Gorodetsky, ed., *Soviet Foreign Policy 1917–1991: Retrospective*. London: Frank Cass, 1994.

Chevardnadze, Edouard. *L'Avenir s'écrit liberté*. Paris: Odile Jacob, 1991.

Delors, Jacques. *Mémoires*. Paris: Plon, 2004.

Dobrynin, Anatoly. *In Confidence: Moscow's Ambassador to America's Six Cold War Presidents*. New York: Random House, 1995.

Doubinine, Youri. *Paris-Moscou. Dans un tourbillon diplomatique*. Paris: Kliopa-Imaginaria, 2002.

Dufourcq, Bertrand. '2 + 4 ou la négociation atypique,' *Politique étrangère* 2 (2000): 467–484.

Dumas, Roland. *Le Fil et la pelote. Mémoires*. Paris: Plon, 1996.

———. 'Un projet mort-né: la Confédération européenne,' *Politique étrangère* 3 (2001): 687–703.

———. *Affaires étrangères 1981–1988*. Paris: Fayard, 2007.

Elbe, Frank. 'Resolving the External Aspects of German Unification: The "two-plus-four" Process', *German Yearbook of International Law* 36 (1993): 371–384.

Froment-Meurice, Henri. *Vu du Quai. Mémoires 1945–1983*. Paris: Fayard, 1998.

Falin, Valentin M. *Politische Erinnerungen*. Munich: Droemer Knaurr, 1993.

———. *Konflikte im Kreml. Zur Vorgeschichte der deutschen Einheit und Auflösung der Sowjetunion*. Munich: Karl Blessing Verlag, 1997.

Gates, Robert M. *From the Shadows: The Ultimate Insider's Story of Five Presidents and How They Won the Cold War*. New York: Simon & Schuster, 1996.

Genscher, Hans-Dietrich. *Erinnerungen*. Berlin: Siedler Verlag, 1995.

Giscard d'Estaing, Valéry. *Le Pouvoir et la vie*, vol. 2, 'L'affrontement'. Paris: Compagnie 12, 1991.

Gorbatchev, Mikhaïl. *Mémoires*. Monaco: Editions du Rocher, 1997.

Gorbatschow, Michail. *Wie es war. Die deutsche Wiedervereinigung*. Berlin: Ullstein, 1999.

Grachev, Andrei, *Gorbachev's Gamble: Soviet Foreign Policy and the End of the Cold War*. Cambridge: Polity, 2008.

Gratchev, Andreï. *L'Histoire vraie de la fin de l'URSS: Le naufrage de Gorbatchev*. Monaco: Editions du Rocher, 1992.

Hurd, Douglas. *Memoirs*. London: Little & Brown, 2003.

Kiessler, Richard, and Frank Elbe. *Ein runder Tisch mit scharfen Ecken. Der diplomatische Weg zur deutschen Einheit*. Nomos: Baden-Baden, 1993.

Kohl, Helmut. *Erinnerungen 1982–1990*. Munich: Droemer Verlag, 2005.

———. *Erinnerungen 1990–1994*. Munich: Droemer Verlag, 2007.

Kohl, Helmut, Kai Diekmann and Ralf Georg Reuth. *Je voulais l'unité de l'Allemagne*. Paris: De Fallois, 1997.

Kotschemassow, Wjatscheslaw. *Meine letzte Mission. Fakten, Erinnerungen, Überlegungen*. Berlin: Dietz Verlag, 1994.

Kwitsinskij, Julij A. *Vor dem Sturm. Erinnerungen eines Diplomaten*. Berlin: Siedler, 1993.

Lanxade, Jacques. *Quand le monde a basculé*. Paris: Nil, 2001.

Major, John. *The Autobiography*. London: HarperCollins, 1999.

Matlock, Jack F. *Autopsy of an Empire: The American Ambassador's Account of the Collapse of the Soviet Union*. New York: Random House, 1995.

Mitterrand, François. *Réflexions sur la politique étrangère de la France. Introduction à vingt-cinq discours (1981–1985)*. Paris: Fayard, 1986.

———. *De l'Allemagne, de la France*. Paris: Odile Jacob, 1996.

Palazchenko, Pavel. *My Years with Gorbachev and Shevarnadze: The Memoirs of a Soviet Interpreter*. University Park: Pennsylvania State University Press, 1997.

Pfeffer, Franz. *Ein Amt und eine meinung. Botschafter in Polen und Frankreich*. Frankfurt am Main: Societäts-Verlag, 2006.

Raimond, Jean-Bernard. *Le Quai d'Orsay à l'épreuve de la cohabitation*. Paris: Flammarion, 1989.

Reagan, Ronald. *An American Life*. New York: Simon and Schuster, 1990.

Shultz, George P. *Turmoil and Triumph: My Years as Secretary of State*. New York: Scribner's, 1993.

Teltschik, Horst. *329 Tage. Innenansichten der Einigung*. Berlin: Siedler, 1991.

Thatcher, Margaret. *The Downing Street Years*. New York: HarperCollins, 1993.

Védrine, Hubert. *Les Mondes de François Mitterrand. À l'Elysée 1981–1995*. Fayard, 1996.

Walters, Vernon A. *Die Vereinigung war vorraussehbar. Hinter den Kulissen eines entscheidenden Jahres.* Berlin: Siedler, 1994.

Personal Interviews

Gilles Andréani, Paris, 6 March 2002.
Jacques Andréani, Paris, 30 July 2002.
Jean-Louis Bianco, Paris, 13 March 2003.
Joachim Bitterlich, Paris, 8 June 2004.
Serge Boidevaix, Paris, 1 August 2002.
James Dobbins, Washington, D.C., 3 October 2002.
Bertrand Dufourcq, Paris, 16 March 2001 and 13 September 2002.
Roland Dumas, Paris, 21 January 2005.
Henri Froment-Meurice, Paris, 9 October 2002.
Roland Galharague, Paris, 2 May 2002.
Nicole Gnesotto, Paris, 13 February 2002.
David Gompert, Washington, D.C., 2 October 2002.
Andreï Gratchev, Paris, 19 November 2004.
Elisabeth Guigou, Paris, 30 March 2004.
Robert L. Hutchings, Washington, D.C., 28 May 2004.
Pierre Joxe, Paris, 6 June 2004.
Jacques Lanxade, Paris, 22 March 2004.
Jean Musitelli, Paris, 21 January 2003 and 11 June 2004.
Caroline de Margerie, Paris, 3 October 2000, 4 September 2002 and 1 April 2004.
Marc Perrin de Brichambaut, Paris, 11 March 2004.
Franz Pfeffer, Paris, 19 May 2003.
Christian Quesnot, Paris, 25 March 2004.
Jean-Bernard Raimond, Neuilly, 10 October 2002.
Hermann von Richthoffen, Ditchley, 22 February 2003.
Gabriel Robin, Paris, 21 December 2001.
Kori N. Schake, Washington, D.C., 26 May 2004.
Brent Scowcroft, Ditchley, 22 February 2003.
Philippe de Suremain, Paris, 29 April 2002.
Horst Teltschik, Berlin, 7 October 2004.
Marisol Touraine, Paris, 16 May 2003.
Hubert Védrine, Paris, 13 May 2003.
Vernon Walters, Paris, 27 November 2001.
Philip Zelikow, Washington, D.C., 26 May 2004.
Robert B. Zoellick, Washington, 27 May 2004.

Secondary Sources

Adomeit, Hannes. *Imperial Overstretch: Germany in Soviet Policy from Stalin to Gorbachev.* Baden-Baden: Nomos, 1998.

Berstein, Serge, Pierre Milza and Jean-Louis Bianco, eds. *François Mitterrand. Les années du changement, 1981–1984.* Paris: Perrin, 2001.

Beschloss, Michael R., and Strobe Talbott. *At the Highest Levels: The Inside Story of the End of the Cold War.* Boston: Little & Brown, 1993.

Bozo, Frédéric. *La France et l'OTAN. De la guerre froide au nouvel ordre européen.* Paris: Masson, 1991.

———. *La Politique étrangère de la France depuis 1945.* Paris: La Découverte, 1997.

———. 'La France, fille aînée de l'Alliance? La politique atlantique de François Mitterrand 1981–1984', in Serge Berstein, Pierre Milza and Jean-Louis Bianco, eds., *François Mitterrand. Les Années du changement, 1981–1984.* Paris: Perrin, 2001.

———. 'Before the Wall: French Diplomacy and the Last Decade of the Cold War,' in Olav Njølstad, ed., *The Last Decade of the Cold War: From Conflict Escalation to Conflict Transformation.* London: Frank Cass, 2004.

———. 'Mitterrand's France, the End of the Cold War, and German Unification.' *Cold War History* 7, no. 4 (November 2007): 455–478.

———. 'The Failure of a Grand Design: Mitterrand's European Confederation (1989–1991).' *Contemporary European History* 17, no. 3 (2008): 391–412.

———. '"Winners" and "Losers": France, the United States, and the End of the Cold War.' *Diplomatic History*, forthcoming.

———. 'France, "Gaullism", and the Cold War', in Melvyn P. Leffler and Odd Arne Westad, eds., *Cambridge History of the Cold War*, vol. 2. Cambridge, Cambridge University Press, forthcoming.

Bozo, Frédéric, Marie-Pierre Rey, N. Piers Ludlow and Leopoldo Nuti. *Europe and the End of the Cold War: A Reappraisal.* London: Routledge, 2008.

Brand Crémieux, Marie-Noëlle. *Les Français face à la réunification allemande, automne 1989–automne 1990.* Paris: L'Harmattan, 2004.

Cogan, Charles. *Alliés éternels, amis ombrageux. Les Etats-Unis et la France depuis 1940.* Brussels: Bruylant, 1999.

Cohen, Samy, ed. *Mitterrand et la sortie de la guerre froide.* Paris: Presses universitaires de France, 1998.

Cold War International History Project Bulletin 12/13 (autumn/winter 2001), 'The End of the Cold War'.

Cox, Michael. 'His Finest Hour? George Bush and the Diplomacy of German Unification.' *Diplomacy and Statecraft* 12 (2002): 123–150.

Favier, Pierre, and Michel Martin-Roland. *La Décennie Mitterrand*, vol. 1, 'Les Ruptures', 1981–1984. Paris: Seuil, 1990.

———. *La Décennie Mitterrand*, vol. 2, 'Les Épreuves', 1984–1988. Paris: Seuil, 1991.

———. *La Décennie Mitterrand*, vol. 3, 'Les Défis', 1988–1991. Paris: Seuil, 1996.

———. *La Décennie Mitterrand*, vol. 4, 'Les Déchirements', 1991–1995. Paris: Seuil, 1999.

Fischer, Beth A. *The Reagan Reversal: Foreign Policy and the End of the Cold War*. Columbia: University of Missouri Press, 1997.

FitzGerald, Frances. *Way Out There in the Blue: Reagan, Star Wars and the End of the Cold War*. New York: Touchstone, 2000.

Fritsch-Bournazel, Renata. *L'Union soviétique et les Allemagnes*. Paris: Presses de la FNSP, 1979.

———. *L'Allemagne unie dans la nouvelle Europe*. Brussels: Complexe, 1991.

Fröhlich, Stefan. *„Auf den Kanzler kommt es an". Helmut Kohl und die deutsche Außenpolitik*. Paderborn: Schöningh, 2001.

Gaddis, John Lewis. *The Long Peace: Inquiries into the History of the Cold War*. New York: Oxford University Press, 1987.

———. *The United States and the End of the Cold War: Implications, Reconsiderations, Provocations*. New York: Oxford University Press, 1992.

———. *We Now Know: Rethinking Cold War History*. Oxford: Clarendon Press, 1997.

———. *The Cold War: A New History*. New York: Penguin Books, 2005.

Garthoff, Raymond L. *The Great Transition: American-Soviet Relations and the End of the Cold War*. Washington, D.C.: Brookings, 1994.

Garton-Ash, Timothy. *In Europe's Name: Germany and the Divided Continent*. New York: Random House, 1993.

Gautier, Louis. *Mitterrand et son armée 1990–1995*. Paris: Grasset, 1999.

Ghébali, Victor-Yves. *La Diplomatie de la détente. La CSCE, d'Helsinki à Vienne (1973–1989)*. Brussels: Bruylant, 1989.

———. *L'OSCE dans l'Europe post-communiste, 1991–1996. Vers une identité paneuropéenne de sécurité*. Brussels: Bruylant, 1996.

Gordon, Philip H. *A Certain Idea of France: French Security Policy and the Gaullist Legacy*. Princeton, NJ: Princeton University Press, 1993.

———. *France, Germany and the Western Alliance*. Boulder, CO: Westview Press, 1995.

Gorodetsky, Gabriel, ed. *Soviet Foreign Policy 1917–1991: A Retrospective*. London: Frank Cass, 1994.

Guérin-Sendelbach, Valérie. *Frankreich und das Vereinigte Deutschland. Interessen und Perzeptionen im Spannungsfeld*. Opladen: Leske + Budrich, 1999.

Hacke, Christian. *Die Außenpolitik der Bundesrepublik Deutschland. Weltmacht wider Willen?* Berlin: Ullstein, 1997.

Haftendorn, Helga. *Deutsche Außenpolitik zwischen Selbstbeschränkung und Selbstbehauptung 1945–2000*. Stuttgart and Munich: Deutsche Verlags-Anstalt, 2001.

Haine, Jean-Yves. *L'Eurocorps et les identités européennes de défense. Du gage franco-allemand à la promesse européenne*. Documents du C2SD, n°33. Paris, 2001.

———. *Les États-Unis ont-ils besoin d'alliés? Les États-Unis et leurs alliés européens, de la guerre froide à l'Irak*. Paris: Payot, 2004.

Hertle, Hans-Hermann. 'The Fall of the Wall: The Unintended Dissolution of East Germany's Ruling Regime,' *Cold War International History Project Bulletin* 2/13 (autumn/winter 2001): 131–140.

Hoffmann, Stanley. 'La France dans le nouvel ordre européen'. *Politique étrangère* 2 (1990): 503–513.

Hohwart, Jean. *Nécessités franco-allemandes et défense en Europe*. Paris: FEDN, 1988.

Hutchings, Robert L. *American Diplomacy and the End of the Cold War: An Insider's Account of U.S. Policy in Europe, 1989–1992*. Washington, D.C.: Woodrow Wilson Center Press, 1997.

Jessel, Jacques. *La double défaite de Mitterrand. De Berlin à Moscou, les faillites d'une diplomatie*. Paris: Albin Michel 1992.

Kaiser, Karl. *Deutschlands Vereinigung. Die internationalen Aspekte*. Bergisch Gladbach: Gustav Lübbe, 1991.

Kissinger, Henry. *Diplomacy*. New York: Simon & Schuster, 1994.

Klein, Jean. *Sécurité et désarmement en Europe*. Paris, 1987.

Kolboom, Ingo. *Vom geteilten Deutschland zum vereinten Deutschland. Deutschland-Bilder in Frankreich*. Bonn, DGAP, Arbeitspapiere zur internationalen Politik, n° 61, April 1991.

Krause, Axel. *Inside the New Europe*. New York: HarperCollins, 1991.

Lacouture, Jean. *Mitterrand. Une histoire de Français*. 2 vols. Paris: Seuil, 1998.

Lacouture, Jean, and Patrick Rotman. *Mitterrand. Le roman du pouvoir*. Paris: Seuil, 2000.

Le Gloannec, Anne-Marie. *La Nation orpheline. Les Allemands en Europe*. Paris: Calmann-Lévy, 1989.

Leimbacher, Urs. *Die unverzichtbare Allianz. Deutsch-französiche sicherheitspolitische Zusammenarbeit, 1982–1989*. Baden-Baden: Nomos, 1982.

Lévesque, Jacques. *L'URSS et sa politique internationale de Lénine à Gorbatchev*. Paris: Armand Colin, 1988.

———. *1989, la fin d'un empire. L'URSS et la libération de l'Europe de l'Est*. Paris: Presses de la FNSP, 1995.

———. 'Soviet Approaches to Eastern Europe at the Beginning of 1989', *Cold War International History Project Bulletin* 12/13 (autumn/winter 2001): 5–23 and 49–72.

Loth, Wilfried. *Ost-West-Konflikt und deutsche Frage*. Munich: DTV, 1989.

Lundestad, Geir, ed. *No End to Alliance: The United States and Western Europe, Past and Future*. New York: Saint Martin's Press, 1998.

———. *The United States and Western Europe since 1945*. Oxford: Oxford University Press, 2003.

Moens, Alexander. 'American Diplomacy and German Unification'. *Survival* 33, no. 6 (November-December 1991): 531–545.

Moravcsik, Andrew. *The Choice for Europe: Social Purpose and State Power from Messina to Maastricht*. Ithaca, NY: Cornell University Press, 1998.

Newton, Julie. *Russia, France and the Idea of Europe*. London: Palgrave, 2003.

Njølstad, Olav, ed. *The Last Decade of the Cold War: From Conflict Escalation to Conflict Transformation*. London: Frank Cass, 2004.

Oberdorfer, Don. *From the Cold War to a New Era: The United States and the Soviet Union 1983–1991*. Baltimore, MD: Johns Hopkins University Press, 1998.

Pond, Elizabeth. *Beyond the Wall: Germany's Road to Unification*. Washington, D.C.: Brookings, 1993.

Rey, Marie-Pierre. 'Le Département international du Comité Central du PCUS, le MID et la politique extérieure soviétique de 1953 à 1991'. *Communisme* 74/75 (2003): 179–215.

———. '"Europe is Our Common Home": A Study of Gorbachev's Diplomatic Concept.' *Cold War History* 4, no. 2 (January 2004): 33–65.

Riché, Pascal, and Eric Aeschimann. *La Guerre de sept ans. Histoire secrète du franc fort 1989–1996*. Paris: Calmann-Lévy, 1996.

Rouget, Werner. *Schwierige Nachbarschaft am Rhein: Frankreich-Deutschland*. Bonn: Bouvier, 1998.

Sarotte, Mary Elise. *1989: The Struggle to Create Post-Cold War Europe*. Princeton, NJ: Princeton University Press, forthcoming.

Schabert, Tilo. *Wie Weltgeschichte gemacht wird. Frankreich und die deutsche Einheit*. Stuttgart: Klett-Cotta, 2002.

Schake, Kori. 'NATO after the Cold War 1991–1995: Institutional Competition and the Collapse of the French Alternative.' *Contemporary European History* 7, no. 3 (1998): 379–407.

Schmidt, Gustav. *A History of NATO: The First Fifty Years*. 3 vols. London: Palgrave, 2001.

Shumaker, David H. *Gorbachev and the German Question: Soviet-West German Relations, 1985–1990*. Westport, CT: Praeger, 1995.

Smyser, W.R. *From Yalta to Berlin: The Cold War Struggle Over Germany*. New York: St. Martin's Griffin, 1999.

Sodaro, Michael J. *Moscow, Germany and the West: From Khrushchev to Gorbachev*. London: I.B. Tauris & Co., 1991.

Soutou, Georges-Henri. *L'Alliance incertaine. Les rapports politico-stratégiques franco-allemands, 1954–1996*. Paris: Fayard, 1996.

———. *La Guerre de cinquante ans. Les relations Est-Ouest 1943–1990*. Paris: Fayard, 2001.

Stark, Hans. *Kohl, l'Allemagne et l'Europe. La politique d'intégration européenne de la République fédérale 1982–1998*. Paris: L'Harmattan, 2004.

Stent, Angela E. *Russia and Germany Reborn: Unification, the Soviet Collapse and the New Europe*. Princeton, NJ: Princeton University Press, 1999.

Sutton, Michael. *France and the Construction of Europe, 1994–2007*. New York: Berghahn Books, 2007.

Szabo, Stephen F. *The Diplomacy of German Unification*. New York: Saint Martin's Press, 1992.

Tiersky, Ronald. *François Mitterrand: The Last French President*. New York: Saint Martin's Press, 2000.

Thomas, Daniel C. *The Helsinki Effect: International Norms, Human Rights, and the Demise of Communism*. Princeton, NJ: Princeton University Press, 2001.

Vernet, Daniel. *La Renaissance allemande*. Paris: Flammarion, 1992.

Weidenfeld, Werner. *Außenpolitik für die deutsche Einheit. Die Entscheidungsjahre 1989/1990*. Stuttgart: DVA, 1998.

Westad, Odd Arne, ed. *Reviewing the Cold War: Approaches, Interpretations, Theory*. London: Frank Cass, 2000.

Zelikow, Philip, and Condoleezza Rice. *Germany Unified and Europe Transformed: A Study in Statecraft*. Cambridge, MA: Harvard University Press, 1995.

Zubok, Vladislav M. 'New Evidence on the Soviet Factor in the Peaceful Revolutions of 1989', *Cold War International History Project Bulletin* 12/13 (Fall/Winter 2001): 5–23.

Index

2+4. *See* Two Plus Four
Adamishin, Anatoly, 259
Adenauer, Konrad, 6, 182
Adomeit, Hannes, 92
Afghanistan, 2, 3, 12, 16, 32
Akhromeyev, Sergei, 254
Alexander, Michael, 333
'*Alliance de revers*', xxii, 10, 25, 297
Allied Control Council. *See* Germany
Atlantic Alliance. *See* NATO
Andréani, Jacques, 246, 247, 279
Andreotti, Giulio, 92, 96, 128, 132, 179, 180, 187, 256, 314, 329
Antall, Joszef, 357
Arche de la Défense (G-7 Summit), 34, 41, 68, 86, 163
ABC weapons. *See* FRG
Attali, Jacques, 49, 120, 125, 158, 227, 235, 238, 246
    Verbatim, xiii, xxviii, xxx, 275
Augstein, Rudolf, 119
Austria, 66, 86, 184, 347, 390
Azerbaijan, 171

Bahr, Egon, 58, 92, 94, 197
Baker, James, 43, 44, 87, 89, 95, 128, 133, 139, 141, 144–5, 175–180, 194, 217, 241, 247, 249, 251–3, 255, 280–1, 283, 286, 288, 291, 293, 317, 318, 319, 339, 342, 345, 346, 356
    Baker-Genscher declaration, 319, 356
    Berlin speeches, 141, 144–5, 317, 342, 356
    'Four Principles', 133, 144
    and Two Plus Four, 175–8, 180–1, 217, 293

Baltic Republics, 171, 240, 345, 378, 382
Bartholomew, Reginald, 256, 318, 338
Belgium, 134
Berlin, 91, 112–4, 137–9, 173–4, 230, 232, 284
    allied initiative on, 138
Berlin Wall
    fall of, xi xiii, xvi, xxi, 84, 104, 111–9, 120, 125, 135, 140, 146, 148, 181, 182, 330, 342, 389, 392
    opening of Brandenburg Gate, xxii, 143
Bertinotti, Dominique, xxix
Bianco, Jean-Louis, xxx, 124, 145, 148, 172, 236, 297, 322
Byelorussia, 383
Bitterlich, Joachim, xxv, 100, 129, 186, 235, 238, 321
Blackwill, Robert, 259, 331
Blot, Jacques, 34, 102–3, 116, 125–6, 173, 176
Boidevaix, Serge, 56, 58, 89–90, 138–9
Borders
    of Germany. *See* Germany
    Intangibility/inviolability of, 13, 103, 108, 155, 156, 223, 225, 231, 232, 265–6, 269–70
Brandt, Willy, xxi, 56, 64, 93, 115, 148
Brezhnev, Leonid, 2
    Brezhnev doctrine, 38, 41, 83
Brzezinski, Zbigniew, xiv, 79
Bulgaria, 38, 39, 86
Bundestag, 45, 53, 115, 121, 122, 123, 224, 225, 226, 227, 232, 287, 297, 298
    Mitterrand speech in. *See* Mitterrand, François
Bundeswehr. *See* Germany
Bush, George H. W., xvi, xix, xxiii, xxiv, 33,

40, 41, 44, 46, 56, 114, 127, 128, 180, 190, 223, 240, 242, 247, 339, 344, 345
  and German unity, 89, 95, 98, 113, 127, 133, 137, 178, 293
  and Gorbachev, 30, 35, 114, 135, 221, 254–5, 282, 378, 379–80, 381, 383, 384
  and Kohl, 115, 130, 192–3, 222, 228, 231, 243
  Mainz speech, 48, 60
  and Mitterrand, 46–48, 58, 59–60, 86, 111, 118, 133–4, 145, 216, 223, 240–41, 247, 248–52, 253, 256–8, 318, 321, 331, 338, 342, 344, 378, 379–80, 383, 384
  and Thatcher, 216, 234

Camp David (Bush-Kohl meeting), 192–3, 194, 219, 243, 303
Canada, 64, 65, 348, 351
Carter, Jimmy, xiv
Caucasus (Kohl-Gorbachev meeting), 283–92
CDU/CSU, 6, 53, 58, 88, 89, 93, 141, 168, 192, 214, 232, 233
Ceausescu, Nicolae, 73, 146
CEEC. *See* Eastern Europe
CFE Negotiations, 43, 46–7, 64, 214, 251, 255, 282–3, 291–2, 298
CFSP. *See* European Community
Cheney, Richard, 339
Chernyaev, Anatoly, 171, 177, 254, 275
Chernenko, Konstantin, 10
Chevènement, Jean-Pierre, 92, 257–8, 302
Chirac, Jacques, 16–18, 370
Chrétien, Jean, 382
Cohen, Samy, xiii
Collor, Fernando, 193
Council of Europe, 41, 63, 65, 352–3
Cossiga, Francesco, 169
CPSU, 31, 87, 177, 283–4, 377–8, 382
  Nineteenth conference of, 31
  Twenty-eighth congress of, 377–8
Croatia, 326–7
CSCE, xvii, 8, 33, 43, 64–5, 85, 103, 123, 126, 127, 132, 137, 144–6, 175, 177, 180, 214, 217, 248, 251–2, 255, 257, 258, 279–80, 282, 289, 293, 297, 298–9, 315, 317, 342, 345, 348, 349, 352–3, 356, 359, 360
  Paris Charter, 146, 300, 367
  Paris summit, 258, 280, 297–300, 312, 317, 349, 360
Czechoslovakia, 39, 86, 87, 349, 355, 357, 359

d'Aboville, Benoît, 26
d'Haussy, Marie-Reine, 259
de Boissieu, Pierre, 314
de Gaulle, Charles, xiv, xv, xxi, xxii, xxiii, xxv, 3, 6, 8 ,14, 16, 35, 37, 59, 64, 67, 103, 223, 343
  and German unity, xxii, xxiii, 59, 62, 64, 81, 103
Dana, Thierry, 259
De Michelis, Gianni, 200, 323–4
De Mita, Ciriaco, 36
Delors, Jacques, 53–55, 65, 183, 184–5, 187–8, 235, 236, 239
  and German unity, 184–5, 187–8
Deutsche Bank, 241
Dienstbier, Jiři, 39
Diplomatic archives (Archives diplomatiques), xvii
Dobbins, James, 363
Dubinin, Yuri, 385
Dresden (Kohl visit to). *See* Kohl, Helmut
Dresdner Bank, 241
Dublin (European Council meetings), 166
  Dublin I, 188, 209, 236, 237, 238, 239
  Dublin II, 209, 238, 239, 242–3, 283
Duclos, Michel, 170
Dufourcq, Bertrand, 32, 116, 131, 173, 210, 211, 212, 215, 219, 220, 229, 231, 255, 287, 289, 293–5, 336, 348, 355, 382
Dumas, Roland, 30, 31, 32, 37, 38, 58, 85, 97, 114, 116, 121, 122, 132, 138–40, 172, 174, 224, 239, 250, 292, 299, 300, 327, 339, 350, 352, 354, 380
  and Baker, 145, 176, 217, 241
  and German unity, 113, 133, 180, 189, 201, 210–2, 214, 234, 286
  and Oder-Neisse line, 224, 226, 230, 232, 288–9
  personal history of, xxi
  personal style of, 211
  relations with Shevardnadze, 31, 48, 89, 90, 136, 181, 215, 244
  relations with Genscher, 53, 54, 88, 122, 124–6, 132, 211, 235, 237, 283, 285, 287, 293, 295, 296, 297, 299, 313, 314
  and Two Plus Four, 176, 210–7, 288–9

Eastern Europe, 36–42, 62–5, 83–5, 87, 97, 98, 99, 100, 101, 115, 117, 119, 120, 123, 131, 132, 134, 135, 145, 169, 227, 247, 251,

Index 411

256, 257, 258, 282, 283, 297, 311, 333, 342, 345, 347–61
   Democratic transition in, xxvi, 33, 40, 63, 84, 123, 140, 350, 358
   and the European Confederation, xiii, xxiii, 63, 65, 147, 311, 347–61
   integration into the European Community. *See* European Community
Eastern European countries. *See* Eastern Europe
EBRD, 120, 146, 353
EFTA, 66
Elbe, Frank, 259
Élysée (dinner of the Twelve at), 116–120
Élysée Treaty, 5, 21–2, 51
Euro-missiles, 1, 4–5, 21
European Common Home. *See* Gorbachev
European Community
   CFSP, 313–6, 320–5, 328–30, 333, 336, 339, 343
   enlargement to Eastern European countries, xvi, 101, 146–7, 347, 358, 391, 392
   European Commission, 41, 53, 65, 86, 184–5, 236–9, 243, 313, 316
   European Council, 184–7, 236–40, 313–4, 321, 324, 330, 337
   EMU, xxv, 30, 53–5, 100–1, 119–22, 126, 130, 132, 133, 144, 185–8, 235–6, 238, 240, 311, 313, 316, 328–30, 391
   European Parliament, 100, 121, 130, 186–7, 236–8, 313–4, 320, 325, 328, 330
   European Union, xvi, xvii, xxv, xxvi, 122, 185, 187, 236, 238–9, 312, 324, 329, 335, 339, 340, 356, 390–2
   Franco-German relaunch of, 183–8, 234–43, 295, 297, 312–31
   IGC, 54–5, 100, 120–2, 129–33, 137, 187–8, 235–40, 314–5, 317, 323–4, 329–30, 333, 335–7, 352
   Political union, 66, 101, 119, 122, 130, 185–8, 209, 235–40, 257, 311–8, 320–4, 327–30, 333, 336, 337, 340
   relations with the United States, 144–5, 317
   support of German unity, 131–3, 151
European Confederation, xiii, xxiii–xxvi, 63, 65, 147, 298, 311, 319–20, 346, 347–361
   assises of, 349–361
   failure of, 357–61

European Defence, 8, 51, 64, 65, 67, 245–6, 281, 295, 311, 315–21, 329, 332, 334, 335, 336, 338, 339, 341, 345
European Monetary Union (EMU). *See* European Community
European Single Act, 12, 66
European Union. *See* European Community

Fabius, Laurent, 54
Falin, Valentin, 171, 198, 254, 303, 307
Favier, Pierre, xiv
FDP, 6, 244
FFA, 281, 297, 321, 322, 332, 343, 344
Fischer, Oskar, 140, 162
Fontainebleau (European Council meeting), 9
Foucher, Michel, 350
Fouchet plan, 8, 313, 330
France
   Relations with Eastern European countries, 7, 36–42, 49–51, 85–6, 311, 347–61
   Relations with the FRG, xxvi, 2–3, 5–6, 12, 21–2, 49–55, 61–2, 100–4, 129–34, 181–90, 213, 233–243, 281, 295, 296–7, 312–31, 388, 392
   Relations with Great Britain, xxii, 168–70, 233–4, 316
   Relations with NATO, 45–9, 51, 195, 280–1, 331–346, 389
   Relations with the Soviet Union, 3, 9–17, 30–6, 59, 213, 214–5, 297
   Relations with the United States, 7–8, 9, 11–12, 46–47, 247–50, 318, 331–9, 342–3, 364
   and Yugoslav crisis, 326–8
Franco-German corps, 301, 321, 324–5, 344
FRG
   Basic Law, 214, 230–2, 287, 290
   domestic politics, 61, 89–90, 93, 112, 115, 122–124, 225, 327
   and NATO, 51, 128, 244–5
   and the European confederation, 355–6
   and European integration, 53–5, 78, 119–122, 295
   neutralism, 6–7, 19, 20
   pacifism, 6–7
   relations with the GDR, 20–1, 88, 93–5, 122–4, 148, 166, 290

economic and monetary union with the GDR, xxi, 187, 221
  See also *Ostpolitik*
FRG-GDR Contractual Community (*Vertragsgemeinschaft*). See Modrow, Hans.
Froment-Meurice, Henri, 23

G-7, 11, 34, 242, 283, 379
Galharague, Roland, 350
Galvin, John, 341
Gambetta, Léon, 60
Gauer, Denis, 259
GDR, xix, xxi, xxii, 57, 58, 87, 88, 89, 91, 93, 94, 96, 97, 112, 123, 124, 140, 141, 142, 143, 167, 172, 179, 181, 181, 184, 214, 237, 290, 298, 323
  and the EEC, 120, 184–5, 239
  collapse of, xxi, 103, 141, 148, 165, 167, 173, 179, 180
  elections, xxii, 123, 172, 186, 187, 210, 214, 215, 216, 224, 225
  reforms, 88, 90, 92, 94, 95, 98, 102, 115, 116, 165
  refugees, 84, 86–7
  Stasi, 87, 167
  status of ex-GDR territory in NATO, 191–3, 243, 252, 255, 279, 284, 285, 286, 291, 292
  Volkskammer, 214, 224, 232, 287, 290, 297
Genscher, Hans-Dietrich, xix, 15, 18, 19, 20, 37, 42, 45, 46, 53, 61, 68, 87, 88, 135, 136, 139, 173, 191, 251, 279, 283, 291, 297, 319, 355, 356
  and European integration, 54, 55, 122, 133, 235, 237, 313, 314, 315
  and German unity, 90, 94, 96, 101, 115, 122–3, 125, 148, 178–9, 283, 285–6, 294–5, 296
  and Oder-Neisse line, 222–5, 232, 287–8
  relations with Shevardnadze, 218, 221, 255, 290
  Tutzing speech, 175, 191–2, 194
  and Two Plus Four, 176, 177, 180, 211, 218, 293, 299
  and Yugoslav crisis, 327
Georgia, 171
Geremek, Bronislaw, 39
Gerlach, Manfred, 142

Germany
  Allied Control Council, 138–9
  borders, 13, 117, 126, 127, 128, 131,132, 136, 189, 190, 222–233, 286, 289
  confederation between the two Germanys, 104, 172
  and the European Community, 183–6, 295, 312–331
  manpower of Bundeswehr, 251, 255, 283–4, 298–99
  meeting of Four Powers representatives in Berlin, 137–9
  and military alliances, 129, 168, 190–195, 243–58, 282–85
  neutrality, 19, 20, 179, 191, 194
  quadripartite rights and responsibilities, 88, 134, 137, 138, 142, 159, 175, 177, 198–9, 212, 213, 218, 220, 224, 232, 279, 287, 290, 291, 298
  renunciation of ABC weapons, xxiii, 190, 211, 212, 252, 282, 284, 291, 295, 301–2
  final settlement, 286, 289
  German-Polish treaty, 225, 228, 230, 233, 287, 298
  peace settlement, 213, 215, 220, 286, 288
  peace treaty, 177, 212, 216, 294
Giraud, André, 18, 20
Giscard d'Estaing, Valéry, 2–4, 6, 113, 381
Gompert, David, 332
Gonzalez, Felipe, 96, 118, 132, 343
Gorbachev, Mikhaïl, xii, xvi, xxi, xxiv, 10–21, 29–36, 38–46, 48, 55, 84, 85, 91–2, 97, 111, 114, 117–8, 127, 132, 134–8, 145, 165, 168, 170, 190, 194, 209, 212, 223, 240, 242, 243, 244, 252–4, 256, 284, 293, 297, 377–84
  ascent to power, 1–2, 10–12
  and Bush, 35–6, 127–129, 135, 221, 222, 254–5, 282
  and Kohl, 57, 283–285, 290, 296
  Common European Home concept, 33, 35, 56, 64–65, 67, 92
  and Eastern Europe, 117, 283
  and German unity, 92–94, 115–6, 171–2, 175, 177–180, 190–2
  visits to France, 12–14, 34–36, 59–61, 68, 297
  visit to the FRG, 56–58, 60
Great Britain, i, xii, xiii, 16, 19, 45, 211, 298, 313, 316, 319, 322, 324, 326, 328, 329

and German unity, 68, 113, 134, 295
Grachev, Andrei, 159
Gromyko, Andrei, 11, 31
Grosz, Karoly, 38
Guéhenno, Jean-Marie, 61, 101–2, 125, 141, 167, 173
Guelluy, Philippe, 257
Guigou, Elisabeth, xxix–xxx, 37, 54, 100, 119, 121–2, 129–30, 145, 183–9, 235–9, 242, 313, 315–6, 347–8, 350

Hadès missile, 43, 45, 48, 52
The Hague (1948 European Congress), 349, 357
Hanover (European Council meeting), 53
Harmel, Pierre. *See* NATO
Hassner, Pierre, xxviii
Hajek, Jiří, 39
Hartmann, Peter, 259
Haughey, Charles, 237–8
Havel, Václav, 39, 73, 349, 353–5, 358, 360
    and the European confederation, 349, 353–5, 358, 360
Helsinki Final Act, 128, 132–3, 253, 254
Helsinki process. *See also* CSCE, 104, 127, 145, 146, 298–300
Hennekinne, Loïc, xxx, 221, 321
Hertle, Hans-Hermann, 162
Honecker, Erich, 20, 84, 91–7, 140–1
Hungary, 36, 41, 83, 85, 86–7, 94, 100, 117, 120, 348, 355, 357, 391
Höynck, Wilhelm, 376
Horn, Gyula, 87
Houston (G-7 summit), 242–3, 283, 287, 379
Hurd, Douglas, 139, 176, 196, 234, 286, 287, 288, 291, 293, 323–4
Husak, Gustáv, 39

IGC. *See* European Community
INF. *See* Euro-missiles
    zero option, 4, 17–8, 42–3, 45, 47
Iraq, 279, 332, 339
Iron curtain, 86
Italy, 16, 128, 180, 212

Jakeš, Miloš, 39
Jaruzelski, Vojtech, 12, 37, 40, 63, 84, 92, 225, 226
Joxe, Pierre, xxviii
Julliard, Jacques, 79

Kadar, Janos, 38
Kastrup, Dieter, 88, 89, 131, 177, 210, 211, 229, 287, 292, 355
Kennebunkport (Bush-Mitterrand meeting), 35, 46–7, 58–9, 249
Kessedjian, Bernard, 198
Key Largo (Bush-Mitterrand meeting), 216, 223, 249, 247, 248–50, 256, 258, 279, 280, 318, 319, 331
Kiev (Gorbachev-Mitterrand meeting), xiv, xviii, xxi, 112, 132, 134–8, 139, 146, 181, 298
Kimmit, Robert, 107
Kissinger, Henry, 40
Kohl, Helmut, xiii, xvi, xix, xxi, xxii, xxiii, xxiv, xxv, 6, 19, 33, 37, 44–7, 50, 61, 68, 87, 88, 233
    and European construction, xxv, 12, 97–8, 100, 117, 120–2, 129–31, 175, 184, 186–7, 235–8, 310–331
    and Oder-Neisse line, 209, 222–33, 234
    and Mitterrand, 21, 51, 52, 53, 97–8, 100, 113–4, 118, 121–2, 125, 129–31, 133, 138–40, 143, 166–7, 168–71, 181–3, 188–90, 216, 234, 239, 241, 283, 296, 314–6, 324, 328–30, 379, 389
    Ten Point plan, xxi, 122–8, 136
    proposes confederative structures with GDR, 123, 141, 167
    and EMU, 53–5
    and Franco-German relations, 181–3, 188, 234, 239, 320–22, 326–27
    and Germany's status in NATO, 190–3, 209, 243, 251
    and German unity, xxii, 5, 21, 84, 88–90, 93–6, 111–2, 115, 118–9, 141, 148–9, 167–8, 180, 219
    visit to the GDR, 140, 142, 149
    visits to the Soviet Union, 55–8, 165, 177, 178–80, 183, 209, 279, 281–5
    and the Yugoslav crisis, 326–7
Kochemassov, Vyacheslav, 137–9
Kozyrev, Andrei, 380
Krenz, Egon, 84, 91, 92–3, 94, 95, 115, 140, 141
    meeting with Gorbachev, 92–3
Kvitsinski, Yuly, 220, 259, 283, 292

Lafontaine, Oskar, 227, 234, 235, 244
Lambsdorff, Otto, 53, 54
Lance missile, 42, 44, 47, 251

Landsbergis, Vytautas, 241
Lanxade, Jacques, 194, 244, 246, 248, 257, 279, 280, 321, 331–2, 338, 339
Latché, Gorbachev-Mitterrand meeting, 383
    Kohl-Mitterrand meeting, 166–7, 168–9, 170, 181–3, 188, 223,
Legge, Michael, 331, 332, 333, 340
Lévy, Jean, 378
Lithuania, 209, 240–2, 252, 378
London, NATO summit, 254, 255, 256, 257, 258, 278–84, 286, 299, 331–2, 340, 341, 343, 346
    G-7 summit, 379
Lubbers, Ruud, 118, 132, 229, 317, 324

Madrid (European Council meeting), 54–55
Major, John, 96, 316, 323, 324, 328, 329, 338, 386
Mallaby, Christopher, 160
Malta (Bush-Gorbachev summit), 35, 112, 114, 126–9, 133, 135, 143, 146, 168
Maastricht (European Council meeting and treaty), xxv, xxvi, 186, 236, 240, 295, 312, 314, 322–30, 343–5, 360, 361, 384, 388, 390, 391, 392
Maizière, Lothar de, 255, 291
Margerie, Caroline de, xxx, 140–1, 211, 221, 225, 288, 315, 321, 325, 331, 349, 353, 355
Martens, Wilfrid, 118
Martin-Roland, Michel, xiv
Martinique (Mitterrand-Bush meeting), 318–9, 338, 339, 340, 342, 378
Mainz (Bush speech). *See* Bush, George H. W.
Mazowiecki, Tadeusz, 84, 224, 225, 228, 231
Mérillon, Jean-Marie, 34, 58, 135
Mexico, 35
Minc, Alain, 179, 152
Misselwitz, Hans, 10
Mitterrand, François
    Bundestag speech, 3, 6, 7, 9, 11, 51
    and disarmament, 16, 18–9, 33, 42–9
    and Bush, 46–8, 133–4, 248–50, 252, 318–9, 321–2, 338–9, 344–5, 379–80, 384
    and Eastern Europe, 7, 36–42, 62–5, 145–7, 311, 347–61
    and Euromissiles, 3–4
    and the European Confederation, xiii, 147, 347–61
    and European construction, xxii, xxv, xxvi, 8–9, 22, 53–5, 65–7, 99–100, 118, 120–1, 129–34, 147, 168, 183–8, 235–40, 312–31
    and Franco-British relations, 169, 233–4, 316
    and Franco-German relations, xxii, 22, 53–5, 181–3, 188, 233–43, 295–6, 312–32
    and Franco-Soviet relations, 9–15, 30–6, 136, 297
    and Franco-German strategic cooperation, 9, 10, 11–12, 51–3, 319–24
    and the CSCE, 145–6, 258, 298–300
    and EMU, xxv, 53–5, 99–101, 120–2, 130–2, 185, 187–8, 236, 329
    and European defense, 245–6, 281, 318–25, 329
    and German unity, xx–xiii, 5, 20–2, 25, 57–62, 90–91, 96–9, 112–3, 116–9, 121, 125–6, 134, 136, 141–3, 147–9, 158–9, 168–70, 171, 171, 182–4, 187, 188, 223–4, 226, 233, 253, 293, 296
    and Germany's status in NATO, 193–5, 252–4
    and Gorbachev, xiv, 2, 10–11, 13–15, 18, 35–6, 134–36, 252–54, 378–84
    meetings with Gorbachev, 10–11, 12–15, 32–3, 33–5, 134–36, 252–4, 383
    and Kohl, 5, 6, 12, 53, 129–31, 181–3, 223, 225, 227–8, 235–43, 296, 320, 328–31
    concerns over Kohl's policy, 53–4, 121–2, 125–6, 168–70, 173, 187
    reactions to Kohl's Ten Point plan, 124–6
    and Oder-Neisse line, xxiii, 98, 117, 132, 136, 190, 209, 222–35, 349
    and NATO, 3–4, 18, 193–5, 245–50, 252–4, 257–8, 280–2, 318–9, 342–3, 344–46
    personal history of, xiii, xvi, xix–xx
    and quadripartite rights and responsibilities over Germany, 126, 138–9, 142, 174–5, 180–1, 183, 210
    and Thatcher, xiii, xxii, 9, 46–7, 133, 138, 168–70, 174–5, 183–4, 196, 229, 234, 251, 281, 316
    and Two Plus Four, xiv, xxiii–xxiv, 176, 180–1, 209, 210, 227–8

vision of the end of 'Yalta', xv, xxi, 8, 14, 22, 62–9
visits to Eastern European countries, 36–42, 73, 86, 348–49
visits to the FRG (official visits), 21, 323
visit to the GDR, xiv, xviii, xxi, 111, 134, 139–43, 182
visits to the Soviet Union, 9–10, 10–11, 14–15, 32–3, 50, 252–4
Modrow, Hans, xxiv, 91, 94, 112, 115, 123,124, 140, 141, 142, 165, 167–8, 172, 174, 177, 178, 179, 189, 191
    proposes a contractual community with the FRG (*Vertragsgemeinschaft*), 94, 114, 115, 123–4, 166, 168, 172, 173
Momper, Walter, 172–3
Morel, Pierre, xxx, 299, 321, 344, 356
Moscow (Two Plus Four ministerial meeting), 278–9, 289, 291–4
Musitelli, Jean, 350–1, 355, 358, 359, 360

NACC. *See* NATO
National archives (Archives nationales), xvi
NATO
    cooperation with Eastern countries, 345–6, 354–5
    creation of NACC, 345
    dual-track decision, 2–6
    French-American rapprochement, 331–9
    Harmel report, 128, 247
    ministerial meetings, 157, 255–6, 334–6, 340, 345,
    status of ex-GDR territory. *See* GDR
    summits, 18, 42, 45–8, 53, 61, 111, 127, 128–9, 133, 144, 168, 248–51, 254–8, 278–82, 283, 286, 299, 325, 331, 338, 340, 341, 343–6, 361, 383
Nemeth, Miklos, 86–7
Netherlands, 134, 180, 212, 322, 391

Oder-Neisse line. *See* Germany: borders
Ostpolitik
    Franco-German Ostpolitik, 49–50, 56, 101, 186, 240–1, 355
Ottawa ('Open Skies' conference), 180

Pankin, Boris, 383
Paris (CSCE Charter). *See* CSCE
Paris (CSCE summit). *See* CSCE

Paris (Two Plus Four ministerial meeting), 279, 282, 285, 286–90
Pavlov, Valentin, 379
Perestroika, xxiv, 1, 11, 31, 34, 36, 39, 84, 94, 179, 171, 240, 242, 294, 377, 378
Pershing missiles, 4, 9, 10, 11, 17, 19
Persian Gulf crisis and war, 279, 296, 312, 315, 315, 319, 339, 341, 389
Peter the Great, 384
Ploetz, Hans-Friedrich von, 333, 344
Pluton missile, 43
Poland, 1–3, 7, 16, 36, 40, 41, 83, 84, 85, 86, 94, 100, 103, 113, 117, 120, 132, 224, 225, 355, 357, 359, 391
    and Oder-Neisse line, 224–227, 228, 230, 232, 288
    leaders meet with Mitterrand, 224–7
Political Union. *See* European Community
Pompidou, Georges, 3
Portugalov, Nikolai, 87, 153
Potsdam agreements, 108, 159, 286
Prunskiene, Kazimiera, 241

Quad group (Four Western Powers' consultation mechanism), 211, 254, 260, 283, 285, 333, 336
Quadripartite rights and responsibilities. *See* Germany
Quesnot, Christian, 321, 341, 344

Raimond, Jean-Bernard, 18, 20
Rao, Narasimha, 383,
Reagan, Ronald, xxi, 4, 7, 9, 11, 15, 17, 32, 33, 35
Reykjavik (Reagan-Gorbachev meeting), 15–8
Rice, Condoleezza, xii, xxvii
Robin, Gabriel, 194, 248, 256, 282, 331–40, 342, 344
Roman, Petre, 360, 378
Rome (NATO summit), 325, 343–6, 361, 383
Rosenzweig, Luc, 125
Ross, Dennis, 175
RRF, 319–20, 341–3
Rupnik, Jacques, 73
Russia. *See also* Soviet Union

Saint-Martin (Bush-Mitterrand meeting), 111, 133–4, 145, 147
Sakharov, Andrei, 10, 32

Santer, Jacques, 118
Sauzay-Stoffaës, Brigitte, xxix
Schabert, Tilo, xiv–xv
Scheer, François, 50
Schmidt, Helmut, 2, 4, 5, 6, 7, 51
Schmitt, Maurice, 251
Scholz, Rupert, 273
Scowcroft, Brent, 60, 95, 246, 250, 322, 323, 325, 331, 332, 344, 383
SDI, 11–3, 15, 17
SED, 88, 91, 93, 140
Seiters, Rudolf, 94
Seitz, Raymond, 89
Shevardnadze, Eduard, 11, 31, 48, 87, 89, 90, 133, 134–6, 138, 171, 173, 177, 180, 181, 214, 215, 216, 217, 218, 220, 221, 244, 251, 255, 283, 285, 290, 293, 297, 377
   resignation of, 377
Skubiszewski, Krzystof, 231, 287, 288, 289
Slovenia, 326–7
SNF, 17–8, 42–9, 52–4, 61, 251
Solidarnosc/Solidarity, 40–1, 84–5
Solzhenitsyn, Alexander, 4, 16
Soviet Union
   attempted coup in, 379–83
   collapse of, 377–84
   economic and financial aid to, 35–6, 170–1, 209, 241–43, 279, 283, 294, 378–9
   human rights in, 12, 32–3, 346
   and united Germany's membership in NATO, 191–5, 244–5, 250–8, 280, 282–6
   and German unity, 57–8, 89, 92–3, 123, 135–7, 147, 170–3, 178–9, 283–5, 289–93
   nationalities, 34, 135, 171, 383
   relations with Eastern Europe, 36, 39–40, 41–42, 63, 85–7
   relations with the GDR, 89, 91–3, 171–2
SPD, 6, 46, 58, 88, 89, 124, 141, 148, 168, 172, 192, 214, 222, 223, 233, 244, 290
SS20, 2, 3
Stalin, Josef, 284
Stasi. See GDR
Stoltenberg, Gerhard, 192, 251
Strasbourg (European Council meeting), xxv, 86, 98, 100, 111, 117, 120–2, 126, 127, 129–33, 137, 138, 139, 140, 141, 143, 145, 146, 168, 181, 182, 184, 185, 186, 187, 188, 235, 237, 313, 320
Streibl, Max, 228
Sudhoff, Jürgen, 139
Sulek, Jerzy, 286–7
Süssmuth, Rita, 224
Szuros, Mathias, 348

Taft, Robert, 331–4, 344
Teltschik, Horst, 49, 50, 118, 124, 125, 133, 167, 179, 227, 228, 235, 238, 241–2, 284, 296
Thatcher, Margaret, xiii, xvi, xxii, 9, 10, 19, 44, 46, 47, 92, 114, 118, 128, 129, 132, 133, 138, 168–9, 174, 175, 183, 184, 212, 216, 223, 229, 234, 242, 243, 251, 256, 281, 295
   and Germany, xiii, xxii, 92, 118, 128, 133, 168–9, 183, 212, 216, 234, 295, 316
Timsit, Joëlle, 87, 162
Tréan, Claire, 102
Two Plus Four process, 173–181, 209–22, 286–95
   intersection with NATO, 211–2, 247
   intersection with the Quad group, 211
   balance sheet of, 293–5
   mandate of, 180
   politico-military questions, 212–3, 215, 216, 218, 219, 220, 244, 245, 255, 282, 289, 291, 293, 294, 298, 317
   British approach, 212
   French approach, 209–22
   FRG approach, 212
   Soviet approach, 212–3
   U.S. approach, 212
   sequence of the settlement, 218, 219, 229

Ukraine, 382–3
United States
   and German unity, 95–6, 113, 115–6, 128–9, 178, 294–5
   and the European confederation, 351, 356–7
   and European defence, 317–20, 323–5, 333–9, 343–5
   and relaunch of the European Community, 317–20
   and NATO, 43–4, 48–9, 128–9, 144–5, 246–58, 280–2, 331–2, 341–3
   relations with Eastern Europe, 40–1, 87

relations with France, 7, 12, 46–48, 133–4, 247–250, 331–3
relations with the FRG, 44–5, 48, 95–6, 192–3, 215, 219, 294, 319
relations with the Soviet Union, 33–4, 35–6, 127–8, 242
relations with Western Europe, 144–5, 317–8, 389
'victory' in Cold War, xii, xxvi

Volkskammer. *See* GDR
Védrine, Hubert, xiv, xx, xxiii,, xxx, 10, 21, 37, 39, 41, 42, 65, 85, 90, 96, 99, 116, 129, 145, 146, 148, 176, 189, 191, 194, 244, 245, 247, 248, 252, 300, 322–3, 324, 327, 339, 345, 347, 348, 354, 355, 380
Vertriebene, 108, 222
Vinocur, John, 27

Waigel, Theo, 54, 119, 304
Walesa, Lech, 39, 84
Walters, Vernon, 58, 102, 134, 139
Warsaw Pact, 84, 85, 92, 129, 145, 184, 190, 192, 221, 251, 258, 293, 297, 342, 345, 354, 391
Weizsäcker, Richard von, 19, 57, 316, 319
Weston, John, 259
WEU, 9, 314, 315, 317, 318, 321–325, 329, 333–38, 342–3
Woerner, Manfred, 44

Yakovlev, Alexander, 31, 171
Yalta conference, xxii
Yanaev, Gennady, 379–81
Year of Europe, 317
Yeltsin, Boris, 377, 378, 379, 380, 382, 383
Yugoslavia, xxiii, 312, 322, 326–328, 361, 382, 383, 384, 388, 390
    Franco-German disagreement over, 326–8

Zelikow, Philip, xii, xxvii, 332, 336
Zero option. *See* INF
Zhelednovosk. *See* Caucasus
Zoellick, Robert, 175, 215, 251, 254, 319

www.ingramcontent.com/pod-product-compliance
Lightning Source LLC
Chambersburg PA
CBHW071213080526
44587CB00013BA/1353